Russians in Alaska

1732–1867

Russians in Alaska

1732–1867

LYDIA T. BLACK

UNIVERSITY OF ALASKA PRESS • FAIRBANKS, ALASKA

Box 756240
Fairbanks, AK 99775-6240
fypress@uaf.edu
www.uaf.edu/uapress

This paper meets the requirements of ANSI/NISO Z39.48-1992 (Permanence of Paper).

Publication design and production by Sue Mitchell, Inkworks.
Cover design by Dixon J. Jones.

Publication of *Russians in Alaska, 1732–1867* was supported by a generous grant from the Rasmuson Foundation, Anchorage, Alaska.

Library of Congress Cataloging-in-Publication Data

Black, Lydia.
Russians in Alaska, 1732–1867 / by Lydia T. Black.
p. cm.
Includes bibliographical references and index.
ISBN 1-889963-04-6 (cloth : alk. paper)—ISBN 1-889963-05-4 (pbk.)
1. Alaska—History—To 1867. 2. Alaska—Discovery and exploration—Russian. 3. Russians—Alaska—History—18th century. 4. Russians—Alaska—History—19th century. 5. Fur trade—Alaska—History—18th century. 6. Fur trade—Alaska—History—19th century. 7. Baranov, Aleksandr Andreevich, 1745–1819. 8. Rossiisko-amerikanskaia kompaniia. 9. Frontier and pioneer life—Alaska. I. Title.
F907.B53 2004
979.8'02—dc22

2003024662

Cover: Petropavlovsk on Kamchatka, Avacha Bay. Watercolor by Luka Voronin, Billings-Sarychev Expedition, 1786–1795.

Back cover: Lomonosov's map of 1763, indicating proposed polar routes from the White Sea to Alaska and India.

In memory of ordinary citizens of the Russian Empire who came to Alaska,

came to love her, made her their home, and now rest in forgotten graves;

and to their descendants in Alaska and Russia.

Contents

ILLUSTRATIONS

Acknowledgments

This book could not have been published without the assistance of Dr. Katherine L. Arndt, who acted as editor, proofreader, and nursemaid to this poor manuscript, a child neglected for almost ten years. My old friend and colleague Professor Richard A. Pierce read several early drafts, gave moral support for years, and provided many rare photographs. James A. Ketz provided the index. Jennifer Robin Collier, of the University of Alaska Press, obtained funds that permitted publication of several important charts and illustrations in color. Dr. Erica Hill, of the University of Alaska Press, supervised the last stages of the publishing process. Matthew L. Ganley helped to computer-enhance several rare color maps and drawings. I gratefully acknowledge their help, as well as the financial support of the Rasmuson Foundation, which assisted with the costs of publication.

Introduction

In 1959, Alaska ("The Great Land," as Alaskans often call their homeland) became the forty-ninth state of the United States of America. Before 1867, Alaska was part of the Russian Empire and was called Russian America or, in official documents, the Russian-American Colonies. Russian sovereignty in Alaska was based on the "right of discovery" established by the naval squadrons commanded by Mikhail S. Gvozdev in 1732 and Vitus Bering in 1741 and the "right of occupation" established in the eighteenth century by Russian entrepreneurs.

In literature and political speeches, the period when Alaska was under the Russian scepter is stereotypically represented as a time of unbridled exploitation—indeed, *enslavement*—of Native peoples, and wanton rape and robbery of Alaska's natural resources. In reality, the Russians (who seldom exceeded 500 persons at any one time) were vastly outnumbered by the Natives. By the 1830s the Russian Crown forbade permanent settlement in Alaska, and only those Russians who legally married Native persons (either men or women) were entitled to petition for permission to remain in Alaska lifelong. The Russian military did not put in an appearance in Alaska until the Crimean War in the 1850s, when a troop of soldiers was stationed at Sitka for defense in case of an attack by British forces.

Russian relationships with the majority of the Native groups were determined by the desirability of continuous, uninterrupted trade. Consequently, the dynamics of intergroup (Russian-Native) and personal relationships and attitudes were qualitatively different from those established later between the people of the United States and Alaska's indigenous peoples. The United States acquired Alaska at a time when major conflicts with Indians were being played out in the western territories. Military occupation and control were the order of business. The attitudes and expectations of military personnel were dictated by the Indian experience. These attitudes were projected, retroactively, onto the Russian scene. Civilians who flocked to Alaska operated under the laissez-faire policies of the time. These policies were in stark contrast to the government-controlled Russian-American Company, where, in return for a monopoly grant to Alaska's resources, the Imperial Russian government demanded that the company provide social services: public health and education, as well as old age, survivors', and disability pensions for their employees. In Alaska, during the Russian period, experimental social legislation was tried out.

What happened in Alaska under Russian sovereignty was very different, not only in the sense that colonization had a different character from the British, American, French, or Spanish pattern, but also in that there were differences over time. Changes in Russia's internal political, social, and economic situation affected events in Alaska. The geopolitical context of the eighteenth century was different from that of the early nineteenth century, and changed dramatically in the second half of that century. The United States of America, which did not exist when Russia first claimed Alaska, emerged as a continental power. The Russian emperor, Alexander II, expected the United States to absorb Canada one day—or wished that this would happen. He would have preferred to share a border with the United States and not with a British colony. Much happened in the course of this century and a half.

The origin of the stereotypic view of the Russian period may be safely laid at the doors of Hubert H. Bancroft and William H. Dall, who desired Alaska's rapid Americanization. This view was challenged by the end of the nineteenth century by a pioneer historian of Alaska, Clarence L. Andrews (1862–1948). Andrews came to Alaska when Russian culture was still very much alive. He became fascinated with the Russian period, "one of the most colorful and least known periods of North American history."[1] Andrews taught himself Russian and began to amass archival and primary sources on various aspects of the Russian period. Eventually he published two pioneering works: *The Story of Sitka* (1922) and *The Story of Alaska* (1931). In 1942, Andrews completed a biography of one of the great movers and shakers in Alaska—Aleksandr Andreevich Baranov (in Alaska 1790–1818)—but the work was never published. Andrews came in contact with radio commentator and writer (newspaper, script, and fiction) Hector Chevigny (1904–1965) in 1938. Until Andrews' death, these two men maintained a lively correspondence on the subject of Russian America. Chevigny, too, became fascinated with Alaska, specifically with the Russian period, after his contact with the eminent historian Edmund Meany. In 1937 Chevigny's first book dealing with Russian America, *Lost Empire* (a highly romanticized account of the life and times of N. P. Rezanov), was published. There followed in 1942 the somewhat unreliable and also romanticized account of Baranov, *Lord of Alaska*. A believer in the "great men" theory of history, which illuminated his approach in general, Chevigny planned to write his next biography on Grigorii Shelikhov, Baranov's employer. Writing, by his own admission, without direct access to Russian sources, like Andrews he was nevertheless able to amass a wealth of materials. Even after he lost his eyesight (and for this reason abandoned the projected biography of Shelikhov), his interest continued. After visiting Alaska twice (in 1959 and 1960) and encountering local enthusiasm for his work, Chevigny wrote the first popular synthesis dealing with the whole of the Russian period, *Russian America* (published in 1965, shortly before his death). This little publication, which largely follows the outline laid down by the historian of the Russian-American Company, Tikhmenev (d. 1888), has established the view among modern readers of a disorderly and violent period when private entrepreneurs competed for Alaska's wealth, followed by the establishment of order, first by Grigorii Shelikhov, then by his heirs, and eventually by the monopolistic Russian-American Company.[2] In the 1940s a Canadian historian, Stuart Tompkins, who had a long-standing interest in the Russian Far East and Siberia, became interested in the Russian adventure in Alaska. This interest is reflected in his work *Alaska: Promyshlennik and Sourdough* (1945).

These three pioneers in the study of Russian America opened the field for scholarly exploration by American and Canadian scholars, who produced a body of literature on specialized topics that began to grow in the late 1950s, continued through the 1960s, and has come into its own in the subsequent decades. The study became enriched when Richard A. Pierce, a specialist in Russian history, through his association with Chevigny, joined the field in the early 1960s. Realizing that a wealth of material was not accessible to anglophone scholars, he initiated a translation series of Russian primary sources on Alaska. However, no comprehensive study has been attempted since the pioneering work of Chevigny.

This book presents to the public a new synthesis, based primarily on archival materials in Russia and the United States. Unless otherwise indicated, all translations of Russian sources are my own. In this volume, I attempt to present the Russian advance to the American continent in historic perspective, including the changing geopolitical context, while focusing on the social and cultural data on the Russians who were active in Alaska. This focus includes the northern skippers of the fur-procuring vessels; the great merchants of the Russian north and, later, of Irkutsk in Siberia; the churchmen who brought to Alaska the lasting heritage of the Orthodox faith; the rank-and-file laborers of various ethnic origins, such as the Yakut, the Kamchadal, the Koriak, and the Tungus (Evenk and Even); the imperial naval officers who had their own point of view on how Alaska should be governed (and in the end came to govern her); and the creoles, the social class deliberately created in order to have a bicultural stratum, members of which would be loyal to their native land, Alaska, and to the Russian cultural heritage brought to Alaska by an ancestor or ancestress.

In the process, I came to re-evaluate the role of the "great men" who fascinated Chevigny so much. A great deal of what I have to say, based on the perusal of documents not readily accessible, is contrary to the received wisdom. In a sense, this book is not simply a new synthesis, it is also a reinterpretation. It is focused on the Russians in Alaska—their motivations, views of life, and attitudes. I truly hope that this book will contribute to a better understanding of the history of the forty-ninth state—our beloved Great Land, Alaska—and perhaps to a better knowledge of a fascinating shared chapter in the history of Russia and the United States.

NOTES

1. Richard A. Pierce, "Hector Chevigny: Historian of Russian America," *Alaska Journal* 15, no. 4 (1985): 33.
2. Ibid., 33–37.

МЫ ЕКАТЕРИНА ВТОРАЯ
ИМПЕРАТРИЦА И САМОДЕРЖИЦА
ВСЕРОССІЙСКАЯ.
Московская, Кіевская, Владимир-
ская, Новгородская, Царица Казанская, Царица
Астраханская, Царица Сибирская, Государыня
Псковская и Великая Княгиня Смоленская,

Plate 1. The charter of nobility.

Plates 1–3. Shortly after ascension to the throne, Catherine the Great granted noble status to Sven Waxell, who in 1742 brought home the survivors of Bering's ship, and to his posterity. The charter of nobility, richly illuminated, is now in the hands of an unknown collector, but in 1979 the late V. V. Ushanoff photographed it (when it was in the hands of an earlier owner) and published the images in the magazine *Alaska Journal.* Reproduced here are the title page of the charter (Plate 1) and, from the same document, two miniatures representing Bering's two vessels, the *Sv. Petr* (Plate 2), commanded by Waxell, and its consort, the *Sv. Pavel* (Plate 3), commanded by Aleksei Chirikov, who safely returned home from the American coast late in 1741.

Plates 1–3 courtesy Robert Henning, Alaska Northwest Publishing Company.

Plate 2. The *Sv. Petr* (*St. Peter*).

Plate 3. The *Sv. Pavel* (*St. Paul*).

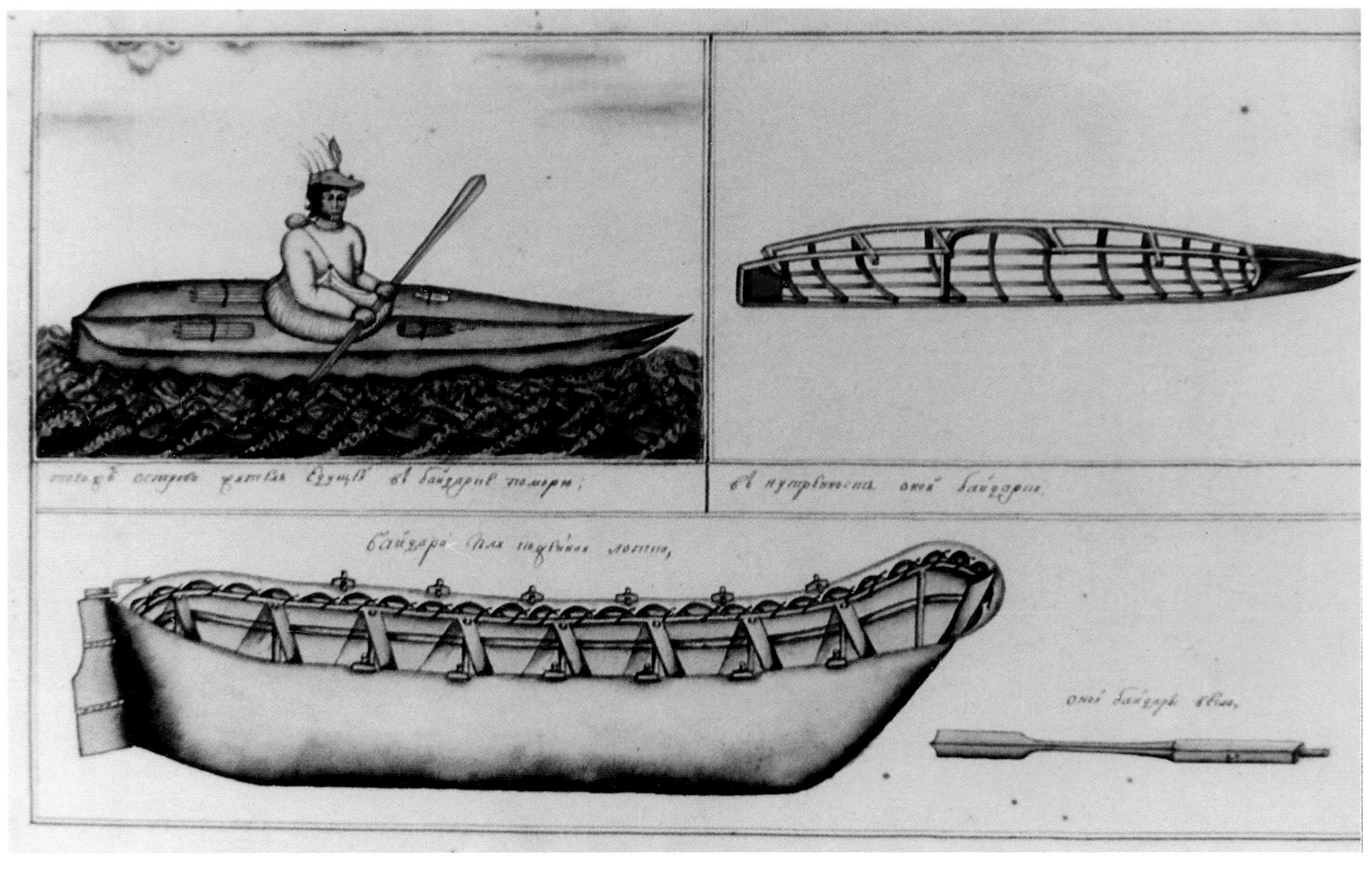

Plate 4. Watercraft: An Aleut hunter in a single-hatch kayak (top left); Aleut kayak frame with a bifurcate bow and a rudder (top right); Aleut baidara, a large skin boat with a rudder and paddle (bottom). Watercolor by Captain Mikhail Levashov, Unalaska, 1768–1769.

Courtesy RGAVMF.

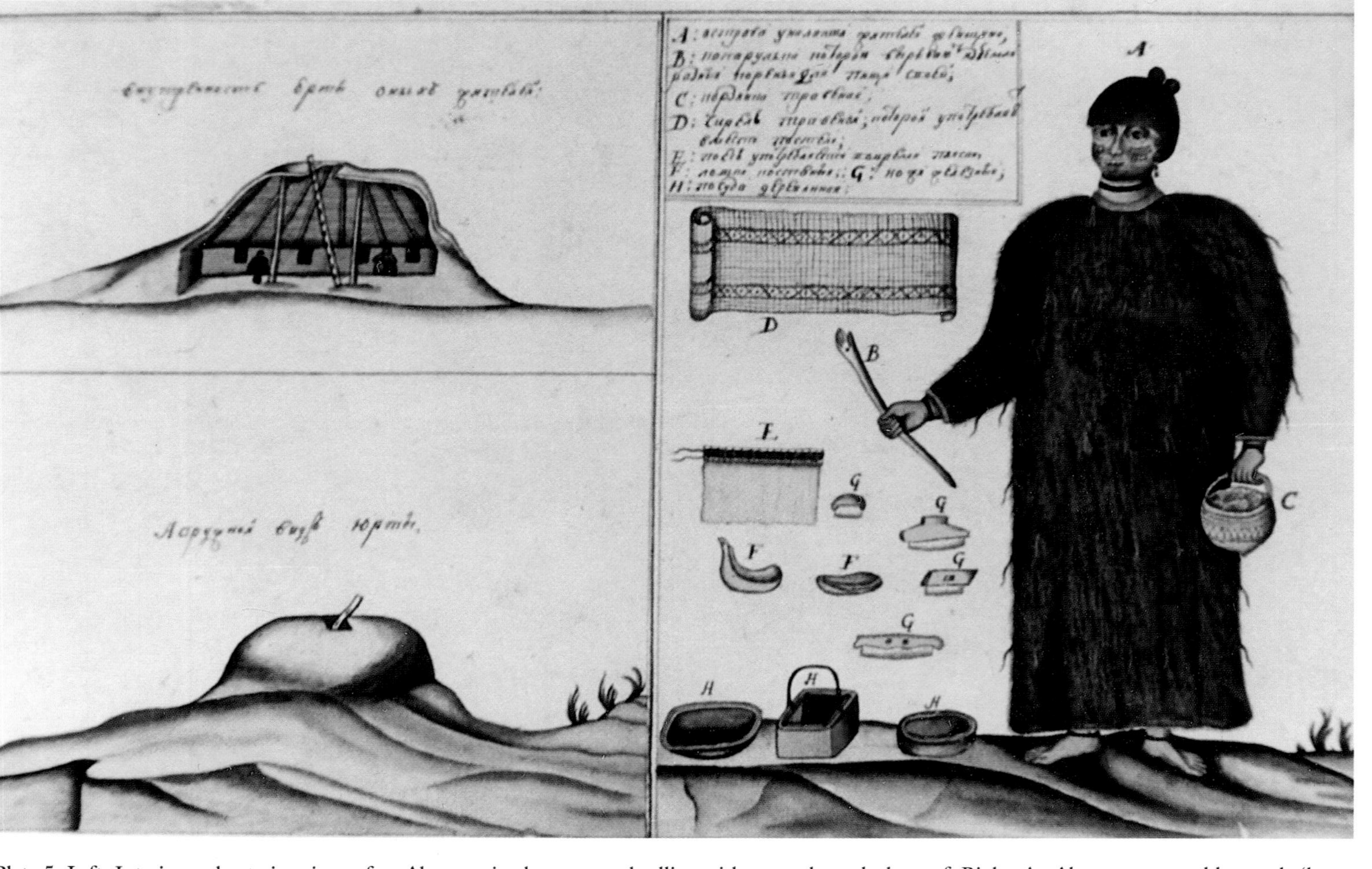

Plate 5. Left: Interior and exterior views of an Aleut semi-subterranean dwelling with entry through the roof. Right: An Aleut woman and her tools (bentwood and grass baskets, scraping tools and knives, digging stick, and bone spoon). A grass mat (D) and a dancing belt (E) are also shown. Watercolor by Captain Mikhail Levashov, Unalaska, 1768–1769.

Courtesy RGAVMF.

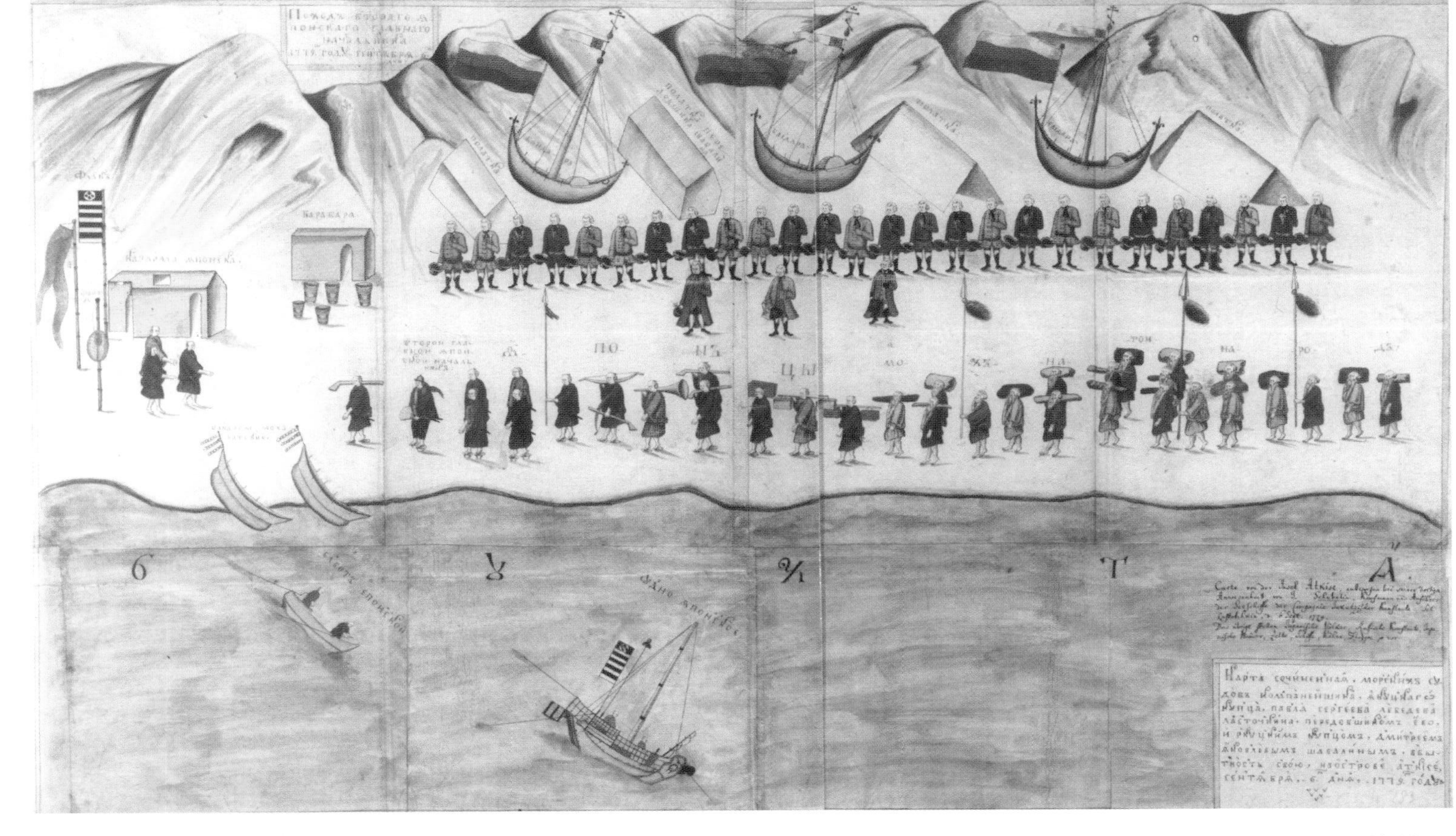

Plate 6. In 1779, Dmitrii Shabalin, merchant of Irkutsk, an agent of Yakutsk merchant P. S. Lebedev-Lastochkin, traded with the Japanese on Hokkaido, possibly in Abashiri Bay. In this watercolor and ink sketch, Shabalin himself illustrated a trade meeting. Russian baidaras (skin boats equipped with sails) are shown at the top; the mast of each vessel ends in a cross, with pennant icons fluttering in the wind. A Japanese vessel and landing boats are shown at bottom. A Russian warehouse is at the top; Japanese storage structures are on the left. Russians are shown awaiting their partners at parade-rest, with the peredovshchiks and interpreter in front. Japanese merchants of various ranks (left and bottom) are followed by Ainu carrying burdens.

Courtesy University of Göttingen Library, Rare Books and Manuscripts, von Asch Collection, no. 283.

Plates 7–12. Ink and watercolor paintings by Japanese merchant Kodayu. Shipwrecked on Amchitka Island in the Aleutians several years earlier, Kodayu was brought home by the Laksman-Lovtsov expedition to Japan in 1792. This set of his drawings and paintings illustrates features of the Russian stay on Hokkaido.
Photo series no. 33; published by Tenri Central Library. Courtesy Tenri University Library, Tenri, Nara, Japan.

Plate 7. Crown vessel *Sv. Ekaterina*, out of Okhotsk, commanded by navigator Vasilii Lovtsov.

Plate 8. *Sv. Ekaterina* at anchor in winter. Note the Russians hauling wood to the vessel with a sled.

Plate 9. Russian camp on Hokkaido.

Plate 10. Detail of the main buildings within the Russian camp.

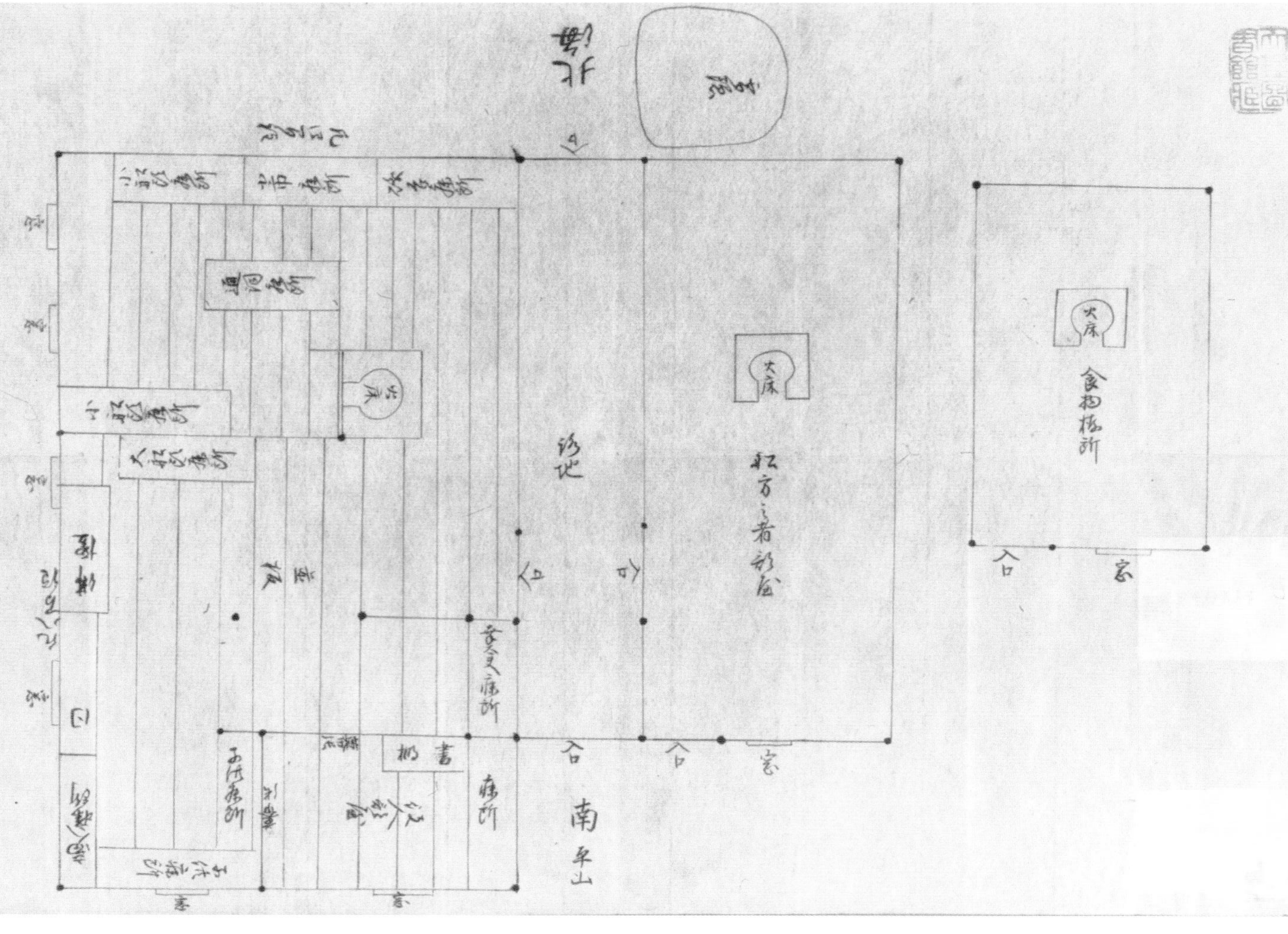

Plate 11. Plan of the Russian quarters.

Plate 12. The party relaxes in quarters at the Russian camp on Hokkaido. Ambassador Laksman is seated on the right wearing a green coat; navigator Lovtsov, fourth from right, enjoys what appears to be a glass of wine.

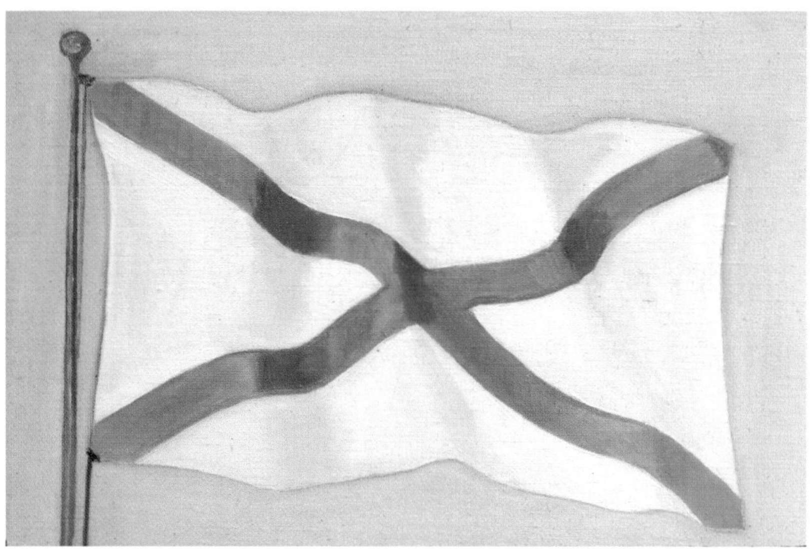

Plate 13. The Cross of St. Andrew (Andreevskii flag) was the flag of the Russian Imperial Navy until 1917. In 1992, the flag was reinstated by the Russian Navy.

Courtesy Richard A. Pierce.

Plate 14. Flag of the Russian-American Company. Watercolor by an unknown artist, 1805.

Original in RGIA, Fond 1329, op. 1, delo 291, fol. 594. Courtesy Richard A. Pierce.

Plate 15. Modern icon of St. Iakov (priest Iakov Netsvetov) Enlightener of Alaska Native Peoples.
Personal collection of the author.

Plate 16. The late Father Ismail Gromoff, Rector of the Cathedral of the Holy Ascension of Our Lord, Unalaska, blesses Christmas stars. During Christmas week, the stars will be carried from house to house by young men, followed by the choir and parishioners.

Courtesy Lewis Moses, 1983.

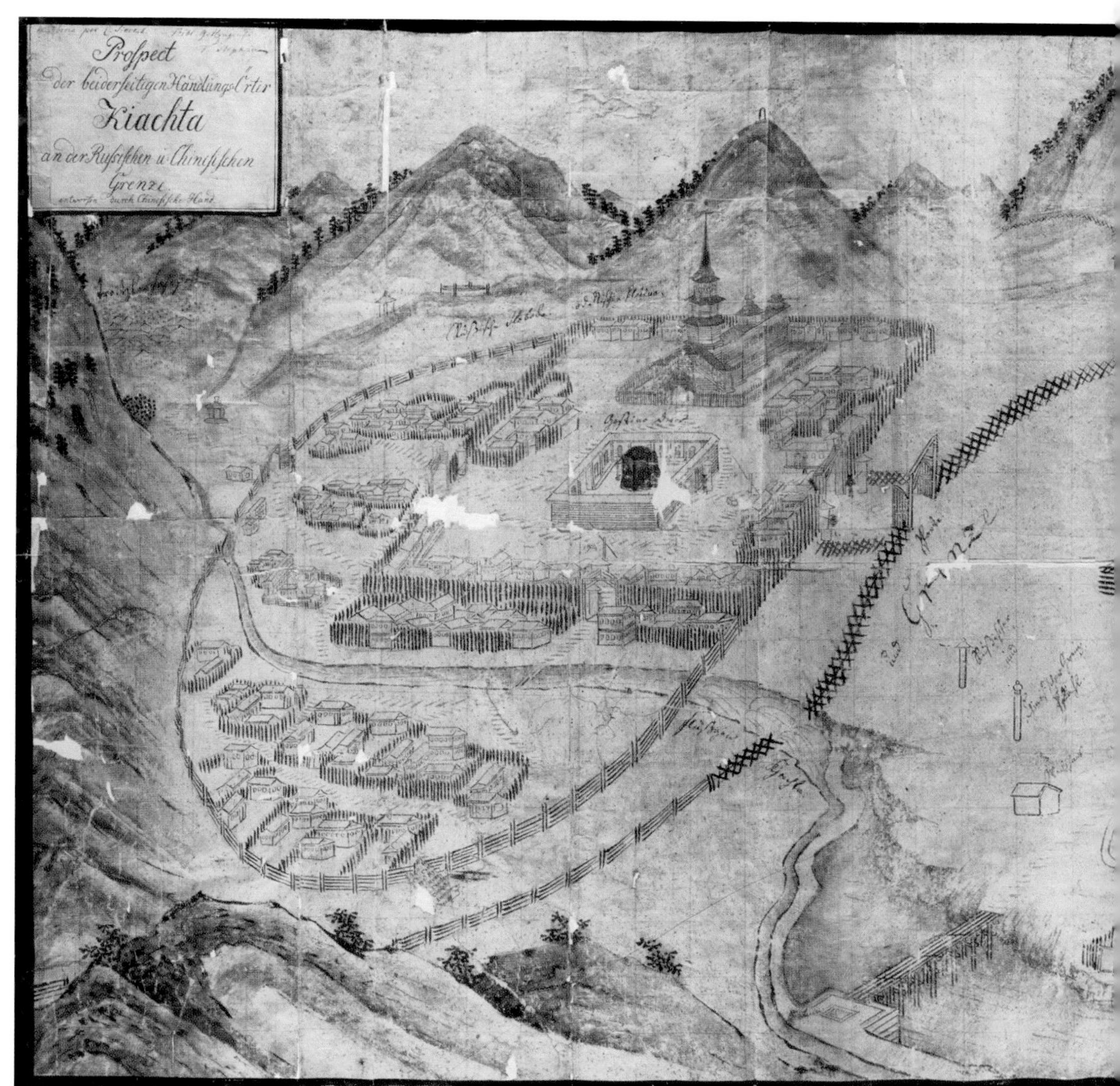

Plate 18. Kiakhta, the trading center on the Russian-Chinese border and entry and checkpoint for caravans traveling to settlements. Ink and watercolor by an unnamed Chinese artist.

Courtesy University of Göttingen Library, Rare Books and Manuscripts, von Asch Collection, no. 269.

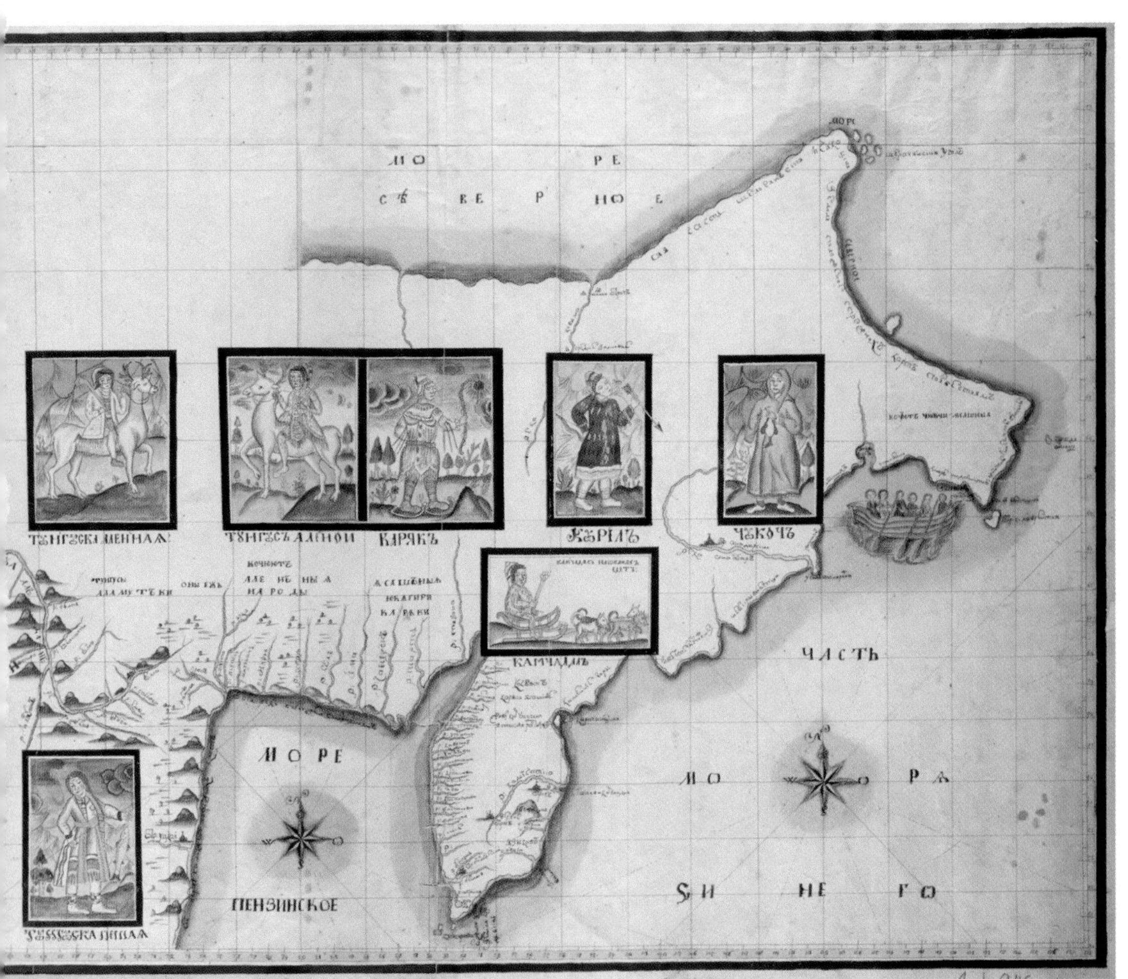

Bering's 1728 voyage. Possibly original; hand colored, 59.5 by 137 cm.

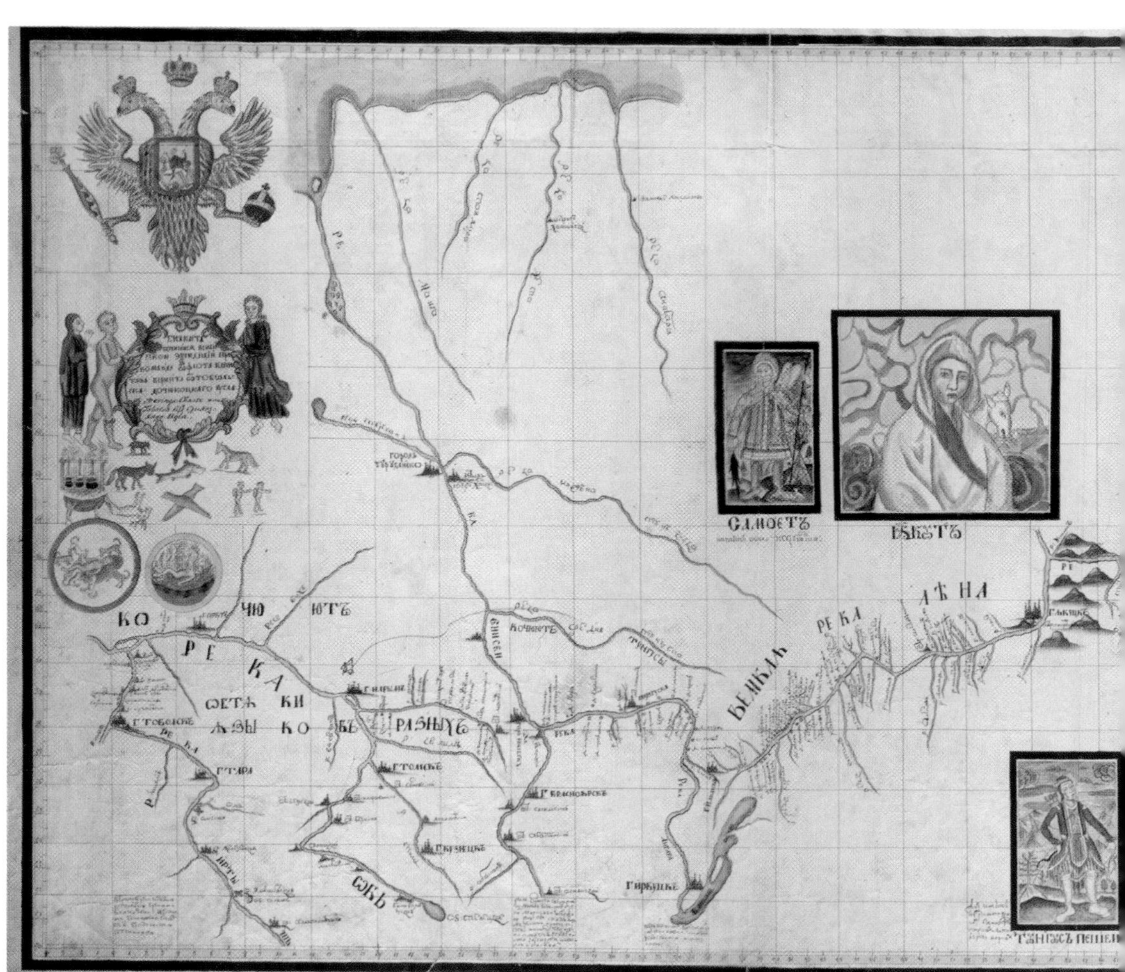

Plate 17. An ethnographic map of Siberia from Tobol'sk to Bering Strait, compiled no later than 1729 by a member o

Courtesy University of Göttingen Library, Rare Books and Manuscripts, von Asch Collection, no. 246.

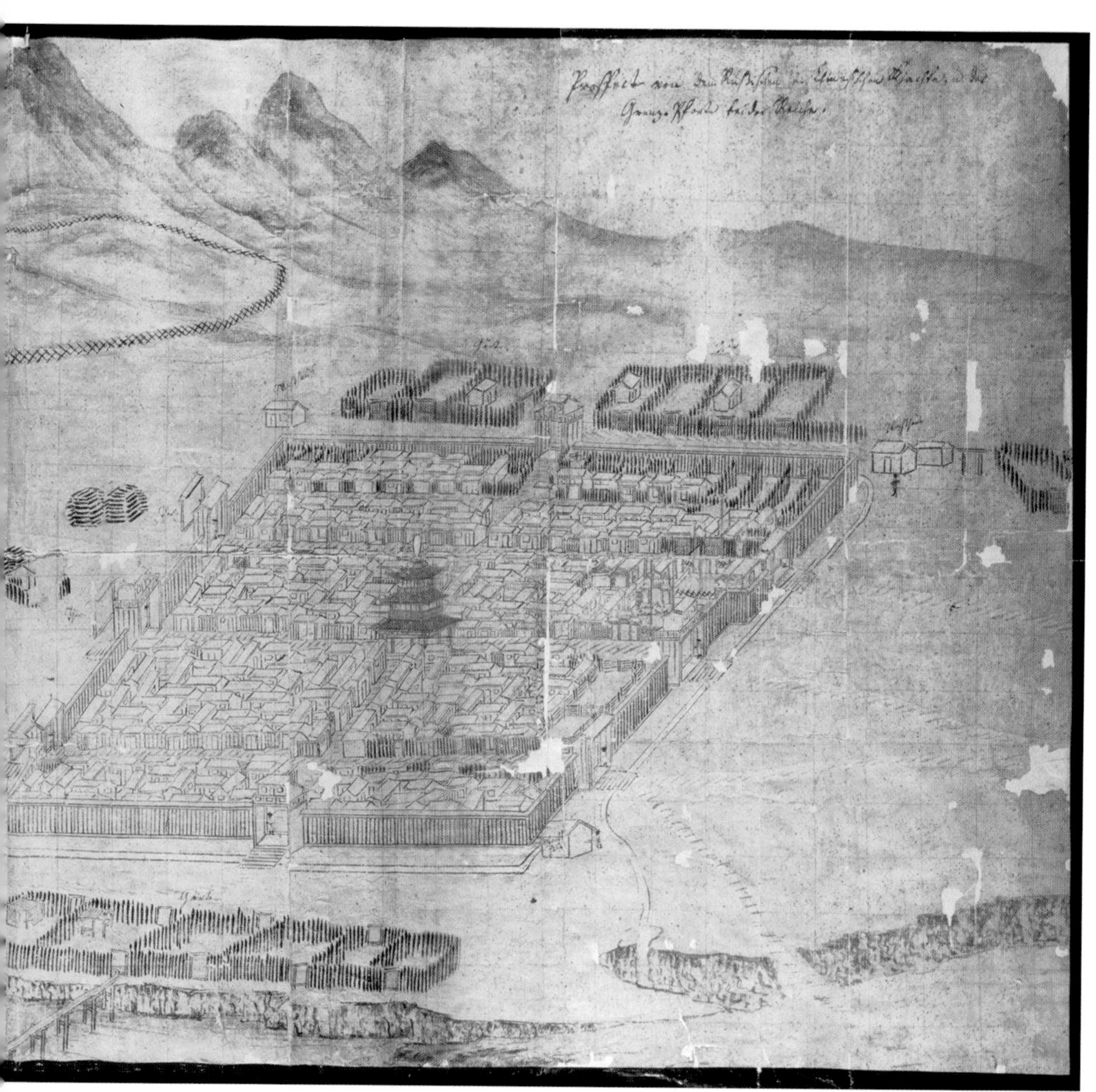

Beijing from the late seventeenth through the eighteenth centuries. Note the gate linking the Russian and Chinese

Chapter One

A Long-Established Pattern

Russian America, the portion of the Russian Empire that appeared, flowered, and withered on the North American continent all within little more than a century, was in several respects a logical outgrowth of patterns established in the Russian homeland from its earliest days. For many centuries, the Russians had looked to the north in search of new lands to settle and new opportunities to exploit. Slavic raiders, entrepreneurs, and settlers had already expanded to the shores of the White Sea in the tenth century. By the fourteenth century, they were arctic sailors, marine mammal hunters and fishermen, and hunters of forest animals. In the following three centuries, these northern settlers spearheaded Russian expansion eastward, across Siberia to the Pacific Ocean, and to the North American continent. This chapter briefly examines this complex process and how it played itself out from the earliest times to the seventeenth century.

As was the case with European overseas expansion, Russian expansion and colonization succeeded because of concerted effort by both private and governmental interests. The patterns of their interaction and the dynamics of the expansion process varied from one European nation to another as well as over time. In Russia this dynamic had very deep historical roots, extending back many centuries and following a long-established traditional pattern. S. V. Bakhrushin, the late historian of Siberia and the Russian north, aptly characterized this pattern:

> Thus, the Russian advance beyond the Urals, in the early times, insofar as it may be characterized on the basis of rather meager sources, was two-pronged. In the forefront were the merchants and hunters engaged in procurement. Year by year they blazed the trail along which there gradually grew hunting settlements and wintering places. The large-scale entrepreneur followed in their footsteps, established himself in the newly opened lands and, from the township he founded in the border zone and which he used as a base of operations, continued the conquest of the territory. The state's intention to subject the new lands followed much later... [it] acted very cautiously, preferring to exploit the results of private activity.[1]

To understand this pattern, and how it changed over time, we must turn to the beginnings of the Russian state and focus particularly on the Russian north, that is, the shores of the Baltic, the White and the Barents Seas, and the lake areas and river basins of this region, extending to the Upper Volga, Kama, and Pechora Rivers. Russian settlement in the north is very ancient and subject to scholarly discussion. However, there is a general agreement on the following sequence.

In prehistoric times, certainly in the Neolithic period of the second millennium B.C. and probably earlier, this vast region was inhabited by peoples speaking Finno-Ugric languages. The population was heterogeneous, however, and it included Saami and some Finnic peoples. The settlements of all these peoples probably were interspersed, especially in the northern areas; in all likelihood they were the first inhabitants of this region. A small influx of ancient Palaeoasiatic peoples, possibly Yukagir, may have occurred. All were foragers, hunters, and fishermen. Also in the second millennium B.C. there appeared in the Baltic regions a culture based on cattle-keeping and incipient agriculture. The ethnicity of the bearers of this culture has not been determined.

In the first millennium B.C., Germanic peoples, probably the ancestors of the later Scandinavians, settled on the Baltic coasts, eventually expanding to southwestern Finland and into modern Scandinavia. Eastern Slavs, a more southern people, began to arrive here also about the first half of the first millennium A.D. They moved in small groups and settled among the local Baltic and Finnish populations. Historians believe that this "voting with the feet" was one of the results of the ever-increasing pressure of the expanding Turkic peoples in the steppe belt.[2] The Slavs were of diverse tribal origins, each group tending to cluster together in the newly occupied territories. In subsequent centuries some expanded not only north but also to the east and northeast. The Nentsy and Entsy (or the Samoyed peoples in general) are believed to have penetrated this area only in the first millennium A.D. (not much earlier than, and possibly at the same time as, the early Slav settlers).

Meanwhile, the Scandinavians—seafarers, traders, and formidable military raiders—were penetrating the Baltic areas and, by the eighth century, expanding out of Norway along the northern shores of the Kola Peninsula. Sometime in the ninth or tenth century A.D., they moved into the White Sea region. (In fact, the Russian word *murman* from which derive both the name of Murmansk, the famous Russian northern seaport, and the Murman, or the Arctic Ocean coast of Russia to the Norwegian border, means precisely that—a Norman, presumably a Swede or sometimes a Dane.) The Norse movement into what today is the Russian north was motivated by the desire to control the trade routes from the Arctic Ocean and Baltic Sea shores to the Black and Caspian Seas, which followed the major waterways through the Slav territories.

From their bases on the Baltic, the Norsemen very rapidly gained dominance of the Oka-Volga trade route to the Caspian Sea, giving them access to Persia and the great caravan routes to the east, and eventually of the route along the Dniepr River to the Black Sea and hence to Byzantium and the Mediterranean. In 856, the Norseman Roric (in Russian sources called Riurik) took control of the Slav trading city of Novgorod and in 862 built a fortified stronghold at Ladoga.[3]

The Norsemen, a military and mercantile elite, as historian Vernadsky points out, "were comparatively few in number . . . and were consequently easily and rapidly absorbed by the Slavs . . . they mingled freely with the people whom they now ruled. . . ." On the other hand, the Slavs who fell under Norse dominion in Novgorod (and also in Kiev) readily adapted to the trade-and-raid operations of their overlords. Their trading caravans, by horse or by ship, were formidable fighting units.

The goods sent along the trade routes from the north were products of the forest and the sea: honey and beeswax, fish and marine mammal oil and skins, walrus ivory (which Novgorodian craftsmen transformed into skillfully carved objects of art), and, above all, furs.[4] Procurement of these trade goods played a role in the rapid expansion of the mixed Slav groups to the shores of the White and Barents Seas, though a northward trickle of individuals and small groups had begun much earlier, would continue through the centuries, and would increase in the wake of Mongol conquest in the middle of the thirteenth century.

True to the long-established pattern, "both before and after the Norse invasion the eastern Slavs mixed freely with peoples of Ural-Altaic family. . . ."[5] Each group often adopted the others' customs, and each learned from the other. It was from the Vikings that the northern Russians probably learned to utilize their waterways to the utmost—the rivers, the lakes, and the sea—and to master the fine art of shipbuilding that eventually carried them along the coasts of the Arctic Ocean eastward and to the shores of arctic America.[6]

It was not long before Novgorod merchants were sending out armed bands to the White Sea and Arctic Ocean shores for barter and to impose and collect tribute. This tribute, paid in furs, besides bringing in much-desired trade goods, also served as a basis for the later legal claims of overlordship by the city called "The Lord Great Novgorod." Not far behind were bands of freebooters (*ushkuiniki* and *vatagi*) who raided aborigines and Slav settlers alike to obtain furs. Often, to legitimize their actions, these freebooters delivered part of their booty to the rulers of Novgorod as "collected tribute."

By the end of the thirteenth century, most of the coastal areas, the Pomor'ie, were settled. People of all classes came to these "new lands," as they were called, but the majority were independent peasants. By the sixteenth century the descendants of these settlers, who as usual mixed with local populations, had fully adapted to the northern coastal environment. They adopted fishing and marine mammal hunting, especially of walrus, as far away as Novaia Zemlia and the mouth of the Yenisei River; whaling, as far away as Spitsbergen; and bird hunting, for skins, meat, and down, as their main occupations.[7] A distinct culture, lifestyle, and dialect emerged. The people who, in another 200 years, would provide the majority of Alaska pioneers came into being as a distinct ethnic entity, the Pomory, with their own identity and maritime traditions.[8] The settlers actively participated in international trade, channeling their take not only through Novgorod but also through the new trading centers, which rapidly developed into cities, such as Arkhangel'sk, Kholmogory, Ustiug, and many others. A glance at a map of the trade network of the city of Ustiug in the seventeenth century (Figure 1) demonstrates the role these cities played in northern Russian commerce.[9]

The Komi, a Finno-Ugric people called Zyriane in earlier Russian sources, were not displaced. The immigrants who settled among them and with whom they freely mixed learned many new skills from them, including how to construct new types of watercraft. The Komi population was concentrated in several areas, notably in the orbit of the city of Ustiug, with its center at Yarensk. The Komi also learned from the newcomers and soon became active in international trade. (Later, they were active participants in the Russian expansion into Siberia and even to Russian America. Several Komi participated in the voyage of Semeon Dezhnev through Bering Strait, and Stepan Glotov of Yarensk, a famous skipper active in the early years of the Aleutian trade, may have been a Komi.)[10]

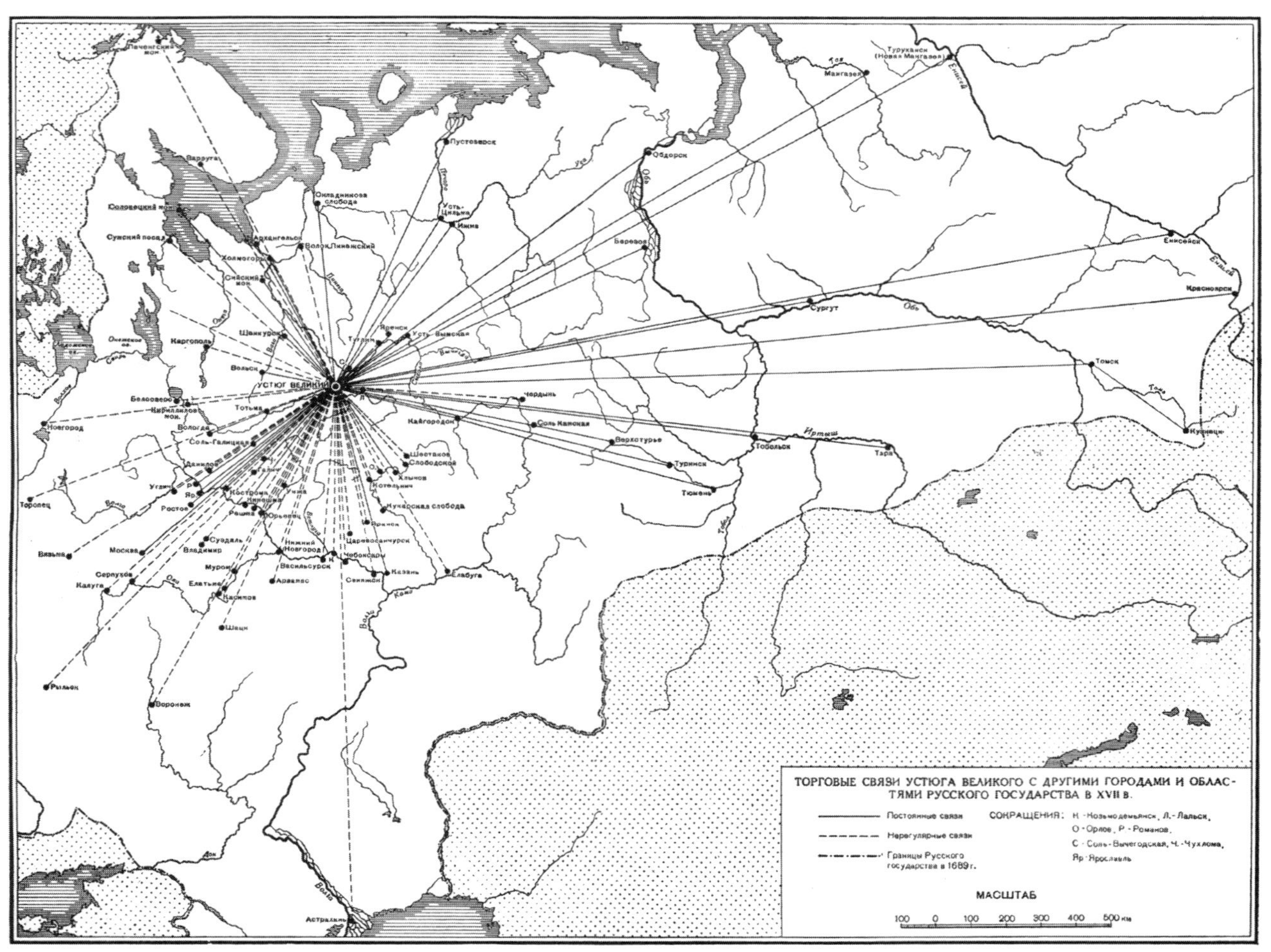

FIGURE 1. Trade network of the city of Ustiug the Great in the seventeenth century.
From Merzon and Tikhonov, 1960, p. 240.

Trade was a major factor in the economic life of the region.[11] From ancient times, no other trade item was as important as fur. Furs were the principal item of export and medium of exchange; they often constituted marriage settlements, war indemnity payments, and dispute settlements. In early times, squirrel fur dominated the market, followed by marten and sable, also lynx, fox, wolf, and bear. In later times sable became the dominant item in the fur trade.

The main suppliers of furs were the independent peasant settlers and their neighbors, the Komi. All combined in their household economy agriculture, cottage industries or crafts, fishing and hunting for subsistence and household needs, and fur trapping for the market. In later centuries this type of complex economic activity was carried to Siberia. The pattern persisted until the twentieth century, up to the introduction of compulsory economic change in postrevolutionary times.[12] Thus, northern Russians had their own social order and their own labor traditions, and some of these were transplanted eventually to Russian America.[13]

The growth of settlements and of agriculture rapidly deforested many regions and consequently reduced furbearer species. To maintain the Novgorodian fur trade, new and more distant hunting grounds had to be brought into the city's orbit. From the tenth century on, this was accomplished by claims over an ever-widening span of territories, and not only by Novgorodian peasants and other Slav settlers, but also by Novgorodian high nobles and heads of trading houses who claimed overlordship of northern areas where they had established themselves as vassals of Novgorod. Among other northern centers founded directly by the Novgorodian great merchants and nobles (the boiars) was Vaga.[14] The Stroganovs, the famous merchants and founders of the salt industry at Sol'vychegodsk on the Vychegda River, and in later ages staunch supporters of Moscow's expansion, established themselves originally in Novgorod but then moved to the north like many other Novgorodians of their class. Eventually, Lord Great Novgorod laid direct claim to overlordship over the expanding Russian north, including the burgeoning maritime trading centers such as Kholmogory on the northern Dvina River and Ustiug.[15] The town of Ustiug, however, staunchly defended its independence. The men of Ustiug fought many wars against the Novgorodians, defeating them in an early contest in 1032. In the end, hard-pressed, they chose to throw in their lot with Rostov-Suzdal, another Russian principality intent on exploiting the lucrative fur trade. The Rostov-Suzdal principality was now formally advancing its own claims to overlordship of the northern territories, and its rivalry with Novgorod for primacy in the north was long-standing, beginning possibly as early as the late eleventh and early twelfth centuries.[16]

In the thirteenth century, Moscow began to interest itself in the area and its fur trade. In the fourteenth century, Moscow brought Suzdal and Rostov into its domain and thus established itself as the overlord of a portion of the northern territories. The allegiances of local territorial units and their relations with the overlords often shifted, until the fifteenth century, when Moscow defeated the Lord Great Novgorod and emerged as the dominant power in the Russian land.

Perhaps the shift in allegiance of several northern settlement areas from Novgorod to Rostov-Suzdal, and thus ultimately to Moscow, in some measure contributed to Novgorod's eventual defeat and the establishment of Moscow's firm control over the Russian north. By then Russians were active, and probably had small enclaves, in northwestern Siberia, in the territory of the Iugra (a term believed to be of Komi origin). These were the

Finno-Ugric-speaking tribes of the Ob' River basin and its major tributary, the Taz. Particularly affected were the Khanty and the Mansi.[17] Both Novgorod and the Russian principalities warred with a number of the Ugric tribes, with varied success. Often, the tribesmen, under the skilled and centralized military leadership of their princes, as the Russian chronicles call them, defeated the Novgorodians, the men of Ustiug, Komi, and other invaders.[18] Among the latter were the Samoyed tribes, Nentsy and Entsy, whom the Khanty and Mansi raided in turn. When making peace or establishing trade relations, all tried to secure hostages—*amanaty*. This ancient practice, too, was carried to Alaska in the eighteenth century.

The earliest record of such hostile contact dates to the eleventh century. The first Muscovite military expeditions date to 1465 when Ivan III, of Moscow, ordered the Ustiug host under Vasilii Skriaba to invade the Iugra territory. Its incorporation into the Moscow-led Russian state was later dated from this event. The Ustiug chronicler also mentions a joint Russian-Ustiug military expedition in 1483 in which they "conquered Near Siberia from Pelema to the Ob' River, returning with much booty without loss of a single man."[19] Soon thereafter, in 1499–1500, Prince Kurbskii led a large army composed of the men of Pomor'ie to the mouth of the Pechora and beyond the Urals where they founded Berezovo (Berezov).

When victorious, Novgorod and others exacted tribute (*dan'*) from the defeated, as was the custom of the times. The take, however, was small, the collection uneven and insufficient to satisfy the demands of the expanding market, which was predominantly European but also Asiatic.[20] Raiders—freebooters who often entered the pay of great merchants—staged lightning raids into the Ob'-Ugrian territories and beyond, even to the Yenisei River, in order to obtain furs by indiscriminate plunder.[21] Men of Ustiug frequently staged veritable invasions, claiming victory even when they lost, and obtaining furs as war indemnities. But trade with the indigenous inhabitants also flourished, especially in the long intervals between hostilities.[22] Moscow had gained the upper hand over the Russian north and Novgorod in the fifteenth century and by the late sixteenth century had systematized collection of tribute in the form of furs. The institution of the *iasak* came to the north. Iasak, a term derived from the Turkic languages, designated the tribute imposed by conquerors upon the conquered. Russians paid iasak to the Mongols after the Mongol conquest in the thirteenth century. The Mongols also exacted iasak from most of the Siberian tribes. Those tribes, when gaining dominance over their neighbors, in turn followed the same practice. Delivery of the iasak, collected in pelts, signified submission to the higher authority. It was a well-understood institution throughout Siberia. Especially in the early period of Muscovite expansion in Siberia, iasak was also a source of state revenue, a form of taxation, to be collected annually.

In older Russian historiography, as well as in modern Western interpretations, this method of obtaining state revenues and the role of the state as fur merchant are overstressed, while the role of the peasant/serviceman/fur trapper and trader (also heavily taxed) is grossly underestimated.[23] The role of the iasak collector was often performed by the settler/fur trapper turned serviceman. This was a peculiar factor which colored the state/private entrepreneur cooperation and which, in the eighteenth century, loomed large as proof of the role of the state in the process of expansion to Alaska.

If private initiative played the leading role in the early centuries of Russian expansion in Siberia, the balance had begun to shift by the reign of Ivan III (1462–1507), and in the reign of Boris Godunov (1598–1605) it definitely shifted from the settler and entrepreneur to the state. At first, Moscow dealt with Siberian indigenous principalities as with foreign powers, diplomatically or by making war. Thus, in 1505, Ivan III sent out a military expedition under Vasilii Kover to the city of Tiumen', residence of the Khan of Sibir'. In his and the subsequent reign, to the end of the sixteenth century (1594), Moscow's foreign office (*Posol'skii prikaz*) handled Siberian affairs. In the reign of Boris Godunov, the burden was shifted to domestic agencies and by 1599 there was an office of Siberian affairs (*Sibirskii stol*). By 1637, in the reign of Tsar Aleksei Mikhailovich, a special department, the *Sibirskii prikaz,* was created.[24] Moscow by now considered practically all of Siberia to be Russian territory.

From the beginning of this period, the state controlled the policy and, beginning with the reign of Ivan IV (the Terrible, 1547–1582), established governmental administration in the newly conquered areas. This included creation of administrative centers and in some instances government-initiated mass resettlement—for instance, in 1630, 500 men and 150 women of Vologda, Tot'ma, Sol'vychegodsk, and Ustiug were resettled in Tobol'sk in order to reinforce the cossacks and servicemen living in "the newly conquered localities." The tsar himself signed the resettlement order and the settlers were conveyed to Tobol'sk in government-owned transport. The government wished to foster agriculture and so began to resettle peasants in Siberia. The shortage of women among the settlers caused the government to recruit single women for resettlement and to concern itself with marital regulations.[25] To maintain communications and to supply the newly created towns, roads were constructed and postal service instituted.

Trade, however, was not neglected. Around 1600, Mangazeia, a major government-sponsored seaport and commercial center, came into being at the Taz River mouth; the government effectively controlled access to it by prohibiting foreign shipping and information flow about this port, and the prescribed routes there were to be used only by Russian subjects. Sea access especially was curtailed.[26]

Nevertheless, the flow of private settlers continued. The rank and file continued to enter the region freely. Thus, after Novgorod's destruction, refugees of all classes, but led by Novgorodian merchants, founded Lal'sk in 1555. Descendants of Russian settlers on the Indigirka River and some on the Yana River maintained in the early twentieth century and even today that their forefathers fled from Novgorodian lands in the reign of Ivan IV, that the refugees included men from different localities, including at least one Komi, and that they traveled by sea in *kochi* (see below) until they reached safety in remote eastern Siberia.[27]

It should be emphasized that colonization of Siberia proceeded eastward mainly along the Arctic Ocean's shores and from north to south along the major waterways.[28] By the time of Ivan IV, the Russian north was famous for its shipbuilding industry. Arkhangel'sk, Kholmogory, and especially Mezen' were major shipbuilding centers. Specialized vessels were developed, such as the *koch* (plural *kochi*), suited to navigating arctic, ice-choked waters. Long-distance seafaring was commonplace. Oral tradition ascribes the leading role in this development to the Solovetskii monastery,[29] which had been founded in 1429 by Saints Savvatii, Zosima, and German. No settlement built by the pioneers lacked a chapel or church, and local saints emerged and were venerated in folk traditions. The pioneers also carried this northern spiritual tradition to Siberia and eventually to Russian America.

The growing, complex interplay between private interests, from great entrepreneurs to rank-and-file volunteers, is best exemplified by the conquest of Sibir' by the Cossack host led by Ermak. This conquest is usually cited as the benchmark in the Russian advance eastward: in 1582 the Cossack chieftain Ermark, sponsored in his enterprise by the merchants Stroganov but having conducted his campaign without royal sanction, laid the spoils of the campaign and the nominal title to the conquered lands at the feet of Tsar Ivan IV.[30] Merchants and their agents,[31] peasants and servicemen, continued their push eastward, but they had become accountable for their actions to the authorities, to be rewarded or punished.[32]

Toward the middle of the seventeenth century they fought their way through to the Eastern Ocean—the bodies of water that would be known as the Bering and Okhotsk Seas of the Pacific. Before 1650 they had passed through Bering Strait, made landfall in the Diomede Islands, ascended the Anadyr' River, discovered a portage from the Kolyma to Anadyr' that offered a safer route than the trek around the Chukchi Peninsula, and had a winter camp near the modern port of Okhotsk. Soon there were pilots who claimed to guide vessels around the Chukchi Peninsula.[33] They penetrated the Amur River basin and encountered and engaged the might of the Chinese empire. In the last half of the seventeenth century, the merchants and their men fought for mastery over the numerous, well-organized, and efficient inhabitants of the Kamchatka Peninsula, the Koriak, the Itel'men (Kamchadal), and their mainland neighbors and enemies, the Chukchi.

By the end of the seventeenth century and during the first decade of the eighteenth, they were exploring, and exploiting as a hunting ground, the Kuril Islands, and had amassed considerable knowledge of the Japanese territories to the south.[34] Tsar Alexis and, soon after his death, his heir and successor, Peter the Great, felt it was high time the government took a hand. Russian expansion into the North American continent in the eighteenth century took place when cooperation between private entrepreneurs and the government was entering a new phase. Peter the Great set the goal of building an empire able to compete with other powerful European nations on a global scale. He dreamed of a Pacific fleet with home ports in the North Pacific and systematic government-sponsored exploration of the arctic coasts of Eurasia, testing the feasibility of the Northeast Passage to China, Japan, and India, and extending sovereignty over the North American coast from Bering Strait to the Spanish possessions in California. The private entrepreneur, however, remained indispensable. He was to be encouraged, but his efforts were to yield to official governmental policies. In the end the private entrepreneur was to serve the state.

NOTES

1. S. V. Bakhrushin, "Russkoe prodvizhenie za Ural," in *S. V. Bakhrushin: Nauchnye trudy,* vol. 3, pt. 1 (Moscow: Izdatel'stvo Akademii nauk SSSR, 1955), 139; and idem, "Istoricheskii ocherk zaseleniia Sibiri do poloviny XIX veka," in *Ocherki po istorii kolonizatsii Severa i Sibiri* (Petrograd, 1922), 2: 32–34.

2. On the prehistoric population shifts I follow V. V. Bunak, ed., *Proiskhozhdenie i etnicheskaia istoriia russkogo naroda po antropologicheskim dannym,* Trudy Instituta etnografii, n.s., 88 (Moscow: Izdatel'stvo "Nauka," 1965); D. A. Machinskii, "Etnosotsial'nye i etnokul'turnye protsessy v Severnoi Rusi (period zarozhdeniia drevnerusskoi narodnosti)," in *Russkii Sever: Problemy etnokul'turnoi istorii, etnografii, fol'kloristiki,* ed. T. A. Bernshtam and K. V. Chistov (Leningrad: Izdatel'stvo "Nauka," 1986); T. A. Bernshtam, *Pomory: Formirovanie gruppy i sistema khoziaistva* (Leningrad: Izdatel'stvo "Nauka," 1978); and M. I. Belov, *Arkticheskoe moreplavanie s drevneishikh vremen do serediny XIX veka,* vol. 1 of *Istoriia otkrytiia i osvoeniia Severnogo morskogo puti,* ed.

Ia. Ia. Gakkel' et al. (Moscow: Morskoi transport, 1956), 21–37. On early Russian history, I follow George Vernadsky, *A History of Russia,* 3d rev. ed. (New Haven: Yale University Press, 1951), 2–26; Vernadsky's multivolume work of the same title, particularly vol. 1, *Ancient Russia,* and vol. 2, *Kievan Russia* (New Haven: Yale University Press, 1943–1948); and Nicholas V. Riasanovsky, *A History of Russia,* 3d ed. (New York: Oxford University Press, 1977). On the formation of the Russian White Sea littoral population, the Pomory, see Bernshtam, *Pomory.* See also A. P. Engelhardt, "The Murman," chap. 5 in *A Russian Province of the North* (Westminster: Archibald Constable and Company, 1899), and Bakhrushin's essays "Russkoe prodvizhenie za Ural" and "Istoricheskii ocherk."

3. Norse- or Norman-established trading centers and principalities probably existed earlier, such as Staraia Russa on Lake Il'men' and another one near the area of modern Astrakhan' (later shifted to the Taman' Peninsula, see Vernadsky, *History of Russia* [1951], 23–24), but traditionally the establishment of a Russian state is dated by historians to Riurik's taking control of Novgorod. There is some uncertainty about the dating of this latter event. Bernshtam, in her book *Pomory,* relying on the Ipat'evskaia chronicle, claims that Riurik first established himself at Ladoga in 862 and only later moved on to Novgorod. Ladoga remained the home ground; in 922, Oleg returned home from Kiev, died, and was buried there (*Pomory,* 21). Thus, the center of Scandinavian activity is placed in Ladoga, with Novgorod as a secondary base, and Kiev coming into prominence somewhat later. On this question see also A. V. Kuza, "Novgorodskaia zemlia," in *Drevnerusskie kniazhestva X–XIII vv.,* ed. L. G. Beskrovnyi (Moscow: Izdatel'stvo "Nauka," 1975), 144–201.

4. See Vernadsky, *History of Russia* (1951). Among major Russian historians who emphasized the commercial origin of the earliest Russian states were S. M. Solov'ev and V. O. Kliuchevskii. See also E. A. Rybina, *Arkheologicheskie ocherki istorii novgorodskoi torgovli X–XIV vv.* (Moscow: Izdatel'stvo Moskovskogo gosudarstvennogo universiteta, 1978).

5. Vernadsky, *History of Russia* (1951).

6. Robert J. Kerner quite rightly stresses the importance of utilization of waterways by Russians throughout their history, "from tribal community to world empire." He wrote: "The railroad, canal, and motor highway have followed through the portages chiefly along the lines laid down by this process" (*The Urge to the Sea* [Berkeley and Los Angeles: University of California Press, 1948], 103). Russian historians by and large take the role of waterways in Russian expansion for granted. Among those who emphasize this factor are S. V. Bakhrushin and his younger colleague M. I. Belov. An earlier author who stresses the importance of waterways is N. P. Zagoskin, *Russkie vodnye puti i sudovoe delo v dopetrovskoi Rusi (Materialy dlia opisaniia russkikh rek i istorii uluchsheniia ikh sudokhodnykh uslovii),* no. 16 (Kazan', 1910). For water routes to eastern Siberia, including those from the Upper Kama and Pechora Rivers, as well as the sea route to the Ob' and Yenisei in western Siberia, see S. V. Bakhrushin, "Puti v Sibir' v XVI–XVII vv.," in *Nauchnye trudy,* 3 (1): 72–136. On the homelands and traditions of Russian pioneers in Alaska, the early *promyshlenniki,* see Lydia T. Black, "Promyshlenniki... Who Were They?" in *Bering and Chirikov: The American Voyages and Their Impact,* ed. O. W. Frost (Anchorage: Alaska Historical Society, 1992), 279–290.

7. N. Ozertskovskoi, "Opisanie morzhovago promysla," *Sobranie sochinenii vybrannykh iz mesiatseslovov na raznye gody* (St. Petersburg: Imperatorskaia akademiia nauk, 1793), 10: 138–184; Osip Belomorskii, "Vzgliad na zapasy ptitselovnago promysla v Pomor'ie," *Morskoi sbornik* 36, no. 8 (1858): 121–140; Nils Storå, "Russian Walrus Hunting in Spitsbergen," *Etudes/Inuit/Studies* 11, no. 2 (1987): 117–137; Vadim Starkov et al., "Russkie poseleniia XVI v. na Spitzbergene," *Vestnik Akademii nauk SSSR,* no. 12 (1983): 109–113; K. V. Chistov and T. A. Bernshtam, eds., *Russkii Sever: Problemy etnografii i fol'klora* (Leningrad: Izdatel'stvo "Nauka," 1981); M. I. Belov, "Russkie poliarnye plavaniia i morskie promysly na evropeiskom severe Rossii v XVI–XVII vekakh: Pokhody na Novuiu Zemliu i Spitsbergen," chap. 3 in *Arkticheskoe moreplavanie,* 46–70; B. D. Emerov, "K istorii kitoboinogo promysla na russkom Severe," *Letopis' Severa* 3 (1962): 188–200; L. L. Breitfus, *Morskoi zverinyi promysel v Belom more i severnom Ledovitom okeane* (St. Petersburg, 1905).

8. On transplantation of the maritime traditions of the Pomory to eastern Siberia, see M. I. Belov, "Pervye morskie i sukhoputnye ekspeditsii v severo-vostochnuiu Sibir': Vostochno-sibirskie poliarnye morekhody," chap. 9 in *Arkticheskoe moreplavanie,* 146–148.

9. S. F. Platonov, "Inozemtsy na Russkom Severe v XVI–XVII vv.," in *Ocherki po istorii kolonizatsii Severa i Sibiri* (Petrograd, 1923), 7–17; A. Ts. Merzon and Iu. A. Tikhonov, *Rynok Ustiuga Velikogo v period skladyvaniia vserossiiskogo rynka (XVII vek)* (Moscow: Izdatel'stvo Akademii nauk SSSR, 1960), 240–241.

10. Bunak, *Proiskhozhdenie i etnicheskaia istoriia,* 261–265; V. V. Politov, *Iarensk: istoricheskii ocherk* (Leningrad: Izdatel'stvo "Nauka," 1978); N. D. Konakov, ed., *Genezis i evoliutsiia traditsionnoi kul'tury komi,* Trudy Instituta iazyka, literatury i istorii, no. 43 (Syktyvkar: Akademiia nauk SSSR, Ural'skoe otdelenie, Komi nauchnyi tsentr, 1989); N. D. Konakov, *Komi: Okhotniki i rybolovy vo vtoroi polovine XIX–nachale XX v.* (Moscow: Izdatel'stvo "Nauka," 1983); idem, *Etnicheskaia ekologiia i traditsionnaia kul'tura komi,* Seriia preprintov "Nauchnye doklady," no. 107 (Syktyvkar: Akademiia nauk SSSR, Komi filial, 1984); idem, *Vodnye sredstva soobshcheniia naroda komi,* Seriia preprintov "Nauchnye doklady," no. 45 (Syktyvkar: Akademiia nauk SSSR, Komi filial, 1979); L. P. Lashuk, *Formirovanie narodnosti komi* (Moscow: Izdatel'stvo Moskovskogo gosudarstvennogo universiteta, 1972); V. A. Semenov, *Etnografiia komi (zyrian)* (Syktyvkar: Permskii universitet, 1986); L. N. Zherebtsov, *Istoriko-kul'turnye vzaimootnosheniia komi s sosednimi narodami* (Moscow: Izdatel'stvo "Nauka," 1982); E. A. Savel'eva, *Perm' Vychegodskaia: K voprosu o proiskhozhdenii naroda komi* (Moscow: Izdatel'stvo "Nauka," 1971). For specific data on Komi participation in the expansion into Siberia, including to Anadyr' and Penzhina Bay (Koriak territory in the Siberian northeast), see A. Napalkov et al., eds., *Rodniki parmy* (Syktykvar: Komi knizhnoe izdatel'stvo, 1989).

11. The trading activity of the city of Ustiug is an excellent example. See Merzon and Tikhonov, *Rynok Ustiuga Velikogo;* S. V. Bakhrushin, "Pokruta na sobolinykh promyslakh XVII v.," in *Nauchnye trudy,* 3 (1): 198–211; idem, "Torgovye krest'iane v XVII v.," in *Nauchnye trudy,* vol. 2 (Moscow: Izdatel'stvo Akademii nauk SSSR, 1954), 118–133; idem, "Promyshlennye predpriiatiia russkikh torgovykh liudei v XVII v.," in ibid., 224–253; V. A. Oborin, "Permskie posadskie liudi v XVI–XVIII vv. (k voprosu o formirovanii torgovo-promyshlennoi verkhushki)," in *Promyshlennost' i torgovlia v Rossii XVII–XVIII vv.,* ed. A. A. Preobrazhenskii (Moscow: Izdatel'stvo "Nauka," 1983), 27–42; P. A. Kolesnikov, "Promyslovo-remeslennaia deiatel'nost' severnogo krest'ianstva v XVIII v.," in ibid., 138–153; V. S. Barashkova, "Torgovlia ryboi i sol'iu belozerskikh posadskikh liudei i krest'ian v kontse XVI–nachale XVII v.," in ibid., 192–202.

12. A. L. Khoroshkevich, *Torgovlia Velikogo Novgoroda s pribaltikoi i zapadnoi Evropoi v XIV–XV vekakh* (Moscow: Izdatel'stvo Akademii nauk SSSR, 1963); Oleg V. Bychkov, "Russian Fur Gathering Traditions in the Eighteenth Century," *Pacifica* 2, no. 2 (1990): 80–87; Bernshtam, *Pomory.* See also R. V. Kamenetskaia, "Russkie starozhily poliarnogo areala," in *Russkii Sever: Problemy etnokul'turnoi istorii, etnografii, fol'kloristiki,* ed. T. A. Bernshtam and K. V. Chistov (Leningrad: Izdatel'stvo "Nauka," 1986), 67–81, for an extensive listing of literature on this subject.

13. On the social order of the northern settlers see S. V. Bakhrushin, "Mangazeiskaia mirskaia obshchina v XVII v.," in *Nauchnye trudy,* 3 (1): 297–330. On the financing and labor relations of the fur hunting enterprises in Siberia, see Bakhrushin, "Pokruta." On the organization and social order of the fur-procuring *artels* in Siberia, see Oleg V. Bychkov, "Russian Hunters in eastern Siberia in the Seventeenth Century: Lifestyle and Economy," *Arctic Anthropology* 31, no. 1 (1994): 72–85.

    On the structure of marine mammal hunting associated with long-distance voyaging, see "O kotliannykh ili artel'nykh promyslakh," a copy of the set of customary labor rules written down by walrus hunters of the Mezen' district for Count Petr Shuvalov and transmitted to N. Ozertskovskoi by Arkhangel'sk notary public Aleksandr Fomin. Ozertskovskoi published this set of rules as part of his article "Opisanie morzhovago promysla." On the transfer to Alaska, see Lydia T. Black, "Creoles in Russian America," *Pacifica* 2, no. 2 (1990): 142–155, and idem, "Promyshlenniki... Who Were They?"

14. S. F. Platonov, "Proshloe russkogo Severa," in *Ocherki po istorii kolonizatsii Severa i Sibiri* (Petrograd, 1923); Bakhrushin, "Russkoe prodvizhenie za Ural," 137–160.

15. Iakov Iakovlevich Friz, "Khronologicheskaia letopis' goroda Ustiuga Velikago," *Severnyi arkhiv* 11 (June 1822): 321–332; K. N. Serbina, ed., *Ustiuzhskii letopisnyi svod (arkhangelogorodskii letopisets)* (Moscow-Leningrad: Izdatel'stvo Akademii nauk SSSR, 1950); A. A. Titov, *Letopis' Velikoustiuzhskaia,* pt. 1 (Moscow: A. K. Trapeznikov, 1889), pt. 2 (Moscow: Bragin, 1905?); "Rossiiskaia istoriia: Nechto o 'piatinakh Novgorodskikh' i v osobennosti o strane, izvestnoi izdrevle pod imenem 'Vagi,'" *Severnyi arkhiv* 9 (1827): 3–34; 10 (1827): 89–120; 11 (1827): 189–209; 12 (1827): 271–289.

16. George V. Lantzeff and Richard A. Pierce, *Eastward to Empire: Exploration and Conquest on the Russian Open Frontier, to 1750* (Montreal: McGill-Queen's University Press, 1973), 81–107. Kerner, *Urge to the Sea;* Khoroshkevich, *Torgovlia Velikogo Novgoroda;* Kuza, "Novgorodskaia zemlia."

17. The Khanty and Mansi are known as the Ostyak/Vogul in early sources. Their territory at one time extended to the west of the Urals, to the Upper Pechora River basin and in all probability to the Upper Vychegda (S. V. Bakhrushin, "Ostiatskie i vogul'skie kniazhestva v XVI–XVII vv.," in *Nauchnye trudy,* vol. 3, pt. 2 [Moscow: Izdatel'stvo Akademii nauk SSSR, 1955], 86–152).

18. On the leadership and military technology and the military raids and trade of the Ob'-Ugrians see Bakhrushin, "Ostiatskie i vogul'skie kniazhestva."

19. M. I. Belov, *Mangazeia* (Leningrad: Gidrometeoizdat, 1969), 22.

20. Khoroshkevich, *Torgovlia Velikogo Novgoroda,* 51–52; Bakhrushin, "Russkoe prodvizhenie za Ural."

21. Lantzeff and Pierce, *Eastward to Empire,* 36–37. On Russian penetration to the Yenisei by the late 1500s, see Bakhrushin, "Russkoe prodvizhenie za Ural," 142.

22. Serbina, *Ustiuzhskii letopisnyi svod;* Kuza, "Novgorodskaia zemlia," 144–201; Friz, "Khronologicheskaia letopis'," *Severnyi arkhiv* 11 (June 1822): 321–332; 12 (June 1822): 401–412; 13 (July 1822): 19–29, 103–118, 221–234. On trade as a primary means of interaction, see Raymond H. Fisher, *The Russian Fur Trade, 1550–1700* (Berkeley and Los Angeles: University of California Press, 1943), 18–19.

23. See the benchmark publication by Raymond Fisher, *The Russian Fur Trade, 1550–1700,* specifically chap. 4, "The Acquisition of Furs by the Muscovite State"; Lantzeff and Pierce, *Eastward to Empire;* and the works of James R. Gibson, *Feeding the Russian Fur Trade: Provisionment of the Okhotsk Seaboard and the Kamchatka Peninsula, 1639–1856* (Madison: University of Wisconsin Press, 1969) and *Imperial Russia in Frontier America: The Changing Geography of Supply of Russian America, 1784–1867* (New York: Oxford University Press, 1976). Though Gibson does not focus specifically on the iasak as the major source of furs for the Russian Crown, this assumption is implicit in his presentation. For a specific discussion of the iasak as a mechanism of fur acquisition by the state, see George V. Lantzeff, *Siberia in the Seventeenth Century: A Study of the Colonial Administration* (Berkeley and Los Angeles: University of California Press, 1943), 123–132, and Fisher, *Russian Fur Trade,* 49–61. For a fundamental analysis of the iasak, see S. V. Bakhrushin, "Iasak v Sibiri v XVII v.," in *Nauchnye trudy,* 3 (2): 49–85, first published in *Sibirskie ogni* (Novosibirsk), no. 3 (1927): 95–129.

24. Lantzeff, *Siberia in the Seventeenth Century,* 4–18.

25. N. N. Ogloblin, "'Zhenskii vopros' v Sibiri v XVII veke," *Istoricheskii vestnik* (July 1890): 194–207; I. S. Gurvich, "Russkie na severo-vostoke Sibiri v XVII v.," in *Sibirskii etnograficheskii sbornik* 5, Trudy Instituta etnografii, n.s., 84 (Moscow: Izdatel'stvo Akademii nauk SSSR, 1963), 71–91, gender relations discussed on pp. 78–81; V. A. Aleksandrov, "Cherty semeinogo stroia u russkogo naseleniia," chap. 5 in *Russkoe naselenie Sibiri XVII–nachala XVIII v. (Eniseiskii krai),* Trudy Instituta etnografii, n.s., 87 (Moscow: Izdatel'stvo "Nauka," 1964), 119–139.

26. Belov, *Mangazeia.*

27. Vladimir Mikhailovich Zenzinov, *Russkoe ust'e Iakutskoi oblasti, Verkhoianskago okruga* (Moscow: P. P. Riabushinskii, 1913), 113–114.

28. This is taken for granted by all specialists. See Bakhrushin as cited; Terence E. Armstrong, *Russian Settlement in the North* (Cambridge, England: Cambridge University Press, 1965) and inter alia Aleksandrov, *Russkoe naselenie Sibiri.*

29. The main complex, constructed on the largest island of the Solovetskii archipelago in the White Sea, where prehistoric Saami erected their sacred stone cairns, eventually became a formidable fortress. It withstood attempts by foreign intruders (Englishmen, Dutchmen, and Swedes) and the forces of Moscow sent to subdue the rebellious monks who in the seventeenth century took a stand to the death in defense of the Old Belief against the church reform of Patriarch Nikon. Though younger in age than many other northern monasteries and churches, to this day it remains the symbol of Orthodox and Old Believer spirituality. S. V. Bakhrushin, "Legenda o Vasilii Mangazeiskom," in *Nauchnye trudy,* 3 (1): 331–354; Black, "Promyshlenniki ... Who Were They?"

30. On the role of the Stroganov family and Ermak's expedition, see George Vernadsky, *A History of Russia,* vol. 5, *The Tsardom of Moscow, 1547–1682* (New Haven: Yale University Press, 1969), 175–182; Lantzeff and Pierce, *Eastward to Empire,* 81–107; and Fisher, *Russian Fur Trade,* 23–27. See also Vasilii Shishenko, comp., *Permskaia letopis' s 1263–1881 g.,* 2 pts. (Perm': Gubernskaia zemskaia uprava, 1881–1882); D. Smyshliaev, comp., *Istochniki i posobiia dlia izucheniia Permskago kraia* (Perm': Gubernskaia zemskaia uprava, 1876); A. A. Dmitriev, *Istoricheskii ocherk Permskago kraia* (Perm': Gubernskaia zemskaia uprava, 1896); Aleksandr Dmitriev, *Permskaia starina: Sbornik istoricheskikh statei i materialov preimushchestvenno o Permskom krae,* 2 vols., 8 pts. (Perm', 1889–1900). These are also very useful general sources on the Russian North, including the expansion eastward beyond the Urals, regional economics, peasantry questions, and extensive listings of rare materials.

31. S. V. Bakhrushin, "Agenty russkikh torgovykh liudei v XVII v.," in *Nauchnye trudy,* 2: 134–153, first published in 1929, and idem, "Torgovye krest'iane v XVII v.," first published in 1928.

32. Gurvich, "Russkie na severo-vostoke Sibiri."

33. A. V. Efimov, ed., *Otkrytiia russkikh zemleprokhodtsev i poliarnykh morekhodov XVII veka na severo-vostoke Azii: Sbornik dokumentov,* comp. N. S. Orlova (Moscow: Gosudarstvennoe izdatel'stvo geograficheskoi literatury, 1951), 44.

34. S. V. Bakhrushin, "Puti v Vostochnuiu Sibir'," in *Nauchnye trudy,* 3 (1): 111–136. Lantzeff and Pierce, *Eastward to Empire.*

FIGURE 2. Alexis (Aleksei Mikhailovich; 1629–1676), tsar of Russia 1645–1676.
Courtesy Slavic and Baltic Division, New York Public Library, Astor, Lenox, and Tilden Foundations.

CHAPTER TWO

The Hand of Moscow

THE PRINCES OF MOSCOW HAD SHOWN AN INTEREST IN NORTHEAST expansion as early as the beginning of the fourteenth century, when Ivan Kalita, grand prince of Moscow (1328–1341), advanced a claim to the Pechora region. To support the claim, he reportedly sent a twenty-man hunting crew to the mouth of the Pechora River by sea every year, and Novgorod issued them a safe conduct.[1] In the fifteenth century, following the conquest of the remnants of the Mongolian Golden Horde, the Moscow rulers of the growing centralized Russian state began to look toward the territories beyond the Ural Mountains. In 1483, Ivan III sent a large expedition which reached the confluence of the Irtysh and Ob' Rivers. A few years later another Moscow force reached the future location of Berezovo on the Ob' River. According to some eighteenth-century Russian historians, Ivan the Terrible also sent an expedition to Siberia, and this expedition, which finally returned in the reign of Ivan's son, Fedor, reported that mighty seas washed the northern and—more significantly—the eastern shores of Siberia.

During the reign of Vasilii III (following that of Ivan III), Moscow created two iasak collection districts in the region beyond the Urals.[2] A system of establishing small fortified outposts (*ostrog* or sometimes *krepost'*), garrisoned by the tsar's servicemen or cossacks, came into being. Moscow levied customs duties on internal trade, and soon many of these ostrogs served as customs stations as well as iasak collection centers. By the time the Romanov dynasty came to occupy the Russian throne in 1613, the private entrepreneurs, organizers and participants of fur-gathering expeditions, and traders had to surrender one-tenth of their catch or cargo as customs dues. Almost simultaneously, there arose the practice of licensing trading expeditions, including those that penetrated new lands. Customs clearance was required for any goods carried on such expeditions.[3]

In 1626, Tsar Mikhail Romanov ordered the compilation of the first official map of Siberia.[4] As early as the fifteenth century, the government's interest in Siberian territories had exceeded the acquisition of new fur procurement areas. The location of silver, gold, copper, and other mineral wealth received increasing priority. By the seventeenth century, although fur collection continued to be an important source of state revenue, the search for raw materials became a dominant motivation.[5]

International trade considerations also played a role. About 1600, Mangazeia on the Taz Arm at the mouth of the Ob' River, an old outpost of the Pomory fur hunters and traders, was rebuilt as a fortified, state-supported port. It also served as a trading center and a base for military expansion eastward to the Yenisei and beyond. Moscow worried about foreigners' penetration of the Russian north and specifically forbade foreign entry into Mangazeia. To prevent foreign access to furs, mineral resources, and, above all, to new trade routes, Moscow forbade sea voyaging along the northern coasts east of the northern Dvina,[6] though the Pomory continued to use it clandestinely. Behind the fear of foreign intrusion was the fear that foreigners might succeed in navigating a route to the Orient along the Siberian coast.

The idea of a northern sea route from Europe to China along Russia's northern coasts was current in Russia from the sixteenth century. In 1525, it was introduced into Western European discourse. When in Rome, Moscow's envoy Dmitrii Gerasimov discussed this possibility and it was published almost immediately by the Italian historian Paulo Giovio. Giovio even stated that Ivan the Terrible planned such an expedition.[7] In England, the idea was put forward by John Dee about 1577,[8] followed by many proposals for a northern ship route, and in 1652 the Swedish trade agent Johan Rodes mentioned a plan to dispatch foreign, non-Russian officers "on a voyage to America" via Siberia. A generation later, a high Russian official discussed the Siberian route to America with a visiting Jesuit, Philip Avril.[9]

Unable to initiate such an expedition, or unwilling to commit the required resources, the central government in Moscow began to dispatch small units of cossacks and servicemen on explorations (on which the latter could collect furs for private sale as part of their recompense for service). More often the government assigned its agents, almost without exception cossacks or servicemen on active duty, to selected, privately launched trading expeditions. The duties of these governmental agents included collecting iasak from aboriginal inhabitants in the newly penetrated areas, and keeping records of furs obtained by the party in barter or hunting in order to ensure that the traders would pay the proper one-tenth tax. They were required to keep notes or journals and report to the government authorities on geography, environmental conditions, and population in the visited areas. As the main thrust of the expansion proceeded along the coast and the river systems, pilots were licensed by the government, and shipbuilders transferred from the northern Russian shipbuilding centers to various launching areas throughout Siberia. Yakutsk, founded on the Lena River in 1632, was such a center, as were Zashiversk on the Indigirka River, which the Russians explored by 1633, and fortified Nizhnekolymsk and other ostrogs established later on the Kolyma River.

These governmentally supported outposts served also as centers of Russian-Siberian native trade. At several sites annual fairs were held, a practice encouraged by the government (eventually, in the eighteenth century, the fairs operated under governmental supervision). At Zashiversk, beyond the walls of the ostrog,

> annual fairs attracted a multitude of traders carrying priceless furs from far and wide, from the taiga (the forest), the tundra and the forested tundra belt. They were met by the merchants emerging from the gates in colorful dress, decorated with bright seed beads, carrying iron and drinking pitchers...and then both the priest and the shaman, each in his own manner, would bless the goods disposed upon the snow and the trade would commence.[10]

Yeniseisk and Yakutsk were the garrison towns, home bases of the Cossack detachments. By 1649, 350 servicemen were stationed at Yakutsk. From there exploration parties were dispatched by local officials and *voevodas* (military governors) in rapid succession along the Arctic Ocean coast and into the interior, where these quasi-trading, quasi-governmental and military parties ascended the major rivers and explored the tributaries and portages to river basins farther east and south.

It was not long before routes to the Pacific were found. Starting in 1638 out of Butalskii ostrog on the Aldan, a tributary of the Lena, Ivan Iur'iev Moskvitin reached the Sea of Okhotsk in 1639 and in 1640–1641 the mouth of the Amur River and possibly Sakhalin Island.[11] Between 1643 and 1646, Vasilii Poiarkov crossed the divide between the upper reaches of the Aldan and the Zeia, a tributary of the Amur River. His party eventually descended the Amur to the Sea of Okhotsk and proceeded along the coast northward, reaching the location of Moskvitin's camp. Consequently, expeditions were planned almost immediately thereafter to reach the Pacific Ocean by sea, from the north. The staging areas were on major rivers: the Lena, Yana, Indigirka, and Kolyma. The first documented attempt to round the Chukchi Peninsula was made in 1646 under the command of Isai Ignatii Mezenets (a native of the Mezen' region on the White Sea). He sailed probably as far as Chaun Bay.[12] Ogloblin, analyzing primary documents of the eighteenth century, believed that Mikhail Stadukhin reached Anadyr' from the Kolyma by sea, went overland from Anadyr' to Penzhina Bay, an arm of the northern Okhotsk Sea, and again by sea reached the Okhota River.[13] He also indicated that Ivan Erastov reached Anadyr' by sea from Kolyma in 1646, though modern scholars believe that this expedition was only planned, never executed.[14] Several other attempts were made which, as far as is known, were unsuccessful—the documentation is inconclusive. Then, in 1647, the Cossack Semeon Dezhnev took his turn at reaching the Pacific from the Arctic. His story, similar to that of many lesser known explorers, is worth recounting here.

Semeon Dezhnev,[15] a native of the Russian north, had been recruited in 1630 for Siberian service in Ustiug the Great. For eight years he served in Tobol'sk and Yeniseisk (becoming a Cossack), then was sent to Yakutiia in 1639 or perhaps even earlier. In fact, he is said to have been a member of the Cossack detachment under Beketov, who is credited with founding Yakutsk in 1632. Dezhnev married a Yakut woman, Abaikada Siuchi of Barogonskaia district. (Their son, Liubim, thanks to his father a hereditary Cossack, served later in the Siberian east.) In 1643 Dezhnev, together with Mikhail Stadukhin and Dmitrii Zyrian, sailed along the seacoast as far as the Kolyma River mouth, at that time the easternmost Russian frontier. Stadukhin was a fellow northerner and Cossack who had been active in eastern Siberia since 1630. He was also a nephew of Gusel'nikov, a wealthy, well-known merchant with interests in the Siberian and international trade.[16] Stadukhin pioneered Russian penetration of the Kolyma River basin, in 1643 founding Srednekolymsk, the first Russian settlement on that river,[17] and learned about the river Pogycha, which was the local, probably Yukagir, name for the Anadyr' River.[18]

Dezhnev, together with Fedot Alekseev, set out in 1647 on such an expedition, but they were unable to round the Chukchi Peninsula. Alekseev (also known as Popov and Kholmogorets), a native of Kholmogory, an ancient city of the White Sea region, and an associate of the great Moscow merchant Usov who was active in the Ustiug trade, immediately embarked on a second attempt in 1648. Dezhnev was attached to Alekseev's merchant expedition as a government agent. Two other participants, Andreev and Astaf'iev, agents of the Gusel'nikov merchant house, provided their own vessel and men, while Alekseev provided five vessels and the majority of the men (their exact number is not known). Dezhnev himself, in keeping with the custom of the times, recruited and equipped a group of men (eighteen or nineteen) for fur gathering for private profit. The expedition was joined by another group, mustering thirty men, led by the serviceman Gerasim Ankudinov, who earlier had tried to have Dezhnev's appointment rescinded. Ankudinov traveled without a license or authorization but had his own vessel. The combined total is believed to have been 89 men, but may have been as high as 121. The party traveled in seven vessels, the traditional koch.[19] At least one woman, Alekseev's Yakut wife, was with the party.[20] Except for Dezhnev, none of the organizers and leaders of the expedition survived to tell their tale. He rounded the northeastern extremity of Asia, made landfall at the Diomede Islands, sailed through Bering Strait, reached the mouth of the Anadyr' River, which empties into the Bering Sea, and, ascending this river, founded the Anadyr' ostrog.

Dezhnev reported that sixty-four out of eighty-nine men perished. This total probably does not include losses from Ankudinov's koch, as he was not an official member of the expedition. Four out of seven vessels were lost before the party reached Bering Strait (two wrecked in a storm, two others lost without a trace).[21] Ankudinov's koch was wrecked on the Chukchi Peninsula in or near Bering Strait.[22] Alekseev's vessel was carried south beyond the mouth of the Anadyr' River, and was believed to have made landfall on

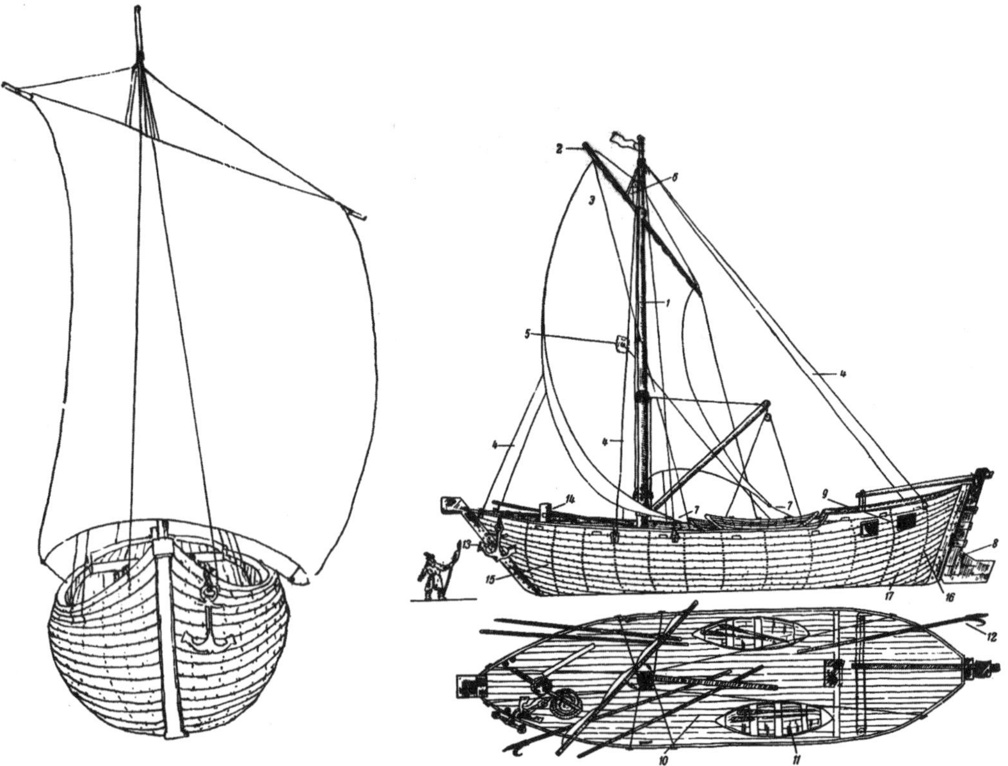

FIGURE 3. Russian koch, designed for sailing in ice-infested waters.
From Belov, 1951, pp. 73, 75.

the eastern shore of the Kamchatka Peninsula in the vicinity of the Kamchatka River.[23] The fate of the other two vessels is disputed by scholars to this day. Locally, in Siberia, it was widely believed that the lost vessels reached safety on the American continent and there either founded a settlement of their own or found succor among the Inuit and eventually became assimilated by them. Denied by many scholars (though by no means all), this legend refuses to die.[24] Some believe that seventeenth-century Russian sailors visited Alaska more than once.[25]

Many attempts were made to sail the same route after Dezhnev's voyage and several attempted the route in the opposite direction, from the mouth of the Anadyr' River to the Kolyma or Lena, traveling north and west. M. I. Belov compiled a chronological table of such sea voyages between 1633 and 1689, in which he lists 177 voyages of record, most of them apparently uncompleted. One attempt to round the Chukchi Peninsula by traveling from the mouth of the Anadyr' River may have been completed.[26] Belov, like Efimov, another well-known Soviet historian of arctic exploration and cartography, frequently notes that the surviving records represent only a portion of the sea traffic east of the Lena. Mostly, the records concern the voyages to which cossacks or Cossack detachments were assigned. Purely commercial voyages may not be represented in the surviving official records. Belov notes that in 1645 alone the Yakutsk customs office issued fifty-one travel documents authorizing sea voyaging and transport of goods to the northeast. Between June and July 1647 the same office issued 404 travel documents authorizing travel "down the Lena and by sea to the Indigirka and Kolyma for trade and industry."[27]

At least one individual, Nikita Voropaev, was for many years a pilot for the sea route from the Lena to Zanos'ie, the region beyond the Chukchi Peninsula.[28] In 1662, Ivan Rubets, with two kochi, rounded the Chukchi Peninsula for the express purpose of taking walrus ivory at the mouth of the Anadyr'. From there he sailed on and reached the Kamchatka River. It appears that he traveled from the Lena River to Kamchatka in one navigational season. The next year, having wintered on the Kamchatka, he sailed north to the Anadyr', and in the fall of 1663 ascended the Anadyr' River and took over the command of the ostrog there.[29] Recently, a Russian geographer proposed that Taras Stadukhin and his crew of ninety (whose voyage in 1668 or 1669 has for many years mystified researchers) landed in Kotzebue Sound in Alaska and crossed the Seward Peninsula from the Buckland River to the Koyuk River, which empties into Norton Sound.[30]

Some scholars believe that Dezhnev himself might have touched upon Alaska's shores, and not only at the Diomede Islands in Bering Strait; if not Dezhnev, then someone else must have made landfall there. This hypothesis derives from the late seventeenth to early eighteenth-century European (as well as Russian) cartography of northeast Asia.[31] Proponents of this hypothesis also believe that the cartographic evidence refutes another myth, firmly entrenched in the literature, that Dezhnev's voyage and information about the strait were not known to Russian authorities until G. F. Müller found documents pertaining to the voyage in the Yakutsk archives in 1736.[32]

Within a year of Dezhnev's voyage (and possibly even prior to his exploit)[33] there was local talk about the "New" or "Great Land" to the east of the Chukchi Peninsula, to be reached by sea. This land was often identified with America. In fact, the eastern Siberian servicemen and promyshlenniki believed (and this belief spread very rapidly among Russian sailors and certainly must have reached the capital) that the islands they sighted along

Siberia's Arctic Ocean shores formed part of the American mainland. They believed that this mainland stretched in a belt from east to west. On the other hand, there was talk about an "Impassable Cape" between the "Lena and Amur Seas," and this apparently resulted in representations of a land link between America and Asia on some European maps. Most scholars believed that this designation applied to the Chukchi Peninsula, but in reality, as Polevoi argued, it is much more likely that it referred to Kamchatka.[34] The arguments are likely to continue for many years to come.

On Russian maps from as early as 1667, primitive and inaccurate as many were, northeastern Siberia is shown as bounded by the sea on the north and east. When Peter the Great acted to establish a Russian naval presence in eastern and northeastern Siberia, he must have been cognizant of this. In fact, in 1710, on his orders, the Siberian voevoda (military administrator of a region and troop commander) Trauernikht dispatched Ivan L'vov to the northeast for more precise information. On his heels traveled the Cossack Petr Popov and comrades, out of Anadyr' to the Chukchi Peninsula. Popov collected considerable information about the Great Land beyond the strait and about the islands between the two continents.[35] But by 1710 "The Great Land" (Alaska) was already shown beyond Bering Strait on several Russian manuscript charts, and inscriptions on these charts, as well as the recorded testimonies by servicemen preserved in Russian archives, leave no doubt that some accurate information was known about the inhabitants of northwestern Alaska.[36]

By the beginning of the eighteenth century this land was shown as well on some European maps derived from Russian sources. There is little doubt that information supplied by Dezhnev was incorporated in several European maps, notably those by Nicolaas Witsen (1687, 1698, and 1705) and Homann in his famous atlas (1725).[37] Significantly, these European maps showing the strait and the Diomede Islands all appeared during the reign of Peter the Great when the proposals for reaching China, Japan, and India via the northern sea route were being renewed and when a major governmental effort was being initiated to launch naval expeditions to explore and chart the entire Siberian polar and Pacific coasts and to reach America from Siberia.[38] Peter and his close associates must have been aware of the available knowledge about this region: the map of the Chukchi Peninsula and Bering Strait that appears in Homann's atlas had been transmitted to the cartographer by Iakov Brius in 1722 on direct orders of Peter the Great.[39]

FIGURE 4. Peter the Great (1672–1725), tsar of Russia 1682–1721, emperor of Russia 1721–1725.
Courtesy Slavic and Baltic Division, New York Public Library, Astor, Lenox, and Tilden Foundations.

It was Peter's close collaborator Ivan Kirilov who eventually formulated plans for exploration of and Russian expansion to the

American continent, plans no doubt supported by Peter himself. Peter, however, did not live to see these plans carried out, except for the establishment of the first Russian Pacific port, that of Okhotsk,[40] as a springboard for overseas expansion.

Meanwhile, parallel to the growth in interest in the extreme north and east had come a Russian push to the Sea of Okhotsk with a view toward establishing a route to Japan. The Russians had reached the Okhotsk or Lama Sea, as they called it, in 1639 (see above). This movement was associated with the Russian penetration of the Amur River basin. That same year they built an ostrog at the mouth of the Ul'ia River, south of modern Okhotsk, and soon gained the upper hand over the local Evenk and Even (Tungus and Lamut) population. In 1646, they explored the Shantar Islands and Sakhalin. In the same year, they moved along the coast northward to the mouth of the Okhota River, where they won a major battle over the Evenk. Two winter outposts (*zimov'ie*) were eventually established. One of these was on the site where in 1642 Ivan Moskvitin had built a small outpost, one that had been soon destroyed.[41]

In 1652, Ivan Nagiba, traveling by sea out of the mouth of the Amur River northward, founded a winter outpost on the Tugur River. Four years later, Mikhail Stadukhin, Dezhnev's sometime comrade but more often rival, spearheaded a movement to the northern Okhotsk Sea coast from the northeast, out of Kamchatka, where he arrived in 1656 out of Anadyr' by sea. He founded the Tauiskii ostrog that year. Beginning in 1661, the Yakutsk administration maintained a command or a small garrison at the Okhotsk ostrog for defense against the Evenk. In 1665, the ostrog was rebuilt and enlarged at another location in the same vicinity and the garrison strengthened.

Armed conflict with the Evenk was incessant; between 1662 and 1680 more than 365 Russian servicemen were killed. In response the government enlarged the garrison at Okhotsk ostrog in 1681 and founded a fortified winter outpost (which later became an ostrog) at the mouth of the Uda River. In 1688, the Okhotsk ostrog was again enlarged and significant fortifications were built; it had become a town, one that remained relatively unchanged until the establishment of the naval port in 1711. By that time the Kamchatka Peninsula was under Russian rule. The Koriak accepted the Russians as allies in defense against the Chukchi while the Itel'men (Kamchadal) had been largely subjugated, though major uprisings were yet to come. The Russians were also moving into the northern Kuril Islands.[42]

Overland communications with the administrative and supply centers presented major problems and a southern sea route to settlements on Kamchatka was deemed essential. The first attempt, made in 1711, out of Tauiskii ostrog, was unsuccessful, largely because no suitable vessels had been constructed for the expedition.[43] In 1713, Peter the Great issued a special order to establish a sea route to Kamchatka, and the Siberian Governor Matvei Gagarin immediately ordered the Yakutsk voevoda to carry out the order. The next year, 1714, again on Peter's direct orders, four White Sea (Arkhangel'sk) navigators, among them Nikifor Treska and Kondratii Moshkov, were dispatched to Okhotsk, and two Swedish prisoners of war with seagoing experience who were then in Siberia were recruited to go there as well. Sailors and an experienced shipwright and two assistants were dispatched, and equipment and supplies sent for outfitting seagoing vessels. In May 1714, the first vessel of the Pacific flotilla was built. It was an Arkhangel'sk type *lod'ia*, built in the manner of those preferred by the Mezen' sailors who traveled to Novaia Zemlia and Spitsbergen. Skippered by the Arkhangel'sk navigator Treska, under the overall command of the Cossack Kuz'ma Sokolov,[44] this vessel accomplished the first round-trip between Okhotsk and Kamchatka in two seasons (1716–1717). At this time, too, the Yakut commander, voevoda Ya. A. El'chin, was to head a large expedition (aborted 1719) whose task was to map Eastern Siberia from Kolyma and the Chukchi Peninsula to the Amur River.[45]

In 1719, Peter dispatched two geodesists (surveyors or topographers), Evreinov and Luzhin, to chart the Kamchatka coasts and the Kuril Islands. Locating the American coasts in relation to Kamchatka was specifically mentioned in their instruction; in fact, Peter appears to have been convinced that America lay not too far beyond the eastern horizon.[46] The Russian empire was set to assert its presence in the northern Pacific waters.

During the 1720s, preparations for broader efforts continued. One of El'chin's subordinates from the planned 1719 mapping expedition to the Amur, Navigator Prokopii Nagiba, in 1720 proposed an expedition to the Great Land. He was ready to sail out of the Anadyr' in 1725, but his vessel was crushed by the spring ice. Two other Anadyr' servicemen, Afanasii Mel'nikov and Vasilii Shipitsyn, attempted during the same season to reach the Great Land, but were apparently unsuccessful. White Sea navigators and shipwrights continued to arrive at Okhotsk. Ivan Butin of Mezen', who, like Treska and Moshkov, later served under Bering and participated in the Shestakov expedition, had arrived in 1723.

Peter the Great, in preparation for dispatching the Russian Naval Expedition to the strait between Asia and America, was building up Okhotsk as the expedition's base and had his navigators testing the sea route from Okhotsk to Kamchatka's western and eastern coasts. The expedition was to be commanded by Vitus Bering.

On 23 December 1724, Peter the Great, mortally ill, signed Bering's instructions.[47] The instruction was implemented after Peter's death, during the reign of his widow, Catherine I, who ruled 1725–1727, and his grandson, Peter II (1727–1730), while most of Peter's close collaborators were still in office.[48]

Officially, Bering's first voyage lasted from 6 February 1725 to 1 March 1730. Bering arrived in Okhotsk in October 1726. There F. Galkin of Yakutsk had been engaged since 1724 in building a vessel for Bering, and Bering's own officer, Chaplin, had begun construction of a sewn-plank vessel (*shitik*), the *Fortuna*, one of two in which Bering sailed in 1727 to Kamchatka, directly to the east coast, to Nizhne-Kamchatsk's outpost. At Nizhne-Kamchatsk, Bering built the *Sv. Arkhangel Gavriil* (*Saint Gabriel the Archangel*). That summer, the sturdy little vessel sailed out of Nizhne-Kamchatsk and passed through the strait from the Bering Sea to the Arctic Ocean. In 1730, members of the expedition were back home in St. Petersburg.

FIGURE 5. Catherine I (1684–1727), wife of Peter the Great, empress of Russia 1725–1727.
Courtesy Slavic and Baltic Division, New York Public Library, Astor, Lenox, and Tilden Foundations.

That year, in 1730, Anna, the daughter of Peter the Great's brother Ioann, ascended the throne. In this new reign Peter's men were falling from power. Some died on the scaffold, others under torture, and a small number, some of them branded and mutilated, were exiled. Three of these men, Grigorii Skorniakov-Pisarev, Anton Dev'ier, and Fedor Soimonov, were to play major roles in the development of Russian Pacific seafaring and the push to Alaska.[49] Skorniakov-Pisarev and Dev'ier would take part in Bering's much more ambitious second expedition (1741). Skorniakov-Pisarev would receive the reports of the last returning detachment of the Afanasii Shestakov expedition, to which we now turn.

The Shestakov expedition, much less known than Bering's expedition, was incorporated into the overall plan of northern exploration. With greater luck, it might have surpassed Bering's achievements. This expedition resulted from proposals originating in Siberia, and utilized local knowledge. The plan had been presented to the ruling senate in 1725 by a Yakutsk Cossack officer (*golova*), Afanasii Shestakov, who had traveled to St. Petersburg especially for that purpose. The proposal was not the first one offered by Shestakov and his Siberian superiors, the princes Cherkasskii and Dolgorukov. Basing their proposal on local knowledge, these men urged the imperial government to support by all available means expeditions of discovery in the Northern and Eastern Oceans. Such expeditions would claim for Russia the islands lying in the Pacific and the Great Land to the east of Kamchatka. In fact, Shestakov brought along with him to St. Petersburg a hand-drawn map that showed the Great Land beyond Bering Strait.[50]

Shestakov's pleas found willing ears in the capital. On 23 March 1727 an edict authorizing the expedition was issued. It contained a detailed outline of the goals of the expedition and general instructions to Shestakov. A copy of the order was given to the governor of Siberia, local authorities in Okhotsk, and to Vitus Bering. All officials were ordered to cooperate with Shestakov; this expedition had as much support as Bering's was to have, if not more. Supplemental instructions were issued on 31 March 1727. The expedition was to proceed by sea, with other detachments proceeding by land. Shestakov was assigned 400 servicemen out of the Yakutsk garrison (which was increased to 1,500 men) to be commanded by Major Dmitrii Pavlutskii, a figure well known to historians of Siberia, primarily for his role in the so-called pacification of Kamchatka and the Chukchi Peninsula. Pavlutskii was to head the forces operating on the Chukchi Peninsula, out of Anadyr' outpost.

Shestakov was also authorized to recruit volunteers, from among both the "Cossack sons" and Siberian natives: Yukagir, Koriak, Yakut, Kamchadal, and Even. Military instructors were to join the party to train the troops in managing the artillery (cannon and mortars). The admiralty seconded to the expedition Simon Gardebol, a mining specialist and assayer of ores, navigator Iakov Gens, subnavigator Ivan Fedorov, topographer Mikhail Gvozdev, shipwright Speshnev, and a number of sailors. An auxiliary expedition, led by Ivan Kozyrevskii, a veteran of the early explorations in the Kuril Islands, was to attempt Dezhnev's route. Kozyrevskii was to start not from the Kolyma but from the Lena River. For this purpose he built a vessel, the *Evers*, and attempted to sail down the Lena to the Arctic Ocean, but the vessel was crushed by ice.

Shestakov arrived in Okhotsk in 1729 and that same summer he built two vessels, the *Vostochnyi Gavriil* and the *Lev*. Bering's two vessels, the *Fortuna* and the *Sv. Arkhangel Gavriil*, were put under his authority. Two vessels of this flotilla were to proceed to the northern shores of the Sea of Okhotsk and from there, in the next navigation season, to round the Lopatka, the southern Kamchatka cape, and sail to Anadyr'. The *Fortuna* was to sail directly to Bol'sheretsk, in Kamchatka, and from there explore the Kuril Islands, while the flagship, the *Sv. Arkhangel Gavriil*, was to sail out of Okhotsk south and to the Shantar Islands. This vessel was to chart the entire coast and then proceed to Kamchatka along the Kuril Island chain, measuring the distance from the Udskii ostrog on the Okhotsk Sea shore to Bol'sheretsk, proceed to Nizhne-Kamchatsk and thence to the Great Land, to America. She carried a crew of sixty-one, under the command of Navigator Moshkov, with Ivan Shestakov (a nephew of the expedition leader) in charge of the detachment. The detachment aboard the *Fortuna* was commanded by the leader's son, Vasilii Shestakov. Serviceman Shergin (a name later found among the Aleutian traders) was on board. The next summer, 1730, they investigated the northern Kuril Islands. (In later years, Shergin, Vasilii Shestakov, and Navigator Butin repeatedly sailed to the Kurils to collect iasak.) Basov also may have been on board. He apparently was with Kozyrevskii, on the Lena River, aboard the *Evers*. Basov became the first entrepreneur to attempt the penetration of the Aleutian Islands, in 1743, and was known to have taken sea otters in the Kurils and to have been a trusted subordinate of Skorniakov-Pisarev.[51]

Cossack Chernyi, well known for his later activities in the Kuril Islands, was aboard the *Sv. Arkhangel Gavriil*. He kept the ship's log and was on board in the late summer of 1730 when this vessel investigated the Amur River estuary and the Shantar Islands. Afanasii Shestakov himself sailed north on the *Vostochnyi Gavriil*, a large vessel (*bot*), commanded by Navigator Treska and carrying a crew of ninety-three. He went ashore at Talak and made his way to Tauiskii ostrog. He ordered construction of additional vessels on the Urak River (where Shelikhov would build his fleet in 1783), while he himself set out with a large detachment by land to subdue part of the Koriak, who had mounted a massive military effort against the Russians. At this point, Shestakov reiterated his orders that the Great Land "across from the mouth of the Anadyr'" was to be investigated and the inhabitants "brought under the Russian hand." Shestakov marched through the Koriak territory without difficulty, but then became embroiled with the Chukchi. In a pitched battle on 14 March 1730, where Shestakov commanded the Russian center (the right wing being composed of Evenk and Even, the left wing of friendly Koriak), his forces were defeated and Shestakov himself was killed. While the Chukchi turned their wrath against the Koriak, the surviving Russians made their way to Anadyr'. There, another land detachment, under Major Pavlutskii, was about to engage the Chukchi.

Pavlutskii had collected a report from a Cossack stationed at Anadyr', who in 1726 had undertaken a sea voyage in the north and had encountered two visitors from the islands in the strait who gave information about the Great Land. It was planned to send a party, by sea, to "investigate the islands in the sea and the Great Land."[52]

In the meantime, another detachment, this one commanded by Ivan Lebedev, sailed on the *Lev*, following the tracks of the *Vostochnyi Gavriil*. Lebedev missed the rendezvous with Afanasii Shestakov's vessel at Tauiskii ostrog, and the *Lev* wintered at the Yama River. Here the detachment came under attack by hostile Koriak, who burned the vessel and the Yama zimov'ie. As the news of Afanasii Shestakov's death and of the unhappy fate of Lebedev and his men reached Okhotsk, Gens, Gvozdev, and Fedorov tried to ascertain what their next tasks would be and who would lead the enterprise. The great Shestakov expedition, now leaderless, had lost its momentum. Nevertheless, some of Shestakov's men would be the first Russian subjects to make a landfall on Alaskan shores.

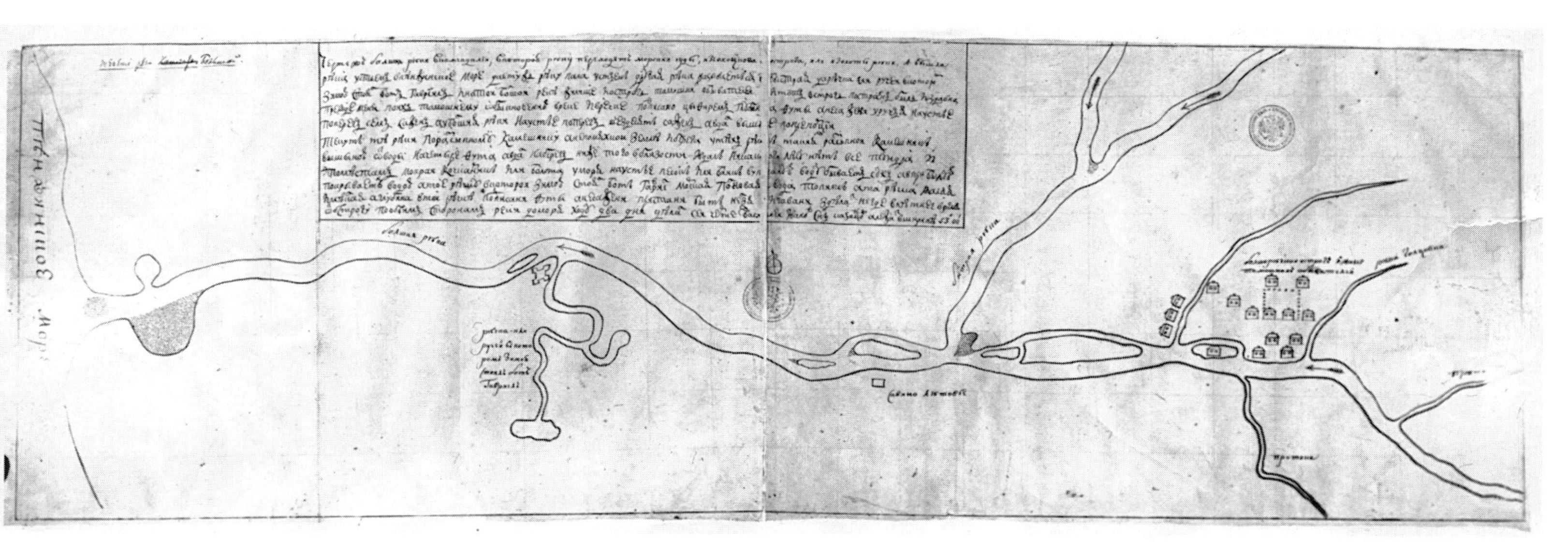

FIGURE 6. Sketch map of the mouth of the Bol'shaia River (western coast of Kamchatka) and the town of Bol'sheretsk, established in 1704 by Russian pioneers. It was the main port on the Okhotsk route in the early eighteenth century.

Original in RGADA, Fond 192, no. 30. Courtesy Richard A. Pierce.

On 3 September 1730, in Okhotsk, Iakov Gens formally assumed command of thirty-two men previously in Shestakov's detachment, and two days later, Ivan Shestakov, son of the dead expedition leader, handed over to Gens the vessel *Sv. Arkhangel Gavriil*, just arrived in Okhotsk from Bol'sheretsk on Kamchatka. The command of the vessel *Vostochnyi Gavriil* was assumed by subnavigator Fedorov, and the two vessels sailed on 18 September for Kamchatka. Only the *Sv. Arkhangel Gavriil* reached Bol'sheretsk safely. The *Vostochnyi Gavriil* was wrecked to the north of the Bol'sheretsk River when driven on shore by a storm; the crew members were saved. At Bol'sheretsk, Gens and Gvozdev waited for orders from Pavlutskii, who was the senior officer of the expedition after Shestakov's death. The order arrived 28 December 1730. Gens and Fedorov, with their entire command, were to proceed by sea to Anadyr' as soon as possible and thence to the Great Land. Gens began preparation to depart that summer, and sailed from Bol'sheretsk for Nizhne-Kamchatsk on 23 June 1731. On 20 July, he cleared the Kamchatka River mouth and stood at anchor in the estuary when news reached him that the Itel'men had risen against the Russians and were burning the outposts. Fifty-two men, including Gvozdev, the expedition's geodesist, were sent from the vessel to aid the beleaguered cossacks.

Thus, pressing military need delayed the sailing until the next year. In the spring of 1732, Pavlutskii relieved Gens of command and entrusted the expedition to the Great Land to Gvozdev. Subnavigator Fedorov was to navigate the ship, according to Pavlutskii's order of 13 July 1732. Fedorov was in poor health, in fact so very ill that he had to be carried aboard ship. The *Sv. Arkhangel Gavriil* sailed on 23 July 1732 with a crew of thirty-nine, including navigator Moshkov. The course was northward, along the Asiatic shore. They reached the Chukchi Peninsula (the exact location is in dispute) from the south on 5 August. Gvozdev, accompanied by a few sailors, went ashore for the first time on 7 August. They continued to sail along the Chukchi Peninsula shores until 15 August, when the promontory known in modern times as Cape Dezhnev was reached and possibly the Eskimo settlement of Naukan. They also visited one of the Diomede Islands.

On 20 August, the vessel stood at anchor off the second Diomede Island, later named Kruzenshtern Island. Here the ship's boat was met by a hail of arrows from Eskimos on shore. The next day, 21 August 1732, the *Sv. Arkhangel Gavriil* hove to close to the American shore. Gvozdev and his comrades stood off Cape Prince of Wales. This was the first landfall made on Alaska by a Russian naval vessel. From then on, all Russian charts would carry an outline of a portion of the Alaskan coast with the notation "Geodesist Gvozdev was here in the year 1732," and for a while the site of his landfall on the Alaska coast was designated "Cape Gvozdev" and the islands he visited in the strait—now known as the Diomedes, as Bering named them—became briefly known as the Gvozdev Islands. The basis for a claim of sovereignty over the Great Land was being prepared.

Soon thereafter, the *Sv. Arkhangel Gavriil* stood off King Island. There, the crew encountered an Alaskan who approached the vessel in a kayak equipped with a sealskin float. Late in September 1732, on the twenty-eighth or twenty-ninth, the expedition returned to the Kamchatka River. The Afanasii Shestakov expedition was coming to its end. Subnavigator Fedorov, gravely ill throughout the trip, died soon after the vessel's return.[53]

Gvozdev had to report to new superiors. Far away, in St. Petersburg, under the new Empress Anna Ioannovna, major governmental reorganization was in progress. The far northeast, like the rest of the empire, was about to become subject to a new administrative

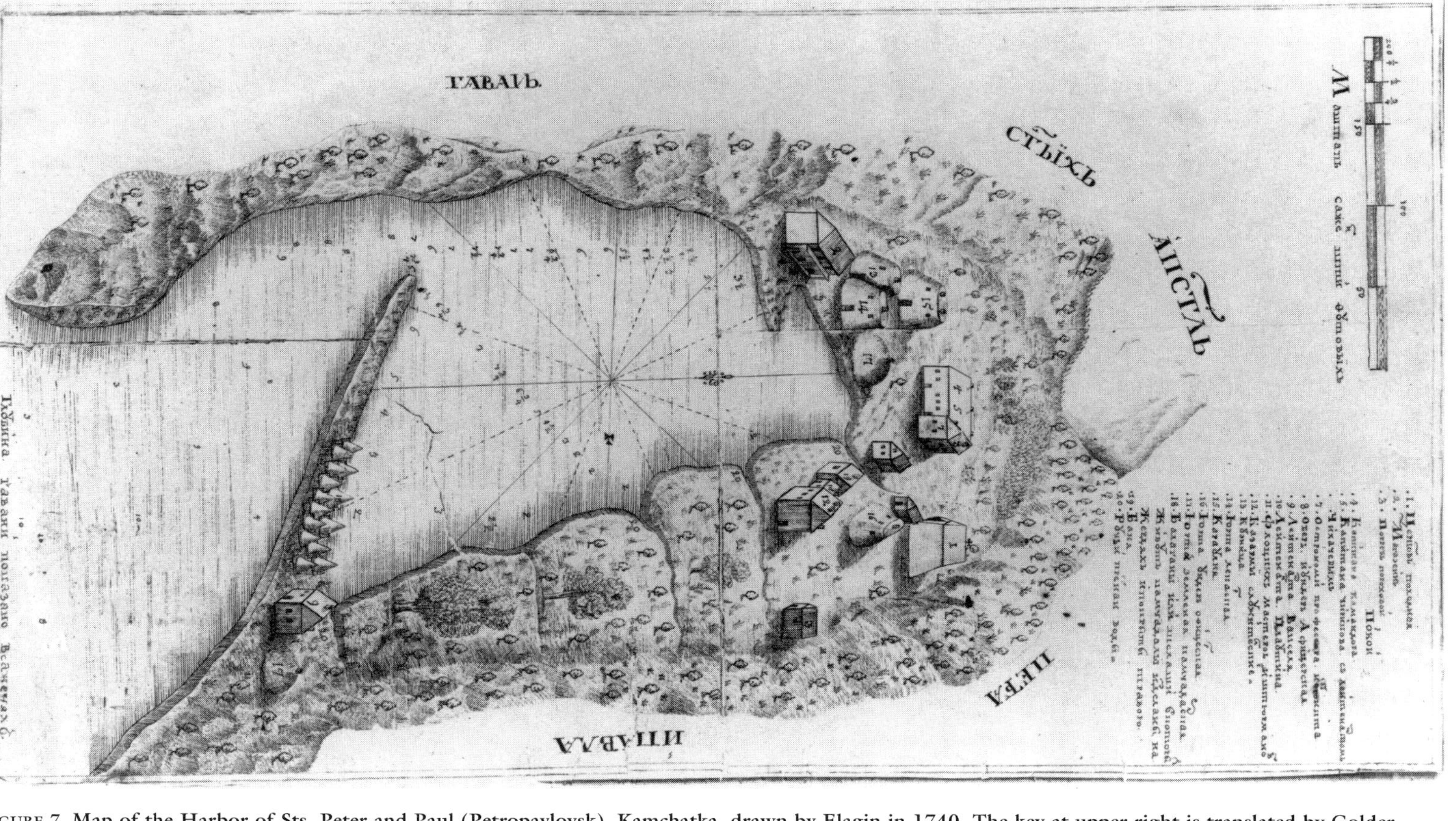

FIGURE 7. Map of the Harbor of Sts. Peter and Paul (Petropavlovsk), Kamchatka, drawn by Elagin in 1740. The key at upper right is translated by Golder (1922, facing p. 34) as follows: (1) traveling church, (2) warehouse, (3) powder house, (4) Captain Commander, (5) Captain Chirikov and Lieutenant Chikhachev, (7) professor of astronomy and adjunct, (8) higher and lower officers, (9) Lieutenant Waxel, (10) Lieutenant Plautin, (11) fleet-masters and navigators, (12) quarters for the crew and workmen, (13) blacksmith shop, (14) medical quarters, (15) guard house, (16) lower officers, (17) native Kamchadal earthen hut, (18) native summer houses raised on a platform and covered with grass, (19) bath house, (20) freshwater spring.

Courtesy Library of Congress, Manuscript Division, former Golder Collection.

FIGURE 8. Okhotsk, the naval base on the Pacific established by Peter the Great in 1711, as pictured by Luka Voronin, staff artist of the Billings-Sarychev naval expedition, 1786–1795.

Courtesy RGAVMF, Fond 1331, op. 4, delo 704, fol. 15.

order. Bering himself was responsible, at least in part, for the new way the government proposed to deal with the region. Upon his return to the capital after the expedition of 1728, Bering had submitted a list of proposals for reorganization of the Kamchatka region, probably having in mind the development of an adequate support base for future naval activities. One of these proposals was the creation of an Okhotsk administrative office, independent of Yakutsk, to which Kamchatka would be subordinate. This recommendation was implemented by imperial orders of 29 April, 10 May, and 22 July 1731. Settlers were to be sent to Okhotsk, a permanent shipyard opened, and merchants brought in to develop commerce, with at least ten years' relief from customs duties and taxation of profits as inducement. Skorniakov-Pisarev, the former commandant of the naval academy, now a state felon settled at Zhigansk in Siberia, was appointed the administrator of the Port of Okhotsk and of Kamchatka. Three hundred Cossack families were moved to Okhotsk and personnel were sent to teach the sons of Siberian cossacks navigation and seamanship.[54]

Bering's Second Expedition was about to be launched, and once again Okhotsk and Kamchatka were to be the jumping-off points. Gens was recalled from Kamchatka to Okhotsk, once again to sail the *Sv. Arkhangel Gavriil.* The *Fortuna*, arriving in Kamchatka in 1733, was also put under his command. On 25 September 1733, the first naval vessel to stand off Alaska's shore entered the port of Okhotsk. She was to resume her duties as the transport vessel on the Kamchatka route. In 1736, repaired and refitted, she would, like her consort, the *Fortuna*, join the flotilla of Bering's Second Kamchatka Expedition. Shestakov's men, like his ships, were reassigned to Bering's new enterprise. Gvozdev was one of them, the mining specialist Simon Gardebol another. Enormous resources in men and material were committed to this expedition, which consisted of several sea and land arms and several auxiliary expeditions. The men of the Russian navy were at last to set out to explore and chart the entire arctic coast from the Kola Peninsula and the White Sea to Anadyr', rounding the Chukchi Peninsula.[55] In addition, the navy was to chart the coasts of the Bering and Okhotsk Seas. Scientific data on geology and mineralogy, flora and fauna, and ethnography were to be collected. The admiralty and the Academy of Sciences joined forces, and a number of scholar-academicians were assigned to the expedition. Besides these scientific tasks, the expedition had geopolitical aims: Bering himself was to sail to America until he touched upon the territory controlled by the Spanish out of Mexico (or any other European power), while one of his senior officers, Martin Spangsberg, was to explore routes to Japan and Korea. Establishment of international trade was one of the long-range goals.

In 1740, at Okhotsk, while the *Sv. Petr* and the *Sv. Pavel* were being outfitted, Bering's second in command, Aleksei Chirikov, proposed that he be allowed to sail on a vessel constructed earlier for Spangsberg to investigate the American coast "north by east from Kamchatka," but Bering refused permission.[56] Had he been allowed to sail, the history of Russia's penetration of Alaska could have taken a different course.

Though Okhotsk was the main staging area for Spangsberg's and Bering's flotillas, Bering chose as his point of departure for America one of the best harbors in the North Pacific, Avacha Bay on southern Kamchatka. On 8 September 1740, the two vessels left Okhotsk for Bol'sheretsk and from there sailed for Avacha Bay, arriving 6 October 1740. There they wintered. It was thus that the great port of Petropavlovsk-Kamchatskii, named for Bering's two vessels, was founded: the Harbor of the Holy Apostles Saint Peter and Saint Paul.

On 4 May 1741, Bering called a council to determine their course on the voyage to America. Chirikov and the majority of the officers argued for a course eastward, within the latitudes of fifty to sixty-five degrees. They were overruled on the basis of representations by Louis Delisle de la Croyère. Assigned to the expedition through the influence of his brother, Joseph Nicolas Delisle, then member of the Academy of Sciences, this officer of the French navy, fresh from service in Canada, may have had his own agenda.[57] Apparently on the basis of his representations, Bering decided first to sail southeast by east in search of the mythical de Gama Land and Company Land, prominent features of Delisle's map. On 21 May 1741, the vessels were ready to sail and stood in the roads in Avacha Bay. On 4 June, the vessels cleared the bay and sailed into the open sea, course southeast. Finding none of the land represented on Delisle's chart, by 13 June the captains of both vessels were ready to change their course to northeast.

On 20 June the two vessels lost sight of each other, and from this point on their course and fate played themselves out differently. The *Sv. Pavel*, commanded by Chirikov, sailed east by north by east and then, on 26 June, sighted what the crew believed to be a mountain range to the northeast, but then resumed the old compass heading. By the end of the first week of July there were definite signs of land. On 15 July 1741, in the vicinity of 55°30' north latitude, Chirikov sighted the coast of America. Two days later, many miles to the north and west, Bering sighted the coast of the Gulf of Alaska. Some members of his crew, including the captain of the flagship, the *Sv. Petr*, Sven Waxell, and the naturalist Georg Steller went ashore on Kayak Island. Years later, these landfalls would determine the boundary of Russian America—and the state of Alaska.

NOTES

1. Belov, *Arkticheskoe moreplavanie.*
2. Ibid., 35–37.
3. Raymond H. Fisher, *The Voyage of Semen Dezhnev in 1648: Bering's Precursor, with Selected Documents* (London: Hakluyt Society, 1981), 147.
4. Leo Bagrow, "Sparwenfeld's Map of Siberia," *Imago Mundi* 4 (1947): 67; K. N. Serbina, "Kniga Bolshogo Chertezha i ego redaktsiia," *Istoricheskie zapiski* 14 (1945): 129–147; idem, "Istochniki knigi Bolshogo Chertezha," *Istoricheskie zapiski* 23 (1947): 290–324; idem, *Kniga Bolshomu Chertezhu* (Moscow and Leningrad, 1950). Bagrow and Serbina are in some disagreement. Bagrow insists that the map ordered by Mikhail was never completed, not even the description ("*eksplikatsiia*"). The data which do appear in the "Kniga Bolshomu Chertezhu" he believes to be only an "itinerary." Bagrow maintains that the Petr Godunov map of 1667 (redrawn by Ul'ian Remezov, father of the famous Russian pioneer cartographer Semeon Remezov) was the first official general map of Siberia.
5. Belov, *Arkticheskoe moreplavanie,* 62–66; A. Pokrovskii, comp. and ed., *Ekspeditsiia Beringa (sbornik dokumentov)* (Moscow: Glavnoe arkhivnoe upravlenie NKVD SSSR, 1941), 6. A good analysis of incipient mercantilism and the growing importance of the search for metals in Russia has been done by Mark Bassin, "Expansion and Colonialism on the Eastern Frontier: Views of Siberia and the Far East in Pre-Petrine Russia," *Journal of Historical Geography* 14, no. 1 (1988): 3–21.
6. Belov, "Mangazeiskoe moreplavanie," chap. 6 in *Arkticheskoe moreplavanie,* 106–123; Bakhrushin, "Mangazeiskaia mirskaia obshchina."
7. On information provided to Giovio by Gerasimov see Leo Bagrow, *A History of the Cartography of Russia Up to 1800,* vol. 1, ed. Henry W. Castner (Wolfe Island, Ontario: Walker Press, 1975), 61–64. For a discussion of a number of projects, see L. S. Berg, *Ocherki po istorii russkikh geograficheskikh*

otkrytii (Moscow and Leningrad: Izdatel'stvo Akademii nauk SSSR, 1946), 10–19; Belov, *Arkticheskoe moreplavanie,* 40–45, 71–95.

8. E.G.R. Taylor, "John Dee and the Map of North-East Asia," *Imago Mundi* 12 (1955): 103–106.
9. The Jesuit Ph. Avril published this information in 1697 in his *Voyage en divers états d'Europe et d'Asie* (Paris), 210–211, cited after Bakhrushin, "Russkoe prodvizhenie za Ural," 157 n. 42.
10. A. P. Okladnikov, Z. V. Gogolev, and E. A. Ashchepkov, *Drevnii Zashiversk: Drevnerusskii zapoliarnyi gorod* (Moscow: Izdatel'stvo "Nauka," 1977), 33–35. Quotation my translation.
11. Boris P. Polevoi, "Pervyi russkii pokhod na Tikhii okean v 1639–1641 gg., v svete etnograficheskikh dannykh," *Sovetskaia etnografiia,* 1991, no. 3: 56–69; idem, "Novyi dokument o pervom russkom pokhode na Tikhii okean," *Trudy Tomskogo kraevedcheskogo muzeia* 6, no. 2 (1963): 27; idem, "Predystoriia Russkoi Ameriki," chap. 1 in *Osnovanie Russkoi Ameriki, 1732–1799,* vol. 1 of *Istoriia Russkoi Ameriki, 1732–1867,* ed. N. N. Bolkhovitinov (Moscow: "Mezhdunarodnye otnosheniia," 1997), 16–19.
12. Fisher, *Voyage of Semen Dezhnev,* 141; Belov, *Arkticheskoe moreplavanie,* 159.
13. Raymond H. Fisher disputes Ogloblin's conclusion in that he follows the Russian scholar Boris P. Polevoi (letter to author, 20 April 1992).
14. N. N. Ogloblin, "Vostochno-Sibirskie poliarnye morekhody XVII veka," *Zhurnal Ministerstva narodnago prosveshcheniia,* no. 5 (1903): 38–62.
15. The Russian-language literature on Semeon Dezhnev is massive; no complete listing is presented here. The first accounts were penned by the academician G. F. Miller (Müller) in the eighteenth century. In the nineteenth century N. N. Ogloblin pioneered the Dezhnev studies on the basis of documents he uncovered in the archives of the *Sibirskii prikaz* (the Department of Siberian Affairs), now housed in the RGADA (Russian State Archive of Ancient Documents). See N. N. Ogloblin, "Semeon Dezhnev (1638–1671): Novye dannye i peresmotr starykh," *Zhurnal Ministerstva narodnago prosveshcheniia,* 1890, no. 12; idem, "Smert' S. Dezhneva v Moskve v 1673 g.," *Bibliograf,* 1891, nos. 3–4; idem, *Semeon Dezhnev* (St. Petersburg, 1890). Among the contemporary Soviet writers who published much of the new material on Dezhnev's voyage are Boris P. Polevoi and the late M. I. Belov. It must be noted that the two scholars are in some disagreement on several points.

    L. M. Demin recently published a readable biography of Dezhnev. See his *Semen Dezhnev* (Moscow: "Molodaia gvardiia," 1990). For extensive scholarly discussion, see M. I. Belov, *Semeon Dezhnev, 1648–1948: K stoletiiu otkrytiia proliva mezhdu Aziei i Amerikoi* (Moscow-Leningrad, 1948); idem, *Semeon Dezhnev,* 2d rev. ed. (Moscow: Morskoi transport, 1955); idem, *Podvig Semeona Dezhneva,* 3d rev. ed. (Moscow: Mysl', 1973). See also Belov's "Istoricheskoe plavanie Semeona Dezhneva," "Semeon Dezhnev i amerikanskaia literatura" and "Novoe li eto slovo o plavanii S. I. Dezhneva?" *Izvestiia Vsesoiuznogo geograficheskogo obshchestva* 79 (1949): 459–472; 89 (1957): 482–485; and 95 (1963): 443–446; T. D. Lavrentsova, "Podlinnye dokumenty o plavanii S. I. Dezhneva," in *Russkie arkticheskie ekspeditsii XVII–XX vv.,* ed. M. I. Belov (Leningrad: Gidrometeorologicheskoe izdatel'stvo, 1964), 127–143; V. A. Samoilov, *Semeon Dezhnev i ego vremia, s prilozheniem otpisok chelobitnykh Semeona Dezhneva o ego pokhodakh i otkrytiiakh* (Moscow: Glavsevmorput', 1945). For an assessment of Soviet scholarship on Dezhnev up to 1973, see Raymond H. Fisher, "Dezhnev's Voyage of 1648 in the Light of Soviet Scholarship," *Terrae incognitae* 1 (1973): 7–26, and idem, *Voyage of Semen Dezhnev.*
16. Belov, *Arkticheskoe moreplavanie,* 155.
17. Boris P. Polevoi, "O mestopolozhenii pervogo russkogo poseleniia na Kolyme," *Doklady Instituta geografii Sibiri i Dal'nego Vostoka* 2 (1962): 66–75; idem, "Nakhodka chelobit'ia pervootkryvatelei Kolymy," in *Ekonomika, upravlenie i kul'tura Sibiri XVI–XIX vv.,* ed. Oleg N. Vilkov (Novosibirsk: Izdatel'stvo "Nauka," 1966), 285–291.
18. There is some scholarly disagreement on this point. The weight of the evidence, however, suggests that Pogycha, indeed, was another name for the Anadyr' River. The problem of identification is complicated, as the cossacks collected information about distant places from indigenous people but did not always indicate the ethnic identity of their informants. These were Yukagir, Evenk, Even,

and, in some instances, Chukchi. The nineteenth-century Russian historian Captain A. Sgibnev, who had access to archival materials now destroyed or lost, identifies Pogycha as Anadyr' without any equivocation. M. I. Belov also had no doubts that Pogycha and Anadyr' are identical (see, for example, his *Russkie morekhody v Ledovitom i Tikhom okeanakh* [Moscow-Leningrad: Glavsevmorput', 1952], 61 n. 3, 64–67). Here he cites in support original reports by Stadukhin and statements by the voevoda, Fransbekov, who spoke of "Pogycha, same as Anadyr'." However, in a later publication (*Arkticheskoe moreplavanie,* 159), Belov seems to opt for the identification of Pogycha with the Chaun River. Polevoi identifies Pogycha with the Pokhacha River, within the territory of the Koriak in northern Kamchatka (Boris P. Polevoi, "O 'Pogyche'—Pokhache [o samom rannem russkom izvestii, otnosiashchemsia k sovremennoi Kamchatskoi oblasti]," *Voprosy geografii Kamchatki* 6 [1970]: 82–86). See Fisher, *Voyage of Semen Dezhnev,* for a discussion of this as he takes a somewhat different position from Polevoi's. I consider Polevoi's interpretation untenable.

19. For a discussion of the number of men and vessels, and an excellent analysis of published data, documents, and interpretations by Russian scholars, see Fisher, *Voyage of Semen Dezhnev,* 160.

20. In official contemporary documents in Russian archives, women are not mentioned at all, except that Dezhnev mentions in one of his later reports that in 1654 he recaptured Alekseev's wife from the Koriak.

21. L. M. Demin, *Semen Dezhnev,* 197; Fisher, *Voyage of Semen Dezhnev;* Belov, cited in Demin, p. 211, claims that only two, not four, vessels were lost before reaching Bering Strait.

22. Demin, *Semen Dezhnev,* 201, 210.

23. Fisher believes that references to an early Russian landing at the Kamchatka River are based not on the Dezhnev-Alekseev voyage but on a later one by Rubets (see below; Raymond H. Fisher, letter to the author, 11 June 1992). Other scholars disagree. Dezhnev's recapture of Alekseev's wife from the Koriak argues for a Kamchatka landing by Alekseev.

24. S. G. Fedorova, "K voprosu o rannikh russkikh poseleniiakh na Aliaske," *Letopis' Severa* 4 (1964): 97–112 and table; idem, *Russkoe naselenie Aliaski i Kalifornii: Konets XVIII veka–1867 g.* (Moscow: Izdatel'stvo "Nauka," 1971), 45–96, English translation by Richard A. Pierce and Alton S. Donnelly, eds., *The Russian Population in Alaska and California, Late 18th Century–1867* (Kingston, Ontario: Limestone Press, 1973), 39–99; see also Polevoi, "Predystoriia Russkoi Ameriki," 19–21; M. B. Chernenko, "Puteshestviia po Chukotskoi zemle i plavanie na Aliasku kazach'ego sotnika Ivana Kobeleva v 1779 i 1789–1791 gg.," *Letopis' Severa* 2 (1957): 121–141. Efimov argues that such early "settlements" did, indeed, occur. See A. V. Efimov, *Iz istorii russkikh ekspeditsii na Tikhom okeane, pervaia polovina XVIII veka* (Moscow: Voennoe izdatel'stvo Ministerstva vooruzhennykh sil Soiuza SSR, 1948); idem, *Iz istorii velikikh russkikh geograficheskikh otkrytii,* abridged and rev. ed. of 1948 (Moscow, 1949); idem, *Iz istorii velikikh russkikh geograficheskikh otkrytii v Severnom Ledovitom i Tikhom okeanakh XVII–pervaia polovina XVIII v.* (Moscow: Gosudarstvennoe izdatel'stvo geograficheskoi literatury, 1950); idem, *Iz istorii velikikh russkikh geograficheskikh otkrytii* (Moscow: Izdatel'stvo "Nauka," 1971).

25. Among American anthropologists none was as strongly opposed to the idea as Dorothy Jean Ray, who went so far as to deny that Dezhnev ever succeeded in rounding Cape Dezhnev at all (see *The Eskimos of Bering Strait, 1650–1898* [Seattle: University of Washington Press, 1975], 11–13). In this interpretation, Ray, who allegedly recently changed her position (Raymond H. Fisher, letter to the author, 20 April 1992), followed the American historian Frank A. Golder, who in the early twentieth century pioneered the studies of Russian expansion to the Pacific and to Alaska. See specifically Golder's "Some reasons for doubting Deshnev's voyage," *The Geographical Journal* (London) 36 (1910): 81–83, and his *Russian Expansion on the Pacific, 1641–1850 . . .,* (1914; reprint, Gloucester, Mass.: Peter Smith, 1960), where the conclusion that Dezhnev did not make the voyage is presented in chap. 3, "A Critical Examination of Dezhnev's Voyage," 67–95. Golder's position is not accepted by modern scholarship. In the United States, his conclusion has been analyzed and refuted by Raymond H. Fisher in "Semen Dezhnev and Professor Golder," *Pacific Historical Review* 25 (1956): 281–292; idem, *Voyage of Semen Dezhnev;* and idem, "The Early Cartography of the Bering Strait Region," *Arctic* 37, no. 4 (1984): 574–589.

The possibility of an early seventeenth-century Russian settlement on Alaska by shipwrecked mariners is nowadays not debated in public. Some archaeologists, historians, and anthropologists privately believe that there were such settlements, or at least concede such a possibility, but in America none has stated such beliefs in print. Earlier hypotheses, such as those expressed by T. S. Farrelly in "A Lost Colony of Novgorod in Alaska," *Slavonic and East European Review* 22 (October 1944): 33–38, and by S. R. Tompkins and M. L. Moorhead in "Russia's Approach to America," *British Columbia Historical Quarterly* (1949, April/July/October), 338 (as cited in Fedorova, *Russkoe naselenie,* 18), have been critically discussed by Fedorova in "K voprosu," and *Russkoe naselenie,* 45–96. Fedorova leaves the question open. Dorothy Jean Ray rejects even the possibility of such an occurrence. In addition to her work cited above, see "The Kheuveren Legend," in *Ethnohistory in the Arctic: The Bering Strait Eskimo* (Kingston, Ontario: Limestone Press, 1983), 67–77, reprinted from *Alaska Journal* (summer 1976), and "Kauwerak: Lost Village of Alaska," *The Beaver* 295 (Autumn 1964): 4–13. On the other hand, L. M. Sverdlov, a Russian arctic geographer, believes such an event did take place (see note 30, below). Sverdlov is the most ardent proponent of the need to examine archaeologically sites which he claims can be predetermined on the basis of geographical considerations. He was very active in organizing a joint U.S.-Russian archaeological expedition to the Seward Peninsula, particularly to the Kotzebue Sound area and the route along the Buckland River to Norton Sound. See bibliography for Sverdlov's publications on the subject.

26. Belov, *Russkie morekhody,* 328–339.

27. Belov, *Arkticheskoe moreplavanie,* 155–156.

28. A. V. Efimov, "Dokumenty ob otkrytiiakh russkikh zemleprokhodtsev i poliarnykh morekhodov v XVII veke na severo-vostoke Azii," in *Otkrytiia russkikh zemleprokhodtsev i poliarnykh morekhodov XVII veka na severo-vostoke Azii: Sbornik dokumentov,* ed. A. V. Efimov, comp. N. S. Orlova (Moscow: Gosudarstvennoe izdatel'stvo geograficheskoi literatury, 1951), 41–44; idem, *Iz istorii russkikh ekspeditsii;* idem, *Iz istorii... otkrytii* (1949); idem, *Iz istorii... otkrytii v Severnom;* idem, *Iz istorii... otkrytii* (1971); A. I. Andreev, *Ocherki po istochnikovedeniiu Sibiri,* vol. 1, *XVII vek,* vol. 2, *XVIII vek (pervaia polovina)* (Moscow and Leningrad: Izdatel'stvo "Nauka," 1960–1965); L. S. Berg, *Ocherki po istorii russkikh geograficheskikh otkrytii,* 2d rev. and enl. ed. (Moscow and Leningrad: Izdatel'stvo Akademii nauk SSSR, 1949); idem, *Otkrytie Kamchatki i ekspeditsii Beringa 1725–1742 gg.* (Moscow and Leningrad: Izdatel'stvo Akademii nauk SSSR, 1946); idem, *Ocherki po istorii* (1946); Belov, *Russkie morekhody;* V. I. Grekov, *Ocherki po istorii russkikh geograficheskikh issledovanii v 1725–1765 gg.* (Moscow: Izdatel'stvo Akademii nauk SSSR, 1960).

29. Boris P. Polevoi, "Plaval li I. M. Rubets ot Leny do Kamchatki v 1662 g.?" in *Istoriia nauki* 6, Izvestiia Akademii nauk SSSR, Seriia geograficheskaia (Moscow: Izdatel'stvo Akademii nauk SSSR, 1981), 130–140; idem, "Zabytoe plavanie s Leny do r. Kamchatki v 1661–1662 gg. Itogi arkhivnykh izyskanii 1948–1991 gg.," *Izvestiia Rossiiskogo geograficheskogo obshchestva* 125, no. 2 (1993): 35–42; idem, "Predystoriia Russkoi Ameriki," 34.

30. See note 25, above; L. M. Sverdlov, "Odin iz putei vozmozhnogo proniknoveniia russkikh na Aliasku v XVII veke," typescript (Moscow: Russian Geographic Society at Russian Academy of Sciences, 1990). Sverdlov's argument is based on considerations of weather, currents, winds, ice conditions, etc., in the Bering Strait region; on the fact that T. Stadukhin, after traversing an area overland, was in a locality where timber for shipbuilding was available; and on the examination of documents of the seventeenth and early eighteenth century that talk about the New or Great Land eastward of the northeastern shores of Asia. There are no reports by Stadukhin himself nor by any of his crew. The only information is contained in the testimony rendered by a Cossack (whose evidence was hearsay) at Yakutsk in 1710 in response to an inquiry by the authorities. The informant alleged that he heard the tale from Stadukhin himself. It was reported that Taras Stadukhin rounded the Chukchi Peninsula (Cape Dezhnev) in six vessels (kochi).

31. Raymond H. Fisher believes that these early charts were based not on direct Russian knowledge but on hearsay, information obtained from the Chukchi, or Alaska Inuit prisoners among the Chukchi (letter to the author, 1992).

32. For a detailed examination of this question, see Fisher, *Voyage of Semen Dezhnev,* 252–276.

33. See discussion in Boris P. Polevoi, "Iz istorii otkrytiia severo-zapadnoi chasti Ameriki (ot pervogo izvestiia sibirskikh zemleprokhodtsev ob Aliaske do petrovskogo plana poiska morskogo puti k Amerike)," in *Ot Aliaski do Ognennoi Zemli* (Moscow: Izdatel'stvo "Nauka," 1967), 107–120.

34. Boris P. Polevoi, "K istorii formirovaniia geograficheskikh predstavlenii o severo-vostochnoi okonechnosti Azii v XVII v.," in *Sibirskii geograficheskii sbornik*, vol. 3 (Moscow and Leningrad: Akademiia nauk SSSR, Sibirskoe otdelenie, Institut geografii Sibiri i Dal'nego Vostoka, 1964), 224–270. See also Polevoi, "Predystoriia Russkoi Ameriki," 21–24, 40–42.

35. Efimov, *Iz istorii... otkrytii* (1971), 155–178.

36. Much of the ethnographic information contained in the servicemen's testimonies is confirmed by data collected on the Seward Peninsula as recently as the 1990s by my graduate students and others.

37. Leo Bagrow, "Sparwenfeld's Map of Siberia," 65–69; idem, "The First Russian Maps of Siberia and Their Influence on the West-European Cartography of N.E. Asia," *Imago Mundi* 9 (1952): 83–93; Johannes Keuning, "Nicolaas Witsen as Cartographer," *Imago Mundi* 11 (1954): 95–110; L. Breitfuss, "Early Maps of North-Eastern Asia and of the Lands around the North Pacific: Controversy between G. F. Müller and N. Delisle," *Imago Mundi* 3 (1939): 87–99; Polevoi, "K istorii formirovaniia"; idem, "Predystoriia Russkoi Ameriki," 42–45.

38. Berg, *Ocherki po istorii* (1946), 20–26; Raymond H. Fisher, *Bering's Voyages: Whither and Why* (Seattle: University of Washington Press, 1977), 8–11. Documents on the project to open a northern sea route to China by master shipwright Fedor Saltykov (1713) were published in A. L. Narochnitskii et al., eds., *Russkie ekspeditsii po izucheniiu severnoi chasti Tikhogo okeana v pervoi polovine XVIII v. (sbornik dokumentov)*, comp. T. S. Fedorova et al. (Moscow: Izdatel'stvo "Nauka," 1984), 21–24, and in V. A. Divin, *Russkaia Tikhookeanskaia epopeiia* (Khabarovsk: Khabarovskoe knizhnoe izdatel'stvo, 1979), 131–133.

39. A. V. Efimov, ed., *Atlas of Geographical Discoveries in Siberia and North-Western America, XVII–XVIII Centuries*, comp. A. V. Efimov, M. I. Belov, and O. M. Medushevskaia (Moscow: Izdatel'stvo "Nauka," 1964), charts 48, 50, 54, 55, 58; Leo Bagrow, *A History of the Cartography of Russia*, vol. 2, 73–76; Fisher, *Voyage of Semen Dezhnev*, 252–271.

40. Russia, Gosudarstvennyi admiralteiskii departament, "Nekotoryia izvestiia ob Okhotskom porte i uezde onago, dostavlennyia kapitan-leitenantom Minitskim v 1809 godu," *Zapiski izdavaemyia Gosudarstvennym admiralteiskim departamentom otnosiashchiesia k moreplavaniiu, naukam i slovesnosti* 3, no. 3 (1815): 87–103; idem, "Prodolzhenie izvestii ob Okhotskom porte, dostavlennykh kapitan-leitenantom Minitskim v 1811 godu," ibid., 3, no. 5 (1815): 137–150; idem, "Ob Okhotskom porte," ibid., 7, no. 3 (1824): 86–97; "Vzgliad na torgovliu proizvodimuiu chrez Okhotskii port," *Severnyi arkhiv* 7, no. 13 (July 1823): 28–45; "Okhotsk (po zapiskam G. Savina, 1846 goda)," *Zapiski Gidrograficheskago departamenta Morskago ministerstva* 9 (1851): 148–161 with map; A. S. Sgibnev, "Okhotskii port 1649 po 1852 g. (istoricheskii ocherk)," *Morskoi sbornik* 105, no. 11 (1869): 1–92; 105, no. 12 (1869): 1–63 (especially pp. 55–63, "Vedomost' sudam Sibirskoi flotilii s 1714 po 1853 god"); A. I. Alekseev, *Okhotsk–kolybel' russkogo Tikhookeanskogo flota* (Khabarovsk: Khabarovskoe knizhnoe izdatel'stvo, 1958).

41. M. I. Belov, "Novye dannye o sluzhbakh Vladimira Atlasova i pervykh pokhodakh russkikh na Kamchatku," *Letopis' Severa* 2 (1957): 89–106.

42. *Pamiatniki Sibirskoi istorii XVIII veka*, vol. 1, *1700–1713* (St. Petersburg: Tipografiia Ministerstva vnutrennikh del, 1882); Boris P. Polevoi, *Pervootkryvateli Sakhalina* (Iuzhno-Sakhalinsk: Sakhalinskoe knizhnoe izdatel'stvo, 1959); Narochnitskii et al., *Russkie ekspeditsii* (1984), 25–29.

43. Sgibnev, "Okhotskii port." Sgibnev used archival materials no longer available. For the early history of the area he also utilized church records and an account based on local documentation by Metropolitan Savva published as "letopis'" in *Vestnik Russkago geograficheskago obshchestva za 1853*, vol. 2, pt. 7, cited in A. S. Sgibnev, "Istoricheskii ocherk glavneishikh sobytii v Kamchatke s 1650 po 1856 g.," *Morskoi sbornik* 101, no. 4 (1869): 65–142; Alekseev, *Okhotsk–kolybel'*.

44. Narochnitskii et al., *Russkie ekspeditsii* (1984), 24–25.

45. This expedition is known as *Bolshoi kamchatskii nariad.* See A. S. Sgibnev, "Bol'shoi kamchatskii nariad (ekspeditsiia El'china)," *Morskoi sbornik* 99, no. 12 (December 1868): 131–139; Fisher, *Bering's Voyages,* 58, 163–164; Lantzeff and Pierce, *Eastward to Empire,* 208; Narochnitskii et al., *Russkie ekspeditsii* (1984), 28–30 (docs. 7–9); Divin, *Russkaia Tikhookeanskaia epopeia,* 134–140 (docs. 18–19). El'chin's expedition is discussed in detail by scholars whose work I have listed in note 28, above.

46. Narochnitskii et al., *Russkie ekspeditsii* (1984), 30–32 (docs. 10–15); Fisher, *Bering's Voyages,* 57–64; L. A. Gol'denberg, *Katorzhanin—sibirskii gubernator: Zhizn' i trudy F. I. Soimonova* (Magadan: Magadanskoe knizhnoe izdatel'stvo, 1979), 45–48; Divin, *Russkaia Tikhookeanskaia epopeia,* 133–134; A. I. Andreev, "Izuchenie Sibiri v pervoi chetverti XVIII v.: Ekspeditsii na vostok do Beringa—I. Evreinov, F. Luzhin, P. Meller i dr.," in *Ocherki po istochnikovedeniiu Sibiri,* vol. 2, *XVIII vek (pervaia polovina)* (Moscow and Leningrad: Izdatel'stvo "Nauka," 1965), 11–32.

47. Today, scholars argue about the exact meaning of Peter's instructions. On this question, see specifically the conflicting views of Polevoi, Fisher, and Carol Urness.

48. The Russian literature on Bering's voyages is enormous and growing. In the United States, we must list Hubert Howe Bancroft, *History of Alaska, 1730–1885* (San Francisco: A. L. Bancroft and Company, 1886; reprint, Darien, Conn.: Hafner Publishing Company, 1970); William H. Dall, "A Critical Review of Bering's First Expedition, 1725–30, Together with a Translation of His Original Report on It (with a Map)," *National Geographic Magazine* 2 (1890): 111–166; idem, "Notes on an Original Manuscript Chart of Bering's Expedition of 1725–1730, and on an Original Manuscript Chart of His Second Expedition; Together with a Summary of a Journal of the First Expedition, Kept by Peter Chaplin, and Now First Rendered into English from Bergh's Russian Version," appendix 19 in *Report of the Superintendent of the U.S. Coast and Geodetic Survey Showing the Progress of Work During the Fiscal Year Ending with June, 1890* (Washington, D.C.: Government Printing Office, 1890), 759–774; George Davidson, *The Tracks and Landfalls of Bering and Chirikof on the Northwest Coast of America. From the Point of Their Separation in Latitude 49° 10', Longitude 176° 40' West, to Their Return to the Same Meridian. June, July, August, September, October 1741* (San Francisco: John Partridge, 1901); F. A. Golder, *Bering's Voyages: An Account of the Efforts of the Russians to Determine the Relation of Asia and America,* vol. 1, *The Log Books and Official Reports of the First and Second Expeditions, 1725–1730 and 1733–1742, with a Chart of the Second Voyage by Ellsworth P. Bertholf,* vol. 2, *Steller's Journal of the Sea Voyage from Kamchatka and Return on the Second Expedition, 1741–1742,* trans. and in part annotated by Leonhard Stejneger (New York: American Geographic Society of New York, 1922–1925); idem, *Russian Expansion on the Pacific.* For a modern interpretation see Fisher, *Bering's Voyages;* and Gerhard Friedrich Müller, *Bering's Voyages: The Reports from Russia by Gerhard Friedrich Müller,* trans. and ed. Carol Urness (Fairbanks: University of Alaska Press, 1986), originally published as *Nachrichten von Seereisen, und zur See gemachten Entdeckungen, die von Russland aus langt den Kuesten des Eismeeres und auf dem ostlichen Weltmeere gegen Japon und Amerika geschehen sind* (St. Petersburg: Akademiia nauk, 1758); a Russian edition was also published that same year (1758). Published accounts by participants are: (1) Georg Wilhelm Steller, *Journal of a Voyage with Bering, 1741–1742,* ed. O. W. Frost, trans. Margritt A. Engel and O. W. Frost (Stanford, Calif.: Stanford University Press, 1988), first published as *Reise von Kamtschatka nach Amerika mit dem Commandeur-Capitän Bering* (St. Petersburg: Johann Zacharias Logan, 1793), and also known as "Tagebuch einer Reise. . . ." Excerpts were published earlier in *Neue nordische Beyträge zur physikalischen und geographischen Erd- und Völkerbeschreibung, Naturgeschichte und Ökonomie,* ed. Peter Pallas (1781, 1793), and reprinted in facsimile, ed. Hanno Beck (Stuttgart: F. A. Brockhaus, 1974). See also *Steller's Manuscript Journal: Facsimile Edition and Transliteration,* ed. O. W. Frost, with transliteration by Margritt A. Engel and Karen Willmore, Alaska Historical Commission Studies in History, no. 114 (Anchorage, 1984), a reproduction of the 1743 manuscript upon which the Engel and Frost translation of 1988 is based. (2) Sven Waxell, *The American Expedition,* trans. from Danish version of Johan Skalberg by M. A. Michael (London: William Hodge, 1952), Russian-language edition published as *Vtoraia Kamchatskaia ekspeditsiia Vitusa Beringa,* trans. from the German manuscript by Iu. I. Bronshtein, ed. A. I. Andreev (Leningrad and Moscow: Glavsevmorput', 1940). Documentary materials published in Russia: Aleksandr I. Andreev, ed. and comp., *Russkie otkrytiia v Tikhom*

okeane i Severnoi Amerike v XVIII–XIX vekakh (Moscow and Leningrad: Izdatel'stvo Akademii nauk SSSR, 1944), English-language edition published as *Russian Discoveries in the Pacific and in North America in the Eighteenth and Nineteenth Centuries: A Collection of Materials,* trans. Carl Ginsberg (Ann Arbor, Mich.: J. W. Edwards for American Council of Learned Societies, 1952); idem, *Russkie otkrytiia v Tikhom okeane i v Severnoi Amerike v XVIII veke* (Moscow: Ogiz, 1948). See also parts 2 and 3 of A. I. Andreev's *Ocherki,* vol. 2 (1965): 45–310 for an analysis of sources. Additional documents were published by Divin, *Russkaia Tikhookeanskaia epopeia;* D. M. Lebedev, *Plavanie A. I. Chirikova na paketbote "Sv. Pavel" k poberezh'iam Ameriki, s prilozheniem zhurnala 1741 g.* (Moscow: Izdatel'stvo Akademii nauk SSSR, 1951); Narochnitskii et al., *Russkie ekspeditsii* (1984); Pokrovskii, ed., *Ekspeditsiia Beringa.* Biographies of the main participants (Bering, Chirikov, Steller) and numerous analyses and commentaries are not listed.

49. A. S. Sgibnev, "Skorniakov-Pisarev i Dev'ier v Sibiri: 1727–1743," *Russkaia starina* 2 (February 1876): 444–450; Gol'denberg, *Katorzhanin—sibirskii gubernator.* Skorniakov-Pisarev and Soimonov were former high-ranking naval officers.

50. This hand-sketched map was published by Breitfuss, "Early Maps," 90 pl. 90, and by N. N. Zubov, *Otechestvennye moreplavateli—issledovateli morei i okeanov* (Moscow: Gosudarstvennoe izdatel'stvo geograficheskoi literatury, 1954), 57. A copy of a portion of this map was published in Efimov, ed., *Atlas,* Map 68. It is my opinion, in agreement with Breitfuss, that this map shows not only a portion of the northwest coast of Alaska but also Wrangell Island. For additional data on Shestakov's map see Divin, *Russkaia Tikhookeanskaia epopeia,* 134–139 (doc. 18), and Narochnitskii et al., *Russkie ekspeditsii* (1984), 55 (doc. 34). A. S. Sgibnev, in his article "Materialy dlia istorii Kamchatki: Ekspeditsiia Shestakova," *Morskoi sbornik* 100, no. 2 (1869): 1–34, discusses a variant of Shestakov's map which was, he states, copied in Paris by Delisle and Buache (ibid., 3). Sgibnev's article, based on archival sources now lost, is one of the most detailed accounts of Shestakov's expedition. He provides additional information in his essay "Okhotskii port," 11–12. For a modern discussion of Shestakov's expedition see L. A. Gol'denberg, *Mezhdu dvumia ekspeditsiiami Beringa* (Magadan: Magadanskoe knizhnoe izdatel'stvo, 1984), 1–3, 8–13. Shestakov's map is discussed by Gol'denberg in a separate publication, "Karta Shestakova 1724 g.," in *Ispol'zovanie starykh kart v geograficheskikh i istoricheskikh issledovaniiakh* (Moscow: Moskovskii filial Geograficheskogo obshchestva, 1980). In my exposition of Shestakov's expedition I follow Sgibnev and Gol'denberg (as cited) and utilize published documents (as cited) as well as Pokrovskii, ed., *Ekspeditsiia Beringa,* 71–80.

51. A. Polonskii, "Perechen' puteshestvii russkikh promyshlennikov v Vostochnom okeane," n.d., Archive of the Russian Geographic Society, St. Petersburg, r. 60, op. 1, no. 2. Basov's career is discussed in detail in chap. 4, below.

52. Gol'denberg, *Mezhdu dvumia,* 81–84.

53. In addition to the works of Sgibnev, cited repeatedly in this chapter, the best sources on the Gvozdev-Fedorov expedition to American shores are A. Sokolov, "Pervyi pokhod russkikh k Amerike 1732 goda," *Zapiski Gidrograficheskago departamenta Morskago ministerstva* 9 (1851): 78–107, and Gol'denberg, *Mezhdu dvumia,* 114–224. Sokolov's article, following a brief introduction by the author, contains a report to Spangsberg by Gvozdev, rendered 1 September 1743, and a brief testimony of the Cossack Skurikhin, a participant. A. Polonskii, "Pokhod geodezista Mikhaila Gvozdeva v Beringov proliv, 1732 goda," *Morskoi sbornik* 4 (November 1850): 389–402, contains some interesting details, but Polonskii, as was his practice, does not indicate his sources. Moreover, as Sokolov points out ("Pervyi pokhod," 87 and nn. on pp. 95, 97, 106), Polonskii interpolates information not present in the archival copies of the documents. As a rule, these interpolations are inimical to the Russians; for example, burning of two Native dwellings and taking of whale oil from others, robbing Native dwellings of caribou skins, burning of a Native dwelling on American shores, etc. These interpolations have not been substantiated by any other researchers.

54. The first navigational school in Siberia, created in response to Bering's representations, was opened in 1735 in Yakutsk. The Second Kamchatka Expedition expressed continued interest in the school and recruited its graduates ("Navigatskiia shkoly Sibiri," *Zapiski Gidrograficheskago departamenta Morskago ministerstva* 8 [1850]: 563–573).

55. For a brief, popular, and readable account, see Jeannette Mirsky, *To the Arctic! The Story of Northern Exploration from Earliest Times to the Present* (Chicago: University of Chicago Press, 1970), 68–85. For synoptic scholarly accounts see Belov, *Arkticheskoe moreplavanie,* and Zubov, *Otechestvennye moreplavateli.*

56. Lebedev, *Plavanie A. I. Chirikova,* 25.

57. See Lydia T. Black, "The Question of Maps: Exploration of the Bering Sea in the Eighteenth Century," in *The Sea in Alaska's Past: Conference Proceedings,* History and Archaeology Publications Series, no. 25 (Anchorage: Office of History and Archaeology, Alaska Division of Parks, 1979), 6–50. On Joseph Nicolas Delisle as a French spy, see V. A. Kordt, *Materialy po istorii kartografii Ukrainy* (Kiev: Izdatel'stvo Akademii nauk, 1931). Waxell specifically blamed "that damnable map" for the misfortunes that befell Bering. Müller, to whom is traditionally ascribed the anonymous publication (in several languages simultaneously) of *A Letter from a Russian Sea-Officer, to a Person of Distinction at the Court of St. Petersburgh; containing His Remarks upon Mr. de l'Isle's Chart and Memoir, relative to the New Discoveries Northward and Eastward from Kamtschatka. Together with Some Observations on that Letter by Arthur Dobbs, Esq.; Governor of North-Carolina. To which is added, Mr. de l'Isle's Explanatory Memoir on his Chart Published at Paris and now Translated from the Original French* (London, 1754), was extremely negative about the role of Delisle de la Croyère and his brother. It should be noted that Delisle was dismissed from the Academy in 1747 and his name was struck from the list of members. L. Breitfuss has no doubts that the Delisle brothers were spying for France; see Breitfuss, "Early Maps." Delisle's map showing de Gama Land to the southeast of Kamchatka is reproduced. Delisle de la Croyère died in 1741 on the return voyage from America.

FIGURE 9. Anna Ioannovna (1693–1740), niece of Peter the Great, empress of Russia 1730–1740.
Courtesy Slavic and Baltic Division, New York Public Library, Astor, Lenox, and Tilden Foundations.

Chapter Three

The Great Land—New Russia—Is Claimed

Russian sovereignty in Alaska traditionally is dated to 1741, when the naval squadron, under Captains Bering and Chirikov, made landfalls on its coasts. Later, the international recognition of Alaska's territorial extent took into account Bering's passage through Bering Strait in 1728, his landfall on St. Lawrence Island, and Gvozdev's landfall on Cape Prince of Wales in 1732. The Russian Imperial Navy provided, by right of discovery, the basis for a claim that for nearly a century would make the Bering Sea a Russian lake. It was left to the private entrepreneurs to validate this claim by the right of occupancy. Those developments were closely linked to Russian policies under the immediate successors of Peter the Great and to governmental changes in the years 1740–1762; while Bering, Shestakov, and their rivals (and colleagues) undertook expeditions, adventures of a more purely political sort were under way in St. Petersburg and other world capitals.

Though the overall design of the naval expeditions and orders to raise the flag on the American continent originated with Peter the Great, the plan was developed and the tasks carried out primarily in the reign of his widow, Catherine I (1725–1727), his young grandson, Peter II (1727–1730), and his niece, Anna (1730–1740).

Anna was a daughter of Peter's brother Ioann, who was co-tsar with Peter from 1682 to 1696 and died young. Anna's reign is remembered most for the political persecution of the opposition among the gentry and of the Old Believers,[1] the novel use of distant Siberian regions as places for political exile, and the advancement of various favorites, most of whom were of German origin and who exercised arbitrary power. Anna herself is usually portrayed as a nonentity under the thumb of her lover, Biron, an adventurer of Swedish descent who made his fortune in the Duchy of Courland, the patrimony of Anna's dead husband.[2] The very solid accomplishments of her reign are seldom mentioned. Notable among those accomplishments was the Great Northern Expedition, a massive undertaking whose contribution to geographic knowledge has never been surpassed. A decade spent mapping the entire Russian Arctic coast and gathering extensive scientific knowledge of Siberia is now little known outside of Russia except for the climax of the expedition, the voyage to America. Of importance, too, were the pioneering of Russia's thrust toward Japan, with the goal of establishing trade,[3] and strengthening commercial and diplomatic relations with China.

Anna's government was particularly concerned with the implementation of trade agreements with China following the Treaty of Kiakhta (21 October 1727, ratified 14 June 1728). This treaty established Kiakhta as the point of entry for Russian trade caravans that traveled to Peking and as an international trading center where Russian and Chinese merchants met and traded on a regular basis.

Russian merchants found a lucrative market in China, especially for furs. From this trade the Russian Crown derived hard currency, gold and silver. Anna's government saw to it that the state maintained a monopoly at Kiakhta on the sale of furs, the commodity the Chinese most desired.[4] The state's monopoly of the fur trade with China first had been promulgated in the reign of Peter's widow, Catherine I, on 30 December 1726 and 26 June 1727. Under Anna, in 1731, governmental control over the China caravan trade was implemented.[5]

Bering's expedition to America's Pacific coast, the Second Kamchatka Expedition, also commenced in Anna's reign but did not end until soon after Peter's daughter Elizabeth ascended the throne (1741–1762).[6]

Two vessels were built for the expedition and Petropavlovsk-Kamchatskii on Avacha Bay established as a base. Bering's *Sv. Petr* and Chirikov's *Sv. Pavel* cleared Avacha Bay on 4 June 1741. That was the last that was seen of them until 12 October, when only the *Sv. Pavel* returned. Of the seventy-five men, officers, sailors, and servants, who had started out aboard her, twenty-one had lost their lives.[7] Six, including two senior officers, had died on the return voyage; Louis Delisle de la Croyère, the French officer of the marine and the expedition's astronomer, had died just as the vessel was entering Avacha Bay.

The story of each vessel was very different. The two vessels had sailed southeast by south for latitude 46° N, following (as instructed by the senate) the chart compiled in 1733 by Joseph N. Delisle and presented by Delisle de la Croyère to Bering and his officers at Petropavlovsk. On 21 June the two vessels were parted in a storm and fog in the latitude of 50° N.

From then on, Chirikov had sailed on his own, reaching southeastern Alaska's panhandle. In the vicinity of Iakobii Island (Yakobi on U.S. maps), possibly at Takanis Bay,[8] Chirikov sent quartermaster Avram Dement'iev with the longboat and a crew of ten men, including two Kamchadal (Itel'men) interpreters, to reconnoiter the shore and replenish drinking water. Every man was armed, and the longboat carried one cannon. Dement'iev was to try to establish contact with native inhabitants and to find out "under whose sovereignty they are." He carried gifts, such as copper kettles, beads, and, from Chirikov's own store, ten-ruble coins. The party did not return.

Chirikov believed that Dement'iev might have suffered an accident and that the fires he observed on shore had been lit by survivors, especially as whoever had lit the fires responded to the firing of the ship's cannon by fanning the flame. After six days, on 24 July, he sent boatswain Sidor Savel'iev, with three men, ashore in the last small craft aboard the *Sv. Pavel*, to assist Dement'iev's crew. They, too, vanished. The next day, 25 July, Chirikov observed two wooden watercraft, of different sizes, approaching his vessel. At first he thought his men were returning safe and sound; however, he soon realized the craft were of a different construction and were not rowed but paddled. The smaller craft, which approached the vessel closer than the large one, carried four men, one in the stern,

Figure 10. Petropavlovsk on Kamchatka, Avacha Bay. Founded as a naval base by Bering in 1740. Watercolor by Luka Voronin, Billings-Sarychev expedition, 1786–1795. The caption on the painting reads: "We arrived in that harbor on 7th November 1789."

Courtesy RGAVMF, Fond 1331, op. 4, delo 704, fol. 16.

the other three paddling. One was dressed in red. Distance prevented discernment of their faces, but their shouts of "*agai, agai*" were heard. Gestures intended to encourage the craft to come closer had no effect and soon the craft turned back to land. Because of a lack of wind, Chirikov was unable to follow. The Savel'iev and Dement'iev parties had to be abandoned. It is surmised that these fifteen men were either killed or captured by the Tlingit. In later years, myths about blond, blue-eyed Indians on the Northwest Coast, alleged descendants of these men, would arise persistently, adding an additional dimension to the more ancient story of a Russian settlement on northern Alaskan shores.[9]

Shorthanded, no longer able to go ashore for water, and bitterly blaming himself, Chirikov consulted his officers and decided on an immediate return to Kamchatka.[10] The *Sv. Pavel* sailed along the coast, sighting Cape Spencer, Mt. Fairweather, the St. Elias Mountains, and Lituya Bay. On 27 July, Chirikov sighted Ocean Cape at the entry into Yakutat Bay. On 1 August, he sighted Cape Elizabeth at the entry into Cook Inlet and the outer, eastern Kenai Peninsula shore. Chirikov turned south, passing Afognak and Kodiak Islands, and then headed toward the Trinity Islands. He passed south of the Shumagin Islands, sighted Unalaska and Umnak Islands in the eastern Aleutians, and at least one of the Islands of Four Mountains group. On 9 September, Chirikov's vessel stood in a bay at Adak in the central Aleutians where the Russian expedition encountered Aleuts. Several times they came out to the ship in single-hatch kayaks, refusing to come aboard but staying near the vessel, sometimes for three or four hours. Chirikov noted in his log that these men resembled Tartars in appearance. The Aleuts proferred, as an opening gift, some edible vegetable roots, in return for which Chirikov offered ship's biscuits. They also offered pieces of a mineral wrapped in kelp, which Chirikov identified as *antimonium crudum*. He traded with them for water, spears (which the Aleuts carried on the decks of their kayaks), and one Aleut wooden hat, offering a china cup and cloth (which the Aleuts threw into the water), a copper kettle (which the Aleuts returned), Chinese pipes and tobacco, needles, and beads (all of which they accepted), knives (which the Aleuts asked for by gesture), and one old axe for the wooden hat (which the Aleuts accepted with expressions of great pleasure). Chirikov noted that the Aleuts were shrewd traders, driving a hard bargain, as they refused to trade one bladder (sea-mammal-stomach water container) for one knife, but demanded several knives for each container.

Chirikov sailed on the same day, passing another island, sighted one of the Rat Islands, probably Kiska, and on 21 and 22 September sighted another group of islands, believed by most investigators to have been Agattu and the Semichi Islands in the Near Islands group. However, there is a strong possibility that on that date he was near Kiska and then off Buldir. The weather was turning stormy with increasing frequency. Fog, heavy seas, rain, and snow added to the hardship. Drinking water was very low, and many of the crew suffered from scurvy. Between 16 September and 10 October, when the vessel entered Avacha Bay, six of Chirikov's men died of scurvy, including, as mentioned, Delisle de la Croyère. Except for him, all of the dead were buried at sea. When the vessel dropped anchor, Sublieutenant Levashov came aboard, bringing the news that Bering's *Sv. Petr* was still at sea. Chirikov, deathly ill with scurvy and unable to walk, was carried to the boat that took him off the ship.

By the next spring, Bering had not returned, and Chirikov, though not yet fully recovered, determined to sail once again to the islands he had sighted the previous summer.[11] In his report to the admiralty dated 18 October 1742, Chirikov wrote about the natural conditions he had observed in the Aleutians, such as the lack of tree growth and the relative scarcity of driftwood, the mountainous terrain, the rocky shores, submerged rocks and shoals, difficulty in locating good and safe anchorages, and weather conditions. The weather, he pointed out, interfered with astronomical measurements and adversely affected the quality of descriptions of the land formations sighted. He was particularly concerned about frequent fogs. He considered that because of "constant thick fogs" any future "navigation must take into account the constant danger of the vessels' loss."[12]

Chirikov left the harbor of Avacha Bay on 25 May 1742 and sighted the island Sv. Fedor (St. Theodore) on 9 June. He described the island as consisting of high, snow-covered mountains with steep shores all around, lacking good anchorage. After determining the trend of the coast, and having rounded the island and standing off its eastern shore, he was carried by a strong wind northward, and then continued to sail eastward for approximately 66 to 70 miles. On 17 June, he turned back, setting his course to the north of the Aleutian Chain.[13] On 22 and 23 June, he passed Bering Island, sailing from west to east, establishing its location and distances from points of reference on the Kamchatka Peninsula. He observed a multitude of fur seals. He named this island Sv. Iulian (St. Julian). On 2 July, Chirikov safely made port in the harbor of Sts. Peter and Paul (Petropavlovsk) that he and Bering had founded. Bering's ship had not yet returned. Chirikov collected the expedition personnel left on shore, plus equipment and material, and on 11 July 1742 sailed for Okhotsk, arriving safely on 16 August. Assuming Bering to be lost, Chirikov took over the command of the expedition.

The fate of Bering's ship was very different.[14] At the beginning of the voyage, 4 June 1741,[15] the flagship *Sv. Petr* was the second vessel to clear Avacha Bay. Chirikov's *Sv. Pavel* had overtaken her but awaited her in the open sea. Together the two vessels sailed southeast by south for the 46° latitude, as noted earlier, following the Delisle chart. (Waxell, master of the *Sv. Petr*, later bitterly blamed this chart for the loss of time and, thus, loss of life among his crew.) The two vessels lost sight of each other at about 50° N latitude. After three days' search for the other vessel, Bering continued on the set course. Only at 45° N latitude did he abandon the fruitless search for the mythical de Gama Land and Company Land on Delisle's chart and change his course to east by north and east-northeast. On 17 July, they sighted land: in the distance, to the northwest, rose towering, snow-covered mountains; the next day equally high mountain ridges appeared to the northeast. Bering named the ridge for St. Afinogen and the land to the northwest for St. Marina. On the nineteenth they were among offshore islets and semisubmerged rocks. By midnight an island was sighted, which Bering named for St. Elias. On 20 July,[16] they anchored off the island now called Kayak Island. The mountains on the mainland and an erupting volcano in the distance inspired awe.[17]

Fleet Master Sofron Khitrovo[18] took the longboat out to reconnoiter other small islands and channels nearby. A dory was dispatched to the nearest and largest island (Kayak Island), with orders to locate a source of fresh water. The expedition's naturalist, Steller, whose official duty was to report on any minerals and ores discovered in the new lands, but whose strong points were botany and zoology, went with the watering party. The dory soon returned, reporting that, indeed, water was available, and that they found two smoldering fires and many paths which showed that people had passed that way not long before, and wood stacked and prepared for use. Here also was a large quantity of smoked fish (the sailors brought back five or so strips) which proved to be very tasty. A number of red foxes, unafraid of men, were observed.

The next day, 21 July, Steller went on shore once again with the watering party and explored a bit farther afield.[19] Soon he found further signs of human occupancy. At the remnants of a fire he saw indications that meat had been boiled by the hot stone method and he identified the bones scattered around as those of a caribou. He also found dried fish strips, and razorback clam and blue mussel shells. He found an herb, called by Russians sweet grass (*Heracleum lanatum* Michx., called in Alaska wild celery), being prepared for use in the same manner as was done in Kamchatka: bundles of this herb were being soaked in water and then the stems scraped with sea shells. One of the parties found a wooden fire drill. All observers remarked that the fire drill was identical to the ones used in Kamchatka by the Itel'men. Steller noted, however, that the tinder used by the Americans was different: a sort of dried algae, he wrote (probably reindeer moss). Around the camp were many tree stumps that showed the marks of stone axes. Steller concluded that the Americans had felled the trees as building material. Trees stripped of their bark were even more numerous. Somewhat farther inland, Steller came upon a spot covered with cut grass. He removed the grass cover and found a storage pit, secured on the outside with rocks, then with tree bark placed in a quadrangle over horizontal pole supports. In the storage pit were several baskets of bark containing quantities of sweet grass, the inner layers of various fiber plants (some of which Steller identified as nettles), rolled-up bundles of the inner bark of cedar or spruce trees, and great bundles of kelp ropes. Underneath it all Steller found several rather long arrows (longer, he said, than those of the Itel'men and close to those of the Evenk of eastern Siberia), with shafts colored black. Bering ordered that several lengths of green-colored cloth, two knife blades, two metal tobacco pipes, about a pound of tobacco, and twenty Chinese trade beads be left at the storage pit as recompense for the several items Steller had taken.[20]

Khitrovo arrived on board soon thereafter. He reported that in the channel beyond the islands were safe anchorages where the vessel could find shelter. He also said that on one of the smaller islands he had come across a fish-processing camp with several structures for drying and storage. One structure was of planks covered with earth, with a plank floor. It was obvious, said Khitrovo, that the inhabitants had knives, axes, and other tools, as the wood was well worked and decorated with carved designs. He surmised that people were living on the mainland but came to the small islands to fish and to hunt sea mammals. From this camp Khitrovo brought a wooden basket, a shovel, a whetstone with traces of copper on it, and a stone with a slit (presumably a net weight).

In the afternoon of the same day Bering set the vessel on a western course, toward home. On 25 July, he consulted with his officers, Waxell, Khitrovo, and navigator Andris Eiselberg (a name found also spelled Geiselberg or Heiselberg), and the decision was made to continue sailing with the easterly winds, course between south and west[21] and, weather permitting, to explore the coast lying to the north. They passed the Kodiak archipelago, sighting the coast of Kodiak or possibly Sitkalidak Island on 26 July. During the night of 2 August, they passed an island in the fog which they named Tumannoi, the Foggy One, now called either Chirikof Island, after Vancouver renamed it in 1794 for his fellow navigator, or by the name derived from the Native one, Ukamak.[22] At 7 A.M. the next day, 3 August, they stood off an island that they named for Archdeacon Stephan.[23]

On 4 August they saw five small islands (now called the Semidi Islands), which Bering named Evdokievskie, for St. Eudoxia.[24] On 29 August at 8 A.M. they sighted a large group of islands, and in the early hours of 30 August they observed a fire on the shore of one of the islands. At 7 A.M. a boat was sent to one of the larger islands[25] where a freshwater lake was located and two water samples taken. Because of a lack of time, Bering decided to replenish the water supply from this somewhat brackish lake, a decision severely criticized by Steller in his journal.[26] This was Nagai, the island where the next day the sick were taken for a rest on shore and where seaman Nikita Shumagin died and was buried. Bering gave the sailor's name to the archipelago, and these islands still are known as the Shumagins. Steller spent his time collecting plant materials, among them several medicinal plants including an antiscorbutic,[27] and noting animal, bird, and fish species. Many sea and land birds and fish were familiar. The same or very similar species were found on Kamchatka and in Siberia—cod, Dolly Varden (char) or steelhead,[28] sculpin, halibut, and salmon. He noted the presence of fur seals in the sea. On land he saw red foxes, a black fox, marmots or ground squirrels, and tracks of an animal Steller presumed to have been a large wolf.[29] He also noted the presence of slate on Nagai Island.[30]

The anchorage was rather dangerous, as it was open to the winds from the Pacific. Bering was anxious to leave as soon as possible, unsure whether the anchor cables would hold, because the wind was rising. Nevertheless, Khitrovo asked to be sent to the island where fire had been observed on the previous night. Bering granted permission, and Khitrovo took out the yawl at 11 A.M. His assignment was to find the people and try to communicate with them. For this purpose he carried gifts: tobacco, needles, mirrors, knives, beads, and red cloth. Heavy seas prevented the yawl's return, and Khitrovo was forced to make his way to another island nearby, where he landed in heavy surf. The wind continued to freshen. On 2 September, the vessel was moved to a safer anchorage, sheltered from the wind by an island. On the third the longboat was dispatched to Khitrovo's camp. In heavy surf he and his men waded out to the longboat, up to their necks in icy water. The yawl was abandoned on shore, as the seas were too dangerous for a small boat.[31] Khitrovo reported that on the first island he visited, he found remnants of a fire, still warm, but did not meet any people. A southwesterly wind was blowing, accompanied by heavy rain, but the anchors held through the night.

The next day the vessel continued to sail among the islands. Iushin, in the longboat, was sounding depth and determining the fairway. In the evening the longboat was taken on board. "It appears that it is impossible to get clear of the islands and it is very dangerous to be here under sail in night time," noted Navigator Iushin. The experienced seamen longed for the safety of the open sea.[32]

Toward the evening of 5 September, Khitrovo's party returned to the island on which they had spent the previous night and dropped anchor in a relatively safe place. The wind blew strongly again, this time from the southeast. In the night the sailors heard voices and once again saw a fire on shore. The next day two single-hatch kayaks approached within shouting distance. The interpreter shouted in the Koriak and Chukchi languages, but it was obvious that the Americans did not understand them. Nevertheless, the two kayakers came closer to the ship, one maintaining a greater distance than the other. Before approaching, this man painted his face "from the wings of his nose across the cheeks in the shape of two pears" with an "iron- or lead-colored shiny earth." This may have indicated "caution, but no hostile intent."[33] Trade goods were tied to a board and thrown into the water: red cloth, mirrors, three Chinese metal pipes, beads, and one bronze or copper bell.[34] The gifts were accepted, and in return the Natives threw the sailors two polished staffs, to one of which was tied a bundle of feathers, to the other a bird's foot surrounded with feathers. Steller says, however, that it was not the islander's intent to give the sailors the second stick. Rather, he wanted the Koriak interpreter to place a piece of red Chinese silk, which he displayed, onto the claw. When the Koriak held on to the stick, the Native let go and paddled away from the vessel. No matter how the sailors tried, the Natives would not go on board, to Waxell's great disappointment. In the meantime, the Americans indicated by gesture that *their* visitors should come to land. By then a group of Natives was observed on shore. These, too, gestured invitingly.

At 7 PM, Waxell himself took out the longboat. Nine sailors, including the Chukchi interpreter, all armed but hiding their weapons, came along. Steller was included in the party.[35] They could not land because of the heavy surf. Waxell dropped a grapnel to hold the boat in place and cautiously advanced closer to shore among the rocks. Three men, two Russians and a Chukchi, waded to shore. One of the elders or leaders of the Americans entered his kayak (which he had lifted with one hand and carried down to the water)[36] and came close to Waxell's boat. Waxell offered him a drink of vodka (the visitors having demonstrated that it was a palatable drink), which the American tried but spat out. He then refused the gifts Waxell offered, except for a pipe, and returned to shore. Steller, who earlier had thought a few dwellings could be seen on shore from the ship,[37] now felt the Americans were urging the visitors to come ashore and visit their habitation.

In the meantime, Waxell's men wandered around for about an hour but never ventured out of sight of the boat. They later reported that they had counted nine single-hatch kayaks and gave the first detailed description of the Aleut speed kayak with bifurcated bow (including the wooden piece inserted into it, presumably to prevent sea weeds from clogging it up) and drip skirt used to keep water out of the kayak. Waxell and Steller also observed in great detail the construction of this craft and later gave very good descriptions of it. Waxell particularly noted how the drip skirt was secured by a cord over the shoulder of the person riding the kayak.[38] On the kayaks' decks were red-colored shafts (presumably spears thrown by means of a throwing stick, used by both the Aleuts and Kodiak Islanders as well as by the Chugach of Prince William Sound, which the visitors failed to identify).

There were nine men in the group of Americans.[39] No armament was observed; the absence of bows and arrows was noted in particular. The Russians also noted that one or two men had iron knives (one of the Americans split a bladder with one). The men wore their knives in sheaths suspended from belts. These knives, not made in the European manner, were approximately eight inches long, broad, with rather thick blades. Steller was puzzled but surmised that the knives were obtained through Native trade, as he knew that the Chukchi traded knives and axes from the Russians which they exchanged with American Natives for pelts, and then traded the latter to the Russians at Anadyr'.[40] The men wore whale-gut, water-resistant shirts, which are now called by the Russian word *kamleika* and which served as the prototype for our modern rain gear and, since the eighteenth century, for sailors' water-resistant clothing. These shirts were calf length. Some wore them loose, others belted with a cord. The Aleuts wore pants of sealskin, colored red (Steller assumed the coloration was by means of alder bark dye). Two men wore boots.[41] Steller characterized the pants and boots as being of Itel'men fashion.[42] They wore hats of sea lion skin decorated predominantly with falcon feathers.[43] Their nostrils were stuffed with grass. Some had their faces painted in red, others in blue. They offered whale blubber and roots which they dug out while the visitors watched.

The visit was going well, but as the wind was rising, Waxell recalled his men to the boat. The Americans grabbed the Chukchi and would not let him go. Waxell ordered that muskets be fired into the air. The shots echoed loudly, and the Americans released their captive, who plunged into the sea and made it to the boat safely, though very scared. The Americans, who at the noise had fallen to the ground, picked themselves up and saw no damage, nor did they show any signs of fear. Waxell concluded that they were unfamiliar with firearms.

The next morning, 6 September, seven[44] kayaks came out single file, the men shouting in what the observers assumed to be a ritual fashion because they had shouted in this manner on previous occasions. They wore wooden visors decorated with feathers. Two approached the vessel, making fast to the rope ladder (*falrep*). The Americans offered gifts: two wooden visors, colored green and red on the inside (one decorated with a bone figurine of a man), and a five-foot-long staff decorated at one end with various bird feathers, the metallic face paint, and a human figurine of bone.[45] The sailors also gave gifts, a metal kettle and needles. Waxell thought the Americans would come on board, but the wind was freshening rapidly, a storm was approaching, and all the Americans hurried to land. Waxell proposed to capture all nine men, but Bering forbade any such action.

The vessel hoisted sails and headed for the open sea. As they passed the island, the Americans stood in a group, shouting in the same ritual manner as when they had greeted the new arrivals. Thus ended the first encounter between Russian sailors and the American inhabitants of southwestern Alaska. They were the last human beings Bering's men would meet until the survivors reached Kamchatka a year later.

The season was late, the weather gloomy with high winds, rain, and sleet. The ship fought continually against the wind. Supplies were dwindling. The number of sick increased every day. Bering and his officers had but one thought: to make it safely to home port. Navigation was difficult because clouds hid the sun during the day and the stars in the night sky. In addition, they soon noticed that there were magnetic disturbances and consequently the compass was unreliable. Waxell was to write later:

> We had to sail in an unknown ocean, not described by anyone, like blind men, not knowing if we were sailing too fast or too slow and unable to determine our location. I do not know if there is anything more joyless, or a more desperate condition, than sailing in undescribed waters. From my own experience I am able to maintain that during the five months' voyage in the region unexplored as yet by anyone I had seldom had a few uninterrupted hours of sleep; I was under constant tension, anticipating dangers and misfortunes.[46]

They kept well to the south to be clear of the dangerous, unknown coast. In the distance, far inland, they saw on 25 September a high volcano, which they named for St. John the Baptist, whose feast day was approaching.[47]

The vessel continued to beat her way westward. Several more islands were sighted and named: the islands of St. Markian, St. Stephan (with three other small islands nearby),[48] and St. Abraham, presumably one of the Near Islands, at the western end of the Aleutian Chain. They sighted the Semichi Islands, a low, small island now called Shemya, and several islets and offshore rocks.

Deaths followed one after the other; burials at sea took place almost every day. Severe storms came without respite, and the weather was getting colder: snow and hail fell almost every day. On 4 November at eight o'clock in the morning, land was sighted. The next day three men died. Bering and several of his officers were extremely ill. Thirty-three men of all ranks were sick. The next morning, Waxell, in actual command but operating on Bering's instructions, called a meeting of all hands in Bering's cabin, as the captain was unable to leave his bed. The men discussed whether to sail on in hope of reaching their home port, the Kamchatkan harbor of Sts. Peter and Paul. Since most of the crew were unable to perform their duties, the ship's company voted to proceed toward the land that was in sight, find a safe anchorage, and save both the vessel and the men.

Many among the crew hoped they were landing on the Kamchatkan coast. Wrote Waxell:

> In the five months of our voyage we never came to explored or known land. Thus, we had no opportunity to correct and bring into order our logs and reckoning. After all, we did not even have a sea chart to guide us, but went ahead like blind men, by feel, not knowing where we were headed. Our sole aid was a blank Mercator grid we drew ourselves before leaving Kamchatka on which we daily marked our route of twenty-four hours proceeding eastward [by dead reckoning] and the same on our return trek.[49]

Next day, they found an open bay, under the circumstances the best possible anchorage. An anchor was dropped, but the cable parted, and the wind and strong seas carried the vessel through the surf into the shallow water. The vessel was secured and the longboat sent out. The weather was foul. From 6 to 22 November, when weather permitted, the sick were transported to land. Those who were still on their feet constructed shelter, using the house depressions of what we now know to have been the remains of a Neolithic village.[50] By 22 November no one remained on the vessel, which they believed was securely anchored. In the meantime, Waxell sent out Constable Boris Roselius, accompanied by two Kamchatkan residents who had once lived in the vicinity of Karagin Island, to reconnoiter the area to the north. After six days they returned, having walked about thirty miles over arduous terrain, but finding no sign of human habitation. In the meantime, a severe Aleutian autumn storm tore the vessel off her cables and drove her onto the beach. She was heavily damaged below the water line and her rudder was torn off.

On 8 December 1741, Bering died. Sailor Anchugov and the Kamchatkan residents, among them Petr Verkhoturov, set out once again, this time to reconnoiter the area to the south. They were away for four weeks. When they returned, they reported that the ship's company was on an island, one not known to the Kamchatkans. It was clear they could not count on rescue and would have to spend the winter on this newly found, uninhabited island. Provisions were scarce, and Waxell ordered a large portion of them to be saved for the return home in the spring. Rations were assigned to each man "without distinction of rank or station." Waxell's twelve-year-old son was to share his father's ration because he was not an official member of the expedition. Orders were issued that, come spring, everyone would dig edible roots and collect edible plants for subsistence. Luckily, there was a food source available: Anchugov reported large groups of sea otters. Those able to keep on their feet clubbed the animals on land and brought the carcasses to the camp to share with the sick and weak. They ate the entire carcass; entrails were boiled to make broth for the very ill. A drift whale was a godsend, though the carcass was rather rank; the meat was boiled and the blubber swallowed raw in small pieces.

By March sea otters were not found so easily on shore, but soon a new source of food began to arrive—fur seals. The island on which the expedition had stranded itself is one of the major rookeries, or breeding grounds, of the northern fur seal. Fur seals as food were not as palatable as sea otters, but with the fur seals came sea lions, and young sea lions became a favorite dish. In the spring, when men were recovering from scurvy by eating nutritious, new green plant food, they ventured to kill several young sea cows. This animal's meat was a real delicacy.[51]

Procurement of driftwood, a needed fuel for warmth and cooking, was a continuing problem. In the winter, digging driftwood from under deep snow was onerous labor and the quantity was small. As time went on, men were forced to wander ever farther from camp to collect it, a great hardship in winter. As the weather became more clement and the men felt stronger, this task was less formidable, even if the men had to go far from camp on their search. Arctic foxes, numerous and hated pests, stole food and gnawed on the bodies of the dead, even sniffed and bit the men who were too sick and weak to drive them off. With the men's improved health they now were able to scare the predators away or, on occasion, kill them.

With spring, too, the men's thoughts turned to the trip home. They believed their homeland was not too far away: in winter, on the island's western shore, they had found items of Russian and Itel'men manufacture, and in clear weather saw high mountains on the horizon. On the eastern shore, among driftwood, they found American-style spear shafts and double-bladed paddles.

The beached ship was inspected and found wanting. Not only had the vessel suffered considerable structural damage, but sand had drifted over it up to seven or eight feet deep. By vote, they decided to cannibalize their vessel and construct a smaller one in which they would set out for Kamchatka. Among the officers was one dissenting vote: Dmitrii Ovtsyn, formerly a naval officer and leader of a detachment of the Great Northern Expedition operating along the Arctic Ocean coast. He had been cashiered because he befriended a member of the opposition to the government, Prince Dolgorukii, who was in exile on the Ob' River. Ovtsyn, who served as Bering's adjutant (having the rank of able seaman, first class), argued for refloating the vessel and against damage and destruction of naval property. Waxell and Khitrovo overruled his objections.

Construction of the new vessel commenced on 6 May 1742, following a party for the entire crew hosted by Waxell. Everyone was busy. There was no time for leisure, and card games, their only recreation, were a thing of the past. Waxell had permitted these games to alleviate boredom when the men were growing stronger, although Steller had strenuously objected, citing admiralty regulations forbidding games of chance.

One-third of the men went hunting every day to provide food for the carpenters. They found a drift whale and carried blubber and meat on their shoulders to those who worked on constructing the new vessel or dismantling the old *paketbot*. At this time, they took their first adult sea cow; the giant animal was hooked from a boat, and forty men, wading into the water, held on to the line while the boat crew continued to stab the wounded animal with spears and swords, then pulled the exhausted beast to shore.[52] This animal provided such quantities of meat that men previously employed in hunting and other means of food procurement could be assigned to the building crew.

Other tasks were repairing water barrels, making new barrels, and constructing a dory capable of carrying up to ten men. Masts, tackle, rigging, and sails had to be repaired and a rudder made. Khitrovo and Iushin charted the coast and offshore islands. By 10 August, the new single-masted vessel, of the hooker type (*gukor*), was afloat and christened in honor of their old ship, *Sv. Petr.* This vessel proved to be so well constructed and maneuverable that, upon their return to Kamchatka, it became part of the Okhotsk port flotilla and, as late as 1752, carried cargo on the Kamchatka run.[53] The vessel was loaded and the forty-six survivors were on board by 13 August. Most of the men carried bundles of the precious sea otter furs, a total of 700 skins, of which 200 belonged to Dr. Steller.[54] They sailed on 14 August. On shore they left some of their equipment in a shed, and they also left their dead, whose resting place was marked by a large Orthodox cross. As they sailed away, arctic foxes were overrunning their camp and devouring anything chewable or edible that had been left behind.[55]

The next day they encountered a severe storm and had to abandon the longboat which they had had in tow. The new vessel sprang a leak, and all hands took turns at the pumps. They jettisoned the cannon balls and shot they carried as part of the ballast and some of the personal luggage to lighten the vessel. The leak was repaired, and on 17 August they sighted the Kamchatkan coast. On 26 August 1742 they entered their home port, the Harbor of Sts. Peter and Paul. Of the seventy-six souls who had started the voyage, thirty-one had perished.

The survivors arrived in port only to find that Chirikov had given up waiting for them and sailed for Okhotsk. Waxell thought to follow him, but the vessel had sprung a new leak and, as the season was late, he decided to winter in Petropavlovsk. On 6 November 1742, he dispatched a detailed report about the voyage of the *Sv. Petr*, along with the charts and logs, to the Admiralty College in St. Petersburg. In the report he stated that Bering and his officers had intended "following the example of other European nations" to name the newly discovered American coast New Russia.[56]

Chirikov and Waxell fully expected there would be a follow-up to the expedition and that they would sail to New Russia again soon. Chirikov especially kept submitting proposals for the renewal of the expedition. In St. Petersburg, however, a new government, that of the young Empress Elizabeth, had other concerns. On 24 September 1743, in St. Petersburg, the empress signed the recommendation of her government to close the matter. In her own hand she wrote, "So be it." For the next twenty years, exploration and gaining footholds on the American continent would be left solely to Russian private entrepreneurs and frontiersmen.

NOTES

1. The number of political exiles, however, was very small. The total number of "some twenty to thirty thousand" (Riasanovsky, *A History of Russia,* 3d ed. New York: Oxford University Press, 1977: 271) includes the Old Believers. At the end of the seventeenth–early eighteenth century, Pomor'ie, the White Sea littoral and, in general, the regions of the Russian North were the main strongholds of the Old Belief (centered on the Solovetskii Monastery).
2. Some documents pertaining to Biron's elevation to the ranks of the nobility, his antecedents, and early career are in the Manuscript Division, Library of Congress ("Russia: Miscellaneous").
3. On Russian interest in Japan see N. N. Ogloblin, "Pervyi iaponets v Rossii, 1701–1705 gg.," *Russkaia starina* 72, no. 10 (October 1891): 11–24; A. S. Sgibnev, "Ob obuchenii v Rossii iaponskomu iazyku," *Morskoi sbornik* 99, no. 12 (1868): 55–61; idem, "Popytki russkikh k zavedeniiu torgovykh snoshenii s Iaponieiu v XVIII i nachale XIX stoletii," *Morskoi sbornik* 101, no. 1 (1869): 37–72. Highly recommended works by a prominent American historian, George Alexander Lensen, are: *The Russian Push Toward Japan: Russo-Japanese Relations, 1697–1875* (New York: Octagon Books, 1971); "Early Russo-Japanese Relations," *Far Eastern Quarterly* 10, no. 1 (November 1950): 2–37; and *Report from Hokkaido: The Remains of Russian Culture in Northern Japan* (Hakodate, Japan: Municipal Library of Hakodate, 1954).
4. Two excellent treatments of the topic in English are Clifford M. Foust, *Muscovite and Mandarin: Russia's Trade with China and Its Setting, 1727–1805* (Chapel Hill: University of North Carolina Press, 1969), and M. I. Sladkovsky, *The Long Road: Sino-Russian Economic Contacts from Ancient Times to 1917,* translation of the revised Russian text by Liv Tudge (Moscow: Progress Publishers, 1981), originally published in Russian as *Istoriia torgovo-ekonomicheskikh otnoshenii narodov Rossii s Kitaem do 1917 goda* (Moscow: Izdatel'stvo "Nauka," 1974). See especially Foust, *Muscovite and Mandarin,* 68–163.
5. These monopolistic economic policies continued under Elizabeth (1741–1761), affecting the structure of the early private fur trade in the Russian Far East and the fur procurement expeditions to the Aleutians. The restriction on the private sale of furs in the Chinese trade was not lifted until 1762, when the reign of Catherine the Great commenced. On this topic see Foust, *Muscovite and Mandarin,* 286. On government regulations and restrictions on private and government trade in Siberia in the seventeenth century, see Lantzeff, *Siberia in the Seventeenth Century,* 146–149.
6. Peter the Great changed the rules of monarchical succession, establishing the right of females to the throne and that of the ruling monarch to designate his or her heir. Because he was unable, in his last illness, to indicate clearly whom he designated as his heir, king makers had a free field from 1725 to the reign of Catherine the Great (1762). Anna was childless and designated her

great-nephew Ioann as her heir. At the time of Anna's death, Ioann was an infant, two months old. By Anna's will, her lover, Biron, was to be regent. Soon, however, Biron was overthrown in a coup, and Anna Leopoldovna, mother of Ioann V, became regent. In less than a year, in another coup, Peter's younger daughter, Elizabeth, was placed on the throne. See Riasanovsky, *A History of Russia*, 268–275; Vernadsky, *A History of Russia* (1951).

7. In the literature there is a discrepancy in the number of casualties among Chirikov's crew. Golder gives the number as twenty-two, while Lebedev claims there were twenty-four, based on Chirikov's report to the admiralty of 7 December 1741. The figure includes men who landed in Tlingit territory and did not return and six men who died on the return voyage.

8. The exact location where Chirikov lost his men has been an object of scholarly dispute for decades. I chose to follow the reconstruction of D. M. Lebedev, *Plavanie A. I. Chirikova*, 49–61. Reconstruction by Ellsworth P. Bertholf (Golder, *Bering's Voyages*, vol. 2, map) places the event in the vicinity of Yakobi Island also, but Golder identifies the location as Lisianski Strait (ibid., vol. 1, 314). Davidson, *Tracks and Landfalls*, places the event in Sitka Sound. It should be noted that the name Iakobii (Yakobi) Island was given by A. A. Baranov to the island Takhanes, prior to 1797 (RGIA, St. Petersburg, Fond 1374, op. 2, delo 1672, fol. 1r–1v).

9. The Tlingit oral tradition maintains that Chirikov's men married into Tlingit society. See Wallace M. Olson, *The Tlingi: An Introduction to Their Culture and History*, 2d ed. (Auke Bay, Alaska: Heritage Research, 1991), 51.

10. On the loss of the two boats, see Chirikov's report to the Admiralty College dated 7 December 1741 in Narochnitskii et al., *Russkie ekspeditsii* (1984), 222–231 (doc. 142); Pokrovskii, *Ekspeditsiia Beringa*, 273–285; Müller, *Bering's Voyages*, 101–102. On Chirikov's self-blame, see his letter to Spangsberg dated October 1741 (Pokrovskii, *Ekspeditsiia Beringa*, 334–335, also cited in Lebedev, *Plavanie A. I. Chirikova*, 64).

11. The log of Chirikov's 1742 voyage has never been published. The only published documents I was able to locate were Chirikov's reports to the Admiralty College of 18 October 1742 (Pokrovskii, *Ekspeditsiia Beringa*, 290–297). His 1742 charts also were never published. Conventional wisdom states that Chirikov did not sail farther than the Near Islands, specifically Attu, naming the island Sv. Fedor (St. Theodore). Attu and Agattu were first identified as Chirikov's landfalls by Golder, *Bering's Voyages*, vol. 1, chart by Bertholf. This identification is repeated by Lebedev, *Plavanie A. I. Chirikova*, 96–103, and by Grekov, *Ocherki po istorii*, 128–129. Chirikov's description of the island in the report cited above does not fit either Attu or Agattu Islands. The description suggests Buldir Island. However, the configuration of the island of St. Theodore, as it is represented on early eighteenth-century charts of the Aleutians, suggests Kiska in the Rat Islands (Lydia T. Black, *The Lovtsov Atlas of the North Pacific Ocean* [Kingston, Ontario; Fairbanks, Alaska: Limestone Press, 1991]). The cartographic information on his tracks is presented in the composite chart compiled in 1767 by Admiral Nagaev. Interestingly, Nagaev shows Chirikov's tracks outward bound beyond the Near Islands, to the east, as far as the Rat Islands group, to Amchitka (Efimov, ed., *Atlas*, chart 140).

12. Pokrovskii, *Ekspeditsiia Beringa*, 291–292.

13. See note 11, above.

14. In recounting the events of Bering's voyage, I relied on available published primary materials. For the voyage of the *Sv. Petr*, under the command of Bering himself, see P. Pekarskii, "Arkhivnye razyskaniia ob izobrazhenii nesushchestvuiushchago nyne zhivotnago *Rhytina borealis* (so snimkom starinnago izobrazheniia *Rhytina borealis*)," *Zapiski Imperatorskoi akademii nauk* (St. Petersburg) 15, suppl. 1 (1869): 1–33; A. Sokolov, "Severnaia ekspeditsiia 1733–1741 godov," *Zapiski Gidrograficheskago departamenta Morskogo ministerstva* 9 (1851): 190–469 and charts; V. Andreev, "Dokumenty po ekspeditsii kapitan-komandora Beringa v Ameriku v 1741," *Morskoi sbornik* 255, no. 5 (1893); Pokrovskii, *Ekspeditsiia Beringa;* Golder, *Bering's Voyages;* Divin, *Russkaia Tikhookeanskaia epopeia;* Narochnitskii et al., *Russkie ekspeditsii* (1984); Waxell, *Vtoraia Kamchatskaia ekspeditsiia;* Steller, *Journal of a Voyage;* idem, *Manuscript Journal;* Müller, *Nachrichten von Seereisen*. It should be noted that A. I. Andreev, in his introduction to the Russian-language edition of Waxell's account, stated that Müller had access to it and used excerpts from it, without attribution (Waxell, *Vtoraia*

Kamchatskaia ekspeditsiia, 8–9). Documents pertaining to the voyage are also found in vols. 8 and 9 of *Polnoe sobranie zakonov Rossiiskoi Imperii s 1649 goda.* In addition, I used charts published by Grekov, *Ocherki po istorii;* Efimov (as cited previously); and Berg, *Otkrytie Kamchatki,* 254–257. The earliest accounts about this expedition were those of 1747, in Danish, based on a report by Waxell to the Russian admiralty, found in Johann Georg Gmelin, *D. Johann Georg Gmelins... Reise durch Sibirien, von dem Jahr 1733 bis 1743...,* 4 vols. (Göttingen, 1751–1752). Another, written in 1753, is a highly unreliable and distorted version by J. N. Delisle to which Müller responded anonymously in his famous *Lettre d'un officier de la marine Russienne* (cited above in its English version).

15. All dates pertaining to Bering's voyage are given in the Julian calendar. In the eighteenth century, the Julian calendar was eleven days behind the Gregorian one, twelve days behind in the nineteenth century, and thirteen days behind the twentieth century. The ship's log began at noon. To recalculate dates in the logs of Bering's vessels for a contemporary calendar, we must add thirteen days and then subtract one, as there was no international date line in Bering's time.

16. There are discrepancies in the primary sources about the time when Bering ordered the vessel to hoist anchor the next day, 21 July. According to the logs, two boats were sent out on 20 July, the first of more than one trip for water nearby. Khitrovo returned to the vessel on 21 July; Steller, who went with the yawl or dory to Kayak Island, also returned on 21 July but somewhat earlier than Khitrovo. Waxell, writing in 1758 (*Vtoraia Kamchatskaia ekspeditsiia,* 58) stated that the vessel sailed promptly at 6:00 AM. In Iushin's log (supported by Khitrovo's log in Pokrovskii, *Ekspeditsiia Beringa,* 347) Khitrovo returned in the longboat at "9 o'clock after midday" (Narochnitskii et al., *Russkie ekspeditsii* [1984], 237).

17. On a chart drawn by Waxell in 1741 (published in *Vtoraia Kamchatskaia ekspeditsiia*) a huge erupting volcano was indicated due north of Kayak Island. Traditionally, it is assumed that this was Mt. St. Elias.

18. Died 1756 with the rank of vice admiral.

19. It is clear from the ship's log kept by Subnavigator Iushin that Steller went ashore twice, on 20 and 21 July, with the watering party on Kayak Island. Steller's accounts, found in his *Journal of a Voyage* and in Golder, *Bering's Voyages,* vol. 2, suggested that he went ashore only once and then for six hours. It should be noted that Steller's accounts, including his "journal," are composites. The journal was compiled by Steller in Kamchatka upon the expedition's return. The available logs are often in disagreement with Steller's assertions. There is scholarly disagreement as to how many logs were kept aboard the *Sv. Petr:* whether one log was kept in which several officers recorded events, or if each officer kept his own log. Narochnitskii et al. discuss this question in detail in note 93 (*Russkie ekspeditsii* [1984], 298). They incline to the opinion that there were three logs. One of these was a composite, compiled on the basis of notations made by various officers during the voyage. It was signed by Waxell and Khitrovo and presented to their commanding officer, Chirikov, and eventually to the admiralty as the official log of the expedition. The original did not survive, but there are four contemporary copies signed by the two officers. The other two journals are by Iushin and Khitrovo, respectively. Excerpts of Khitrovo's journal are available in several publications of documents pertaining to Bering's voyages, but the full text has never been published. Golder (*Bering's Voyages,* vol. 1) used in part Iushin's and in part Khitrovo's journal. Narochnitskii et al. consider, however, that Iushin's journal has the greatest detail and accuracy with respect to observations made on American shores. Excerpts from the Iushin journal are presented by Narochnitskii et al., *Russkie ekspeditsii* (1984), 232–249.

20. Bering's officers' and Steller's version of this event do not agree. According to Steller (*Journal of a Voyage,* 72), he suggested to Bering that gifts should be left behind. The gifts were sent, and only then were items taken from the storage pit.

21. Waxell's report of 15 November 1742 in Golder, *Bering's Voyages,* vol. 1, 270–282; Narochnitskii et al., *Russkie ekspeditsii* (1984), 262–270 (doc. 156).

22. Traditionally, Tumannoi is identified as Chirikof Island. Khitrovo, however, drew an outline of Tumannoi Island and indicated its trend; this rough map does not correspond to Chirikof Island

but is in concordance with Tugidak Island. It appears that Chirikof Island was the one they sighted the next day and named for Archdeacon Stephan; see note 23.

23. Iushin's log in Narochnitskii et al., *Russkie ekspeditsii* (1984), 239. The Feast of Archdeacon Stephan is, indeed, celebrated on 2 August according to the Orthodox ecclesiastical calendar. However, there is a second entry in Iushin's log (ibid., 246) for 28 October, to the effect that at 7:30 AM they sighted an island, which they named for *Prepodobnyi Stephan.*
24. Iushin's log in Narochnitskii et al., *Russkie ekspeditsii* (1984), 240.
25. Waxell, *Vtoraia Kamchatskaia ekspeditsiia,* 59. Waxell's chart (facing p. 128) shows twelve islands and several very small ones. The trend of Nagai Island and the concentration of islands to the east of Nagai are indicated correctly. To the north and west of Nagai is shown Unga, probably only part of its coast. Khitrovo's sketch (reproduced in Golder, *Bering's Voyages,* vol. 2, 76, and in Steller, *Journal of a Voyage,* 88) shows the vessel's anchorage off Nagai and a group of islands to the east of Nagai. It does not represent all the islands the expedition sighted in the Shumagin group.
26. Steller went ashore on Nagai, according to his journal, but this fact is not noted in the two logs by Iushin and Khitrovo.
27. Steller, in his journal, noted that he collected these "for my use and the Captain-Commander's" (*Journal of a Voyage,* 93). Contrary to the established belief, Steller was not the expedition's physician. Assistant physician Mathias Bet'ie (also spelled Betge in some sources) served in that capacity. It is worth noting that Bet'ie shared the "German dugout" with Steller (see below). Like Steller, he survived the voyage. He is barely mentioned in Steller's journal. As noted by Dr. Robert Fortuine in his presentation at the Bering/Chirikov 250th Anniversary Symposium, held in Anchorage, Alaska, in August 1991, Steller was highly selective concerning whom he treated for scurvy and with whom he shared medicines and food. On Bering Island Steller claimed to have organized a majority of the Germans (five in all) to share a dugout. Steller's two servants or assistants, Bering's former servants (before his death), and one other Russian eventually came to share the dugout, but only as servants and subordinates who had to follow without question the orders given by the Germans (ibid., 133, and more explicitly in the manuscript version, Steller's *Manuscript Journal*). Steller's journal and reports to the Academy of Sciences are self-serving. The journal, originally published in 1793, is at the core of the belief, reinforced by Steller's biographers (see editor's introduction to *Journal of a Voyage*), that his were the main achievements and that survival of the crew was solely due to him. Interestingly, Steller also claims that the only sailor aboard who understood navigation, weather, and so on was a fellow German, Navigator Andreas Eserlberkh or Eselberg (Eiselberg). The latter, who shared the dugout with Waxell, died on Bering Island. Waxell's accounts have to be compared to that of Steller in order to achieve a more balanced picture.
28. Steelheads and Dolly Varden do not occur in the same locations, but both are called by the same term in Russian.
29. Local residents surmise that Steller may have seen a land otter or a young bear or bear cub, though wolves are known to appear sometimes in the Shumagins, crossing from the Alaskan mainland probably on winter ice. See Steller, *Journal of a Voyage,* 91, 201–202, ed. n. 24.
30. This is a very important archaeological datum. Slate tools have been found in the Aleutian Islands, but the site of the slate quarries is not known. The presence of slate on Nagai Island is confirmed by local elders.
31. Waxell, *Vtoraia Kamchatskaia ekspeditsiia,* 62–63; Waxell's report of 15 November 1742 to the admiralty in Narochnitskii et al., *Russkie ekspeditsii* (1984), 264.
32. The Shumagin Island group consists of more than thirty islands. The straits (in Alaska "passes") between these islands are still extremely dangerous to navigate, even with today's charts, electronic equipment, and *The Coast Pilot.* There is little doubt that night sailing in the then-uncharted waters of the Shumagins was a harrowing experience for the crew. Steller's accusations of cowardice against the vessel's officers provoke Homeric laughter among modern fishermen who sail out of Sand Point on Popov Island in the Shumagins.

33. Steller, *Journal of a Voyage*, 98. Waxell, *Vtoraia Kamchatskaia ekspeditsiia*, 67, observed that the men he encountered on shore had their faces painted red and blue, traditional Kodiak Islanders' war colors. According to Hieromonk Gedeon, who was on Kodiak 1803–1807, Kodiak Islanders often painted their faces, and black was used only in times of sorrow or in war (*The Round the World Voyage of Hieromonk Gideon, 1803–1809*, trans. Lydia T. Black, ed. Richard A. Pierce [Kingston, Ontario; Fairbanks, Alaska: Limestone Press, 1989], 58–59). The so-called glitter paint found archaeologically on several Kodiak Island artifacts is not a true black, but grayish-blue. For other mention of face painting on Kodiak see Grigorii I. Shelikhov, *A Voyage to America, 1783–1786*, trans. Marina Ramsay, ed. Richard A. Pierce (Kingston, Ontario: Limestone Press, 1981), 54; Carl Heinrich Merck, *Siberia and Northwestern America, 1788–1792: The Journal of Carl Heinrich Merck, Naturalist with the Russian Scientific Expedition Led by Captains Joseph Billings and Gavriil Sarychev*, trans. from the German manuscript by Fritz Jaensch, ed. Richard A. Pierce (Kingston, Ontario: Limestone Press, 1980), 100–101. All early observers agree that while Kodiak men painted their faces in many contexts, only women were heavily tattooed. Tattooing by both sexes was observed among the Aleuts in the eighteenth century east of the Near Islands (where, too, only women were tattooed). On Kodiak, men with facial tattoos were encountered rarely. These were transvestites, and probably shamans.

34. Thus in Waxell's report in Narochnitskii et al., *Russkie ekspeditsii* (1984), 264. Steller does not list the gifts that were offered. In Khitrovo's log, as published by Pokrovskii (*Ekspeditsiia Beringa*, 352) "three metal bowls" are listed. This is probably a misreading of *ganza* (pipe) as *taz* (bowl). Iushin's log (Narochnitskii et al., *Russkie ekspeditsii* [1984], 244) reads "3 Chinese *gamza*."

35. Steller's (*Journal of a Voyage* and *Manuscript Journal*) and Waxell's (*Vtoraia Kamchatskaia ekspeditsiia*) accounts supplement each other. Their detailed observations are of extreme importance to ethnographers, indicating significant cultural variation among the groups inhabiting the Aleutian area. Some details indicate a strong influence, probably via eastern Alaska Peninsula settlers from Kodiak Island (Alutiiq). Another indication of Kodiak Island influence is the suggestion that at first contact Shumagin Islanders were whalers. There is another possibility, however, suggested by the description of details of clothing and face painting, namely, that the "Aleuts" encountered in the outer Shumagin Islands by the men of the *Sv. Petr* were sea mammal hunters and whalers from the Alaska Peninsula or even Kodiak Island raiders. Local Shumagin archipelago lore focuses sharply on wars with and raids by the Kodiak Islanders. Facial paint is characteristic of Kodiak Islanders' usage, especially when on a war party.

36. Steller, *Manuscript Journal*, 192.

37. Ibid.

38. Waxell's description (*Vtoraia Kamchatskaia ekspeditsiia*, 66–67) is the most detailed. He and Khitrovo also illustrated the kayak on the charts they drew. Steller's description of the kayak was not as precise as Waxell's, but he included the description of the double-bladed kayak paddles characteristically in use by the Aleuts. For the best discussion of the Aleut kayak and of the bifurcated-bow feature see George Dyson, *Baidarka* (Edmonds, Wash.: Alaska Northwest Publishing Company, 1986).

39. Steller's note that both men and women were present, but that he had difficulty distinguishing one from the other because they were dressed alike, is not borne out by his later discussion of nine men and their dress (*Journal of a Voyage*, 103–104).

40. Steller, *Manuscript Journal*, 197–198.

41. Steller, *Journal of a Voyage*, 103.

42. Ibid.

43. Waxell, *Vtoraia Kamchatskaia ekspeditsiia*, 66.

44. In some documents it is stated that there were nine kayaks in all, of which seven remained at a distance while two approached the vessel.

45. See Lydia T. Black, *Glory Remembered: Wooden Headgear of Alaska Sea Hunters* (Juneau: Alaska State Museums, 1991). Steller (*Journal of a Voyage*, 105, and *Manuscript Journal*, 199) said that

he had collected and delivered several hats of this type on Kamchatka; that Koriak and Kamchadal wear identical hats. He said: "And here again I found a clear indication that the Americans originated in Asia since the Kamchadals and Koriaks are accustomed to wear the same kinds of hats, of which I acquired several for the Kunstkammer" (*Journal of a Voyage,* 105). Steller's statement is unique and a puzzle. No other observer, to my knowledge, ever reported such use among the Itel'men and Koriak. I was unable to locate any evidence substantiating Steller's statement, nor are any of the wooden hats in collections in Russian and Baltic museums documented for any area other than southwestern Alaska.

46. Waxell (*Vtoraia Kamchatskaia ekspeditsiia,* 68), my translation. See also the passage in the 1952 English-language translation from the Danish.

47. This sighting remains unidentified. Bertholf, in his reconstruction of Bering's tracks, places the vessel due south of Atka Island in the Andreanof Island group (central Aleutians). Khitrovo's logs bear an annotation, in a different hand, to that effect and specifically identify the volcano as the one on Atka Island, today called the Korovinskii (Korovin) Volcano (Pokrovskii, *Ekspeditsiia Beringa,* nn. 1, 3). The problem arises with Waxell's account and his chart (*Vtoraia Kamchatskaia ekspeditsiia,* 68 and chart facing 128). Waxell reports that to the south of the high mountain ridge and the great volcano which dominated the landscape in the distance were "a multitude of islands at a considerable distance from the [mainland] shore." This does not fit Atka, unless one assumes that Waxell erroneously placed on the chart Great Sitkin and adjacent islands, which lie to the west of Atka. The time factor is also puzzling. If we assume that, indeed, the *Sv. Petr* was off Atka on 25 September, it means that the vessel made it from the Shumagins to Atka, sailing way to the south, tacking, and beating against the wind, in fourteen days, but covered the much shorter distance to the Rat Islands (if the identification of the island of Sv. Markian as Kiska is accepted) in *thirty* days, from 25 September to 25 October. I am inclined to the idea that on 25 September the *Sv. Petr* was south of the Alaska Peninsula/Unimak Island: here, the topography as stated by Waxell makes sense.

48. Bertholf (in Golder, *Bering's Voyages,* vol. 1, chart) identifies this *second* Island of St. Stephan (cf. note 23) as Buldir. However, there are no other islands near Buldir, certainly not to the south, as indicated on Waxell's and other expedition charts. Moreover, the outline of the island is elongated, trending east to west. Buldir is an extinct submarine volcano and is almost round in shape.

49. Waxell, *Vtoraia Kamchatskaia ekspeditsiia,* 71–72.

50. Russian archaeologists, assisted by Danish colleagues, have conducted several seasons of archaeological excavations at the site of Bering's camp. See V. D. Len'kov, G. L. Silant'iev, and A. K. Staniukovich, *Komandorskii lager' ekspeditsii Beringa (Opyt kompleksnogo izucheniia)* (Moscow: Izdatel'stvo "Nauka," 1988), and the English ed., *The Komandorskii Camp of the Bering Expedition (An Experiment in Complex Study),* trans. Katherine L. Arndt, ed. O. W. Frost (Anchorage: Alaska Historical Society, 1992).

51. *Hydrodamalis gigas,* in older literature sometimes *Rytina* or *Rhytina stelleri* (Steller's sea cow), was, together with *Trichechidae* (*Manatee* species) and *Dugongidae,* a member of the Sirenia order. A littoral sea mammal subsisting mainly on kelp and other seaweeds, found in great numbers in the Commander Islands by members of Bering's expedition, it was soon hunted out (see next chapter). Occasional sightings and taking of sea cows were reported by early Russian fur traders in the Near Islands. Fossilized skeletons have been found even in the eastern Aleutians (Unalaska, not dated) and a Late Pleistocene skeleton was found on Amchitka in the Rat Island group (see Frank C. Whitmore, Jr., and L. M. Gard, Jr., *Steller's Sea Cow* [Hydrodamalis gigas] *of Late Pleistocene Age from Amchitka, Aleutian Islands, Alaska,* Geological Survey Professional Paper 1036 [Washington, D.C.: U.S. Government Printing Office, 1977]). Steller, who provided a careful description of the animal, mistakenly thought it to be a manatee.

52. For a description of the first successful taking of a sea cow by Bering's crewmen, see Steller, *Journal of a Voyage,* 159–164, and Waxell, *Vtoraia Kamchatskaia ekspeditsiia,* 94–96. O. W. Frost ascribes the initiative and the invention of the method of taking the sea cows to Steller, on the basis of a description of the "Greenland whale fishery" by Adam Olearius ("Adam Olearius, the Greenland

Eskimos, and the First Slaughter of Bering Island Sea Cows, 1742: An Elucidation of a Statement in Steller's Journal," in *Russia in North America: Proceedings of the 2nd International Conference on Russian America, Sitka, Alaska, August 19–22, 1987,* ed. Richard A. Pierce [Kingston, Ontario; Fairbanks, Alaska: Limestone Press, 1990], 121–135). I find no substantiation for Frost's ascription of the initiative to Steller.

53. Waxell, *Vtoraia Kamchatskaia ekspeditsiia,* 100.

54. According to Steller, about 700 sea otters were killed by the ship's company for food from November 1741 to the middle of August 1742. How many pelts were taken to Kamchatka is not known. Space was at a premium and each man was allowed to take only a certain weight in personal baggage (see *Manuscript Journal,* 252–258, 283). That Steller claimed 200 skins is stated in a letter from him to Gmelin, 4 November 1742 (cited after Frost, "Adam Olearius," 130, 133 n. 35).

55. Steller, *Manuscript Journal,* 284–285.

56. Narochnitskii et al., *Russkie ekspeditsii* (1984), 269.

Figure 11. Elizabeth I (Elizaveta; 1709–1761), empress of Russia 1741–1761.
Courtesy Slavic and Baltic Division, New York Public Library, Astor, Lenox, and Tilden Foundations.

Chapter Four

Toward the Unknown Islands

Though small-scale entrepreneurs had been active in fur procurement, specifically sea otters, in Kamchatka and the Kuril Islands for several decades, and had taken some fur seals in the Shantar Islands, there is little doubt that the return of the Bering-Chirikov expedition of 1741–1742 triggered what amounted to a run on America and opened the way for the expansion of the sea otter and fur seal trade. Members of the expedition confirmed that the Great Land, rumored for nearly a century, was indeed America, that the coasts they had reached resembled Kamchatka in many respects, that there were many offshore islands, and, indeed, a chain of islands that stretched from east to west toward Kamchatka. The people they encountered, though they spoke languages different from those of the Itel'men, Koriak, and Chukchi, looked very much like the inhabitants of northeastern Asia. There was an abundance of marine mammals—whales, walrus, dolphins, sea lions, and, above all, the fur seals and sea otters coveted by the Chinese.

The rush to the newfound islands began soon after the return of Bering's men to Kamchatka, in a rather modest way. On 1 August 1743, a small vessel owned by Emel'ian Basov cleared the mouth of the Kamchatka River and sailed out into the Eastern Ocean. Her skipper, Cossack Evtikhii Sannikov, navigating by dead reckoning with the aid of a compass, set her course east by southeast, toward the Unknown Islands. The vessel, the *Sv. Apostol Petr*,[1] was named for Bering's flagship, whose crew had returned only the previous fall from the fabled Great Land. Sannikov's voyage was but a small, early expression of a growing idea. The news of the Bering expeditionary party's winter on Commander (now Bering) Island, where sea mammals and fur bearers were abundant, quickly had become common knowledge throughout Kamchatka, in Okhotsk, and at the settlements on the Anadyr'. There were plenty of men ready to risk their estates, fortunes, and lives for a chance to strike it rich in the search for furs, the "soft goods." Success could bring not only riches but advancement in rank, which could make it possible for a peasant or workingman to enter one of the powerful merchant guilds in distant cities of metropolitan Russia and, most important, bring honors and special privileges in recognition of service to the Crown. The service that counted most was opening new lands and bringing new subjects under the Russian imperial scepter.

Neither the sea nor the danger of hostile encounters held much of a threat, as life on the empire's eastern frontier was already full of daily hazards. Many had sailed time and time again along the Siberian rivers and Siberia's arctic shores, on the sea off Kamchatka, to Anadyr' in the north and the Kuril Islands in the south. Many regularly sailed the Okhotsk-Kamchatka routes, to Penzhina Bay off the northern Okhotsk Sea, to the dangerous entry to Bol'sheretsk harbor on Kamchatka's western coast, or to Nizhne-Kamchatsk or the harbor of the Apostles, Sts. Peter and Paul, in Avacha Bay. Most had at times, and at a moment's notice, become fighters. They had fought for their lives, their families, their possessions, their catch, and, when called, for the Crown. Occasionally they rebelled, not against the Crown, but against the agents of the Crown, the local administrators and their immediate superiors. There was no peace in Kamchatka. The very year Bering sailed for America, 1741, the Itel'men of Kamchatka's western shores attacked Russian outposts.[2] The year the keel of the *Sv. Apostol Petr* was laid, many kinsmen and friends of the members of her crew were called to subdue the Itel'men. Others had fought (and would fight in the future) in the north against the Chukchi. Soon, many would fight the Koriak.[3] These men were rough and unruly, ready to face any hardship, even death, their physical courage and endurance unquestioned. But they bowed before ancient customs of their northern homeland. They could be generous to family and friends, humble in their faith in God, hospitable to visiting strangers, ruthless to their competitors, and cruel or magnanimous by turn to their enemies. They dreamed of riches and advancement, but above all they cherished their free life. Life on the frontier gave them hope and, sometimes, a chance to escape the government's heavy hand. For this chance, they were ready to pay a heavy price.[4] The men who sailed to the Unknown Islands were cast in that mold.

The organizer of the enterprise that sent Sannikov's vessel seaward, and chief mover in the construction of the first vessel in the future Aleutian Islands merchant fleet, was, as mentioned, Emel'ian Basov. A peasant's son from a small village near Tobol'sk in Siberia, Basov had participated in the Shestakov expedition. At that time he served under Ivan Kozyrevskii. Kozyrevskii was a Cossack and rebel, one of the first to venture into the Kuril Islands; later he became (against his will, it is said) a monk, Ignatii, but when needed was recalled to the tsar's service.[5] Basov rose through the ranks and became a sergeant of the Okhotsk command. A trusted subordinate of Skorniakov-Pisarev, the Okhotsk commander, he had planned an enterprise in the Kuril Islands, with government assistance, for which he obtained authorization and promise of support while in Moscow as Skorniakov's courier. When he returned to Okhotsk, the new area commander, Dev'ier, found various reasons to deny Basov the opportunity to go to the Kurils, but in 1741 granted permission to launch such fur-procuring voyages from Kamchatka, provided Basov equipped the vessels at his own cost.[6] Basov, who had little capital except what he could muster from relatives and friends, was hard-pressed to equip even a single vessel, though he undertook to send out at least two.

The *Sv. Apostol Petr* was built in the winter of 1742–1743 by a Kamchatka serviceman, Petr Kolokol'nikov, on the Yelovka, a tributary of the Kamchatka River. In the spring of 1743, Kolokol'nikov brought the vessel downriver to Nizhne-Kamchatsk and delivered her to her owners. She was of sewn-plank construction, built of local materials, tamarack and spruce wood, with sea mammal skin lashings, moss and nettle for caulking, and nettle fiber for ropes. She was forty-two feet long along the keel, but not wide, and of little displacement, and thus small even by the standards of the time. Nevertheless, she proved well suited for her purpose. Her flexible hull helped her withstand the pounding of the heavy seas and she was well constructed by a fine craftsman. This sturdy vessel was to make five voyages. On her fifth voyage, 1750–1752, she was said to have reached the island of Atka in the central Aleutians, collected the first iasak payments in that area, and brought to Kamchatka a young hostage named Khaliunsan who was baptized to the Christian name Il'ia (Elias). On the return voyage, the vessel was wrecked at Attu Island.[7]

Basov and his companions had financed the venture on shares, each contributing equally (except Basov, who provided more funds than his ordinary share required). The venture consisted of twenty shares. Among the shareholders were Basov's brother, Vasilii, and Dmitrii Nakvasin, brother-in-law of the Kamchatka townsman Nikifor Trapeznikov. In later years Nakvasin would become a well-known and much respected skipper and navigator, while Trapeznikov would go down in history as one of the most famous of the entrepreneurs and merchants engaged in the Aleutian trade. Each of the companions put up about 370 rubles per share for construction materials and equipment. The builder was to be paid from the proceeds of the voyage; if the vessel were to be wrecked, he had to bear his losses. All participants in the voyage were to share equally in defraying all the costs, including additional equipment, such as compasses and the cloth sails Emel'ian Basov had acquired. Other small vessels built at that time in Kamchatka and Okhotsk usually carried reindeer-skin sails.

Even though an earlier government had ordered the local administrators to encourage private enterprise, by remission of taxes, customs duties, and highway tolls for ten years for any merchant who would undertake such voyages,[8] under Elizabeth, the new sovereign, government support was scant. Specifically, there was no remission of the tax equal to one-tenth of the entire take (i.e., the catch). However, when the *Sv. Apostol Petr* was being outfitted, the government provided two anchors salvaged in 1729 from a wrecked Japanese trading vessel.

FIGURE 12. A shitik, a vessel of sewn-plank construction.
From Belov, 1951, p. 464.

This was by no means an inconsiderable gesture and it merits an explanatory digression. Anchors, indispensable on any sea voyage, and often making the difference between survival and death in the dangerous waters of uncharted shores, presented a very special problem for the Kamchatkans. Iron was not locally available. In the seventeenth and early eighteenth centuries, the Russian outposts on the eastern seaboard were supplied overland from the Kolyma settlements via the Anui River to Anadyr' and from the Lena River via the Aldan River to the Sea of Okhotsk and to the Amur River.[9] Transport of anchors overland from Siberian foundries to Okhotsk had been one of the greatest difficulties Bering had to solve on his two expeditions to the North Pacific. By the time the Aleutian trade was under way, supplies were shipped from Irkutsk to the Lena River, floated down the Lena to Yakutsk and from there taken to Okhotsk over arduous routes, winter and summer. From there, supplies were shipped to Bol'sheretsk, the western Kamchatkan port located on the Bol'shaia River, and from there, once again overland, to the settlements on Kamchatka's Pacific coast. The anchors, even for small vessels, weighed no less than five or six pud (a pud is equivalent to 36.11 pounds in English system units) and often as much as ten pud. It was not feasible to transport ready-made anchors overland; therefore, they usually were forged locally of bar iron shipped in smaller weight units.

From Okhotsk, the anchors forged there, or the iron for anchors, would be shipped most often aboard Crown vessels for a fee. The high transport costs had to be added to the already high cost of iron, twenty rubles and higher per pud. The cost of ropes for rigging, but especially for anchor cables, was even more formidable.[10] Even the locally manufactured nettle rope fiber cost fifteen rubles per pud.[11]

To repair or replace a lost anchor, almost every fur-trading vessel carried aboard a forge and, if a competent specialist could be found, a blacksmith. As a rule, the blacksmith received one share in a venture, a recompense equal to that normally given to the skipper/navigator (*morekhod*) and to the foreman (*peredovshchik*) who was responsible for the organization of fur procurement, labor relations, record keeping, and the delivery of the proper tax and accounting to the authorities.[12]

When the *Sv. Apostol Petr* sailed on this first Aleutian trade voyage, almost all shareholders came along as ordinary laborers. Only one, Kholshchevnikov, hired laborers, three men whom he was obliged to pay in furs from his share of the catch. At that time there was little currency in Kamchatka and all trade was conducted against furs, the red fox pelts providing a basic standard of valuation. Also on board was the real pioneer of the Aleutian trade, Petr Verkhoturov. A Kamchatkan cossack's son, he had served under Shestakov and was with Bering and Waxell on the voyage of 1741–1742. He was to show the way to the islands. He would go on to sail again many times and would meet his death, in 1761, at the hands of the Aleuts of Agattu Island.[13]

In five days they reached Bering Island where they wintered, hunting arctic foxes and sea otters. Sometime during their stay on the island, they saw land to the west. They returned home to Kamchatka, first sailing south and east, sighting on the return voyage the Near Islands of the Aleutian Chain in August 1744.

One-tenth of the catch was taken by the local office as tax for the treasury, and participants in the voyage donated fifty sea otter skins to the Nizhne-Kamchatsk Church of St. Nicholas,[14] the patron of northern hunters, fishermen, and sailors. The money received for these skins was used to purchase bells, censers, votive lights, altar cloths, and priest's vestments brought from the old northern Russian city of Tot'ma in 1746.[15]

The next summer, Basov, joined in this new venture by several more shareholders, sailed on 30 July with a crew of thirty-two, this time directly to the island to the west of Bering Island, sighted the previous summer. He reached his goal on 6 August and erected a cross on the shore of the island now called Copper or Mednoi. Because of the lack of a good harbor there, he returned to the familiar Bering Island to winter near Bering's old camp. The following year, after a futile attempt to reach the Aleutians, he moved to Mednoi, and then returned to Kamchatka in 1747. This time, after payment of the one-tenth tax to the treasury, the catch was divided into thirty-three shares. One full share was donated to the Nizhne-Kamchatsk Church of St. Nicholas.

Basov was not a good businessman, and some former companions sold their shares to his competitors. Nevertheless, his obvious success in finding furbearers attracted the attention of important Moscow merchants, among them Andrei Shelikhov and Andrei Serebrennikov,[16] who put up capital for his third venture. This marked the first instance of the entry of outside capital into the island fur trade. A number of locals also joined the venture. Among them was Andrean Tolstykh, of Selenga in Siberia, later one of the most famous trading skippers sailing the Aleutian waters. To undermine the competition, which

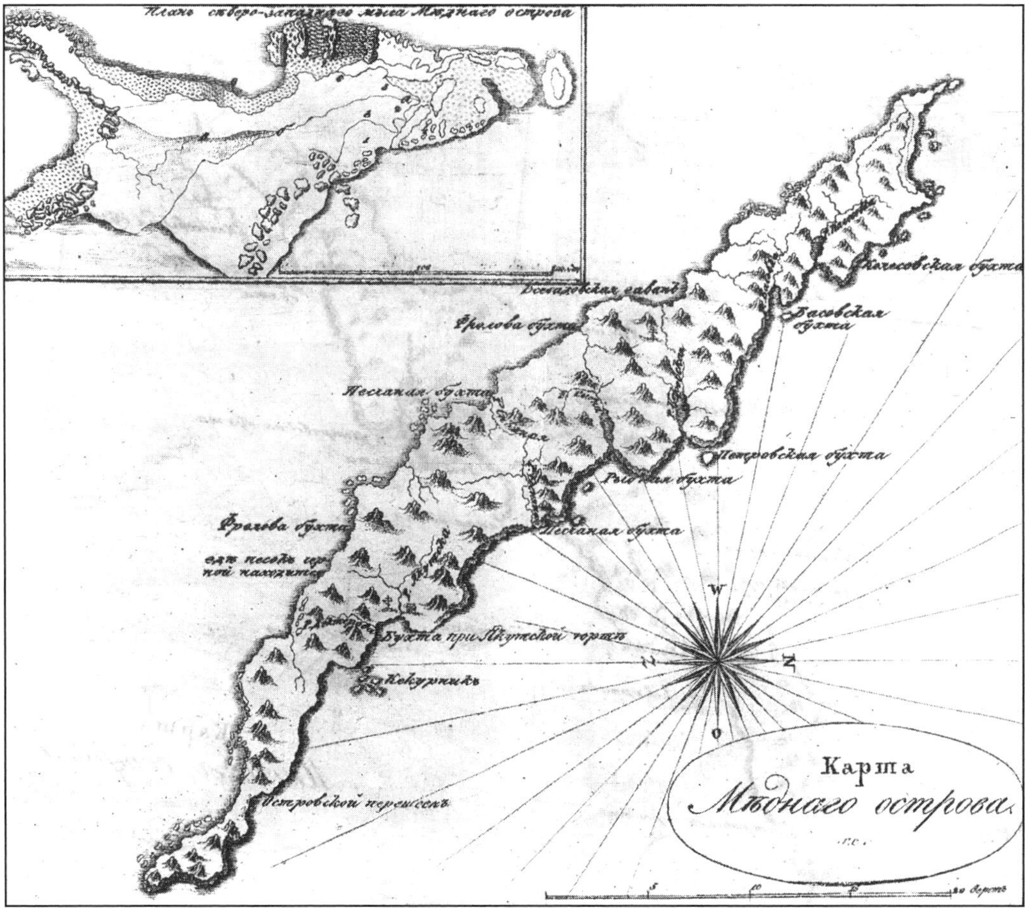

FIGURE 13. **Map of Mednoi Island (Copper Island) by Dmitrii Nakvasin, 1755, showing locations of copper ore. Inset shows detail of northwest end of the island.**

From Spasskii, 1822.

was growing (one vessel had already reached the Near Islands, hunting there from 1745 to 1747), Basov made it known that his vessel would seek new islands to the east, and urged that hunting be prohibited in the Commander Islands. He argued that government property left there by Bering's crew would be endangered through pilfering of iron. Needless to say, he secured permission to land there himself,[17] unknowingly laying himself open, on this very same basis, to later charges of misconduct. It was on this voyage, Basov's third, that Dmitrii Nakvasin discovered copper while exploring Mednoi Island. Basov, upon his return, made much of this find. On the next sailing of the *Sv. Apostol Petr* he remained behind, urging the government's attention to his contribution, the discovery of a promising ore deposit. Nakvasin, in the meantime, took the vessel once again to the Commander Islands. Of the thirty-eight crew members, thirteen were Russians, and twenty-five were hired Itel'men laborers. Already, the character of the participants in the trade was changing.

Basov continued to stress the importance of the discovery of copper. All other merchants—and by now there was a considerable number of them sending out fur-hunting vessels to the Aleutian Chain—were prohibited from landing on Mednoi. By Basov's orders Nakvasin was to provide an exact description and chart of the island and the copper deposits. This Nakvasin did, probably on the vessel's last voyage, when she was under totally new ownership; Basov's business had been dissolved. Nakvasin's involvement with Mednoi Island continued. In 1755, he took there a government mining team, headed by Petr Iakovlev (whose brief description of the island was published by Pallas in 1781).[18] Basov, in the meantime, totally lost his standing, and his capital was exhausted. Nevertheless, he attempted to acquire an interest in the vessel on which the mining team was to sail.

This was not a lucky vessel and had already once been wrecked on an experimental voyage. In 1746, an Ustiug merchant, Ivan Bakhov, and two companions, Nikita Shalaurov and Yakutsk merchant Semeon Novikov, who all contemplated revival of the old sea route from the Arctic Ocean to the Pacific, built the vessel which they named for the northern saints: *Sv. Perkun i Zanat*. Their first aim was to test the sea route from Anadyr' to Kamchatka. They left the mouth of the Anadyr' River and were carried eventually to Bering Island, where, on a fierce November day, the vessel was cast ashore by a high wave and smashed by the surf. Out of the wreckage and driftwood, the shipwrecked men built a new vessel,[19] helping themselves to some supplies from the expedition stores left by Bering's crew in 1742. They renamed the rebuilt craft *Sv. Kapiton*.

When Bakhov, Shalaurov, and Novikov returned to Kamchatka, the effective ownership of the *Sv. Kapiton* was acquired by their partner, the Sol'vychegodsk merchant Ivan Zhilkin, as the main shareholder. Basov had promised Zhilkin 1,000 rubles for the controlling interest in the vessel, but somehow, Basov's promissory note to Zhilkin and other records disappeared; the vessel's ownership was in dispute. Iakovlev, the head of the government mining team, sided against Basov and delivered the vessel to Zhilkin.

Basov was penniless. Facing a cheerless Christmas, and concerned for his wife and children, he forged some coins and bought for the holiday some berries, milk, salt fish, and, for himself, fifty kopeks' worth of tobacco. His inept forgery was soon discovered; he was arrested, tried, and, in 1762, sentenced to hard labor at the Nerchinsk mines and a public flogging. He died soon thereafter, a convicted felon, an old and broken man,[20] his long service to the state forgotten.

In the meantime, the tempo of the commercial penetration of the Aleutian Islands continued to grow and the character of the trade was changing rapidly. At the time of

Basov's first venture, and in the first few years following it, the participants were local, mainly Kamchatkan servicemen and settlers who themselves sailed on the fur-procuring voyages, each contributing his labor as well as capital, each holding only one or very few shares in the venture. However, within a decade a different situation emerged. One of the factors affecting the development of the Aleutian trade was the prohibition of merchants' travel to the Kuril Islands, a restriction in effect until 1761.[21] Another important factor was the changing market conditions. The great fur merchants of the Russian north traded furs internally in Russia and on the European and Chinese markets. Each market dealt in different furs. At first there was practically no domestic or European market for sea otter or fur seal pelts (though demand for fur seals grew and resulted in international competition),[22] but Chinese demand for these furs was great, indeed. Capital was attracted from the old traditional centers of the fur industry in the Russian north, from the new cities of Siberia, and from Moscow, the main center of commerce, but the most lucrative internal Russian trade focused on sable, marten, and fox furs. Above all, black fox was the luxury good, commanding exceedingly high prices, higher by far than the prices paid by the Chinese for sea otter furs. Until the end of the 1750s and the early 1760s, the American territory did not provide any land animal furs, but with the discovery of foxes and penetration of the American mainland, which provided river otter, marten, and beaver, profits began to be made on other than sea otter and fur seal pelts.

The major financial risks were borne by the merchants who financed the ventures. If the vessel was lost, their investment, naturally, was gone. But this possibility, only too often realized, was not the only risk. Preservation, storage, and transport of furs from Kamchatka (usually Nizhne-Kamchatsk) either to Russian fur-market centers, such as Sol'vychegodsk and Moscow, or to the Chinese entry port of Kiakhta for transport to Beijing (Peking), were major problems. Storage facilities in Kamchatka and Okhotsk were meager. The merchants had to move the furs rapidly. Preservation, following scraping of the skin, required use of salt. The major investors had to see to it that salt, indispensable if skins were to keep for the market, was available. An alternative, boiling sea water for salt, required large, expensive kettles, an expenditure of wood (a scarce commodity in the treeless Aleutian Islands), and the expenditure of extra labor. Even so, some crews relied exclusively on this method.

Marketing under the government monopoly in the China trade was also a problem. The small investor and ordinary laborer sold his share of the catch at Kamchatkan prices. The big entrepreneurs preferred to transport their goods to Okhotsk, where prices were higher, or, best of all, to Kiakhta, where the Chinese market was growing. Sea otters were sold at Kiakhta for from 14 to 25 rubles, depending on the pelt's quality, and in 1727 at Beijing, from 14.95 to 19.55 rubles.[23] In 1760, a sea otter pelt was selling in Kamchatka for 20 rubles while at Kiakhta the going price was 40 rubles.[24] Toward the end of the century the Chinese were willing to pay even more, but to get the Chinese prices and reap the rumored fabulous profits, the pelts had to be transported overland at great expense. In the end only the major competitors and the exceptionally successful (or lucky) local entrepreneurs could stay in the game.

Toward the end of the century the competition in the Aleutian trade became intense, in some cases vicious. Eventually, the small, independent entrepreneurs were forced out, and only four or five great merchant companies were left to compete for the American trade. By 1780, formal proposals had been put before the government to establish a monopoly modeled on the British Hudson's Bay Company or the East India Company, but this was not to be while Catherine the Great, a firm believer in free enterprise, was on the throne.

In the beginning, though, a number of merchants were testing the waters. Usually these were members of the great merchant families of Ustiug, Sol'vychegodsk, Tot'ma, Arkhangel'sk, and Vologda. They held, sometimes through the *prikazchiks*, their representatives and business managers, several shares in a venture and, more often than not, they sponsored several ventures simultaneously.[25] The prikazchiks[26] of the great merchant houses sometimes held shares in their own right and gained the status of independent merchants themselves. Small investors were encouraged to participate in these ventures. Even Itel'men and Koriak were sometimes shareholders. Many a small investor, when his luck held and his first venture brought him a handsome profit, invested this profit in other fur-procuring ventures. A few grew rich and retired from the trade, choosing less risky activities. Some, like Basov, ran afoul of the imperial law and lost their estates, status, and freedom. Some lost their shirts and died paupers, their brothers, sons, and nephews hiring themselves out as ordinary laborers in an effort to recoup the family fortunes.

Some of these men did not sail on the ships they financed, while others did. Some sailed at the beginning of their trading careers, then retired to the counting houses. Others, especially the natives of the Pomor'ie, continued to sail for decades, established families in the Aleutians, and returned home only in their old age to die and be buried in their homeland. Some chose to stay in America. Once in a while, an "Old Voyager," as they became known later, finding that there was no going home again, returned to the Great Land and died there. During the voyages, many died in the islands, from hunger, from illness, in accidents, drowning or falling off cliffs, in shipwrecks, or at the hand of the Aleuts. In the islands the lifestyle and the lot of a great merchant who chose to sail on a venture and that of the laborer he had hired were much the same.

The ventures were organized on the model long established in the Pomor'ie. Following the centuries-old custom, each shareholder had to provide a laborer for each share he owned unless he himself came along and worked as a crew member. The laborers were paid by the shareholder out of his share of the catch by agreement, but most often a general contract signed by all concerned regulated the division of the catch and the individual recompense, as well as all other financial matters.[27] Sometimes the shares were divided fifty-fifty between the owners who financed the venture and the crew. Though the foreman and the skipper-navigator were each usually assigned a full share, and occasionally more, an ordinary laborer was likely to sail on a half share. This was especially true of the local Itel'men and Koriak who were hired in great numbers, particularly in the early decades of the Aleutian trade. Some crews mustered more Itel'men than Russians. The Kamchatkan Natives were not only cheap labor, it was believed they were less prone to diseases and, because of their diet, were especially resistant to scurvy. Moreover, they were often hired as a sort of marines: as their warfare tactics and techniques were similar to those of the Aleuts, some skippers liked to have the Itel'men along as a fighting force. At times the practice backfired; the Itel'men's aggressive behavior provoked several conflicts.

Some owners, however, preferred to hire their crews on wages. By 1760, the fair rate was considered to be 50 rubles per year if a man was hired in a Siberian town, and 100 rubles per year if hired in Kamchatka, where there was a labor shortage. The men preferred payment in furs, especially after Catherine the Great abolished the government monopoly on the sale of certain furs at Kiakhta. When paid in furs, the laborer could realize more than the usual going rate of recompense.

In the early decades most of the laborers were either local Kamchatkan or Okhotsk littoral settlers, long-time Siberian residents engaged in the fur industry, or natives of the Russian north. Many were married to Siberian native women, or were children or grandchildren of mixed unions. A number were, as mentioned, Itel'men or Koriak. The climate and landscapes of Alaska, the subsistence on fish and marine mammal products, presented no surprises to them. All these northern-rooted laborers had survival skills and were expert at a variety of tasks, from boat and ship building to land and marine animal hunting and trapping. Often, when shipwrecked in unfamiliar waters, they survived on drift whales, seaweeds, and marine mammals until they were able to build a new vessel. Such was the case of the *Sv. Kapiton*, itself rebuilt from the wrecked vessel *Sv. Perkun i Zanat*, which sailed once again in 1757. She was wrecked in 1758 on Rat Island (Hawadax̂) and rebuilt once again, returning in 1760 to Attu where the crew was disbanded.[28] Sometimes, when such a vessel was rebuilt, the crew chose not to return home but to sail on. Thus Petr Bashmakov, a native of Arkhangel'sk, skippered the *Sv. Ieremiia*, built on Mednoi Island in 1751 out of the wreckage of the *Sv. Semeon i Anna*, wrecked there on her second voyage. Bashmakov sailed the *Sv. Ieremiia* westward, suffered shipwreck on Adak Island in the central Aleutians, and built there another vessel, which he named *Sv. Petr i Pavel.* He brought her safely home to Kamchatka and sailed her again in 1756 to the central Aleutians, and in 1758, searching for twelve Kamchadal who had deserted in a *baidara* (a skin-covered open boat) and taken with them a considerable number of weapons and precious metal utensils, he went as far as the Distant (later known as Fox) Islands, probably as far as the Krenitzin archipelago.[29]

Since a voyage lasted a minimum of two years, an owner who did not employ his men on shares had to have on hand, for the average crew of fifty, from 2,500 to 5,000 rubles per year and to provide food, such as flour, for which payment had to be in cash or its equivalent. Because provisions were scarce in Kamchatka and Okhotsk, and shipment of provisions from European Russia was prohibitively expensive, the vessels were minimally provisioned with Kamchatkan products (dried fish, dried reindeer meat, etc.), just about enough to get them to the Commander Islands and make camp there. Crew and vessel then spent at least one year in the Commander Islands, where sea mammals, seal and sea lion meat, blubber and oil, fur seal meat, sea otter meat, and, above all, sea cow products were put up for the long voyage to the Distant Islands and eventually to the American mainland itself. Sea mammal skin and fur clothing was made, as well as *torbasy*—boots of seal, sea lion, and sea cow skins. Here, too, the crew prepared skin boat covers for the baidaras, used in lightering from ship to shore, near-shore navigation, procuring driftwood, hunting, and transporting the work and hunting crews to their outlying camps. The inner frame of these boats was constructed at Kamchatka and carried along in parts, to be reassembled when needed. In the early days, the skin covers were made in the Commander Islands out of sea cow skin. Vasilii Shilov, one of the entrepreneurs who himself sailed at least twice to the Aleutians, testified in 1765 before the Admiralty College:

> As the merchant companies by now know some of the islands more distant from Kamchatka than the Northern Commander and Mednoi, and as when one thinks about Kamchatka [it is clear] that it cannot provide food supplies needed for such distant voyages and for

> the prolonged stay, it has been decided to take advantage of the abundance of Commander and Mednoi Islands, except for flour, which we take on in Kamchatka. Every vessel which has as her destination the Distant Islands takes on in Kamchatka (except for flour) only so much of food supplies and fresh water as is sufficient to reach the above-named islands even if the weather turns foul; they consider that there will be no need whatsoever of flour in the future. There they winter. During the wintering, they procure furs and prepare food supplies for the long voyage. This consists mostly in taking sea cows, whose meat is very filling and healthy, and when dried is a bread substitute. As this cattle has lots of blubber, the oil is preserved in casks and is used instead of good butter. This oil may also be drunk like the best vegetable oil without any danger to health. It also serves for lighting in lamps, instead of candles. The skins of the said cows are used as covers for boats.[30]

Skin boats were in wide use in the Russian north and among eastern Siberian natives, and they became the only small craft used by the fur traders. Shilov and another skipper, Stepan Cherepanov, founder of a prominent Aleut family in the Krenitzin Islands, stated their case well. A skin boat, said Cherepanov, was light, strong, and maneuverable. Among the offshore rocks it was easily handled, and it was great when landing in the surf. It was easily portaged. The wooden dories were clumsy by comparison, too deep for shallow waters where there were many submerged rocks, too difficult to steer, and not as fast. Wooden dories, said Shilov, could be much more easily capsized in rough water. A single sea cow skin was enough for a boat cover. One did not have to piece together several skins, and thus there was no danger that a seam might spring a leak.[31]

Sea cows were hunted in clement weather, when the sea was calm. A baidara, manned by a crew of eight or ten, went out in search of a feeding or preferably a sleeping animal. The animal was of giant proportions, measuring more than forty-two feet in length. The meat alone, without bones, often weighed over 7,000 pounds, between three and a half and four tons; according to the engineer Iakovlev in 1755, "enough to feed thirty-three men for a month." A disturbed sea cow could easily overturn or wreck the boat and had to be approached cautiously. One or two men armed with a very long pike with a long metal blade stood in the stern, which was the first portion of the vessel to reach the sea cow. The man or men armed with the makeshift lance stabbed the cow. The oarsmen began to pull away the moment the cow was struck (that was the reason for approaching stern forward, for easier getaway from the thrashing animal). The wounded beast would move away, slowly, not into deep water but always following the shore, and the boat would follow. If the thrust was well placed, the animal would soon belly-up; if not, it would be struck again, this time with a stabbing weapon to which a rope was attached. When the animal ceased to struggle, the men would pull it close in to shore by the rope and butcher the carcass at low tide (the animal was much too heavy to be pulled up on the beach).[32] By 1754, when Iakovlev visited Mednoi Island, the sea cows were growing scarce. He sounded the alarm, warning that if the hunters' practices were not stopped, the animal would soon be extinct. His warning was prophetic. By the mid-1780s, sea cows were not mentioned any more. Today, only sketches by Waxell and Steller and a few other Russian mariners, and several skeletons in various museums, testify that this unique animal was once abundant in the waters of the northern Pacific.

Leaving the Commanders, the vessel would sail to the Aleutians, Kodiak archipelago, Alaska Peninsula, or Prince William Sound. As the years passed, the vessels traveled for ever greater distances and the voyages grew longer. If the early voyages lasted from one to two years, in later times a voyage of five or so years was commonplace, and at least one lasted almost a decade. The lure that prompted the mariners was the discovery of foxes in the eastern Aleutians, from Unimak to the Islands of Four Mountains group, and the presence of valuable land animals on the Alaska Peninsula, Kodiak, and on the American mainland itself. Sea otters, of course, were a staple of the trade, but the discovery of silver and, above all, black foxes (whose pelts were valued twice as much as a sea otter pelt in Kiakhta and were considered the royal fur in Moscow) was a very important event. The merchants who brought the first Alaskan black fox furs to the empress were awarded medals, released from various service obligations to the state, and their indebtedness to the treasury (money borrowed to outfit the vessels) was forgiven.[33]

In general, in terms of volume, fox pelts were probably the most important item in the Russian trade. Red fox skins were a standard of valuation in Kamchatka; not as abundant, but still taken in great volume, were various varieties of arctic fox. This animal was present in great numbers in the Commander Islands and was an excellent fallback when sea otter hunting was not very productive. The importance of arctic foxes in the trade was well recognized. In 1750, Andrean Tolstykh, on his second voyage in the vessel *Sv. Ioann*, in which he was a major shareholder,[34] brought a litter of young arctic foxes from the Commander Islands to Attu to start a new and secure fur crop there. He also distributed the traps with which Russian fur procurers habitually took foxes. Within six years the Aleuts were taking arctic foxes on Attu Island for the Russian market.[35] Today, tourist shops in Alaska sell models of these "Aleut" fox traps.

FIGURE 14. Detail from a chart dated 1774, drawn by or for Capt. Shmalev at Okhotsk, showing Glotov's landfall on Kodiak (present-day Russian Harbor) in 1762–1763 and a large Native village on Aiaktalik Island.
Original formerly in AVPRI. Courtesy V. A. Postnikov.

Once a vessel reached her destination, reconnoitering parties were sent out. The main object was to locate a convenient and safe harbor where the vessel could be dragged ashore and put up on rollers for the winter and to find salmon streams—a steady source of food—and places where driftwood was abundant. As a rule, the skippers staked out a convenient harbor and the hunting grounds to which they returned again and again. Many names that appear on modern maps mark such bays and harbors, and bear names of Russian promyshlenniki, skippers, or foremen: Pan'kov Harbor on Amlia, Korovin Harbor or Bay on Atka, Bechevin Harbor (Bechevin Bay) on the tip of the Alaska Peninsula, Nizovtsev and Basov Harbors on Mednoi Island, and so on. Some localities were later named by the Natives "Russian harbors," as is the case with the location where Glotov spent a winter on Kodiak Island in 1762–1763, the first recorded stay by a Russian merchantman in the Kodiak archipelago. These names derive from usages of long ago, based on oral historical data, testifying to a skipper's presence in a locality at some time, as the skippers themselves used and designated localities on their charts by Native names.[36]

At the main camp a semisubterranean dwelling was constructed. It differed from the Aleut semisubterranean house, which was entered through the roof by means of a notched-log ladder, in that it had a side entry, sometimes an anteroom, a window or two, and a stone fireplace or stove inside (Aleut houses had no central fireplaces or hearths). Also constructed were racks for drying and smoking fish, store structures (called by an Itel'men-derived word, *barabara*), and the indispensable wet steam bath, the *bania,* today a venerable institution in all areas of Alaska once influenced by Russian contact. Then the crew divided into the artels, the work crews, each under a leader, called the *baidarshchik*, who traveled by baidara to distant areas where they would spend a season or two hunting independently. They made camps, smaller and less elaborate replicas of the main camp, usually apart from but often in relatively close proximity to Aleut settlements. Following the customary Siberian practice, the work crews as well as the men who remained at the main camp tried to obtain hostages to ensure relative safety. Hostage taking was a centuries-old practice in Siberia as well as customary among the indigenous peoples of Alaska.

Aleuts were formidable fighters, and the Russians had a healthy respect for them. A prudent skipper usually tried to make camp on an island where the population was small and in a sheltered bay where there was no Aleut village nearby. The artels, on the other hand, appear to have lodged themselves rather often near Aleut villages; one of the reasons for choosing such locations may be surmised to have been the potential for female company. Sometimes, this potential was realized amicably, through gifts, but frequently there were abductions. Needless to say, such situations led to conflict in which the Russians did not always win.

Often the isolated work units became easy prey for hostile Aleuts. For example, the Itel'men who left Bashmakov's camp (see above) were all killed by the Aleuts. In July 1761, the vessel *Sv. Vladimir* lost a labor crew of twelve on the island of Adak, including the foreman, the skipper and the iasak collector, veterans of several voyages to the Aleutians. Most of the vessels in the early period had but a few firearms, five or six muzzle-loaders, and in the later period more and somewhat more sophisticated semirifled weapons. As a rule, in contrast to other European merchantmen, they did not carry any cannon. Special permission and support of the authorities in obtaining cannon were needed, and such permission was rarely granted. However, the crews were all armed with lances and knives, and some carried a type of sidearm they called *shpaga*, a narrow sword with a hilt cup. The word has entered the Aleut language and is used in stories when describing Russian weapons. In terms of weapons, the Aleuts and the Russians were matched more or less evenly.[37]

As a rule, the sea animals they took were hunted by means of harpoons at sea or clubbed on shore. Firearms were seldom used, as powder was scarce, and pelts could be damaged. Clubbing the sea otters was feasible only on their hauling grounds; otherwise, these animals were taken mainly by nets. Netting sea mammals was an ancient practice in northern Eurasia, widespread in Kamchatka, and probably practiced also by some Alaska groups. It was not known, however, in the western Aleutians. Here, Andrean Tolstykh introduced the practice when he gave several large sea otter nets as a present to an Aleut leader on Attu. The technique soon spread to other areas in the Aleutian archipelago and by 1820–1830 was practiced by most Aleuts. Sea otter nets had to be of very strong but thin fiber; up to twenty pounds of fiber was needed for a single net. Most commonly, the net was attached to a frame or had wooden floats on the upper edge while the bottom edge was weighted. The wood of the frame and of the floats was darkened, usually by fire, as the hunters believed that sea otters had very acute vision and would shy away from the light color of raw wood. For the same reason the hunters used thin fibers for the nets. The nets were then positioned vertically near submerged or semisubmerged caves and among offshore rocks where sea otters were likely to feed or rest. Entangled animals that did not drown were finished with a blow of a club. Nets were also spread on kelp beds, but this method was much less productive. Today, on Kodiak Island, old men recollect that, long ago, sea otters were netted in the open water by means of a net suspended between two boats.[38] Sea otters were hunted in spring and summer beginning about the middle of March and, weather permitting, ending sometimes as late as November. They were hunted only on calm, preferably sunny days, as rough water, especially breakers, could damage the expensive and often irreplaceable nets.[39]

Each crew leader was responsible for keeping track of the fur animal take, disciplining his crew (especially assuring that they not provoke armed conflict with the Aleuts), and maintaining good relations among the crew. Maintaining communication with the foreman and delivering iasak, the tribute payment, to the foreman at the main camp were also part of a crew leader's responsibilities. It was much easier to obtain permission from the authorities for the next voyage if the local administrator was presented with a number of iasak furs. Very early in the development of the Aleutian trade, servicemen were assigned to each vessel. Their job was to collect iasak and report on the number of new imperial subjects. Moreover, the foremen and skippers, as well as collectors, were issued instructions to collect information on languages, customs, subsistence means, social organization, religion, military potential, and any signs of contact with other European powers on the part of the indigenous peoples. They were also responsible for collecting examples of the indigenous material culture items for the Kunstkamera in St. Petersburg, one of the oldest, if not *the* oldest, ethnographic museum in the world.[40] As the voyages grew longer, artels were sometimes left on the islands to the west, on the Commanders, Attu, Amchitka, in the central Aleutians, and in other localities, to be picked up on the vessel's return trek.

At the end of the hunting season, or of the voyage, everyone assembled at the main camp. Often Aleuts came to see the vessels off. Amid feasting, presents were exchanged and hostages, if any, were released. If crew members from other vessels wanted to take passage home, or if shipwrecked competitors were picked up, room was made for them and their chattels. This, too, was regulated by the centuries-old customary practices of Pomor'ie. Sometimes crews from more than one vessel, meeting in the islands, decided to procure furs jointly. In accordance with ancient practices, such agreements were formalized, often in writing, and were then reported to port commanders and owners upon return to home port.

The vessels left Alaska usually in May or the summer months, to sail with the favorable winds. They stopped at various locations to pick up labor crews who had been left to shift for themselves, sometimes for two or three years or more. If they planned to stop at Attu or Shemya, they prayed for safe passage through the offshore rocks, shoals, riptides, and heavy breakers encountered there during storms.[41] The greatest dangers were at the approaches to the harbors, the mouth of the Kamchatka River, the Bol'shaia River on the Okhotsk Sea side of the Kamchatka Peninsula, and the shoals at Okhotsk. When they made the harbor safely they went to church, perhaps for the first time in years, to offer thanks for a safe return. Later the foreman and the skipper reported to the port authorities, delivered the tribute furs (if any had been collected), presented the "bound books" in which they had entered the names and home villages of the tribute-paying Alaskans, and reported to the owners or to their agents on the catch (which was inspected and appraised by government agents). They also surrendered any curiosities, Native artifacts, samples of rocks and minerals, and rare animal or bird skins. After waiting for the division of the catch, they would make their way to their homes. They would spend their money freely for a time, traveling to Moscow or to Arkhangel'sk, making lavish gifts, drinking, and feasting. But soon, many of them would sail again to the now known but ever more Distant Islands in search of soft gold.[42]

NOTES

1. See Vasilii Berkh, *Khronologicheskaia istoriia otkrytiia Aleutskikh ostrovov, ili podvigi Rossiiskogo kupechestva* (St. Petersburg: N. Grech, 1823), English ed., *A Chronological History of the Discovery of the Aleutian Islands, or, The Exploits of Russian Merchants with a Supplement of Historical Data on the Fur Trade,* trans. Dmitri Krenov, ed. Richard A. Pierce (Kingston, Ontario: Limestone Press, 1974), 1–2. Berkh erroneously gives the name of Basov's vessel as the *Sv. Kapiton.*
2. The two Kamchatka expeditions under Bering created unbearable burdens and caused much suffering among the native populations of the Okhotsk area and Kamchatka as well as for the Russian settlers. Skorniakov-Pisarev and his successor, Dev'ier, tried in vain to mitigate this suffering. Unrest among the Even and Evenk along the Okhotsk Sea littoral and the Itel'men and Koriak of Kamchatka may be attributed to the economic hardships inflicted upon the population by the Bering expeditions, as well as (as it often is) to the arbitrary and occasionally brutal actions of local Russian detachments and administrators. In 1741–1743, Bering, and later Chirikov and Spangsberg (ultimately commander of the squadron, under Bering, that was assigned the exploration of the Kuril Islands and contact with Japan), were directly involved in quelling (or preventing by strong measures) native unrest. On this question see Sgibnev, "Istoricheskii ocherk"; idem, "Okhotskii port"; S. B. Okun, *Kolonial'naia politika tsarizma na Kamchatke i Chukotke v XVIII veke: Sbornik arkhivnykh materialov*, ed. Ia. P. Al'kor and A. K. Drezen (Leningrad: Institut narodov Severa, TsIK SSSR, 1935), 81–86.
3. Two major Koriak uprisings occurred during the early stages of Russian penetration into the Aleutians, one in 1745–1749 and the second in 1751–1754. The Chukchi did not accept their de facto

submission to Russia until the end of the eighteenth century. See Okun, *Kolonial'naia politika tsarizma*; Sgibnev, "Istoricheskii ocherk," 5 pts., *Morskoi sbornik* 101, no. 4 (1869): 65–142; 102, no. 5 (1869): 53–84; no. 6 (1869): 37–69; 103, no. 7 (1869): 1–29; no. 8 (1869): 33–110.

4. The Russian frontier, without question, attracted many by this dream of freedom. The government at various times recognized this and allowed those who settled in remote areas (and later those who sailed to Alaska) to exist without valid internal passports, or with expired documents, residence permits, forgiveness of past-due taxes, etc. Cossack uprisings were frequent. See Okun, *Kolonial'naia politika tsarizma,* and Sgibnev, "Istoricheskii ocherk," for information on outbreaks in Kamchatka and the remote northeast. For a good general introduction to Cossack rebellions in Russia in the seventeenth and eighteenth centuries, see Paul Avrich, *Russian Rebels, 1600–1800* (New York: W. W. Norton and Company, 1972).

5. Kozyrevskii was recalled to participate in the Shestakov expedition. On the Shestakov expedition, see chap. 2, this volume. Also, Vasilii N. Berkh, "Puteshestvie kozach'iago golovy Afanasiia Shestakova, i pokhod maiora Pavlutskago v 1729 i 1730 godakh," *Syn Otechestva* 54, no. 20 (1819): 3–17; Sgibnev, "Materialy"; Gol'denberg, *Mezhdu dvumia*; Grekov, *Ocherki po istorii,* 45–54. On Kozyrevskii, see K. E. Cherevko, "Ignatii Kozyrevskii—avtor opisaniia Iaponskago gosudarstva," *Problemy Dal'nego Vostoka* 2 (1975). Documents pertaining to Kozyrevskii's travels to the Kuril Islands have been published in *Pamiatniki Sibirskoi istorii XVIII veka,* vol. 1, *1700–1713* (St. Petersburg: Tipografiia Ministerstva vnutrennikh del, 1882), 459–464 (doc. 109), 472–486 (doc. 111), 487–491 (doc. 112), 495–508 (doc. 117), 527–551 (doc. 123), and vol. 2, *1713–1724* (St. Petersburg: Tipografiia Ministerstva vnutrennikh del, 1885), 46 ff., 268–278 (doc. 65); Narochnitskii et al., *Russkie ekspeditsii* (1984), 33–35 (doc. 17).

6. Data on Basov and the vessel he commissioned are from Polonskii, "Perechen'," fols. 2r–10v. Unfortunately, Polonskii does not indicate his sources. So far, I have been unable to confirm them through an independent source.

7. Early historians of the Aleutian trade, Vasilii Berkh, *Khronologicheskaia istoriia,* and J.L.S., *Neue Nachrichten von denen neuentdekten Insuln in der See zwischen Asien und Amerika; aus mitgetheilten Urkunden und Auszügen verfasset* (Hamburg and Leipzig: Friedrich Ludwig Gleditsch, 1776), ascribed this event to the voyage of the vessel *Sv. Boris i Gleb,* owned by Nikifor Trapeznikov and company, either on her first (1749–1750) or second (1752–1757) voyage. The crew of the wrecked *Sv. Apostol Petr* returned to Kamchatka from Attu aboard this vessel in 1752, according to Polonskii. Modern historians tend to date Russian penetration of the central Aleutians to the late 1750s (under Bashmakov, see below) or even to the early 1760s (under Pan'kov, Bechevin, and Andrean Tolstykh, see below). However, in the eighteenth century, and even in the nineteenth, Russian settlers in Alaska believed that the central Aleutians were reached in the early 1740s. For example, Ioann Veniaminov, the first parish priest to reside in the Aleutians, attributed the founding of the Atka church (in the sense of the community of the faithful, not a building) to 1743 ("Sostoianie russkoi pravoslavnoi tserkvi v Rossiiskoi Amerike," compiled 1840, published in Aleksandr Sturdza, ed., *Pamiatnik trudov pravoslavnykh blagovestnikov russkikh s 1793 po 1853 goda* [Moscow: Got'ie, 1857], 209). Veniaminov specifically stated that the first church *building* was constructed there in 1827, but that the community had existed since 1743 (if one postulates a possible typographical error, 1745 or 1748).

8. Paragraph 24 of the governmental order (*ukaz*) issued on 10 May 1731 to Okhotsk Governor Grigorii Skorniakov-Pisarev, quoted in Sgibnev, "Okhotskii port," 22.

9. The earliest document on the regular supply route I was able to locate is dated 24 October 1719. Published in *Pamiatniki Sibirskoi istorii,* vol. 2, 260–261 (doc. 60).

10. James R. Gibson, *Feeding the Russian Fur Trade*; Mikhail Chulkov, *Istoricheskoe opisanie rossiiskoi kommertsii pri vsekh portakh i granitsakh ot drevneishikh vremen do nyne nastoiashchago i vsekh preimushchestvennykh uzakonenii po onoi Gosudaria Imperatora Petra Velikago i nyne blagopoluchno tsarstvuiushchei Gosudariny Imperatritsy Ekateriny Velikoi,* vol. 3 (Moscow: Universitetskaia tipografiia N. Novikova, 1785).

11. The overland provisioning of the Pacific seaboard was so difficult and expensive, even for the Crown, that the generally unresponsive government of Empress Elizabeth was ready to offer support, in 1755, to Nikita Shalaurov, who attempted to reopen the sea route to Kamchatka pioneered by Dezhnev. Dezhnev had sailed from the Kolyma, which lies to the east of the Lena River. Shalaurov proposed to start at the Lena River, making for a much longer trek. Kozyrevskii had made an attempt to sail from the Lena a generation earlier as part of Shestakov's expedition but had failed. Shalaurov also failed. He and his companions died on the Chukotka coast. The route was not successfully navigated until the twentieth century. Today, with the development of icebreaker technology, it is traversed regularly by Russian fleets as part of the Great Northern Sea Route.

12. Ivan Dmitrievich Vsevidov, a blacksmith (died late 1762 or early 1763 at Bol'sheretsk), was assigned such a share in the venture of 1758–1762.

13. Polonskii relates that Verkhoturov was on Agattu collecting iasak where he was killed for some "sad transgression" and that his body was then lowered over a cliff into the sea and that his firearm and powder measure were also thrown into the sea. The Aleut village elder then allegedly reported to the Russians that Verkhoturov was lost in a storm ("Perechen'," fol. 31v). Raisa Makarova, *Russkie na Tikhom okeane vo vtoroi polovine XVIII veka* (Moscow: Izdatel'stvo "Nauka," 1968), English ed., *Russians on the Pacific, 1763–1799,* trans. and ed. Richard A. Pierce and Alton S. Donnelly (Kingston, Ontario: Limestone Press, 1975), 240 n. 14, mentions Verkhoturov's death but gives no details and cites no source, though she used Polonskii's manuscript as well as archival documents in her work. I question that the body would have been thrown into the sea, as Aleuts were very careful not to pollute the sea spiritually; they took great care to bury their slain enemies to prevent such pollution.

14. This church, destroyed in the Soviet period, was rebuilt and consecrated in August 1993. A delegation from the City of Unalaska and members of the Aleut community participated in the event. Father George Pletnikoff, then priest of St. Paul, Alaska, co-officiated with the local priest. Jointly, the two clergymen baptized and administered communion to several hundred local residents. Nikolai Lekhanoff, *Starosta* (elder) of the Unalaska Church of the Holy Ascension of Christ, on behalf of the city and the Aleut community of Alaska, presented the Nizhne-Kamchatsk church with the print of an icon of the Four Alaska Saints painted by well-known Alaska artist Byron Birdsall.

15. Polonskii, "Perechen'," fol. 5v n. 2. Many early pioneers in the Aleutian trade, particularly the navigators, came from Tot'ma. The outside walls of the cathederal in that city are decorated with their commemorative crests. See Lydia Cheshkova, "Kartushi starykh morekhodov," *Vokrug sveta* 3 (March 1992): 14–20.

16. Polonskii, "Perechen'," fol. 6v. Andrei Serebrennikov was later an active participant in the Aleutian trade. The name of Andrei Shelikhov does not appear in any other source available to me. It is not clear whether this early participant in the Aleutian trade was a member of the merchant family to which Grigorii Shelikhov, the major force in Russian settlement on the American continent, belonged. However, Shelikhov's recent biographer does point out that one of his uncles was a merchant of Moscow (L. A. Sitnikov, *Grigorii Shelikhov* [Irkutsk: Vostochno-Sibirskoe knizhnoe izdatel'stvo, 1990], 42, 331 n. 19).

17. Polonskii, "Perechen'," fol. 7. This prohibition did not last long (though there was a brief time when a monopoly was granted to merchant Iugov). Moreover, it was difficult to enforce and eventually lapsed.

18. Peter S. Pallas, "Kurze Beschreibung der sogenannten Kupferinsel (Mednoi ostrof) im Kamtschatkischen Meere," *Neue nordische Beyträge* 2 (1781): 302–307. Nakvasin's map, often attributed to Iakovlev, was published in 1822 in G. Spasskii, "Opisanie Mednago ostrova, lezhashchago v Kamchatskom more i proizvodimykh na onom gornykh rabot," *Sibirskii vestnik* 18 (1822): 281–290, map.

19. This habit of rebuilding a vessel out of wreckage, or constructing a new one out of driftwood and sea mammal skin, can be traced to the ancient Pomory practice. The pattern was repeated again and again in Alaskan waters throughout the eighteenth century. Some of us who work at present in the Aleutians refer to the practice as "hull recycling."

20. Polonskii, "Perechen'," fol. 9.

21. Order of the Ruling Senate dated 24 August 1761, revoking the prohibition, was issued on the urging of the Governor-General (former Admiral) Soimonov, an advocate of industrial and commercial development of Siberia and Russia's Pacific northeast coasts (A. L. Narochnitskii et al., eds., *Russkie ekspeditsii po izucheniiu severnoi chasti Tikhogo okeana vo vtoroi polovine XVIII v. (sbornik dokumentov)*, comp. T. S. Fedorova et al. [Moscow: Izdatel'stvo "Nauka," 1989], 58–59; Chulkov, *Istoricheskoe opisanie*, 420–421).

22. The Russians began to exploit the northern fur seals early in the eighteenth century (on the rookeries off Sakhalin Island near the Amur delta) and then in the Commander Islands. The Alaskan fur seal rookeries in the Pribilof Islands began to be exploited in the third quarter of the eighteenth century. Russian fur-procuring vessels observed the spring and fall migration of the fur seals and sought their rookeries. In 1786 and 1787, Gavriil Pribylov, a naval navigator serving with the merchant fleet in Alaska, put these islands on the map (see below). However, from the fact that at least two vessels returned from Alaska with over 20,000 fur seal skins aboard, it is probable that these rookeries were found by the Russians at an earlier date; it is not possible to obtain such numbers of pelts pelagically during the migrations. Moreover, traces of European presence on the islands were observed by Pribylov's crews. Fur seals, first cousins of the sea lion, have bipolar distribution. The southern fur seals are found in South American waters, south of Peru, on the Galapagos Islands in the Pacific, and off the coast of southern Brazil, Argentina, and on Falkland and Staten Islands; they live also on the south and southwest African coasts. Varieties of fur seal are found on the isolated islands in the Indian and southern Atlantic Ocean and on the southern and southwestern coasts of Australia, New Zealand, and Tasmania. Beginning with the late eighteenth century, the fur seal industry in southern waters, both in the Pacific and the Atlantic, was an important part of the American maritime economy. By 1840, the herds suffered a collapse due to overhunting and also possibly due to a pestilence. Today, only Uruguay harvests southern fur seals (Judith E. King, *Seals of the World* [London: Trustees of the British Museum (Natural History), 1964]). For an excellent account of American fur sealing in the early nineteenth century, see Capt. Benjamin Morrell, Jr., *A Narrative of Four Voyages, to the South Sea, North and South Pacific Ocean, Chinese Sea, Ethiopic and Southern Atlantic Ocean, Indian and Antarctic Ocean: From the Year 1823 to 1831* (New York: J. & J. Harper, 1832). It should be noted that American fur sealers were known to poach in the "Russian" waters off California and later in the Pribilof Islands. On that point see Peter Corney, *Voyages in the Northern Pacific: Narrative of Several Trading Voyages from 1813 to 1818, between the Northwest Coast of America, the Hawaiian Islands and China, with a Description of the Russian Establishments on the Northwest Coast* (Honolulu: Thos. G. Thrum, 1896, reprinted from *The London Literary Gazette*, 1821).

23. The first set of figures has been extracted from doc. 82 in *Pamiatniki Sibirskoi istorii*, vol. 2, 374–386; the second set of figures has been computed on the basis of price given in liang and fen in "Account of the Tretiakov-Molokov Caravan on its Departure for Peking, September 1727," in Foust, *Muscovite and Mandarin*, 368 app. 2, and the conversion to rubles based on "Weights, Measures, and Currencies," ibid., 366 app. 1.

24. Chulkov, *Istoricheskoe opisanie*, 424.

25. An overwhelming majority of the merchants and their agents came from the old Russian north, Pomor'ie. It should not come as a surprise that the skippers whom they recruited, also in an overwhelming majority, were Pomory as well. It should be noted that at this time the Russian navy, especially the Okhotsk flotilla, liked to recruit navigators from the Russian north. For example, Ivan Butin, a Crown skipper who later was hired to navigate an Aleutian merchant vessel, was from Mezen', the center of Spitsbergen and Novaia Zemlia navigation.

26. "*Prikazchiki* were persons possessing personal freedom, who served as entrepreneurs on the basis of free hire, under specified conditions, in accordance with a contract, and were recompensed either by a certain salary 'on a year's hire' or by part of the profits" (S. V. Bakhrushin, "Torgi gostia Nikitina v Sibiri i Kitae," in *Nauchnye trudy*, 3 [1]: 226–251).

27. On the structure and organization of the fur industry, labor relations, social antecedents, and social mobility of the participants, see Bakhrushin, "Pokruta." This article contains specific reference to the Pomor'ie origin of the labor recruitment practice and conditions of labor known as *pokruta*, and the persistence of the same in Pomor'ie until the twentieth century. Valuable data are also contained in the works of P. N. Pavlov, *Pushnoi promysel v Sibiri XVII v.* (Krasnoiarsk: Krasnoiarskii gosudarstvennyi pedagogicheskii institut, 1972), and idem, *Promyslovaia kolonizatsiia Sibiri v XVII v.* (Krasnoiarsk: Krasnoiarskii gosudarstvennyi pedagogicheskii institut, 1974). For an example of a general contract, dated 15 September 1773, see app. to Makarova, *Russkie na Tikhom okeane*, 171–198.

28. Narochnitskii et al., *Russkie ekspeditsii* (1989), 55–57 (doc. 14).

29. Narochnitskii et al., *Russkie ekspeditsii* (1989), 50–52, 347 nn. 12–14. This voyage sometimes is ascribed to Vsevidov, who served as foreman. See J.L.S., *Neue Nachrichten*, 33–40, 58–59. It should be noted that in all standard texts the discovery of the Fox Islands is attributed to a somewhat later voyage, that of the *Sv. Iulian*, Stepan Glotov of Yarensk commanding.

30. Cited after Pekarskii, "Arkhivnye razyskaniia," 32.

31. Shilov, in Pekarskii, "Arkhivnye razyskaniia," 32–33; Stepan Cherepanov, report rendered at Bol'sheretsk office on 3 August 1762, in A. I. Andreev, ed., *Russkie otkrytiia* (1948), 113–120.

32. Stepan Cherepanov, report rendered at Bol'sheretsk office on 3 August 1762, in A. I. Andreev, ed., *Russkie otkrytiia* (1948), 113–120; P. Pekarskii, "O rechi v pamiat' Lomonosova, proiznesennoi v Akademii nauk doktorom LeKlerkom," *Zapiski Imperatorskoi akademii nauk* 10, no. 2 (1866): 184–186.

33. These merchants were Il'iia Snigirev, Ivan Burenin, and Ivan Nikiforov, owners of the vessel commanded by Stepan Glotov who brought a breeding pair of black foxes from his 1762–1764 voyage. See Narochnitskii et al., *Russkie ekspeditsii* (1989), 84 (doc. 25).

34. Tolstykh was one of the shareholders in a company headed by Kholodilov of Tot'ma. This vessel sailed first in 1747–1748, her destination unknown, though she sailed a great distance to the east, possibly as far as the central Aleutians (Polonskii, "Perechen'," fol. 13v; J.L.S., *Neue Nachrichten*, 19; Berkh, *Chronological History*, 6–7).

35. Later on, during the days of the Russian-American Company, a variety of foxes were planted on different islands, and traps were distributed to the Alaska Natives who took the animals for market. Seal carcasses were often left for these introduced foxes to feed upon. Still later, though for the most part in the years after 1867, ground squirrels were introduced from Alaska's mainland as prey for the foxes. The practice of feeding the foxes stocked on various islands persisted through the Russian period. It formed the basis for fox farming in southwestern Alaska, which diminished only with the collapse of fox pelt prices in the twentieth century, during the Great Depression, and ceased completely only after World War II.

36. The toponymic information found on the early charts of Alaskan shores compiled by the merchant skippers awaits detailed study by an interested researcher.

37. Joan B. Townsend, "Firearms Against Native Arms: A Study in Comparative Efficiencies with an Alaskan Example," *Arctic Anthropology* 20, no. 2 (1983): 1–33.

38. Information supplied orally by Jacob Semionoff of Akhiok, Kodiak Island. I believe that this was practiced by sea otter schooners in the American period when a laissez-faire policy was adopted. It should be noted that on Kodiak sea mammals, including whales, were caught by means of long seine-like nets. Some scholars, including Heizer, believed that the practice might have been introduced by Itel'men on Russian vessels, though there is no direct evidence that this was not an aboriginal practice.

39. Cherepanov, in A. I. Andreev, ed., *Russkie otkrytiia* (1948), 119; Iakov Netsvetov, *The Journals of Iakov Netsvetov: The Atkha Years, 1828–1844*, trans. Lydia T. Black and ed. Richard A. Pierce (Kingston, Ontario: Limestone Press, 1980), 42–48.

40. Today, Museum of Peter the Great, Kunstkamera, Russian Academy of Sciences, also known as MAE.

41. To appreciate how dangerous these waters are, refer to United States, Department of Commerce, Coast and Geodetic Survey, *United States Coast Pilot 9: Alaska, Cape Spencer to Arctic Ocean,* 6th ed. (Washington, D.C.: U.S. Government Printing Office, 1954).

42. The term "soft gold" appears in recent American literature; the early Russian term was *miagkaia rukhliad'*, or "soft goods."

FIGURE 15. Catherine II (Ekaterina, or Catherine the Great; 1729–1796), empress of Russia 1762–1796.

Courtesy Slavic and Baltic Division, New York Public Library, Astor, Lenox, and Tilden Foundations.

CHAPTER FIVE

A Game for High Stakes

The Age of Catherine the Great, 1762–1796

THE EFFORTS OF RUSSIAN PIONEERS LAID THE FOUNDATION FOR RUSSIA'S CLAIM of occupancy to Alaska, to add to the claim of discovery by Gvozdev in 1732 and Bering and Chirikov in 1741. To the pioneers Alaska was Russian territory and theirs to exploit. But the field the entrepreneurs believed to be wide open was about to be contested by a number of international players, and the Crown was stepping in. Geopolitics during the late eighteenth century were to affect the North Pacific in many ways.

Almost immediately after the accession of Catherine II to the throne, following the brief reign of her unpopular husband, Peter III, her government took on a very active role with respect to the American territories claimed by Russia. This involvement, and the empress's personal interest in America, did not abate until the end of Catherine's reign.

The foundation for this involvement, however, stemmed from the reign of her predecessor, Empress Elizabeth (1741–1761). Though Elizabeth's government did not reactivate the Great Northern Expeditions carried out in the previous reigns, probably because of the empire's disastrous financial situation due to improvident fiscal policies and, toward the end of Elizabeth's reign, Russia's involvement in the Seven Years' War in Europe, her government did pay attention to the economic development of Siberia, particularly the establishment of communications and transport systems. There was also an interest in establishing trade and diplomatic relations with Japan. Elizabeth consistently followed the policy of bringing back from exile or penal servitude and reinstating in office men formerly associated with her father, Peter the Great, and appointing them to positions of responsibility. Thus, on 29 March 1753, Admiral Vasilii Miatlev was appointed governor-general of Siberia. He was to facilitate the settlement and agricultural development of Siberia, ensure safe, uninterrupted navigation down the Amur River (more of a wish than a reality in view of the Treaty of Nerchinsk[1]) and in the Okhotsk Sea, and invigorate shipbuilding and commerce in the Eastern Ocean. Detailed cartographic and hydrographic work was to be conducted.

Miatlev, an exceptionally able man, was one of Peter's fosterlings. He chose as his assistant another high-ranking officer who had served Peter the Great, Fedor Soimonov, a fellow navy man who, during the reign of Anna, had suffered torture, the lash, and exile. In 1757, Soimonov succeeded Miatlev as governor-general when the latter was needed on active duty in the Seven Years' War. Soimonov served as governor until 1762. When he returned to St. Petersburg he was offered an appointment as a member of the ruling senate. He declined this appointment and asked that Mikhail Soimonov, his son who had been with him in Siberia, serve instead. Still, his interest in the development of the economy of Siberia and maritime activity on the Pacific was respected. He was asked to serve at the senate whenever any matter concerning Siberia arose, and in the end he did accept the appointment as senator.[2] His was an authoritative voice, and his opinions carried weight with Catherine, her government, and the admiralty. He was influential in the creation of a special commission whose task it was to evaluate and reform the imposition and collection of iasak. He was also instrumental in the liquidation of the old governmental agency dealing with Siberia, the *Sibirskii prikaz*.[3] Both Miatlev and Soimonov took an active interest in the activities of private entrepreneurs in the Eastern Ocean. Both, but especially Soimonov, were concerned with economic development of the northeast coasts and strengthening of Russia's seagoing capability. Soimonov was especially interested in cartography and exploration, as well as the development of Siberia's economic potential. On this topic he published several influential essays in addition to reports and presentations to the ruling senate and to the Empress Catherine.[4]

While in Siberia Soimonov and Miatlev were instrumental in establishing in 1754 the navigational school at Irkutsk where navigators, geodesists, mining engineers, and Japanese language specialists were trained. Of the navigators in the first graduating class of 1756, sixteen were assigned to Okhotsk.[5] In 1765, as a senator, Soimonov saw to it that a navigation school was opened at Yakutsk.

On his watch Soimonov collected detailed information on the results of the voyages of the fur-trading skippers and actively supported Shalaurov's plan to revitalize the northern sea route from the Arctic to the Pacific Oceans, as well as Ivan Bechevin's ambitious plan to explore the Pacific Basin.[6] That plan misfired, as Bechevin never carried out his proposals but instead created a major conflict between the Russians and Aleuts because of wanton violence by members of his crew while in the Aleutian Islands, from Atka in the central Aleutians to the Alaska Peninsula. Soimonov advocated, and in several cases succeeded in obtaining, government subsidies for private entrepreneurs active in the Aleutian trade and advocated governmental supply of armaments for their vessels and powder for their firearms. At the same time he attempted to regulate their activities. He proposed shipboard regulations and guidelines for shipbuilding and equipment, and also tried to set limits (on grounds of safety) as to how far the traders were permitted to sail (see Figure 16). These restrictions were proposed in 1761 and lifted in 1762.[7]

Soimonov sought appointments of competent men to administer remote northeastern regions, among them F. Plenisner, a veteran of Bering's 1741–1742 expedition, as administrator of Kamchatka; he supported the exploration of the Kurils, the Anadyr' area, and the Chukchi Peninsula, the latter conducted by the famous Chukchi Nikolai Daurkin, who would bring reports of the Great Land—North America—which lay to the east. In 1761, Soimonov instructed Lt. Ivan Sindt, another veteran of Bering's voyage to America, to sail from Okhotsk to Bering Strait via Kamchatka, Anadyr', and St. Lawrence Island, then to the American mainland. Sindt was specifically instructed to chart and describe the coasts. Hydrographic work and charting of the coasts were, at all times, Soimonov's priorities. Several charts of the Aleutians were compiled either by him (he was an expert cartographer) or for him under his guidance and supervision. One such chart is mentioned in a note of

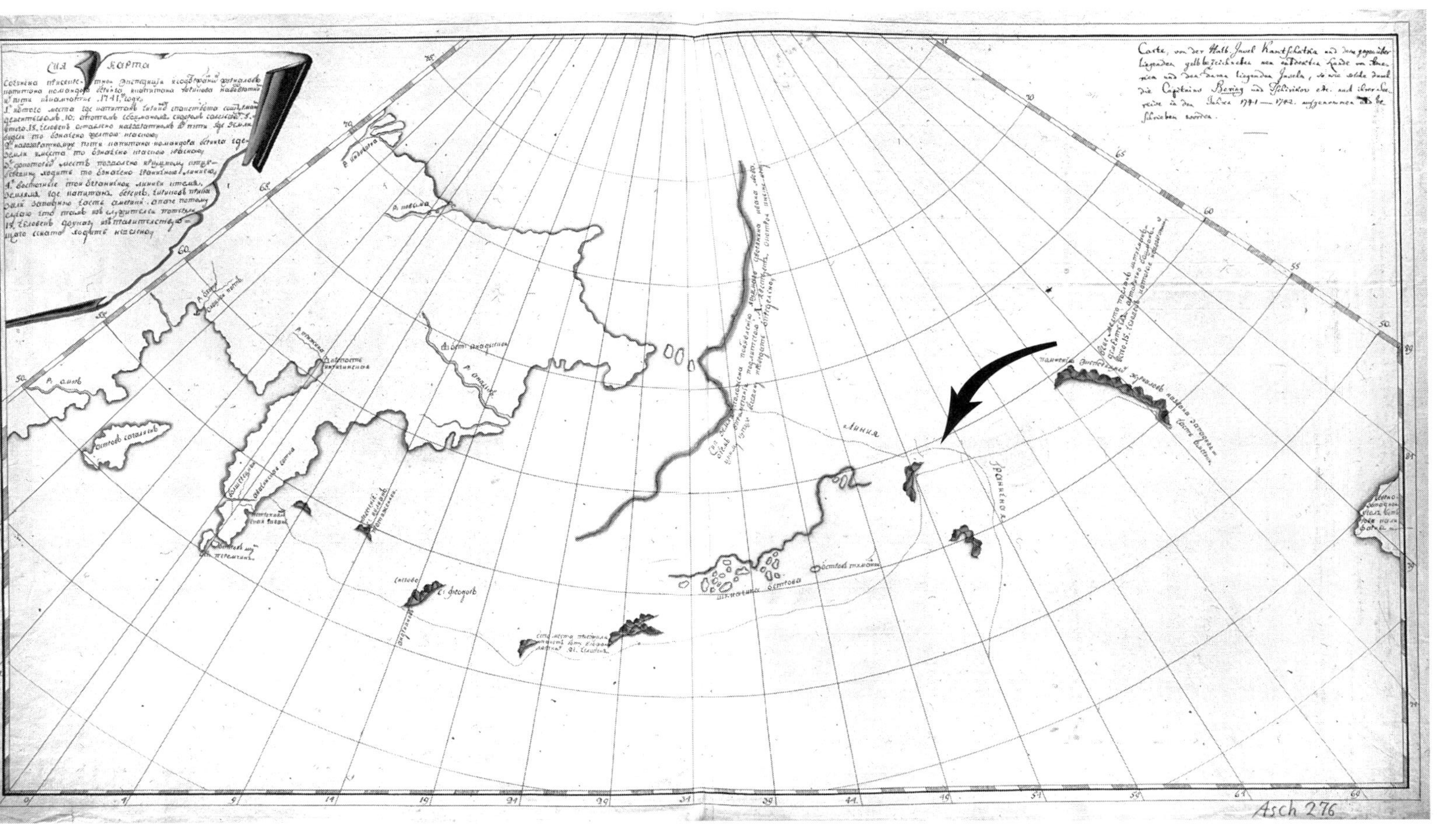

FIGURE 16. Chart compiled by Governor-General F. I. Soimonov. It includes Gvozdev's voyage of 1732, but is based primarily on the charts and logs of Bering's 1741 voyage. The dotted line (arrow added) indicates the boundary beyond which Soimonov prohibited Russian merchantmen, specifically Irkutsk merchant Bechevin, to sail. The inscription on the right indicates where Chirikov lost fifteen men.

Courtesy University of Göttingen Library, Rare Books and Manuscripts, von Asch Collection, no. 276.

FIGURE 17. Mikhail Vasil'ievich Lomonosov's map of 1763, executed by Lomonosov's student Il'ia Abramov. The map indicates proposed cross-polar routes from the White Sea to Alaska and India.
From Lomonosov, 1952, facing 424.

28 May 1764 addressed to him by Empress Catherine. In a postscript the empress says: "I know that these islands [eastern Aleutians] were discovered through your efforts."[8] In Moscow and in the capital, he continued to keep in touch with the Aleutian mariners and kept himself well informed. He also was in touch with the scholars associated with Bering's second expedition, G. F. Müller and Ia. I. Lindenau.[9]

In 1764, the proposal Soimonov had initiated in 1760 for an official expedition to the Pacific, the Aleutian Islands, and the American mainland was approved. It is not clear whether the naval expedition led by Krenitsyn and Levashov, which reached the Aleutians in 1768 (the first since Bering's voyage of 1741), was planned in accordance with Soimonov's ideas, but it is certain he was consulted. In any case, the empress sent a chart of the Aleutian area drawn by Mikhail Lomonosov, the famous Russian scientist, to Soimonov

FIGURE 18. Mikhail Vasil'ievich Lomonosov (1711–1765)—a peasant's son from the remote Russian north, a Pomor, and initially self-taught—came to Moscow in 1728 and commenced his formal education in Russia and abroad. Eventually, under the patronage of Academician Shumakher (Schumacher), he joined the Russian Imperial Academy of Sciences. A scholar of colossal erudition and competence in several natural sciences, he calculated that the shortest route from Europe to the American continent was across the North Pole and that if ice-free passage could be found, it would be the most efficient route of intercontinental communication. Today, airlines essentially follow the route mapped out by Lomonosov in the 1760s.
Courtesy Richard A. Pierce.

for comment. In acknowledging the receipt of the chart, Soimonov stated that a detailed description of the islands (presumably accompanied by the most accurate charts) would be completed by the end of summer.[10]

Also prominent in planning the new naval effort was Mikhail Lomonosov, one of the founders, with Count Shuvalov, of Moscow University. A native of the Russian north, a Pomor, fully aware of the role of the Pomory navigators in the expansion along the northern coast of Siberia, Lomonosov was deeply interested in the problems and development of arctic navigation. As early as 1747, he spoke in a poem of "the Russian Columbuses," sailing eastward among the ice.[11] In 1755, he wrote an essay entitled "Letter about the Northern Route to East India via the Siberian Ocean."[12] Lomonosov wrote several other essays in the late 1750s and early 1760s devoted to such problems as the need for greater precision in navigational practice, arctic ice formations and types, and the aurora borealis. On 20 September 1763, he addressed to Crown Prince Paul (then nine years old but the official president of the Admiralty College) a lengthy manuscript entitled "A Brief Description of Various Voyages in the Northern Seas and Demonstration of the Feasibility of a Passage via the Siberian Ocean to East India."[13] In this work Lomonosov proposed that the shortest route from northern Russia to America, from the Kola Peninsula to the Aleutians, lay across the polar region. In fact, he proposed at least two alternate routes. One would extend from either the Kola Peninsula or the Siberian coast in the vicinity of the Ob' River via Novaia Zemlia to Bering Strait and into the North Pacific. The other proposed route was from the Kola Peninsula via Spitsbergen, past Greenland, to Bering Strait and into the North Pacific Ocean (this route is followed by Aeroflot today, from Moscow to San Francisco). Catherine sent Lomonosov's manuscript for review to Soimonov, who, based on his Siberian experience, stated that polar ice precluded the successful completion of the proposed sailing routes.[14] Waxell, too, was extremely negative. The admiralty, however, was interested; the then Vice-Admiral Nagaev, in particular, found it intriguing. By the end of December 1763, Lomonosov's proposal had been heard by the recently created naval commission charged with the revitalization of the Russian navy. The admirals were determined to make the attempt, in spite of the negative reactions by such experienced men as Soimonov and Waxell. Lomonosov's essay became a basis for the planning of an expedition along the polar route, known as the Chichagov expedition, and the dispatch to the Aleutians of a navy squadron under the overall command of Captain Krenitsyn.

The naval commission, upon hearing Lomonosov's arguments, ordered that experienced northern seafarers be interviewed. Men of the Pomor'ie who had sailed to Spitsbergen and Novaia Zemlia were summoned. Naval personnel who had sailed in the Barents Sea and Old Voyagers who had returned from the Aleutian Islands were ordered to report to St. Petersburg. The admirals interviewed the mariners at length. Lomonosov also met with them. Although the commission was inclined toward the Spitsbergen route, it did not arrive at a decision and passed the matter to the Admiralty College. Lomonosov continued to argue in favor of his proposal and submitted two "Appendices," the first dealing with the Spitsbergen route, the second with what was then known about the geography of the eastern Aleutians and the southwest Alaskan coast.[15] At this time Lomonosov became officially associated with the Admiralty College. He actively participated in the planning of the Chichagov and the Krenitsyn-Levashov expeditions and was the author of a detailed instruction for both, though he did not live to appreciate the results (he died 15 April 1765). The two expeditions were part of a single plan: Chichagov was expected to sail across the Arctic Ocean via Spitsbergen and Greenland, while Krenitsyn and Levashov were to sail out of Okhotsk and Kamchatka to the American coast. The two squadrons were to meet in Aleutian waters. After an exchange of officers and crew, Krenitsyn was to return to Russia by the Greenland-Spitsbergen route, while Chichagov was to sail to Kamchatka and Okhotsk along the Aleutian Chain. One of the expeditions' objectives was to train mariners in arctic navigation as well as to familiarize them with the two routes.[16]

By 1764 the plan was being put into operation. Lieutenant M. Nemtinov sailed to Spitsbergen in command of a naval vessel and several merchantmen leased from the local Pomory. He carried with him ten prefabricated dwellings, a steam bath, a storage structure, and supplies. He established a camp in Klok Bay (Bell Sound), leaving provisions, equipment, and a small crew. This camp was to function as a support and resupply base for the main expedition, which was to sail the following summer. In May 1765, a three-vessel squadron, commanded by Vasilii Ia. Chichagov, left Kola (where the vessels, built especially for the expedition at Arkhangel'sk, had been moved the previous year), following the course prescribed by the Admiralty College. Among his crews he had recruited more than twenty Pomory steersmen and sailors experienced in sailing to Spitsbergen. Reaching latitude 80° 30' N on 18 July and encountering impassable ice fields and dense fogs, Chichagov turned back. Arriving at Arkhangel'sk 10 September, he reported that the route was not feasible. He found support for this opinion in an interview with a Dutch sealing captain out of Iceland, whom he encountered while standing off Spitsbergen. This sailor, who claimed fifteen years' experience in arctic waters, did not think it was possible to reach Greenland from Spitsbergen; he stated that he had never encountered ice-free waters in the area. Rendering a scientific opinion on the subject, Professor Franz Ulrich T. Epinus of the Imperial Academy of Sciences stated that it was unreasonable to expect ice-free conditions in the high arctic latitudes. The admirals, however, were not convinced.

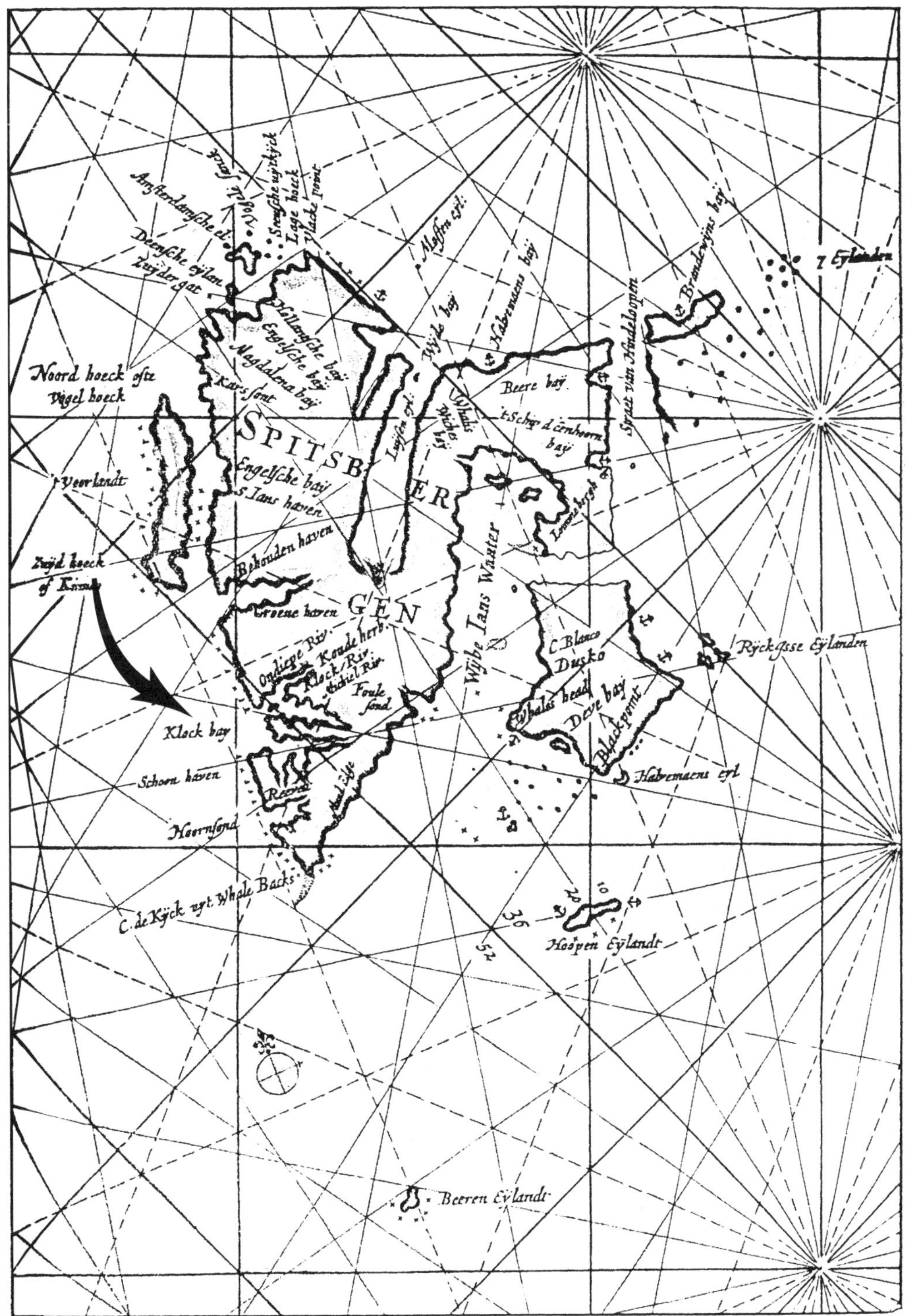

FIGURE 19. Spitsbergen. Arrow (added, center left) indicates Klock Bay.

After Conway, 1906.

Count Chernyshev, in an official letter to Chichagov, was scathing. Perhaps in this they were influenced by Epinus, who, in spite of his considerations of arctic ice, proposed as feasible a somewhat different route from the one suggested by Lomonosov. The Admiralty College expected Chichagov to try again.

The admirals proposed that Chichagov take his vessels to Klok Bay on Spitsbergen for the winter and sail from there the following summer. Chichagov, with relatively broad decision-making powers on this second attempt of the arctic route, found this not feasible. The vessels, once again, were to sail out of Kola.

Chichagov sailed on 19 May 1766, this time having some leeway in determining his course. On 17–18 July he was again above 80° latitude. On this voyage he, too, encountered Dutch whaling vessels and, when calling in at Klok Bay, dispatched an officer to interview the Pomory sea mammal hunters who wintered nearby. Ice, fog, and difficult sailing conditions, as well as what he heard from the skippers he encountered, firmed his conviction that the polar route was impassable. He turned back, collecting the support crew on Spitsbergen, where he found eight of the men had died during the difficult winter there. He reached Arkhangel'sk on 10 September and at once dispatched a report to the Admiralty College. His report was heard there 27 September, and this time accepted. The Admiralty College now awaited reports from the expedition to the American coast.

This expedition had several tasks. While it was planned as an intercept for the Chichagov squadron, should it complete the polar route, a very important part of its mission was to verify information given by the private entrepreneurs about the islands off the American coast. The government paid particular attention to the accounts by those fur hunters who had sailed from 1758 to 1762 aboard the *Sv. Iulian,* which vessel had been commanded by Stepan Glotov of Yarensk, located in the Pomor'ie region and the center of the Komi settlements in that area. Many documents were carefully studied: observations transmitted by the Cossack Ponomarev (who was the iasak collector) and by the foreman and part owner Petr Shishkin; charts and descriptions of the lands farther eastward, especially the Shugattany (Land of the Shugat—the Chugach, Prince William Sound area), obtained from Aleut informants and from Kodiak Island captives among the eastern Aleuts; and reports about the Alaska mainland supplied by members of Ivan Bechevin's crew, who in 1761–1762 wintered on the Alaska Peninsula. These reports triggered anew the government's concern about the possible presence of other Europeans off the American coasts in the North Pacific, notably the Spanish. The Spanish maintained that they had a legal claim to the entire western coast of the North American continent, from Mexico northward to Bering Strait.

In the order authorizing the expedition, dated 4 May 1764, Catherine specifically referred to Governor Chicherin's reports about the voyage of the *Sv. Iulian*. The next day, 5 May, the Admiralty College appointed Captain Petr Krenitsyn as the expedition's commanding officer, and on 26 June issued detailed instructions outlining his mission. Earlier, Governor Chicherin had received orders to support the expedition and prepare supplies, ships, and equipment for it. He also received additional instructions for Krenitsyn, to be handed to him upon his arrival in Irkutsk. Captain Krenitsyn was to make use of any merchant vessels he found suitable for the assigned task and to utilize the knowledge and skills of the fur hunters, the promyshlenniki. In particular, he was to enlist the services of the Cossack Ponomarev as a guide to the island of Umnak in the eastern Aleutians. At his discretion he was to recruit any number of the Old Voyagers to sail with him. He was to ensure that cartography and hydrographic work were carried out, and that demographic data and detailed ethnographic information on the inhabitants were collected. Natural resources, flora, fauna, and mineral wealth were to be described. He was to ascertain how near (or distant) the Shugattany was from any European settlements and if any of the aboriginal groups he might encounter on the American mainland recognized the power of—that is, were subject to—any European nation. Like Chichagov's expedition, Krenitsyn's voyage was considered a state secret. Results of his findings, and especially his charts, were not to be made public or disclosed to any unauthorized persons.

Krenitsyn was supplied with all available information and charts, from those compiled by officers of the Bering-Chirikov expedition to charts of the Aleutian Islands provided by the promyshlenniki, and composites compiled by officers of the admiralty (in the Mercator projection) on the basis of their charts, reports, and oral testimonies.

On 5 March 1765, Krenitsyn, already in Siberia, received supplementary instructions from Governor Chicherin, who informed him that it was not advisable to use merchant vessels for his voyage and that new vessels would be constructed at Okhotsk for his use and under his supervision. Chicherin, apparently skeptical about the Chichagov intercept, stated that the most important tasks before the expedition were describing and charting the coast of the Alaska Peninsula, Kodiak archipelago, and adjacent waters, and reporting on the local populations. He urged Krenitsyn to cooperate with private traders and stressed their usefulness to the expedition. Also, Chicherin highly recommended the enlistment of Old Voyager volunteers. He warned Krenitsyn that reports were reaching Kamchatka that several vessels had suffered shipwrecks or other disasters and instructed Krenitsyn to give relief to the promyshlenniki who might be in adversity. He also assigned to Krenitsyn an Old Voyager, Prokopii Lisenkov, a man who had sailed in the Rat Islands as well as to the eastern Aleutians. In a letter to the empress dated 16 February 1765, Chicherin spoke of his intention to assign Lisenkov to Krenitsyn, with a salary of fifteen rubles per month. He also forwarded to St. Petersburg Lisenkov's detailed description of the Aleuts and their political subdivisions, dialects, armaments, seagoing craft, and war tactics; later he delivered a copy to Krenitsyn. Lisenkov's description remains, to this day, one of the most important early documents on ethnography of the Aleuts.[17] Chicherin noted in his letter that Lisenkov was not interested in amassing riches, that he spent whatever he made on a voyage and embarked as soon as possible on another, and that his one ambition was to become a first-rate skipper. Aleuts, said Chicherin, were warlike, and only the fear of firearms at times kept them from hostile action. Chicherin went on to say that as Krenitsyn would have little armament, he should be authorized to enlist at his discretion a contingent of military men from local garrisons for his expedition. In the end, however, Krenitsyn sailed without a military contingent.

Krenitsyn and his second-in-command, Lt. Mikhail Levashov, arrived in Okhotsk in 1765 and spent the winter there supervising the construction and outfitting of new vessels and the repairing of other, older vessels that they commandeered for their use. Their flotilla sailed for Kamchatka in October 1766, very late in the season. All of the vessels were damaged on approaches to the dangerous (and, to the officers, unfamiliar) Kamchatkan coasts in stormy and inclement weather. Necessary repair and refitting of damaged vessels took time, and delayed the expedition's departure for another year.

In the meantime, in August 1766, two vessels returned from the Aleutians, both commanded by veterans of the Aleutian trade, Stepan Glotov and Ivan Solov'iev. They

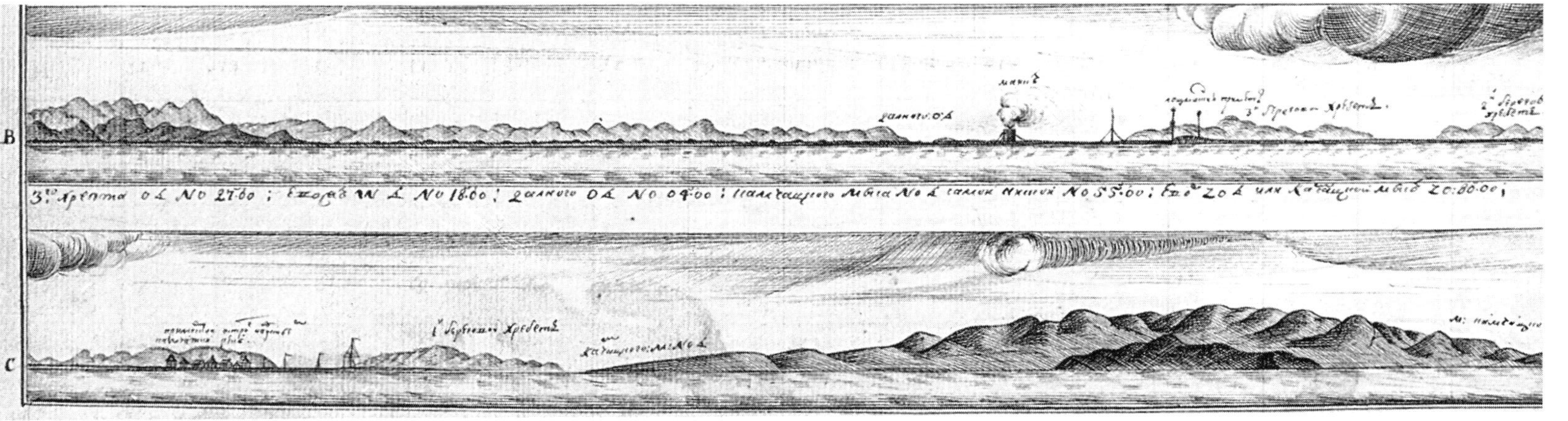

Figure 20. This drawing by Capt. Mikhail Levashov (1768–1769) shows the Kamchatka River estuary off Nizhne-Kamchatsk, the staging port for Russian fur-procuring expeditions from the 1740s to the late 1770s. It is remarkable in showing sophisticated navigational markers: lighthouse, buoys, etc.
Courtesy RGAVMF.

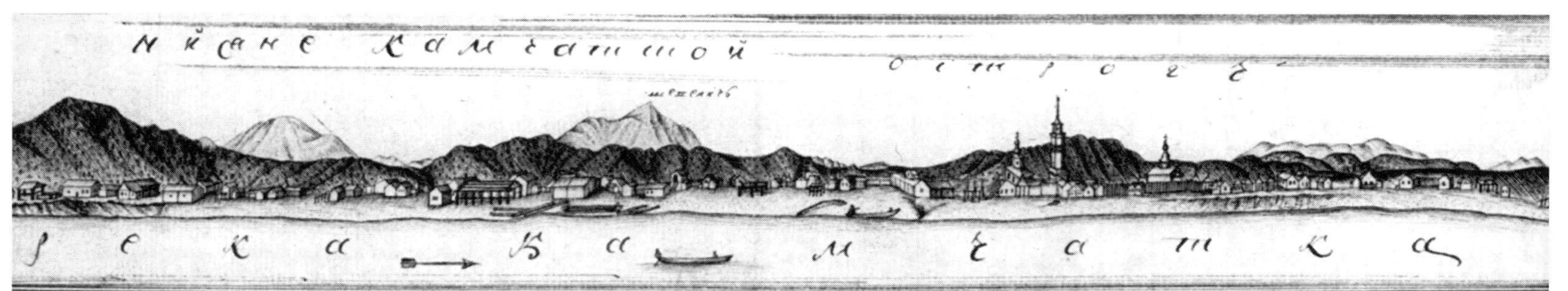

Figure 21. Town of Nizhne-Kamchatsk or Nizhnekamchatskoi ostrog, founded in 1703. Sketch by Capt. Mikhail Levashov, 1768–1769.
Courtesy RGAVMF.

brought disastrous news. The Aleuts, angered by unspeakable and apparently unprovoked atrocities committed in 1761–1762 by Bechevin's men on Unimak Island and the Alaska Peninsula, determined on a war of annihilation against the Russians. In December 1763, the Aleuts had overcome their local political disagreements and had mounted a concerted attack on the Russians hunting in the islands. Four vessels were lost: one on Umnak Island, two on Unalaska, and one on Unimak. Of their crews, which had numbered well over 200 men, only twelve survived from the two ships anchored in two different locations on Unalaska Island. These men were saved only by the timely arrivals of Glotov from Kodiak, where he had wintered, and of Ivan Solov'iev from Kamchatka, both in the summer of 1764. The survivors were led by an experienced skipper, Ivan Korovin. Relieved by Glotov, he joined that crew.

Korovin was bent on revenge, but he received only token support from Glotov, who had parted with the Aleuts of Umnak on friendly terms during his earlier voyage. Solov'iev, on the other hand, was persuaded that if not revenge (which was forbidden by the government), then a preventive strike was justified to ensure his crew's safety. Korovin soon moved to Solov'iev's camp. Several times in the summer of 1764 and through the next year, Solov'iev or Grigorii Korenev (Solov'iev's lieutenant) and Korovin fell upon Aleut villages from Konets Head, on the strait that separates Unalaska from Umnak Island, to Reese Bay, which faces Akutan Island to the north and east, and to Beaver Inlet. These events have entered folk memory as the time of destruction, the beginning of the end of Aleut independence. Solov'iev's image became the incarnation of the destructive force. Even though he himself apparently acted with some restraint and exercised moderation, most of the violent acts committed by the Russians through time have come to be ascribed to this man. Actual casualties will never be known, though the figures given in literature are grossly exaggerated. By Solov'iev's own report, from forty to sixty Aleut men were killed in armed confrontations. This was, indeed, a traumatic event, as Aleut villages deprived of their able-bodied men, the providers, could not survive. Moreover, Solov'iev believed that the most effective means to subdue the Aleuts was to destroy their capability to wage war; therefore, he systematically destroyed all their weapons: bows and arrows, spears, lances, and their kayaks and large skin boats. Without these, the Aleuts were not only powerless in war, they were helpless in the face of hunger: their means of subsistence was gone. The Aleuts had won a major battle by destroying Russian vessels and killing their crews in 1763–1764, but they lost the war. The scorched-earth policy of Solov'iev brought the Umnak-Unalaska political alliance to its knees.

Nevertheless, when he heard the reports of these events in the islands, Krenitsyn felt that he was facing a dangerous situation. He needed the help of experienced Aleutian sailors more than ever. As soon as Krenitsyn arrived in Bol'sheretsk, he interviewed the Cossack Ponomarev, who was very old, having served in Kamchatka before Bering's Second Expedition, and almost blind. Clearly, he could not serve Krenitsyn as a pilot. Krenitsyn then summoned the two newly arrived skippers, Glotov and Solov'iev. Both were enlisted to sail with the expedition. Krenitsyn talked to them at length and listened to their advice: to spend yet another winter in Kamchatka, transfer his vessels from Bol'sheretsk to Nizhne-Kamchatsk, and sail in the spring of 1768. He also carefully noted their accounts of Aleut ferocity.

In September 1767 at Nizhne-Kamchatsk, Krenitsyn interviewed twenty-five Old Voyagers, most of whom he recruited for his expedition. In addition, four young Aleuts, formerly hostages in Russian camps, two of them godsons of Glotov and Solov'iev, were enlisted as interpreters. Both of them had gone to school and were literate in Russian.

The two vessels Krenitsyn had outfitted for the voyage, the *Sv. Ekaterina*, which he commanded, and the *Sv. Pavel*, commanded by Levashov, sailed 21 July 1768 out of Nizhne-Kamchatsk, arriving in Umnak Pass on 20 and 22 August, respectively, and proceeding together to Unalaska Bay. Here Krenitsyn issued his first written order on interaction with the Aleuts, urging caution and avoidance of contact, and, whenever possible, peaceful exchanges. The next day both vessels were off Unalaska Bay, one of the best harbors in the Pacific. Two skin boats were dispatched to the island of Akutan for fresh water, and seventeen casks were filled. Navigator Dudin (Junior), who was dispatched with the watering party, reported to Levashov that he had encountered Aleuts, mostly women, children, and old folk, in a summer dwelling. He also reported that he was given some help in filling the casks and provided concise but accurate ethnographic information on Aleut appearance, adornments, dwellings, and so on. The vessels then proceeded toward the Alaska Peninsula, passing the island group now named the Krenitzin Islands for the expedition's commander, who was the first to chart them. Finding that Isanotski Strait was unsuited for seagoing vessels of deep draft, as in places it is very shallow, they decided to seek harbor for wintering separately. Navigator Dudin (Jr.) completed a preliminary reconnaissance along the Alaska Peninsula's Bering Sea shores. In October, Navigator Dudin (Sr.) completed the charting of the peninsula's Pacific shore.

Krenitsyn chose to remain for the winter near the Bering Sea entry into Isanotski Strait. In the islands Krenitsyn acted with the utmost caution, though not very wisely. Wintering on Unimak, at St. Catherine Cove, he would not permit his men to travel away from the camp for food, nor allow any Aleuts who came in groups to approach. Unable to obtain fresh provisions either through hunting or trade with the Aleuts, Krenitsyn's men suffered from food shortages and scurvy. Thirty-six men out of the seventy-one, among them Stepan Glotov (died 4 May 1769) and, probably, Prokopii Lisenkov, died during the spring. They were buried on the shore of St. Catherine Cove. (The large white cross with their names on it that surviving expedition members placed there has long since gone, and the site of their grave is not known.)

Levashov decided to winter in the inner harbor of Unalaska Bay, now called in his honor Captain Bay. He took another tack. With the help of two Russian skippers who were hunting on Umnak, he obtained a large number of hostages, eventually holding thirty-three Aleuts. One of them, a young boy from the island of Akutan, asked to go with Levashov to Kamchatka and was apparently adopted by him. One of Levashov's first acts was to deliver gifts to important Unalaska Bay Aleut leaders. The excellent charts Levashov directed to be made of Unalaska Bay, completed by Navigator Iakov Shabanov, are still studied today for changes in depth of various portions of the bay. (The place where Levashov made camp on shore is now named Levashov's Landing.)[18]

During the winter, besides conducting hydrographic work, Levashov made ethnographic observations, noting, for the first time as far as we know, autonyms of several local Aleut groups and remarking that the term "Aleut" applied only to the inhabitants of the Near Islands. Other indigenous groups in the Aleutian archipelago were called by the promyshlenniki "Americans." In addition to the compilation of extensive ethnographic notes, Levashov sketched and painted Aleut men and women and their tools, items of personal adornment, weapons, musical instruments, etc. He recorded the manner in which the merchant fur procurers hunted in the islands, specifically how they obtained foxes. He also noted some information about the conflicts still existing between the fur merchants and the Aleuts and casualties on the Russian side, about inter-Aleut conflicts, particularly between the inhabitants of Unalaska and Unimak, and about evidence that in Aleut villages there were many orphaned children who apparently suffered deprivation, hunger, and lack of clothing. In fact, Levashov provided several orphaned boys with warm clothing.

Although Levashov's crew experienced food shortages and many were sick toward the end of their stay in spring 1769, he lost only three men. Having learned through Aleut messengers that Krenitsyn was shorthanded and suffered hardship, he sailed to St. Catherine Cove. From there the squadron sailed on 23 June for home. Levashov arrived at Nizhne-Kamchatsk on 27 July with Krenitsyn following on 30 July. They were gratified to learn that their sojourn in Alaska, hard as it was, had saved them from a smallpox epidemic that had devastated Kamchatka. They wintered in Nizhne-Kamchatsk and in the summer of 1770 were ready to depart for Okhotsk when Krenitsyn, together with Ivan Cherepanov, an Aleut turned Cossack, drowned in the Kamchatka River when their kayak overturned.[19] Levashov assumed command and sailed the two vessels for Okhotsk. He returned to St. Petersburg on 22 October 1771 and on the twenty-fifth rendered his first summary report to the Admiralty College.

To this day the bulk of the documents, including detailed charts of the eastern Aleutian coasts, their descriptions, and ethnographic data remain unanalyzed.[20] The results of the expedition were not greatly appreciated at the time and many Russian naval historians, then and later, dubbed it a failure.

In contrast, outside of Russia, both expeditions, Chichagov's to the north of Spitsbergen and that of Krenitsyn and Levashov to Alaska, linked by rumors to other, earlier government and merchant voyages, aroused immediate interest. This interest was most evident on the part of the Spanish[21] and the British admiralty, but for different reasons. The Spanish were most concerned with the violation of their sovereignty. British concerns were in connection with their search for either a Northwest or Northeast Passage between the Atlantic and the Pacific and also with approaches to Japan. The Spanish worried that the British and the Russians would form a coalition with the objective of taking possession of America's Northwest Coast. Well ahead of the actuality, the Spanish believed that Russians were establishing settlements in California.[22] By 1773, orders went out to Mexico's viceroy, Bucareli, to dispatch an expedition to the Northwest Coast. This, the first of several Spanish expeditions to North American waters, sailed in 1774 under Juan Pérez, but did not go farther north than 55° N latitude. The viceroy immediately ordered a second expedition, which sailed in 1775 under Bruno de Hezeta and Juan Francisco de la Bodega y Quadra. Their orders were not only to explore but to take possession of northwestern America formally, in the name of the king of Spain.

The British admiralty, also aware of Russian activity in the North Pacific and the Arctic Ocean, in 1763 granted permission to Lt. John Blankett to travel to Russia in order to obtain information on their Pacific discoveries. In 1771, Blankett was one of the authors of a proposal submitted to the British admiralty to seek the Pacific entrance to the Northwest Passage.[23] In 1773, the British, having acquired information about Chichagov's secret voyage, dispatched Sir Constantine John Phipps to attempt the route that Chichagov had failed to negotiate.[24] Almost simultaneously with the dispatch of

Phipps's squadron, planning began for the famed James Cook's third voyage, this time to the North Pacific and Bering Strait, incorporating Blankett's proposals to seek entrance to the Northwest Passage. This expedition took place in 1778–1779.

The Russian government was well aware of the British plans. They knew of the ambassadorial interests in the doings of the Russian navy and also kept themselves well informed about their rivals' activities. In fact, the Russians are believed to have fed misinformation to the ambassadors of England, Spain, and France. The release of information to Robertson and, later, Coxe,[25] as well as the publication of grossly incorrect maps of the North Pacific by Shtelin in 1774 (simultaneously in England, France, Germany, and Russia) were calculated measures. The Shtelin map, carried by Cook as an authoritative document, in all probability was intended to mislead.[26]

The Spanish, too, became aware of Cook's impending voyage. The attempted measures designed to abort or at least to impede Cook's efforts,[27] as ordered by the Spanish authorities, were unsuccessful. However, responding to the perceived British threat, the Spanish immediately (in 1779) launched the third Spanish voyage to the Northwest Coast, commanded by Ignacio de Arteaga y Bazán and Bodega y Quadra. This expedition reached Prince William Sound and Cook Inlet.

The Russian response, while not so swift, was determined. The arrival of Cook's two vessels in Alaskan waters in 1778, reported to the government by at least two Russian skippers (one of them navy-trained navigator Gerasim Izmailov), and their subsequent appearance in Petropavlovsk on Kamchatka in 1779, alarmed the Russian government. St. Petersburg received the news, sent from Siberia on 16 July, at the latest by October 1779. Cook had given English names to coastal features in areas that he knew full well were claimed by the Russians. The Russians were in possession of charts purporting to delineate Cook's discoveries and showing his tracks since 1779, when Clerke (who succeeded to the command after Cook's death in Hawaii) and then King (who assumed command after Clerke died at Petropavlovsk) gave simplified versions of their own charts to von Behm, Kamchatka's administrator.

In 1780, at the Irkutsk Navigational School, before Cook's captains reached home and reported to their admiralty, a cartographer of officer's rank, *secund-maior* Tatarinov, compiled a manuscript chart into which he incorporated the data from Cook's third voyage, including a chart of Petropavlovsk Harbor based on the cartographic work of Roberts, one of Cook's officers.[28] The provenance of the data was explicitly stated to stem from "earlier descriptions and the new one by the English Captain-Commander Cook in the years 1778 and 1779." In 1781, three years *before* the British admiralty published the results of Cook's voyage, the Russians produced an engraved chart showing Cook's tracks and also showing tracks and landfalls by Bering, Gvozdev, and Chirikov, as well as some Russian merchant voyagers. In short, Russians were taking steps to assert their claims by right of previous discovery.

However, the Russian government felt no real alarm at this time, as Cook's voyage was not followed up immediately. The political situation in Europe, particularly conflicts with France, the war with the American colonies, and the engagement of British shipping in this connection in the Atlantic were all factors, though development of trade with Asia by means of a Pacific route was at that time very much on the minds of important members of the British government. The commercial potential of northwestern America had been one of the considerations in dispatching Cook's expedition. In 1782, Blankett once more proposed to the British government that a naval expedition be dispatched to secure for Britain trade in Japan, China, and northern Asia.[29] However, the success of Cook's crew members at Canton in selling sea otter skins obtained on the American Northwest Coast incited the British private entrepreneurs, some of them former members of Cook's crews, to initiate systematic fur trade. Other entrepreneurs were ex-naval officers because, with the end of the American conflict and the reduction in naval service, British navy men were seeking other means of subsistence. Some of them entered the Russian naval service and became involved in the Russian advancement in the North Pacific. Of these, Captain Joseph Billings, Captain Robert Hall, and shipbuilder James Shields are the best known.

The first successful British sea otter trader was James Hanna, who sailed to America in 1785. He was followed rapidly by others. In 1786, when Hanna made his second voyage, there were six other British trading ships off the Northwest Coast. The British trading vessels, in contrast to the Russian ones, were, as a rule, large, heavily armed with cannon, and traveled in pairs.[30] Their success depended on intimidating the Natives by a show of arms, thus inducing them to choose trade over hostilities, and offering as trade items firearms (including, sometimes, cannon) and alcohol. In later years this trading policy (forbidden to the Russians) played a role in conflicts between the advancing Russians and the Natives of the Northwest Coast, especially the Tlingit and, to some extent, the Haida of the Queen Charlotte archipelago.

By 1786, and probably earlier, British trade activity, specifically that of Captain Hanna, was being discussed at the highest levels of the Russian government. At the same time proposals were being advanced through Captain Peters of the *Lark*, who put in at Petropavlovsk in 1786 specifically to make contact, for joint British-Russian trade through Canton in cooperation with the British East India Company. His efforts were brief, for Peters's vessel was wrecked on Mednoi Island later the same season, with a loss of all but two men. Another agent active in promoting potential British-Russian cooperation in trade, and possibly more general activity in the Pacific, was Colonel Samuel Bentham, brother of the British economist Jeremy Bentham. In Russia since 1780, he studied the developing Siberian industry and trade, notably with the Chinese via Kiakhta. In 1782, in Irkutsk, he met with several merchants engaged in the Aleutian trade, chiefly Grigorii Shelikhov, the future empire builder in America. Thanks to his having the patronage in St. Petersburg of the all-powerful Potemkin, Catherine's favorite, who gained for Bentham an audience with the empress to discuss Pacific Ocean activities, Bentham was engaged to supervise shipbuilding for the Black Sea fleet. In 1789, he once again went to Siberia, where he apparently avoided meeting and cooperating with Joseph Billings (see below). Traveling widely over Siberia and the northeastern regions, Bentham, in concert with Shelikhov, made proposals for arctic exploration and renewed attempts to round the Chukotka cape, as well as for expeditions to the Kuril Islands and opening trade with Japan, the so-called Pacific Expedition.[31] He was given command of a Siberian battalion. Later on he and Shelikhov urged that Shelikhov depart with a military force, notably 100 of Bentham's soldiers, for America. Bentham also imported British shipbuilders and, in 1790, sent James Shields, with eighty men, to Okhotsk to build large vessels ostensibly for Kodiak.[32] (Later Shields, under Baranov, would take charge of shipbuilding for Shelikhov's company in America.)[33]

In the meantime, however, the Russian government decided to show the flag in American waters. To this end, a circumnavigating expedition was to be dispatched from Kronstadt (St. Petersburg's naval base) to northwestern America, in order to demonstrate Russian dominance over its coast formally and establish a governmental presence there.[34] On 8 August 1785, Empress Catherine authorized the dispatch of a naval expedition, commanded by Joseph Billings, a veteran of Cook's voyages but now in Russian service, out of Okhotsk to North America and the extreme northeast of Siberia, to act as support for the circumnavigating squadron. Improvement of Okhotsk's port facilities and establishment of another, better Pacific port were part of Billings's commission. Captain Fomin, charged specifically with determining the best possible location for the new port, was dispatched to the far eastern regions. The formal orders for the circumnavigating expedition were signed by the empress on 22 December 1786, and six days later the admiralty appointed Captain of the First Rank Grigorii Mulovskii as the expedition's commander.

The squadron mustered four newly built ships of the line and one transport. All were heavily armed. There were 34 officers and 639 crew members, all handpicked, all volunteers. Peter Simon Pallas, a member of the Imperial Academy of Sciences, was appointed fleet historiographer and put in charge of assembling an impressive scientific corps. Georg Forster, a participant in Cook's voyages to the Pacific, was one of the scientists. Scientific and navigational equipment were the best and most modern. All available charts and logs of all known Pacific voyages were provided to the commander and his officers. Four artists were to accompany the expedition. The ships were superbly provisioned, and all possible measures were taken to ensure the well-being of the crew. Special clothing, from socks and underwear to hooded parkas, was provided in ample quantities for each man. Antiscorbutics were plentiful. Water desalinization equipment was secured as well as a hospital facility with a capacity of forty patients. Vegetable and other plant seeds and livestock were to be carried for introduction in the new land. Mulovskii's orders were very clear. He was to claim "that coast from the harbor of Nootka to the point where Chirikov's discovery begins, as possession of the Russian State if no other State is occupying it." In contrast to Spain, which insisted on her claim based solely on the right of discovery, Russia intended to press her claim *by the right of occupancy.* In the instructions, whenever a geographic location was mentioned, Russian or Native names were used, but, when these locations were known to have been mapped by Cook, followed by the statement that it was "called by Cook" so-and-so. Should Mulovskii find any shore installations by foreigners in the Russian territory, he was authorized to destroy them as well as any symbols or markers left by foreigners. Foreign shipping was to be ordered to leave Russian waters and force used against any vessels that refused to obey the order.

In addition, Mulovskii, in concert with Billings, was to investigate the American coast north of Cape Rodney and beyond Bering Strait. He was also to visit the coast to the southeast, to the mouth of the Columbia River and to California. The instructions contained a detailed outline on the formalities to be observed in taking possession of new territory, and detailed symbolic acts signifying Russian sovereignty that were to be performed. The Natives were to be treated with kindness and forbearance at all times and the use of arms against Native Americans was absolutely forbidden, even when provoked by hostile or "bestial" acts. There was to be no retaliation (this no-retaliation policy was later incorporated into the regulations pertaining to the Russian-American Company).[35]

Mulovskii was to sail in late 1787. That summer Turkey and Sweden went to war against Russia, and the navy was needed elsewhere. Reluctantly, on 28 October 1787, Empress Catherine signed the order canceling the expedition. Only Billings's squadron, being readied at Okhotsk, carried out part of the mission and also received additional orders. A number of predominantly British vessels were reported to be active in the North Pacific as privateers, flying the Swedish flag. Billings was to intercept them and prevent harassment of the Native coastal settlements. Specifically, Billings was to intercept the British brig *Mercury*, John Henry Cox commanding, which reportedly had burned Aleut villages in the central Aleutians.[36]

In the meantime, France (which had lost its American colonies on the North Atlantic to England) also showed an interest in the North Pacific coast. In 1786, a French naval squadron, commanded by Jean-François de Galaup, Comte de La Pérouse, put in at Petropavlovsk on Kamchatka and then sailed to North America, putting in at Lituya Bay, which the commander believed to be outside the territory that Spain might claim on the basis of her 1775 voyage as well as beyond the Russian outposts. He claimed this portion of the coast for France.[37]

It is believed that La Pérouse picked up some information, probably rumors, about Russian plans to advance their claims in the eastern North Pacific. In any case, he transmitted this disturbing information to the Spanish.[38] Persons in authority in America were already alarmed by the information about Russian advances supplied to them by La Pérouse while he was in Chile. Besides, at that time the Spanish Californian missions and some merchants had some interest in the sea otter trade. Unsettling information was also being submitted to the authorities by the Spanish ambassador to Russia. Spain had never laid aside the worry about the Russian threat to Spanish interests on the American Northwest Coast, and now the worry seemed more than ever justified. By 1788, Spain sent two warships, one commanded by veteran North Pacific sailor Estéban José Martínez and the other by Gonzalo López de Haro, to Alaskan waters. De Haro on Kodiak Island and Martínez at Unalaska picked up information (from Russian skippers alarmed by the presence of well-armed naval vessels of a foreign power) that the Russian navy was on the move. The news that Mulovskii's circumnavigating expedition was canceled had not yet reached Russians working in Alaska. Martínez was convinced that, indeed, Nootka, the harbor that he knew since the days he had sailed with Juan Pérez (1774), was to be taken by the Russians.

Upon his urgent recommendation, Martínez was authorized to forestall the Russian advance. In 1789, he sailed to Nootka, Vancouver Island, where instead of the Russians he found British and American sea otter trading vessels. Bent upon asserting the Spanish claim, Martínez seized the British vessels, and what is known in American history as the "Nootka incident" began. The conflict, settled by the British and Spanish governments far from the American shore, eventually gave England possession of the coast from north of the Columbia River to Alaska's present-day southeastern boundary line. In 1792, George Vancouver showed the flag for England. Spain was effectively eliminated from the Alaskan arena and, in the wake of the French revolution, so was France. In the future, the high-stakes game for the Alaska territory, her people, and her resources would be played out among Russia, England, and the United States of America.[39]

NOTES

1. The Treaty of Nerchinsk, 1689, established the Russian-Chinese boundary along the Argun and Gorbitsa Rivers (tributaries of the Amur) and the Stanovoi Mountain Range. Thus, the Amur was, in Miatlev's day, a Chinese river.
2. Gol'denberg, *Katorzhanin—sibirskii gubernator,* 221–222.
3. Ibid., 223.
4. [F. I. Soimonov], "Drevniaia poslovitsa: Sibir'—zolotoe dno," *Sochineniia i perevody k pol'ze i uveseleniiu sluzhashchiia* 14, no. 3 (November 1761): 449–467; idem, "Prodolzhenie o drevnei poslovitse: Sibir'—zolotoe dno," *Ezhemesiachnyia sochineniia i izvestiia o uchenykh delakh* 19, no. 2 (January–June 1764): 44–59; "Iz"iasnenie o sposobakh k proizvedeniiu Rossiiskoi kommertsii iz Orenburga s Bukharskoiu, a iz onoi i s Indiiskimi oblastiami," *Ezhemesiachnyia sochineniia i izvestiia o uchenykh delakh* 18, no. 2 (July–December 1763): 401–408.
5. Gol'denberg, *Katorzhanin—sibirskii gubernator,* 113.
6. Soimonov to the Senate, 24 February 1758, in Narochnitskii et al., *Russkie ekspeditsii* (1989), 46 (doc. 10).
7. Some archival materials pertaining to Soimonov's interests in the exploration of the North Pacific by private entrepreneurs may be found in RGADA, Fond 24, Sibirskii prikaz i upravlenie Sibiri, no. 34, fols. 1–7v (four documents, only one dated to 17 June 1764, the other three, by context, probably 1763 to early 1764); also Fond 248, op. 113, no. 1557, fols. 139–146v, 16 February 1759; Fond 24, op. 113, no. 1557, fols. 297–301v, 24 April 1759, and fols. 273–277v, 14 August 1760; Fond 263, no. 21, fols. 229–239v, 17 November 1763; Fond 199, portfel' 528, pt. 2, no. 10 (the last item cited after Gol'denberg, *Katorzhanin—sibirskii gubernator,* 285 n. 51). The chart indicating the line beyond which Soimonov prohibited merchant vessels to travel was compiled in 1758 or 1759, confirmed by the Ruling Senate (RGADA, Fond 248, chart 1912, a variant published by Efimov, *Iz istorii... otkrytii* [1971], 171–173), and printed in 1762 (RGADA, Fond 192, maps of Irkutsk guberniia no. 65a, published by Grekov, *Ocherki iz istorii,* 173 fig. 34). Several documents were published by Divin, *Russkaia Tikhookeanskaia epopeia,* 306–311 (doc. 64) (cf. Narochnitskii et al., *Russkie ekspeditsii* [1989], 46–50 [doc. 10]), 312–314 (doc. 66), and by Narochnitskii et al., *Russkie ekspeditsii* (1989), 52–53 (doc. 12, Soimonov's instructions to Sindt), 58–59 (doc. 15, Senate order of 24 August 1761, regarding merchantman travel in the Kuril Islands), which state that Soimonov had the responsibility to issue regulations for merchant navigation in the North Pacific.
8. V. A. Perevalov, *Lomonosov i Arktika* (Moscow and Leningrad: Izdatel'stvo Glavsevmorputi, 1949), 312.
9. Jacob Johann Lindenau was assigned as an assistant to the more widely known Johann Eberhard Fischer; he is known as an ethnographer and scholar in his own right. His data on the Evenk, Even, Buriat, Yakut, Koriak, and Iukagir are widely appreciated by modern ethnologists. For data on Lindenau see (in addition to Gol'denberg, *Katorzhanin—sibirskii gubernator*) Ia. I. Lindenau, *Opisanie narodov Sibiri (pervaia polovina XVIII veka): Istoriko-etnograficheskie materialy o narodakh Sibiri i Severo-Vostoka,* trans. from the German manuscript, ed. Z. D. Titova (Magadan: Magadanskoe knizhnoe izdatel'stvo, 1983).
10. Soimonov to Catherine, 2 September 1769, RGADA, Fond 24, no. 34, fols. 6r–6v.
11. This image, repeated by Lomonosov in several other poems, became a motto and part of the inscription on the grave monument to Grigorii Shelikhov, founder of the first permanent Russian settlement in Alaska.
12. "Pis'mo o severnom khodu v Ost-Indiiu Sibirskim okeanom," cited after Perevalov, *Lomonosov i Arktika,* 10. See also Mikhail Lomonosov's collected works, *Trudy po russkoi istorii, obshchestvenno-ekonomicheskim voprosam i geografii, 1747–1765 gg.,* vol. 6 (Moscow and Leningrad: Izdatel'stvo Akademii nauk SSSR, 1952), 603. According to the editors, this letter formed the basis for section three of Lomonosov's 1763 outline of all the arctic voyages in search of the Northwest and Northeast Passages.

13. "Kratkoe opisanie raznykh puteshestvii po severnym moriam i pokazanie vozmozhnago prokhodu Sibirskim okeanom v vostochnuiu Indiiu," original, with map, in the State Public Library (formerly the M. E. Saltykov-Shchedrin Public Library), St. Petersburg (Q IV, no. 415), first published by the naval historian A. P. Sokolov in 1847. For a full discussion of the manuscript material and the publication history of this work, prior to 1949, see Perevalov, *Lomonosov i Arktika,* 32–36. Perevalov republished this work, together with Lomonosov's circumpolar map with proposed routes from Russia to America via the polar region, with extensive commentary (ibid., 37–141). Unfortunately, in this version Lomonosov's syntax and spelling have been modernized. Republished in Lomonosov, *Trudy po russkoi istorii,* vol. 6, 602.

14. Vasilii Berkh, "Dopolnenie k zhizneopisaniiu M. V. Lomonosova," *Moskovskii telegraf* 11 (1828): 290, cited after Perevalov, *Lomonosov i Arktika,* 232 n. 1.

15. (1) "Pribavlenie o severnom moreplavanii na vostok po Sibirskomu okeanu," March 1764, submitted to the Admiralty College. Alternative title "Pribavlenie pervoe...," published in Perevalov, *Lomonosov i Arktika,* 254–259, and in Lomonosov, *Trudy po russkoi istorii,* vol. 6, 506. (2) "Pribavlenie vtoroe, sochinennoe po novym izvestiiam promyshlennikov iz ostrovov amerikanskikh i po vysprosu kompaneishchikov, tobol'skago kuptsa Il'i Snigireva i vologodskago kuptsa Ivana Burenina," published in Perevalov, *Lomonosov i Arktika,* 284–288, and in Lomonosov, *Trudy po russkoi istorii,* vol. 6, 509–514.

16. On the Chichagov expedition see Gerhard Friedrich Müller, "Nachrichten von den neuesten Schiffahrten im Eissmeer und in der Kamtschatkischen See, seit dem Jahr 1742; da die zweite Kamtschatkische Ekspedition aufgehört hat: Ein Stück aus der regierungs-Geschichte der grosser Kayserinn Katharina II," *Neue nordische Beyträge* 5 (1793): 15–104, which includes a discussion of the voyage by Phipps (see below) and excerpts from the logs of Chichagov's ships, German-language manuscript (51 folios and versos) in RGADA, Moscow, Fond 199 "Portfeli Millera," op. 2, no. 534, pt. 2, no. 1; A. Sokolov, "Proekt Lomonosova i ekspeditsiia Chichagova 1765 i 1766 goda," *Zapiski Gidrograficheskago departamenta Morskago ministerstva* 5 (1847): 240–251; idem, "Raznye svedeniia otnosiashchiiasia k ekspeditsii Chichagova," *Zapiski Gidrograficheskago departamenta Morskago ministerstva* 6 (1848): 100–141; 9 (1851): 108–147; "Zapiski P. V. Chichagova," *Russkaia starina* 50 (1886): 221–252, 463–488; V. A. Perevalov, "Plavaniia ekspeditsii severo-zapadnogo prokhoda pod nachal'stvom kapitana V. Ia. Chichagova, 1765–1766," pt. 3, sec. 1 of *Lomonosov i Arktika,* 385–431; V. A. Divin, "Ekspeditsii V. Ia. Chichagova i Krenitsyna-Levashova," chap. 10 in *Russkaia Tikhookeanskaia epopeia,* 333–362; Lydia T. Black, "The Best Route to America Lies Across the Pole" (paper presented at Cook Inlet Historical Society Symposium "Science Under Sail: Russian Exploration in the North Pacific, 1728–1867," Anchorage, Alaska, October 2000, and forthcoming in the symposium proceedings); see also *Arkhiv Admirala P. V. Chichagova* (St. Petersburg, 1885). Archival materials, in part in the Russian State Naval Archive (RGAVMF), St. Petersburg, Arkhiv gidrografii, Fond 913, op. 1, nos. 90–91, 98, and in RGADA, Moscow, Fond 199, op. 2, no. 540 (15 fols.).

On the Krenitsyn-Levashov expedition see William Coxe, *Account of the Russian Discoveries between Asia and America, to which are added, The Conquest of Siberia, and The History of the Transactions and Commerce between Russia and China* (London: T. Cadell, 1780), 251–266 app. 1, with chart (see also later editions). This is the earliest published account of this voyage and represents a very brief summary based on materials put at the disposal of the historian William Robertson by Catherine's government. Published in Russia in German translation and with annotations by P. S. Pallas, "Bericht von der in den Jahren 1768 und 1769 auf allerhöchsten Befehl der russischen Monarchinn unter Anführung des Capitains Krenitzyn und Lieutenants Lewaschef von Kamtschatka nach den neuentdeckten Inseln und bis an Aläska oder das feste Land von America vollbrachten Seereise," *Neue nordische Beyträge* 1, no. 2 (1781): 249–272, with a chart by Pallas incorporating some data from Cook's charts of 1778–1779 in Russian archives. See also A. Sokolov, "Ekspeditsiia k Aleutskim ostrovam kapitanov Krenitsyna i Levashova, 1764–69 gg.," *Zapiski Gidrograficheskago departamenta Morskago ministerstva* 10 (1852): 70–103; Perevalov, *Lomonosov i Arktika,* 435–459; Divin, *Russkaia Tikhookeanskaia epopeia,* 333–362; Narochnitskii et al., *Russkie ekspeditsii* (1989), 76–83 (docs. 22–24), 97–101 (doc. 28), 110–116 (docs. 30–32), 118–132 (docs. 34–45), 141 (doc. 47); I. V. Glushankov, "Aleutskaia ekspeditsiia Krenitsyna i Levasheva," *Priroda* 12 (1969): 84–92, in English translation by Mary Sadouski and Richard A. Pierce, "The Aleutian Expedition of Krenitsyn and Levashov," *Alaska Journal* 3, no. 4 (1973): 204–210; and the journals and documents of this expedition in the Russian State Naval Archive (RGAVMF), St. Petersburg (Arkhiv gidrografii), Fond 913, op. 1, 1724–1885, delo 34, dela 109–116, dela 119–122, dela 124–132, dela 136–143. In addition, RGAVMF holds an album of watercolors by Levashov illustrating the material culture of the eastern Aleuts. Selected illustrations in black-and-white have appeared in various publications dealing with Alaska, but the spectacular color paintings have not been available to the reading public.

17. A copy of Chicherin's synopsis of Lisenkov's testimony survives in the Russian State Archive of Ancient Documents in Moscow (RGADA). The version published by Divin in *Russkaia Tikhookeanskaia epopeia,* 344–349 (doc. 76), has very significant omissions. Specifically, all passages dealing with Russian-Aleut conflicts are omitted.

18. Personal oral communication from Rufina Shaiashnikov of Unalaska, owner of the land at the head of Captain Bay.

19. Narochnitskii et al., *Russkie ekspeditsii* (1989), 141 (doc. 47); Russian State Naval Archive (RGAVMF), Fond 216, op. 1, delo 77, fol. 376.

20. For an assessment of Levashov's published ethnographic data and his drawings as an ethnographic source see Roza G. Liapunova, "Etnograficheskoe znachenie ekspeditsii kapitanov P. K. Krenitsyna i M. D. Levashova na Aleutskie ostrova (1764–1769)," *Sovetskaia etnografiia,* no. 6 (1971): 67–78. Levashov's watercolor sketches have been published several times in black-and-white. Recently color reproductions have been made by the Russian State Naval Archive (RGAVMF). Funds are being sought for publication in the United States of Levashov's album in full, in color, accompanied not only by a translation of his ethnographic essays but also by excerpts from the expedition journals containing navigational, ethnographic, hydrographic, and ecological data.

21. See Warren L. Cook, *Flood Tide of Empire: Spain and the Pacific Northwest, 1543–1819* (New Haven: Yale University Press, 1973), 24; Christon I. Archer, "The Political and Military Context of the Spanish Advance into the Pacific Northwest," in *Spain and the Northwest Coast: Essays in Recognition of the Bicentennial of the Malaspina Expedition, 1791–1792,* ed. Robin Inglis (Vancouver, B.C.: Vancouver Maritime Museum, 1992).

22. Cook, *Flood Tide,* 134–136; Archer, "Political and Military Context," 10–11. On Spanish expeditions to Alaskan waters see also Wallace M. Olson, *Through Spanish Eyes: Spanish Voyages to Alaska, 1774–1792* (Auke Bay, Alaska: Heritage Research, 2002).

23. Alan Frost, "British Ambitions and the Western Coasts of the Americas, 1763–1793," in *Spain and the Northwest Coast: Essays in Recognition of the Bicentennial of the Malaspina Expedition, 1791–1792,* ed. Robin Inglis (Vancouver, B.C.: Vancouver Maritime Museum, 1992), 36–37.

24. Constantine John Phipps, *A Voyage Towards the North Pole Undertaken by His Majesty's Command, 1773* (London: Nourse, 1774; reprint, Dublin: Sleater et al. Publishers, 1775; 1774 ed. reprint, Whitby, Yorkshire: Caedmon of Whitby Press, 1978); idem, *The Journal of a Voyage Undertaken by Order of His Present Majesty, for Making Discoveries Towards the North Pole by the Hon. Commodore Phipps, and Captain Lutwidge, in his Majesty's Sloops* Racehorse *and* Carcase*: To Which is Prefixed an Account of the Several Voyages Undertaken for the Discovery of a North-East Passage to China and Japan* (London: Printed for F. Newbery, 1774).

25. William Robertson, *The History of America,* 2 vols. (London: W. Strahan, T. Cadell, 1777); William Coxe, *Account of the Russian Discoveries* (1780; 3d, revised and corrected ed., 1787). Coxe's work is based mainly on J. L. S., *Neue Nachrichten.* Other information was supplied to him in a synopsis in French.

26. Black, "The Question of Maps," pt. 2, "Shtelin," 23–36 nn. 21–31.

27. Barry M. Gough, *Distant Dominion: Britain and the Northwest Coast of North America, 1579–1809* (Vancouver: University of British Columbia Press, 1980).

28. Andrew C. F. David, "Russian Charts and Captain Cook's Third Voyage," *The Map Collector* 52 (Autumn 1990): 2–6.

29. Alan Frost, "British Ambitions," 38.

30. For the best concise account of the British (and then American) sea otter trade see James R. Gibson, *Otter Skins, Boston Ships, and China Goods: The Maritime Fur Trade of the Northwest Coast, 1785–1841* (Seattle: University of Washington Press, 1992). For information on number, size, and take by British ships in the early period of trade, see ibid., 23–35.

31. R. A. Kristi and L. A. Sitnikov, "Novoe ob istorii osvoeniia severnoi chasti basseina Tikhogo okeana (stat'ia pervaia)," in *Istochniki po istorii Sibiri dosovetskogo perioda: Sbornik nauchnykh trudov,* ed. N. N. Pokrovskii (Novosibirsk: Izdatel'stvo "Nauka," Sibirskoe otdelenie, 1988), 163–197.

32. This fleet was never built. There is a whiff of suspicion that it was intended for other purposes than transport of men and cargo to and from Kodiak. Documents pertaining to Bentham and Shields are scattered in various Russian archives (Irkutsk State Regional Archive; Russian State Historical Archive, St. Petersburg [RGIA]; and Russian State Naval Archive [RGAVMF]) as well as in the British Library.

33. For information on Samuel Bentham in Russia see Richard A. Pierce's introduction to Shelikhov, *A Voyage to America,* 24–26. More detailed information can be found in L. A. Sitnikov, *Grigorii Shelikhov,* 191–212. See also Walther Kirchner, "Samuel Bentham and Siberia," chap. 9 in *Commercial Relations between Russia and Europe, 1400 to 1800: Collected Essays* (Bloomington: Indiana University, 1966), 218–230. Samuel Bentham's Russian adventures await special study.

34. The material presented here is based on an article published by the author, "The Russians Were Coming…," in *Spain and the North Pacific Coast: Essays in Recognition of the Bicentennial of the Malaspina Expedition, 1791–1792,* ed. Robin Inglis (Vancouver, B.C.: Vancouver Maritime Museum, 1992), 29–34. It should be noted that this planned expedition is not discussed even in such authoritative sources as Cook's *Flood Tide.*

35. Later, this "no retaliation" policy would be interpreted by the American military as weakness.

36. For a highly sanitized account of the *Mercury* voyage, see Lieutenant of the Marines George Mortimer, *Observations and Remarks Made During a Voyage to the Islands of Tenerife, Amsterdam, Maria's Islands near Van Diemen's Land; Otaheite, Sandwich Islands; Owhyhee, the Fox Islands on the North West Coast of America, Tinian, and from thence to Canton in the Brig* Mercury, *Commanded by John Henry Cox, Esq.* (Dublin: Printed for J. Byrne et al., 1791). In the foreword, Mortimer states that the voyage was undertaken out of "curiosity," secondarily with a view toward fur trade, and besides, Cox had business in Canton. He is aware that "others" considered the reasons for the sailing of the *Mercury* to have been very different.

37. Jean-François de Galaup, Comte de La Pérouse, *Voyage de La Pérouse autour du Monde, publié conformément au décrêt du 22 avril 1791, et rédigé par M. L. A. Milet-Mureau,* 4 vols., atlas (Paris: Imprimerie de la République, An 5 [1797]). The account of the voyage itself appeared in English the following year as *A Voyage Round the World, Performed in the Years 1785, 1786, 1787, and 1788 by the "Boussole" and "Astrolabe" under the command of J. F. G. de la Pérouse,* 2 vols. (London: Printed for J. Stockdale, 1798); the atlas was published in English under the title *Charts and Plates to La Pérouse's Voyage* (London: G. G. and J. Robinson, 1798). Jean Baptiste Barthelemy, Baron de Lesseps, *Journal historique du voyage de M. de Lesseps, Consul de France, employé dans l'expédition de M. le comte de la Pérouse, en qualité d'interprète du Roi: Depuis l'instant où il a quitté les frégates Françoises au port Saint-Pierre & Saint-Paul du Kamtschatka, jusqu'à son arrivée en France, le 17 octobre 1788,* 2 vols. (Paris: Imprimerie Royale, 1790), English translation, *Travels in Kamtschatka, during the Years 1787 and 1788,* 2 vols. (London: J. Johnson, 1790).

38. Robin Inglis, "The Effect of Lapérouse on Spanish Thinking about the Northwest Coast," in *Spain and the North Pacific Coast: Essays in Recognition of the Bicentennial of the Malaspina Expedition, 1791–1792,* ed. Robin Inglis (Vancouver, B.C.: Vancouver Maritime Museum, 1992), 46–52.

39. Vancouver's expedition took place in 1791–1794. Readers interested in the diplomatic history of the territorial claims, divisions, and border adjudication should consult the extensive specialized literature on the subject.

FIGURE 22. Official portrait of Grigorii I. Shelikhov (1748–1795).
Courtesy Richard A. Pierce.

Chapter Six

The Empire Builders

P. S. Lebedev-Lastochkin and G. I. Shelikhov

The geopolitical context of the late eighteenth century—international political realignments and changes in international trade—constituted part of the forces that affected Alaska. Internal developments in Russia, changes in governmental trade policies, and policies that structured the Russian settlement of Siberia also played a major role in reformulation of the state's policies toward its American territory. The liberalization of trade in the reign of Catherine the Great (following legislation favoring the merchant class passed in the previous reign), particularly rescission in 1762 of the state monopoly on trade with China, including sale of furs, and in 1774 of the previously obligatory tax of ten percent of the catch, made participation in the Aleutian fur-procurement enterprise very attractive to large merchant houses. New capital from such large trading centers as Moscow, Tobol'sk, and Irkutsk began to fuel the trade. Large-scale entrepreneurs, with interests in many ventures, courted and found governmental support. They squeezed out the smaller companies, resulting in progressively less individual and local participation in the ventures. This led to the gradual disappearance of small individual fur-procuring enterprises and eventually to creation of a monopolistic company granted the right to exploit all of Alaska's resources. The destruction of four Russian vessels by the Aleuts in 1763–1764 undoubtedly had contributed to the downfall of some early fur traders, even such notable and well-connected ones as Nikifor Trapeznikov, who had been a major shareholder in three of the four lost vessels.

Of importance also in changing the nature of Aleutian enterprises was the interruption in the Kiakhta trade with the Chinese from 1763 to 1768, due to a major political conflict with China, with the level of trade not recovering until 1780. Even in the late 1780s, however, Aleutian merchants, such as Shelikhov, complained about the state of the fur trade at Kiakhta. In 1789, discussing the market conditions and the situation at Kiakhta with his employee and partner Evstrat Delarov, Shelikhov followed advice of the commander of the naval expedition, Joseph Billings, by suggesting that Delarov dispatch a vessel to Macao where illegal trade in furs for the China market was flourishing.[1] Moreover, the fur market at Kiakhta had changed, with squirrel, ermine, and sable now topping the list of items in greatest demand. The demand for sea otters had fallen, especially after 1785 when British (and soon also American) traders brought them to Canton in large quantities at cheaper prices.[2]

Toward the end of Catherine's reign, only four large merchant companies were involved in the Aleutian fur trade. Of these, the company of the Panov brothers, from the northern Russian city of Tot'ma, was operating on the American mainland from bases on the upper Alaska Peninsula and modern Bristol Bay.[3] Before the end of the eighteenth century, however, the Panovs sold their interests to the Lebedev-Lastochkin Company. Lebedev-Lastochkin, a Yakutsk merchant residing in Irkutsk, had a long-standing interest in the Pacific fur trade, both in the Aleutians and in the Kuril Islands, and had succeeded in trading with the Japanese on Hokkaido. He also acted for the government in exploring possibilities for trade and diplomatic relations with Japan (see below). His crews had been exploiting fur seal rookeries in the Pribilof Islands since 1786. His main rival by that time was the Shelikhov-Golikov Company, which established a permanent base and jumping-off point on Kodiak Island in 1784. Also remaining in the field, but a distant third, was the Kiselev Brothers Company with headquarters on Unalaska Island. The three fought it out to the end.

The end came in 1799, when Emperor Paul I granted the monopoly for the eastern North Pacific fur trade to the heirs of Grigorii Shelikhov, creating the Russian-American Company, and Lebedev-Lastochkin and the Kiselevs had to withdraw by government edict. What precisely led to the emperor's decision is now unknown. This period of Alaskan history is very sketchily understood, as the only documentary evidence on hand is that provided by the victors: the Russian-American Company and Shelikhov's heirs.[4] The two decades at the end of the eighteenth century were a time of great activity but, in retrospect, little clarity exists. Nevertheless, specialists agree that the chief loser in the struggle for the Alaska fur trade, Pavel Sergeevich Lebedev-Lastochkin, was an important historical figure.

Little is known about him. In 1796, aged fifty-eight, he lived in Irkutsk with his wife, Anna, his junior by thirty years, using the name Lastochkin. They belonged to one of the few city (as opposed to suburban) parishes dedicated to two northern Russian saints, Prokopii and Ioann of Ustiug. The couple had no children.[5] He died in Irkutsk in 1800.[6]

Lebedev-Lastochkin apparently first came to Kamchatka about 1773 as an agent of the Moscow merchant Ivan Savel'ev.[7] At that time, the newly appointed Kamchatkan governor von Behm was seeking volunteers to take a vessel to Hokkaido (then called Atkis[8]) to contact Japanese merchants reportedly trading there in Ainu territory.[9] Lebedev-Lastochkin is known to have traveled in 1774 from Okhotsk to Kamchatka aboard a Crown vessel, carrying supplies for this project. Grigorii Shelikhov, then a young merchant of Ryl'sk who had been residing in Irkutsk since 1773, was at that time in Okhotsk and in Kamchatka, probably from late 1773 to sometime in 1775. Apparently, the two men met in this period. In 1775, they, with assistance from the authorities, acquired the use and later the ownership of the *Sv. Nikolai*, a vessel of the *bot* type, forty-five feet along the keel, then idle in the harbor of Petropavlovsk. (The major shareholders in the *Sv. Nikolai*, merchants Mukhin and Zasypkin, were in court, ownership of the vessel being disputed.)[10]

At the same time, Shelikhov was possibly assessing the fur trading situation for merchant Ivan Golikov; it is believed that Shelikhov started his career in Siberia as Golikov's agent, though this relationship is documented only from 1778. Later, Shelikhov and Golikov would become partners in forming major fur trading companies in Alaska, Kamchatka, and the Kuril Islands. In the meantime, Lebedev-Lastochkin allegedly invited Shelikhov to join him in this government-sponsored effort to establish contact and trade with the Japanese. Lebedev-Lastochkin's contact with the Japanese, secretly sponsored by the imperial government, and the information his men provided, laid the foundation for the official government embassy to Japan under Laksman and Lovtsov in 1792.

Trade and fur procurement were to mask the fact that this expedition was government sponsored. The vessel was to be skippered by apprentice navigator Putintsev, one of a number of navigators trained in the government navigation schools in Siberia and, since the days of Soimonov's administration, seconded for duty aboard the merchant vessels. The real head of this secret expedition was the Siberian nobleman Ivan M. Antipin, who spoke Japanese. Japanese interpreter I. Ocheredin was to assist him. The vessel carried cannon.[11] Part of their mission was to be on the lookout for the Crown vessel *Sv. Petr*, pirated at Bol'sheretsk in 1771 by the Polish prisoner of war Moritz August Beniovskii.

The Beniovskii epic, though peripheral to the story of Russian America, has engaged the imagination of a number of Russian and foreign authors and has been made the subject of very colorful accounts and fictional romances. Beniovskii was a prisoner of war who, after an attempt to escape in 1769, was sent to Kamchatka "to earn his living by his own efforts" by order of Catherine the Great. When Beniovskii left Kamchatka, with him were sixty-three men and seven women, some of them taken against their will. Among those were navy-trained navigators Dmitrii Bocharov and Gerasim Izmailov, major figures in the history of eighteenth-century Alaska. Both later commanded vessels in Alaskan waters and are famous for their investigation of the Northwest Coast, possibly as far as Glacier Bay, in 1788. Beniovskii sailed the *Sv. Petr* along the Kuril Chain where some of the involuntary mutineers attempted either to seize the vessel or escape. Becoming aware of the plot, Beniovskii had some of them flogged and put Izmailov and the Kamchadal Paranchin and his wife ashore in an uninhabited place. They survived on roots and mollusks for a while but, luckily, soon stumbled upon a camp of a Russian fur-hunting artel. The next year, 1772, they were brought back to Kamchatka aboard another fur-hunting vessel that put in at the Kurils.

In the meantime, Beniovskii sailed on. He reached Taiwan, where two of his men were killed and four wounded in a conflict with natives. In retaliation, Beniovskii burned a native settlement and all native boats, killing several men. On 12 September 1771, he reached Macao, where he sold the vessel. He and his crew remained in Macao until 4 January 1772, but fifteen of his people died there of fever. Survivors were placed on two French vessels chartered by Beniovskii and reached France 7 July 1772, with five more casualties suffered en route. Only thirty-seven men and three women remained of those who had left Kamchatka with Beniovskii. Of these, seventeen, among them navigator Dmitrii Bocharov (whose wife had died on the voyage), made their way to Paris, where they asked the Russian representative to return them home. Others entered foreign service or settled abroad. Beniovskii himself went to Madagascar accompanied by eleven men, including the veteran Aleutian voyager Chuloshnikov (the former foreman of merchant Kholodilov and probably Kamchadal) and a woman who sailed with him from Kamchatka. At various times Beniovskii threatened to sail to Alaska and establish an independent republic there or, alternatively, to return to Kamchatka and take it for himself and his cohorts. Foreign, that is, European, attempts upon the Kuril Islands were also not ruled out (with or without Beniovskii's assistance).[12]

Moreover, in 1777 Beniovskii proposed to the Continental Congress of the United States that Madagascar be used as an American base for naval operations. He did raise some funding from private sources in the United States for his Madagascar adventure. Some historians, among them the prominent Russian historian N. N. Bolkhovitinov, believe that Beniovskii's threats contributed significantly to Russian suspicions of foreign vessels in North Pacific waters and may have planted the idea that the Americans might have had their own aims there.[13] But as far as life and events on Kamchatka were concerned, the Beniovskii episode left little trace and things continued as usual. His adventures might have been colorful, but they were not significant to history.[14]

In the long run, the more prosaic struggles of the merchants played the major role in the development of territory on the North Pacific. And struggles they had indeed. The *Sv. Nikolai*, which cost 25,560 rubles to outfit, not counting the assistance from the Crown, reached the southern Kuril Islands, where she was wrecked 30 August 1776. Part of the crew made their way to Bol'sheretsk in skin boats, part remained on the eighteenth Kuril Island procuring furs. Lebedev-Lastochkin dispatched relief, also in skin boats, at a cost of an additional 8,000 rubles[15] and petitioned the government for the use of a government vessel, the brigantine *Sv. Nataliia*, under the command of Crown navigator Petushkov, with Irkutsk merchant Dmitrii Shabalin representing Lebedev-Lastochkin and acting as foreman. Shabalin did reach Hokkaido and in 1778 and 1779 traded there with the Japanese merchants. He left a detailed account, a journal, and a painting of his 1779 meeting with the Japanese (Plate 6).

Shelikhov, however, did not participate in this second voyage in any manner; he sold his shares in the *Sv. Nikolai* to his partner. From then until the 1790s, Shelikhov gave his main attention to the Aleutian trade, while Lebedev-Lastochkin continued to be active in both areas. An uneasy association between the two men continued in some measure. They were partners in outfitting two vessels, the *Sv. Andrei Pervozvannyi*, built in 1777, and the *Sv. Georgii Pobedonosets*, a former Crown vessel of the galiot type, first put at the disposal of Lebedev-Lastochkin for his operations in the Kurils, but then bought by him and his partners. It was this vessel, sailing under Crown navigator Gavriil Pribylov, that is credited with the discoveries of the Bering Sea fur seal rookeries, the islands of St. George and St. Paul (the Pribilof Islands of today).[16] Their main efforts, however, were continued independently. Lebedev-Lastochkin, in company with other merchants, invested in four vessels, while from 1776 to 1780 Shelikhov acquired interest in five, with major financial backing from Ivan Golikov. In fact, in all available documents of the time Golikov is listed as the senior partner. One historian states that between 1777 and 1797 Shelikhov held an interest in fourteen of the thirty-six ships in the field.[17]

In 1782–1783, Shelikhov built three vessels designed to carry a large party to establish a permanent settlement in Alaska. Prior to this time he was the sole owner of only one vessel, which he had built. The sources of his capital remain a mystery. The often-expressed view that he married for money has now been effectively refuted.[18] Most financing, no doubt, was provided by the wealthy Golikov merchant family,[19] his partners, and some may have been provided by Shelikhov's own relatives and possibly by some of his wife's kin, who were engaged in the Aleutian trade (see below). In his plan to establish permanent settlements on American soil, he was supported by Demidov, an industrialist who enjoyed the support of the then–Crown Prince Paul, who loaned him 50,000 rubles.[20] From 1788, an Englishman named James Smith (Iakov Shmit), also a protege of Demidov in St. Petersburg, was Shelikhov's business partner.[21] The influential Demidov family's support for the Shelikhovs continued after Grigorii Shelikhov's death, as his widow's correspondence attests. Their acquaintance, like that of the Shelikhov and Golikov families, is tied in with the circle of G. I. Derzhavin, senator, court poet, and statesman, in 1794–1796 head of the Commerce College, who was close to the entourage of Crown Prince Paul. Shelikhov apparently met Derzhavin through Golikov, his employer and later partner; at one time, the Golikovs and Derzhavin were neighbors. Shelikhov probably made his acquaintance early in his career and used it in presenting his proposals for the development of the Alaska trade to the government.[22] Derzhavin, like Platon Zubov, is known to have been a patron of Nikolai Petrovich Rezanov, who later married the eldest Shelikhov daughter. He was instrumental in gaining Rezanov an entree into Paul's inner circle. In any case, from the late 1770s Shelikhov, assisted by the Golikovs, was tireless in pursuing his advantage in St. Petersburg. One of his major arguments in requesting governmental support was the need for permanent Russian settlement of Alaska.

Though Lebedev-Lastochkin, too, thought in terms of settlement, beginning in the early 1780s the interests of the two men diverged sharply. Eventually, their relationship ended in bitter rivalry, mutual recriminations, and, on the ground, open fighting between Lebedev-Lastochkin and Shelikhov men. Shelikhov may have cheated his partner, and certainly, while in Alaska, he tried to take over the Lebedev-Lastochkin men and operations then headquartered in Unalaska, on the Alaska Peninsula, and the Shumagin Islands, and rapidly expanding into Cook Inlet and Prince William Sound. In an instruction to Bocharov, one of his skippers, dated 19 March 1786, Shelikhov told him to entice Lebedev-Lastochkin's men, Russian and Kamchadal and Yakut, to enter Shelikhov's service. He claimed he had a letter from Lebedev-Lastochkin transferring to him absolutely the management of the Lebedev company and further claimed to have given a copy of this letter to Bocharov.[23] Lebedev-Lastochkin, allegedly in some trouble with the government as of 1794, lived to see himself defeated. After his death, his widow pursued his claims against the new Russian-American Company, apparently in vain.[24]

For a while, as long as Catherine lived, Shelikhov was not successful in gaining governmental support. Within his family, however, he found an able and strong ally. In 1775, he had married Natalia Alekseevna, a Siberian girl only thirteen years of age. She may have been a Kamchatkan settler, sister to Ivan Kozhevin and possibly a relative of the Kamchatkan navigator Aleksei Kozhevin[25] and of Stepan Kozhevin, a navigator and shareholder in several Aleutian ventures.[26] She grew up to be a remarkable woman. She accompanied her husband to Kodiak Island in 1784, with one small child: son Mikhail, who died later in Irkutsk in 1787 at five years of age.[27] Daughter Avdot'ia (Evdokiia) was born probably during the winter the Shelikhovs spent on Mednoi Island.[28]

For years afterwards, as her letters show, she ably supported her husband in his business affairs. After his death she became the moving power in the formation of the joint company that later became the Russian-American Company. The role of Natalia Shelikhov deserves much more attention than it has yet received. Mother to eight children (three sons, of whom only one survived infancy, and five daughters), she preserved her husband's estate for her surviving children, in fact enlarged it, and looked out for their interests to the end of her days.[29]

Not only their daughter Anna, who married Rezanov (the man wrongly credited by many authors with the creation of the Russian-American Company), but three other daughters married well above their station after their father's death. All of their husbands became major shareholders in, and two served as directors of, the Russian-American Company (which Natalia Shelikhov rather than Rezanov was instrumental in founding).[30] Emperor Paul in 1797 elevated Natalia Shelikhov and all her children to the status of hereditary gentry but ordered that they were to retain the privilege of engaging in commerce, normally prohibited to the nobility. She skillfully maintained links to the high and the mighty, including Derzhavin, the Demidovs, and Count Zubov. All, as the correspondence attests, were sincere admirers of Natalia herself. The biography of this woman, who overcame accusations of infidelity and of possibly poisoning her husband,[31] is a task for a future historian. Here, we must return to the affairs of her husband.

Within a decade of entering the Aleutian trade, Grigorii Shelikhov began to argue for a monopoly on fur procurement and for organization of a trading company on the model of the British East India or Hudson's Bay Companies. Proposals of this sort were not new.[32] One such proposal, submitted 4 February 1780 by an anonymous author, was published by Chulkov in 1785 in his massive work on Russian commerce. To judge by the title in the address ("Illustrious Prince!"), the wording of the proposal, and reference to the fact that the proposal was discussed with Golikov, this may be the proposal, initiated as early as 1775, submitted by the merchant Kutyshkin to Prince Viazemskii.[33]

At first Shelikhov requested various forms of governmental support, including massive loans, consistently urging the necessity of colonization as opposed to the long-distance exploitation of resources practiced by the other fur-procurement companies. It is reasonable to suppose that both Shelikhov's and Lebedev-Lastochkin's push for settlement on the American mainland was motivated not only by logistics and the desire to gain substantive government support—which of course played a role—but also by the changes in the Chinese fur trade at Kiakhta; it was known that the mainland was rich in the fur-bearing land animals that commanded high prices both in Russia and in China. This appears likely, especially since Russians had no access to the Chinese markets except through Kiakhta, where land mammal furs were now the main item in demand.

Be that as it may, in 1781, the Golikovs and Shelikhov specifically petitioned the government in St. Petersburg for support of an enterprise that would involve establishment of a permanent settlement in America. To effect these plans, the new partners set a goal of establishing the "American, Northeastern, Northern, and Kuril Company" in ten years. They chose as the location of their future settlement the island of Kodiak, known to the Russians since at least 1762 and possibly earlier. It was the most populous island off the American coast, offering sea and land subsistence resources, timber (absent in the Aleutians), and rich fur-bearer hunting grounds. It was also a convenient base from which to make a push for the mainland. The island's inhabitants were numerous in comparison to the Aleutians, and the men were well known to the Russians as fierce warriors skilled in organized warfare.

Most skippers avoided putting in at Kodiak, as conflict with the Natives there appeared virtually unavoidable; in several confrontations the Russians had come out second best. For most skippers the advantages of potential trade did not outweigh the dangers. Moreover, if the government became aware of violence, skippers, foremen, and crews were investigated, faced trial, and, if convicted, were subject to dire punishment. Though the death penalty was abolished by Empress Elizabeth and reinstated by Catherine only for a very limited number of crimes against the state, the government considered unprovoked violence against Natives to be one of those crimes. The threat of the death penalty appears in several orders issued to the Russians trading in the Aleutians. The government also took steps to inform Native leaders that this was so and that they could seek redress if offered insults, violence, or abuse. Shelikhov, who was personally to lead the Kodiak effort, knew this all too well. It is clear that from the outset, however, Shelikhov—contrary to the government's policy that Native inhabitants were to be brought under the Russian scepter through persuasion, without violence—planned to carve out his niche in the New World by armed conquest. Perhaps he counted in advance on support from Siberian officials (whom he cultivated and bribed) should an investigation follow.

Three vessels of the galiot type named the *Tri Sviatitelia Vasilii Velikii, Grigorii Bogoslov i Ioann Zlatoust*, the *Sv. Simeon Bogopriimets i Anna Prorochitsa*, and the *Sv. Arkhistratig Arkhangel Mikhail*, were built on the Urak River north of Okhotsk, and were ready to sail by summer 1783. All three vessels carried cannon, albeit of a small caliber (in 1788, at Three Saints Bay, the Spanish captain de Haro observed two galiots on rollers, only one of which had four "very small stone-mortars" for armament).[34] Shelikhov engaged the best available navigators in Okhotsk: Gerasim Izmailov, Dmitrii Bocharov, and a man known to history only as Olesov. All were navy trained and seconded to merchant ships. The entire party numbered 192 persons (62 on the *Sv. Mikhail* under Olesov), recruited not locally but in Irkutsk.

The expedition began on 16 August 1783, out of Urak, course set for the Commander Islands. Olesov's vessel became separated from the other two early in the voyage; the others believed she might have been lost. (The *Sv. Mikhail* did not arrive on Kodiak until May 1786, just as Shelikhov was preparing to sail back to Okhotsk. The skipper, immediately relieved of his command and losing his well-paid job with Shelikhov, either was exceptionally unlucky or—and this cannot be excluded—deliberately tried to avoid participation in the planned action, which he knew to be illegal, against the Kodiak Islanders.)

The *Three Saints*, as Izmailov's vessel is popularly known, and the *Sv. Simeon i Anna*, under Bocharov, wintered at Mednoi Island. The next summer, 1784, they set sail for Kodiak, not waiting for the possibly lost *Sv. Mikhail*, under Olesov. They stopped briefly at Unalaska, where twelve Natives were taken on board. Among them were two interpreters, war prisoners taken by the Aleuts from Kodiak Island; one of these men, according to Kodiak Island oral tradition recorded almost a century later, would show the Russians a way to penetrate a Native fortress (*krepost'*) deemed inaccessible to an enemy. On 3 August, the two vessels stood off southwest Kodiak, just off the strait that separates the islands of Kodiak and Sitkalidak. They entered the bay, now called Three Saints Bay, where they would establish the first intended permanent Russian settlement on American soil (earlier, about 1774, the harbor of Illiuliuk or Unalaska Bay had become through usage a permanent outpost).

Almost immediately Shelikhov struck the assembled Kodiak forces, his men storming the refuge rock off Sitkalidak Island with a great loss of life among the Native defenders. The first strike was swift and brutal, followed by several mopping-up operations and assaults on Kodiak forces in outlying areas in the course of the next two years.[35] A palisaded, well-constructed outpost was established on Afognak Island in 1785–1786, and by late summer of the same year on the Kenai Peninsula, in outer Cook Inlet (Redoubt of St. Alexander, or Aleksandrovskoe, modern English Bay or, in Alutiiq, Nanwalek). Aleksandrovskoe was reached via Shuyak and Peregrebnye or, after Cook, the Barren Islands. By May 1786, Izmailov had circumnavigated and charted Kodiak and adjacent islands; outer Cook Inlet was explored.

In 1787, Evstrat Delarov established an outpost at Karluk, on the Shelikof Strait side of Kodiak Island, then sailed along the Pacific coast of the Alaska Peninsula (familiar to him from earlier voyages) and staked out Katmai, a site of Native trading fairs, for a company outpost (in 1787, the artel stationed at Katmai was wiped out by the local people;[36] it was reestablished in the 1790s under Baranov). Delarov had sailed in the Aleutians since 1764, under Solov'iev, and participated in the so-called pacification and preventive strikes against the Umnak-Unalaska Aleut alliance. Eventually he became a skipper of excellent reputation and part owner of fur-trading vessels. Shelikhov had met Delarov in Irkutsk in 1787 and persuaded him to become the chief manager of his establishment on Kodiak. He sailed to Kodiak that same year as foreman aboard the vessel *Three Saints*, commanded by Izmailov. He left the colonies to return to Irkutsk only in 1792. Later, Delarov, since 1789 a merchant of the second guild in Irkutsk, became a partner in the Shelikhov enterprises as a major shareholder, and in 1796 assumed the direction of affairs in Irkutsk. After 1799 he became one of the directors of the Russian-American Company and moved to St. Petersburg.[37]

Immediately, Shelikhov's men also began to expand westward out of Kodiak, specifically establishing artels in the harbor of the island of Unga in the Shumagin archipelago. Here, earlier, Panov's men, including Delarov, were active. Delarov had made this harbor his home away from home on several voyages; for many years it was known as Delarov Harbor, or Greko-Delarovskoe because Delarov was a Greek. It is from here that in 1781–1786, in company with two other skippers, he made a foray into Prince William Sound.

The Shumagin Islands offered several advantages. From there it was easy to reach either side of the Alaska Peninsula, both the eastern, occupied by Alutiit speaking a dialect of the language spoken on Kodiak, and the western, occupied by Aleuts. In addition to Katmai, there was another major traditional Native trading rendezvous at Sutkhum (on or near present-day Sutwik Island). Also readily accessible out of the Shumagins were the island of Unimak and the Sanak Islands, one of the most famous sea otter grounds in Alaska, where in 1774–1776 Ivan Solov'iev fought, traded, and in the end believed that he had made friends with the local Aleuts. In addition, artels from a number of vessels in which Shelikhov had a stake were placed on Unalaska Island and one large artel was dispatched to St. Paul Island in the Pribilofs. Other artels were scattered in the central Aleutians, with a main base on Atka, and in the Near Islands.

Shelikhov reorganized the enterprise, forming the Northeastern Company, operating out of Kodiak; the Northern Company, destined to occupy St. Paul in the Pribilof Islands among other things; and the Predtechenskaia Company, headquartered at Atka.[38] Shelikhov's expansionist plans were, however, much grander. From the start he wanted to expand his sphere of activity to the north, to Bering Strait, issuing instructions to Dmitrii Bocharov to proceed to 65° N latitude and beyond, and to California. The expansion into the latter area was much on his mind: in his instructions to Samoilov, written just prior to his departure from Kodiak in 1786, he mentioned three times that reconnaissance of the Californian coast was imperative. In his report to Governor-General Iakobii of 19 April 1787, soon after his return to Okhotsk, he stated: "I strove, before all else, to succeed [*sic*] along the American coast to the south, toward California, by securing locations for Russian settlements and leaving emblems of our sovereignty in this part of the earth to prevent any attempts by other nations and make our establishments there the first."[39]

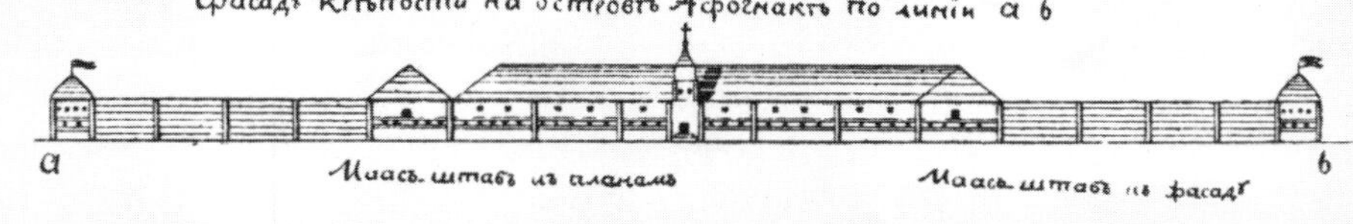

FIGURE 23. Left: Short-lived Three Saints Magazin on Afognak Island. Right: Plan for Shelikhov outpost at English Bay.
From A. I. Andreev, ed., 1948, p. 256.

The number of men Shelikhov had recruited in Siberia was small, and efforts were made to augment them with crews from other vessels owned in part by Golikov and Shelikhov and with men employed by competitors whom Shelikhov managed to persuade to join him. From the outset, Shelikhov used the Kodiak Islanders who had bowed before him in defeat as a source of manpower. From the beginning, the Native men were used not only as hunters for the company but also as fighters in areas other than their own. Thus, Delarov used the Kodiak Islanders from the Pacific side against the settlements on Shelikhov Strait, notably in occupation of the major northern Native center of Karluk. Native enmities, local and intertribal, were skillfully exploited.

Shelikhov, however, realized that in the long run force alone would not suffice. Acts of brutality and intimidation were followed by gifts, unexpected fairness, and occasional kindnesses. In his instruction to K. A. Samoilov, whom he left as manager on Kodiak in 1786, he told Samoilov to take care to impress the Natives with the might and power of the Russian state and the empress who "exterminates those who raise against her" but at the same time directed that the hostages, including women and those used for labor (*kaiury*), be treated fairly, be well fed and clothed, and that the men under his command not be permitted to exploit women in any way. Should they make use of women, severe penalties were to be meted out. In the same instruction he said that the Fox Island Aleuts, who of their free will and with their wives and children had come to live at the Russian establishments on Kodiak, were to be treated in all respects as Russians and, should they desire to return home, were to be provided with the means to do so with all honor. He repeated this in another paragraph (26), mentioning specifically Aleuts from Unga, led by the *toions* (chiefs) Vasilei (*sic*) and Marko, who, upon departure for home, were to be given two Alutiiq skin boats, their accounts settled honorably, and rewards given. A debt due them for twenty-two lavtaks (dehaired sea lion skins) was to be paid in full.[40] In many instances, he spoke of gifts to be distributed and respect to be shown to Native leaders. Moreover, Shelikhov was mindful of his self-defined future mission to establish Russian civilization in Alaska. In his accounts and reports he spoke of his efforts to gain the islanders' friendship, mostly by demonstrating the superiority of Russian technology and knowledge, though his men were under no circumstances to divulge to the Natives the "secret of firearms."[41]

Shelikhov was much concerned with the population question. He instructed his managers to conduct a full census,[42] and suggested that the young unmarried Russian men be married to Native women. In a letter to Evstrat Delarov dated 30 August 1789, he said, "To preserve from venereal disease, permit those who are not married, and want to do so, to marry; God be the judge of the married men, not us; the natural weakness cannot be prevented by anybody in the course of life." This concern was reiterated in a letter to Baranov dated 9 August 1794; speaking of settlers he was dispatching to Alaska, he said, "Make an effort to see to it that the single settlers being sent [to Alaska] presently marry fine upstanding American girls; to this end I have sent you various items, necessary complements to clothing, as gifts for the brides and future wives; at weddings, supply each groom with same."[43]

Shelikhov also claimed that he was the first to teach the Kodiak Islanders the principles of Christianity. He stood godfather to one resident of Kodiak, christened Nikolai, who presumably adopted his godfather's surname (Natalia Shelikhov was godmother to a number of Native women). Upon his return he petitioned the government to assist him in dispatching a clergyman to Alaska. Thus he is customarily credited with establishing the official presence of the Orthodox Church on the American continent, though in reality it was his partner Ivan Golikov who was most energetic in lobbying the government in this matter.[44]

Though Shelikhov's statements are self-serving and have to be taken with a great deal of skepticism, it must be granted that he and his partners financed the building of the first Orthodox church on Kodiak and that he established the first school on Kodiak Island where young boys taken as hostages (and later a number brought by fathers who wished their sons to acquire the foreigners' knowledge) were taught Russian language and literacy, mathematics, and navigation. When leaving in 1786, he instructed Samoilov to maintain the school and stated that he would send books from Okhotsk on the next vessel. The Spanish noted this school in 1788, when de Haro met Delarov and was given a hand-drawn chart of Shelikhov Strait, the entry into Cook Inlet, and Prince William Sound.

In 1789, Shelikhov urged Delarov to see to it that boys were taught "literacy, arithmetic and singing so that in time they would become navigators and fine sailors; it is also necessary to teach them various crafts, but especially carpentry."[45] By 1792, the school had produced nine apprentices in navigation, seven of whom were employed in the colony. The other two were sent out of Okhotsk on a voyage to Japan, under command of navigator Lovtsov and Laksman, who was to represent Russian governmental interests in trade negotiations.[46] After the spiritual mission arrived in 1794, the school passed to the guidance of the clergy, with the consent of Shelikhov, who wrote to Baranov that several brethren were capable of being good teachers, and had expressed interest in becoming such, especially Hieromonk Makarii. With the missionaries, Shelikhov sent books for the school: "classical, historical, mathematical, moral, and on economics." He instructed Baranov to add to this starter set all the books on hand on Kodiak and among the other artels.[47] In 1804–1807, Hieromonk Gedeon, who came to Alaska aboard the *Neva* to inspect the status of the Orthodox Church, reorganized the school.[48]

When Shelikhov left Kodiak in 1786, he took along forty Kodiak Islanders, among them youngsters whom he planned to place in schools in Okhotsk and Irkutsk. There they were to be taught literacy, as well as art and music. (Much later, in 1820, one of these young men, Ivan Poliakov, who spent seven years in school in Irkutsk, would be accused of an attempt to organize a revolt on Kodiak. Reportedly, he used his literacy skills to persuade others to follow his lead.)[49]

Shelikhov was also concerned with introducing various crafts, blacksmithing, joinery and carpentry, fine metalsmithing, and others, and with initiating agriculture. With the next vessel, he sent seeds, pedigreed dogs, rabbits, goats, pigs, and two pairs of cattle as well as male and female calves; in 1794, additional cattle, goats, sheep, and a mare and a foal were shipped.[50] Shipbuilding facilities were to be created immediately.

His was the vision of a settled and developed country. As a young girl, Avdeeva-Polevaia, the daughter of Shelikhov's business partner Aleksei Polevoi, knew Shelikhov personally and wrote that he was a most unusual man, possessed of a powerful intellect and steely will: "His fiery soul coveted not so much riches, but glory; for him, obstacles did not exist, he conquered all with his inflexible iron will; those around him called him 'the scorching flame' for good reason."[51] At the same time, he had, among his peers in Irkutsk, a reputation as a hard and cruel man.

From the start Shelikhov dreamed of his settlements in Alaska as cities, where commerce, trades, crafts, and art would flourish, with all sorts of cultural amenities, fine architecture, music, cathedrals, wide streets, and spacious plazas. In several letters to his subordinates he talked about proper layout of streets, optimal location of buildings, appropriate quality of construction for buildings, and sanitary facilities. Libraries, museums, and art were to be part of life, and he instructed his subordinates to collect ethnographic and natural history specimens for museums in Russia.

These cities were and remained a dream, but Shelikhov must have tried to ensure a certain quality of life in his little settlement on Kodiak. In any case, in 1788 de Haro found the little Three Saints Bay settlement very well appointed. He was especially impressed with the quarters of Delarov and a married officer (probably Izmailov). These were "very well furnished, all hung with the paper printed in China, with a large mirror, many pictures of saints well painted, and rich beds." Russian women were present, if de Haro was correct in his perceptions and did not mistake Aleut wives for Siberians. Some of them wore Chinese-style dresses, "very good clothes of this kind," and served dinner on good china. There were vegetable gardens. In one of the beached vessels there was a chapel, where, according to de Haro, daily services were held.[52]

Shelikhov left Kodiak 22 May 1786 on the *Three Saints* (Gerasim Izmailov commanding), intending to send the vessel back the same season. However, while Shelikhov was on shore during a stop at Bol'sheretsk on Kamchatka, leaving the *Three Saints* at anchor in the mouth of the Bol'shaia River, a storm came up and the vessel was carried out to sea when her anchor cables parted. Instead of making for the harbor, the vessel sailed away for Okhotsk. Natalia Shelikhov was on board. Shelikhov intended immediately to proceed to Okhotsk overland, but when he learned that an English vessel was at Petropavlovsk, he went there instead and met with Captain William Peters of the *Lark*, representing the East India Company. A one-time deal was concluded, but both parties were interested in joint trade in the future (for which Shelikhov needed governmental approval).[53] In the meantime, the *Lark* sailed but was wrecked on Mednoi Island. Shelikhov returned to Bol'sheretsk, then to Tigil' and from there, on 18 November, by dogsled to Okhotsk, which he reached 27 January 1787. Rejoining his wife, who had been separated from him when the vessel was torn off her anchors, he traveled with her to Irkutsk, arriving there on 6 April.[54]

Shelikhov wasted no time in reporting his achievements, which he grossly exaggerated, to the authorities and petitioning again for government support and this time for permission to create a monopolistic trading company. In one document, in which he outlined the privileges he sought, he stated that a military force of up to one hundred men, with supporting personnel, including weaponsmiths, cannoneers, surveyors, and mining engineers, should be put at the company's disposal. In the same paragraph he suggested that two priests and a deacon should be assigned to Alaska. All were to receive salaries from the company under the condition that they be absolutely prohibited from engaging in any kind of trade as individuals. The company was to be authorized to hire as laborers Russian citizens of all stations, holding valid passports or lacking them, and debtors with undischarged debts provided they were repaying twenty-four rubles per year; the company was to be permitted to buy prisoners of war and slaves being held by Native groups and settle the same in various localities, while the Aleuts and the inhabitants of the Kuril Islands were to be employed for hire; the company was to be accountable only to the governor-general of Siberia and to a special government representative designated to supervise its affairs; the company was, for the greater glory of the fatherland, to be permitted to initiate and conduct trade with Japan, China, Korea, India, and the Philippines, and Spaniards and Americans in America; the company, if successful in locating lands not yet occupied by other European states, would have the right to bring the population under the Russian scepter, settle these lands, and introduce agriculture, factories and industry. The final paragraph requested that, in view of large capital expenditures and the closure of the trade at Kiakhta, the imperial government was to loan 500,000 rubles for twenty years; the company would pay interest and provide bond. In the meantime a Crown vessel stationed at Okhotsk would be put at the company's disposal.

By 30 November 1787, Governor Iakobii was writing to St. Petersburg supporting the proposal. By February 1788, Golikov and Shelikhov addressed the empress directly with a petition to grant their request, though their request for a loan was scaled down to 200,000 rubles but now to be made interest free. In March the Commerce College, headed by Vorontsov, reported favorably to the empress, and on 6 April so did the State Council.[55]

Shelikhov was persistent in advancing the notion that one strong, united company, backed by the government, was necessary to prevent foreigners, British or American, from infringing on Russian interests. The American threat at this time became personified in the form of John Ledyard, of Dartmouth, New Hampshire, who had been to Alaska with Cook and was now traveling in Siberia. He and Shelikhov met, and Shelikhov informed him that there were many Russians in Alaska, that the settlements there were long-standing, and that Russia claimed the coast even unto California.[56]

Though there was also some opposition to the proposal, nobody expected Catherine's reaction. Her comments, of three points, with thirteen additional "nota bene," were scathing. All requests were refused. Golikov and Shelikhov were to be given certificates of award, the right to wear swords, and medals, but the government was not to back them. On the contrary, the government was to look into their affairs. The empress wished to know on what basis the company had been collecting iasak. An investigation should be conducted in the matter, since iasak collection had long since been prohibited (this task fell to officers of the Billings expedition; the records of their proceedings are yet to be studied in detail). Catherine's last remark expressed her grave doubts about expansionist aims in the Pacific: "It is one thing to trade, quite a different thing to take possession." The empress also noted that information provided about the American mainland was scant, to say the least, and requested further hard information.[57]

In the meantime, charges of misconduct and brutality toward the Natives were lodged against Shelikhov and his men. These charges were submitted to Captain Billings by an eyewitness to the conquest of Kodiak, forwarded to the admiralty, and, eventually, to the empress herself. But Shelikhov did not give up. While in Irkutsk, he made a point to cultivate the acquaintance of Billings, the naval commander ordered to investigate charges against him.

He also got his name before the reading public. In 1787, he composed "A Note on Shelikhov's Voyages in the Eastern Ocean." Believed to have been addressed to the governor-general, it somehow found its way into print. On 11 October 1791, the government censor Nikita Rublev approved the material for publication. Later, after Shelikhov's death, the family claimed the material was printed without his approval. In 1792, excerpts from the journal kept by the navigators Bocharov and Izmailov, on their voyage in 1788 along Alaska's southeast coast to Lituya Bay and beyond, were added to the 1791 text and published in a new edition, again under Shelikhov's name. Another edition appeared in 1793, as did an English translation of the first and second editions.[58]

Shelikhov did not neglect the government bureaucrats, either. He constantly addressed the governor, the Commerce College, and the empress, extolling his own achievements and "faultless" behavior, and was tireless in pointing out that, on one hand, foreigners were penetrating the North Pacific, and, on the other hand, his competitors (not he) were violating governmental regulations and were guilty of brutality toward the Natives.

We do not know what Lebedev-Lastochkin was doing at this time. It is unlikely that he let all of this propaganda go unchallenged. In Alaska, the competition was played in physical terms. Lebedev-Lastochkin men, led by the very able navigators, the brothers Potap and Stepan Zaikov, secured permanent positions on the Alaska Peninsula's Bering Sea shore and from there penetrated into the interior—the Iliamna and Lake Clark region. In 1791, Bocharov was dispatched, on behalf of the Shelikhov company, to chart the Alaska Peninsula's northern shore. He did that, and then portaged to the peninsula's Pacific shore, charting the large lake that is now called in his honor Becharof (*sic*) Lake. Lebedev-Lastochkin men controlled Kamishak Bay on Cook Inlet, where there was an easy portage to Iliamna Lake, and the routes to the Bering Sea. By 1790, they had outposts on Cook Inlet—St. George on the Kasilof River (established 1787) and a post on the Kaknu (Kenai) River—both on the western shore of the Kenai Peninsula.[59] By 1794, they also controlled upper Cook Inlet, having an outpost at Tyonek and small stations near present-day Anchorage, at Turnagain Arm, and at the Knik River.[60] They controlled all portages from Cook Inlet to Prince William Sound and had outposts off Montague Island as early as 1788,[61] in the vicinity of modern Seward as well as on Hinchinbrook Island and apparently at Cook's Snug Corner Cove off Port Fidalgo, where Meares had wintered in 1786. It is believed that they sent out parties to investigate the Copper River and the Yukon-Kuskokwim drainage. Vasilii Ivanov is supposed to have traveled to the Yukon-Kuskokwim area in 1790.[62]

Although the Lebedev-Lastochkin crews were firmly entrenched on the mainland and penetrating Alaska's interior between 1784 and 1794, the stage was set for the final conflict between the empire builders.

Shelikhov, in the capital, and then from Irkutsk, pressed for assignment of clerics to Alaska (granted), for settlers to establish an agricultural colony (granted, with assignment of a small contingent of serfs, most of them craftsmen, through the agency of Platon Zubov), and for military support, through Samuel Bentham (refused), though Bentham and Billings were apparently instrumental in bringing James Shields to Alaska. Shields, formerly a lieutenant in the British navy and a shipbuilder and navigator associated with Bentham's activity in Siberia, became an employee of the Shelikhov-Golikov Company when an expedition planned by Bentham for a venture in the Pacific failed to materialize.[63]

In 1790, Shelikhov found a man who appeared to share his dream of settlement and was capable of carrying out the grand design. He hired Aleksandr Baranov, who was a native of the Russian north and had been for some time a merchant with a trading post among the warlike Chukchi. It was this man who, in the years following Shelikhov's death, ousted the Lebedev-Lastochkin Company, extended effective Russian presence along Alaska's southeastern shores, checked the advance of the British and American traders, attempted to take possession of the Columbia River estuary, established a settlement in California and, briefly, one in Hawaii. If there were Russian empire builders in Alaska, ones to whom posterity should grant the title, they would be these two men: Grigorii Shelikhov and Aleksandr Baranov.

NOTES

1. Shelikhov to Governor-General Iakobii, 19 April 1787, in A. I. Andreev, ed., *Russkie otkrytiia* (1944), 72 (doc. 6); Shelikhov to Delarov, 30 August 1789, in P. A. Tikhmenev, *A History of the Russian American Company*, vol. 2, *Documents*, trans. Dmitri Krenov, ed. Richard A. Pierce and Alton S. Donnelly (Kingston, Ontario: Limestone Press, 1979), 20 (doc. 5), and also in A. I. Andreev, ed., *Russkie otkrytiia* (1948), 285–289 (doc. 31).
2. Sladkovsky, *The Long Road*, 111–152; Foust, *Muscovite and Mandarin*, 215–329; Gibson, *Otter Skins*, 22–109.
3. Up to 1790 the Panov brothers had controlling interest in fourteen vessels, and held shares in four other vessels financed by their prikazchiks, the Popov brothers. Their papers have never been located. Historian Vasilii Berkh, writing in 1823, lamented: "I also regret that I could not obtain the ships' journals which belonged to the Panov company. These enterprising men also had big establishments and sent their vessels to the Saint Matthew and Saint Lawrence Islands" (cited after English translation by Dmitri Krenov; see Vasilii N. Berkh, *Chronological History*, 72).
4. The papers (if any) of the Lebedev-Lastochkin Company, not to speak of other merchant houses, such as those of the brothers Panov or Kiselev, have never been studied or even located. This task is

yet to be accomplished by younger scholars, should such papers survive in Russian provincial archives or in private collections. On the creation of the Russian-American Company the most recent treatment is by Aleksandr Iu. Petrov, *Obrazovanie Rossiisko-amerikanskoi kompanii* (Moscow: Izdatel'stvo "Nauka," 2000). See also idem, "Obrazovanie Rossiisko-amerikanskoi kompanii (1795–1799)," chap. 9 in *Osnovanie Russkoi Ameriki, 1732–1799,* vol. 1 of *Istoriia Russkoi Ameriki, 1732–1867,* ed. N. N. Bolkhovitinov (Moscow: "Mezhdunarodnye otnosheniia," 1997), 322–363.

5. Irkutsk State Regional Archive, Fond 50, op. 1, t. 1, delo 562 and delo 523, Confessional records of the Church of Sts. Prokopii and Ioann of Ustiug.
6. Polonskii, in his unpublished manuscript about the era of the promyshlenniki, preserved in the Archive of the Russian Geographic Society in St. Petersburg, states that Lebedev-Lastochkin was an escaped felon charged, together with his wife, with murder, and that he fled from Nizhnii Novgorod to Yakutsk where he somehow obtained a false passport. Polonskii alleges that Lebedev-Lastochkin remained under investigation for this matter until 1787 (Polonskii, "Perechen'," fol. 86). No corroborating data have come to light. On the other hand, Ekaterina Avdeeva-Polevaia, daughter of Aleksei Polevoi, a merchant of Ryl'sk and compatriot and business partner of Grigorii Shelikhov, knew both men personally. She mentions Lebedev-Lastochkin as an outstanding citizen, "the old hero of the Siberian industry" (Ekaterina Avdeeva-Polevaia, *Zapiski i zamechaniia o Sibiri, s prilozheniem starinnykh russkikh pesen* [Moscow: N. Stepanov, 1837], reprinted as part of *Zapiski irkutskikh zhitelei,* comp. and ed. M. D. Sergeev [Irkutsk: Vostochno-Sibirskoe knizhnoe izdatel'stvo, 1990], 7–124).
7. Sitnikov, *Grigorii Shelikhov,* 49.
8. *Atkis* was the name used by the Russians for, apparently, modern Abashiri on Hokkaido. Hokkaido was also sometimes called by the Russians the "22nd Kuril Island" and Matsumae.
9. As noted earlier, Russia had looked toward establishment of trade with Japan since the reign of Peter the Great. This topic is explored by George Alexander Lensen in his authoritative *Russian Push toward Japan.* We note that a squadron of Bering's Second Expedition, under the command of Spangsberg and Walton, on governmental orders explored Japanese waters. See Narochnitskii et al., *Russkie ekspeditsii* (1984), 180–185, 189–194 (docs. 117–118, 121) and ibid. (1989), 27–30 (doc. 1), Chirikov's report to the Admiralty, 18 June 1746. See also the account of Spangsberg's part in Bering's Second Expedition recently published by Tatjana Fjodorova et al., *Martin Spangsberg: En dansk opdagelsesrejsende i russisk tjeneste* (Esbjerg, Denmark: Rosendahls Forlag, 1999), available in translation as *Martin Spangsberg: A Danish Explorer in Russian Service* (Esbjerg, Denmark: Fiskeri- og Søfartsmuseet, 2002). On governmental planning of a probe toward Japan by Russian merchantmen, see Narochnitskii et al., *Russkie ekspeditsii* (1989), 142–143 (doc. 48).
10. Narochnitskii et al., *Russkie ekspeditsii* (1989), 143–145 (doc. 49).
11. For governmental instructions to merchants Lebedev-Lastochkin and Shelikhov, and for other documents pertaining to the expedition of the *Sv. Nikolai* to the Kuril Islands and Hokkaido in 1774, see Narochnitskii et al., *Russkie ekspeditsii* (1989), 143–170 (docs. 49–54). For general instructions to traders active in the Kurils and the Aleutians see ibid., 170–176 (doc. 55).
12. Behm to Governor-General in Irkutsk, 13 August 1775, quoted after A. Polonskii, "Kurily," *Zapiski Imperatorskago russkago geograficheskago obshchestva* 4 (1871): 449–450. See Lensen, *Russian Push,* 71–84, on Beniovskii's attempts to interest other powers in opening up Japan and on his false warning to the Japanese about Russian designs upon their country.
13. N. N. Bolkhovitinov, *The Beginnings of Russian-American Relations, 1775–1815,* trans. Elena Levin with intro. by L. H. Butterfield (Cambridge, Mass.: Harvard University Press, 1975), 148–154, original Russian edition published as *Stanovlenie russko-amerikanskikh otnoshenii, 1775–1815* (Moscow: Izdatel'stvo "Nauka," 1966); Lensen, *Russian Push,* 76.
14. Beniovskii's own account of the events, published in *Memoirs and Travels of Mauritius Augustus Count de Benyowsky,* translated from a French printed version by W. Nicholson (London: G. G. J. and J. Robinson, 1790), and almost immediately in all other major European languages, is highly unreliable, fanciful, and in some instances fictitious. There are several accounts in Russian which are based on historical documents of the eighteenth century and one account by a participant.

These are: "Zapiski kantseliarista Riumina o prikliucheniiakh ego s Beniovskim," 3 pts., *Severnyi arkhiv* 2, no. 5 (March 1822): 375–394; 2, no. 6 (March 1822): 447–462; 2, no. 7 (April 1822): 3–18; A. Sgibnev, "Bunt Ben'iovskago v Kamchatke v 1771 g.," 2 pts., *Russkaia starina* 15, no. 3 (March 1876): 526–547; 15, no. 4 (April 1876): 757–769; "Zapiska o bunte, proizvedennom Beniovskim v Bol'sheretskom ostroge i posledstviiakh onago," *Russkii arkhiv* 4 (1865): 417–438; D. N. Bludov, "Zapiska o bunte Beniovskago v pol'zu kniazia Pavla Petrovicha," *Russkii arkhiv* 4 (1865): 657–680; Vasilii N. Berkh, "Pobeg grafa Ben'iovskago iz Kamchatki vo Frantsiiu," *Syn Otechestva* 71, no. 27 (1821): 3–23; 71, no. 28 (1821): 49–79.

Beniovskii's adventure continues to fascinate writers in Russia and in the West. Plays, operas, and fictionalized accounts abound; they are numbered in the hundreds. Relatively recently, Leonid Paseniuk, a Russian fiction writer turned historian, published two excellent essays on Beniovskii: "Pokhozhdeniia barona Beniovskogo: Istoriko-biograficheskii ocherk," in *Kamchatka* (Petropavlovsk-Kamchatskii, 1978), 109–166, which contains an excellent literature review, and "Miatezhnaia sud'ba skital'tsa," in *Belye nochi na reke Mamontovoi* (Krasnodarsk knizhnoe izdatel'stvo, 1988), 194–302. An interesting essay on Beniovskii's activities in the United States was published by E. Dvoichenko-Markova, *Benjamin Franklin and Count M. A. Beniowski* (Philadelphia, 1955). In 1992, a fictionalized account by N. G. Smirnov, originally published in 1928, appeared under the title *Gosudarstvo solntsa* [Country of the sun] (Moscow: Respublika) with an introduction by an eminent Soviet historian, Ia. Svet.

15. Polonskii, "Kurily," 452.

16. Shelikhov, desiring not only to ingratiate himself but also to assert his own claims to these islands, called them the Zubov Islands in honor of Count Platon Zubov, then Empress Catherine's favorite. In fact, in 1786 Shelikhov tried to create an impression that Pribylov was his employee (Instruction to Bocharov, 19 March 1786, Kodiak, in A. I. Andreev, ed., *Russkie otkrytiia* [1944], 43 [doc. 2]).

17. S. B. Okun, *The Russian-American Company,* ed. B. D. Grekov, trans. from Russian by Carl Ginsburg, preface by Robert J. Kerner (Cambridge, Mass.: Harvard University Press, 1951), 23.

18. Sitnikov, *Grigorii Shelikhov,* 38. The usual version is that Shelikhov's wife, Natalia, was a wealthy widow. Sitnikov demonstrates, on the basis of vital statistics, that this is an impossibility due to her early age at marriage to Shelikhov (see below).

19. In the historiography of Russian America the role of the Golikovs is poorly delineated. Archival materials suggest that a reevaluation is in order, especially of Ivan Golikov's activity in connection with the establishment of the first Orthodox mission in Alaska (see below) and creation of the office of the bishop-vicar for Alaska in 1798. Golikov was the *senior* partner.

20. Okun, *Russian-American Company,* 22.

21. See Sitnikov, *Grigorii Shelikhov,* 380–404 (appendix, eighteen letters by Smith to Shelikhov, 1788–1792).

22. The link to Derzhavin, too, held firm after Shelikhov's death. It was Derzhavin who authored the pompous epitaph engraved on Shelikhov's monument and who exercised his influence on behalf of the Shelikhovs before Emperor Paul.

Shelikhov's grave marker in the graveyard of the Znamenskii cathederal in Irkutsk is an obelisk; all four sides are inscribed. Two verses, on two sides, are by Derzhavin and read:

1. "The Russian Columbus here is buried, [who] crossed the seas, discovered unknown countries, and seeing that everything on earth is corrupt, he set his sail to the heavenly ocean, to seek treasures celestial, not earthly. The Treasury of Good, O God, rest his soul";

2. "Here in expectation of the Coming of Christ is buried *the* body [of one] by name Shelikhov, by acts Invaluable, by occupation Citizen, by designs Honorable Man, of broad and strong mind; As during the reign of Catherine the Second Empress and Autocrat of All the *Russias,* glorious and great ruler, who enlarged Her Empire by victories over Her enemies in the west and in the south, He by his daring sea voyages in the east discovered, subdued and added to Her dominion not only the islands Kyktak [Kodiak], Afognak and many others but the mainland of America extending toward the northwest; [he] established on them house building, shipbuilding, agriculture, and through the

protection and intercession at the throne by the patron, Count Platon Alexandrovich Zubov, having procured Archimandrite with brethren and choir [he] proclaimed among the uncivilized people, by unheard of ignorance trampled down, the name of God, unknown to them, and, in the name of the Holy Life-Giving Trinity, implanted [there] the Orthodox Christian faith in the year 1794" (English translation by Marina Ramsay, excerpted from appendix 8 in Shelikhov, *A Voyage to America,* 135–137; division by lines is omitted; my corrections to the translation are italicized).

23. Shelikhov's instruction to apprentice navigator Dmitrii I. Bocharov, 19 March 1786, at Three Saints Bay, Kodiak, in A. I. Andreev, ed., *Russkie otkrytiia* (1944), 43 (doc. 2).

24. Richard A. Pierce, *Russian America: A Biographical Dictionary* (Kingston, Ontario; Fairbanks, Alaska: Limestone Press, 1990), 303.

25. The data on Natalia Shelikhov's age at marriage and her probable maiden name were located by Sitnikov, *Grigorii Shelikhov,* 38, 62–63. Sitnikov's data may suggest that the marriage took place in one of the Kamchatkan settlements and not in Irkutsk, as is widely assumed. A recent search of vital statistic records and preliminary marriage annoucements in the records of the Irkutsk Orthodox churches for the Shelikhovs' marriage record was fruitless. There remains a possibility, however, that Natalia may have been related in some way to the Myl'nikovs, a powerful Irkutsk merchant family. After Shelikhov's death, several members of this family became directors of Shelikhov enterprises (and later of the Russian-American Company). The Myl'nikov-Kozhevin link remains to be investigated.

26. Polonskii, "Perechen'."

27. Irkutsk State Regional Archive, vital statistics of the Church of the Holy Resurrection in Irkutsk for the year 1787. It appears that there was another son, also named Mikhail, who died in 1782 at the age of three years (vital statistics of the Orthodox churches in Irkutsk).

28. Sitnikov, *Grigorii Shelikhov,* 128–129. Data on Shelikhov's children in America presented by Pierce (*Biographical Dictionary,* 459) are derived from *Peterburgskii nekropol'.*

29. R. A. Pierce's editorial note in Shelikhov, *A Voyage to America,* 145.

30. The surviving letters of Natalia Shelikhov, preserved in the Russian State Naval Archive in St. Petersburg and in the Archive of Russia's Foreign Policy (AVPRI) in Moscow, are ample testimony to her abilities and role in creating the Russian-American Company. Assertions in the literature that she was illiterate and Okun's hypothesis that the letters signed by her were in reality written by Rezanov I find to be unsubstantiated by the evidence.

31. See Pierce's introduction to Shelikhov, *A Voyage to America,* 29–31, 138–145 (app. 9). Pierce tends to give the rumors some credence. Sitnikov, aware of these rumors, tends to disregard them as he disregards the unlikely hypothesis advanced by B. Polevoi that Shelikhov committed suicide (Sitnikov, *Grigorii Shelikhov,* 288–292).

32. For a discussion of mercantilism and proposals for the establishment of monopolistic trading companies in eighteenth-century Russia, see Okun, *Russian-American Company,* 18–20, and on Shelikhov's proposals, ibid., 22–33. This section includes an able discussion of the support given to Shelikhov by Siberian governors Pil' and Iakobii and by members of the Commerce College.

33. See Pierce's introduction to Shelikhov, *A Voyage to America,* 6–8, and the text of Kutyshkin's statement addressed to Emperor Paul I, 27 August 1800, ibid., 111–113 (app. 1).

34. Excerpts from de Haro's journals, translated by Katrina H. Moore, "Spain Claims Alaska, 1775: Spanish Exploration of the Alaskan Coast," in *The Sea in Alaska's Past: Conference Proceedings,* History and Archaeology Publications Series, no. 25 (Anchorage: Office of History and Archaeology, Alaska Division of Parks, 1979), 67–70; and in Wallace M. Olson, *Through Spanish Eyes,* 250–268.

35. For a detailed analysis of Shelikhov's assault on the Kodiak Islanders, see Lydia T. Black, "The Russian Conquest of Kodiak," *Anthropological Papers of the University of Alaska* 24, nos. 1–2 (1992): 165–182.

36. Izmailov's log for the voyage Okhotsk-Kodiak 1787, Russian State Naval Archive (RGAVMF), Fond 870, op. 1, delo 1784, fol. 16.

37. Data from church records in Irkutsk State Regional Archive and after Pierce, *Biographical Dictionary,* 115–117.

38. The charters and original contracts (*valovye kontrakty*) for these companies are in the Russian State Historical Archive (RGIA), St. Petersburg, Fond 1374, op. 2, delo 1672: the Northern Company (*Severnaia kompaniia*), fols. 1a–56v; and Predtechenskaia, fols. 1–28v. The same file contains contracts for other forerunners of the Russian-American Company: the Unalashka Company and the Kodiak Company. It is interesting to note that several Aleut men were listed as shareholders, most of them on half-shares like Russian laborers in earlier times, and two toions holding one full share or more. Moreover, the contract for the Kodiak Company includes allocation of half-shares to be offered to men who would switch their employment from the Lebedev-Lastochkin Company to the Kodiak Company.

39. A. I. Andreev, ed., *Russkie otkrytiia* (1944), 71 (doc. 6).

40. Instructions of Shelikhov to K. A. Samoilov, dated 5 May 1786, at Three Saints Bay, Kodiak, ibid., 46–59.

41. Instruction to Samoilov, 5 May 1786, ibid., 49.

42. Instruction, Shelikhov to Samoilov, 4 May 1786, in A. I. Andreev, ed., *Russkie otkrytiia* (1948), 186 (doc. 14); Narochnitskii et al., *Russkie ekspeditsii* (1989), 220 (doc. 69).

43. Shelikhov to Delarov, 30 August 1789, in A. I. Andreev, ed., *Russkie otkrytiia* (1948), 288 (doc. 31); Shelikhov to Baranov, 9 August 1794, in ibid., 344 (doc. 43).

44. Russian State Historical Archive (RGIA), St. Petersburg, Fond 796, op. 74, delo 210, the Diocese of Irkutsk papers.

45. Shelikhov to Delarov, in P. A. Tikhmenev, *Istoricheskoe obozrenie obrazovaniia Rossiisko-Amerikanskoi kompanii i deistvii eiia do nastoiashchago vremeni,* pt. 2 (St. Petersburg: Edvard Veimar, 1863), 23–26 (app.); reprinted in A. I. Andreev, ed., *Russkie otkrytiia* (1948), 288–289 (doc. 31).

46. A. I. Andreev, ed., *Russkie otkrytiia* (1948), 332 (doc. 43).

47. Shelikhov to Baranov, 9 August 1794, ibid., 346 (doc. 43 [44]).

48. See Gideon, *Round the World Voyage,* 74–75, 97–98, 108–109. However, Rezanov in his dispatches falsely claimed to have founded the school.

49. Ianovskii to Main Office, 15 April 1820, No. 62, in Records of the Russian-American Company, Correspondence of the Governors-General, Communications Sent, vol. 2 (reel 26), fol. 17v; Ianovskii to Captain Ushinskii, Port Commander, Okhotsk, 15 April 1820, No. 64, in ibid., fols. 18v–19v.

50. Shelikhov's instructions to Delarov, Irkutsk, 5 May 1787, in A. I. Andreev, ed., *Russkie otkrytiia* (1944), 80 (doc. 8); Letter, Shelikhov to Baranov, 9 August 1794, in Narochnitskii et al., *Russkie ekspeditsii* (1989), 325 (doc. 118).

51. Avdeeva-Polevaia, *Zapiski,* 56.

52. Moore, "Spain Claims Alaska," 69; Olson, *Through Spanish Eyes,* 288–289. De Haro's statement that a priest had his residence at the chapel and that liturgy was conducted daily is in error. No consecrated clergy were present in Alaska at that time and any services must have been conducted by a lay reader, as is done in many Alaskan communities even today.

53. Instruction by Shelikhov to his agent for Kamchatka, Fedor A. Vykhodtsev, in A. I. Andreev, ed., *Russkie otkrytiia* (1944), 59–64 (doc. 4), and idem, *Russkie otkrytiia* (1948), 200–204 (doc. 16); Shelikhov's agreement with Captain Peters, August 1786, in A. I. Andreev, ed., *Russkie otkrytiia* (1948), 199–200 (doc. 15); Shelikhov's official "Note on the manner of trade being considered in Kamchatka with the English," in A. I. Andreev, ed., *Russkie otkrytiia* (1944), 73–77 (doc. 7), and idem, *Russkie otkrytiia* (1948), 214–218 (doc. 19). See also Shelikhov, *A Voyage to America,* 50–51.

54. Shelikhov, *A Voyage to America,* 51–52.

55. Shelikhov to Governor-General Iakobii, 13 April 1787, in A. I. Andreev, ed., *Russkie otkrytiia* (1944), 64–65, and idem, *Russkie otkrytiia* (1948), 205–206; Shelikhov to same, 19 April 1787, in A. I. Andreev, ed., *Russkie otkrytiia* (1944), 66–73, and idem, *Russkie otkrytiia* (1948), 206–214; Shelikhov's "Note on the privileges [requested] for his Company," May–November 1787, in A. I. Andreev, ed., *Russkie otkrytiia* (1944), 81–85, and idem, *Russkie otkrytiia* (1948), 223–226; Report by Iakobii to Empress Catherine, 30 November 1787, and related docs., in A. I. Andreev, ed., *Russkie otkrytiia* (1948), 250–280. For discussion see Okun, *Russian-American Company,* 22–49; and "Note on Shelikhov's voyages in the Eastern Sea," May–Nov 1787, in A. I. Andreev, ed., *Russkie otkrytiia* (1948), 226–249.

56. R. A. Pierce's introduction to Shelikhov, *A Voyage to America,* 19–20. Bolkhovitinov, *Beginnings of Russian-American Relations,* 152–162, 258, 351, 362, 366, 372, contains a useful discussion and references to other analyses of Ledyard's sojourn in Russia. For the text of Shelikhov's account of his conversations with Ledyard, see Narochnitskii et al., *Russkie ekspeditsii* (1989), 246; for an English translation, see Nina N. Bashkina et al., eds., *The United States and Russia: The Beginning of Relations, 1765–1815* (Washington, D.C.: U.S. Government Printing Office, 1980), 232–235. Additional documents pertaining to Ledyard's activity in Russia are found in ibid., 222–223, 225–228, 238–245.

57. Catherine II, April–August 1788, in A. I. Andreev, ed., *Russkie otkrytiia* (1948), 281–282. Her remark on the request for a loan is worth quoting in full: "Two hundred thousand for twenty years, interest free. There never was such a loan even in the time when the Senate freely gave out moneys and installations to volunteers. Having sufficient bond and surety, they can borrow, not from the treasury but from private sources. The proposed loan resembles the proposal of a man who wanted to train an elephant to talk within thirty years. When asked why such a long term, he replied: 'The elephant can die, I can die, or else the person who loaned me money to teach the elephant might die.'"

58. "Bibliography: Editions of G. I. Shelikhov's 'Travels,'" in Shelikhov, *A Voyage to America,* 146–147. The English translation produced by the Limestone Press in 1981 was made from yet another Russian edition, published in 1812. In that translation, "variations from Shelikhov's original report of 1787, and the 1793 edition" are indicated in brackets (editor's note in ibid., vi).

59. In the literature, the latter settlement is identified as that of St. Nicholas on the Kenai River (S. G. Fedorova, *Russkoe naselenie,* 113). In 1993, I was able to establish that this identification is not correct. According to the log by Izmailov, skippering the vessel *Sv. Simeon i Anna* for the year 1793, a Baranov artel was operating on the Kenai Peninsula twenty verst from the St. Nicholas Bay or Harbor (*Nikolaevskaia bukhta*) that Izmailov located and explored (and named) on 9 May 1793. Apparently, this Shelikhov artel was shifted to Nikolaevskaia subsequent to that date.

60. See Archibald Menzies, *The Alaska Travel Journal of Archibald Menzies, 1793–1794,* ed. Wallace M. Olson, with list of botanical collections by John F. Thilenius (Fairbanks: University of Alaska Press, 1993), and George Vancouver, *A Voyage of Discovery to the North Pacific Ocean and Around the World,* in 3 vols., and charts (New York: DaCapo Press, 1967; originally printed in London for G. G. and J. Robinson, 1798).

61. In Izmailov's log for 1794, kept in the Russian State Naval Archive, the Native name of the island where Lebedev-Lastochkin men had an outpost is given. Unfortunately, we were still unable to identify the island. See also Olson, *Through Spanish Eyes,* 254–255.

62. James W. VanStone, ed., *Russian Exploration in Southwest Alaska: The Travel Journals of Petr Korsakovskiy (1818) and Ivan Ya. Vasilev (1829),* trans. David H. Kraus (Fairbanks: University of Alaska Press, 1988), 5–7; Berkh, *Chronological History,* 71–72. Berkh interviewed Ivanov himself and stated that the group led by Ivanov traveled over five hundred verst into Alaska's interior and reached a river several verst in width. More than forty villages were reported on this river.

63. Russian State Historical Archive (RGIA), Fond 1374, op. 2, delo 1672, fol. 20.

FIGURE 24. Aleksandr A. Baranov. Portrait by Mikhail Tikhanov, 1818.
Courtesy Richard A. Pierce.

Chapter Seven

Baranov Arrives

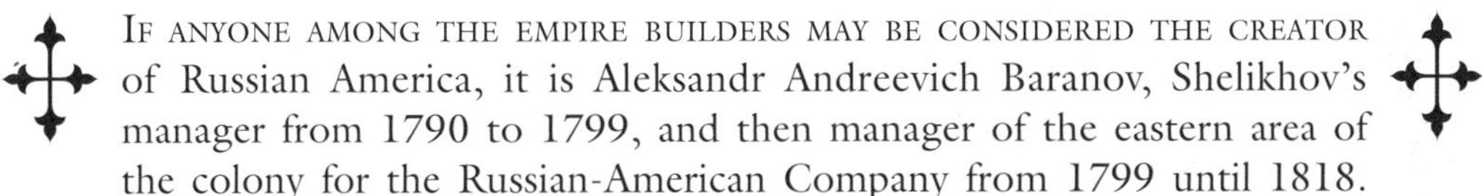

If anyone among the empire builders may be considered the creator of Russian America, it is Aleksandr Andreevich Baranov, Shelikhov's manager from 1790 to 1799, and then manager of the eastern area of the colony for the Russian-American Company from 1799 until 1818.

Baranov, born in 1746 in the provincial town of Kargopol' in the Russian north, was an exceptionally able man. In spite of his lack of formal education, he gained entry into the mercantile circles of St. Petersburg and Moscow. His commercial interests were diverse. He moved to Irkutsk shortly before, or in, 1780, when he became manager of a glass factory for the merchants Vasilii Sitnikov and Aleksei Polevoi, partner of Golikov and later of Shelikhov. Soon, in partnership with Laksman (Sr.), Baranov established another glass factory (which for a time produced mainly glass beads for the native trade), founded a distillery, engaged in tax farming,[1] and with his brother Petr as a partner opened a large trading post on the Anadyr' River primarily for trade with the Chukchi. He also had an office and business interests in Yakutsk. For his part in developing the glass industry in Siberia he was elected, in 1787, to the Free Economic Society. Then, about 1790, Baranov met with severe business reverses. He suffered significant losses when, about that time, Chukchi destroyed his trading post on the Anadyr' River. His family life, too, was disappointing. His wife, Matrona, bore him no sons. His adopted son, Apollonii, was a foundling, left on the doorstep of Baranov's house in Irkutsk in 1787, and so was one of his two daughters. Matrona was godmother to Apollonii.[2] Leaving his brother to wind up their affairs in Siberia, Baranov was preparing to return to his home in Kargopol'. But events took a different turn. Shelikhov asked Baranov to go to Alaska to develop Shelikhov's enterprises there.

It is not known with certainty when Shelikhov made Baranov's acquaintance. There is some evidence that Baranov was one of the Irkutsk merchants who had helped finance Shelikhov's early ventures. Apparently Shelikhov had approached Baranov about Alaska at least twice before, but Baranov had declined the offers. This time, when Baranov's affairs were on a downswing, Shelikhov was offering excellent terms, and the two men signed a detailed contract on 15 August 1790.[3] Presumably Shelikhov, having assessed Baranov's character, chose him to manage affairs in Alaska because he needed a strong man there; Samoilov, who came to Kodiak with Shelikhov in 1784, had proven to be, in his opinion, somewhat soft, and Delarov, who had replaced Samoilov in 1787, had bought

Figure 25. Ivan Kuskov, the founder of the Russian outpost in California.
Courtesy S. G. Fedorova.

into the company and wanted to participate in the business in Irkutsk. Though he had started as an ordinary sailor-laborer aboard fur-procuring vessels in the Aleutian trade, Delarov had become rich enough eventually to register as a Moscow merchant.[4]

According to the contract, Baranov received the title of chief manager, 210 shares in the company, and many additional benefits. In many aspects, for a private contract, this one was a most remarkable document. Some of its provisions, no doubt, were open to government challenge.[5] Baranov would be accountable only to Shelikhov. Article five of the contract specified that he would have absolute discretion in managing Shelikhov's interests in Alaska, subject only to appropriate government regulations, with the caveat that "if the local circumstances prevented [following the governmental regulations] or if the best interests of the company and fatherland were served otherwise, I am not prevented from taking action which I deem fit." In addition, all trade with any foreign nationals, Europeans and Americans, was to be conducted only through Baranov. Article eight contained a provision explicitly authorizing Baranov to expand the territory under his sway and found new colonies. One of the articles stated that Baranov was authorized to select and employ two assistants at his own cost and discretion. One of them was to be selected from among those already on Kodiak or, if he could not find anyone answering his requirements, he was authorized to hire these assistants in Russia. He hired Ivan Kuskov (1765–1823), a burgher of Tot'ma who had fallen on hard times. Kuskov was to remain his chief lieutenant to the end of Baranov's career. An intelligent and able man, in many capacities indispensable to his employer, he was apparently in charge of impressment of the Natives into the labor force in the early years.[6] Baranov's other choice is not known. After 1802, however, he was assisted by Banner, formerly a land and serf owner[7] and mining engineer, later a police chief (*ispravnik*) at Zashiversk, a northern settlement and market town on the Indigirka River.[8]

Other terms of Baranov's contract committed Shelikhov to maintain Baranov's membership in the Irkutsk Merchant Guild and to pay his annual dues to that organization. If Shelikhov incurred any expenses in dealing with authorities on Baranov's behalf, Baranov's agents in various cities or his brother Petr, representing his interests in Yakutsk, were to be presented with the charges. Baranov was to be paid on his 210 shares and the extras not in furs, but in money, after the catch was sold. The term of Baranov's service was unlimited, but he had a right to resign at will, the only stipulation being that should he wish to leave America, he was to give Shelikhov ample notice.

Baranov made financial provisions for his family for the duration of his employment and also in case of his death. One article in the contract specified that his wife and their two daughters would be sent to Kargopol' at Shelikhov's expense. Baranov's adopted son Apollonii was put under the care of Baranov's brother Petr, his partner in the Chukchi trade, and remained in Irkutsk. The contract was duly registered at the proper governmental office two days later, 17 August 1790. Baranov and his wife separated at that time, never to be reunited.

There have been speculations that the marriage partners were estranged, chiefly because soon after his arrival in Alaska Baranov established a liaison with a Kodiak Islander, Anna Grigor'ivna Razkazchikov.[9] But Baranov seems to have been a womanizer, as he was earlier in Irkutsk. In Alaska he admitted to having enjoyed favors of women other than Anna Grigor'evna (out of political necessity, he claimed, such as cementing ties with the Chugach). The relationship, however, became a lasting one, though he accused Anna of being unfaithful (saying in the same breath that he supposed she felt justified in light of his own occasional lapses).[10] It is claimed that out of jealousy he subjected a young man accused of being Anna's lover, an Aleut who had been educated at Shelikhov's school, to running the gauntlet and to ultimate humiliation by ordering his head and eyebrows shaved and his exposure in a public place, his parka split open from head to toe. Then he sent the young man away to an outlying artel where he "works for one recompense: the lash."[11] After Baranov's first wife died in 1806, Anna became his legal wife.[12]

Baranov was sailing for Alaska at a time when the international situation in the North Pacific was tense. The waters claimed by Russia were being penetrated by foreign merchantmen in ever-increasing numbers.[13] In 1786 alone at least seven, but possibly as many as nine, British vessels had been reported along the Northwest Coast, and by 1788 possibly as many as three American vessels entered the trade.[14] Six of the British vessels reported on the coast in 1786 were in Prince William Sound and at least two of these traded in Cook Inlet. Some of them were observed off Kodiak and may have shelled one or two coastal villages on that island's western (Pacific) coast.[15]

British merchantmen sailed in pairs. Two of the vessels entering Russian American territory in 1786, the *Captain Cook* (under Captain Laurie) and the *Experiment*, belonged to a company formed in India by James Strange. They sailed out of Bombay to Nootka (Vancouver Island) and then ascended the coast, making landfalls in the Queen Charlotte Islands, elsewhere in Haida territory, and in Tlingit territory before anchoring in Prince William Sound. Strange considered himself to be acting not only in a private capacity but also as representing the interests of the British Crown. He engaged in symbolic acts, burying in the ground evidence of British presence on what are now the British Columbian and Alaskan coasts, and formally took possession of the territory for England. He later argued for the immediate founding of British settlements on the Northwest Coast. Also, having read the recently published book by Coxe about Russian discoveries in the North Pacific, he dispatched his larger vessel, the *Captain Cook*, westward along the Aleutian Chain to explore and possibly take possession of the purportedly rich copper deposits on Mednoi Island. Due to the stormy weather that late in the season, Captain Laurie was not able to complete the mission and turned toward China, meeting his consort at Macao early in 1787.

Two other British vessels, the *King George* and the *Queen Charlotte*, belonging to the company founded by Richard C. Etches and commanded by Captains Portlock and Dixon, respectively, sailed from England around Cape Horn. They entered Cook Inlet in 1786 (Portlock is credited with the discovery of coal deposits in outer Cook Inlet).

There they encountered Russians, apparently Shelikhov's men who were in the process of establishing an outpost to be known as Aleksandrovskoe (present English Bay). From there they moved to Prince William Sound, then down the coast to the Alexander Archipelago and then to Hawaii. They returned to Prince William Sound in 1787. The third pair, the vessels *Nootka* and *Sea Otter*, owned by a company organized by John Meares, sailed out of Madras, India, under the overall command of Meares. They sailed separately by different routes along the coast of Japan and then along the Aleutian Chain eastward, to meet in Prince William Sound. Meares, in the *Nootka*, stood off Atka by 5 August 1786, and was at Unalaska within a few days, having passed Amukhta and the Islands of Four Mountains, where he observed Aleut collective whaling. Leaving Unalaska on 27 August, he sailed for the Shumagin Islands, where, to his dismay, he learned that the Russians were established on Kodiak. Meares had believed that Russia had not advanced past the islands nearest Unalaska. He sailed to Cook Inlet and found that British vessels were there before him (those were the vessels under Portlock and Dixon). Meares then went on to Prince William Sound where he decided to wait for the *Sea Otter*, Lt. William Tipping commanding, and then to winter there. During the winter he lost twenty-three men to scurvy. In May 1787, he was visited by Captain Dixon of the rival Etches Company. Both of this company's vessels were in Prince William Sound, Portlock having established himself off Montague Island. Meares left Prince William Sound on 21 June 1787, and soon thereafter Portlock and Dixon also sailed away. Tipping never arrived to link up with Meares.

Tipping had been in Prince William Sound earlier, in the summer of 1786, where he met with Strange. On the evening of 6 September his vessel was observed by a lookout from a high mountain in Prince William Sound, heading for Cook Inlet. Strange believed

FIGURE 26. The *King George* at anchor in 1786 at modern English Bay, Kenai Peninsula, where coal was discovered.

From Portlock, 1789, facing p. 108. Courtesy University of Alaska Fairbanks, Rasmuson Library, Alaska and Polar Regions Department, Rare Book Collection, no. B0092.

that Tipping was sailing there to avoid competition in trading with the Natives. The vessel was never seen again. Russian records and Dena'ina (Tanaina Athabaskan or Kenaitsy) traditions indicate that it was taken by the Dena'ina of Cook Inlet. At the time Russians heard that a British vessel was captured. The Dena'ina traditions say that long ago their ancestors captured a foreign vessel, some say by magical means.[16]

As Baranov was preparing to leave for Alaska aboard the trusty *Three Saints*, this time commanded by Bocharov, he received several instructions from I. G. Kohl, the port commander at Okhotsk, acting for Governor-General Pil' of Siberia. One of these instructions stated that navigator Bocharov had reported the presence of foreign vessels, and that one vessel had been taken by the Natives. Reportedly, there were two Englishmen still alive and kept prisoner among the Kenaitsy. Baranov was to make every effort to ransom any survivors and send them to Okhotsk.

It appears that the Russian government became aware of this concerted British effort in short order, because when Evstrat Delarov sailed to Alaska in 1787, he was issued a number of official Russian imperial possession plates and crests and received orders to have them placed along the Northwest Coast.[17] The next year, 1788, Izmailov and Bocharov were dispatched out of Kodiak to explore the coast from Prince William Sound southeastward. On this voyage Russian possession plates and crests were placed at various points. One of these crests was seen by the Malaspina expedition (1791–1792) and sketched by an artist. By 1794, the crest placed at Yakutat, after the death of the chief to whom it was given, had been sold to the Chilkat Tlingit.[18] Another found its way through Native trade networks to the Columbia River area. In 1934, it was found by archaeologists in an Indian grave.[19]

When sailing for Alaska, Baranov also received an instruction that dealt with placing in the American territory claimed by Russia the five numbered possession plates and crests he had been issued. The crests were to be displayed, the plates buried, and Russian territorial rights enforced. This instruction supplemented the one issued earlier to Delarov, of which all provisions remained in force. Yet another instruction, dated 16 August 1790, dealt with the English brig *Mercury*, a privateer under the Swedish flag. It reflected the growing concern on the part of the governor-general with the situation in the North Pacific, now aggravated by the war between Russia and Sweden. On 25 February 1790, the governor reported that Billings, who was ordered to intercept foreign privateers on behalf of Russia, was in the field, and that by the governor's order all merchant vessels sailing in the season of 1790 would carry arms, including as many cannon as could be provided.[20] It was anticipated that the *Mercury*'s Captain Cox would attack Petropavlovsk-on-Kamchatskii, the Kuril Islands, and Japanese settlements, as well as Russian outposts in the Aleutians, particularly Unalaska. Reportedly, the *Mercury* sailed from Tenerife, with stopovers in Canton and

Figure 27. **Russian possession plate.**
Courtesy Richard A. Pierce.

Hawaii. Should Baranov encounter this vessel en route to Alaska, he was to "open fire with muskets and rifles, if distance permits" but to seek safety before everything else, as the *Mercury* was heavily armed, carrying fourteen cannon, and her large crew consisted of handpicked English sailors and additional recruits from Hawaii. Baranov was warned not to be deceived by the flag a vessel might display.[21]

Thus, from the outset of his career in Alaska, Baranov had to deal in some ways on behalf of the Russian government with foreign shipping and foreign nationals and also had to concern himself with safeguarding Russian sovereignty. He was to use this circumstance to the utmost in later dealings with his main competitors, the Lebedev-Lastochkin men.

Another problem from Shelikhov's standpoint, of which Baranov had to be aware, was that the Russian naval expedition led by Joseph Billings, Gavriil Sarychev, and Roman Gall (Robert Hall) was in Alaska that very same year under instructions to investigate Shelikhov's conduct on Kodiak and general charges of brutal and unjust treatment of the Aleuts, leveled by Sergeant Britiukov to Billings himself 2 November 1788.[22] The naval expedition was also to investigate the unauthorized collection of the iasak, which had been abolished by Empress Catherine, the orders to that effect having been repeated several times at various dates, and to conduct a census of Native populations which would enable the government to level iasak payments in the future according to law.[23] The naval commission's eventual reports were far from favorable to Shelikhov's men, though Baranov himself, arriving on Kodiak only in 1791, was not personally involved. It is quite probable that, had Catherine lived longer, Shelikhov's company's activities in America might have had a different end, in spite of the support and protection by Siberian officials, including three successive governors-general.

As far as Shelikhov was concerned, Baranov was above all to safeguard his company's interests. Initially, he was to be in full charge of all business on Kodiak and the Alaska mainland and to expand the company's activities north and southeast: Shelikhov, in letters to Baranov, freely shared his expansionist plans, including another attempt to establish himself in the Kuril Islands. Baranov was to establish an accounting system and would be responsible for the bookkeeping and for keeping up the labor force at 192 men (the original number recruited by Shelikhov for the voyage of 1783–1786); he also was to conduct a census, enhance and extend the company's control on the American mainland, develop settlements, and insure good returns on the investments. In general, Shelikhov's demands and grandiose instructions were such that at one point Baranov complained that Shelikhov was treating him like a serf, not a manager, and charged that he was breaking their agreement. His response—more than once—was to threaten to resign.

It is necessary at this point to digress somewhat and discuss the impact of Shelikhov's labor policies as implemented by Baranov on the coastal peoples of southwestern Alaska. The concern with the Natives implicit in Baranov's instructions had little to do with their hostility. Instead, it reflected the intention to use the Native population as a labor base, and to incorporate it as a whole into the political and economic system Shelikhov sought to establish. In fact, immediately after his return from Alaska in 1787, Shelikhov had requested governmental permission to use Natives as laborers. Governor-General Iakobii granted such permission "provided that every one of them is paid fair wages for his work.... Paying fair wages for their work will benefit the company and enable you to inspire in them a will to be subjects under the Russian scepter."[24]

The labor question was becoming acute, in part because of the great social changes within Russian society, especially the deterioration of the status of the peasantry. In the reign of Catherine the Great, most of the Central Russian and Ukrainian peasantry became serfs. The gentry, a status and social class conceived by Peter the Great to be acquired by achievement through obligatory service to the state, had become for the most part instead a land- and serf-owning hereditary, though minor, nobility through grants by the Crown of titles and lands (with the people who were bound to that land). There was no more mass "voting with the feet," and recruitment for Alaska became more difficult. There were now very few Russian northerners, skilled seafarers, and experienced shipwrights among those who hired themselves out, nor were there many skilled fur hunters and trappers. Thus, Russian laborers were employed as skilled craftsmen, crew chiefs, lower-level administrators, and supervisors (some of them, new to the enterprise, learning on the job). In fact, at the time of Baranov's arrival on Kodiak, there were in his command "about 150 men, peasants and burghers of various provinces."[25] Shelikhov, and later his heirs, with governmental cooperation, hired navigators and ships' commanders who were serving in the navy and a few Old Voyagers like Izmailov, Bocharov, and Pribylov who were near retirement. As far as skilled hunters and fur processors were concerned, they saw that the best source of this kind of labor was the Native population. Writing to Delarov on 30 August 1787, Shelikhov said: "[U]pon receiving this letter, send 25 Russians up north, with them 104 Americans who[m] you will have to hire to hunt sea otters, fur seals, foxes, whales, and walrus tusks."[26]

This was the labor-shortage situation the new company manager found in Alaska. Thus, soon after his arrival Baranov instituted large-scale recruitment of Native laborers. Each Native settlement under his control had to provide "several persons of both genders" as laborers. This class of laborers was designated kaiury (a term used in Kamchatka to designate hired dog-team drivers). Their numbers were augmented by former slaves of the Aleuts, war captives, and their descendants, who were thus technically liberated. These practices, which violated the orders issued by the government especially in regard to fair payment for labor,[27] were stopped immediately upon Baranov's removal in 1818 and from then on Aleuts who had, in Russian terms, the status of free peasants were hired for wages, the terms of their employment strictly regulated. Men were paid from 100 to 180 rubles per year and more, depending on their position; the women earned from 60 to 120 rubles per year, a wage not far behind what the Russian rank and file received.[28]

As the government adamantly refused to supply troops for the colony, there was also need for additional manpower for defense purposes. It was taken for granted that Natives could be used in this capacity also. Precedents existed for this practice: at some point in the late 1770s some skippers began to recruit Aleuts, allegedly volunteers, not only as laborers or hunters of sea mammals, but also to augment the available defense force. Native tradition has preserved accounts of conflicts between Unangan (Aleuts) of the Aleutian Chain, coming to Kodiak aboard the Russian vessels, and the Alutiit of Kodiak Island. In the early 1780s, Aleuts participated in a conflict (which apparently ended in a trade agreement) between the crews of two Russian vessels and the Alutiit of the eastern Alaska Peninsula, a conflict in which a major role was allegedly played by Aleuts and in which an Aleut chief from Akun Island was captured by Alutiit and put to death.[29] In Baranov's time the impressed Native sea hunters, like the Russian laborers, were warriors on demand.

These practices carried a heavy social cost. In the late 1780s and into the 1790s, Shelikhov's skippers were the worst offenders, dislocating large numbers of people with very grave results to their home settlements. This draining away of young, able-bodied people, especially the males, left the home villages defenseless and without means of subsistence, as only old men, women, and young children remained. Hunger and hardship were a frequent result.[30] This practice in the last two decades of the eighteenth century must be considered one of the most disruptive factors affecting the population of the Aleutian archipelago, perhaps much more so than introduced or epidemic diseases: no epidemics were reported until after the turn of that century.

The question of how deleterious the Russian presence in Alaska was to the Natives is muddled by uncertainty about what their population actually was. The population numbers prior to contact and the scale of the diminution of the Alaskan population soon after contact as cited in current literature are based on various items of second-hand testimony or late-nineteenth-century projections, actually guesses, which remain in dispute. Recently, some primary documentation has come to light. The first official census of the Aleut population in the central and eastern Aleutians was conducted in 1791–1792 by members of the Billings-Sarychev expedition in connection with the investigation of iasak collection practices. Consequently, only able-bodied males, the hunters, were listed. As the expedition chaplain, Vasilii Sivtsov, baptized and chrizmated (a rite akin to being confirmed in the faith) a large number of persons in the Unalaska area, some of these Christians were omitted from the rolls (following an old practice in Siberia of exempting newly baptized, indigenous males from taxes for three years; the admiralty instruction directed the commission to establish a basis for regularizing iasak collection should the government decide to reinstitute it). The western Aleutians, Near and Rat Islands, Shumagin Islands, and men on various Russian merchant vessels, on Kodiak, and in the Pribilof Islands were not counted. Thus, the census is incomplete, even for the adult male population, but nevertheless it provides a basis for a reasonable estimate and demonstrates that at the end of the eighteenth century the archipelago population was substantial. This census lists, for the eastern Aleutians, from the Alaska Peninsula to the island of Samalga, west of Umnak, forty-four villages, with 950 able-bodied males. This permits us to estimate the population range roughly from 3,800 to 4,750 persons for the eastern Aleutians alone. On the seven islands in the central Aleutians for which the rather sketchy census data were given there are listed thirteen villages with 249 able-bodied males, resulting in an estimated population range for these islands of 996 to 1,245, or a total population for the census area of 4,796 to 5,995 persons.[31]

En route to Kodiak, Baranov was delayed at Unalaska until 1791 because of shipwreck in Kashega harbor. In accordance with Shelikhov's instructions, he attempted a census of able-bodied males on Unalaska, Umnak, and Krenitzin Islands. His data are very sketchy and far less reliable than data compiled in the same year by the naval commission and those published in synoptic form in 1802 by Sarychev. Sarychev lists in his published work for the same area forty villages and 916 able-bodied males, apparently excluding young hunters considered minors by Russian standards. Sarychev's figures give a top estimate of more than 4,500 persons. Baranov gives a total of twenty-six villages and 583 able-bodied males, permitting an estimate of the population for this limited area of 2,332 to 2,915.

After analyzing population data reported in the earliest Russian sources, including reports on iasak collection, Russian ethnographer Roza G. Liapunova concluded that at the time of contact the population of the entire Aleutian archipelago, from Attu to the Shumagins, numbered at maximum an estimated 7,500 to 9,500 persons.[32] If one takes into account that a significant number of able-bodied males were absent at the time of the census, either on board various vessels or transported to the Pribilofs, Kodiak, or Cook Inlet, and that the Shumagin Islands were not covered, the estimate must be somewhat increased. It appears then that the population indeed had decreased (if we take the range suggested by Liapunova to be correct) in the first half-century when the independent promyshlenniki reigned supreme, but not to the extent usually postulated in the literature. Moreover, some of this drop was due to out-migration. A more drastic drop must be attributed to a later time, with a considerable decrease taking place during the Baranov era. This result emerges from comparison of the 1791–1792 figures for the eastern Aleutians of from close to 5,000 to almost 6,000 persons (not counting the Shumagins and the absentees) to those given by Fedor Burenin as of 1 January 1806 of 1,898 adults of both genders; by Ivan Kriukov for 1 May 1813, counting adults and minors of both sexes and those transported to Kodiak and the Pribilofs in 1810, of 1,508 total; by Captain Vasil'iev for 1821, which lists twenty-eight settlements in the eastern Aleutians including one on Unga and two on the Alaska Peninsula not listed in previous data (cf. above, forty-four villages in 1791–1792), with a population of 1,700 (both genders, age breakdown not given); and Veniaminov in 1834 of slightly over 2,000 persons for the eastern and central Aleutians combined.[33]

For the eastern and central Aleutians, in the years 1806–1807 an epidemic was reported of hacking cough, chest pains, and bloody flux, from which many people died. Khlebnikov calculated that losses were 390 "souls of both genders and all ages."[34]

By 1821, the situation was so serious, and several villages became so small, that Vasil'iev organized a transfer of population from three villages on Umnak Island and one on Samalga to Recheshnoe (modern Nikolski, Umnak Island), and of one village from the Bering Sea shore of the Alaska Peninsula to the settlement on Unga in the Shumagin Islands.

For the Kodiak area the picture is similar and the data are less controversial. Shelikhov reported in the 1790s fantastic precontact figures of 50,000 or 40,000, which are discounted by specialists. It is generally assumed that Shelikhov gave these grossly exaggerated figures in order to enhance his accomplishments before the officials of the imperial government. Modern scholars postulate the Kodiak archipelago population to have been in the vicinity of 10,000 or somewhat lower.[35] When Baranov conducted the first census in 1792, immediately after his arrival, he found 6,510 Alutiiq persons inhabiting the Kodiak archipelago and the eastern Alaska Peninsula. The additional figures given for Prince William Sound (423 persons of both sexes) represent three principal Chugach villages. It is not clear if the figures given for Cook Inlet (176 persons of both sexes) refer to the local Chugach settlements, or represent a portion of the coastal Athabaskans, or show the numbers of Kodiak Alutiit sent off by Baranov to these areas. The total population of the settlements Baranov could reach numbered, by the census, 7,109.

According to Natalia Shelikhov, another census of the mainland population in Cook Inlet and Prince William Sound was conducted in 1793 and 1794. A second census on Kodiak, in 1796, recorded a total of 7,093 persons. These data are close to (though somewhat at odds with) the data for the years from 1795 to the end of 1807 collected or copied by Gedeon (on Kodiak 1804–1807). Gedeon listed thirty-six (possibly thirty-seven) settlements in the Kodiak archipelago with a population of 6,418 in 1795 and 4,850 in 1804 (both genders counted, no breakdown by age given). Gedeon's note appended to his census data challenged the "50,000 souls" figure given by Shelikhov for the 1780s in the published account of 1793. Gedeon suggested that this figure perhaps was meant to indicate indigenous populations in all areas where the Russian fur merchants were trading.[36] In 1817, when Baranov was about to be relieved of his duties, a new census was conducted under the supervision of naval officers. The population of the Kodiak, eastern Alaska Peninsula, Cook Inlet, and Prince William Sound villages together then reportedly numbered 6,642 persons.

Khlebnikov, serving in Russian America from 1817 until the end of 1832, calculated that between the years 1792 and 1817 Kodiak alone lost 2,412 "souls." He pointed out, however, that this number included 217 people, 179 men and 38 women, who were resettled in Sitka.[37]

The Russian intrusion affected not only the population numbers; the gender balance, too, was disturbed. Early Russian reports indicate that in all Aleutian archipelago villages (and on Kodiak also) women outnumbered men. But the Baranov census of 1792 for Kodiak, and all subsequent ones except for the census of 1806 indicate that men outnumbered women. There is no documentary evidence that permits us to explain such a change in gender figures. Based on supposition and circumstantial evidence, the taking of women as wives, concubines, and laborers, and higher mortality from the introduced stressful conditions may be a partial explanation.

Another complicating factor was the shifting of large numbers of people from one ethnic area to another. The practice, begun by the independent skippers in the late 1770s, was recognized by the imperial government as insidious and detrimental to the Aleuts and was expressly forbidden by an order issued to all skippers and foremen by the Okhotsk Port Commander G. K. Ugrenin on 15 June 1787. On the same date Ugrenin sent a manifesto addressed to the Aleut people and their leaders informing them of their rights, specifically of their right to remain in their settlements unmolested.[38] Nevertheless, the practice of relocation was widely used by Shelikhov, begun systematically under his orders of 1786. Gedeon claimed that in 1786 Shelikhov brought seventy families to Kodiak from the eastern Aleutians.[39] During the Baranov era, the number of Aleuts resettled elsewhere grew. Eastern Aleuts and Kodiak Islanders suffered the most, when large groups came from Unalaska and the Shumagins to Kodiak, from Kodiak to the Alaska Peninsula (notably at the outpost at Katmai, which had been established by Baranov soon after his arrival in the colony), to the Chugach area and eventually into Tlingit territory.

The settling of the Pribilof Islands was very important. Uninhabited at the time the Russians located them, though known to the Aleuts as Amiq, these islands are a major breeding ground of the northern fur seal. The Russians, acquainted with the species' migratory patterns since 1741 in the Commander Islands, knew of the seasonal movements of fur seal herds from the Pacific to the Bering Sea by way of the eastern Aleutians and searched for the rookeries or the breeding grounds. They probably located them in the 1770s, to judge by the enormous fur seal catches brought in by some vessels, but the first official report was rendered by Gavriil Pribylov, a naval navigator seconded to the Lebedev-Lastochkin Company, who in 1789 joined the Billings expedition. His vessel, the *Sv. Georgii Pobedonosets* (St. George the Victorious), sailed in the eastern Aleutians 1781–1789. In 1786, Pribylov found the smaller island, which he named St. George for his vessel, and left a crew there. In 1787, on a clear day, another island was observed from St. George and reached by members of this crew in a skin boat. This larger island was named for the Sts. Peter and Paul whose feast the promyshlenniki were celebrating that day (modern St. Paul Island and city). The government became aware of this valuable island group only in 1789. By 1790, Shelikhov was making every effort to establish firm control of this area, which provided a lucrative fur catch and which he considered also a springboard for expansion northward along the American coast of the Bering Sea.[40] That year he was already dispatching his men, and a large number of Aleuts, to the Pribilofs.

In 1794, Shelikhov ordered that the artel operating on Unalaska (under foreman Kochutin) be united with the Predtechenskaia Company, which operated out of Atka and which had a large crew on St. George in the Pribilofs under Ivan Fomich Popov, merging them to form the Northern Company (also known in the literature as the Severo-Amerikanskaia, that is, the North American Company). Shelikhov wanted to station at least 140 men on both islands. (It was at this time that Shelikhov attempted to name the islands for his patron, Platon Zubov, but the name was later changed by Chief Manager Murav'iev, seconded by the navy for service with the Russian-American Company 1820–1825, in honor of navigator Pribylov.)

The activity of this new company was to be headed by Vasilii Petrovich Merkul'iev, a burgher of Tomsk, assisted by Popov. Merkul'iev was a trusted Shelikhov employee who in 1786 was left in charge of the stores on Kodiak (and was accused by the Russian laborers of shortchanging them when settling their accounts).[41] He may have been a brother or son of Petr Merkul'iev, also a trusted and literate employee, who came to Alaska with Shelikhov in 1783–1784. In 1799, Merkul'iev became the first manager of the Pribilof Islands operation for the new Russian-American Company. That year he was sailing a baidara from St. George to St. Paul, with a large group of men, when they were carried by a storm to the Alaska mainland. Trying to land, they encountered hostile Yup'ik (Central Alaska Eskimo) warriors. After a brief encounter, in which the intruders were bested, Merkul'iev was forced to sail on, seeking shelter elsewhere.[42] He had married an Aleut woman, possibly from Umnak Island. She was baptized by lay baptism in 1786, Natalia Shelikhov standing as the godmother, and was named Ekaterina. The marriage was solemnized by Priest Vasilii Sivtsov, chaplain to the Billings-Sarychev expedition, on 5 July 1790, at a Kodiak settlement called Shettaq (or Sheshtaq), near Three Saints Bay. At the same time, their two sons, Dmitrii and Iakov, aged two and four years, also baptized by laymen, were chrizmated.[43] Vasilii Merkul'iev died in 1828 in the Aleutians when the baidara in which he traveled was caught in a riptide in the strait separating Akutan Island from Unalaska.

The Russian-American Company's main base was to be the Pribilofs, and from that base their sphere of operations was to expand northward toward Bering Strait and the Chukchi Peninsula. Here, the two foremen were to organize trade and establish an annual trading rendezvous. At first, the two foremen were independent of Baranov. Later, after 1797, they would be subordinated to a major shareholder, Emel'ian Larionov, assigned to manage the newly created Unalaska District of the reorganized Shelikhov enterprise, the United American Company.

In 1790, the skipper of one of Shelikhov's vessels, Daniil Ivanovich Shirokii, took fifty men and thirty women from Unalaska to St. Paul Island in the Pribilofs. They were to strengthen the Aleut contingent from Atka under Popov. Aleuts today claim that the speech of St. George islanders differs from the Unalaskan dialect spoken on St. Paul and is closer to the Atkan Aleut speech. Merkul'iev (whose surname today is the name of several prominent Aleut families on both St. George and St. Paul Islands) was to bring reinforcements to the Pribilofs, a minimum of seventy men, most of them Aleuts from Unalaska and adjacent islands, notably Umnak.[44] In 1810, an additional 200 souls (men, women, and children) were brought from the eastern Aleutians to the Pribilof Islands, while the number of Russian laborers was reduced to a minimum. In subsequent years only one or two Russians resided in the islands. The Pribilofs became home to a large number of Aleuts, and have remained so for more than 200 years. Today the two Pribilof Islands communities are the largest and most viable Aleut settlements.

Aleuts were used by other skippers not only as laborers. Some acted as foremen and were shareholders, but the majority were employed as expert hunters of sea otters for some time before Shelikhov established himself on Kodiak. This practice, too, was continued. By 1786, some Kodiak Islanders were so employed, as reported by Captains Portlock and Dixon, who observed while in Cook Inlet that most of the fur take of the Russians was obtained by Aleut hunters rather than through trade with the local peoples. In Baranov's time this practice grew out of all proportion. Large baidarka (Aleut kayak) fleets were dispatched along the coast, in later years as far as California, and even as far as Baja California for salt. The dispatch of the large kayak parties was initiated by Baranov in 1792–1794. The first party, commanded by Egor Purtov, traveled to Yakutat Bay where Purtov had hunted in 1792 with a fleet of 170 kayaks, the first "experiment in hunting beyond Cape St. Elias."[45] The experiment was repeated in 1794 when Purtov took his kayaks well beyond Yakutat. Soon thereafter, much larger parties were being dispatched farther afield. One party consisted of 500 kayaks, presumably two-hatch—that is, 1,000 men. Parties hunting closer to home were smaller; they numbered from 100 to 200 kayaks. The largest total that could be mustered is stated to have been 700 kayaks, engaging up to 1,400 men, not counting support personnel who may have traveled in the large skin boats.[46] The pressure on the available manpower, especially the Kodiak Islanders, was enormous.

As Baranov expanded his operations along the Northwest Coast, his demands grew for both hunters and warriors (to check the Tlingit). By 1804, Kodiak could not provide the number of men he needed. Aleuts from the Unalaska area were once again impressed for resettlement. By 1807, ninety kayaks were brought over. Khlebnikov believed these were single-hatch kayaks and, therefore, estimates the total number to have been about 150 souls, as he assumed that families were brought along. Using the demographic rule of thumb of four to five dependents for each adult male, the figure should be from 360 to 450 persons, provided families were moved. If the kayaks were double-hatches, it is probable that 180 men were relocated. Relocation of a large number of dependents is not reflected in the available evidence. It is much more likely that only a small number of dependents accompanied the relocated men. The disruption in family and village life must have been devastating.

Another factor in population reduction in the Baranov era is the heavy losses suffered by these expeditionary parties from accidents and in hostile encounters with the Tlingit.

It must be kept in mind that when Baranov expanded operations to the continent, into the Chugach region, and then into the Tlingit area, the Aleuts, mainly men from Kodiak, constituted the bulk of his fighting force.[47] Khlebnikov[48] provided a list of casualties from 1792–1805 and Gedeon[49] provided additional though sketchy data. According to these sources, in seven years 195 Aleut men were killed or captured in battles with the Tlingit, 280 or 290 drowned, with an additional 100 drowning in baidara accidents during stormy weather at Kodiak, and, according to Gedeon, 64 drowned in 1800 off Tugidok Island. In addition, in 1799, 135 to 140 men died near Sitka from shellfish poisoning and an additional number (the highest figure given by Gedeon at 40) died of illness en route. The total number of able-bodied men lost was likely at least 751 (Khlebnikov data) or well over 800 (if one incorporates additional data from Gedeon).[50] This represents a loss of ten percent of the total population reported for Kodiak by Baranov's census of 1792 and a third of the male population. The social dislocation can hardly be imagined.

The methods to secure the Aleut labor employed in Baranov's time, described in detail by Hieromonk Gedeon, were brutal. The term *impressment* describes it best. Baranov, apparently, had some pretensions to establishing a quasi-military order and used methods current at that time in all the European navies and in the Russian army: the lash and running the gauntlet (where, instead of rods, he used baleen staves).[51]

The lash was also used to punish transgressions by Russian laborers against company policies, and not by Baranov alone. Demid Il'ich Kulikalov, a long-term veteran and one of the first to lead hunting parties into the Tlingit territory, administered the Pribilof Islands for a time and then took charge of operations in the central Aleutians. He was described by his contemporaries as a man of fine and upstanding character, mild and of quiet demeanor, a fond father of his Alutiiq son. When he visited Unalaska on business in 1805, Kulikalov was publicly flogged on Rezanov's orders for alleged brutality to an Aleut woman and her child. He was put in irons and shipped to Okhotsk, apparently separated forever from his family. Rezanov, in his own words, used this method to show the Aleuts that before his power even a Russian foreman is very low indeed, though in a letter to the emperor he described the event as a demonstration of imperial justice.

It must be noted at this point that at no time were Shelikhov, Baranov, or later the Russian-American Company or any of the company's representatives authorized to administer justice (nor did they have power to tax), one of the cardinal determinants of sovereign power, but Rezanov (like, allegedly, Shelikhov before him) attempted to claim such judicial power. Baranov had asserted this claim for himself on at least one occasion at the beginning of 1801, a claim disputed by the clergy and by at least one naval officer, Talin.[52] In Russian America, if a crime was committed, the perpetrators and all witnesses had to be transported to metropolitan Russia for proper judicial investigation and trial. So few crimes occurred in Alaska during the Russian period that, to the end in 1867, there was not a single jailhouse. Native communities, as was the custom throughout imperial Russia, followed their own traditional legal codes in adjudicating disputes and punishing grievous offenders. Disputes between Native communities and the Russian establishment were, preferably, also settled by Native custom, such as payment of indemnities in goods.

However, in Baranov's time disobedience and refusal to join long-distance hunting (and raiding) parties were settled by the lash. Death could be inflicted in this manner, avoiding legal complications with the government: deliberate infliction of death was a punishable, capital offense by the imperial code, but it could be argued that death after a severe flogging was due to constitutional weakness of the victim, an unintended consequence, or attributable to other causes. In Aleut and Alutiiq societies corporal punishment was the most shameful event that could befall an individual. There were instances in which men subjected to the lash later committed suicide. To this day, the memory of flogging is preserved in oral traditions and constitutes a heavy black mark on the Russian escutcheon, though the period as a whole is remembered in rather fond terms.

Russian laborers were flogged (on rare occasions) in outlying outposts, where the transgressions were judged and punishment prescribed by captains of the company vessels who fell back on the law of the sea of that time. This was the case up to 1860, when corporal punishment was abolished throughout the Russian empire. The flogging of Natives was forbidden after Baranov's removal, though Baranov himself fairly soon had understood the Native attitude toward corporal punishment and tried to eliminate it, especially in regard to high-ranking men. In his instruction (dated 1800) to Medvednikov, the head of the settlement of Novo-Arkhangel'sk at Sitka, he expressly directed that Aleut leaders should never be subjected to corporal and not even to verbal abuse and that respect must be shown them at all times.[53]

The political structure of Native communities, both at international and internal levels, was also changed irreversibly. Aleut, Alutiiq, and Tlingit societies all had a hereditary ranking system, which included the ruling or leadership elite kin groups, nobles, commoners, and slaves, that approached class stratification. With the Russian intrusion came changes in leadership structure, in some instances through internal Native reassessment of the situation, and in some instances through Russian imposition, as on Kodiak after Shelikhov's arrival. There are several documented cases where leadership passed from one kin group to another, because the successors were better able to manipulate the contact situations and deal with the Russians. Sometimes, as in the case of Shelikhov on Kodiak from 1784 to 1786, the change of leadership was effected through the execution of the captive chiefs and appointment of a member of the elite willing to cooperate. Sometimes the leadership passed from the older, experienced men to the younger ones who either looked for accommodation and change or, as was the case in the Pribilofs soon after Baranov's removal, who attempted to lead an armed revolt (with the older and wiser heads quashing such attempts which they judged, by experience, to be futile).

The impressment, especially on Kodiak and in the eastern Aleutians, of all ranks and the subjugation of high-status males to corporal punishment grievously affected the ranking system, which soon survived only in memory. Nevertheless, Native leadership remained, by and large, self-selecting and quasi-hereditary. Appointments by the Russian authorities were, in almost all cases, confirmation of the election or acceptance of a recognized consensus within the Native community. Until the promulgation of the company's Third Charter, the Russian authorities accepted that Native communities were governed by their traditional kin-group toions. Only rarely were men first selected by the Russian authorities and then accepted by the Native communities as leaders.

Russian intrusion also affected the balance of power between various Native communities. In the relatively early history of the Russians in the Aleutian archipelago, some Native leaders sought to ally themselves with the Russians against their traditional enemies. On the other hand, sometimes formerly independent political units allied themselves in a common front against the Russians, as had been the case in 1763 and 1764 in the eastern Aleutians, when four vessels and their crews were taken and destroyed. Later, particular Aleut communities formed alliances with particular Russian skippers and became involved in conflicts between the skippers over hunting territories. In the 1790s, Baranov and Lebedev-Lastochkin men used Natives in their own power struggle. Until the competition between the Russian merchant houses was eliminated by the granting of the monopoly to exploit Alaskan resources to Shelikhov's heirs in the Russian-American Company in 1799, the Native communities (outside Kodiak) preserved in large measure their political independence, playing off one company against the other. After 1799, there was no room for maneuvering, and political independence in external affairs was lost to all nations within the immediate control of the company. These were the Aleuts of the Aleutian archipelago, Alutiiq peoples of the Kodiak archipelago and eastern Alaska Peninsula, the Chugach of Prince William Sound and outer Cook Inlet, and coastal communities of the Cook Inlet Athabaskans, the Dena'ina. *Pax Rossiia* was imposed (and accepted) and Native international relations changed.

In sum, the Baranov era must be considered as a time of tremendous impact, producing early on fundamental changes and long-lasting effects on the Native communities of Alaska's Southwest. It is not an exaggeration to say that for the Alaska Natives of this region, the Baranov era was their darkest hour.

NOTES

1. Acted as a tax collector for a fee or percentage of receipts.
2. Records of the Orthodox Churches, Church of the Resurrection, Irkutsk, Irkutsk State Regional Archive, Fond 50, op. 3, delo 37, fol. 6; I. P. Kazantsev, ed., *Irkutskiia letopisi* (Irkutsk, 1911).
3. Kiril T. Khlebnikov, *Zhizneopisanie Aleksandra Andreevicha Baranova, glavnago pravitelia Rossiiskikh kolonii v Amerike* (St. Petersburg: Morskaia tipografiia, 1835), English-language edition, *Baranov: Chief Manager of the Russian Colonies in America,* trans. Colin Bearne, ed. Richard A. Pierce (Kingston, Ontario: Limestone Press, 1973). A copy of the contract signed by Baranov and Shelikhov, from the papers of the late A. Dolgopolov, has been put at my disposal by Richard A. Pierce. Published in part in Narochnitskii et al., *Russkie ekspeditsii* (1989), 277–280 (doc. 92).
4. Records of the Orthodox Churches, Church of Sts. Prokopii and Ioann of Ustiug, Irkutsk, matrimonial records for 1796.
5. Baranov's removal in 1818 by the navy, representing the government, probably rested in part on legal questions arising from this contract.
6. Kuskov also did not hesitate to act when threatened with incipient rebellion and labor unrest. His name is remembered on Kodiak Island even today: disobedient children are told "Kuskov will get you." Historians remember Kuskov as the founder of Settlement Ross in California in 1812. Dismissed not long after Baranov's removal, in 1822 he legally married an American Indian girl baptized Ekaterina, and took her to Tot'ma in 1823. Kuskov died shortly after his return home, and Ekaterina married another Russian. Her portrait and that of her husband survive and are on display in Kuskov's house in Tot'ma, now a museum.
7. One of Banner's serfs gained manumission on Kodiak in 1807.
8. Shelikhov hired Banner to take charge of the planned expansion of the Shelikhov commercial enterprise in Alaska to the north along the sea coast to Bering Strait. Banner sailed to Alaska ca. 1797, stopping at Unalaska. The company shareholder and manager of the Unalaska office, Larionov, found the plan not feasible for various reasons and detained Banner at Unalaska. Sometime later, Banner went to Kodiak. When Baranov transferred his main residence to Sitka in 1804, Banner was left in sole control of the Kodiak archipelago and adjacent areas. He remained on Kodiak, serving until his death in 1816; his two sons repatriated to Russia in 1821. His wife, who had accompanied him to Alaska, died on Kodiak in 1806.

9. Styled by many romantic writers an Indian princess from the Kenai Peninsula. In this guise she appears in a recently published novel by Ethel Roesch.

10. Letter, Baranov to Shelikhov and Polevoi, 20 May 1795, in Tikhmenev, *A History,* vol. 2, 68 (doc. 18).

11. Letter by Archimandrite Ioasaf, head of Religious Mission, Kodiak, to Shelikhov, 18 May 1795, Yudin Collection, Box 1, Folder 1, Manuscript Division, Library of Congress.

12. They had three children of which the eldest, a son, Antipatr, was born in 1797 (he died in 1821 in St. Petersburg). Their two daughters, Irina (born 1804) and Ekaterina (born 1808), married Russians and went with their husbands to Russia. Irina married a naval officer, Lieutenant Ianovskii, one of the first naval managers of the colony. Anna Baranov outlived her husband by many years, and is said to have remarried, dying on Kodiak sometime after 1836. She spent the last years of her life on Spruce Island, under the protection of St. Herman of Alaska, and was buried there.

13. For an excellent analysis of foreign shipping, see Agnes T. Sirridge, "Spanish, British and French Activities in the Sea Otter Trade of the Far North Pacific, 1774–1790" (Ph.D. diss., St. Louis University, 1954). For American Northwest Coast trade, see Mary Malloy, *"Boston Men" on the Northwest Coast: The American Maritime Fur Trade, 1788–1844* (Kingston, Ontario; Fairbanks, Alaska: Limestone Press, 1998).

14. F. W. Howay, *A List of Trading Vessels in the Maritime Fur Trade, 1785–1825,* ed. Richard A. Pierce (Kingston, Ontario: Limestone Press, 1973), originally published in *Proceedings and Transactions,* Royal Society of Canada, 24–28 (1930–1934).

15. Recently, an archaeologist has found East India (Bengal) Company cannon balls (Richard Knecht, telephone conversation with the author); however, these cannon balls may just as well belong to the brig *Mercury,* the privateer that shelled Native villages, according to official Russian documents.

16. James Strange, *James Strange's Journal and Narrative of the Commercial Expedition from Bombay to the North-West Coast of America together with a Chart Showing the Tract of the Expedition with an Introduction by A. V. Venkatarama Ayyar, Curator, Madras Record Office* (Madras: Government Press, 1928); Nathaniel Portlock, *A Voyage Round the World; But More Particularly to the North-West Coast of America: Performed in 1785, 1786, 1787, and 1788 in the* King George *and* Queen Charlotte, *Captains Portlock and Dixon* (London: John Stockdale and George Goulding, 1789); George Dixon, ed., *A Voyage Round the World; But More Particularly to the North-West Coast of America: Performed in 1785, 1786, 1787, and 1788 in the* King George *and* Queen Charlotte, *Captains Portlock and Dixon* (London: George Goulding, 1789); John Meares, *Voyages Made in the Years 1788 and 1789 from China to the North West Coast of America, to Which Are Prefixed, an Introductory Narrative of a Voyage Performed in 1786, from Bengal, in the Ship* Nootka*; Observations on the Probable Existence of a North West Passage; and Some Account of the Trade between the North West Coast of America and China, and the Latter Country and Great Britain* (London: Logographic Press, 1790). Dena'ina traditions: Dr. James Kari, Alaska Native Language Center, University of Alaska Fairbanks, and Mr. Paul Zacar, Nondalton, Alaska, conversations with the author.

17. Instructions, I. V. Iakobii, Governor-General of Siberia, to Samoilov and Delarov, 21 June 1787, in Tikhmenev, *A History,* vol. 2, 17–18 (doc. 4).

18. Purtov and Kulikalov to Baranov, 9 August 1794, in ibid., 50 (doc. 16).

19. William W. Fitzhugh and Aron Crowell, eds., *Crossroads of Continents: Cultures of Siberia and Alaska* (Washington, D.C.: Smithsonian Institution Press, 1988), 70, fig. 70. The artifact is now in the Smithsonian Institution (NMAH 420307).

20. Ivan Pil' to Empress Catherine II, 25 February 1790, in Narochnitskii et al., *Russkie ekspeditsii* (1989), 263–264 (doc. 85).

21. Tikhmenev, *A History,* vol. 2, 22–27 (docs. 6–8).

22. Photostat copy of documents from the Russian Naval Archive, Golder Collection, University of Washington, Seattle.

23. The iasak was never imposed. Unfortunately, no published documents deal with this matter. Recently, the Russian State Naval Archive (RGAVMF) put at the disposal of the Rasmuson Library,

University of Alaska Fairbanks, microfilms of the logs of Captains Billings and Sarychev as well as several other related documents. This material is yet to be studied.

24. Instructions, Iakobii to Samoilov and Delarov, 21 June 1787, in Tikhmenev, *A History*, vol. 2, 17–18 (doc. 4).
25. Khlebnikov, *Baranov*, 7.
26. Letter in Tikhmenev, *A History*, vol. 2, 19–21 (doc. 5).
27. Cf. point 6 of Instructions, Iakobii to Samoilov and Delarov, 21 June 1787, in Tikhmenev, *A History*, vol. 2, 17–18.
28. Kiril T. Khlebnikov, *Russkaia Amerika v neopublikovannykh zapiskakh K. T. Khlebnikova*, ed. R. G. Liapunova and S. G. Fedorova (Leningrad: Izdatel'stvo "Nauka," 1979), 60.
29. Polonskii, "Perechen'," fols. 79v–82, confirmed by native tradition recorded by Patricia Partnow; see Partnow's "Alutiiq Ethnicity" (Ph.D. diss., University of Alaska Fairbanks, December 1993).
30. Excerpt from the journal of Captain Robert Hall (R. R. Gall), 31 July–4 August 1791, in Narochnitskii et al., *Russkie ekspeditsii* (1989), 293–294 (doc. 101); and protocol, Billings Commission, Yudin Collection, Box 2, Folder 23, Manuscript Division, Library of Congress. See also the journal of Christian Bering, in the Aleutians with Sarychev 1790–1792, manuscript, Russian State Naval Archive.
31. Russian State Archive of Ancient Documents (RGADA), Fond 24, no. 67.
32. In the literature, the most frequently cited precontact population figure is that of 16,000 (from an estimate by Mooney). Other estimates range from 20,000 to 40,000, a fantastic figure. More modest estimates go as low as 5,000 to 12,000. For Liapunova's assessment, see Roza G. Liapunova, "The Aleuts Before Contact with the Russians: Some Demographic and Cultural Aspects," *Pacifica* 2, no. 2 (November 1990): 8–23.
33. The census data obtained by Baranov, Burenin, and Kriukov, and Sarychev's data published in 1802, are cited in Khlebnikov, *Russkaia Amerika v neopublikovannykh*, 99, 102, 109–110. For the 1834 data see Ioann Veniaminov, *Zapiski ob ostrovakh Unalashkinskago otdela* (St. Petersburg: Rossiisko-amerikanskaia kompaniia, 1840), English-language edition, *Notes on the Islands of the Unalashka District*, trans. Lydia T. Black and R. H. Geoghegan, ed. Richard A. Pierce (Fairbanks: Elmer E. Rasmuson Library Translation Program, University of Alaska Fairbanks; Kingston, Ontario: Limestone Press, 1984), xix–xxi. For the census by Vasil'iev, see Russian State Naval Archive (RGAVMF), Fond 213, op. 1, delo 45, fols. 1–3v.
34. Khlebnikov, *Russkaia Amerika v neopublikovannykh*, 109–110.
35. After careful consideration of all available data, Lydia Black and Donald Clark (work in progress) propose a figure somewhat in excess of 8,000.
36. Adelung Fond, op. 1, delo 136, no. 7, Manuscript Division, State Public Library, St. Petersburg, Russia.
37. Khlebnikov, *Russkaia Amerika v neopublikovannykh*, 24.
38. Tikhmenev, *A History*, vol. 2, 15–17 (doc. 3). Synoptic account, in Khlebnikov, *Russkaia Amerika v neopublikovannykh*, 189.
39. Gideon, *Round the World Voyage*, 68–69.
40. Shelikhov to Baranov, 9 August 1794, in Narochnitskii et al., *Russkie ekspeditsii* (1989), 328; Khlebnikov, *Russkaia Amerika v neopublikovannykh*, 193.
41. P. N. Pavlov, ed., *K istorii Rossiisko-amerikanskoi kompanii* (Krasnoiarsk: Krasnoiarskii gosudarstvennyi arkhiv; Krasnoiarskii gosudarstvennyi pedagogicheskii institut, 1957), 63–73 (doc. 5), specifically pp. 65–68.
42. The story of this attempted landing and the hardships suffered by the men in the baidara before they found safety is preserved both in Russian-American Company documents and Yup'ik oral tradition. For a brief synoptic mention see Khlebnikov, *Russkaia Amerika v neopublikovannykh*, 193–194.

43. Report of Priest Vasilii Sivtsov to Captain Billings, Russian State Naval Archive (RGAVMF), Fond 214, op. 1, delo 28, fols. 83, 85.

44. On removal to the Pribilof Islands under Merkul'iev and Popov, see Robert Hall (Gall), log, 31 July–4 August 1791, in Narochnitskii et al., *Russkie ekspeditsii* (1989), 293–294 (doc. 101); Shelikhov and Polevoi to I. F. Popov, 31 July 1794, in Pavlov, ed., *K istorii Rossiisko-amerikanskoi kompanii,* 52–61 (doc. 3), English-language edition, *Documents on the History of the Russian-American Company,* trans. Marina Ramsay, ed. Richard A. Pierce (Kingston, Ontario: Limestone Press, 1976), 60–70 (doc. 3). In these documents Merkul'iev's name is spelled *Merkur'iev.* Veniaminov, *Notes,* 256, states that Merkul'iev took eighty families to the Pribilof Islands and that forty-two men were lost in a baidara accident in 1812; others were killed by sea lions. On Merkul'iev's death, see Veniaminov, *Notes,* 178, and Records of the Russian Orthodox Church, Vital Statistics, Unalaska parish. Information on Umnak Island's providing a large contingent for the Pribilofs under Merkul'iev is drawn from Lydia T. Black, unpublished field data.

45. Baranov to Shelikhov, 24 July 1793, in Tikhmenev, *A History,* vol. 2, 32.

46. Kiril T. Khlebnikov, *Russkaia Amerika v "zapiskakh" Kirila Khlebnikova: Novo-Arkhangel'sk,* ed. Svetlana G. Fedorova (Moscow: Izdatel'stvo "Nauka," 1985), 41. Later writers, such as F. Vrangel' (Wrangell) (in Khlebnikov, *Russkaia Amerika v neopublikovannykh,* 247–248) exaggerated the number by at least a factor of two. A description of the dispatch and structure of these hunting parties (1804–1806) is given in considerable detail by Gideon, *Round the World Voyage,* 62–64.

47. Tlingit tradition preserves memories of the "Aleut" (probably Chugach and Kodiak Islander) raids. See Frederica de Laguna, *Under Mount St. Elias: The History and Culture of the Yakutat Tlingit,* Smithsonian Contributions to Anthropology, vol. 7, pt. 1 (Washington, D.C.: Smithsonian Institution Press, 1972), 256–258.

48. Khlebnikov, *Russkaia Amerika v neopublikovannykh,* 25.

49. Gideon, *Round the World Voyage,* 69.

50. Khlebnikov, *Russkaia Amerika v neopublikovannykh,* 25; Gideon, *Round the World Voyage,* 69.

51. Gideon, *Round the World Voyage,* 69–70.

52. Letter, Baranov to Larionov, 22 March 1801, in Tikhmenev, *A History,* vol. 2, 123–125 (doc. 31).

53. Point 5 of Instructions, Baranov to Medvednikov, 19 April 1800, in Pavlov, ed., *K istorii Rossiisko-amerikanskoi kompanii,* 101–102 (doc. 8). Khlebnikov, in his biography of Baranov, also mentions his understanding of the Aleut and Alutiiq attitudes.

Figure 28. This undated pencil sketch by an unknown artist may be the earliest representation of St. Paul Harbor (Kodiak), established by Baranov in 1792. Since the building on the right has a cupola and thus may indicate a chapel or residence of clergy, the sketch may date to 1794 or 1795.
Courtesy Richard A. Pierce.

Chapter Eight

Baranov Takes Hold

Many of the long-term effects of Baranov's managerial reign on the Native communities were far in the future in 1790, when Baranov wintered on Unalaska where his ship had been wrecked in Kashega Bay.[1] The next spring he traveled to Kodiak by skin boat. The journey took from 25 April to 27 June and was a grueling one. Earlier he had attempted to get help from Kodiak, but the party he dispatched to seek aid there encountered hostile Alaska Peninsula Alutiit and was forced to take shelter in the Shumagins on Unga. Five Fox Islanders were killed in this encounter.

Once he reached Kodiak, Baranov almost immediately dispatched Dmitrii Bocharov, skipper of the wrecked *Three Saints*, to chart the Bering Sea shore of the Alaska Peninsula, a task he accomplished with great success, producing the first detailed (and excellent) charts. He portaged his skin boats across the Alaska Peninsula and then sailed for Kodiak, where he arrived 27 September 1791. Here Bocharov took over the command of the vessel *Sv. Mikhail* and sailed her to Okhotsk (where soon thereafter he changed his employment and became a navigator for the brothers Kiselev). The second vessel at Baranov's disposal, the *Sv. Simeon i Anna*, was commanded by Izmailov and provided support for Baranov's subsequent activity in Prince William Sound.

Baranov at once realized that the main Shelikhov settlement, the one founded in 1784 at Three Saints Bay, could no longer serve as headquarters. In 1788, an earthquake and a tsunami had made the harbor there unsuitable for seagoing vessels. By the time he arrived, the company vessels sought anchorage in another harbor, known today as Old Harbor.[2] Moreover, the end of Kodiak Island where the original settlement had been located lacked timber and thus new construction, or addition to or replacement of the eight structures then in existence, would be difficult.[3] Therefore, Baranov almost immediately decided to relocate, selecting for this purpose Chiniak Bay and in May 1792 naming the new location, in honor of Crown Prince Paul, Pavlovskaia Harbor (now the site of the modern city of Kodiak). After Baranov transferred his headquarters to Sitka at the end of 1808, it would become the center for the Kodiak District of the Russian-American Company and was, until 1867, the second largest Russian settlement in Alaska. Shelikhov, pleased with the move, instructed that this settlement had to look from the start like a town, and urged careful planning and good quality construction, "to be beautiful and pleasant to live in."[4]

By 1796, the Kodiak settlement, now named the Harbor of St. Paul, had a church, extensive vegetable gardens where agricultural experiments were conducted, docks, storage structures, barracks for the workers, private houses, and many workshops, including an iron smelter where experiments with producing iron locally were conducted and bricks were manufactured.[5]

The second vital task Baranov put into execution almost immediately upon his arrival was the consolidation of his company's bases on the mainland, where 263 Lebedev-Lastochkin men allegedly lived in several permanent settlements.[6] There was at the time, however, an internal dispute between Petr Kolomin (or Kolomein), foreman in charge of the Lebedev-Lastochkin vessel *Sv. Pavel*, and Konovalov, the skipper of a newly arrived vessel, the *Sv. Georgii*. A third vessel, the *Sv. Ioann*,[7] was under the command of Stepan Zaikov, a trained navigator and brother of the renowned Potap Zaikov (who by this time had died at Unalaska); Stepan Zaikov remained loyal to his employer, Lebedev-Lastochkin. The dispute escalated, Native communities became involved, Kolomin complained to Lebedev-Lastochkin and, apprised of Baranov's arrival on Kodiak, appealed to Baranov for help (21 November 1791 and again 11 March 1792). The next year, Lebedev-Lastochkin and Shelikhov jointly appealed to the head of the ecclesiastical mission, who was preparing to sail to Kodiak, to investigate the matter and adjudicate the dispute.

To Baranov the situation seemed opportune for a takeover, or at least for gaining a foothold on the mainland. Thus, Baranov felt he had full justification in personally proceeding to Prince William Sound and Cook Inlet.[8] But his plan to consolidate control of the mainland outposts in his own hands had larger aims than weakening or eliminating competition: it was a necessary prerequisite to planned expansion to the southeast. For Baranov, all other considerations aside, such expansion meant new sea otter hunting grounds, as he believed the area around Kodiak, Cook Inlet, and Prince William Sound to be near exhaustion in the wake of intensive exploitation by his and the Lebedev-Lastochkin companies and by the Natives who were engaging in massive trade with the English.

Shelikhov, too, pressed for expansion, stressing the necessity to interdict British trade along the coast and to forestall, if possible, any British settlement, especially at Nootka. It appears that Delarov had discussed the situation with the Spanish (Malaspina expedition, 1791) and understood that at this time the Spaniards would welcome Russian expansion along the coast, would cooperate with the Russians, and had no objection to Russian fur gathering, a practice in which the Spanish stated they had no interest. What mattered to them was preventing the establishment of a permanent British foothold on the American Northwest Coast.[9] Shelikhov particularly was concerned with the British threat, as one British vessel had stopped in the Pribilofs and three of her crew members were left on St. George Island. One of the Englishmen left behind died on St. George; the fate of the other two is not known, but it is possible they entered Baranov's employ (several Englishmen served Baranov very ably, three of them coming to Alaska in 1792 with James Shields; the origin of most is not known).

This unknown vessel's captain had visited Shelikhov's establishment in the Pribilofs, under Ivan Popov, at Popov's invitation. Shelikhov feared that the British would attempt to wrest the fur seal trade from the Russians as he believed they were doing with the sea otter trade. In a letter to Popov dated 31 July 1794, he would express his displeasure at Popov's action and discuss at length how detrimental the British penetration of the North Pacific was, and would continue to be in the future, to Russian interests.[10]

Thus, when Baranov set out for Prince William Sound on 23 May 1792, he was planning to establish a permanent outpost there as a base for further expansion. He investigated most of the sound, conducted a population census in three main Chugach villages, and took twenty hostages. Baranov also claimed to have taken a census of the local Athabaskans, whom he recognized as oriented in their subsistence not toward the sea, as were the Chugach, but toward exploitation of the Interior. He saw them as potential allies in any expansion to the north from the coast.

He claimed that he had "annexed" the Chugach villages in the sound and took umbrage when that same summer the Lebedev-Lastochkin men moved the people of one village from Cook Inlet to Prince William Sound in order to establish another settlement there. Baranov wrote that they interfered with his hunting parties and his establishment at English Bay (Aleksandrovsk) and "tried to deny us Chugach Bay."[11] Nevertheless, he proceeded to move into upper Cook Inlet and Prince William Sound. He was supported by two company vessels, the *Sv. Simeon i Anna* under Izmailov and the *Orel*, just arrived from Okhotsk where she had been built, and commanded on her maiden voyage by James

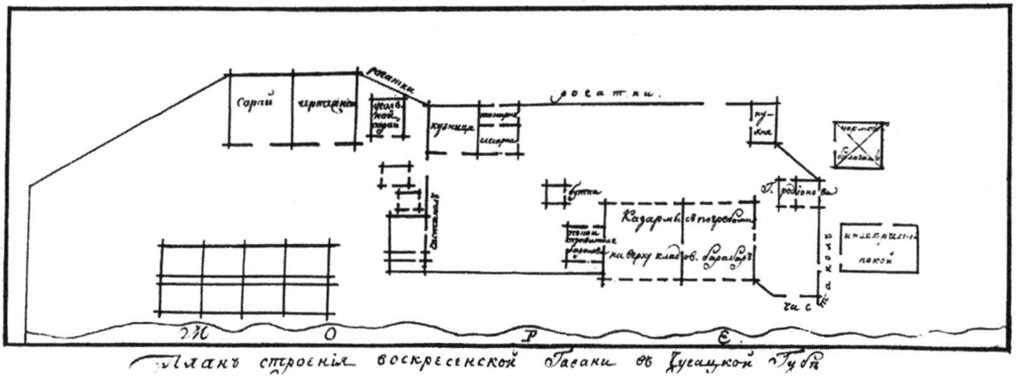

FIGURE 29. Voskresenskaia Gavan' (Seward) shipyard. From a watercolor by James Shields.
Original in AVPRI. Courtesy A. V. Postnikov.

Shields. Both skippers were charting and exploring the sound in 1792. That year Baranov had already determined a place suitable for establishing a shipyard: a locality on the Kenai Peninsula coast (*Voskresenskaia Gavan'* or Resurrection Bay, in Izmailov's log *Kudalia naganok* bay, site of the modern city of Seward). Baranov claimed that he chose this site to disrupt the portage traffic between Cook Inlet and Prince William Sound maintained by the Lebedev-Lastochkin crews.[12] Construction commenced and was completed in 1793, the year in which Baranov spent the entire winter in Prince William Sound.

Baranov's activity of 1792 greatly alarmed the Lebedev-Lastochkin men. They intercepted twenty Aleut kayaks sent out from Kodiak to Prince William Sound and moved some of the Chugach from lower Cook Inlet to an outpost in the sound. In the meantime, in May 1793, Izmailov sailed to Cook Inlet and placed an artel in a sheltered bay on the Kenai Peninsula coast and named it *Nikolaevskaia bukhta*. From there Izmailov proceded to Prince William Sound to rendezvous with Baranov and the *Orel* under Shields. By the end of May construction of the Resurrection Bay settlement and shipyard commenced. The two skippers continued to explore the sound. On 15 June both men went to visit the Lebedev-Lastochkin artel on one of the islands in the western portion of the sound, which Izmailov called in his log *Nikataxla*. He wrote that a fortified outpost had been built here in former years (1780s) by navigator Dmitrii Polutov "who wintered here together with the Greek [Delarov]." This fortified outpost was repaired and refurbished by the Lebedev-Lastochkin contingent. The two skippers delivered to the Lebedev-Lastochkin crew a letter from Baranov which demanded that the Chugach "from whom he had collected iasak," and thus had brought under Russian sovereignty in 1792, be returned to him. In response, the outpost crew accused Baranov of selling four Chugach hostages to the Tlingit and uttered very uncomplimentary remarks about the manager. The two men reported their failure to Baranov. He arrived on the scene a week later and attempted to land at the outpost in a three-hatch kayak. He was met by abuse and threats of force of arms. Then Shields and Izmailov were sent to the outpost once again, this time to read "orders sent by Okhotsk and higher" authorities and Baranov's understanding about the allegedly government-mandated relationship between the rival companies. They found the gates of the outpost closed and all men within fully armed with pistols and sidearms. Under threats, they retreated to their baidara where they were joined by several Aleuts fleeing the camp. Next day, Lebedev-Lastochkin foreman Balushin came to talk with Baranov. Instead of talking, Baranov ordered Izmailov to read to Balushin a rude and insulting, in places unprintable, "Announcement" composed by Baranov (dated "28 June 1793 at the Island of Nika'ta'luk"). Baranov stated that he had secret appointment to the highest office in the territory and secret instructions "in regard to matters of State." What those instructions were he was unable to reveal to anyone unless they took, on the spot, an oath of unquestioned obedience to him. The reading of this document was met with ridicule, and Balushin and his men departed discharging firearms, which were echoed by guns and cannon fired in the air from their outpost.[13]

It is certain that the Lebedev-Lastochkin men had, in addition to this island fortress, an outpost manned by twenty men at Tatlek (Tatitlek, near Cordova), another one on Hinchinbrook Island, and they also claimed control of the mouth of the Copper River.[14] Though his Russian competitors in Alaska were thus well entrenched, Baranov was determined to drive them out. Nevertheless, it would take him almost six years to gain the upper hand over the Lebedev-Lastochkin contingents, setting Natives to attack the competition's outposts, and, on Shelikhov's advice, enticing the Russians to change their employers by hook or by crook.[15]

In 1792 and 1793, Baranov devoted most of his attention to Prince William Sound. It was here that he encountered the British vessel *Phoenix* and made friends with Captain Moore, who presented him with a Hindu slave (for his friendly intercourse with the British, Baranov was soundly chastised by his employers).[16] Here, too, in 1792 he had his first encounter with Tlingit warriors. On the night of 20 June, Baranov's camp on a spit off the Bay of Sts. Constantine and Elena was attacked by a combined force of Yakutat Tlingit and Eyak. The attackers came up in six large war canoes, intending to take revenge upon the Chugach who had inflicted some injury on the Yakutat people the previous year. Having stumbled on the Russian camp, they attacked (so stated Baranov and Izmailov) in hopes of booty. The encounter ended in a standoff. Both sides suffered casualties, and both took a few prisoners. Baranov took several suits of Tlingit armor, one of which he sent to Shelikhov and another to the Okhotsk commandant.[17] The Yakutat Tlingit in this attack used their Native weapons, though the Russians knew that some Tlingit groups to the southeast already possessed firearms supplied by the British.[18] Baranov had ample firearms and cannon. He also had support from Izmailov's vessel—additional men, weapons, and ammunition. Izmailov took on board the wounded, the dead, and the sick from Baranov's party, who were replaced by healthy members of Izmailov's crew.[19]

At this same time, a large hunting party, mustering 170 kayaks, under Egor Purtov, accompanied by three other Russians and protected by the *Orel*, made a probe into Yakutat Bay and beyond, reaching possibly as far as Lituya Bay. On the return trek, Purtov encountered a three-masted British vessel, probably the *Jenny* under James Baker.[20]

In 1794, a larger party was sent beyond Yakutat Bay, once again under Purtov; this party encountered Vancouver and Puget several times at various locations. The Russians believed that Vancouver stated to them English claims to Cook Inlet and Prince William Sound and added that soon several British warships would arrive. As a consequence, Baranov asked for governmental instructions on how far below Lituya Bay he should advance. Natalia Shelikhov urged Count Zubov, in a letter written soon after her husband's death, that "now is the time to settle the question as to the boundary line between the Russian possessions and the English as there is a danger that they might make us abandon them altogether."[21]

In the meantime, Baranov steadily pushed southeast. Purtov, in order to hunt in the Tlingit land, exchanged hostages, in some cases leaving behind Kodiak Islanders and, in at least one instance, Russians. The Purtov party interacted with the Tlingit and Eyak. They also met the Tlingit chief from Akoi Bay (Dry Bay). There was at that time at Yakutat a British trading vessel, the *Jackal*, under William Brown, who stood by (and provided armed escort) for Purtov in some of his dealings with the Tlingit in respect to hostage exchanges. It must be noted that the Tlingit considered the taking of sea otters in their territory by the Russian hunting parties a grievous transgression of their territorial rights.

The weight Baranov gave to the affairs on the mainland could be gauged by the fact that for the three years 1792–1794, he spent most of his time in Prince William Sound. The probes deep into Tlingit territory, and the establishment of a settlement there, required a mainland base and sufficient marine transport.

FIGURE 30. **Launching of the *Feniks* (*Phoenix*) at Voskresenskaia Gavan' (Resurrection Bay, modern town of Seward), from a watercolor by James Shields, 1794.**
Courtesy Library of Congress, Manuscript Division, former Golder Collection.

Though Shelikhov continued to build new vessels that sailed regularly each year to Alaska with supplies and men, taking away furs and those who were leaving company employ, ships were badly needed within the colony. Baranov, now ably assisted by Shields, started an ambitious ship construction program within his domain. By the summer of 1793, Shields was busy on the construction of a three-masted ship, later christened the *Phoenix*, at Voskresenskaia adjacent to Prince William Sound. This vessel was launched in the summer of 1794 (but was to be lost with all hands in 1799). A smaller shipyard operated at the same time on Lesnoi (Woody) Island at Kodiak, where two small vessels, the *Del'fin* and the *Ol'ga* (which Baranov skippered himself), were built in the winter of 1794–1795. By 1795, Baranov was so confident he could develop shipbuilding in the colony that he advised Shelikhov there was no need to build any new vessels for Alaska in Okhotsk. His confidence was misplaced: the shortage of shipping continued and grew ever more acute, as Baranov's needs increased due to the expansion of his activities while support for the colony from the Russian mainland waned with the reorganization of the company following Shelikhov's death in 1795, loss of the *Phoenix* in 1799, and the greater and greater involvement of Russia in the Napoleonic Wars in Europe. Thus, the availability of shipping was a continuing concern.

In 1795, plans for a settlement at Yakutat were put into execution, and the possibility of another outpost farther southeast, in Sitka Bay near Mt. Edgecumbe, was being considered.

Also in 1795, Shields was dispatched in the little *Del'fin* southeast to the Queen Charlotte Islands; he then sailed back north to Sea Otter Bay ("called by the Spanish Bucareli") in the Prince of Wales archipelago, then to Sitka Sound where he traded for

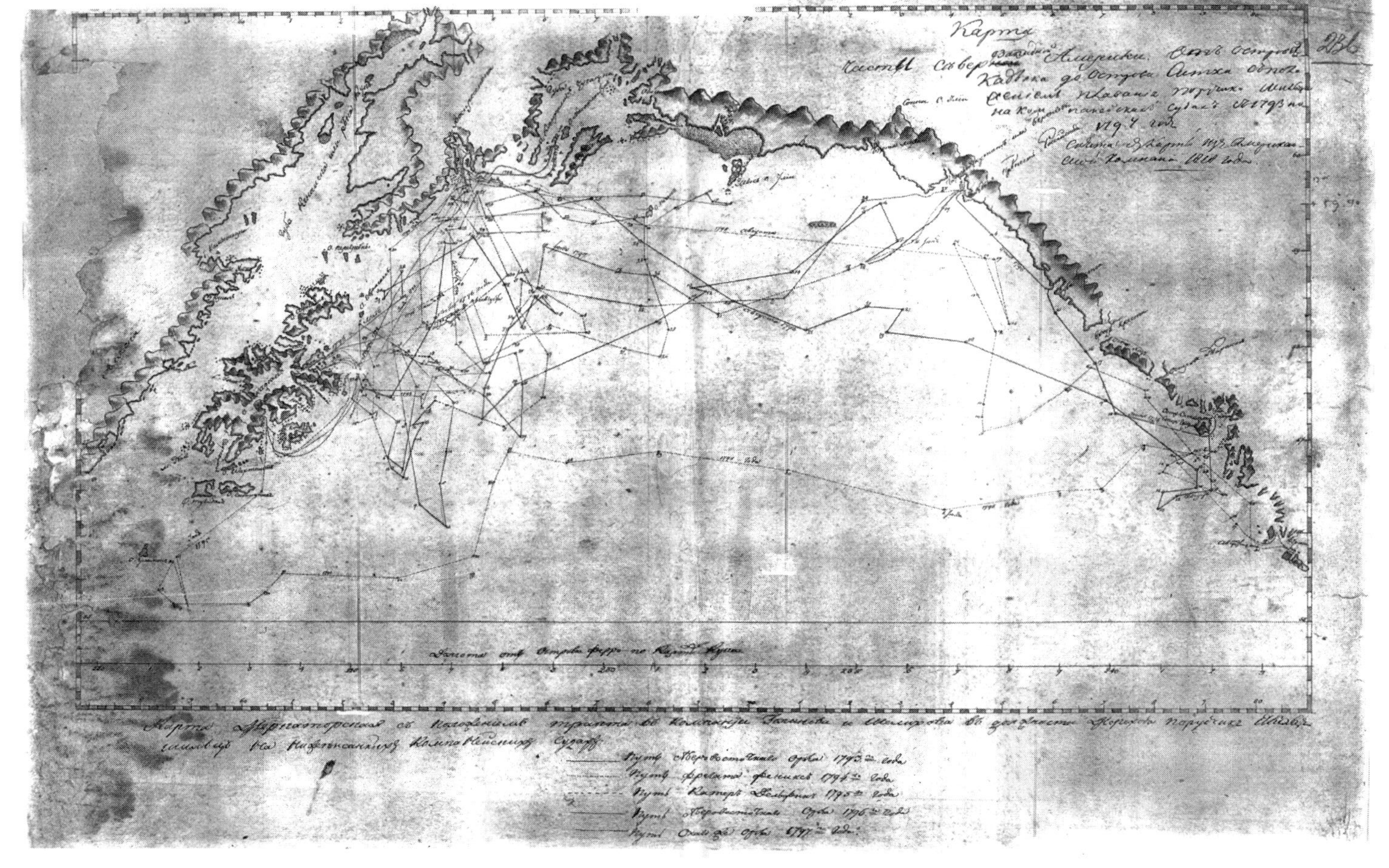

FIGURE 31. Mercator chart showing the tracks of the voyages of Lt. Iakov Shil'ts (James Shields) between Kodiak Island and the Alexander Archipelago aboard vessels of the Shelikhov-Golikov Company, 1793–1797. The key at the bottom of the chart distinguishes between Shields's voyages aboard the *Severovostochnyi Orel* (1793, 1796, 1797), the frigate *Feniks* (*Phoenix*; 1794), and the cutter *Del'fin* (1795).

Original in RGAVMF, Fond 1331, op. 4, delo 152. Courtesy Richard A. Pierce.

sea otter skins with a small group of Tlingit (seeing live sea otter pups in the Tlingit canoes). His crew did not observe any firearms among the Tlingit they met nor did they encounter any foreign shipping, except for the *Arthur*, a British snow out of Bengal, commanded by Captain Barber. Shields reported the complaint of a Tlingit chief that at one time Barber had put him in irons, demanding sea otter skins.[22] The Russians knew not only that the waters in this area by this time were being frequented by the British, who had called here in great numbers since 1786, but that the French also probed here (in 1791, Etienne Marchand, *La Solide*), and that at least fifteen American vessels had traded here prior to 1795, supplying the Natives with firearms and rum. Thus, Shields was to report not only on the availability of sea otters and Native trade, but on any foreign shipping in the area. He was in the southeast region again in 1796.

Baranov, at the same time, was exploring the Tlingit coast in the *Ol'ga*. He reached Chastye Islands (Bay of Islands) and Icy Strait (Cross Sound), noted the Wall of Ice in modern Glacier Bay, and was in Lynn Canal. He claimed that he had been in the land of the Kaigane, the Haida of the Queen Charlotte archipelago. He also was in Sitka Bay.[23] Then he sailed to Yakutat. Between 1795 and 1798, Baranov, again in command of his *Ol'ga*, would visit the coast beyond Lituya Bay several times, put in at Chilkat Bay (modern Haines), and claim friendship with the people at Sitka.[24]

In the fall of 1794, a group of settlers (serfs) put at the disposal of the Shelikhov-Golikov Company through the efforts of Count Zubov (a necessary move, because merchants were forbidden to own serfs) had arrived at Kodiak, and Baranov had ordered that the settlement at Yakutat commence the following year.[25] He would be on hand to supervise the initial effort. The thirty or thirty-two settler families (among them the Kashevarovs, parents of young Filip whom Baranov had apprenticed to Shields to study navigation) were augmented by fifty Russian promyshlenniki and a number of Kodiak Islanders. Each group had its own appointed leader, a future source of conflict. They traveled in the new vessel, named also for *The Three Saints*, built by Shelikhov in 1793 to replace the one that had brought Baranov to Alaska and had been wrecked in 1790 at Unalaska. On her maiden voyage in 1794, commanded by Izmailov, she had carried to Alaska the first ecclesiastical mission as well as the group of would-be settlers. In 1796, when Yakutat was being settled, she was commanded by the aging and ailing navigator Gavriil Pribylov, whom Shelikhov had hired after the Billings-Sarychev expedition was disbanded. Pribylov sailed only as far as Hinchinbrook Island in Prince William Sound and then returned to Kodiak (where he died the same year of 1796). Baranov, after waiting at Yakutat in vain for Pribylov's arrival, exchanged hostages with the local Tlingit leader, leaving behind a large number of hostages of his own, nine (six, according to Filip Kashevarov) of them Russians, among them a government mining expert, Dmitrii Tarkhanov. The next year Tarkhanov would travel with a mixed Tlingit/Eyak party from Yakutat, over the Malaspina Glacier to the Copper River. His journal, preserved in the holdings of the Public Library in St. Petersburg, Russia, but never published in full, is the earliest ethnographic and linguistic record on hand of the Yakutat Tlingit, the Eyak, and the Ahtna, the Athabaskan group of the middle and upper Copper River.[26]

The settlement was effected in 1796–1797 at the same time that Baranov dispatched a small party to occupy the territory between the mouth of the Copper River and Cape St. Elias, in order to prevent Lebedev-Lastochkin men from establishing themselves there. From then on, this settlement would serve as a transshipment point for the furs collected by the long-distance hunting parties along the southeastern coast of Alaska and Kodiak and a resting place for the hunters.

All was not calm in the new settlement. In the previous year there had been unrest bordering on rebellion among the settlers, and several men with their families had been sent to an isolated artel at Igak (modern Ugak Bay) on Kodiak, out of harm's way, while others went to the Kenai Peninsula where they were expected to experiment with agriculture. Three of the leaders of this near-rebellion were flogged. Hardship and poor leadership in the new, poorly provided-for settlement bred discontent. From the start, Ivan Grigor'evich Polomoshnyi, the *starshina* assigned by Shelikhov to be in charge of the settlers, could not get along either with the settlers or with Stepan Larionov, the foreman of the promyshlenniki. By 1799, he had to be removed (he and his family were drowned on their voyage from Yakutat when the *Orel* was wrecked off Montague Island).

But the Yakutat settlement was not the only activity engaging Baranov's attention during this period. He sent Vasilii Medvednikov and Filip Kashevarov to reconnoiter the Lake Iliamna region of the Alaska Peninsula interior. This was the second trip to that region for Medvednikov, who had explored it in 1792 by baidara, out of Unalaska, perhaps as a member of the Bocharov party. He traveled up the Kvichak River, which debouches into the Bering Sea, traversed Lake Iliamna, visited Lake Clark, and was on the Newhalen River. This region was occupied by a Lebedev-Lastochkin crew (who, sometime before April 1798, were killed by the Athabaskans). It was from here that Ivanov traveled into the Interior and to the Kuskokwim River.[27]

Baranov also was collecting intelligence about the Yup'ik peoples of the Bristol Bay area and preparing to take over the Lebedev-Lastochkin establishments in Cook Inlet, anticipating Stepan Zaikov's decision to leave. In 1797 he took over the Lebedev-Lastochkin outpost on Hinchinbrook Island. The settlement of *Sv. Konstantin i Elena* (Sts. Konstantin and Elena), which controlled access to the Copper River, was his. In 1798, he dispatched a volunteer, Patochkin, to explore the Copper River basin and to find the source of the native raw copper. Patochkin wintered there, probably at Taral, near the Chitina River, returning in 1799.[28] The plans to establish a settlement on Sitka were ready to be put into execution, but Baranov had had to deal with several side issues during the same period.

In 1797, the company was reorganized, and Emel'ian Larionov, a shareholder in the Shelikhov-Golikov enterprises, accompanied by his wife, soon arrived at Unalaska to take charge of the business there and in the Pribilofs. It seemed as if Baranov's authority had been reduced. In his correspondence with this new and influential company manager, Baranov showed his finest diplomatic skill, breaking in a novice, instructing without seeming to instruct.

Another rival company, that of the brothers Kiselev, still operated on Unalaska and in the central Aleutians. Bocharov, as mentioned earlier, had defected to them, and Izmailov followed his friend's lead. Bocharov had died at Unalaska on 18 November 1793; Pribylov had died on Kodiak in 1796; Izmailov died sometime between 1795 and 1797, apparently in Okhotsk.[29] Experienced skippers now were sadly lacking and were badly needed. The Russian-American Company began hiring naval officers.

Three naval officers, released to take service with the company, arrived in Alaska and soon Baranov was at loggerheads with them. Naval officers were not receptive to taking orders from, and following the instructions of, a mere provincial merchant. This situation would arise again and again in the future, and, eventually, the combined negative reports of the navy men would carry enough weight to topple Baranov from power.[30]

In addition, the spiritual mission that arrived on Kodiak in 1794 was energetically taking a stand in defense of Native rights. In this the clerics were supported by some of the staff at Kodiak and several Russian laborers, whom Baranov termed "radicals," as well as by some naval officers in company service. The church, too, would prove a very effective critic of Baranov's management. Native unrest on Kodiak, supported by the mission, was suppressed by Kuskov, an action that earned him his long-lasting bad reputation. There was unrest in Cook Inlet (suppressed by Kuskov also). At Unalaska the Aleuts found a defender in Father Makarii, who took a delegation to Russia to lodge a complaint about their treatment before the emperor.[31]

Baranov must have wondered about his future position with the company. In 1799, while he was busy establishing the Russian presence at Sitka, the Russian-American Company was formed, and administration was restructured once more (with the central and western Aleutians and the Commander Islands placed under the supervision of the company's Okhotsk office). In 1800, it appeared that the board of directors had instructed Emel'ian Larionov, manager of Unalaska, to replace Baranov should he desire to resign. He did, indeed, submit his resignation to Larionov,[32] though he rescinded it the same day.[33] Though Baranov's position at that time may have been ambiguous and he was troubled by a lawsuit instigated by Lebedev-Lastochkin, he persevered in the pursuit of his larger goals. Whatever the situation, Baranov proceeded with implementation of his plans, reminding his correspondents that he was serving the higher interests of the state.[34]

NOTES

1. A veritable mythology exists about this wreck and, from time to time, schemes to dive for Baranov's "gold treasure" or to raise the wreck are proposed. Fortunately, a detailed account exists: the skipper's log. The vessel, the *Three Saints,* built by Shelikhov in 1783 and commanded by Dmitrii Bocharov, was anchored (with Baranov's concurrence or on his insistence) in the inner part of Kashega Bay, Unalaska. On 1 October 1790, a storm hit the coast and continued unabated for several days. The vessel was battered by the surf against the bottom. Most of the crew were ordered to shore. Efforts to save the vessel failed. From 8 to 16 October the crew was busy breaking up the vessel in order to salvage valuable materials. On 16 October the cables were cut and what remained of the wreck was battered to smithereens (Russian State Naval Archive [RGAVMF], Fond 870, op. 1, delo 1942, Log of the vessel *Three Saints,* kept by skipper Bocharov, 1790).
2. Local oral tradition, Sven Haakanson, Sr., Old Harbor. The tsunami that devastated Three Saints harbor is briefly mentioned in Shelikhov's letter to Baranov, 9 August 1794, in Narochnitskii et al., *Russkie ekspeditsii* (1989), 322. Bottom changes resulting from the earthquake are mentioned by Baranov in a letter to Shelikhov dated 24 July 1793 (Tikhmenev, *A History,* vol. 2, 36).
3. On the number of structures at Three Saints harbor in 1790, see the sketch in Sarychev's journal, microfilm courtesy RGAVMF, St. Petersburg; in repository at the Rasmuson Library, University of Alaska Fairbanks; and Gavriil A. Sarychev, *Puteshestvie flota kapitana Sarycheva po severovostochnoi chasti Sibiri, Ledovitomu moriu i Vostochnomu okeanu ... pod nachal'stvom flota kapitana Billingsa s 1785 po 1793 god,* atlas (St. Petersburg: Tipografiia Shnora, 1802).
4. Shelikhov and Polevoi to Baranov, 9 August 1794, in Tikhmenev, *A History,* vol. 2, 54–55 (doc. 17). This settlement remained Baranov's main base until 1804–1808, when he moved his headquarters to Sitka in Tlingit territory.
5. Baranov to Shelikhov and Polevoi, 20 May 1795, in ibid., 59–77 (doc. 18). The brick works were actually on Long Island.

6. The log of John Sheriff, Master's Mate, with the Vancouver expedition, 1791–1795. Public Records Office, Kew, Richmond, Surrey, England, Adm. 53/334, fol. 152v. Datum courtesy Wallace M. Olson.
7. The official name of this vessel is unclear—the *Sv. Ioann Bogoslov* (John the Theologian), as it appears in one document, or *Sv. Ioann Predtecha* (John the Precursor), as it is sometimes referred to in the literature.
8. Tikhmenev, *A History,* vol. 2, 27–37, 39–46, 52–85 (docs. 9, 11–15, 17–19).
9. Excerpt from a report by Governor-General I. A. Pil' to Empress Catherine, dated 29 September 1792, in Divin, *Russkaia Tikhookeanskaia epopeia,* 411–413 (doc. 94).
10. Pavlov, ed., *K istorii Rossiisko-amerikanskoi kompanii,* 52–61, specifically paragraph 4, pp. 55–56; Shelikhov and Polevoi to Baranov, 9 August 1794, in Tikhmenev, *A History,* vol. 2, 57 (doc. 17).
11. Baranov to Shelikhov, 24 July 1793, in Tikhmenev, *A History,* vol. 2, 32–35 (doc. 9).
12. Baranov to Shelikhov and Polevoi, 20 May 1795, in ibid., 66 (doc. 18).
13. Russian State Naval Archive, Fond 870, op. 1, delo 1784, Izmailov's log for 1793, in which Baranov's "announcement" is reproduced in full (fols. 59v–60r). Baranov charged that Balushin and his men, instead of respectfully reading his letters, advised him to wipe his arse with them.
14. Report, Purtov and Kulikalov to Baranov, 9 August 1794, in Tikhmenev, *A History,* vol. 2, 46–52 (doc. 16).
15. Shelikhov and Polevoi to Baranov, 9 August 1794, in ibid., 53–54 (doc. 17).
16. Ibid., 57.
17. Letter, Baranov to Shelikhov, 24 July 1793, in Tikhmenev, *A History,* vol. 2, 27–37 (doc. 9).
18. Archimandrite Ioasaf (Bolotov), Head of the Northeastern American Mission, "Kratkiia ob"iasneniia sdelannye sootvetstvenno zapiske prislannoi ot Sviateishago Pravitel'stvuiushchago Sinoda, ob Amerikanskom ostrove Kadiake" and more extensive manuscript (n.d., ca. 1797), Yudin Collection and Russian collections (formerly Golder Collection), Manuscript Division, Library of Congress, photostat; original in RGAVMF, St. Petersburg. An abridged version is published in *Drug prosviashcheniia* 10 (1805): 89–106. An English translation of the latter by Lydia T. Black is published in "The Konyag (The Inhabitants of the Island of Kodiak) by Ioasaf [Bolotov], 1794–1799, and by Gideon, 1804–1807," *Arctic Anthropology* 14, no. 2 (1977): 82–87. The reference to firearms is found on p. 86 of Black's translation.
19. Russian State Naval Archive, Fond 870, op. 1, delo 1784, Izmailov's log for 1792, fol. 42, contains a description of the incident, as far as is known the only testimony besides Baranov's own account.
20. Pierce, *Biographical Dictionary,* 414–415.
21. Nataliia Shelikhov to Count Platon Zubov, 22 November 1795, in Tikhmenev, *A History,* vol. 2, 88 (doc. 20).
22. Kiril T. Khlebnikov, "Pervonachal'noe poselenie Russkikh v Amerike," parts 1–3, *Raduga,* Special supplement, 2 (1833): 313; 3 (1833): 15–24; 5 (1833): 69–85.
23. Baranov to Shelikhov and Polevoi, 20 May 1795, in Tikhmenev, *A History,* vol. 2, 64 (doc. 18).
24. Baranov to E. Larionov, 3 March 1798, in ibid., 95 (doc. 24).
25. A partial list of these settlers, arranged in thirty family units, contains data on ages and the family heads' occupations. See Russian State Naval Archive (RGAVMF), Papers of Count Kushelev, Fond 198, op. 1, delo 71, fols. 42v–44r.
26. See Tarkhanov's manuscript, sbornik Q IV.311, fols. 1–76, Manuscript Division, Russian National Library, St. Petersburg, and also A. V. Grinev, "Zabytaia ekspeditsiia Dmitriia Tarkhanova na Mednuiu reku," *Sovetskaia etnografiia,* 1987, no. 4: 88–110, published in English translation by Richard Bland as "The Forgotten Expedition of Dmitrii Tarkhanov on the Copper River," *Alaska History* 12, no. 1 (1997): 1–17.

27. Baranov to Polomoshnoi, 28 April 1798, in Tikhmenev, *A History,* vol. 2, 92 (doc. 23); Filip Kashevarov, [Answers to Kiril Khlebnikov's questions on the history of the Russian American colonies, 10 June 1822], microfilmed copy in Shur Collection, reel 2, item 13, Rasmuson Library, University of Alaska Fairbanks (original in State Archive of the Perm' Region, Perm', Russia, Fond 445, op. 1, delo 75).

28. Khlebnikov, *Baranov,* 23; G. I. Davydov, *Dvukhkratnoe puteshestvie v Ameriku morskikh ofitserov Khvostova i Davydova, pisannoe sim poslednim,* 2 pts. (St. Petersburg: Morskaia tipografiia, 1810–1812), English edition, *Two Voyages to Russian America, 1802–1807,* trans. Colin Bearne, ed. Richard A. Pierce (Kingston, Ontario: Limestone Press, 1977), 200; Khlebnikov, *Russkaia Amerika v neopublikovannykh,* 53–55.

29. Concerning the date of Izmailov's death, see Pierce, *Biographical Dictionary,* 207; L. M. Paseniuk, "Morekhod Gerasim Izmailov," in *Amerikanskii ezhegodnik 1994* (Moscow: Izdatel'stvo "Nauka," 1995), 115.

30. Baranov to Navigator Talin, May 1799, in Tikhmenev, *A History,* vol. 2, 98–101 (doc. 25). On the navy's attitudes toward the Russian-American Company see Glynn Barratt, *Russia in Pacific Waters, 1715–1825* (Vancouver: University of British Columbia Press, 1981).

31. Baranov to Larionov, 24 July 1800, in Tikhmenev, *A History,* vol. 2, 115–117 (doc. 29).

32. Ibid., 117–120 (doc. 29).

33. In another letter to Larionov (ibid., 120–122 [doc. 30]), written the same day, Baranov apparently retracted his resignation.

34. Ibid.

FIGURE 32. Paul I (1754–1801), emperor of Russia 1796–1801. He authorized the establishment of the Russian-American Company.
Courtesy Slavic and Baltic Division, New York Public Library, Astor, Lenox, and Tilden Foundations.

FIGURE 33. Alexander I (1777–1825), emperor of Russia 1801–1825. He initiated the navy circumnavigating expeditions beginning in 1803, and in 1818 he established the practice of seconding senior naval officers to serve as managers of the Russian American colony.
Courtesy Slavic and Baltic Division, New York Public Library, Astor, Lenox, and Tilden Foundations.

Chapter Nine

Baranov Extends the Empire

In spite of the seemingly never-ending difficulties facing the energetic manager, Baranov kept extending the reach of his commercial empire, coming into conflict with the Tlingit, and coping with emissaries from the new Russian-American Company, skippers from foreign nations who sometimes became his allies, and, eventually, the high-ranking Russian naval officers who worked for the government.

These and other vicissitudes made the imperial extension a slow and irregular process, even from its early stages. By 1799, the Sitka-Angoon region had become a regular port of call for Baranov's long-distance hunting parties. Shields's probes into this area had become regular visits. He and other navigators now escorted the large baidarka hunting parties in order to give them cover when Tlingits attacked. In 1797, Shields in the *Orel* had escorted such a party to Sitka Sound and in 1798 Navigator Talin, who took over the *Orel*'s command from Shields, was dispatched to chart the sound and adjacent waterways. A hunting party operated there under Dem'ianenkov at the same time. In 1799, Vasilii Medvednikov, who had been selected to head the new settlement, went to Sitka on the *Orel*. The *Sv. Ekaterina*, under Podgash, explored the Queen Charlotte Islands and then sailed to Sitka, transporting necessary building materials, and Baranov himself sailed there on the *Ol'ga*. An Aleut hunting party of 550 kayaks was dispatched from Kodiak in April and was at Sitka that summer, but departed for Kodiak before construction of the new outpost commenced. It was on this journey that more than 100 Aleuts died in Peril Strait of shellfish poisoning. That summer shellfish poisoning had occurred also in Cook Inlet; it is the earliest documented occurrence of the red tide in Alaska.

Baranov negotiated with three Tlingit chiefs, representing the two Tlingit moieties, who headed the settlement centered on the great rocky outcrop where Baranov later was to build his own headquarters. He pretended that the Tlingit agreed to permit establishment of a settlement in return for trade and alliance against common enemies, though he himself realized that the Tlingit would oppose a *permanent* establishment. On 15 July 1799 construction commenced. The settlement was named Novo-Arkhangel'sk in honor of the ancient center of northern Russian seafaring and trade, and, like the old city on the White Sea, was placed under the protection of the Archistrategos Archangel Michael. Sometime in early 1800, a formal ceremony, including a procession, an improvised religious service, a quasi-military parade, and a great many volleys from firearms and cannon was held to mark the taking of possession and incorporation of the territory under the Russian scepter. A possession plate and crest were buried, together with various folk symbols, as tangible proof of Russian sovereignty. Tlingit chiefs and their retinue came to witness the event,[1] but Baranov was not present at this ceremony; he had already left Sitka. He had remained at Sitka only until spring, supervising the progress of the work and cultivating Tlingit leadership not only by offering gifts but also by holding dances and feasts. Apparently he stood godfather to one of the Tlingit leaders, as was the custom of the time, in lay baptism. This leader is known in Russian records by his baptismal name, Mikhail, as well as by his Tlingit name, Skautlel't (Shk'awulyeil of the Kiks.adi clan, Raven moiety). He also tried to cultivate the friendship of Katleyan, Skautlel't's nephew and at that time the Tlingit military leader (K'alyaan, later the chief of the Sitka Tlingit). On 25 March 1800, Baranov ceremoniously presented Chief Mikhail with an imperial crest and a formal written testimonial in which it was stated that the territory had been ceded to the Russians freely and for recompense, though Baranov clearly realized that the Tlingit "did not expect us to settle permanently."[2]

By the time Baranov left Sitka, 22 April 1800, the two-story-high main building and an octagonal *kazhim* (communal and ceremonial house) for the Aleuts and barracks for the men were completed, as were several temporary structures that Baranov intended to replace with more permanent ones (steam bath, blacksmith shop, separate warehouse, etc.). Two blockhouses were under construction as well as the palisade, of which only forty-two feet were completed. It was never finished, apparently because Medvednikov, the man in charge, felt himself to be secure, in spite of several indications of tension and dissatisfaction with the Russian presence, at least among a part of the Tlingit leadership, including Katleyan. While Baranov was still at Sitka, there had been several attempts at surprise attacks by warriors visiting his camp, which he was able to forestall. At one point, when a Tlingit woman Baranov sent to invite the chiefs to attend festivities was badly beaten, he felt compelled to display a show of force. He marched to the Tlingit settlement with his entire Russian force of twenty-two men, dragging two cannons, and fired two volleys over the main house. There were no casualties, no blood was shed, and at the end courtesies were exchanged, food was shared, and the uneasy truce preserved.

The tensions were aggravated by the fact that several English and American vessels were in the vicinity prior to Baranov's arrival, during his stay there, and in the next two to three years. Baranov went on board several vessels and remarked on the hospitality he was offered on an American one. Podgash, in command of a company vessel, also made visits and his visit was remarked on by the skipper of the *Hancock*.[3] The presence of heavily armed foreign merchantmen in considerable numbers and their mode of operation when dealing with the Natives disturbed Baranov greatly. Upon his return to Kodiak, he wrote to Emel'ian Larionov at Unalaska on 24 July 1800:

> The inhabitants have guns, cannons and ammunition in abundance from the English and from the American Republicans from Boston who aim not only at trading but at occupation of this territory as well. Only the revolution in France and wars are keeping them from doing so, but as soon as they have peace we will find ourselves in danger of losing this territory which was explored by our seafarers a long time ago.... I myself saw in neighboring villages, four cannons of one pounder caliber and heard that in other villages they have more of them of heavier caliber.[4]

Earlier, probably in the fall of 1798, Baranov had reported to the governor of Siberia at Irkutsk his concern that the British were planning to claim the coast that he considered part of Russian territory. He stated that the British were presenting medals to the Natives, buttons for their festive clothing (now known as "button blankets"), and hats "resembling those of grenadiers decorated with English crest." One such crest that Baranov had collected in southeastern Alaska arrived in Irkutsk together with his report. He also reported that he had formally taken possession for the Russian Crown of the "inhabited island *Taxanas*, which is named Iakobii" (for a former governor-general of Siberia). A Russian possession crest "together with an appropriate charter" had been presented to the local toion.[5]

To complicate matters further, a number of foreign sailors were left on the coast by their skippers. Around 1799 at least eleven sailors had been left at Sitka by their skippers as punishment: three of them are known to have been off the American vessel *Jenny*, and seven probably off the *Hancock*; three of these joined the Russians, and the other eight stayed with the Tlingit. Later, the Russians would maintain that these sailors were left to incite the concerted attack upon the Russian contingents in 1802.

Baranov was also concerned with the economic competition, as the Americans paid highly for sea otter skins in guns, ammunition, powder, and iron. It was also rumored that the Americans traded African slaves to the Tlingit.[6] Their generosity (which, as Baranov clearly saw, they compensated for by transporting Chinese goods, obtained in trade at Canton for the furs, to the eastern seaboard) affected even the British who would soon, almost within a decade, relinquish the field.

The distribution of liquor to the Natives was also a sore point. There was never any abundant supply of liquor in Russian America. In Baranov's time he and a few high-ranking officials, predominantly navigators who sailed to Okhotsk, occasionally had access to government-controlled "white vodka." Otherwise, Baranov claimed, only he (and in the early years Navigator Izmailov) brewed liquor from local berries in limited quantities, drinking it usually to mark a special feast day. This absence of liquor was noted by British seafarers, such as Portlock and officers aboard Vancouver's ships, and explains the eagerness with which some Russians accepted British and American hospitality, where liquor was dispensed with a liberal hand.

Baranov hoped in vain that, due to the political situation in Europe, Spain would rescind the agreement ceding Nootka to the British, the situation would be eased, and his hold on the territory Russia claimed would remain secure. His letters and his instructions to Medvednikov of 19 April 1800 clearly show how worried he was about the safety of his remote outpost.[7]

The so-called garrison of Novo-Arkhangel'sk was manned by twenty-five to thirty Russians, fifty-five Alaskans from the Kodiak-Prince William Sound area, and Aleuts recruited from as far away as the Andreanof Islands (central Aleutians). The men spent their time improving and constructing buildings and hunting and fishing for their subsistence. In summer, most Aleuts, with a few Russians, were sent out to hunt sea otters. There were a few women, wives of the Aleuts and of some Russians; later some men married Tlingit women. They were low on supplies and Baranov could not help, as the supply ships from Okhotsk did not arrive, and the main supply ship, the *Phoenix*, had been lost in 1799.[8] Baranov claimed that because of this lack, he was forced to give away his own clothing as presents to the Tlingit at Sitka. Perhaps he was referring here to the chain-mail shirt he gave to Chief Mikhail of Sitka that now reposes in the National Museum of American History of the Smithsonian Institution in Washington, D.C.

But in the immediate future, in 1802, Baranov was faced with great reversal, bordering on catastrophe. That summer, Captain Barber, commanding the *Unicorn*, put into St. Paul Harbor on Kodiak, bringing news that Novo-Arkhangel'sk had been destroyed.

In spite of his earlier misgivings, Baranov had not anticipated this. Sitka, like Yakutat, had become a base for the sea otter hunting parties that now could probe even as far as the Queen Charlotte Islands. The previous year, a long-distance sea otter hunting party out of Kodiak, under Kuskov, had hunted in the Alexander Archipelago and farther to the southeast with great success, obtaining through hunting and trade about 5,000 sea otter skins; they used Novo-Arkhangel'sk as their base and rallying point.[9] In April 1802, Baranov once again detailed Kuskov to lead a long-distance hunting party beyond Sitka. After a stopover at Yakutat, he sailed to the Tlingit settlement the Russians called Akoi (Dry Bay), on the Alsek River, where he found a great many Tlingit men from various coastal settlements as distant as Hoonah and Kaknu, and the mood decidedly unfriendly. A group of Tlingit leaders addressed Kuskov with long speeches reciting grievances against the Russians, among them the alleged robbery of a grave site of Kuiu by members of the Sitka hunting party and the murder of the Kuiu chief and his wife. The latter was from the Stikine region (the vicinity of modern Wrangell), and Kuskov believed this was one of the reasons for the involvement of this remote Tlingit group in the conflict.[10] Another item in this indictment was that Russian hunting activities in their waters interfered with the Tlingit's European trade. By the evening of 22 May, the Tlingit were taking hunting and fishing implements away from Aleuts and Chugach who ventured to go out by themselves; then, by force of arms, they took several kayaks and fired muskets or rifles at a small detachment sent to the rescue of the stragglers. The capture of two Tlingit nobles stopped the conflict; a representative of the Kaknu settlement came to bargain for their freedom. Kuskov set the nobles free, but the next day the Tlingit attacked his camp, violating the agreement Kuskov believed he had reached. There were casualties on both sides. Yakutat, Hoonah, Kaknu, Akoi, and Tlingit from other settlements, some very distant, participated in the fight. The Stikine Tlingit were also involved (and allegedly would later participate in the attack on Novo-Arkhangel'sk). The party that attacked Kuskov was led by a high-ranking Tlingit from Angoon. The Angoon and the Stikine people were involved, in Kuskov's opinion, because the Angoon chief's nephew had been seized by the Russians and held for a long time in irons in either 1800 or 1801, in reprisal for the seizure of hunting implements from two members of the long-distance hunting party. The Stikine involvement rested on Tlingit kinship obligations. There had been a recent marriage between an Angoon chief's daughter and the son of the Stikine chief, which, at least for a time, changed the relationship between these two traditionally hostile groups.[11] Kuskov lost much of his equipment and supplies in the retreat to the boats but managed to establish a makeshift though defensible camp. After failing to take it, the Tlingit opened negotiations while sending messengers along the coast southward to their allies.

On 30 May Kuskov sailed back to Yakutat where he left the sick, the wounded, and the Tlingit captives, and then set out again for Icy Strait. Here Kuskov met several Tlingit who asked about one of their own who had died in the fighting; Kuskov disclaimed any knowledge of his fate. One of the old men told Kuskov that a large group of warriors, among whom the Angoon people mustered ten canoes and Sitka Tlingit at least two, waited in ambush for his party farther south along the coast, ostensibly to trade. Kuskov also obtained information that the Stikine River Tlingit, in concert with others, were going to attack at Sitka but, said Kuskov, he was not clear whether the attack was intended upon the Sitka Tlingit or against the Russian outpost there. He sent six kayaks, commanded by the Kodiak Aleut Eremei Kochergin, to Novo-Arkhangel'sk to ascertain the situation there and to see if the hunting party out of Sitka could rendezvous with Kuskov at Kaknu or in Chilkat Bay. Kuskov hoped to obtain from Novo-Arkhangel'sk one cannon for his party, additional firearms, and a Tlingit interpreter. Kuskov himself proceeded toward Chichagof Island. From there he dispatched part of his men among the islands off Sitka (now Baranof) Island. Here, on 20 June, five of the six Kochergin kayaks rejoined him and reported that Novo-Arkhangel'sk was a smoking ruin.

One of Kuskov's kayaks rescued a Kodiak Islander, from Alitak, who had been stationed at Novo-Arkhangel'sk and had witnessed the attack upon the outpost. Afraid that now the Tlingit would attack Yakutat, Kuskov sailed back with all possible speed and sent Baranov a report about the disaster. According to information gathered by Kuskov, Chief Mikhail had warned the outpost repeatedly of the impending attack by Tlingit from as far away as the Stikine region and, in fact, an anonymous warrior delivered a warning almost on the eve of the attack. Medvednikov had ignored all warnings. Though he was aware of the possibility of Tlingit seeking revenge for the killing of several important Tlingit men by the Aleuts in the previous summer (presumably as partial retaliation for the death by shellfish poisoning of so many Aleuts, which they had interpreted as being due to sorcery), he probably did not believe that any revenge would take the form of an all-out attack. Most of his men were dispatched in ninety double-hatch kayaks under the leadership of Urbanov to Bucareli Bay and Frederick Sound, the territory of the Kake Tlingit, to hunt sea otters. There were left at Novo-Arkhangel'sk twenty-nine Russians and three Englishmen, fewer than twenty Aleuts, and an unspecified number of women and children. Shortly before the day of the attack, sixteen men set out to hunt seals and sea lions. Medvednikov apparently did not foresee that any revenge would take the form of an attack on the outpost.

The Tlingit, knowing Russian habits and the day-to-day situation through information supplied by Tlingit women living in the outpost, attacked on Sunday afternoon, while most of the Russian men were either napping, fishing, or attending to their own private tasks. Only sixteen men were in the main building, which the Tlingit stormed. There were forty-two survivors, mostly women and children, and five or six men. Many more died when the Tlingit attacked the Urbanov party near Kake. Of the nearly 200 men in the Urbanov party, only Urbanov himself and twenty-two Aleuts made their way back to Yakutat.

The Russians firmly believed that the attack would never have taken place had not the American and British skippers agitated for it by threatening to stop trading with the Tlingit unless the Russians were destroyed, and by supplying firearms, including cannon, in quantity.[12] In fact, the *Unicorn* under Barber appeared at Novo-Arkhangel'sk when the flames had barely died down. According to Barber's account, almost immediately "the Chief of the Sound" (Skautlel't) came aboard his vessel, accompanied by three American seamen who said that three more Americans were with the Tlingit and that the Tlingit had plundered more than 4,000 sea otter skins from the Russian factory. When Chief

Skautlel't and Katleyan came aboard the *Unicorn*, they were seized, put in irons, and tied to the yardarm. Barber threatened to hang both of them unless the Tlingit gave up any survivors and all the Russian sea otter pelts taken from the warehouse. The next day, Barber was joined off Novo-Arkhangel'sk by two American vessels out of Boston, the *Alert* and the *Globe*, commanded by Ebbets and Cunningham, respectively. The three captains "concluded…that the most effectual way to effect the business would be to make as many prisoners as possible.…Those taken aboard the *Globe* and *Alert*, fought with their knives and daggers, till most of them were wounded and overpowered, several Indians lost their lives, the Chief's wife and six men were made prisoners, and five of the middling sized canoes taken." Then the three captains and seven of their officers formed a court-martial and, as a public example, condemned one of the Tlingit prisoners to death. He was hanged forthwith aboard the *Globe* "in the presence of the Chief of Shetka."[13] Barber had all the Russian and Aleut survivors transferred to his vessel and sailed for Kodiak. There, training his twenty guns on the town, Barber demanded that Baranov pay ransom for the five (Barber says eight) men and eighteen women and children (Barber says seventeen women and three children). Baranov got ready to defend the town but he did pay the ransom—in sea otter skins—less than Barber demanded but valued at no less than 10,000 rubles.[14]

Baranov took the loss of Novo-Arkhangel'sk very hard. Not only were the manpower and materiel losses stupendous, he lost some of his best men, men to whom he

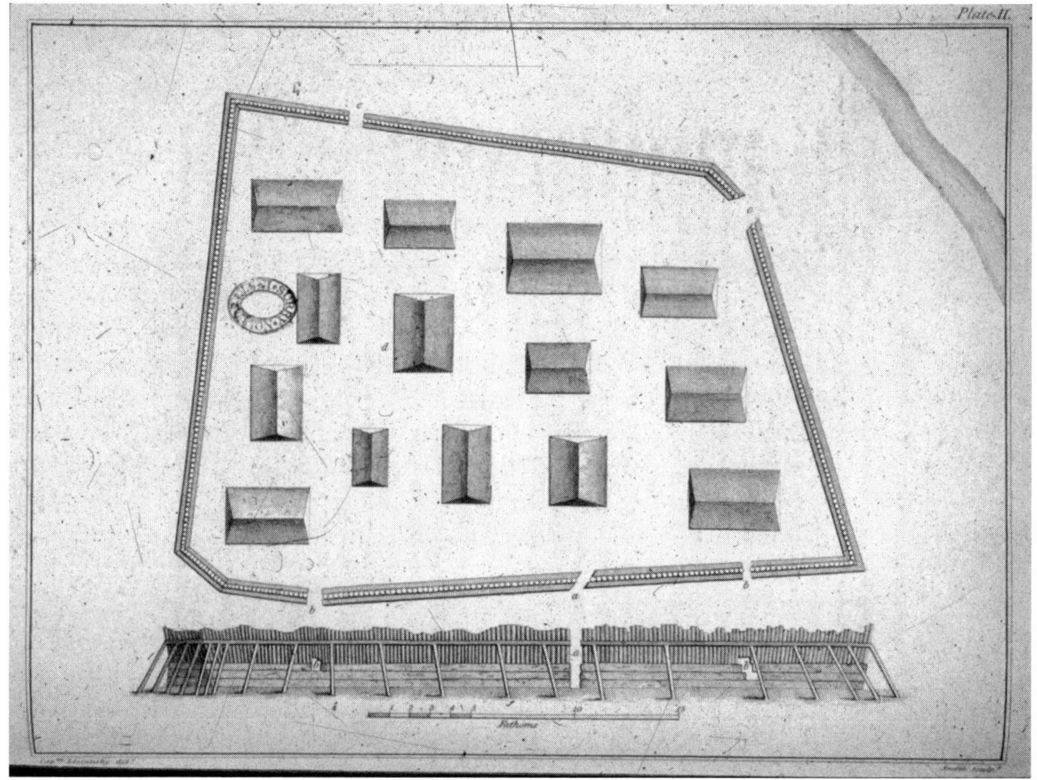

Figure 34. Tlingit fort at Sitka, taken by the Russians in 1804. Drawing by Captain-Lieutenant Iurii F. Lisianskii.

Courtesy University of Alaska Fairbanks, Rasmuson Library, Alaska and Polar Regions Department, Rare Book Collection, no. A0915, p. 163.

was bound by ties of friendship. Moreover, his best sea otter hunting grounds were in danger. There was, at the moment, no sea otter hunting in the Tlingit territory south of Yakutat. Baranov thus was ready to give a willing ear to the suggestion of an American, Joseph O'Cain, that he be lent Aleuts for sea otter hunting in California. Shvetsov, put in charge of the Aleut detachment, had orders to collect all information he could about the Californian coast, trade with the local inhabitants, and presence (or absence) of foreign shipping. When O'Cain returned, Shvetsov was able to report to Baranov about California as far south as San Diego.

Baranov was also concerned that the loss of this forward Russian establishment would preclude the possibility of any action on his part to advance Russian claims as far as possible southward toward Nootka. He was afraid the British and the Americans would seize the moment to establish permanent settlements on the coast.

Baranov was determined to retake Sitka and establish an upper hand within the Tlingit territory. For this he needed ships. Two new vessels, the *Ermak* and the *Sv. Rostislav*, were constructed at Yakutat for use in the planned counterattack. By April 1804, Baranov was ready to recover the ground he had lost. A large long-distance party, consisting of 300 kayaks, was dispatched under Dem'ianenkov, under the protection of the *Sv. Rostislav*. The *Sv. Ekaterina* and the *Sv. Aleksandr* were ordered to Sitka, while Baranov, in the *Ermak*, sailed to Cross Sound, where he joined the hunting party and the *Sv. Rostislav*. The two vessels and the hunting party proceeded through Chatham Strait to Lynn Canal and farther southeast past Auk, Kake, and Stikine. Baranov ordered Kake and Kui (Kuiu) burned because it was here that the Urbanov party had been ambushed and destroyed almost to the last man.[15] These operations lasted through the summer. Baranov then proceeded to Sitka Sound, where he arrived on 2 September 1804 and, to his great relief, found that a navy frigate, the *Neva*, under Captain-Lieutenant Iurii F. Lisianskii, was there, ready to assist him.

In short order the Tlingit stronghold was stormed but the Tlingit repulsed the attack. Complicated negotiations ensued, and on the night of 7 October the Tlingit abandoned their camp, having killed babies and dogs to avoid alerting the enemy. Baranov later conducted formal peace negotiations, and a modus vivendi was established which lasted to the end of Russian America, with few interruptions and only one short-lived armed outbreak at Sitka in the period of the Crimean War. Novo-Arkhangel'sk was rebuilt in a new location and became the capital of Russian America and an international port.

When Baranov reestablished himself firmly at Sitka in 1804, a shipyard was created there also, and in 1806 the first vessel, the *Avos'*, was launched. That year, he hired an American shipwright[16] who built three vessels there and retimbered and repaired two others. He also trained several Russians, among them Grudinin, who later built vessels at the Russian settlement in California. For many years afterward, the Novo-Arkhangel'sk (Sitka) shipyard was the only shipbuilding and ship repair facility on the North American west coast. In addition, when the Americans made contact with the Russians in Alaska, Baranov purchased several vessels from them and at least one from the British (the *Myrtle*, Captain Barber).[17]

In the north of the Tlingit territory, however, another serious conflict erupted. About 20 September 1805 the settlement at Yakutat was destroyed and the entire population killed, with the exception of a few children and women (there were also, in the area of the Copper River, several killings of individual employees who went off alone on errands).[18]

Figure 35. Iurii F. Lisianskii in full uniform. Lisianskii is responsible not only for a succinct account of the second battle for Sitka but also for very good ethnographic descriptions of the Kodiak Aleutian way of life and Kodiak whalers, and the first systematic collection of artifacts from Alaska. Engraving by A.Ukhtomskii, 1812.
Courtesy Richard A. Pierce.

Some survivors were ransomed or rescued with the assistance of the American Captain Kimball, but the settlement known as Slava Rossii at Yakutat Bay was never reestablished.

The Tlingit people remained politically independent; however, they not only tolerated the Russians' presence and traded with them, but in later years supplied Novo-Arkhangel'sk with food and even grew potatoes in quantity specifically for sale to the Russian colony.[19] Russians did not interfere in Tlingit internal affairs. When slaves were to be sacrificed, Russians tried to purchase the intended victims, usually at high price, and set them free (these captives then often entered the company's service). Chief managers, high-ranking officials, and their wives attended Tlingit feasts (now called potlatches) and in turn gave feasts for Tlingit leaders and their retinue. Intermarriage, which took place in a number of instances from the very beginning,[20] increased and so did Tlingit conversion to Orthodoxy.[21]

The supply situation at this time was approaching a critical state throughout the colony. Even at

Figure 36. Grave of Captain Iurii F. Lisianskii (2 April 1773–22 February 1837), Sv. Aleksandr Nevskii Lavra, St. Petersburg.
Photo by Nikolai Turkin.

Kodiak and Unalaska supplies were running low. Shipping furs to market also presented new difficulties. Baranov's thoughts turned more and more toward the possibility of marketing his furs directly at Canton. An opportunity presented itself when an American vessel, the *Enterprise*, under Captain Ezekiel Hubbell, called at Sitka and then entered St. Paul Harbor on Kodiak. Baranov traded for supplies. On board was Joseph O'Cain, who realized a business opportunity when he saw it. He was back at Kodiak in 1803, on a new vessel named *O'Cain*, with his business partner Jonathan Winship in command. They brought supplies and entered into an agreement with Baranov by which he was to supply Aleut hunters and kayaks, which O'Cain and Winship would transport for sea otter

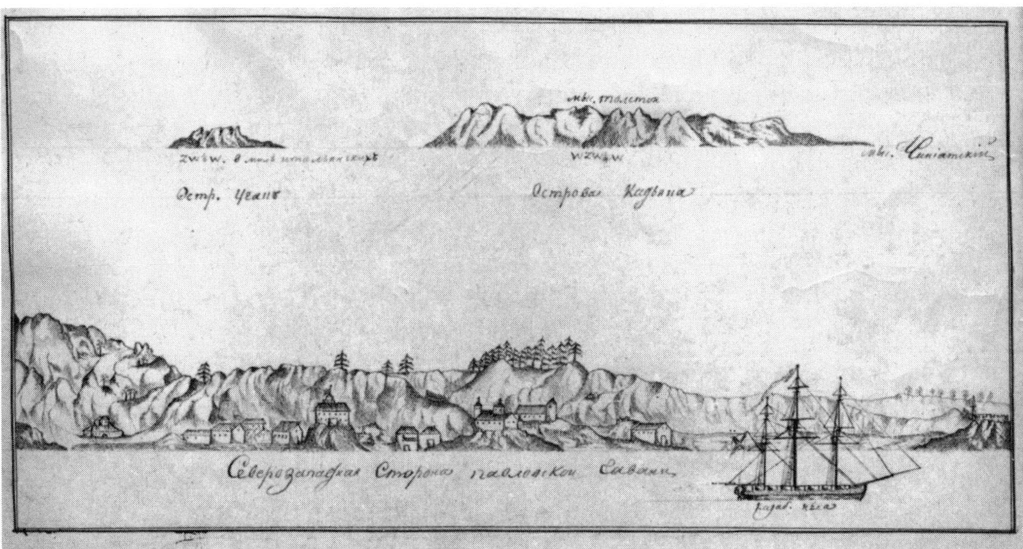

Figure 37. View of St. Paul Harbor (modern Kodiak) from the north. Sketch by Iurii Lisianskii, commander of the ship *Neva* (lower right), which, in 1804, was the first Russian naval circumnavigating vessel to come to Alaska. Hieromonk Gedeon, empowered by the synod to investigate conditions of the church in Alaska, traveled aboard the *Neva* and remained on Kodiak 1804–1807.
Courtesy Richard A. Pierce.

Figure 38. Sketch of Sitka (Novo-Arkhangel'sk) site, 1805, by Lisianskii, showing the three-masted *Neva* and Baranov's *Ermak* and *Sv. Rostislav*.
Courtesy Richard A. Pierce.

hunting along the coast of California. The catch would be sold in Canton and the profits divided between the Americans and the company. In 1806, O'Cain, now in command of his own *Eclipse*, undertook to carry Baranov's furs to Canton. On the return voyage, in 1807, he was wrecked off Sanak Island in the eastern Aleutians. He repaired his vessel with Aleut and Russian help and refloated her. Unfortunately, the vessel was caught in a storm off Unimak and wrecked once again. O'Cain drowned in the mishap.

Several other American skippers soon followed in quick succession and entered into agreements similar to the one O'Cain had attempted: Ayres, Kimball (in command of the *Peacock*, who in 1805 aided Baranov in regaining prisoners taken by the Tlingit at Yakutat and captured a Chilkat chief), Whittmore, Blanchard, the brothers Meek. Through the Americans, Baranov established contact with several rulers in the Hawaiian Islands, which later culminated in his attempt to establish a Russian outpost there.

But Baranov was not entirely abandoned by the home front during this difficult period. Not only did he receive official recognition in the form of the Order of St. Vladimir, but he was also elevated to the status of Active Collegiate Councillor. More to the point, two vessels arrived from Okhotsk, bringing an additional 120 newly hired men and some badly needed supplies. Another vessel arrived early in 1804. Banner arrived from Unalaska and took some of the burden from Baranov in managing his by now far-flung and growing empire. The main office, dissatisfied with the poor results in the Unalaska District managed by the shareholder Larionov, put the district under Baranov's control. The Pribilofs, too, were now under his management. Larionov, who considered the fur seal trade the mainstay of company business, had overhunted the herd. Masses of fur seal pelts were inadequately cured and stored. When shipped to the Chinese market, these inferior skins were refused. It was at this time that Baranov ordered the first stoppage of fur seal harvest to replenish the herd and also to improve the market. In later years

Figure 39. Lisianskii brought to Kodiak, in 1804, gifts to the capital of Russian America, including this bust of Emperor Alexander I and a set of communion vessels, gift of Count Rumiantsev. The bust is preserved in the Baranov Museum in Kodiak. The communion service is kept in Kodiak's Church of the Holy Resurrection.
Courtesy Richard A. Pierce.

regular stoppages of harvest and the selective harvesting of nonbreeding three- to five-year-old males would be instituted and followed systematically. This practice, followed until modern times, preserved the fur seal herds as a renewable resource, the take maintained at sustainable level until it was stopped in the Pribilofs by U.S. Congressional action in the 1970s; the fur seal harvest continued in the Commander Islands.[22]

The year 1804, however, brought Baranov complications of a different sort. Lisianskii, representing the navy, which traditionally acted for the Crown in the North Pacific, was expected to render an independent report about the situation in the colony. He must have informed Baranov that Nikolai P. Rezanov, invested with all sorts of important-sounding titles and representing the company's board of directors, was in Kamchatka preparing to sail to Alaska. Rezanov claimed to have authority and wide-ranging powers to reorganize the colony from the Emperor Alexander I himself. Moreover, Lisianskii brought to Kodiak aboard his own *Neva* Hieromonk Gedeon, a representative of the church, with a mandate to report on the conditions in the colony, specifically the state of the spiritual mission (with whose members Baranov had had sharp disagreements over his treatment of the Natives) and to report directly to Metropolitan Gavriil, of Novgorod and St. Petersburg, and the emperor. Though according to the Russian proverb, allegedly often quoted by Baranov's men, "God dwells high, and the tsar is too far," the Crown was asserting its authority.

NOTES

1. Baranov to Medvednikov, Order of Ceremonial Procession held at Sitka in the year 1799, October [day omitted], RGADA, Fond 796, op. 1, delo 356, no. 13, fols. 1r–7v; Baranov to Larionov, 24 July 1800, in Tikhmenev, *A History,* vol. 2, 113–114 (doc. 29).
2. Baranov to Larionov, 24 July 1800, in Tikhmenev, *A History,* vol. 2, 113 (doc. 29).
3. Ibid., 109; Howay, *List of Trading Vessels,* 38–39.
4. Tikhmenev, *A History,* vol. 2, 108, 113 (doc. 29).
5. Russian State Historical Archive (RGIA), St. Petersburg, Fond 1374, op. 2, delo 1672, fols. 1r–1v, Summary of information by Governor Tolstoi for the Office of the Procurator-General of the Ruling Senate, 3 March 1799.
6. Report, Kuskov to Baranov, 1 July 1802 from Yakutat, in Pavlov, ed., *K istorii Rossiisko-amerikanskoi kompanii,* 119 (doc. 9).
7. Instruction to Medvednikov, ibid., 95–106 (doc. 8).
8. Baranov to Fedor Rodionov, Foreman at Hinchenbrook Island, 14 May 1800, in Tikhmenev, *A History,* vol. 2, 102–103 (doc. 26); Baranov to Emel'ian Larionov, 24 July 1800, in ibid., 106–120 (doc. 29); Khlebnikov, "Pervonachal'noe poselenie," 3–11; idem, *Russkaia Amerika v "zapiskakh,"* 41–43; W. Wilfried Schuhmacher, "Aftermath of the Sitka Massacre of 1802: Contemporary Documents with an Introduction and Afterword by W. Wilfried Schuhmacher," *Alaska Journal* 9, no. 1 (1979): 58–61.
9. Khlebnikov, *Zhizneopisanie,* 65–66.
10. Report, Kuskov to Baranov, 1 July 1802 from Yakutat, in Pavlov, ed., *K istorii Rossiisko-amerikanskoi kompanii,* 107, 120 (doc. 9). It is not clear (as Kuskov used a Russian adjectival form in his report) whether the term Kuiu refers to a locality, or to a clan at Auk Bay (near modern Juneau).
11. The imprisonment of an important Tlingit noble is reflected in Tlingit oral traditions, although in the one available version the man who suffers is from Chilkat, not Angoon. See Nora Marks Dauenhauer and Richard Dauenhauer, "The Battles of Sitka, 1802 and 1804, from Tlingit, Russian, and Other Points of View," in *Russia in North America: Proceedings of the 2nd International*

Conference on Russian America, Sitka, Alaska, August 19–22, 1987, ed. Richard A. Pierce (Kingston, Ontario; Fairbanks, Alaska: Limestone Press, 1990), 6–24.

12. Khlebnikov, "Pervonachal'noe poselenie," and idem, *Zhizneopisanie.* See also instruction to Baranov from the Board of Directors, 29 April 1805, to supply information immediately on the reasons for the attack on Novo-Arkhangel'sk, as the Board had received independent information that the English vessel (Barber's *Unicorn*) was instrumental in inciting the attack (Tikhmenev, *A History,* vol. 2, 163). For modern scholarly assessments of the significance of the American sea otter trade in shaping Russian-American relations see Gibson, *Otter Skins,* particularly chap. 3, "The American Takeover," and N. N. Bolkhovitinov, *Beginnings of Russian-American Relations,* 171–193. In this relationship there were competition, tension, and cooperation. A provocative view on this question was advanced by Howard I. Kushner (*American-Russian Rivalry in the Pacific Northwest, 1790–1867* [Ann Arbor, Mich.: University Microfilms, 1970], and *Conflict on the Northwest Coast: American-Russian Rivalry in the Pacific Northwest, 1790–1867* [Westport, Conn.: Greenwood Press, 1975]), who postulated that throughout the eighteenth and nineteenth centuries the relationship of conflict was dominant. A more balanced view is presented by Gibson, and Wheeler stresses cooperation and mutual dependency. See James R. Gibson, "Bostonians and Muscovites on the Northwest Coast, 1788–1841," in *The Western Shore: Oregon Country Essays Honoring the American Revolution,* ed. Thomas Vaughan (Portland: Oregon Historical Society, 1975), 81–119; and Mary Wheeler, "Empires in Conflict and Cooperation: The 'Bostonians' and the Russian-American Company," *Pacific Historical Review* 40, no. 4 (1971): 419–441. For an assessment of American scholarship on this question, see Bolkhovitinov, *Russko-Amerikanskie otnosheniia i prodazha Aliaski, 1834–1867* (Moscow: Izdatel'stvo "Nauka," 1990), 17–22.

13. Advertisement in the Sydney *Gazette,* 9 December 1804; Schuhmacher, "Aftermath of the Sitka Massacre," 58–61.

14. Khlebnikov, "Pervonachal'noe poselenie," 24; idem, *Zhizneopisanie,* 69–70; Baranov to his men, 15 February 1803, in Pavlov, ed., *K istorii Rossiisko-amerikanskoi kompanii,* 124 (doc. 10).

15. Khlebnikov, *Zhizneopisanie,* 81–82.

16. Khlebnikov, *Russkaia Amerika v "zapiskakh,"* 50, gives the name of the American shipwright as Linken (Lincoln).

17. Filip Kashevarov [Answers to Kiril Khlebnikov's questions].

18. A. V. Grinev, "The Eyak Indians and the Fate of a Russian Settlement at Yakutat," *European Review of Native American Studies* 3, no. 2 (1989): 1–6; William S. Hanable, "New Russia," *Alaska Journal* 3, no. 2 (1973): 77–80. The last-mentioned source, though containing several errors of historical fact, indicates archaeological efforts to locate the site of the Russian outpost.

19. James R. Gibson, "Russian Dependence upon the Natives of Alaska," in *Russia's American Colony,* ed. S. Frederick Starr (Durham: Duke University Press, 1987), 77–104.

20. See Dauenhauer and Dauenhauer, "Battles of Sitka," 15–16, on Abrosim (Amvrosii) Plotnikov, one of the few survivors of the 1802 destruction of Novo-Arkhangel'sk. According to Robert Martin, a direct descendant (and Chairman of the Board of Trustees of Sealaska Heritage Foundation), Plotnikov was saved by his Tlingit brothers-in-law who chased him through the woods with great show of bloodthirsty enthusiasm. Mr. Martin says "they kept chasing him back into the woods to avoid having to fight him" (ibid., 16).

21. Today, a large segment of the Tlingit population is Orthodox. On the significance of Orthodoxy in Tlingit society, see the publications of Sergei Kan, including "Memory Eternal: Orthodox Christianity and the Tlingit Mortuary Complex," *Arctic Anthropology* 24, no. 1 (1987): 32–55; "Russian Orthodox Missionaries and the Tlingit Indians of Alaska, 1880–1900," in *New Dimensions in Ethnohistory: Papers of the Second Laurier Conference on North American Ethnohistory and Ethnology,* ed. Barry Gough and Laird Christie (Hull, Quebec: Canadian Museum of Civilization, 1991), 128–160; and "Russian Orthodox Brotherhoods among the Tlingit: Missionary Goals and Native Response," *Ethnohistory* 32, no. 3 (1985): 196–222.

Several Tlingit men who were closely associated with the Russian-American Company and held positions of importance emigrated to Russia with their families after 1867, and one man is known to have chosen to go to Russia shortly before the revolution of 1917; in 1937 he wrote to his relatives at Sitka asking them for help to return to the United States (Personal archives of Richard A. Pierce, University of Alaska Fairbanks).

22. See Bering Sea Tribunal of Arbitration, *Fur Seal Arbitration, Proceedings of the Tribunal of Arbitration, Convened at Paris,* 16 vols. (Washington, D.C., 1895), particularly vol. 8, which contains translations of relevant Russian-American Company documents. See also Katherine L. Arndt, "Preserving the Future Hunt: The Russian-American Company and Marine Mammal Conservation Policies" (paper presented at Cook Inlet Historical Society Symposium "Science Under Sail: Russian Exploration in the North Pacific, 1728–1867," Anchorage, Alaska, October 2000).

From A. I. Andreev, ed., 1944, facing p. 134. Courtesy Glynn Barratt.

Courtesy Hokkaido University Library, Northern Studies Collection.

Figure 40. Portraits of Nikolai Petrovich Rezanov (1764–1807). Rezanov was born into a burgher family in Irkutsk. He climbed the social ladder, serving in the civil service and intermittently in the army, eventually gaining the rank of lieutenant colonel. In 1794, he came to Irkutsk apparently to audit Grigorii Shelikhov's books and instead married his fifteen-year-old daughter Anna. Romanticized by Russian historians and authors in Russia and America as a great man, he was in reality ambitious, irresponsible, and of very questionable character. One mystery is his relation to Emperor Alexander I—Rezanov was closely involved with Count Palen, chief architect of the coup in which Alexander's father, Paul I, was murdered. The official portrait of Rezanov by a Russian artist (left) contrasts with the way the Japanese saw him in this 1804–1805 painting (right).

Chapter Ten

Rezanov's Tour and Baranov's Final Years

The story of Nikolai P. Rezanov's voyage to Alaska is complicated and closely tied to the dispatch of the first Russian circumnavigating voyage (1803–1806). Two navy vessels, the *Nadezhda* and the *Neva*, purchased in England and outfitted with funds largely provided by the Russian-American Company, were under the overall command of Captain Ivan F. Kruzenshtern. The idea for a circumnavigating voyage originated with Kruzenshtern, who had served under Admiral Chichagov and Captain Mulovskii in 1788. Along with Iurii F. Lisianskii and several other Russian officers, he had served in the English navy from 1793 to 1799 where he became interested in the East India and China trade conducted by England. Both Kruzenshtern and his second in command Lisianskii, captain of the *Neva*, had sailed in what are now Canadian and U.S. waters, in the Atlantic, in the West Indies, off Africa, and to India. Kruzenshtern, on his own, traveled to China. In 1799, he devised a proposal for circumnavigating voyages to supply Russian outposts in Alaska and to market furs in China. In 1802, he outlined his project to Admiral Mordvinov, the minister of the navy, and to Count Rumiantsev, the minister of commerce.[1] The proposal was shown to Rezanov, since 1799 company "correspondent"—that is, the lobbyist whose job it was to argue for the company's interest before officialdom.[2] Rezanov succeeded in gaining Rumiantsev's confidence, and the company undertook the expedition's financing. In the eyes of Rezanov, the expedition became a company enterprise. Rezanov believed that Rumiantsev's instruction to him had put him in charge, with the navy playing the subordinate role. The naval officers commanding the ships, and having their own instructions from the admiralty and Alexander I himself, had a very different view of their role. Nevertheless, it appears that Kruzenshtern was to be responsible to the admiralty *and* to the company, with whom Kruzenshtern and Lisianskii had signed a contract. Rumiantsev's and royal instructions to Rezanov, indeed, put Kruzenshtern into an ambiguous position and probably laid the ground for the future open conflict between the two men. Rumiantsev considered that the chief purpose of the mission was "trade of the Russian-American Company, at whose own expense they [the vessels] were bought, armed, and supplied with appropriate cargoes."[3] Nevertheless, the two vessels were sailing under the flag of St. Andrew, the flag of the imperial navy.

Rumiantsev's instructions to Rezanov in respect to the role he was to play in Alaska also included a most extraordinary passage, which gave him to understand that he had the power to administer the law: "administer courts and punishments as much as possible, remove all burdens from the inhabitants, lay firm foundations for every good order."[4] Rezanov freely exercised the first prerogative, though Rumiantsev, of course, had no power to grant it. The expedition also was supposed to establish diplomatic and trade relations with Japan: Alexander I had appointed Rezanov as an envoy to the Japanese court (and in this connection conferred on Rezanov the rather high rank of Active State Councillor, Chamberlain and Cavalier of the Order of St. Anna). It is to be surmised that the reason for this appointment lay in the fact that "in 1800, Emperor Paul stated that all further attempts to establish relations with Japan be left in the hands of the Russian-American Company."[5] Rezanov also had made several representations that the Russian colony in America would be best supplied from Japan.[6]

From the very beginning Rezanov made himself unpopular with the expedition's naval commander. One of the expedition's artists had to be left behind, as well as some staff and senior officers, because Rezanov's large retinue made both ships overcrowded, especially the flagship *Nadezhda*.[7] Neither was he courteous enough to inform Kruzenshtern of the amount of cargo he would bring along.[8] The tension between Rezanov and Kruzenshtern grew steadily, presumably due to Rezanov's consistent attempts to assert his authority over Kruzenshtern, to the extent that at one point naval officers were suggesting that he be court-martialed. Most of the officers developed a negative attitude toward Rezanov not only out of feelings of loyalty to their commander but in large measure due to Rezanov's personality and his seemingly unsavory personal relations. One of these relations was his link to the young Lt. Golovachev who became his close friend. Eventually, Golovachev committed suicide on the homeward-bound voyage, shortly after he had asked the company agent Shemelin to deliver a portrait bust sculpted of him in Canton to Rezanov who, said Golovachev, "will know the reason why I do this."[9]

When the *Nadezhda* reached Kamchatka, Rezanov appealed to the administrator at Nizhne-Kamchatsk, charging mutiny and requesting an immediate investigation and removal of Kruzenshtern from command. Otherwise, Rezanov threatened to cancel the embassy to Japan. He even offered command to Kruzenshtern's lieutenants, clearly overstepping the bounds of his authority and proposing an action that the admiralty would never countenance.[10] Kruzenshtern was forced to apologize publicly. Moreover, Rezanov wrote to Admiral Chichagov, then assistant minister of the navy, a letter full of oblique accusations against Kruzenshtern.[11] Interestingly, in a letter addressed to the emperor, he very carefully refrained from any accusations, but blamed the discord he had reported earlier to the emperor on his subordinate, young Fedor Tolstoi, a member of his own retinue.[12] It appears that Rezanov was in the habit of accusing subordinates when his own actions threatened adverse government reaction. Tolstoi was sent home under pressure from the Kamchatkan commandant.

One cannot help but wonder if Kruzenshtern's negative reports about the activities of the Russian-American Company in Kamchatka and in Alaska (of which he had no firsthand knowledge whatsoever) were colored by his personal dislike of and conflict with Rezanov. On the other hand, Rezanov's later vituperation of all naval officers in the company's service in Alaska (with the exception of Davydov) may reflect the general long-standing grudge against the navy which he developed while aboard the *Nadezhda*.[13]

In September 1804, while the *Neva* under Lisianskii was preparing to spend the winter at Kodiak, the *Nadezhda* carried Rezanov to Nagasaki. The emperor's envoy proved to be singularly unsuccessful; later, in one of his letters, Rezanov laid the blame on the interpreter, the survivor of a Japanese vessel wrecked in the Aleutians in 1790. The negotiations with the Japanese proved to be very difficult, and Rezanov was not a good diplomat. Arrogant, tactless, and inept, he lost his temper on more than one occasion and felt himself deeply insulted. He threatened the Japanese by stating to their officials that the Russian emperor had means at his disposal to teach them respect and told the Japanese not to expand north of Hokkaido.[14] He carried away a grudge against the Japanese, dreamed of revenge, and eventually proposed military action to teach the Japanese a lesson; at the same time he continued to write about the necessity and advantages of trade with Japan. Without waiting for a response from St. Petersburg, on 29 August 1805 Rezanov informed Baranov that he had ordered such an action against Japan. He also informed Minister of Commerce Rumiantsev to that effect,[15] and issued highly controversial instructions to Lieutenants Khvostov and Davydov to destroy Japanese settlements on Hokkaido and northern Japan.[16]

Earlier that year, Rezanov prepared to travel to Alaska aboard the company vessel *Mariia Magdalina*, commanded by Lt. Mashin, another navy man in company service. Among the passengers were Khvostov and Davydov. These young naval officers, Davydov still in his teens, Khvostov about ten years his senior, had entered the service of the Russian-American Company as navigators in 1802. This move was suggested to Khvostov by Rezanov, who knew him well. Khvostov and Rezanov then persuaded Davydov to come along. They arrived on Kodiak in the fall of 1802 and spent the winter there. In the summer of 1803, they sailed to Okhotsk and from there went for a visit to St. Petersburg where they became shareholders of the Russian-American Company. In 1804, they returned to Okhotsk and sailed the *Mariia* (as the vessel is popularly referred to in the literature) to Petropavlovsk, where they decided to winter. When the *Nadezhda* with Rezanov on board arrived in Petropavlovsk in late May 1805, the two inseparable young men "joined forces with Rezanov and came directly under his disposition and command."[17] The group was joined by a member of the circumnavigating expedition under Kruzenshtern, Georg Langsdorff, whom Rezanov engaged as his personal physician. Khvostov noted on the occasion: "I do not know if good or bad fate let us come together with N. P. Rezanov in the most remote point of the Russian State."[18]

Figure 41. Georg Langsdorff.
Courtesy Richard A. Pierce.

They sailed out of Petropavlovsk, Kamchatka, on 25 June, put in at the Pribilof Islands, and reached Unalaska on 16 July 1805. Their stay there lasted a week. If Rezanov's letters to the board of directors and to the high and mighty officials in St. Petersburg are to be believed, the week sufficed for him to acquire extensive knowledge of the district's affairs: he rewarded the incompetent (and some say mentally deranged) Emel'ian Larionov and flogged Baranov's trusted helper Demid Kulikalov and expelled him from the colony.

Rezanov and his party left Unalaska on 25 July, arriving at Kodiak on 31 July, leaving on 20 August. In less than three weeks, Rezanov claimed to have organized a school (which actually was long in existence and run by the missionaries), a boarding school for orphaned girls, and to have made enduring friendships with Native leaders. By 26 August he was in Sitka. By 29 August he wrote his first letter (instruction) to Khvostov and Davydov indicating that he intended them to take a punitive expedition to Japan. It was from Sitka that Rezanov began to dispatch lengthy letters and memoranda to the board of directors, the emperor, Rumiantsev, Chichagov, and others, letters full of complaints about the state of affairs in the colony and proposals for remedying its alleged abysmal condition. In these letters he slandered everyone except Baranov and Kuskov, but especially the officers manning the company's ships and the clergy (whom he had praised so highly in his letters from Irkutsk in 1794), ascribing to himself their achievements in education, compilation of Native dictionaries, and experiments in agriculture. He stressed the suffering and privation he had to endure and his bravery and resoluteness. He was vicious in denouncing the mission and leveled false accusations against the clergy, especially against Father Herman, beloved by the Natives. But his main complaint was that the clergy were remiss, in his view, because they "have never followed the path of the Jesuits in Paraguay by trying to develop the mentality of the savages, and have never known how to enter into the extensive plans of the Government or company."[19] (At the time, the clergy were not only critical of Baranov's policies, they were attempting to defend the Natives against exploitation and were gaining popularity and ever-increasing support from the Russian laborers.)

Figure 42. The vessel *Mariia*, with Rezanov on board, off the island of St. George approximately 6 July 1805.
From Langsdorff, 1812, vol. 2, facing p. 26. Courtesy University of Alaska Fairbanks, Rasmuson Library, Alaska and Polar Regions Dept., Rare Book Collection, no. A0907.

Rezanov proposed that the government organize the settlement of the territory by serfs, drunkards of whom the landowners would be glad to be rid, and who, in the absence of liquor in Alaska, would become good and useful citizens (and on the next page he says that Baranov wept tears that Rezanov, Emissary Plenipotentiary, "found here a drunken republic").[20] The company could pay the landowners from 25 to 50 rubles per unwanted soul. In return the landowners would sign a paper that they would never require the return of their serfs. He proposed that the government send each year 200 men condemned to exile, to be settled in Alaska in perpetuity, for whom "women could be shipped from Unalaska." On the other hand, men currently in Alaska and having Native families should be forbidden to take their wives and children with them when they left. In fact, marriage with Natives should be forbidden to all employees if they did not want to remain in Alaska forever. A third source of settlers, according to Rezanov, would be bankrupts, who would be shipped by the government to Alaska to stay forever and whose entire earnings would be assigned to pay their creditors. He argued that "the dread that this law would produce would keep people from dishonoring themselves and would promote confidence and trust toward trade." He highly recommended the British practice of settling "criminals and men of bad morals" at Botany Bay. While in London in 1803, he had visited Newgate prison and learned how "in this way the state is getting rid of its unwelcome citizens and at the same time is building towns with their help in the colonies."[21]

FIGURE 43. Unalaska, briefly visited by Rezanov in 1805.
From Langsdorff, 1812, vol. 2, facing p. 28. Courtesy University of Alaska Fairbanks, Rasmuson Library, Alaska and Polar Regions Dept., Rare Book Collection, no. A0907.

One can only imagine the reaction of such men as Count Rumiantsev as they read these proposals. To the everlasting honor of the imperial government and of the company's board of directors, Rezanov's suggestions were ignored. Unfortunately, they have served to establish the firmly entrenched myth that in the Russian period Alaska was settled by criminals and the Natives were slaves.

Rezanov also wanted to see a military presence in Alaska. Writing from Unalaska to the emperor, he not only told Alexander I that he would dispatch Khvostov and Davydov to "ravage" Japanese coasts and "push them off Sakhalin" as well as destroy their settlements on Hokkaido, he implored the emperor to send navy vessels and artillery in order to expel all Bostonians by military force from North Pacific waters.[22] This suggestion was also ignored. In order to prove his point that military force was needed, he spoke of constant murders of all Russians "everywhere," another myth he created that refuses to die.

He bemoaned the high salaries the company was paying naval officers seconded to its service and suggested that a new system of hiring be instituted in which candidates would be offered a certain pay and could not bargain for better terms. He would prefer foreigners or retired naval officers, so that there would be no invoking of the Crown. A military-type discipline should reign in the colonies: at present, the hunters had too much freedom to do as they pleased. Everyone was insubordinate, claiming the status of free men. If the company business was to prosper, measures must be taken to insure that orders were obeyed above all else. Poor Baranov suffered from insubordination and must be given the status of provincial governor, as otherwise he had no authority whatsoever. He had to have the power to punish: "Impose penalties for disorder and they will know their duties better." Rezanov exhorted the board of directors to disregard reports from others and especially any complaints by the labor force. "Do not think, My dear Sirs, that their debts are due to high prices."[23]

At the same time, Rezanov apparently interfered in Baranov's decisions. Specifically, Khlebnikov reported that Rezanov's presence put a stop to Baranov's profitable dealings with the American skippers.[24]

It is interesting that, while Rezanov praised Baranov and Kuskov, he constantly harped on the state of disorder, anarchy, and the lack of organization, as well as prophesying that financial losses to the company would lead to bankruptcy if the management continued as it was. One wonders whether Baranov's resignation tendered to Rezanov at this time, and Kuskov's refusal to accept the position of manager offered to him, as Rezanov claims, may not have been tied to Rezanov's reorganizational efforts. He did write, after all, "I will admit that my orders of reorganization may not entirely please the local administration. . . ." In a reorganization plan received by Baranov on 9 September 1805 (barely three weeks after Rezanov's arrival), in seventeen acerbic paragraphs Rezanov told the man who had been running the colony for thirteen years all that was wrong with his management (better treatment of the rank-and-file labor force formed no part of it) and instructed him to proceed with grandiose development of industries, agriculture, and business, which Baranov had absolutely no means to accomplish and which were totally unfeasible in Alaskan conditions.[25]

Rezanov's instructions to Baranov, issued 20 July 1806, shortly before his departure from Alaska, must have left the old man wondering. He was given much unasked-for and impractical advice and suggestions for the future he must have known to be fantasies.

One such was Rezanov's statement that he would organize supplies for the colony out of Japan and "make the necessary arrangements for the emigration of the Japanese to America." Baranov was instructed how to treat such Japanese settlers, grant them free ownership of land, guarantee freedom of religion, etc.[26]

Rezanov found the living conditions at Novo-Arkhangel'sk, which Baranov was constructing with great speed, not much to his liking, and complained at length of discomforts he suffered there. In August of 1805, John D'Wolf, an American from Bristol, Rhode Island, arrived at Sitka, and in short order became a member of the select group composed of Khvostov, Davydov, Langsdorff, and, of course, Rezanov. D'Wolf was willing to sell his vessel, the *Juno*. On Baranov's advice Rezanov bought her. Soon thereafter, he dispatched her under Khvostov, with D'Wolf on board, to the Three Saints settlement on Kodiak to seize all fish supplies there and bring them to Sitka, along with a sufficient supply of women. (This episode, reported by Langsdorff, led that author to conclude that the Aleuts were slaves, a conviction that exists in some quarters to this day.) One wonders how Baranov reacted to such high-handed methods of "reorganization." Certainly, neither the Kodiak Islanders nor the Russian *baidarshchik* (crew chief) at Three Saints Bay appreciated the raid.

Khvostov returned from Kodiak not only with dried fish and women, but also with news of new losses: the destruction of Yakutat, the loss of six baidaras off Kodiak, and of 200 men from the long-distance sea otter hunting party under Dem'ianenkov. He also had learned that the Chugach, having asked the Yakutat Tlingit to a potlatch, had killed their guests during the feast almost to the last man. All of these misfortunes were grist for Rezanov's mill in his reporting about the dismal prospects of the American enterprise unless the whole mode of operations be changed in accordance with his proposals. At the same time, in Sitka, he publicly expressed his support and admiration for Baranov.

FIGURE 44. **Lieutenant junior grade (*michman*) Gavriil Davydov.**
Courtesy Richard A. Pierce.

In 1806, aboard the *Iunona* (formerly the *Juno*), Rezanov undertook a voyage to California to obtain supplies and to establish a trade relationship with the Spanish. En route, he planned to take possession of the Columbia River, but Khvostov was not able to bring his vessel past the famous Columbia bar.[27] Rezanov bitterly blamed Khvostov for this failure. By this time his cordial relations with Khvostov were a thing of the past. The reasons for the quarrels may only be inferred: in Sitka, young Davydov left Khvostov and moved into Rezanov's quarters.[28]

Rezanov is usually credited with the California initiative, but, as we have seen, Baranov had been reconnoitering the situation since 1803–1804. Rezanov informed the Spanish commandant, Arguello, that he "received from the Emperor the command over all the American territories," that he was "Commandant General." He was careful in

FIGURE 45. Grave monument of Anna Shelikhov Rezanov and her sister Aleksandra Shelikhov Politkovskii, in the historic cemetery of Sv. Aleksandr Nevskii Lavra, St. Petersburg. It was erected by G. I. Politkovskii, Aleksandra's widower, in 1816. *Photo by Nikolai Turkin.*

his letters to officials in Russia to point out that he made this claim solely in order to impress the Spanish, being fully aware that he had no such authority. In order to ingratiate himself with Arguello, this forty-two-year-old widower (who kept an underage Tlingit girl at Novo-Arkhangel'sk as his mistress) proceeded to court the fifteen-year-old daughter of his Spanish host, Concepción, going so far as making a marriage proposal which, by his own admission, he had no intention of keeping. This fictitious "romance" has become part of the mythology associated with Russian America, made famous by Chevigny in his *Lost Empire*, and the subject of a sentimental novel by the American writer Gertrude Atherton, several novels and a rock opera in Russia, and at least one master's thesis in which the fate of these allegedly star-crossed lovers is discussed.[29] Rezanov, in a letter to company director M. M. Buldakov, wrote that should Buldakov have heard of his alleged romance, it was naught but "another sacrifice on my part for the glory of the fatherland."[30]

Rezanov was less than candid with Arguello in other matters as well. In the meantime, his sailors were jumping ship. Asking the Spanish commandant to permit a search for two Russians, a party under Khvostov explored the north side of San Francisco Bay. The deserters were not found, but one German and three American sailors were recaptured and then marooned, on Rezanov's orders, on a barren and rocky island in the bay until the *Iunona* was ready to depart. As the eminent historian Richard A. Pierce put it, "the four men may have been the first men to sit out a sentence on Alcatraz."[31] Here Rezanov also quarreled with Langsdorff, who shortly after his return to Sitka departed from America by himself.[32]

Rezanov also left Alaska shortly after his return from California on 8 June, boarding the *Iunona* on 24 June 1806, announcing that he would travel to Japan. Rezanov made known that he would lead the punitive expedition to northern Japanese settlements himself, but on 8 August 1806 changed his mind, stating that his presence was needed in St. Petersburg. He left Khvostov's vessel at Okhotsk, issuing yet another rather vague instruction to Khvostov.[33] The two young men, Khvostov and Davydov, were left holding the bag. They carried out several raids in 1806–1807, burning and pillaging several Japanese settlements. On 18 October 1806, Khvostov formally declared Sakhalin to be a Russian possession. These actions brought them arrest, a court-martial, and almost cost them their careers. They saved themselves when they volunteered for service with the fleet in the war with Sweden and through bravery expiated their sins. In the end, it cost Rezanov the patronage of Rumiantsev,[34] and Russian-Japanese relations were soured. There is little doubt that these unprovoked raids within Japanese territory were a cause for the imprisonment by the Japanese from 1811 to 1813 of Captain Vasilii Golovnin and several members of his crew, who spent a considerable time in cages.[35] Golovnin, like Kruzenshtern, developed a negative attitude toward the company's administration of Russia's American possessions and it was he who in 1818 effected Baranov's removal.[36]

After parting with his men and vessel in Okhotsk, Rezanov set out ostensibly for St. Petersburg with all possible speed (the romantics claim it was in order to obtain permission to marry his Spanish sweetheart, a permission he did not need). Instead, he stopped at his native Irkutsk where he spent almost three months, from the end of November to 13 February of the next year, engaging in a very active social life. On 10 January, he dazzled local society with a breakfast and dance which began at eleven o'clock in the morning and ended in the early hours of the next day; the lavishness of food, drink, and entertainment became a local legend.[37] He moved on to Krasnoyarsk, where he contracted a fever and died 1 March 1807. In Irkutsk, he was remembered for this "breakfast," and as a compatriot who became ambassador to Japan, but not for either his business acumen or his role as a member of the Russian-American Company. His meteoric stay in Alaska left no tangible traces, but his voluminous letters to the powers that be created, after his death, an impression that he was a great empire builder who significantly and beneficially affected the developments in Alaska. Controversial in his lifetime, he remains a controversial figure, like many legends sometimes painted larger than life. A realistic biography of this man has yet to be written.

In the meantime, even while Rezanov was in Sitka issuing directives for the future that could not be executed even with the best of will, Baranov was running the colony's affairs. While Rezanov was in California, Baranov took the opportunity to pursue his own efforts there. He contracted with Jonathan Winship of Boston, who called in 1806 at Sitka, for joint sea otter hunting off the coasts of California. He sent along fifty Aleut kayaks under one of his able subordinates, Sysoi Slobodchikov. They sailed to the Columbia River. Slobodchikov is credited with compiling the first Russian chart of that river's estuary. Then he proceeded to California. At Trinidad Bay, Slobodchikov buried a Russian imperial possession plate (on his second voyage to California, in 1807, he placed such a plate at Humboldt Bay). While in California, he parted company with Winship (it is said they had a disagreement), bought an American schooner, the *Tamana*, which he renamed the *Sv. Nikolai*, and sailed to Hawaii where, on Baranov's behalf, he concluded the first trade agreement with King Kamehameha I. He returned to Sitka, bringing to Baranov Kamehameha's gifts of a helmet and splendid feather cloak "off his own shoulders." (To the end of Baranov's tenure, the two rulers exchanged gifts, and Kamehameha even granted Baranov land in his domain.)[38] At the same time, Baranov commissioned O'Cain to negotiate for him with the Japanese at Nagasaki, the Dutch at Batavia (Java), and the Chinese at Canton. After Rezanov's departure, trade with California was conducted by Baranov indirectly through American skippers.

Baranov went to Kodiak, where affairs were not being run to his liking under "the kind and good hearted Banner." The general tenor was not in tune with the stern measures expected by the chief manager.[39] Here Baranov met with Hieromonk Gedeon, who was inspecting the general situation on Kodiak and the situation of the spiritual mission. Here, too, in May 1807, Baranov bought the *Myrtle* from the ill-famed Captain Barber, who had fallen on hard times. The vessel was renamed the *Kad'iak* and put under the command of Navigator Bulygin. One of Bulygin's first missions was to ransom survivors of the Slava Rossii settlement at Yakutat (he rescued three women and their children, including the widow of the settlement manager Stepan Larionov, cousin of the Unalaska manager). A year later, Baranov sent the American Captain Kimball on the same errand. Kimball captured a Chilkat chief, who had taken possession of Yakutat (badly weakened by the Chugach killing of almost 200 men at a potlatch), and rescued an Aleut and his wife. Two hostages, nephews of the Chilkat chief, were taken to Kodiak and later served the company at Sitka as interpreters.[40]

Baranov continued to use Yankee skippers for his own ends, driving hard bargains, including in the contracts clauses for protection and just recompense to the Aleut hunters (and indemnities for widows or orphans), and always placing a trusty subordinate, such as Slobodchikov, Tarakanov, or Shvetsov, to be his eyes and ears among the Yankees. His interest in the Columbia River grew, especially after Shvetsov, aboard the vessel *Mercury* under Captain Ayres, reported that he had encountered there "two American officials" with an armed escort, who were issuing to the Natives "medals with the likeness of Washington." It appears that Baranov had been made aware in short order of the Lewis and Clark expedition's success in crossing the continent.

Baranov's fleet was increasing through construction in Sitka shipyards and purchases from Americans, and in 1808 he decided to send his own vessels to the Columbia River and California. Under Nikolai I. Bulygin, the *Sv. Nikolai* was to explore the coast of Vancouver Island and select a site for a settlement on what is today the Oregon coast.[41] The expedition of the *Nikolai* did not succeed; the vessel was driven ashore at the mouth of the Quillayute River,[42] and the survivors (including Bulygin's wife and the foreman Timofei Tarakanov) were captured by the Indians. Two years later, a Yankee skipper ransomed thirteen of the survivors and, sometime later, another skipper ransomed two more. The rest perished in captivity.

Tarakanov, like Shvetsov, had been to California with O'Cain in 1803 and with Kimball in 1806. His remarkable American career is worth a brief digression here: an astute, intelligent man, who led "through discussion and informed assent," Tarakanov was a serf set free in Alaska in 1817 by an official decree. While in captivity, he was formally recognized by the Macah Indians as a chief because of his knowledge and leadership qualities.[43] He continued in positions of responsibility, frequently serving in California, and in 1816 sailed with a group of Aleuts aboard an American vessel to Hawaii, where Dr. Georg Schaeffer, on Baranov's behalf, attempted to establish control over the Hawaiian Islands but botched the job (see below). In 1817, Tarakanov, left behind in Hawaii, brought a large contingent of men, Russians and Aleuts, back to Alaska with the aid of the Boston skipper W. H. Davis, an old friend from California days. He sailed in 1818 to St. Petersburg to report on the Hawaiian affair, then returned to Alaska, where he had a family, but was sent to Okhotsk in 1820.[44] At that time, Baranov's old hands were dismissed one by one from service under one pretext or another and shipped out of Alaska.

Ivan Kuskov, in the second vessel, made his way to California, where he remained hunting in and near Bodega Bay, returning to Sitka in October 1809. After receiving Kuskov's report, Baranov began to plan a permanent settlement in California.

In the meantime, the company had instituted a new and uniform order of recompense for all its employees in Alaska (previously paid by a share of the catch), a measure by no means favorably received and which almost immediately caused renewed labor unrest. There were other grievances. Baranov had to cope with a conspiracy against him on the

FIGURE 46. **Kodiak, ca. 1808–1809.**

Original in RGAVMF, Fond 1331, op. 4, delo 132. Courtesy Richard A. Pierce.

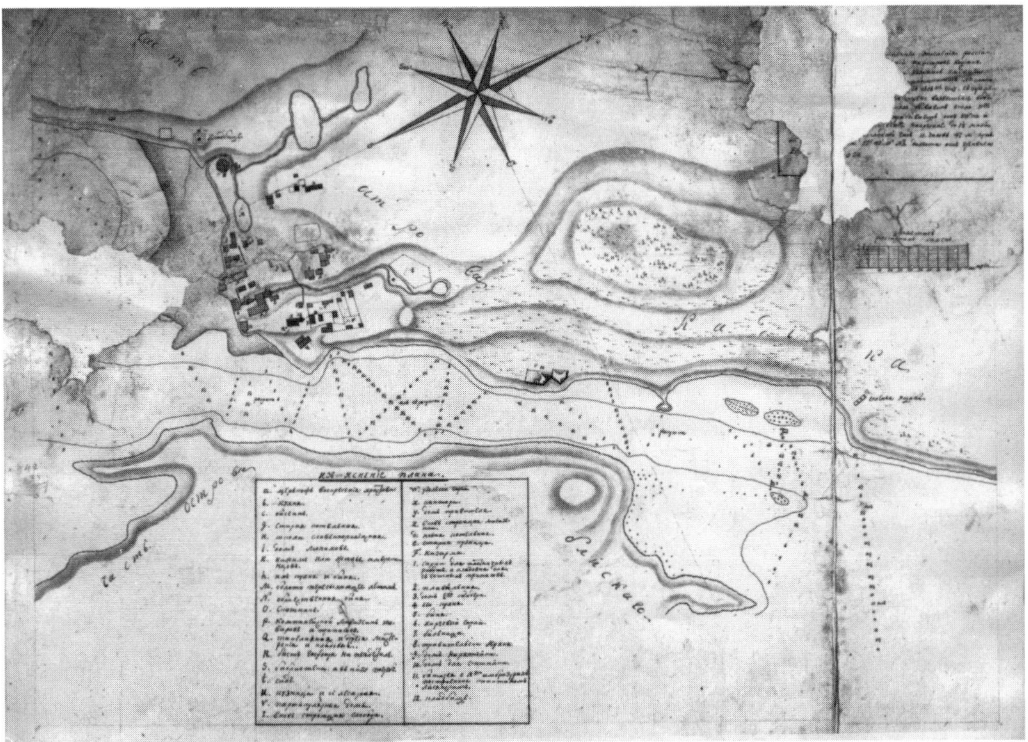

FIGURE 47. **Kodiak, 1808–1809.**

Original in RGAVMF, Fond 1331, op. 1, delo 211. Courtesy Richard A. Pierce.

part of discontented employees. Allegedly, they even planned his murder. Khlebnikov asserted that this conspiracy motivated the aging Baranov to submit his resignation in earnest. Once again, it was not accepted by the board of directors, though they promised to send an assistant and eventually choose a successor (Koch, who died en route to Alaska in 1811).

Baranov continued to direct the colony's affairs as best he could under a changing political situation. The Napoleonic Wars were at their height in Europe, alliances and fortunes of war were constantly shifting, and Russia's alliance with England had come to an end in 1807. This meant there would be difficulties in provisioning the colony by sea from the Baltic ports. Baranov's ties with the American skippers permitted him to keep the colony supplied with the necessities. In the years between 1809 and 1812 alone, he collaborated with six "Bostonian" ships. When the War of 1812 broke out between England and the United States, five American vessels were at Sitka (Baranov bought two of them). In spite of the difficult international situation, the Russian-American Company was able to maintain regular communication with the colony from Okhotsk and Kamchatka.

Nevertheless, Russia sent out naval circumnavigating expeditions to supply the colony and explore the Pacific. In 1808, the *Neva* under Hagemeister arrived in Sitka, and in 1810, much later than expected, the *Diana,* under Vasilii M. Golovnin (she sailed in 1807 but was detained by the British at Cape Town for more than a year, from 1808 to 1809). Baranov's relations with Hagemeister had been amicable, and he dispatched him to the Hawaiian Islands, possibly to reconnoiter the potential for establishing a permanent settlement there.[45] Not so his relationship with Golovnin, whose mission was to show the imperial flag in the North Pacific and who, like Kruzenshtern before him, had developed a very negative attitude toward the Russian-American Company, strongly objecting to the quasi-governmental role its chief manager played in Alaska. Golovnin officially represented the government. He also believed that no commercial company should represent Russian interests in the Pacific. He was not kindly disposed toward Baranov. Baranov's difficulties with the navy kept growing. One historian believes that only Golovnin's captivity in Japan "delayed the final ousting of the Company [represented by the local manager] from its position of executive authority over the settlements."[46]

Figure 48. V. M. Golovnin (1776–1831). A high-ranking naval officer, he was authorized to remove Baranov.
Courtesy Richard A. Pierce.

By 1809, Baranov had entered into negotiations with John Jacob Astor. The government, concerned about the colony, tried to aid in the establishment of a formal agreement with Astor. Letters from Astor and Dashkov, the Russian envoy in the United States, were brought to Baranov in 1810 by Captain Ebbets of the *Enterprise.* The negotiations eventually culminated in a formal agreement of 20 May 1812, under which Astor was obliged to supply Russia's American colony and take Russian furs to Canton. In this, the imperial government gave Baranov its full support, officially petitioning the United States government to control the free-wheeling American traders operating on the Northwest Coast (it was hoped that Astor would be granted exclusive rights by the United States government to trade in the Russian territories). Baranov did not sign this agreement, hoping that the war with England would not last and that the colony would be supplied from St. Petersburg by circumnavigating vessels. Instead he concluded a separate agreement with Ebbets for a one-time effort to ship furs to China and bring back provisions and trade goods.[47] This venture ended in disaster, as the *Enterprise* was wrecked near Okhotsk. The attempt at formal Russian-American economic cooperation came to naught with the elimination of Astor's Columbia River factory, Astoria, in the War of 1812; Astor also lost two other vessels in the Pacific. Moreover, the United States government refused (and in all probability was not able) to restrict the New England seamen and intervene in U.S. citizens' business activities.

The Russian government, however, had been motivated at this time not solely by concern for the company's well-being, but, more significantly, by concern with any potential territorial dispute with the United States, because the Americans had penetrated and claimed the Columbia River region.[48]

In 1811, Baranov received from the main office of the company a go-ahead for settlement in California. In November, Ivan Kuskov, with a party of Russian laborers and Aleuts (forty kayaks), departed on the vessel *Chirikov* (built at Sitka by Lincoln, an American shipwright in Baranov's service), commanded by Khristofor Benzeman. The winter was spent preparing timbers and clearing the site, and Settlement Ross was founded in June 1812.[49] By 1818, Ross was producing vegetables and fruit, including grapes (introduced from Chile), watermelons, muskmelons, apples, peaches, and significant numbers of domestic cattle, pigs, and horses. The settlement's population numbered 26 Russians and 102 "Aleuts," Alaska Natives, including some Athabaskans from the Kenai Peninsula.

During the War of 1812, several Americans entered Baranov's service, as did several Englishmen. Long-distance sea otter hunting parties continued to be dispatched to California. By this time, the Spanish authorities were taking a dim view of the situation and on several occasions captured a number of men, Russians, Aleuts, Americans, and English, including the man known as "Elliott" (Eliot de Castro, formerly advisor to King Kamehameha I of Hawaii). The Spanish were also seizing the American ships that were provisioning Ross out of Hawaii, accusing them of poaching.[50] That year, the main office did appoint a replacement for Baranov. T. S. Bornovolokov sailed from Okhotsk in the fall of 1812. After a stopover at Resurrection Bay near Prince William Sound, his vessel sailed to Sitka, where on 8 January 1813 she was driven onto rocks near Mt. Edgecumbe. The vessel broke up in the surf; of seventy-seven men on board, thirty-nine drowned, among them Bornovolokov.[51] Peaceful retirement was not to be Baranov's destiny.

With the end of the Napoleonic Wars in 1814, the annual Russian circumnavigating voyages to the colony were resumed. Moreover, Rumiantsev sponsored the voyage of the *Riurik*, commanded by young Otto Kotzebue (1814–1818). Kotzebue sailed through Bering Strait and turned eastward along Alaska's coast, where he discovered the large bay now called Kotzebue Sound. In 1814, the *Suvorov* arrived. When she sailed the next year homeward bound, she left behind her surgeon, one Dr. Georg Schaeffer. Baranov, glad to

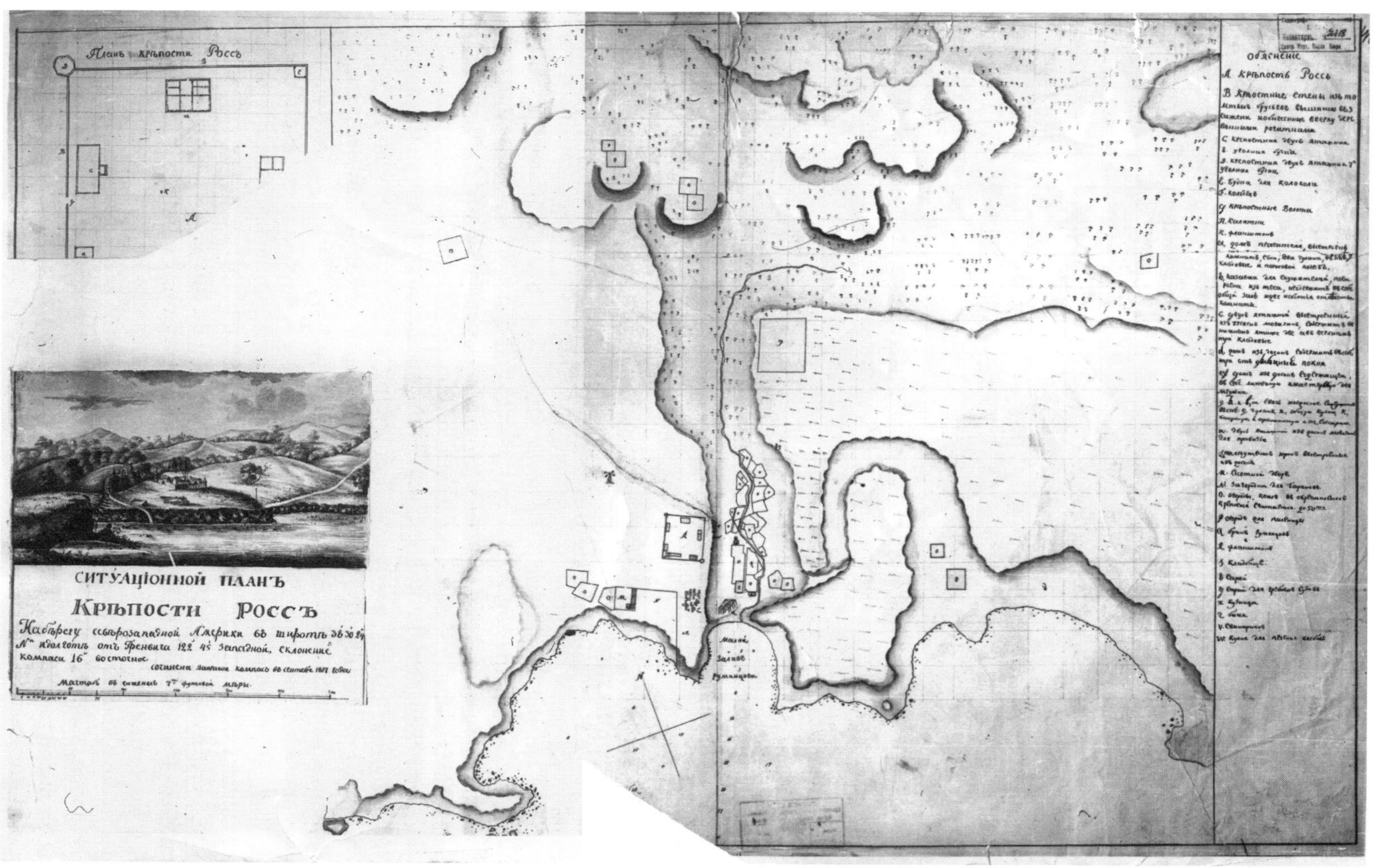

FIGURE 49. **Ross, September 1817.**

Original in RGAVMF, Fond 1331, op. 1, delo 221. Courtesy Richard A. Pierce.

have the services of an educated person, dispatched him to Hawaii to represent Russian interests and to negotiate an agreement in regard to the lucrative sandalwood trade. In a letter to Kamehameha, Baranov had hinted that he would support him if needed in military action against his rival, King Kaumualii. But Schaeffer alienated Kamehameha and entered into a dubious relationship with Kaumualii. He then proceeded to build a fortified settlement and establish plantations. Upon receipt of Schaeffer's reports Baranov was aghast and ordered him to refrain from any further "speculations."[52] Schaeffer badly miscalculated Hawaiian politics, telling Kaumualii that he would be under the protection of the Russian emperor (and allegedly infuriated the Hawaiians by desecrating one of their shrines, the *morai*). He also circulated rumors that the Russian navy would soon come to his support. His credibility, however, was at a low point with both Hawaiian rulers.

Perhaps the change of attitude toward Baranov's emissary was in some measure due to the fact that in 1816, Kotzebue, while in Hawaii, told Kamehameha that Schaeffer's efforts were not supported by the Russian government in any shape or manner. Schaeffer was forced to leave Hawaii in 1817.[53] In 1818, Emperor Alexander I ruled: "Acquisition of these islands and their admission under [imperial] protection out of their free will cannot bring Russia any substantial benefits; on the contrary in many respects it will prove to be seriously inconvenient."[54] Thus, Baranov's plans to establish the Hawaiian connection and, possibly, join Hawaii to Alaska as Russian domain came to naught. The Russian navy was in open opposition to him on this issue, and the government listened to the naval officers and diplomats stationed in foreign capitals.

Kotzebue also put in his oar in California, leaving the impression with the Spanish authorities there that he believed, as the Spaniards maintained, that Kuskov was in violation of Spanish sovereignty. In this, however, in contrast to the situation in Hawaii, he had no support from other naval commanders. Hagemeister, in 1817, met at Ross with the local Indian leaders to establish the legality of occupation, and a formal protocol was drawn up. The senior Indian leader, Ch-gu-an, received a silver medal.[55]

The lines had been drawn between the navy and the company. Influential senior officers such as Sarychev and Golovnin were powerful adversaries.[56] The end of the Baranov era in Alaska was determined in St. Petersburg long before Baranov's actual removal by Hagemeister on 11 January 1818. On that day, Hagemeister assumed the status of chief manager. Forthwith, until the end of Russian America in 1867, the colony would be governed by a high-ranking officer of the navy, accountable first of all to the government and concerned primarily with matters of state.

The main office in St. Petersburg had acquiesced in this move. As a face-saving device, it cited Baranov's advanced age, his long service, poor health, and his own desire, expressed so many times, to retire. Baranov was directed to surrender all business records and inventories. An audit was instituted. Kiril Khlebnikov, whose job it was to conduct the audit, came to the conclusion that Baranov always acted in the best interest of the company and the state. He became one of the greatest admirers of the fallen chief and would write his first biography.[57]

"The 72-year-old elder," wrote Khlebnikov, "wished only for peace but hesitated where to spend the last days of his life." He thought of settling down with his Alaskan family on Kodiak, or at Ozerskoi Redoubt in Sitka Bay where allegedly a "fine house has been built for him,"[58] or in the Hawaiian Islands near his friend Kamehameha. However, Golovnin, in America with the *Kamchatka*, counseled that he go to Russia. It was rumored (and is so represented in history books) that the navy men were afraid that as long as Baranov was near, no new order, no new style of management, would be implemented: the old man's authority was too great. He finally agreed to go, parting with family and friends, after twenty-eight years of ruling Alaska. "Old, grey-haired men, his comrades in glorious deeds and voyages, sobbed like children at parting with their beloved leader. Many in his entourage grew up during his tenure, others were born while he was boss. He was godfather to one and almost all of the young ones were trained under him. Even the Tlingit who trembled before him, but who respected his brave and decisive spirit, took leave of him with ambivalent feelings in which fear and joy were mingled," wrote an eyewitness. Katleyan ceremoniously made his peace with him.[59]

Baranov was a tough taskmaster and certainly guilty at times of great brutality. But this complex man could also lead and inspire unquestioning loyalty on the part of his Russian subordinates and also among his Native forces. He himself never skirted danger or shirked hard work, and bore hardship with fortitude. He never failed to reward achievement, kept his promises, and when his men—Russians or Natives—were captured by hostiles he made every effort to ransom them. He also showed some care for the men's families. In the later years of his leadership, when he instituted the practice of loaning Aleut hunters to Yankee or other foreign skippers, who took them as far away as southern California, he made sure that the contract specified indemnities to widows and orphans of any men lost on such voyages. He recognized ability and helped advance able young men, Russian, Native, and those born of international parentage in the colony. (Filip Kashevarov, born a serf, was one such man. One of his Alutiiq sons, Aleksandr, became an explorer and eventually served in the Russian navy with flag rank.)

Some men no doubt hated Baranov, and in 1809 there had been a conspiracy to murder him; he spoke also of an attempt on his life by Russian laborers sometime prior to May 1795.[60] Members of the ecclesiastical mission who arrived on Kodiak in 1794 opposed him, especially in regard to his treatment of Kodiak islanders. In fact, in 1795, Archimandrite Ioasaf, writing to Shelikhov, urged that Baranov be removed and a decent and kind person be appointed in his stead. He was in violent conflict with Lebedev-Lastochkin crews and skippers and wrote most derogatory reports about them, accusing them of being criminals.

High-ranking naval officers who came to Alaska on circumnavigating expeditions, ever more frequently following the 1803 expedition under Kruzenshtern and Lisianskii, were highly critical, not to say contemptuous of him and no doubt were instrumental in his eventual removal.[61] Yet, he was respected and even admired by people who knew him best, by many of his lieutenants, by the Yankee skippers with whom he dealt, by British visitors, by the Hindu slave presented to him by a British captain in 1792 and whom he later set free to return to his homeland, by King Kamehameha of Hawaii, and even by his enemies, the Tlingit.[62]

The Tlingit war leader Katleyan, who at one time had defeated Baranov, came to see him off with honor when he learned that Baranov, now seventy-two years old, was leaving Alaska. The chain-link mail shirt, said to have been Baranov's gift to Katleyan's uncle, the leader of the Sitka Tlingit in 1796, for a long time was considered one of the family's treasures. (It is now, as noted earlier, in the National Museum of Natural History, Smithsonian Institution, Washington, D.C.).

Baranov sailed on the *Kutuzov* 27 November 1818. In reality, despite the honors attending his departure, he was under judicial investigation and was to face charges and, in all likelihood, a trial. As early as the end of 1817 or beginning of 1818, the government had determined on such an investigation; on 21 February 1818 Golovnin, on the admiralty's recommendation and with the consent of the finance minister, was appointed as the state's attorney. In effect, he was to act as the prosecutor, jury, and judge.

The *Kutuzov* put in in March 1819 at Batavia (Dutch East Indies) where she remained for thirty-six days. There, Baranov fell ill. He died at sea, in the Sunda Strait, 16 April 1819, and the next day his body was lowered into the sea. Only on 23 September 1821 would the admiralty and the Ruling Senate close the case against Baranov due to the accused's death.[63]

In Alaska an era had come to an end. Baranov had built the foundation and established the extent of Russia's American possession. Whatever happened afterward was built on that foundation.

NOTES

1. Several writers, among them S. G. Fedorova, have incorrectly ascribed authorship of this plan to Nikolai P. Rezanov.
2. I find no evidence to support Sarafian's inference that the position of *correspondent* meant that the holder of this office supervised company activities on behalf of the government. Sarafian's interpretation rests, apparently, on Rezanov's actions in the colony in 1805–1806. The office was abolished in 1804 while Rezanov was on his way to Japan and Alaska. A governmental committee was established to supervise the affairs of the company, especially in regard to the impact of its activities on foreign relations. From 1813 to 1844 the committee included the Ministers of the Navy, Interior, and Finance. See Winston L. Sarafian, *Russian-American Company Employee Policies and Practices, 1799–1867* (Ann Arbor, Mich.: University Microfilms, 1971).
3. "From an Instruction of Nikolai P. Rumiantsev to the Representative of the Russian-American Company, Nikolai P. Rezanov," in Bashkina et al., *The United States and Russia,* 370.
4. Ibid., 370–375, specifically task 1 (p. 370), and task 7 (pp. 371–372).
5. Lensen, *Russian Push,* 122.
6. Ibid., 126–127.
7. Gideon, *Round the World Voyage,* 1.
8. Kruzenshtern, cited after Barratt, *Russia in Pacific Waters,* 117.
9. Fedor Shemelin, *Zhurnal pervago puteshestviia rossiian vokrug Zemnago shara,* pt. 2 (St. Petersburg: Meditsinskaia tipografiia, 1818), 423. Additional, previously unpublished, information on Rezanov's relations with captain and crew is found in Hermann Ludwig von Löwenstern, *The First Russian Voyage around the World: The Journal of Hermann Ludwig von Löwenstern, 1803–1806,* trans. and ed. Victoria Joan Moessner (Fairbanks: University of Alaska Press, 2003).
10. Barratt, *Russia in Pacific Waters,* 129–130.
11. Rezanov to Chichagov, 17 May 1804, in Tikhmenev, *A History,* vol. 2, 144–145 (doc. 38).
12. Rezanov to Alexander I, 16 August 1804, in ibid., 148–149 (doc. 39).
13. Rezanov to the Board of Directors, 15 February 1806, in ibid., 190–193 (doc. 44).
14. A. Sgibnev, "Popytki russkikh," 37–72.
15. Ibid., 61.
16. See A. L. Narochnitskii et al., eds., *Rossiisko-amerikanskaia kompaniia i izuchenie Tikhookeanskogo Severa, 1799–1815 (sbornik dokumentov),* comp. L. I. Spiridonova et al. (Moscow: Izdatel'stvo "Nauka," 1994), 151–154 (doc. 91). On the raids on Japanese settlements, see also Davydov to

Admiral Chichagov, 20 April 1807, in ibid., 167–169 (doc. 102) and Davydov's journal, excerpt, in ibid., 172–182 (doc. 106).

17. Introduction by Vice-Admiral Shishkov to Davydov's notes, published in Russian in two parts, 1810–1812, cited after the English translation, Davydov, *Two Voyages,* 6; A. Sokolov, "Khvostov i Davydov," *Zapiski Gidrograficheskago departamenta Morskago ministerstva* 10 (1852): 408–409.

18. Sokolov, "Khvostov i Davydov," 409.

19. Rezanov to the Board of Directors, 6 November 1805, in Tikhmenev, *A History,* vol. 2, 167.

20. On the absence of liquor in Russian Alaska, see Shemelin, *Zhurnal.*

21. Rezanov to the Board of Directors, 6 November 1805, in Tikhmenev, *A History,* vol. 2, 160–161.

22. Rezanov to Alexander I, 18 July 1805, from Unalaska, in ibid., 149–150 (doc. 40).

23. Rezanov to the Board of Directors, 6 November 1805, in ibid., 169–170.

24. Khlebnikov, *Russkaia Amerika v "zapiskakh,"* 46.

25. Khlebnikov, *Zhizneopisanie,* 91–97.

26. Yudin Collection, Box 1, Folder 11, Manuscript Division, Library of Congress. Published in Alaska History Research Project, *Documents Relative to the History of Alaska,* vol. 3 (College, Alaska, 1938), 176–185, and in part in Bashkina et al., *The United States and Russia,* 455–457 (doc. 233). I do not consider that documentary evidence supports Barratt's conclusion that "Rezanov and Baranov understood each other well" and that they were enthusiastic collaborators (Barratt, *Russia in Pacific Waters,* 148–149, 152).

    The only suggestions by Rezanov that were ever implemented were the incorporation of the central and western Aleutians and the Commander Islands under a single Alaska management and the renewal of the settlement in the Kuril Islands. These actions were taken in the 1820s, after the company's charter was renewed for another twenty years. His advice to the board of directors that it begin negotiations immediately for extension of the monopoly charter for another twenty years was hardly necessary. No doubt the directors would have acted on that matter even if Rezanov's letters had never been written (Rezanov's letters of 6 November 1805 and 15 February 1806, in Tikhmenev, *A History,* vol. 2, 153–197 [docs. 42–44]).

27. On Rezanov's voyage to California see his letter to Rumiantsev, Minister of Commerce, 17 June 1806, in Tikhmenev, *A History,* vol. 2, 199–227 (doc. 46).

28. On the peculiar friendship between Davydov, born 1784, and Khvostov, born 1776, see Sokolov, "Khvostov i Davydov," 391–433, and Sokolov's brief article of the same title in *Morskoi sbornik* 9, no. 5 (1853): 349–357. See also remarks by Avdeeva-Polevaia in her *Zapiski,* 60–61. Their stormy relationship (and Khvostov's violent jealousy) are reflected even in the very brief excerpts from Khvostov's diary published by Sokolov in 1852. Rezanov, in his letters and reports from Alaska, initially praised them both to the skies, but later became ambivalent, even hostile, toward Khvostov. Khvostov reciprocated in kind. Rezanov's hostility is best evident in his letter to the board of directors, 15 February 1806, in Tikhmenev, *A History,* vol. 2, 192–196 (doc. 44). The circumstances of Khvostov's and Davydov's simultaneous deaths, following a party in St. Petersburg in early October 1806, hosted by Langsdorff and attended by D'Wolf, are also peculiar. They drowned in the Neva River. It is supposed that they had tried to jump onto a passing barge when the bridge they were crossing was raised (physically a more than improbable event given the construction of this bridge).

29. For a recent treatment of this topic see Eve Iverson, *The Romance of Nikolai Rezanov and Concepción Argüello: A Literary Legend and Its Effect on California History,* ed. Richard A. Pierce (Kingston, Ontario: Limestone Press, 1998).

30. A. P. Surnik, "Rezanov's Documents in G. V. Yudin's Collection" (paper presented at Second St. Innocent Readings, Russia and Russian America, Petropavlovsk-Kamchatskii, Russia, 9–11 August 1993). There is some circumstantial evidence (oblique statements in Rezanov's letters to a relative) that he may have seduced the girl. The point is being argued by Rezanov's partisans.

31. Richard A. Pierce, ed., *Rezanov Reconnoiters California, 1806: A New Translation of Rezanov's Letter, Parts of Lieutenant Khvostov's Log of the Ship* Juno, *and Dr. Georg von Langsdorff Observations* (San Francisco: Book Club of California, 1972), specifically Pierce's introduction, p. xv.
32. It is significant that Langsdorff dedicated his book about the voyage to America to Rezanov's "enemy," Kruzenshtern.
33. A. Sgibnev, "Popytki russkikh," 61–63.
34. Surnik, "Rezanov's Documents," Rezanov's letter to Buldakov written in Krasnoyarsk, shortly before Rezanov's death. Rezanov bitterly complains that he has been abandoned by his illustrious patrons in the capital.
35. V. M. Golovnin, *Zapiski Vasiliia Mikhailovicha Golovnina v plenu u iapontsev v 1811, 1812 i 1813 godakh i zhizneopisanie avtora* (St. Petersburg: N. Grech, 1851). See also Lensen, *Russian Push,* chap. 6, "Japanese Reaction," and chap. 7, "Wise Counsels," 177–256.
36. Lydia T. Black, "The Imperial Navy, V. M. Golovnin, and Baranov's Removal" (paper presented at International Conference Dedicated to the 200th Anniversary of the Formation of the Russian-American Company and to the Investigation of American Civilization as a Historical Phenomenon, Center for North American Studies, Institute of World History, Russian Academy of Sciences, Moscow, 6–9 September 1999).
37. Ivan Kalashnikov, "Zapiski irkutskago zhitelia," in *Zapiski irkutskikh zhitelei,* ed. M. D. Sergeev (Irkutsk: Vostochno-Sibirskoe knizhnoe izdatel'stvo, 1990), 281.
38. Khlebnikov, *Russkaia Amerika v "zapiskakh,"* 295 (editorial note by Fedorova); Pierce, *Biographical Dictionary,* 475; Khlebnikov, *Zhizneopisanie,* 107–108.
39. Khlebnikov, *Zhizneopisanie,* 117.
40. Richard Dauenhauer and Nora Marks Dauenhauer, "Collisions in Tlingit America: Tlingit Interpreters and the Russian-American Company" (paper presented at the conference "Worlds in Collision: Critically Analyzing Aboriginal and European Contact Narratives," University of Victoria, Victoria, B.C., Canada, February 21–24, 2002).
41. For an excellent account of the voyage of the *Sv. Nikolai,* see Kenneth N. Owens and Alton S. Donnelly, *The Wreck of the* Sv. Nikolai (Portland, Ore.: Western Imprints, The Press of the Oregon Historical Society, 1985). In this account the authors combine the documentary evidence with the Indian traditions.
42. The location of the disaster is so identified by Owens and Donnelly. Pierce, in the biographical sketch of Tarakanov, says the vessel was wrecked at Destruction Island, near Gray's Harbor (*Biographical Dictionary,* 498).
43. Kenneth N. Owens, "Timofei Tarakanov: Frontiersman for the Tsar," in *Russia in North America: Proceedings of the 2nd International Conference on Russian America, Sitka, Alaska, August 19–22, 1987,* ed. Richard A. Pierce (Kingston, Ontario; Fairbanks, Alaska: Limestone Press, 1990), 136–143.
44. Pierce, *Biographical Dictionary,* 497–499. In 1810, shortly after his rescue, Tarakanov met in Sitka Captain Vasilii Golovnin, who later published an account of the wreck of the *Sv. Nikolai.*
45. For a discussion of this controversial question, see Barratt, *Russia in Pacific Waters,* 154–158.
46. Ibid., 164.
47. Khlebnikov, *Zhizneopisanie,* 135–140.
48. See Bashkina et al., *The United States and Russia,* for documents relevant to the Astor agreement and Russian-American diplomatic exchanges in connection with the situation on the Northwest Coast. On the interactions between American merchant skippers and Baranov and on the need to open the Canton trade for the Russians, the Russian reaction to the Lewis and Clark expedition, and the Russian evaluation of the War of 1812, see Bolkhovitinov, *Beginnings of Russian-American Relations,* 146–349.
49. Khlebnikov, *Zhizneopisanie,* 147.

50. Barratt, *Russia in Pacific Waters,* 181.

51. See the accounts of V. N. Berkh and V. M. Golovnin in Antoinette Shalkop, trans. and ed., *The Wreck of the* Neva (Anchorage: Alaska Historical Society and Sitka Historical Society, 1979).

52. Bolkhovitinov, *Beginnings of Russian-American Relations,* 101.

53. See Richard A. Pierce, *Russia's Hawaiian Adventure, 1815–1817* (Berkeley and Los Angeles: University of California Press, 1965); Khlebnikov, *Zhizneopisanie,* 160–169; and N. N. Bolkhovitinov, *Russko-amerikanskie otnosheniia, 1815–1832 gg.* (Moscow: Izdael'stvo "Nauka," 1975), 86–133 ("Hawaiian Adventure of Doctor Schaeffer").

54. Bolkhovitinov, *Russko-Amerikanskie otnosheniia* (1975), 113–117.

55. Ibid., 132–182 (specifically, p. 142).

56. See Barratt, *Russia in Pacific Waters,* 173–189; Black, "The Imperial Navy."

57. Khlebnikov, *Zhizneopisanie.* Later, two Americans became Baranov's ardent admirers. One of them was Hector Chevigny, who wrote a popular account of Baranov's life and times under the title *Lord of Alaska: Baranov and the Russian Adventure* (New York: Viking Press, 1942). That same year, Clarence L. Andrews completed a scholarly biography of Baranov which remains unpublished (Archives, Rasmuson Library, University of Alaska Fairbanks). Andrews came to Alaska in 1892 when Russian influence was still greatly felt. He became fascinated with the period, taught himself to read Russian, and became a pioneer historian of Alaska, focusing on the Russian period. About Baranov he wrote the following in the "Author's Note" prefacing the aforementioned manuscript:

> I have been impelled to write the story of Alexander Andryevich [*sic*] Baranov, as nearly as I can trace it from the Russian Records. I have an intimate knowledge of the land where he worked. His indomitable courage, his resourcefulness in dealing with the new, rugged land and with the primitive people, fascinate me.
>
> Shipwrecked on those inhospitable, nearly uninhabited shores more than one hundred and fifty years ago, he dominated the situation and brought his men through the winter without the loss of a single life. He was Sourdough of the first water, and for twenty-eight years he lived on that frontier, the Russian Colonies in America, without leaving the boundaries of what we now call Alaska—a land just now, coming to its own.
>
> Baranov is one of the world's great, unsung empire builders, seen among wintry storms and tempestuous seas, patient, courageous and unflinching. Adversity only brought his determination to the front.

58. Hagemeister to Kad'iak Office, 30 January 1818, in Richard A. Pierce, ed., *The Russian-American Company: Correspondence of the Governors, Communications Sent, 1818,* trans. Richard A. Pierce (Kingston, Ontario: Limestone Press, 1984), 45 (doc. 38).

59. Khlebnikov, *Zhizneopisanie,* 175–176.

60. Pavlov, ed., *K istorii Rossiisko-amerikanskoi kompanii,* 166–167 (doc. 23); Baranov to Shelikhov and Polevoi, 20 May 1795, in Tikhmenev, *A History,* vol. 2, 60 (doc. 18).

61. For a good analysis of the navy's attitude toward the Russian-American Company and toward Baranov personally, see Barratt, *Russia in Pacific Waters,* 173–239.

62. The Peabody Museum of Salem, Massachusetts (former East India House), has a complete outfit, composed of a richly appliqued, embroidered, waterproof shirt (*kamleika*), trousers, cape, hat, and boots said to have belonged to King Kamehameha, a gift from Baranov. Though one author (Barratt) claims that the relationship between Baranov and Kamehameha soured in the years 1809–1810, it is significant that, when removed, Baranov asked (as mentioned in this chapter) that he be permitted to settle in Hawaii on the land allegedly given him as a gift by Kamehameha (Khlebnikov, *Baranov,* 98).

63. Russian State Naval Archive (RGAVMF), Fond 166, op. 1, delo 4767, fol. 9, for Golovnin's appointment as government investigator; ibid., fols. 31–32, on closure of the case against Baranov.

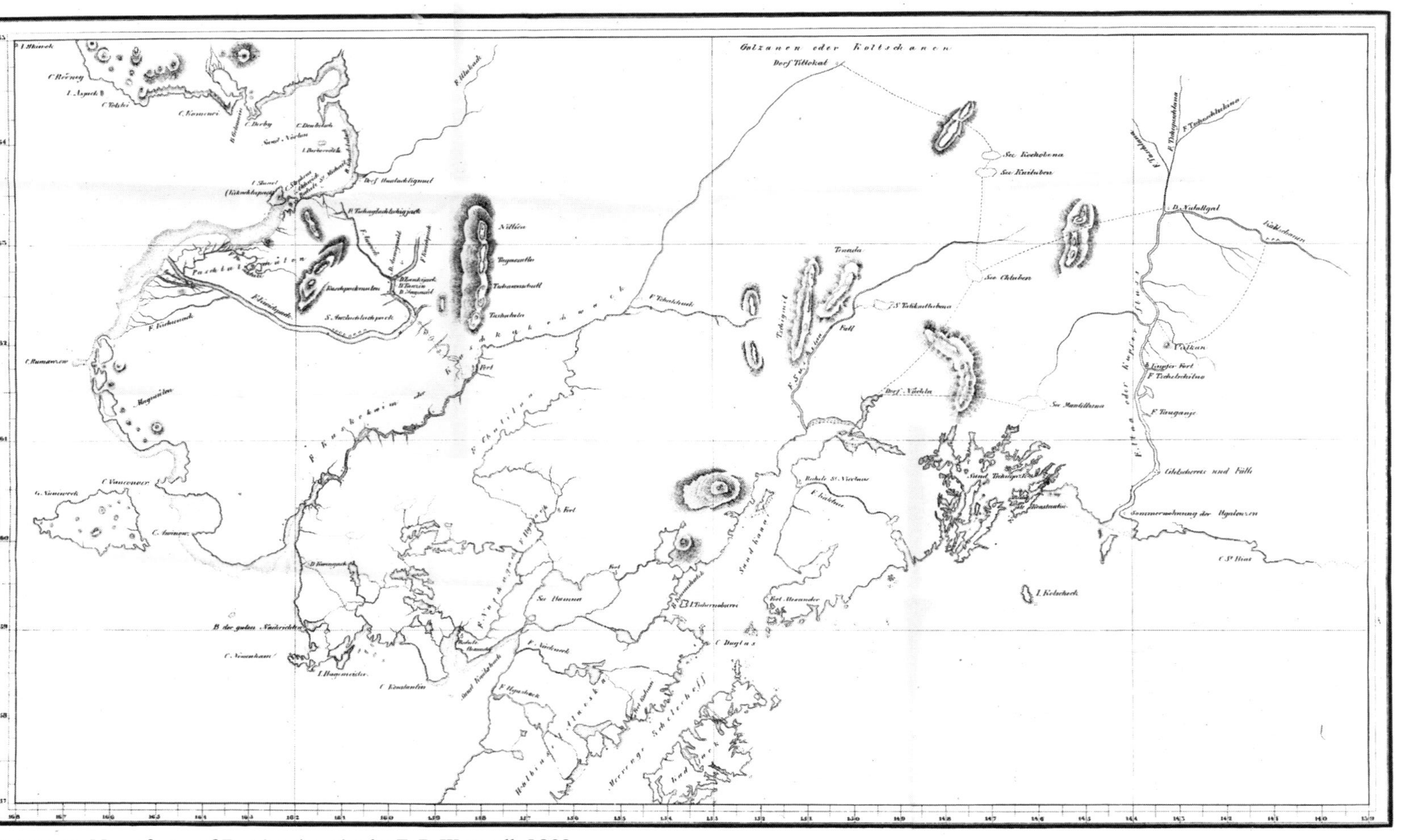

FIGURE 50. Map of part of Russian America by F. P. Wrangell, 1839.

Courtesy University of Alaska Fairbanks, Rasmuson Library, Alaska and Polar Regions Department, Rare Book Collection, no. A0503.

CHAPTER ELEVEN

After Baranov, 1818–1845

ON 11 JANUARY 1818, THE FOLLOWING DISPATCH WAS SENT FROM Novo-Arkhangel'sk to the company's main office in St. Petersburg:

> The commander of the round-the-world expedition, fleet Captain Lieutenant and Cavalier Hagemeister, today in the presence of Messrs. naval officers and before an assembly of various company officials and employees of various ranks, made known the will of the Council established by His Majesty the Emperor in the Main Office of the Company that he is to accept the duty of Chief Manager of the Russian American regions from Mr. Collegiate Councillor and Cavalier Aleksandr Andreevich Baranov. He then informed this office that from this date all matters are subject to his direct order, concerning which the Novo-Arkhangel'sk office has the honor to report to the Main Office.[1]

Perhaps it was at this assembly that the grizzled men wept, the ones who had served Baranov through thick and thin for twenty-eight years as Baranov's biographer Khlebnikov recounts. Perhaps they had every right to weep, as things began to change very rapidly. Soon the world they knew became a very different place, and the order to which they were accustomed vanished. They were to serve under new and unfamiliar rules. Most of those who exercised any authority under Baranov would soon be eased, many none too gently, out of the colony where they had spent most of their lives. Ivan Kuskov, Baranov's right hand and the founder of Ross in California, would be among them. "His influence on the old Russians and even on the Aleuts is well known. He has a bad influence on the disaffected," wrote Chief Manager Murav'iev in 1822 to the manager of the Kodiak District, where Kuskov was stopping en route to Russia. The local manager was told to watch Kuskov closely.[2] Baranov's son-in-law Sungurov, married to his younger daughter Ekaterina, and his nephew Kuglinov also had to leave. The changes in rules and management style commenced almost immediately.

The reasons for Baranov's removal were manifold. Not only did the aging chief manager consistently quarrel with the naval officers dispatched to ensure that all was well in the colony, and with whom he disagreed intensely on governance and relations with foreigners, but there were also complaints about his management by the clergy and by the naval commanders who inspected Alaska.[3] In addition, there had been substantial financial losses to the company, and several changes in employee policies that the board of directors deemed advisable to implement. The company's charter was about to expire, negotiations about charter renewal were in progress, and apparently it was time to clean house. In this instance the board of directors' and the navy's agendas coincided. The view that Baranov had to go, in spite of his long service and well-recognized achievements, was expressed in the orders Hagemeister was issued by the imperially appointed supervisory council of the company before he left St. Petersburg.

When Hagemeister, in command of the navy vessel *Suvorov*, exercised the authority to remove Baranov and assumed the office of chief manager of the colony, he became the first naval officer to occupy this position, commissioned to represent first of all the interests of the state, but at the same time to ensure the economic success of the Russian-American Company. This position, to the end of the Russian period, remained a difficult one, fraught with ambiguity and contradictions. Fortunately, for several decades extremely able men were selected to fill this office.

Hagemeister ordered an audit of all company records in Alaska, both at Novo-Arkhangel'sk and in all the districts and outposts, including the Californian settlement established by Kuskov. Inventories of company property were to be compiled. The employees, who previously had been hired in accordance with the age-old practice of half-shares of the catch (and had disputed more than once during Baranov's time the fairness of the division of the catch), were now to be paid annual salaries, in some cases supplemented with a subsistence allowance in the form either of provisions or of additional money or its equivalent. (The company had tried to implement a similar policy, issuing to the employees the assessed value of their half-shares in money, as early as 1803.)[4] This was to the company's advantage, because when they had furs, the employees had sold theirs at lower prices than the company and thus, in effect, became competitors. Introduction of wages and prohibition of the possession of furs were protested by employees and caused disaffection (which proved to be long lasting: as late as 1822, old-time employees still were asking to be paid in furs[5]). Another advantage to the company from the changes was that the introduction of wages would make the employees even more dependent on company stores. Keeping of accounts, such as the amount of credit given to any employee, his indebtedness, or, in the case of Aleut hunters not employed by the company but who sold their furs to the company at a set rate, their positive balance, would be much easier.[6] Aleut hunters in company employ were to be paid forthwith ten rubles for each sea otter skin, the amount fixed by the main office, and those in the Pribilofs employed by the company were to receive, as of 1 January 1818, thirty kopeks per fur seal skin in addition to other recompense and an annual salary. Under the new regime, by 1822 the Pribilof Aleuts who contracted to stay in the islands for three years would receive an additional twenty-five rubles if they agreed to stay for a fourth year.[7] Trappers of foxes, too, were paid a set price per animal skin.

Payments in cash were not without problems, either. There was a constant shortage of cash in the colony and during Baranov's time rarely were any transactions based on money rather than barter. Baranov's practice of reimbursing some of the employees in Spanish piasters (cash to which he had access through Settlement Ross and its trade with Californian missions) was officially condemned by Hagemeister as being against the law.[8] Quite early in his career, Baranov suggested that some sort of scrip be devised for use in Alaska. This scrip—or tokens, in the company records *marki*—were authorized in 1816 and continued in use to the end of the Russian period.[9]

Hagemeister instituted various personnel changes at outpost manager level, and ships' commanders were changed. Independent actions taken as circumstances demanded by hunting party leaders or foremen (such as Timofei Tarakanov, as noted in the preceding chapter) were discouraged, and the men were charged with overstepping their authority if they did act without instructions. Regulations, old and new, were to be strictly observed. Men who were without passports or held expired passports were required to apply for renewals. Accusations of crime were immediately dealt with: Navigator Demidov, of the *Finliandiia*, who had been accused of manslaughter aboard his vessel, was dispatched to Okhotsk (along with witnesses); foreman Iakov Babin, serving at Ross under Kuskov, was put under close guard and eventually sent to St. Petersburg for investigation and trial for allowing the Kodiak Islanders under his command to slaughter Indians on an island off the southern coast of California. Kuskov was reprimanded for failure to report this violence to Hagemeister when he was at Ross to conduct an audit there.[10] In general, there was a perception that under Baranov the employees, at least the Russian employees, had led a rather free life with little labor discipline. Such discipline would be enforced in the future, at least in theory.

Hagemeister, whom Baranov had sent to Hawaii in 1808 (but who also had been assigned to assess that situation independently for the navy), mopped up the mess left there in the wake of Schaeffer's activities and investigated the conduct of affairs in California, particularly the sea otter hunting detachments hired out to American skippers. He deputized Khristofor Benzeman, skipper of the company brig *Il'mena,* to pay respects to the Californian governor at Monterey, Pablo Vicente de Sola, and to deliver to him, as Hagemeister's personal gift, a carriage built at Settlement Ross. Benzeman was to negotiate with the governor for return of all personnel detained by the Spanish for having been caught hunting with Americans in California, and was to buy provisions for Alaska. In his instructions to Benzeman, Hagemeister asserted (perhaps reaffirmed) the right of the company's vessels, granted by Emperor Paul, to fly the Russian-American Company flag.[11]

Hagemeister ordered that a school be established at Ross in California and that on Kodiak cows belonging to the company "be given free of charge to aged officials and hunters unable to leave for Russia, and who have on Kad'iak their domicile and family, for their support, according to the size of their families."[12] A new population census was ordered and special attention was to be paid to enumerating people of mixed Russian-Alaskan descent. Economies were effected by reducing the number of Russian personnel, outlying work crews, and the artels and outposts. Trade in the Alaskan interior took up much of Hagemeister's attention. Natives and creoles (people claiming a Russian-Alaskan descent) who were trusted employees of the company were used as middlemen in establishing trade links with the peoples of the Interior.

Soon after assuming office, Hagemeister dispatched an expedition to the north, along the shores of the Bering Sea, with some private funds furnished by Count Rumiantsev, who had earlier sponsored the Kotzebue expedition to Bering Strait. (It is unclear whether plans for such an expedition had already been formulated under Baranov's initiative.) Hagemeister, and apparently Kotzebue before him, believed that in the north there were descendants of Russians, and part of the expedition's mission was to find them. The manager of the Kodiak District was to ask for volunteers.[13] This expedition, traveling by kayak, was to follow a probe conducted earlier (1816) by Fedor Kolmakov, manager of the company outpost and trading center at Katmai on the Alaska Peninsula. Young Petr Korsakovskii, accompanied by Fedor Kolmakov, reached the Kuskokwim River[14] and possibly explored the Bering Sea coast north of that river's mouth. On the return trek Korsakovskii followed the Kvichak River to Lake Iliamna, explored this lake, and then Lake Clark. In 1819, Andrei Ustiugov, an Aleut from Unalaska, now a navigator in command of a company vessel, charted the coast up to Cape Newenham; when his brother Nikolai led an abortive revolt in the Pribilofs, he was pardoned out of respect for Andrei's achievements and assigned to the second Korsakovskii expedition in 1819.[15] While Ustiugov sailed that year once again along the coast, Korsakovskii once more went by land. In 1820, Khristofor Benzeman was dispatched along the coasts described by Ustiugov and continued the cartographic work along the coasts north of Bristol Bay.[16] On Hagemeister's orders, but under his successor, Lieutenant Semeon Ianovskii, an outpost was established in 1819 at the mouth of the Nushagak River. It was named Novo-Aleksandrovskii Redoubt.[17]

Exploration of the Copper River also resumed. While Hagemeister was still in Alaska, Navigator Afanasii Il'ich Klimovskii, son of Russian old-timer Il'ia Klimovskii and his Alutiiq wife, was dispatched to reconnoiter the Ahtna territory, far inland. This territory had been visited by Tarkhanov in 1796, explored by Patochkin in 1798–1799, and then visited briefly by Bazhenov in 1805.[18]

The central and western Aleutians and Commander Islands received little or no attention, as they were managed at this time out of the Okhotsk office. In some areas of the Aleutian archipelago not visited by any company vessels for many years, life reverted to purely subsistence mode. This was the case for the Aleuts living in the Rat Islands, and for the very few Russian men living in Aleut communities, or in very small enclaves, as was the case on Atka.

FIGURE 51. Novo-Aleksandrovskii (Nushagak). Old Russian trading post for the Bristol Bay region, founded by Fedor Kolmakov in 1819. Drawing by Henry W. Elliott, ca. 1870s.
Courtesy University of Alaska Fairbanks, Rasmuson Library, Alaska and Polar Regions Department, Archives.

In 1819, an American vessel, sailing from Java, put in at Novo-Arkhangel'sk. The crew was infected with some sort of virulent fever, and soon the epidemic spread to the population at Sitka and eventually was carried to Kodiak.[19] The event illustrated how medical care, or rather lack thereof, was a serious problem in the colony. Care for the sick was mostly limited to the pharmaceutical supplies that Baranov requested and occasional assistance from medical officers aboard circumnavigating vessels. Under Baranov, there

FIGURE 52. View of Captains Harbor (Kapitanskaia Gavan'), modern Unalaska Bay, 1817. Watercolor by Ludwig (Louis) Choris, staff artist with the Otto von Kotzebue expedition, voyage of the *Riurik* (1815–1818).

From Choris, 1822, plate 11 preceding section Iles Aléoutiennes. Courtesy University of Alaska Fairbanks, Rasmuson Library, Alaska and Polar Regions Department, Rare Book Collection, no. B0083.

FIGURE 53. View of Illiuliuk settlement (site of modern city of Unalaska), the Russian-American Company's principal establishment on Unalaska Island, 1817. This watercolor by Ludwig (Louis) Choris, staff artist for the Otto von Kotzebue expedition, voyage of the *Riurik* (1815–1818), is the only work known to feature the Orthodox Chapel of the Ascension of Christ, built before or in 1812.

From Choris, 1822, plate 7 preceding section Iles Aléoutiennes. Courtesy University of Alaska Fairbanks, Rasmuson Library, Alaska and Polar Regions Department, Rare Book Collection, no. B0083.

was a small makeshift hospital at Kodiak, but no long-term resident physician; Baranov himself had often administered home remedies to his sick workers. Several epidemics had occurred, and the mortality rate was high. There was cause for worry. Ianovskii, as Baranov and Hagemeister before him, urged that medical facilities be established and physicians assigned to duty in the colony.

The company management responded and eventually an effective public health system was developed. The first company physician arrived in Novo-Arkhangel'sk in 1820. The first hospital on the Northwest Coast of America was built in Novo-Arkhangel'sk between 1820 and 1826, in the tenure of the first naval chief manager to serve full term, the first under the Second Charter, Captain Matvei I. Murav'iev. The medical services in the colony were supported out of profits, five percent of which was set aside for that purpose.[20] In subsequent years, medical services were considerably improved and expanded. The hospital at Novo-Arkhangel'sk was enlarged (and continued to operate through 1867). The company encouraged young men of mixed Russian-Alaskan ancestry to qualify as medical practitioners, physician's assistants, and paramedics; it employed pharmacists and midwives; Native midwifery was also supported. Small hospitals were established at St. Paul Harbor on Kodiak, at Unalaska, Atka, and, after 1833, at St. Michael on Norton Sound. Precautions against smallpox were taken. Smallpox vaccination was introduced in Alaska quite early (a shipment of vaccine arriving on the *Neva* in 1808) and Father Sokolov, the first resident Orthodox priest, when dispatched to Alaska in 1816, underwent training in administering smallpox vaccination, as all priests were required to do.

Nevertheless, the smallpox pandemic that devastated Alaska between 1836 and 1840 could not be stopped, mostly because of the Native resistance to vaccination (the procedure ran contrary to Native theories of disease causality).[21] The death toll among the Native population was enormous. The administration of vaccine by teams of volunteers in Alaska's interior was interpreted as an intentional spread of infection. An attack on the Russian outpost at Ikogmiut on the Yukon and an attempted attack on an outpost on the Kuskokwim at that time were probably intended as retaliation. Among the Russians and those Natives who were vaccinated, however, the mortality was almost nil. The object lesson was clear and taken to heart. When in the early 1860s another smallpox pandemic was sweeping the North American continent, Alaska escaped because vaccination, conducted by employees of the company, Orthodox clergy, and progressive village chiefs, had found wide acceptance. Smallpox was not the only disease the Russian-American Company managers battled with some success. Sweeping measures were undertaken to check the spread of venereal diseases, especially syphilis.

As noted by Robert Fortuine, a physican long concerned with the problems of public health and an authority on the history of health care and diseases in Alaska:

> By the end of their sojourn in Alaska, the Russians had developed a well-thought-out system of health care extended to all company employees and to many of the native peoples as well. Although ... [the service] was far from perfect, it was a well-organized effort that was effectively adapted to the living conditions and geography of Alaska. Except for the recruitment of physicians and the annual drug and supply shipments from Russia, the system was largely self-sufficient and self-perpetuating. Unfortunately, soon after the American flag unfurled over Baranov's Castle in October 1867, this valuable legacy of experience was allowed to go undeveloped.[22]

Speaking in a public forum in 1991 in Anchorage, Dr. Fortuine remarked: "The proud old hospital [in Sitka] died of a broken heart."

One innovation by Hagemeister, however, had very adverse effects on the colony and probably on the company's finances (in 1822–1823 the company, deeply in debt, stopped paying dividends).[23] He had prohibited trade with foreigners and in 1821 such prohibition was made official by an imperial decree. Murav'iev, who succeeded Ianovskii in 1820, had to bear the consequences of this policy, which many considered ill-advised.

Murav'iev proved an able administrator in a difficult time. It was during Matvei Murav'iev's tenure that the Sitka Tlingit returned to their old habitat, from which Baranov and Lisianskii had dislodged them by force of arms in 1804. They established their settlement adjacent to a section of the Novo-Arkhangel'sk palisade and began to trade with the town under strict rules introduced by Murav'iev. Trade with the Tlingit helped the town survive (or at least have a better standard of living) until the 1867 transfer and beyond.[24] Murav'iev established the policy that a new chief manager should tour the entire domain and visited even Atka and Attu, putting the administration of such distant outposts on a more formal footing. When a new supply crisis arose, not only because of the 1821 prohibition on trade with foreigners but also because the board of directors judged that the colony was now well provisioned and there was no need to send out a circumnavigating vessel with supplies,[25] Murav'iev had to fall back on supplies traded from the Spanish in California and those bought in Hawaii in exchange for fur seal and beaver pelts obtained from Alaska's interior. The situation was complicated by the fact

FIGURE 54. In this lithograph (partial view) dated 1867, the area where Tlingit settled after 1820, outside of the palisade surrounding Novo-Arkhangel'sk, is clearly shown. Today this is Katleyan Street, Sitka. By an unknown artist, published in 1869 by George Davidson.

Courtesy University of Alaska Fairbanks, Rasmuson Library, Rare Book Collection, no. A1868 1st 1869, facing p. 118.

that from 1821 California was part of the independent Republic of Mexico, which the Russian government had not recognized. The newly appointed governor, Arguello, had even challenged the legality of the Ross settlement. And all the time Murav'iev kept arguing against the orders and policies he considered unreasonable and detrimental to the colony's well-being.[26] Finally, in 1825, the *Elena*, commanded by Lt. Petr E. Chistiakov, arrived. Murav'iev took over her command, leaving Chistiakov in Novo-Arkhangel'sk as his replacement.

Petr Chistiakov was a hard-working, poor but honest man who eventually was elevated to the rank of admiral, but lacked the vision for Alaska, or the easy hand, or the initiative to act even in violation of orders from St. Petersburg, of a Murav'iev. An able administrator who followed the letter of the law, he governed affairs in Alaska at a time when the imperial government had signed international conventions with the United States in 1824 and England in 1825. The conventions recognized Alaska's boundaries as extending to 54° 40' N latitude, and running from the southern extremity of Prince of Wales Island along the Portland Canal to 56° N latitude, and then northwesterly along the coastal mountain range, ten nautical leagues (55.5 km) inland to the 141st meridian. For citizens of the United States, the convention guaranteed ten years of free access by vessels to "all inner seas, sounds, harbors and bays" along the Northwest Coast "for fishing and trade with the aboriginal inhabitants of that land," excluding from this trade alcohol and firearms.[27] British subjects were granted the right of free navigation in all the rivers that debouched into the Pacific Ocean through Russian territory. They, too, were granted a ten-year period of freedom of fishing in Russian waters and trade with the Natives, excluding alcohol, firearms, powder, and other military gear. In the opinion of one historian-specialist, in signing this convention the Russian foreign office did not consider the needs or benefits of the company but followed other considerations of state.[28] For the same reasons, the government ignored several proposals presented by junior naval officers and would-be empire builders, such as Romanov and Zavalishin: Romanov proposed drastic measures to check British dominance of the North American interior, while Zavalishin's far-ranging proposal included the annexation of California.[29]

The convention signed with England in 1825 would in the future provide a foundation for an 1838 rapprochement between the Russian-American Company and the Hudson's Bay Company, which in the 1820s was establishing itself in the Pacific Northwest and soon controlled the interior trade of what is now British Columbia and the states of Washington and Oregon.[30]

During Chistiakov's administration the central and western Aleutians, as well as the Commander Islands and the Kuril Islands, were put firmly under management out of Novo-Arkhangel'sk. In 1828, a company settlement was established on Urup in the southern Kuril Islands, manned predominantly by Alutiiq volunteers from Kodiak Island. In 1829 and 1830, Ensign Ivan Ia. Vasil'iev explored the course of the Nushagak River far into the Alaskan interior.[31] Also during Chistiakov's tenure a naval expedition of two vessels, commanded by Mikhail N. Staniukovich (the *Moller*) and Fedor P. Litke (the *Seniavin*), explored the Bering Sea and its coasts (including St. Lawrence Island), engaging in hydrographic and cartographic work. This was a follow-up on the earlier naval expedition to Bering Strait and the Arctic Ocean in 1821–1822 commanded by Captains Mikhail N. Vasil'iev and Gleb S. Shishmarev and the expedition, sponsored by Rumiantsev, of the *Riurik* under Kotzebue. But company vessels were also sent out from time to time to Bering Strait and along Alaska's arctic shore, following the pioneering voyages of A. Adolf Etholen and Vasilii S. Khromchenko in 1821 and 1822.[32] Chistiakov, shortly before the end of his term, sent Etholen out beyond Bering Strait. Under his successor, Wrangell, several voyages to the north were undertaken, and from the 1840s to the end of the Russian regime a ship was sent out annually. The company and the government were well aware of continuing British interest in the Northwest Passage and took singular notice of Beechey's passage through Bering Strait and the ensuing charting of Alaska's northern coasts in 1826 and 1827.[33]

Company vessels were exploring possibilities of Native trade in the north and specifically participation in the trading rendezvous on the Buckland River in Kotzebue Sound. For trade to the Iñupiat they carried predominantly Alaskan products, including whale blubber from Kodiak Island. The company was interested in the flow of Alaskan products, especially furs, through Native trade networks from the Yukon River via the Koyukuk River to the Iñupiat of Alaska's North Slope and from there to the Chukchi and Siberian markets. Acquisition of beaver pelts and beaver castor (the dried perineal glands, in great demand by perfumers) and other land animal furs assumed ever greater importance.

It was during Chistiakov's term that arctic foxes from the Pribilofs and black and silver foxes from the American mainland were transplanted to the central Aleutians and Rat Islands, and that fox farming (which persisted until World War II) had its inception. Fur seal and sea otter conservation practices began to be implemented. In 1828, the Aleut population of Sanak Island, one of the most famous sea otter grounds in Alaska, was moved to the Alaska Peninsula in order to rest the Sanak hunting ground, as almost half a century earlier Maxim Lazarev had moved the people of Amchitka to Adak and Atka to rest the sea otters in the Rat Islands.[34] The Sanak people settled the village of Belkofski, which was inhabited until the late 1980s; Sanak was never reoccupied by the Aleuts.[35] Other sea otter conservation measures were limits on the number of animals to be taken per year in a given district or in specific hunting areas (for example, in the Atka district the number could not exceed 300), prohibition of the taking of female and pup pelts or buying them from the Aleuts, rotation of hunting grounds, and prohibition of settlement near sea otter hauling grounds.[36]

FIGURE 55. **Baron Ferdinand Wrangell (1796–1870). Colonial chief manager of the Russian-American Company, 1830–1835.**
Courtesy Richard A. Pierce.

In 1830, Chistiakov was replaced by one of the ablest chief managers in the history of Russian America, Baron Ferdinand Wrangell, a well-known navigator and arctic explorer. He came to the colony accompanied by his wife, who promptly established friendships with the local women (including several Tlingit ladies in the Tlingit settlement at Novo-Arkhangel'sk) and became very popular with all classes of the town's population. She is credited with introducing a degree of refinement in the social life of Novo-Arkhangel'sk: musical evenings, amateur theatricals, dances, picnics, and visits to the nearby hot springs as a kind of a spa.[37] These practices were continued under Wrangell's successors, apparently with great success and the admiration of foreign visitors, British naval captains as well as shipwrecked Japanese, but ridiculed by Russians, such as Lt. Zagoskin in 1842, who was then fresh out of St. Petersburg.

Under Wrangell, relations with the Tlingit steadily improved, and conservation—or rather the harvesting of marine fur bearers on a sustainable yield basis as introduced piecemeal by Baranov, then more systematically under Chistiakov—became an established practice. The ten-year special relationship between the Russian-American Company in Alaska and American and British citizens, guaranteed by the conventions of 1824 and of 1825, expired, and the company did not wish its renewal. To neutralize the Hudson's Bay Company's activities on the Stikine River, Wrangell authorized the establishment of a redoubt, then called St. Dionysius.[38] (The present-day town near the redoubt site bears Wrangell's name.) In 1834, the British vessel *Dryad*, owned by the Hudson's Bay Company, attempted to sail up the Stikine River and was detained by the Russians. An international incident was in the making. The imperial government urged the Russian-American Company to settle damage claims advanced by the Hudson's Bay Company.[39] The dispute ended with a formal agreement concluded in 1839 in Hamburg, Germany, with Wrangell negotiating on behalf of the Russian-American Company and George Simpson representing the Hudson's Bay Company. The agreement, originally for ten

FIGURE 56. Fort Wrangell, 1876, near the site of Redoubt St. Dionysius, which was established by order of Ferdinand P. Wrangell in 1834.

Courtesy Provincial Archives, Victoria, British Columbia.

years but renewed in 1850, was of benefit to both, so much so that during the Crimean War the Hudson's Bay Company managed to persuade the British government to treat Alaska as neutral territory. From then on the Hudson's Bay Company provided Russian America with goods at moderate prices and part of the furs they obtained as holder of a lease on Redoubt St. Dionysius, which was renamed Fort Stikine.[40] This agreement, in the opinion of some historians, obviated the need to maintain Settlement Ross in California, which was soon liquidated, Wrangell's efforts to the contrary notwithstanding. Ross was sold to John A. Sutter in 1841. It was not long thereafter that California was annexed by the United States.[41]

Wrangell did not neglect company activities in the north. In 1833, St. Michael was founded on Norton Sound, and exploration and the push into the Yukon Basin began immediately. Andrei Glazunov, a navigator and explorer of Russian-Alaskan ancestry, was on the Unalakleet River that same year, anxious to find a convenient route to the middle Yukon. The route to the lower Yukon was closed by determined Yupiit of the Pastolik

FIGURE 57. St. Michael, on the island of the same name in Norton Sound, established 1833. Drawing by Il'ia Voznesenskii, 1842.

Courtesy Richard A. Pierce.

FIGURE 58. Kolmakovskii Redoubt, established by Semeon Lukin in 1841 across the river from a small post founded by Lukin and Fedor Kolmakov eight years earlier.

Lithograph published in 1886 by Henry W. Elliott. Courtesy University of Alaska Fairbanks, Rasmuson Library, Alaska and Polar Regions Department, Rare Book Collection, no. A0463.

FIGURE 59. Arvid Adolf Etholen (in Russian, Adolf Karlovich Etolin). Colonial chief manager 1840–1845. *Courtesy Richard A. Pierce.*

area who held the Apoon channel. The Russians were also aware that there were convenient portages on the middle-lower Yukon to the Kuskokwim River. Glazunov reached the Anvik River, a Yukon tributary, and sailed downriver along the Anvik and the Yukon to a Native trading rendezvous at Anilukhtakhpak (near the site of modern Holy Cross). From there he explored the Innoko River, then crossed over to the Kuskokwim, to the outpost recently established there by Semeon Lukin, another Russian-Alaskan, and went up the Kuskokwim River to Holitna. He attempted to ascend this river and cross the (Alaska) mountain range to Cook Inlet, but lack of game (he and his team ate only whatever they could catch or shoot) forced him and his companions to turn back. In April 1834, he returned to St. Michael Redoubt on Norton Sound. Semeon Lukin and Fedor Kolmakov, pioneer of 1816 and 1818 Russian explorations on the Kuskokwim, investigated the middle and upper course of the Kuskokwim and the upper Innoko River. In the summer of 1834, Aleksandr Kashevarov, a Russian-Alaskan who later became a high-ranking naval officer serving in St. Petersburg, explored the Pastolik River, a water route from St. Michael to the mouth of the Yukon River, and the Yukon delta, charting five of the river's arms. He noted seasonal abundance of king salmon and also that the inhabitants of the settlements on the Yukon delta hunted white whales and bearded seals. His report is a wealth of brief but accurate and very early ethnographic information on the Northern Yup'ik and on trade networks and winter and summer routes of communication.[42]

Under Wrangell's successors, Ivan A. Kupreianov (1835–1840) and A. Adolf Etholen (1840–1845), the exploration and establishment of trade networks in Alaska's interior continued. In 1836, Petr Fedorovich Kolmakov, son of Fedor Kolmakov, once again ascended the Kuskokwim and explored the upper reaches of the Innoko River. In 1838, Aleksandr Kashevarov aboard the brig *Polifem* sailed through Bering Strait and along the Alaskan shore, exploring the coast in skin boats and traveling beyond Point Barrow. Trade was expanded along the Yukon with several outposts (*odinochkas*) established, such as Nulato, Ikogmiut (now Russian Mission), Andreevskaia, and Unalakleet.[43] Kupreianov keenly felt the setbacks suffered by many of these outlying outposts and the devastation wrought by the smallpox epidemic that he was unable to stop. Kupreianov was also host to a British warship, the *Sulphur*, the first foreign warship to put in at the port of Novo-Arkhangel'sk. Her captain, Edward Belcher, and Midshipman Francis G. Simpkinson left accounts of their two visits (in 1837 and 1839, respectively). Their description of the town of Novo-Arkhangel'sk, its defenses, new construction and the old church (later replaced by the Cathedral of St. Michael under Ioann Veniaminov's direction), and the description of Veniaminov himself as a young man, while serving as Novo-Arkhangel'sk parish priest, are extremely valuable. Interestingly, Captain Belcher noted that the local Russians were "a shade lower in civilization by their intermarriage with the natives." But he greatly admired the school and the hospital. He also noted that the local Tlingit

FIGURE 60. **Ikogmiut (Russian Mission), ca. 1890, showing the church built by Fr. Iakov Netsvetov next to the new church built by Fr. Iakov's student, Fr. Zakharii Bel'kov, with the financial assistance of his brothers. Photo by William Gerstle.**

Courtesy University of Alaska Fairbanks, Rasmuson Library, Alaska and Polar Regions Department, Archives, Gerstle Collection, no. 76-132-1001.

chiefs wore ermine capes and that ermine was imported from Siberia for trade with the Natives. Belcher was most impressed with a social evening at the chief manager's house, with the dancing skills of the local ladies and, above all, with Mrs. Kupreianov. Not so Midshipman Simpkinson, who much admired the beauty of Mrs. Rozenberg (Rozenberg was Kupreianov's assistant and a future chief manager), but found much amiss in the ladies' attire, their dancing skills (except in the waltz), and in the men's smoking in the presence of the ladies.[44]

Kupreianov was followed by Arvid Adolf Etholen, a Finn,[45] who served in Alaska for many years; he had arrived in 1818 at the age of nineteen aboard the circumnavigating vessel *Kamchatka*, commanded by the famous Vasilii Golovnin. During Etholen's tenure Lt. Zagoskin was dispatched to map Alaska's interior. The latter, shortly after his return to Russia, published an extensive account of his travels.[46] Most of the sweeping changes in the administration of faraway outposts and in trade with the Natives that Zagoskin proposed, however, were found to be disruptive and were largely ignored. Some were implemented at later dates, others only in part. Nevertheless, slowly and surely, Russian fur trade was developing in the Interior.[47]

On the whole, Etholen's administration may be characterized as a time of consolidation and improvement, not of drastic changes. On Etholen's orders the Kodiak villages depopulated by smallpox were consolidated into a few larger and more viable settlements. It was during his tenure that, as noted above, Ross Settlement in California was liquidated (several Pomo Indian families or women married to Alaskans who served at Ross moved to Kodiak). Strict orders were issued that no one, no matter of what position or rank, could strike a Native, and in self-defense only if one's life depended on it. The policy of nonretaliation for Native attacks, long promulgated by the imperial government, was also reiterated (for this reason, as a face-saving device, in any case of armed conflict the administration assumed provocation on the part of its employees). Relations with the Hudson's Bay Company proceeded smoothly, and by an agreement with Sir George Simpson concluded in 1842, trade in alcohol was stopped (or, more probably, drastically curtailed).

The first Lutheran church on the Northwest Coast was built in Novo-Arkhangel'sk during this administration. Uno Cygnaeus, who came to Alaska in 1840, traveling together with Etholen and his wife, was the first pastor to serve the growing Protestant community in Russian America. This community was composed predominantly of Finns, who since 1809 had entered company service in ever-increasing numbers, and Baltic Germans.[48] The education system was expanded and improved. In this area Etholen had the whole-hearted support and assistance of Ioann Veniaminov who had returned to Alaska as Bishop Innokentii (Innocent), the colony's first bishop of the Orthodox Church. Education, though not universal as it is in the twentieth century, was open to all who desired to attend school. Native children were enrolled in both church and company schools as were, of course, children of Russians and Russian-American Native couples. As U.S. Army Lt. Eli Huggins was to remark in his journal in 1868, "there was no bar to the promotion of these creoles either in church or state, and many of the most honored and responsible officials we met in the territory were creoles who had been educated in Russia."[49] In a sense the middle of the ninteenth century in Alaska could be characterized as the age of the creole.

Figure 61. Uno Cygnaeus.
Courtesy National Museum of Finland.

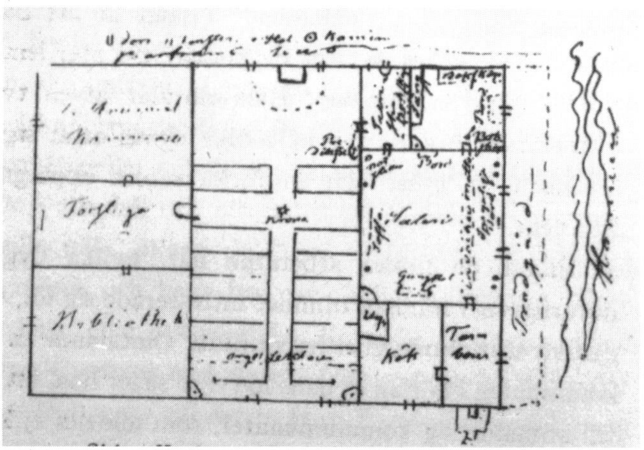

Figure 62. Floor plan of the first Lutheran church in Sitka.
Courtesy Richard A. Pierce.

NOTES

1. Pierce, ed., *Correspondence of the Governors,* 1 (no. 1).
2. Records of the Russian-American Company, Correspondence of the Governors-General (hereafter, RAC), Communications Sent, vol. 3, no. 97, 16 April 1822, National Archives, Washington, D.C.
3. See, for example, Barratt, *Russia in Pacific Waters,* 173–189. For Golovnin's scathing indictment of the company's labor policies (including treatment of the Natives), see "Memorandum of Captain 2nd Rank Golovnin on the Condition of the Aleuts in the Settlements of the Russian-American Company and its *Promyshlenniki,*" trans. Katherine L. Arndt, *Alaska History* 1, no. 2 (Fall/Winter 1985–1986): 59–71.
4. For a detailed discussion of employee policies of the Russian-American Company, see Sarafian, *Employee Policies and Practices.* The discussion by S. B. Okun, "Labor Conditions in the Russian Colonies in America," chap. 8 in *Russian-American Company,* 171–192, is marred by the anti-capitalist bias of the time in which he wrote this work. The stress is on the exploitative character of the company and the indebtedness of the personnel. The social services provided by the company, such as old-age and disability pensions, well in advance of the times and unheard-of elsewhere until the twentieth century, are either ignored or characterized as miserly, as they often appeared to outside visitors unfamiliar with Alaskan conditions.
5. Chief Manager Murav'iev to Main Office, RAC, Communications Sent, vol. 3, no. 88, 15 April 1822, fol. 18v, National Archives, Washington, D.C.
6. On the positive balance of Aleut hunters who sold their pelts at Attu and in the Commander Islands, see Kiril Khlebnikov, "Travel Notes aboard the Brig *Kiakhta* along the Islands of Andreianov, Bering, Near, and Rat [Islands] District, by Manager of the Novoarkhangel'sk Office Khlebnikov, the Year 1827," unpublished translation by Lydia T. Black made from a microfilmed copy (reel 6, no. 52) in the Shur Collection, Rasmuson Library, University of Alaska Fairbanks. The original Russian manuscript is found in the Archive of the Russian Geographic Society, Razriad 99, delo 34.
7. Pierce, ed., *Correspondence of the Governors,* 18 (no. 33), 136 (no. 228); RAC, Communications Received, Main Office to Murav'iev, vol. 4, no. 119, 27 February 1824, fol. 8, National Archives, Washington, D.C., reply to Murav'iev's communication No. 297, 18 November 1822, approving the payment.
8. Pierce, ed., *Correspondence of the Governors,* 9–10 (no. 23).
9. For a detailed account of the history of the Russian-American Company's "skin money" see Richard A. Pierce, "The Russian-American Company Currency," in *Russian America: The Forgotten Frontier,* ed. Barbara S. Smith and Redmond J. Barnett (Tacoma: Washington State Historical Society, 1990), 145–153.
10. Hagemeister to Kuskov, 28 January 1818, in Pierce, ed., *Correspondence of the Governors,* 11 (no. 24). See also related nos. 232 and 301 in ibid., 138–139, 172.

    This episode forms the basis for the popular children's book by Scott O'Dell, *The Island of the Blue Dolphins* (New York: Bantam/Doubleday, Dell Publishing, 1960), and a motion picture of the same name. For a brief synopsis of historical data on this or similar episodes and possible identification of the island, see Pierce, ed., *Correspondence of the Governors,* xi–xii.
11. Pierce, ed., *Correspondence of the Governors,* 5 (no. 17). For the history and a description of the company flag see S. G. Fedorova, "Flag Rossiisko-Amerikanskoi kompanii," in *Ot Aliaski do Ognennoi Zemli* (Moscow: Izdatel'stvo "Nauka," 1967), 121–129.
12. Pierce, ed., *Correspondence of the Governors,* 14–15 (no. 30).
13. Hagemeister to Kad'iak Office, 21 January 1818, in ibid., 7–9 (no. 21).
14. See VanStone, ed., *Russian Exploration in Southwest Alaska.*
15. Hagemeister to Aleut chiefs, no date, in Pierce, ed., *Correspondence of the Governors,* 136–137 (no. 228); Ianovskii to Kad'iak Office, 5 December 1818, in ibid., 164–168 (no. 289). On Korsakovskii's 1819 expedition, see instruction by Ianovskii, 4 December 1818, in ibid., 157–163 (no. 286).
16. Khlebnikov, *Russkaia Amerika v neopublikovannykh,* 54.

17. This redoubt was soon transferred to Hagemeister Island (named so by Ustiugov) and then in 1822 back to the Nushagak River. For a detailed account of the early period of the Novo-Aleksandrovskii Redoubt, see Berkley B. Bailey and Geoffrey C. Orth, "Novo-Aleksandrovskii Redoubt: Hagemeister Island," in *Russia in North America: Proceedings of the 2nd International Conference on Russian America, Sitka, Alaska, August 19–22, 1987,* ed. Richard A. Pierce (Kingston, Ontario; Fairbanks, Alaska: Limestone Press, 1990), 413–425.

18. On Patochkin and Klimovskii see Khlebnikov, *Russkaia Amerika v neopublikovannykh,* 53–54, 63–65. On Bazhenov see Iurii Lisianskii, *Puteshestvie vokrug sveta na korable "Neva" v 1803–1806 godakh* (Moscow: Gosudarstvennoe izdatel'stvo geograficheskoi literatury, 1947), 175; originally published 1812 in Russian and 1814 in English.

19. Richard A. Pierce, *Builders of Alaska: The Russian Governors, 1818–1867* (Kingston, Ontario: Limestone Press, 1986), 5.

20. Robert Fortuine, "Health and Medical Care in Russian America," in *Russian America: The Forgotten Frontier,* ed. Barbara S. Smith and Redmond J. Barnett (Tacoma: Washington State Historical Society, 1990), 121–129.

21. James R. Gibson, "Smallpox on the Northwest Coast, 1835–1838," *BC Studies* 56 (Winter 1982–1983): 61–81. This is an excellent study, though Gibson is in error when he proposes that the 1769 smallpox epidemic which devastated Kamchatka spread to the Aleutian Islands. There is direct evidence (people arriving in Kamchatka from Alaska giving thanks for having escaped the epidemic) that this is not so. Katherine L. Arndt, "The Russian-American Company and the Smallpox Epidemic of 1835 to 1840" (paper presented at twelfth annual meeting of the Alaska Anthropological Association, Anchorage, 2 March 1985), presents an excellent picture of the attempts made to vaccinate the Natives and how some village chiefs often saved their people by compelling them to undergo vaccination. For an alternate interpretation of the Russian vaccination effort, see Don E. Dumond, "Poison in the Cup: The South Alaskan Smallpox Epidemic of 1835," *University of Oregon Anthropological Papers* 52 (1996): 117–129.

22. Fortuine, "Health and Medical Care," 128–129.

23. Bolkhovitinov, *Russko-amerikanskie otnosheniia* (1975), 247.

24. Gibson, "Russian Dependence," 77–103.

25. Pierce, *Builders of Alaska,* 7–9.

26. Wheeler, "Empires in Conflict," 419–441; Bolkhovitinov, *Russko-amerikanskie otnosheniia* (1975), 44–254.

27. Cited after Bolkhovitinov, *Russko-amerikanskie otnosheniia* (1975), 272, my translation.

28. Ibid., 244–307.

29. Barratt, *Russia in Pacific Waters,* 224–232. Zavalishin's request addressed to Emperor Alexander I in 1822 for permission to establish a knightly order for the taking over of California by the Russians (RGIA, Fond 1673, op. 1, delo 26).

30. Gibson, *Otter Skins,* 62–83.

31. VanStone, ed., *Russian Explorations in Southwest Alaska.*

32. James W. VanStone, ed., *V. S. Khromchenko's Coastal Explorations in Southwestern Alaska, 1822,* trans. David H. Kraus, Fieldiana: Anthropology, vol. 64 (Chicago: Field Museum of Natural History, 1973); Bailey and Orth, "Novo-Aleksandrovskii Redoubt."

33. On Beechey's activities, see Frederick W. Beechey, *Narrative of a Voyage to the Pacific and Beering's Strait, to Co-operate with the Polar Expeditions: Performed in His Majesty's Ship* Blossom, *under the Command of Captain F. W. Beechey, R. N., ... in the Years 1825, 26, 27, 28,* 2 pts. (London: Henry Colburn and Richard Bentley, 1831).

34. In 1812, Ivan F. Vasil'iev had transported the Aleut survivors from Atka back home to Amchitka.

35. Early in the American period, people out of Unalaska and the Shumagin Islands hunted at Sanak Island, and for a time a sea otter hunters' settlement, of mixed Scandinavian-Aleut membership, came into being. Today it is a wildlife refuge.

36. On sea otter conservation measures during the Russian period, see Vasilii Kashevarov, Manager of Kodiak District of RAC to Chief Manager Wrangell, Report on Conditions in the District, manuscript, ca. 1833, in Archive of the Russian Geographic Society, St. Petersburg, Razriad 99, op. 1, delo 107; Cedor L. Snigaroff, *Niiĝuĝis maqax̂tazaqangis: Atkan Historical Traditions Told in 1952 by Cedor L. Snigaroff,* trans. and ed. Knut Bergsland, 2d rev. ed. (Fairbanks: Alaska Native Language Center, University of Alaska Fairbanks, 1979), 34–44; C. L. Hooper, *A Report on the Sea-Otter Banks of Alaska* (Washington, D.C.: Government Printing Office, 1897); Arndt, "Preserving the Future Hunt."
37. For Elizabeth Wrangell's own account of her sojourn in the colony, see Alix O'Grady, *From the Baltic to Russian America, 1829–1836,* ed. Richard A. Pierce (Kingston, Ontario: Limestone Press, 2001).
38. On the complex interplay of local Tlingit, Russian, and British interests in this area, see Katherine L. Arndt, "Russian Relations with the Stikine Tlingit, 1833–1867," *Alaska History* 3, no. 1 (1988): 27–43.
39. Bolkhovitinov, *Russko-amerikanskie otnosheniia* (1990), 35–39.
40. James R. Gibson, "The 'Russian Contract': The Agreement of 1838 between the Hudson's Bay and Russian-American Companies," in *Russia in North America: Proceedings of the 2nd International Conference on Russian America, Sitka, Alaska, August 19–22, 1987,* ed. Richard A. Pierce (Kingston, Ontario; Fairbanks, Alaska: Limestone Press, 1990), 157–180.
41. Bolkhovitinov, *Russko-amerikanskie otnosheniia* (1990), 39–49.
42. A. Kashevarov in Khlebnikov, *Russkaia Amerika v neopublikovannykh,* 229–237.
43. On the development of the Russian fur trade in Alaska's interior see Katherine L. Arndt, "Russian-American Company Trade on the Middle Yukon River, 1839–1867," in *Russia in North America: Proceedings of the 2nd International Conference on Russian America, Sitka, Alaska, August 19–22, 1987,* ed. Richard A. Pierce (Kingston, Ontario; Fairbanks, Alaska: Limestone Press, 1990), 180–192; idem, "Russian Exploration and Trade in Alaska's Interior," in *Russian America: The Forgotten Frontier,* ed. Barbara S. Smith and Redmond J. Barnett (Tacoma: Washington State Historical Society, 1990), 95–107; idem, "Dynamics of the Fur Trade on the Middle Yukon River, Alaska, 1837–1867" (Ph.D. diss., University of Alaska Fairbanks, 1996); James A. Ketz and Katherine L. Arndt, "The Russian-American Company and Development of the Alaskan Copper River Fur Trade," in *Le Castor Fait Tout: Selected Papers of the Fifth North American Fur Trade Conference, 1985,* ed. Bruce G. Trigger, Toby Morantz, and Louise Dechêne (Montreal: Lake St. Louis Historical Society, 1987), 438–455.
44. Richard A. Pierce and J. H. Winslow, eds., *H.M.S.* Sulphur *on the Northwest and California Coasts, 1837 and 1839* (Kingston, Ontario: Limestone Press, 1979), 22, 24, 28. For Midshipman Simpkinson's account, see ibid., 91–106.
45. Pierce, *Builders of Alaska,* 22–26; Lydia T. Black and Richard A. Pierce, "Russian America and the Finns," *Terra* 29, nos. 2–3 (December 1990–May 1991): 18–29.
46. Lavrentii Alekseevich Zagoskin, *Puteshestviia i issledovaniia leitenanta Lavrentiia Zagoskina v Russkoi Amerike v 1842–1844 gg.,* ed. M. B. Chernenko et al. (Moscow: Gosudarstvennoe izdatel'stvo geograficheskoi literatury, 1956), available in English translation as *Lieutenant Zagoskin's Travels in Russian America, 1842–1844,* trans. Penelope Rainey, ed. Henry N. Michael, Anthropology of the North: Translations from Russian Sources, no. 7 (Toronto: University of Toronto Press for Arctic Institute of North America, 1967).
47. Arndt, "Dynamics of the Fur Trade."
48. On Finns in Russian America, see Black and Pierce, "Russian America and the Finns."
49. Eli Lundy Huggins, *Kodiak and Afognak Life, 1868–1870* (Kingston, Ontario: Limestone Press, 1981), 2.

FIGURE 63. View of Novo-Arkhangel'sk by Il'ia Voznesenskii, ca. 1843, showing the Church of St. Michael the Archangel before it was replaced by the cathedral built soon thereafter by Bishop Innokentii (Veniaminov, St. Innocent of Alaska and Siberia).

Courtesy Richard A. Pierce.

Chapter Twelve

The Rise of the Creole Class

WHAT DISTINGUISHED RUSSIAN COLONIZATION IN ALASKA FROM OTHER colonial empires on the American continent was that settlement, in the sense of settling people and communities on the land, was not a primary goal. The monopoly granted to the Russian-American Company, under "protection of His Majesty," specified that for twenty years the company had the sole right to trade in Alaska and extract resources (including mineral resources) from the land. The land itself was Russian territory, not the property of the company. Creation and development of a permanent Russian population in Alaska, in spite of Shelikhov's and Rezanov's empire-building dreams, was incidental to maintaining the Russian presence in the face of Native opposition and providing the necessary support for fur extraction, acquisition through trade with the Natives, and marketing activities. There never was a government-sponsored plan for establishing a permanent Russian population in Alaska; in fact, government regulations forbade Russian settlement for the sake of settlement.

The motivation for this prohibition has been debated, with opinions ranging from the government's desire to prevent the displacement of the Natives to the wish to ensure that the peasant serf population would not leave their landlords in Russia (the latter opinion, most forcefully expressed by the late historian Okun, remains the dominant interpretation, though direct evidence for such a conclusion is lacking). For a variety of reasons, the company, from its very inception, had difficulty in recruiting a sufficient number of men for long-term service, and the government interdicted settlement. However, by the time the company came into being there was a relatively large and constantly growing number of persons of mixed parentage, sometimes of the second or third generation, and so the management sought to create from this segment a reliable and loyal permanent labor pool, men and women whose loyalty would be to both Alaskan land and Russian culture and political order. By providing these people with special privileges and education, the Russian-American Company eventually created such a class. To this class were assigned persons who could claim descent from a Russian ancestor in the male line, though theoretically and in law descendants of females could also make such a claim. The marriage of Russian women to Alaska Native men was at times even encouraged, but was rare because throughout the Russian period the number of Russian women relative to the number of men was very small. But, by no means did all Native persons who could claim Russian ancestry belong to this class.[1]

In the early stages of Russian penetration, the era of the promyshlenniki, the men who went to Alaska expected to return to their homes after a hunting season, or two, or three. However, many of these men sailed on many voyages, so that their cumulative stay in Alaska often amounted to decades, while visits home were brief and infrequent (especially as the voyages lasted longer, sometimes eight to ten years).

The overwhelming majority of these men were Russian northerners or Siberian descendants of the Pomory. They were predominantly free peasants, or Siberian townsmen, with their own notions of social order, community, leadership, labor relations, religious community structure, and marriage.[2]

With the change in structure of the American fur procurement, the large merchant companies increasingly hired men from Siberian cities, with the Russian north by now a distant second (the northerners preferred to be participants on shares). Thus, the social composition of the Russian recruits shifted from free peasant to predominantly townsmen and burgher class; the peasants now constituted the second largest group, with a sprinkling of small merchants or merchants' sons and people of other low estates, such as teamsters or factory workers (probably state serfs) and people not assigned to any officially recognized stratum (*raznochintsy*).

Men were now hired either for a single voyage or for a specified number of years. In 1799, the Russian-American Company had been granted the right to recruit "persons of every estate, free and not under any suspicion," and the local administrators were directed to issue such recruits passports valid for seven years. If serfs were to be hired, permission had to be obtained from their masters. The company was obliged to pay all local and state taxes for their employees for the duration of their service.[3] In reality the company continued the practice of hiring predominantly burghers and free peasants, overwhelmingly Siberian residents, who signed on for a minimum of seven years.[4] Sometimes, men were left in remote outposts or Native communities for a very long time indeed. For example, Evstrat Proshev was left on Attu in 1794 by Shelikhov's vessel *Sv. Simeon i Anna* to look out for company business and was collected only in September of 1801, when a vessel of the Russian-American Company, the *Sv. Mikhail*, stopped there briefly.

The Siberians shared many customs and traditions with the northerners. Almost all these men, when hired, were young. As was the case in Siberia, the female question was a problem, and unions with Alaskan women were inevitable. In the beginning, offspring of such unions presumably were absorbed by the Native communities or, if the child was the result of kidnapping and rape and the mother abandoned it, it died.[5] On the other hand, relatively early in the process some men formed permanent unions and considered such unions valid marriages, acknowledged paternity, and brought their Alaskan wives and children to Kamchatka, Okhotsk, or their home towns. To judge by several documented cases, the formation of such unions was often accompanied by observance of Native customs and, therefore, these unions were no doubt considered legal marriages by the Native communities.[6] Customary marriage, by both Alaska Native and Russian tradition, and maintenance of kinship ties were effected by mutual gift exchanges, bride service, giving of bridewealth, mutual support, and hospitality. Such behaviors had the force of customary law; they were obligatory.[7] As far as Russians were concerned, especially the Russian northerners and Siberians, and particularly among the Cossacks,

> marriage remained in the eyes of the common people nothing more than a sort of civil contract, entered into in the presence of community as a sign of its recognition and sanc-

> tion.... The young couple, after previous arrangement, went to the popular assembly of the village ... and declared that they had made up their minds to become husband and wife.... "So be it" chanted the assembly. "We wish you luck and happiness."... The young couple ... thought their union legally established as soon as they were publicly joined to each other in the presence of the community, which was invited on the occasion to a sort of festival.[8]

The offspring of unions so established acquired, in Russian eyes, a right to the father's family name, social estate, and property. The blessing by the clergy was not necessary: "For many centuries the Russian clergy had to fight against the inveterate custom of our lower classes to contract unions without the sanction of the Church."[9] According to the authority cited above, the Russian legal scholar Maxim Kovalevskii, this attitude prevailed in the Russian north even in his own time, the last quarter of the nineteenth century. Early on, Archimandrite Ioasaf, in a letter to Shelikhov of 18 May 1795, had complained that the dissolute promyshlenniki did not wish to be legally married, or lived in sin with local women while they had wives in Russia. In light of the Russian customary marriage form, the archimandrite's complaints take on a rather different dimension. Some men probably thought the church ceremony superfluous, especially when one considers the absence, at that time, of priests in all areas of Alaska outside of Kodiak; some of those who had spouses in Russia may have considered themselves divorced by the centuries-old customary law. The church, on the other hand, by the end of the eighteenth century no longer recognized dissolution of marriages by agreement, though the village customary courts, also recognized by the state, continued to do so.[10] Baranov himself was apparently caught up in this bind and incurred the wrath of the archimandrite.[11] His consequent negative attitude toward the first mission may be explained not only by the cleric's opposition to his labor policies and exploitation of the Natives, but also by a purely personal motive.[12]

However, at the time Russians came to Alaska, the state fully supported the church in its drive to establish the church-sanctioned marriage as the only form of legal matrimony. In the nineteenth century, the state was, indeed, recognizing only this form as a fully legal one. Some of the labor discontent in the Baranov era can be traced to the fact that there were no clergy to serve the men's matrimonial and other needs. Members of the original spiritual mission were confined to Kodiak, and the parish priest sent to Sitka in 1816 remained at Novo-Arkhangel'sk. Men in the distant outposts, scattered over an enormous territory—where communication with the outside world took place, if they were lucky, once a year, but more often once in three, five, or in one case seven years—had no recourse to the clergy. In addition to having difficulty in legalizing their marriages as required by the state, the men felt acutely the absence of a priest to administer communion and perform full burial services. Men who had established families saw to it that their children were baptized by the rite of lay baptism, and were anxious that they be chrizmated, a rite akin to confirmation, performed usually together with baptism, but only by a priest. Sivtsov, a priest assigned to the Billings-Sarychev expedition, baptized, chrizmated, and performed marriages on Kodiak and Unalaska in 1790–1791,[13] and Hieromonk Gedeon, on his way home in 1807, recorded in one day at Unalaska twelve chrizmations of children, ranging in age from nine months to ten years, born to Russians in the settlement of Good Accord (modern Unalaska). In this number were included two elder sons of Egor Netsvetov, whose marriage to Maria Alekseeva of Atka was consecrated on the same day by Hieromonk Gedeon, along with four other Russian-American marriages and thirty-one marriages where both partners were listed as Aleuts. In 1821, Ivan Kriukov, manager at Unalaska, petitioned the commander of the circumnavigating expedition, Captain Mikhail N. Vasil'iev, to permit the expedition's chaplain to perform the necessary services for the local residents, both Russians and Aleuts. A number of marriages were then performed.

In the absence of clergy, men devised and recorded their own marriage contracts. Several such contracts, some witnessed by Baranov himself, have survived. When in July 1827 Khlebnikov visited the Commander Islands, which had been placed under Novo-Arkhangel'sk administration together with the central and western Aleutians, four Russian men presented him with the marriage contracts they had entered into and asked that he grant them official recognition. They stated they would undergo a church marriage ceremony should a priest come to the islands, or they would go to a locality where a priest was in residence. In fact, when, in 1828, a priest was finally assigned to the Atka District of the Russian-American Company (which stretched from the island of Seguam in the east to the Commander Islands in the west and to the northern Kuril Islands in the southwest), on his first visit to the Commanders, in 1830, he performed marriages for six Russians, one creole, and seven Aleut men, among whom were at least two who had petitioned Khlebnikov for recognition. The four men who said they had pledged their word of honor to the kinsmen of their Aleut wives all founded important Aleut families: Burdukovskii, Lestenkov, Paranchin, and Miakishev. The contracts the men drew up followed similar form:

> In the year 1823, the last day of June on Commander [Bering] Island, I, the Head of the lineage from Attu, Tikhon Dorofei Golodov have given this pledge to the townsman of Lal'sk, Vasilii Petr Burdukovskii. That in accordance with our agreement formally and freely concluded in the year 1822, I released to him the maiden brought up by me as my foster child, native of the island under my command [Attu], Melania, daughter of Petr, to enter into lawful marriage. As there is no priest in these islands, there was no one to perform the sacrament of marriage in accordance with the Rules of the Holy Fathers. And he, Burdukovskii, held the said maiden Melania as his future lawful wife and had with her children of both sexes. They constitute a family since that time. This family is to be considered his, Burdukovskii's, [legal] family, and in the confirmation thereof, in order to have this [document] considered lawful, I witness with my own hand. To this certificate, upon the order of my father Tikhon son of Dorofei Golodov, I, Manuil Golodov, appended my signature as a witness.[14]

It should be noted that Chief Golodov was fully literate in Russian, kept historical records for Attu and the Near Islands in general, and thus fully comprehended the significance of the marriage contract. The bridegroom Burdukovskii had come to Alaska in 1790, employed by Shelikhov's company, aboard the vessel *Ioann Predtecha* under Navigator Shirokii. He, along with Mikhail Lestenkov, later manager of the Russian-American outposts on Amchitka and Attu, was left on Bering Island in 1805 under foreman Shipitsyn. They survived in the Commander Islands without any contact with the outside world until 1812, when the *Finliandiia*, under Ivan F. Vasil'iev, came to look for any remains. The entire group volunteered to stay on. At that time, they entered into contact with Attuans who began regularly to visit Bering Island in small groups.[15]

Many of the men, however, took their Alaskan families with them when returning to Russia. Such was the case, in 1827, of the baidarshchik Ivan Serebrennikov, who sailed for Okhotsk with his wife (the daughter of a Russian resident on Atka, Vasilii Mershenin, who was married to an Aleut woman) and children. He had registered all his sons as burghers of the Siberian city of Yeniseisk[16] and paid taxes on their behalf. Thus, legally, through their father, all the Serebrennikov children were Russians. Serebrennikov, however, came back to Alaska and petitioned for a permit to become a permanent resident. After his death two of his sons petitioned to be reclassified as creole since they intended to remain in Alaska and did not want to pay taxes to a city they had never seen. They also did not wish to be drafted for military service.

Even more common was the practice of taking home to Russia children whose paternity the men acknowledged. Archimandrite Ioasaf roundly condemned this practice and argued that such children should be left in the colony and educated in Alaska in the Russian manner. The archimandrite was directly involved in the case of Demid Kulikalov, who had led parties to Yakutat, served in the Pribilofs, and for several years managed the Atka station, only to be publicly flogged at Unalaska and ordered deported by Rezanov. Apparently this last order was not carried out. Kulikalov may have been too valuable to lose, and Rezanov was gone from Unalaska in short order. Later, Baranov put Kulikalov in charge of an experiment in establishing an outpost on St. Matthew Island where the artel spent a winter, returning to Unalaska in 1810. Kulikalov had a young son at Kodiak, whom he wished to send to Russia. Archimandrite Ioasaf asked Shelikhov to return the child to Alaska forthwith, should Kulikalov succeed in taking his son to Okhotsk, as Kulikalov "has legitimate children in Irkutsk." Kulikalov lost this round: the boy was kept by the clergy. Ten years later Baranov succeeded in taking the boy away. He was one of the four young men of mixed Russian-American parentage whom Lisianskii took in 1805 to St. Petersburg for education at the company's expense. Baranov wrote to the boy's father that while on the *Neva* young Kulikalov would be taught English and navigation. The son eventually returned to Alaska, but it is doubtful that his father ever saw him again. Rezanov, while in Alaska in 1805–1806, forbade the men leaving the company's employ and returning to Russia to take along their women and children.[17] By this measure he sought to compel men to remain in Alaska permanently. Indeed, thirty-three men petitioned Rezanov for permission to remain in the colony in perpetuity, all of them family men, heads of households. The company also sought to have taxes due in their home towns rescinded for all who remained in the colonies, but this was not granted.[18]

There are several cases in which company officials separated Russian men from their American families as punishment for perceived transgressions against company interests. Several "Old Hands" who served under Baranov suffered this fate, the most blatant case being that of Semeon Salamatov, in 1827 manager of the company outpost on Attu. Young Etholen (later one of the ablest chief managers of the colony on secondment from the navy), then commanding the company vessel *Chichagov*, called at Attu and heard that Salamatov had sea otter furs in his private possession. Enforcing the company policy that no employee should possess or trade sea otter skins, he searched Salamatov's house during the baidarshchik's absence. When Khlebnikov arrived, another search was made. Among other items, the officials found four pelts and items made or trimmed with sea otter fur, such as a pillow and a woman's parka and two sea otter dancing belts, property of Salamatov's Aleut wife, all of which were confiscated. One wonders if the splendid eider duck parka trimmed with sea otter, now in the Etholen Collection in the National Museum of Finland, did not belong, once upon a time, to the unfortunate Mrs. Salamatov. Khlebnikov reported the case to the then chief manager, Lt. Chistiakov, who ordered Salamatov deported and suggested that the company prosecute him in the courts. The company refused to do so, writing to Chistiakov that separation from his beloved family was punishment enough. Salamatov never saw his wife or children again.[19]

Sometimes Russians who had spent a lifetime in Alaska desired to return to Russia in their old age and were unable to take their Native families. Such was the case of Fedor Burenin, in the early days proud owner of his own vessel and organizer of ventures, after 1799 a hired employee of the Russian-American Company (one surmises that he stayed on because of his family). He was manager on Unalaska 1806–1813, serving earlier as assistant manager, but he did not please Baranov and was replaced by Ivan Kriukov. In Alaska since 1785, Kriukov for many years served as foreman on the island of Unga in the Shumagin Islands. It is not known when he moved to the Fox Islands, but he had family ties in Chaluka or Recheshnoe on Umnak Island, now Nikolski (in Russian sources Nikol'skoe). In 1820, he requested permission to return to Russia and left in 1822, after being awarded a bonus of 2,000 rubles for his service. In Irkutsk he met the young priest Ioann Popov (later Veniaminov) and persuaded him to go to the Aleutians as the priest. It is believed that Kriukov, like Serebrennikov, returned to Alaska and ended his days in the bosom of his Aleut family at Nikol'skoe. His descendants still reside in this village.

How many persons of mixed parentage were absorbed by Native communities, not acknowledged by their fathers or not residing in a Russian settlement or outpost but with their mothers in Native settlements, is not known and cannot be known. Moreover, among the matrilineal Tlingit, children acquired their nationality, ethnic identity, moiety, and clan affiliation through their mother. Hence, an offspring of a Russian man and Tlingit woman was a full-fledged member of Tlingit society, and if the father claimed the child, Tlingit kin might object.

Often such individuals had a double nationality: in one context a creole, in another a Tlingit. Such was the case of Ivan Pavlov, manager of the Russian-American Company outpost at Nulato on the Yukon from 1865 to 1868. He married a local Athabaskan woman and left nine children. His descendants confounded an anthropologist by their insistence that their ancestor (with such an obviously Russian surname as Pavlov) was a Tlingit.

In Baranov's time men of mixed ancestry were joining the company and were used by Baranov in positions of authority at the middle level. It was also in Baranov's time that young men of mixed parentage began to be sent to Russia to obtain a higher and better education. They were sent to navigational schools, to schools of medicine, and were also trained in crafts and skilled trades, such as shipbuilding and mechanics. By 1821, when the second charter was granted to the company for another twenty years, the status of this group, by now known as creoles, became defined through regulations. In Alaska people designated creoles became members of an officially recognized social estate that existed only in Alaska (if a creole moved to Russia, he or she was assigned to the social estate of the father). The numbers of people who were recognized as members of this social estate did not represent the actual number of all peoples of mixed Russian-Alaska Native descent.

It is not known exactly when or by whom the term *creole* was introduced. The earliest usage is found in the church records of the Novo-Arkhangel'sk (Sitka) parish for 1816. It is used in company documents not earlier than 1817 and appears in published sources only in Golovnin's 1822 account of his voyage to Alaska in 1818. The term *creole* derives from the Spanish *criollo*. It was used by the Spanish first at the end of the sixteenth century to designate persons of European descent born in the West Indies. Its basic meaning remains the same today, referring in general to a "descendant of persons not native to the New World." This encompasses not only descendants of Europeans but also descendants of Africans. The Russian usage adheres to descendent of persons not native to the New World and was never applied to Russian citizens outside of Alaska, no matter what their biological parentage, no matter where born. The term was introduced sometime before 1816–1821 for use exclusively in Alaska.

Paragraph 41 of the Second Charter, authorized by Emperor Alexander I on 13 September 1821, states:

> Creoles, who according to the latest information numbered 180 souls of male and 120 of female gender, and all those who should be born in the future are to be registered in the Main Colony; from now on they shall constitute a separate estate under enjoyment of the following rules:
>
> a. Creoles are Russian subjects. As such, they have a right to governmental protection on the same basis as all subjects belonging to the burgher estate, provided that they have not acquired through personal achievement or other exceptional circumstances membership in another [higher] estate.
>
> b. Creoles, while in the Colonies, will not be subject to state taxation or state service of any kind unless new regulations will be issued in this matter.
>
> c. To safeguard their rights, the Company will confirm this to the Chief Manager of the Colonies, in his capacity as an official of the State, that he is to keep vigilant eye in this matter over all local managers in safeguarding their [creoles'] rights and property.
>
> d. Creoles who entered Company service and distinguished themselves by their zeal and natural endowments will enjoy, at their superiors' discretion, all privileges granted other Russian subjects of burgher estate who are in Company service.
>
> e. Creoles educated in Russia at the institutions of higher learning at Company expense and who, upon graduation, have achieved the status of students or physicians with all the rights and privileges granted by universities and academies, may not refuse a sojourn of not less than ten years' duration, to serve the inhabitants of that region for an appropriate salary and subsistence allowance provided by the Company. After the completion of such term, they have the right to leave the colonies, if they so wish, and practice their profession elsewhere.

This regulation, which had the force of a statute, deserves comment on two points. With respect to point "a" it must be noted once again that in Russia a person belonged to the estate of his or her father. However, under certain conditions, such as achievement of officer's rank in military service, state service officialdom, or in the clergy, or for other personal achievements, especially when rewarded with an official medal or order so that a person became a "Cavalier," the person's status was changed to gentry, either personal or hereditary. A person who became a priest or a deacon was assigned to the clerical estate (a separate social estate). The status was also extended to the cleric's family.

With respect to point "e" it should be stressed that the obligation of ten years' service applied, at that time, only to those who graduated from institutions of higher learning, specifically to those who received medical degrees.

The creole status was further defined in the company's Third Charter, granted 5 March 1841, approved by Emperor Nicholas I on 10 October 1844. In appended regulations the status of company employees in Alaska was discussed in detail, including the creole status. Paragraphs 8(1), 8(4), and 8(5) stated that all those serving in the colonies under the auspices of the Russian-American Company were considered on active state (military or government) duty, provided they were members of the estates that were subject to such service. Company employees who belonged to the estates not entitled to state service enjoyed privileges of the estates to which they belonged. If they left company service after serving in the colonies less than ten years, they remained in their original estate upon return to metropolitan Russia. If they honorably completed ten years of service, they received the rank of personal "notable citizenship" (*pochetnye grazhdane*) and, in exceptional circumstances, such status could become hereditary. Paragraph 12 stated that the employees leaving company service who desired to settle in Alaska could not be compelled to leave. This regulation, no doubt, was linked to company policy instituting retirement, old age, disability, and survivors' pensions.

In this third charter, the government recognized five social categories under colonial administration: contract employees, colonial citizens (voluntary settlers), creoles, settled foreigners (Natives, *inorodtsy*), and foreigners of religious faiths other than Orthodox not fully dependent on the company (*inovertsy*). The rights of colonial citizens, a category appearing now for the first time, were defined in sections 2 and 8, the rights of the other categories in section 8. Paragraph 227 defined colonial citizens as "persons of Russian citizenship and other free persons, who have a right to leave America but out of their own free will wish to remain there." This regulation applied mainly to Russians, Finns (who by now served the company in significant numbers), and Siberian natives, but did not exclude the creoles. Paragraph 245 specifically stated that "creoles who leave Company service and choose their own way of life are to be registered as colonial citizens, whose rights are outlined in Section II." It should be noted that by a specific regulation in that section, Russians and Siberians married to American women *and their children* were eligible to become colonial citizens.

Creole status was hereditary, predominantly in the male line. The extension of creole status to subsequent generations was spelled out in Paragraph 236 of the Second Charter: "Those born of a European or Siberian and an American woman, or of a European or Siberian woman and an American, *as well as their children*, will be assigned to the creole estate" (emphasis added).

The rights of creoles as burghers were emphasized in the Third Charter (par. 237), as was freedom from taxation and obligatory (state or military) service (par. 238). The obligations of those who received education at company expense were redefined. Those who were educated in Russia were to serve ten years, but now this regulation applied not only to those in medical professions but also to those who received military or naval and technical (including skilled trades) education. Those who received education in Alaska, which by the time of the Third Charter had a well-established secondary and specialized technical educational system,[20] had to serve for fifteen years, commencing at graduation, that is, at age seventeen (par. 243). In 1863, reduction of terms of service to six years was recommended across the board.

Upon expiration of the obligatory service term, creoles had a right to leave the colony for Russia, where they were counted as members of the burgher estate or in a higher estate they had achieved through personal accomplishments. The company was obligated to provide all those who chose to go to Russia with travel expenses and transportation to their destination (par. 244). Several paragraphs deal with the creoles' right to education. Paragraph 246 specifically states that children born out of wedlock who might be characterized as creoles had to be educated at company expense.

Under the Russian regime neither the term *creole* nor the term *colonial citizen* was a racial category. Both designated social status (estates within the ranked system of the Russian empire). A colonial citizen could be of mixed European-Siberian or European-Siberian-Alaskan ancestry. In keeping with the general Russian custom of social status being inherited agnatically, the creole status became acknowledged usually in the paternal line, the regulations indicating bilateral inheritance of the status to the contrary. The children of a creole woman who married a Native American were almost without exception considered members of their Native father's group: Aleut, Athabaskan, Chugach, Alutiiq, etc. Children of a male creole marrying a Native woman, however, retained their father's creole status. This was specifically noted as an incongruity by company management in 1863. Achievement and position in the company administrative hierarchy also counted. There were several cases in which Alaska Natives occupying important management positions, such as manager of the Pribilof Islands sealing operations Kasian Shaiashnikov, or the manager of Atka District Grigorii Terent'ev,[21] were listed as creoles.

The estate creole existed only in Alaska. Persons assigned to this estate in Alaska, if they chose to settle in Russia, assumed other legally recognized statuses: burgher, cleric, gentry, etc. Even in Alaska some creoles achieved the status of gentry. Such was the case of Grigorii Terent'ev, mentioned above. Several Kashevarov brothers, born to former serf Filip Kashevarov and his Alutiiq (creole) wife, became naval officers and, by virtue of their rank, members of the gentry; others became clergymen, and one was offered a high administrative post of a diplomatic nature in Russian government. The eldest brother, Aleksandr Kashevarov, explored the arctic shores of Alaska, participated in eighteen naval expeditions and campaigns, and during the Crimean War commanded the port of Aian on the Okhotsk Sea; he became the head of the cartographic department of the Imperial Navy, received many commendations and several honorary orders, authored an atlas of the Pacific Ocean, and retired with the rank of general, equivalent to flag rank.

By the end of the Russian period, the number of persons in company service belonging to the creole status was considerable: in 1863, their numbers approached 2,000. Their role in managing the colony was of prime importance. Creoles were managers of remote outposts and of districts. They were teachers, clergy, navigators, cartographers, ship commanders, and artists.

An ordinary creole who did not exercise his right to obtain an education at company expense, or who was educated at family expense, could choose either to earn his own living in Alaska (in a Native community or, after 1844, as a colonial citizen) or enter company service under contract on the same basis as employees of other origins and estates.

In the context of the nineteenth century, creoles in Alaska constituted a privileged class, a fact noted by the company's management in 1862 and 1863. They enjoyed exemption from taxation and obligatory state services, including military service, had a right to education at company expense, and opportunity for social mobility and freedom of choice not open to Russians of lower ranks.

Because of the privileges they enjoyed and because of the positions of responsibility and leadership many occupied in the colony, they were, as a class, resented by the Russians of the lower estates who were denied educational opportunities and were far less socially mobile. On the other hand, some creoles showed just pride in their status and achievements. This sometimes provoked resentment directed at "upstarts" on the part of higher ranking visitors to the colony, who charged them with arrogance and often ridiculed what were perceived as pretensions.

Government officials tended to view the creole status as an anomaly. Kostlivtsev, who inspected the colony on behalf of the government in 1863, when the sale of Alaska was already being contemplated, noted the social mobility of the people called creoles. He remarked on inconsistencies in the rules for ascription both to the creole and colonial citizen's estates, and that there was continuous movement between the two estates as well as to other estates recognized in metropolitan Russia.

Kostlivtsev also noted that, as a class, creoles were a privileged estate, and he felt that their privileges were not justified. He pointed out that individuals of creole status occupied positions of honor and respectability in Alaska, while others belonging to the same estate were hired on the same basis as Alaska Natives and were indistinguishable from them. Kostlivtsev officially suggested that the majority should be encouraged to live the life style of Native Alaskans, to maintain Native skills and crafts. He proposed that the creole estate be abolished and the individuals hitherto designated creoles either join the Native communities or, as would be their right through their fathers, assume membership in the estates of metropolitan Russia. Children born out of wedlock, Kostlivtsev suggested, would be ascribed to the estate of their mother. Indeed, there were cases in which creoles participated in traditional Native occupations. On Kodiak, in the creole settlement of Little Afognak, members of at least three families became whalers. They hunted by traditional Native methods, with Native weapons, participated in rituals, and were considered sorcerers (shamans) as recently as the beginning of the twentieth century.

After the sale of Alaska, the creoles became disenfranchised. Perhaps, of all peoples of all sorts and conditions the Americans found in Alaska in 1867, none suffered such degradation as the creoles. Labeled "half-breeds" by anglophone writers, beginning with William H. Dall's influential *Alaska and Its Resources*, first published in 1870, they were so considered by the military and civilian administrators. They were also presumed to be, as was the tenor of the times in regard to "mixed races," totally depraved. Dall wrote: "In their present condition the Creoles are unfit to exercise franchise, as American citizens."[22]

Though a few educated creoles were employed by the Alaska Commercial Company and its competitors in the fur trade, many chose either to emigrate to Russia or moved to the United States where they passed as Russians, while in Alaska some educated Natives wishing to obtain employment at low-level managerial levels passed as creoles.[23] In the course of time, the majority became reabsorbed by Native communities. They would regain their civil rights, if not the privileges they enjoyed under the Russian regime, only in the last decades of the twentieth century, specifically with the passage of the Alaska Native Claims Settlement Act in 1971.

There was, however, one arena wherein the creoles (and Natives) retained or assumed preeminence, decision-making powers, and leadership: the Russian Orthodox Church. The story of this institution in Alaska is examined in the following chapter.

NOTES

1. Material in this chapter is based, in part, on previously published material, Black, "Creoles in Russian America." See also B. D. Lain, "The Decline of Russian America's Colonial Society," *Western Historical Quarterly* 7, no. 2 (1976): 143–153.
2. For analyses of the social composition of the Russian crews and settlers in Alaska, see O. M. Medushevskaia, "Russkie geograficheskie otkrytiia na Tikhom okeane i v Severnoi Amerike (50-e—nachalo 80-kh godov XVIII v.)" (Ph.D. diss., Moscow State University, 1952), app.; and Fedorova, *Russkoe naselenie,* 153–163.
3. *Polnoe sobranie zakonov Rossiiskoi imperii,* Sobr. 1, vol. 25 (1830), 703–704, doc. 19030, cited after Fedorova, *Russkoe naselenie,* 157–158.
4. As Fedorova has shown, in the period from 1799 to 1829, out of 143 employees for whom data on social and geographic origin are available, only three were "household serfs" and these came from Siberia. In addition, seven employees were Siberian Natives, four were teamsters, four were factory workers, and seven had no assigned status. Only twenty-one came from central and southern Russia (Fedorova, *Russkoe naselenie,* 158–159).
5. I have located in the Archive of Russia's Foreign Policy in Moscow (AVPRI), Fond Rossiisko-amerikanskoi kompanii, "Portfeli Millera," testimony taken from members of the crew of the *Sv. Evdokim,* in the Near Islands 1745–1746. The crew was being investigated on charges of wanton violence and atrocities committed on Attu during their winter there. Aleksei Beliaev, alleged instigator of the mayhem, is said to have abducted a young girl who bore a child. Later on, the girl escaped, leaving the infant behind in Beliaev's camp. The fate of this infant can only be conjectured.
6. On this point, see Michael J. Oleksa, "The Creoles and Their Contributions to the Development of Alaska," in *Russian America: The Forgotten Frontier,* ed. Barbara S. Smith and Redmond J. Barnett (Tacoma: Washington State Historical Society, 1990), 185–195.
7. Maxime Kovalevsky, *Modern Customs and Ancient Laws of Russia, Being the Ilchester Lectures for 1889–1890* (Oxford, 1891; reprint, New York: Burt Franklin, 1970). See specifically Lecture 2, "The State of the Modern Russian Family, and Particularly That of the Joint or Household Community of Great Russia," pp. 32–68.
8. Ibid., 37–38.
9. Ibid., 37.
10. Ibid., 42–44.
11. Fedorova, *Russkoe naselenie,* 187–188, cites several other cases.
12. Archimandrite Ioasaf to Shelikhov, 18 May 1795, Yudin Collection, Box 1, Folder 1, Manuscript Division, Library of Congress.
13. Sivtsov's records are in the Russian State Naval Archive, St. Petersburg, Fond 214, op. 1, delo 28, fols. 79–85.
14. Khlebnikov, "Travel Notes."
15. Khlebnikov, "Travel Notes." For the situation of these Robinson Crusoes of the North Pacific in 1812, see accounts by Ivan F. Vasil'iev, "Vypiska iz zhurnala puteshestviia shturmana Ivana Vasil'ieva k ostrovam Aleutskim v 1811 i 1812 godakh. [Soobshchil] direktor Irkutskago uchilishcha Ivan Miller," *Kazanskie izvestiia,* 1814, no. 11, and idem, "Vypiska iz zhurnala puteshestviia shturmana

Ivana Vasil'ieva k ostrovam Aleutskim v 1811 i 1812 godakh. [Soobshchil] direktor Irkutskago uchilishcha Ivan Miller," *Dukh zhurnalov* 14, no. 41: 675–684; 15, no. 42: 721–732; 15, no. 43: 757–766. Excerpts from Vasil'iev's notes were also published in *Novosti literatury* (1823–1824); these were translated by Lydia T. Black and published, with an introduction and annotations, as Appendix 2 in *Atkha: An Ethnohistory of the Western Aleutians* (Kingston, Ontario: Limestone Press, 1984), 151–170.

16. Pierce, *Biographical Dictionary*, 448, reports in error that the Serebrennikovs were registered as burghers of Tiumen'. The records of the Russian-American Company in the National Archives, Washington, D.C., clearly state that they were burghers of Yeniseisk (RAC, Communications Sent, vol. 13, No. 155, 4 May 1836, fol. 84v; ibid., vol. 16, No. 576, 30 November 1838, fol. 312; and elsewhere).

17. Rezanov to the Board of Directors, 6 November 1805, in Tikhmenev, *A History*, vol. 2, 160 (doc. 42).

18. Fedorova, *Russkoe naselenie,* 143.

19. Ekaterina Salamatov took her children home to Atka, where her sons were educated by Iakov Netsvetov, through his mother himself an Atkan and the first priest of Aleut origin to serve the Orthodox Church in Alaska (Iakov Netsvetov was recognized as a saint of the Russian Orthodox Church in 1994). Salamatov's eldest son, Lavrentii, became a priest, serving his native Atka until his death in 1864. A scholar of the Aleut language, he made an unsurpassed contribution to Aleut linguistics. David and Vasilii became seafarers, David a well-known navigator, Vasilii a cartographer. Both contributed to the famous atlas of Alaska's coasts compiled by former Chief Manager Mikhail D. Teben'kov and published in 1852. One of Semeon Salamatov's grandsons, Moisei (son of Lavrentii), also became a priest and served Alaska all his life. Moisei's daughter, Matrena, became a schoolteacher during the American period; some of this master basket weaver's craft is preserved in the Phoebe A. Hearst Museum of Anthropology, University of California, Berkeley.

20. For a good synopsis, see Richard L. Dauenhauer, "Education in Russian America," in *Russian America: The Forgotten Frontier*, ed. Barbara S. Smith and Redmond J. Barnett (Tacoma: Washington State Historical Society, 1990), 155–163.

21. Terent'ev was an Alutiiq, a native of Kodiak. He ended his career, in retirement from company service, as a member of the Russian gentry. In 1872, at an advanced age, he led a group of Central and Western Aleuts to resettle in the Commander Islands, which after 1867 remained within Russian jurisdiction.

22. William H. Dall, *Alaska and Its Resources* (Boston: Lee and Shepard, 1870; facsimile reprint, New York: Arno Press and New York Times, 1970), 241.

23. Henry W. Elliott married an educated Aleut-Creole lady, A. Milovidov, of the Pribilofs. When he took her home the local paper reported her arrival as that of a "Russian bride." The wedding was in the Orthodox church at Unalaska and performed by Father Innokentii Shaiashnikov, an Aleut (whose daughters had also married Americans). Dall, then at Unalaska, expressed his disgust in his diary. He refused to attend the wedding. On the tribulations suffered by the creoles in the American period, see the judicial opinion of Judge James Wickersham (In re Naturalization of John Minook, 16 May 1904) and other materials discussed in David Hunter Miller, *The Alaska Treaty* (Kingston, Ontario: Limestone Press, 1981), 208–214.

убогїй Германъ

FIGURE 64. **St. Herman of Alaska (German, humble monk of Valaam).**

Courtesy University of Alaska Fairbanks, Rasmuson Library, Alaska and Polar Regions Department, Rare Book Collection, no. A0024.

Chapter Thirteen

The Light of the Spirit

The Orthodox Church in Alaska

As the Russians advanced, they brought with them to Alaska their greatest spiritual treasure: the Orthodox faith. Today, the Russian Orthodox Church is a major Christian denomination not only in Alaska, but throughout the United States and Canada. The Orthodox Church of Alaska is considered the foundation of Orthodoxy on the American continents, north and south. With the exception of the Iñupiat of the Arctic coast and the Athabaskans of the middle and upper Yukon River basin, the majority of Alaska Natives—Aleuts, Alutiit, Yupiit, Tlingits, and some Athabaskans—profess, or until recently professed, Orthodoxy. The conversion to Christianity was peaceful, gradual, and effected in the early contact stages by laymen. In this chapter we shall trace the conversion to and development of the Orthodox Church in Alaska since the eighteenth century, beginning with the first conversions on record.[1]

Sometime between the end of September 1760 and July 1761, while the vessel *Sv. Ioann Ustiuzhskii* was wintering on Attu Island, the Aleut Makuzhan, a chief of the Attuans, brought his young son to the Russian camp. The young man had been grievously injured; his arm was laid open so that the bones could be seen, he was unable to get up from his bed, and the Aleut healers had given him up. Makuzhan asked that the boy be baptized, hoping that in this way he would be healed. The Russians responded that God was great and merciful and soon granted mercy to those who called on him in faith. Makuzhan replied that if the God of the Russians was good, his son would be well again. A lay baptism was held, and the young man received the Christian name Leontii. He got well, and traveled to Okhotsk with the Vologda merchant Fedor Kul'kov aboard the *Sv. Zakharii i Elizaveta*. Later the young man returned home aboard yet another vessel.[2] He was one of the first Aleuts to become an Orthodox Christian who helped spread the faith.

The early promyshlenniki and the Aleuts shared much in matters of faith. Cherepanov, who left us the account of the baptism and healing of Leontii, son of Makuzhan, wrote:

> They live and act in everything simply. Just like we Russians, when we set out on any enterprise, call on the name of the Lord God to aid us and bless [the enterprise] or when at sea in the baidaras on the way to our hunting, all keep silent for a while and then, having

> called on God for aid in hope of His mercy we say "God aid us," likewise these foreign peoples, leaving for the hunt, say the prayer "Lord bless." And when setting out in the baidaras, like ourselves, all keep silent and then say, like we do, "God help us." They are very understanding of the Orthodox Christian faith and do not believe that we are possessed of falsehood because of the singular occurrence with the foreigner Leontii.[3]

For their part, Russians did not discount the power of the shamans. They believed that the shamans could harm them, when invoked by the Aleuts, or help when asked, heal, or change the weather. They believed that the healing power ultimately derived from God and, when ill, sought the shaman's help in the same way that Makuzhan sought baptism for his wounded son.

Leontii's baptism was by no means the first one. Russians considered the act of baptism a great gift they could offer. Young hostages who stayed in their camps for prolonged periods and learned to speak Russian, and especially those whom Russians adopted or brought with them to Siberia for a temporary sojourn, were often baptized. Sometimes baptisms were performed in Okhotsk and Kamchatka. The sponsor, in such a case, bore the expense of the rite performed by a priest. Frequently, the godfathers sent those young Aleuts to school at their expense.

The bestowal of a new, baptismal name probably helped to attract people who wished to undergo baptism. There is ethnographic evidence that Aleuts believed that names had power and each person acquired, in addition to the name given at birth, other names in the course of the life cycle. Sometimes the name signified a newly acquired status, sometimes it commemorated a deed, and sometimes it signified a desired state of being or character. From the earliest baptisms a pattern emerged in the bestowal of Christian names, the same that was followed in Siberia. The newly baptized person was given the name of a saint (usually the name of a saint whose feast fell on or near the date of the baptism), and in addition acquired the patronymic derived from the baptismal name of his or her sponsor and the use of the sponsor's family name. Thus, a young boy from Attu taken to Kamchatka in 1747 aboard the *Sv. Evdokim* became Pavel Mikhailovich Nevodchikov, in honor of his baptismal sponsor, Navigator Mikhail Nevodchikov. It is this naming practice that explains the adoption of Russian names by Aleuts; it became widespread in the Aleutian archipelago in the early decades of the nineteenth century, and in the Kodiak archipelago, Alaska Peninsula, and Prince William Sound by the middle of the same century.

The bond of godparenthood was taken seriously by both the Russians and the Aleuts. To this day, this bond is considered next in importance to the parent-child relationship among Orthodox Alaskans. The best documented case from the middle eighteenth century is that of Ivan Stepanovich Glotov of Umnak Island. As a young boy, a nephew of the local leader, he was baptized by Stepan Glotov, skipper of the vessel *Sv. Iulian*, in 1759. He was taken by Glotov to Kamchatka, and then returned to Alaska, also with Glotov. He traveled in 1762 with his godfather to Kodiak and served as interpreter. In 1763, Ivan Glotov returned to Umnak. At some time he became literate in Russian. Long after Stepan Glotov's death in 1769 on Unimak Island, his godson remained true to his godfather's faith. In 1807, Ivan Glotov, now in his sixties and chief of the modern village of Nikol'skoe, traveled by kayak from Umnak to Unalaska when he heard that a priest was stopping there. He went to confession and received chrizmation at the hands of Hieromonk Gedeon, who was then on his way back to Russia from Kodiak. From

Gedeon we know that Chief Ivan Glotov built a chapel dedicated to St. Nicholas in his settlement of Chalukax̂ and that he himself conducted prayer or reader services (which laymen are entitled to conduct) on Sundays and all the feast days of the church. By that time a majority of the Aleuts professed themselves Christians. They became so without benefit of the presence of the clergy. By 1807, Hieromonk Gedeon could observe: "The inhabitants of the Unalashka Island, as well as of the entire Aleutian Chain, are strongly devoted to the faith. They know and reverently observe all major Feasts, lovingly and very willingly listen to the teachings offered, and follow these in real life."[4]

The Orthodox faith was carried to the Aleuts, and later to other Alaska Natives, not by missionaries dispatched for the task of conversion of the heathens but by ordinary people, first Russians and in later years Natives who considered themselves Orthodox Christians. These Orthodox, or Old Believer Russians, believed and manifested their faith by the use of symbols expressive of that faith in everyday life, through the observance of rituals and special laymen services held on feast days of the church. Each man carried with him a metal traveling icon which would accompany him to his grave, should he die: several such icons, characteristic of northern Russian craftsmanship, dating from the seventeenth and eighteenth centuries, have been found in the Aleutians in association with skeletal remains. If not each man, then each working group or artel carried special peg calendars, on which were marked the ecclesiastical year, major feast days, Sundays, and the feast days of the saints particularly revered by the group or the man who made the calendar.[5]

Their vessels were named for the saints they venerated in the Russian North. On the manifests of their vessels they always listed first the icons and the holy books they carried, and always they had with them the icon of the saint for whom the vessel had been named:

> One icon of the 12 major feasts, with Christ's Holy Resurrection and all the Saints, one icon of the All Holy Theotokos, Joy of All Who Sorrow, with a silver halo; one triptych of the Life Creating Trinity, Blessed Saint Nicholas and the Theotokos, in silver cover,

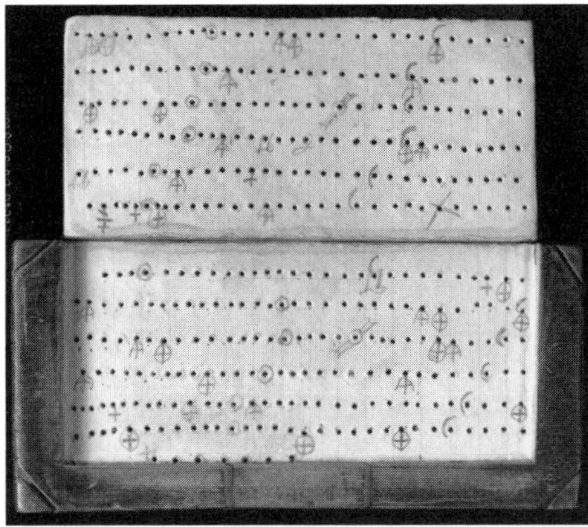

Figure 65. Russian Orthodox peg calendar. Date and collection place unknown; received at University of Alaska Museum 1947.

Courtesy University of Alaska Museum, Fairbanks, no. UA339.

Figure 66. Russian Orthodox peg calendar collected by Otto Geist in Perryville, Alaska Peninsula, in 1933.

Courtesy University of Alaska Museum, Fairbanks, no. UA1/1933-9416.

Traveling icon, front (left), back (right), damaged.

Body cross, side a

Body cross, side b

Figure 67. Metal traveling icon and body cross found by accident during World War II by a U.S. soldier working outside the village of Chernofski, Unalaska Island.

Courtesy Harold Jorgensen, Big Fork, Montana.

> one votive light of green copper, Book of the New Testament, Psalter (colored Triodion), Lives of the Saints, [an icon] of the martyr Holy Hierodeacon Evpl.[6]

Each vessel carried a banner with the image of an angel protector, and even the masts of their skin boats ended at the top in the Orthodox cross.[7] Also on the masts they put up a "mast icon," a metal frame encasing a series of holy paintings (one of which was always St. Nicholas, patron of sailors); a shaped piece of colored cloth was affixed to the end of the frame, forming a pennant. From each catch they made donations to the Church of St. Nicholas at Nizhne-Kamchatsk and to the monasteries revered in the north as holy places, such as the Solovetskii monastery in the White Sea (a center and rallying point for Old Believers). When books were lacking, some men who were literate wrote out the life of a saint they particularly revered, as they remembered. Thus, when Ivan Solov'iev arrived at Unalaska in 1764, he found an abandoned, collapsed dwelling constructed by the Russians who were overwhelmed by attacking Aleuts. The house had been ransacked, but a broken musket stock and the *Life of Saint Nicholas* written out in longhand remained.[8] Many years later, in the American period, when the use of the Aleut language was discouraged in the schools and attempts were made to wean the Aleuts away from Orthodoxy, Aleut Ugorel'nikov, on the island of St. George, would write from memory the *Life of Saint George the Victorious,* using the Aleut script introduced by Orthodox churchmen.[9]

The overwhelming majority of the early promyshlenniki were, as stated often above, from the Russian North.[10] In religious matters, the people of this area were accustomed to great independence. Traditionally, their religious communities were self-governed. Local festivals of pre-Christian origin merged with Christian observances, as was the case with the *radunitsa*, commemoration of the dead. Incorporation of shamanistic practices of the local aboriginal populations into the Russian practices was frequent, the recourse to shamans as healers even more so. In communities where the aboriginal population predominated, such as the Komi settlements, a descendant of shamans sometimes chose to become a priest.[11] More often than not, the daily religious life was conducted by laymen.[12] When a member of the community desired to become a priest, he obtained a supportive charter from the people, traveled to the bishop's see and was consecrated by the bishop. In the seventeenth century, following the schism over church reform, which was introduced during the reign of Tsar Alexis by Patriarch Nikon, many communities refused to accept it and followed what is now called the Old Belief. In these communities the conduct of religious life without benefit of clergy became the rule.

FIGURE 68. Central part of a bronze triptych personal icon. Metal icons such as this were placed in the graves of those who died.

Photograph by Sue Thorson, courtesy Sheldon Jackson Museum, Sitka, no. V.A.9.

The northern tradition of daily religious observances by the community of laymen was carried to Alaska by the earliest Russian fur procurement crews.[13] The settlements they founded were named for and put under the protection of the saints. Not only were prayers said and blessings invoked at the commencement of the day or the task, but religious services were held regularly. A memorable event was always accompanied by a religious service, often

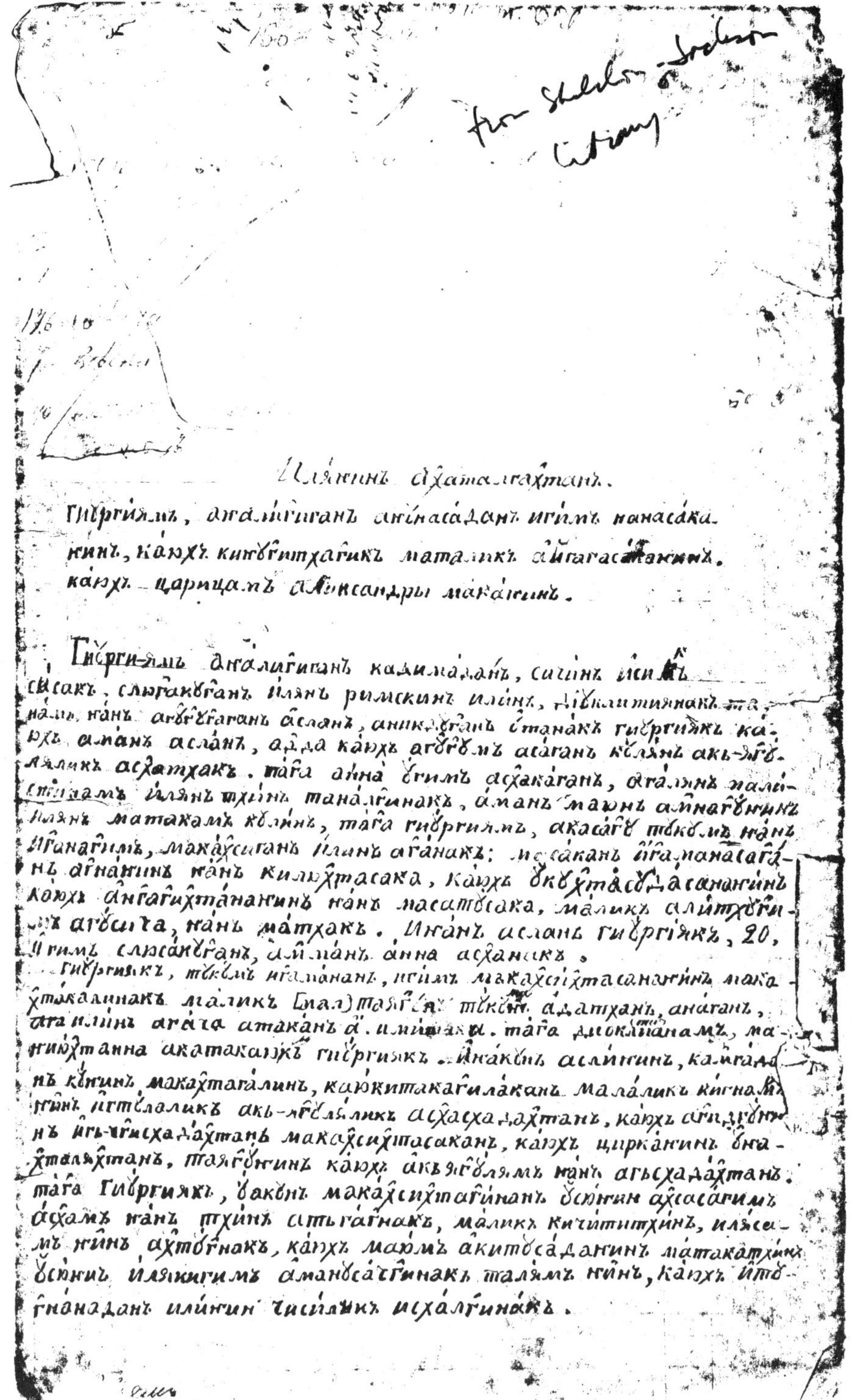

FIGURE 69. Front page of *Life of Saint George the Victorious,* written from memory by the Aleut Ugorel'nikov in Aleut script, 1868.

Courtesy Sheldon Jackson College Library.

improvised, as was the case in 1799 when Baranov devised an order of ceremonies for taking possession of Old Sitka. All services were (and are) sung or chanted. Candles and votive lights are always lit. One can only imagine the effect of the rendering of ancient church hymns and chants by a chorus of male voices in small candlelit rooms with icons placed in the eastern corner and a votive light burning before them. Some modern scholars maintain that just as the body cross was accepted by the Natives as a protective talisman, and the priest assumed aspects of the shaman's role, the icon became a functional equivalent of the mask that provided a window into the worlds of the spirits and of the Spirit.[14] Edward W. Nelson, a late-nineteenth-century American observer, noted explicitly that the Yukon Yup'ik Eskimos identified the Orthodox liturgy with their own masked festivals.[15] Overtly and everywhere, indigenous masked festivals coalesced with masking on the occasion of the Orthodox New Year.

Aleuts, hostages, friends, godchildren, or visitors were included in the services. John Ledyard, an American who sailed on Cook's voyage to the North Pacific in 1778, witnessed such a service at Unalaska:

> After I had lain down the Russians assembled the Indians in a very silent manner, and said prayers after the manner of the Greek Church, which is much like the Roman. I could not but observe with what particular satisfaction the Indians performed their devoirs to God through the medium of their little crucifixes, and with what pleasure they went through the multitude of ceremonies attendant on that sort of worship.[16]

The body cross, worn against bare skin, is considered by the Orthodox to act as protection against evil and misfortune. No doubt this use was congenial to the Aleuts, who had a number of protective talismans. On Kodiak, in 1788, the Spanish navigator de Haro made similar observations. Also, in 1788, at Unalaska, the Russians were delighted when Stepan Mondofía, of Dubrovnik, a pilot aboard the Spanish vessel commanded by Martínez, participated in their prayers, joining the chanting of the Lord's Prayer in Slavonic. Many years later, Ioann Veniaminov (St. Innocent of Alaska), who came to Alaska in 1824 and is revered as the greatest priest to serve the country, would write that the Christian faith was carried to Alaska by ordinary Russians and religious life was maintained in the course of everyday activities. When the clergy came, they found a Christian community already in full bloom, a living church. This was the case when the first priest to come to Alaska, Vasilii Sivtsov, the chaplain with the Billings-Sarychev expedition, visited Three Saints Bay settlement on Kodiak in 1790 and spent the winter of 1790–1791 at Unalaska. He is known to have, in both settlements, chrizmated, baptized, and married people who had asked that these sacraments be performed. In June 1790, he baptized sixty-three men and twenty-nine women from Unalaska and the Krenitzin Islands; in July, while on Kodiak, Sivtsov chrizmated one Alutiiq male, four females, and four children, all baptized earlier by laymen,[17] and baptized twenty-five Native males, among them one Tlingit. The total number of those baptized, by Sivtsov's calculation, was "93 males and 33 females, a total of 126 persons." Sixteen couples were married, fourteen on Unalaska (the majority of them Aleut couples) and two on Kodiak (Russians to Aleut women).[18] However, he did not engage in any missionary activity: it was not his task. At Unalaska, according to Sarychev, he never ventured far from the vessel or the expedition's winter camp.

The Christian faith was adopted by the Aleuts, and later by the Alutiit, the Chugach, the Athabaskans, the Yupiit, and the Tlingit, not through missionary preaching or through incitement by gifts and social advancement. The church, when the clergy came, addressed them in their own languages and did not demand that they abandon their own cultural ways and traditions. Becoming Orthodox did not mean changing one's lifestyle. In the early years even polygyny was tolerated if the marriages were contracted before baptism, and shamans who were healers were not rejected, but even welcomed.[19] In modern jargon, Orthodoxy was not as culturally destructive as some other denominations which demanded that a conversion be accompanied by the use of the dominant language, abandonment of all Native customs, and a change to Western lifestyle.[20] Moreover, some central symbols of the Native populations, especially of the Esk-Aleuts, coincided with those of Orthodoxy. The Aleuts, like the Orthodox, prayed to the east. The symbolism of light was central and associated with good. A bird represented the spirit, the Creator. In both religious systems water was a medium of healing, transformation, and purification. Fasting and abstinence were practiced by participants in both religions. Confession was a requirement for the Orthodox. Among some Native groups, specifically the Yup'ik and Alutiiq speakers, public confession was also practiced as a mode of individual and group purification.[21]

The common ground in religious faith was strengthened by ties of marriage, parenthood, friendships, and personal devotion to the faith by an overwhelming majority of the Russians: they were sinners, to be sure, but unbelievers they were not. For example, Grigorii Shelikhov, when leaving Alaska in 1786, instructed his manager, Samoilov, to take care of his godson Nikolai, physically and spiritually: "Above all teach him about God's Law." He also claimed that he actively explained the principles of the Greek-Catholic (Orthodox) Church to many Kodiak Islanders.[22] When clergy came, they came to serve both the Russian and Native communities. Thus, the establishment and institutional presence of the church did not coincide with the introduction and spread of Orthodox Christianity.

The introduction of the Orthodox Church as an institution derived both from an appreciation of the spiritual needs of the Russian settlers and the more pragmatic aims of the empire builders. Once Shelikhov determined on establishing a permanent settlement, he immediately set about petitioning for assignment of a priest and made plans for building a church—a Russian town was unthinkable without a church. He began to agitate for construction of a church in Alaska as early as 1789. In his letter to Evstrat Delarov, who had replaced Samoilov as manager at Shelikhov's settlement on Kodiak, he wrote: "I am most of all concerned with the need to have a church."[23] Later, in the *Historical Calendar* prepared in 1817, the board of directors of the Russian-American Company would state:

> The founder of the American company Shelikhov, having established a permanent Russian settlement on Kad'iak, and noting that many islanders wished to adopt the Christian religion (by means permitted each layman, when there is no priest) asked the authorities to assign to the company a lay [white or parish] priest to preach the gospel and to permit the establishment of a Church on Kad'iak.[24]

The official request, in the names of both Ivan Golikov and Shelikhov, was forwarded to the Ruling Synod by Gavriil, Metropolitan of Novgorod and St. Petersburg, 20 April

1793. In this petition, the two merchants emphasized the plight of their hired laborers, who were pictured as pious, devoted sons of the church, suffering without a member of the clergy being on hand to tend to their needs, making do on feast days by reading the hours and holding prayer services (*molebny*) as best they could. The Native peoples were also in dire need, wrote the petitioners. Many were Christians baptized by laymen, many were literate in the Russian language. Should the government decide to send a well-educated hieromonk, that is, a monk ordained priest, he could assume the responsibility for education. But a parish priest was needed most of all. The petitioners suggested that one of the Natives educated in the school at Kodiak should be enrolled in the Irkutsk seminary at their expense. After graduation and consecration, this Native priest would return to Alaska to serve the Native peoples. The document concluded with a request for permission to build a church: all necessary church utensils, vestments, and other adornments the petitioners would supply at their own expense.[25] The response to the petition was not what the petitioners expected. Instead of a parish priest, the government, on the instructions of Catherine II, asked the church to dispatch an ecclesiastical mission. Empress Catherine did not think it fitting that the spread of Orthodoxy in her new domain be left in private hands. The missionaries were selected, in 1793, by Metropolitan Gavriil for "excellence of their knowledge, humble and good life." They came from northern Russian monasteries, the Valaam (in Finnish Valaamo in Karelia) and the Konevitsa or Konevskii, both located on islands in Lake Ladoga. Their superior was Ioasaf (elevated to the status of an archimandrite in connection with his assignment to the mission). He was then thirty-six years of age. Born Ivan Bolotov, he graduated from the Tverskaia seminary, where he read theology, philosophy, Latin, and natural sciences. He became a monk in 1786 and eventually chose the life of solitude and contemplation at Valaam monastery. Five other members of the mission were also monks of Valaam.[26] The choice was based on practical considerations, but in Alaska the tie to the ancient monastic community of the Russian North acquired enduring symbolic significance. Eventually, a "New Valaam" would grow up in Alaska, a small hermitage on Spruce Island, where the humblest and best-remembered member of this mission, St. Herman of Alaska, made his abode and where he died in 1836.

The mission numbered ten men, carefully chosen by Metropolitan Gavriil: not only for their good and pious life, as quoted above, but also because all had chosen to live in remote monasteries, were accustomed to solitude, and were adapted to life in the north and subsistence on fish, sea mammals, and products of the land that they gathered or could grow themselves in the northern climate. Besides Ioasaf, three were priests (hieromonks), Afanasii, Makarii, and Iuvenalii; one was a hierodeacon, Nektarii; and one was a lay brother, a humble monk, Herman. Four were postulants. Later that year, in Irkutsk, one of the postulants would become a monk like his brother Iuvenalii, take the name of Stefan, be consecrated hierodeacon, and eventually perish in 1799 in the shipwreck of the *Phoenix* together with Ioasaf and his entourage (see below). Another, Koz'ma Alekseev, would become a monk after arriving on Kodiak and take the name of his ecclesiastical superior, Ioasaf. Of the remaining two postulants, Nikita Semenov, on Kodiak, would leave the clerical estate and Dmitrii Avdeev would suffer shipwreck near Kamishak Bay in 1796. Dmitri Popov, a cousin of St. Innocent of Alaska, may have joined the group in Irkutsk.[27]

They were poor to the point that their clothing (simple worn cassocks, says Metropolitan Gavriil) was threadbare. Metropolitan Gavriil bought them warm overcoats and issued travel money in the sum of 900 rubles from the "Palestinian fund," intended for support of the Orthodox faithful and churches under Turkish domination. The mission was equipped with an impressive number of church books from the synodal publishing house in Moscow (Ioasaf went to Moscow to fetch these books) and a *riznitsa* (group of utensils and vestments for church services) was supplied by Metropolitan Gavriil.

In the meantime, Shelikhov shipped twenty pud of copper to Alaska and asked Baranov that a bell be cast for the church that was yet to be built. As far as the church was concerned, it was to be of two altars, in accordance with a plan drafted at Irkutsk. This plan, wrote Shelikhov,

> has been given by me to the Archimandrite [head of mission], together with all the items for its beautification which should serve for the time being, vessels and garments. The plan may be modified, enlarged or diminished, as circumstances warrant. The first temple is to be dedicated to the Lord's Holy Resurrection, the second to Dormition of Theotokos. The location for the Church is to be selected so that one half of the Church will parallel the settlement or face the dwellings, so that the Church can be entered from this side, without trespassing on the other. The latter is to remain outside of the settlement, in an area protected by a high and sturdy fence, sufficient to accommodate the cells of the Archimandrite and other monks, with service structures, vegetable gardens, and the school for the minor Americans.[28]

Figure 70. This is the earliest depiction of the Church of the Holy Resurrection, completed by the first Orthodox Ecclesiastical Mission in 1796. Watercolor ca. 1798 by Iakov Shil'ts (James Shields), shipbuilder and commander of the *Phoenix*.

Original in AVPRI. Courtesy Richard A. Pierce.

The mission assembled in St. Petersburg, and here Ioasaf received a twenty-four point "admonition" (*nastavlenie*). An instruction modeled on the one issued to the Siberian clergy in 1769 in Tobol'sk was given to the mission as a whole.[29] The missionaries were to convert the heathen not by preaching but by personal example, by exemplary life and human kindness. They were to behave as guests in someone else's house.

Starting out on 25 December 1793, the mission traveled to Moscow. From Moscow they set out 22 January 1794 on the arduous trek across Siberia to Okhotsk. They covered thousands of miles on horseback, forded rivers, went on the Lena by boat, and, as Father Herman wrote from Kodiak to his abbot, encountered great brown bears a number of times. They arrived in Irkutsk 16 March 1794. Here, postulant Mikhail Govorukhin, a former mining engineer from the Nerchinsk works, took monastic vows and was consecrated hierodeacon. According to a letter to Metropolitan Gavriil dispatched by Rezanov from Irkustk, the mission "by their exemplary behavior and piety en route arouse among all a zeal to support their deed and in Irkutsk they became so respected and beloved by the populace that everyone was loath to see them go and shed tears."[30] Departing Irkutsk 2 May, they arrived in Okhotsk 12 July, escorted by one of Shelikhov's partners. Shelikhov and his companions had provided supplies for the mission sufficient for three years. In Okhotsk they boarded the newly built (1793) *Three Saints* (a replacement for the vessel on which Shelikhov himself sailed to Alaska in 1783), commanded by Gerasim Izmailov. She had just completed the run from Kodiak. On board were nine Chugach, and the missionaries met their first Americans. The mission traveled together with the group of serfs assigned to Shelikhov for settlement, whom Shelikhov himself called "thirty families who are to be agriculturalists, selected from the unfortunate ones."[31] The young Filip Kashevarov and his parents were among them. Soon to become apprentice navigator, Filip gained the trust of Archimandrite Ioasaf and carried confidential letters for him.[32]

The vessel put in at Unalaska, where the priests baptized more than 100 people. On 24 September 1794, the mission reached its destination, the harbor of St. Paul on Kodiak. By May 1795 the five priests had baptized several thousand Natives from various localities. They also performed a number of marriages.[33]

The mission, which was supposed to be supplied with all necessities by the company, soon found it necessary for the monks to gain their own subsistence, mostly by fishing (the disposition of supplies shipped for the mission to Kodiak by Shelikhov is not known). It was probably the monks who popularized the Russian type of seining on Kodiak. They also immediately set to experimenting with agriculture, planting vegetable gardens, oats, and wheat and rye (the last two crops were not a success in the maritime southwestern Alaska climate).

Two of the priests, Hieromonk Makarii and Hieromonk Iuvenalii, were assigned to outlying stations: Iuvenalii to Yakutat, Makarii to Unalaska.

Makarii traveled to Unalaska from Kodiak, departing aboard the *Phoenix* (Izmailov commanding, destination Okhotsk) 25 May 1795 via the Alaska Peninsula and the Shumagin Islands. Wherever he stopped, he performed the sacraments of baptism, chrizmation, and marriage. According to the report he submitted to Bishop Veniamin of Irkutsk in 1797, there were fifty settlements in the eastern Aleutians in which 2,472 persons (1,149 men and 1,323 women) were baptized.[34]

Makarii arrived at Unalaska 13 June 1796. He found there a situation most disturbing to a former serf who had come as a volunteer to serve the Natives and "spread the

Light of the Christian Faith" (so he wrote later). By that time only two merchant companies were competing for the fur trade in the eastern Aleutians, the Shelikhov-Golikov Company and that of the Irkutsk merchants Kiselev. Makarii took a firm stand against depredations and abuses of the Natives by Shelikhov-Golikov crews, under then manager at Unalaska Vasilii Merkul'iev and foreman Ivan Kochutin, a burgher of Vologda, and sought support from the rival company. Kiselev's foreman, Ivan Svin'in, burgher of Okhotsk, assigned him an armed guard. Two or three of his men kept watch around the clock at the priest's dwelling. Kochutin, on the other hand, tried to prevent any Aleuts from visiting the priest and more than once threatened violence against Makarii. When a baptized Aleut was dying, the priest was prevented from going to hear his confession. When the man died unconfessed, the priest was prevented from performing the burial service at the cemetery. He sang the service at home. Apparently, the chapel that was to be built at Unalaska at that time was never built, though lumber for its construction was shipped from Kodiak aboard the *Phoenix*.[35] Baptisms, chrizmations, and marriages were all performed in the dwelling where Kiselev's men stood guard. In one instance a fight broke out between Kiselev's men who defended Makarii and the Shelikhov-Golikov men. In a letter Makarii submitted personally to Emperor Paul, he wrote:

> The Shelikhov and Golikov company men threaten other people in a most barbarous way. They lack any human kindness. They take their wives and daughters as mistresses by force, they kill the people. They send out the men to hunt sea otters from the earliest spring, healthy or ailing, it does not matter. Some of those who are ill, die en route. They keep the men hunting until fall and there is no time to put up food for themselves and their families, nor get materials for clothing. They starve to death, and suffer from cold because they lack clothing. When they are subjected to severe floggings, they commit suicide. If an Aleut does not bring in plenty of fox pelts, they strip him and pin him to the ground and beat him with sinew cords, all the time chanting that "we do not tolerate laziness."[36]

The letter was an uncompromising indictment of the exploitation of Unalaska Aleuts by the men of Shelikhov's company. Makarii cited particular cases, naming men who committed acts of violence, such as the severe beating of a minor girl, a baptized Christian, by a man who kept her as his mistress. He squarely laid the blame for Kochutin's men's behavior at the door of Vasilii Merkul'iev. Several Aleut leaders sought redress from Kiselev's agent, Svin'in. As Makarii said in his report, they sought this protection not out of joy but from great sorrow suffered at the hands of others.

Makarii assembled a delegation of several leading men and together with them, aided by Kiselev's foreman Svin'in, boarded Kiselev's vessel, which was sailing to Okhotsk. There the Aleut leaders presented their case to the local authorities in Okhotsk and asked that Svin'in be empowered to offer them protection. They found little satisfaction. Shelikhov's managers at Okhotsk made an attempt to detain them or send Makarii immediately back to Kodiak, but Commandant Minnitskii, upon Makarii's representations, let them proceed to Yakutsk. Makarii then determined to carry their complaint to the highest level of the imperial government, even to Emperor Paul himself. He went to Irkutsk where he reported to Veniamin, Bishop of Irkustsk and Nerchinsk. We do not know what Makarii said in the audience with his bishop, but Veniamin instructed him to proceed to St. Petersburg and lay the case before Emperor Paul. Veniamin contacted the governor, and the latter issued an official travel document, which read in part:

> Those proceeding from here to St. Petersburg, travelers from America, toion Kagolukh, in baptism Elisei Pupyshev and the Aleuts, interpreter Sukanikatanakh, in baptism Nikolai Lukanin, and Changisunakh, in baptism Nikifor Svin'in, accompanied by the Hieromonk Makarii of the American Mission, are to appear before His Imperial Majesty.
>
> From Irkutsk, along the entire tract, they are to be supplied at all post stations with four post horses and guides without any delays whatsoever. They are to be rendered all assistance due them by law and governmental orders, and supplied against recompense from their per diem moneys.
>
> Signed: Ludwig Nagel, etc. etc. etc. at Irkutsk

The document bears an official red wax seal and all titles of Governor Nagel are stated. The bishop forwarded to the synod in St. Petersburg a detailed account of the information supplied by Makarii.[37]

The delegation was afraid that Shelikhov's agents in Irkutsk might attempt to stop them but, with the bishop's and government support, they succeeded in reaching St. Petersburg. Makarii and the Aleuts were heard by Emperor Paul, who ordered that abuses be stopped.[38] Makarii was reassigned to the mission and set out on his way back to America.

In the meantime, Archimandrite Ioasaf, who immediately upon arriving in Alaska wrote to Shelikhov, to his ecclesiastical superiors, and to others about abuses of power he observed on the part of Baranov and his men, was recalled to Irkutsk to be consecrated bishop-vicar for Alaska. In this office his status would be equal to that of a governor of a province and thus no mercantile company manager would be in a position to challenge his authority. This measure had some support from the founders of the company. Ivan Golikov, in particular, had in May 1796 petitioned the Holy Synod to establish an Alaska see. The synod decided in favor of this measure 4 July 1796, and the decision was approved by Catherine the Great. An appropriate governmental edict was issued 19 July 1796: the empress, true to her policy that the mission should be governmentally and not privately supported, assigned to the maintenance of the bishop-vicar's see a sum of 4,030 rubles and 18 kopeks per annum to be paid from the royal treasury. Tobol'sk merchant Osip Prianishnikov, who was married to a Native woman and who served the mission as an interpreter in 1795, received an appointment in this capacity from Catherine herself: he was to be paid an annual salary of 250 rubles by the synod. He was released from the merchant estate and received a title of collegiate interpreter. A new and rich riznitsa (vestments and utensils for the bishop-vicar's church at Kodiak) was assembled and shipped to Moscow from where an agent of the Shelikhov-Golikov Company was to arrange transport to Alaska. Additional supplies necessary for performance of all church rites, such as myrrh, were to be prepared in Irkutsk. In 1797, the synod reported that in addition to the annual sum authorized by the late Empress Catherine for the maintenance of the episcopal vicariate in Alaska, a one-time donation of 2,000 rubles would be made.

The notification of the proposed changes in the status of the mission reached Kodiak early in 1798, and Ioasaf embarked on the trip back to Irkutsk with the next vessel that was sailing to Okhotsk. In expectation of his arrival, 9 October 1797, the synod, disturbed by the information about conditions in the colony and especially about the abuses of the Native peoples, decided to summon Ioasaf to St. Petersburg. It was planned that

Ioasaf would report to Emperor Paul; therefore, the proposal was submitted to Paul. To the chagrin of the synod, but especially Metropolitan Gavriil, Paul prohibited Ioasaf from coming to St. Petersburg. Paul wrote that, because of the distance and expense that would be incurred by such journey and charged to the treasury, there was absolutely no need for it. The synod then instructed Ioasaf upon his arrival in Irkutsk to submit a detailed report about the situation on Kodiak. Guidelines for the report, in the form of twenty-two questions, were sent.[39]

Ioasaf was duly consecrated in Irkutsk on 10 April 1799. In May 1799, at Okhotsk, accompanied by Makarii, who had rejoined him, by the choristers, Hierodeacon Stefan, and the servitors and novices who had accompanied him from Kodiak as well as those who were additionally assigned to the vicariate, Ioasaf boarded the *Phoenix* (James Shields, her builder, commanding). Also on board were the staff of the seminary that Ioasaf planned to establish on Kodiak. Clearly, from the very beginning Ioasaf planned for the creation of Native clergy. He was concerned that the Gospel be preached in the Native languages. Already in 1795, he had recommended to Shelikhov, who then was again petitioning for the assignment of a parish priest to Alaska, that Osip Prianishnikov, the Alutiiq interpreter for the mission (see above), be consecrated as a priest.[40] Ioasaf's vessel sailed for Kodiak, but was caught in a severe storm, in all probability in the western part of Shelikof Strait, and went down with all hands. The spiritual mission at Kodiak was to remain without an ecclesiastical superior, though a natural spiritual leader emerged in the person of the humble monk Herman (now St. Herman of Alaska).

By 1799, the mission was reduced to one priest, Hieromonk Afanasii, who served the Church of the Holy Resurrection at St. Paul Harbor on Kodiak, and Hieromonk Nektarii, who taught school, despite very poor health. They were aided by monks Ioasaf and Herman. Hieromonk Iuvenalii, who in 1795 was assigned to Yakutat but stayed at Nuchek on Hinchinbrook Island in Prince William Sound, decided to go northwest to seek the legendary old Russian settlements on Alaska's north shores. He was very successful in his mission among the Chugach and Cook Inlet Athabaskans; he visited the Lake Iliamna and Lake Clark regions and then proceeded to the Yup'ik Eskimo area on the Kuskokwim River. He and his Athabaskan escort were killed by the Yupiit at Quinhagak on the Bering Sea (Kuskokwim delta).[41]

Reduced in numbers and bearing many hardships, and at times persecuted by Baranov's henchmen, the clergy continued to oppose harsh treatment of the Natives, facing even the wrath of Baranov himself. Thus, according to Baranov, when, sometime prior to July 1800, two Natives from the Lake Iliamna area who had been accused of complicity in the killing of three Russians were brought for punishment to Kodiak:

> they gained the favor of the clergy.... They were freed from irons and treated the same as the Russians.... Kuskov decided to send them to me to Sitka on the *Ekaterina*, but the fathers objected and Mr. Interpreter [Prianishnikov] even wrote a protest which I am enclosing ... the fathers did not stop and insisted that I give the natives their freedom, telling me that I would have to answer for this, prophesying that a government expedition would arrive to investigate the management here. They hope for it, perhaps keeping in mind their and Father Makarii's former complaints.... They [apparently Christian Natives] claimed that the Bishop would not be sent here and that Father Makarii would be in charge of the mission.... There are still more troubles with the restless government

> employees and the monks, who judge everything according to ideas that might be all right for a recluse in a desert.[42]

Baranov, of course, had at the time personal problems with the clergy on account of his second, irregular (in the clergy's view) union with Anna Grigor'ievna. Bitter though he was against the clergy, it was the monks' interference on behalf of the Natives that most provoked his ire. Father Herman came in for special mention:

> We have a hermit here now by the name of Herman, who is worse than Makarii. He is a great talker and likes to write. Even though he keeps himself in his cell most of the time, not even going to church out of fear of worldly temptations, he knows nevertheless everything that we think and do, not only at daytime but even at night. By means of pious cajoling, he extracts all the information that he wants from his pupils, and sometimes from our own men.[43]

And again, in another letter, Baranov wrote:

> I was punished by anxiety and my temper was sorely tried, because the clergy and the government employees were entirely out of bounds and for half the winter tried to instigate an uprising among the hunters and especially among the islanders.[44]

The incident to which Baranov refers in the last passage was a labor dispute involving Russian workers and employees seconded to the company from the navy. Baranov charged that the monks overstepped their authority when they took sides in the dispute. Even more serious was the incident of administering the oath of allegiance to the emperors, first Paul and then Alexander I when he came to the throne in 1801. Baranov wrote that the monks protested dispatch of bird hunting parties and the long-distance sea otter hunting parties. He charged that the monks gave as a poor excuse for this protest that they had to administer the oath of allegiance to the emperor to the men of Kodiak. In imperial Russia, when a sovereign died and the heir to the throne assumed the office of the emperor, all *free* subjects took an oath administered in the presence of or by the clergy. The taking of this oath symbolized full-fledged citizenship and thus protection under imperial law. Baranov objected but could not prohibit outright the taking of the oath. He argued for postponement to a time convenient for the company's hunting schedule. He wanted the monks to show proof that such an oath was authorized by the government, or at least to wait until the arrival of the bishop. Hieromonk Afanasii argued that the islanders were loyal subjects and the oath had to be taken by all, so that no special decree to that effect was necessary. The monks sent an official complaint on this matter to the synod on 31 July 1802. This was a very important matter, not fully settled until the investigation conducted in 1804 by Hieromonk Gedeon. Baranov wrote about the clergy's role: "They promised the islanders independence and freedom to live according to their old customs if they would take the oath of allegiance." He also commented: "Their freedom consists in robbery and in everlasting bloody barbarism."

The clergy, despite Baranov's objections, attempted to carry out their plan to administer the oath to the Natives. They dispatched messengers to outlying villages to tell the men, especially the leaders, to come to St. Paul Harbor for this purpose. Baranov ordered that the Alutiiq leaders (the toions) who did so be seized. Most escaped; only one, the chief from Tugidak, was captured. The clergy actively assisted the escape of the

Alutiiq leaders; in one case Hieromonk Afanasii, dressed in Alutiiq clothing, acted as a decoy. According to Baranov, the clergy were ready to fight his men physically to secure the Natives' escape.

Baranov then proposed either to isolate the clergy, virtually imprisoning them behind a stockade built around their residence, or to ship them out for chastisement at Unalaska. In the wake of this open conflict between the clergy and the company, the priests performed sacraments for the Natives clandestinely outside of the church buildings, in private dwellings or in their quarters, as had been the case with Makarii earlier at Unalaska.[45]

The clergy's resolute stand would, in 1805, bring upon them the venom of Rezanov's pen. He generated letters in which he not only misrepresented their characters and activities (contradicting his earlier, initial letter to Metropolitan Gavriil from Irkutsk, written before he became Shelikhov's son-in-law), but lied about them. He also lied about the nature of his interaction with them during his three-week stay at St. Paul Harbor on Kodiak, particularly with Hieromonk Gedeon, who represented the Holy Synod, the Metropolitan of St. Petersburg, and Emperor Alexander I. The scurrilous remarks about the clergy in Rezanov's letters to the board of directors (absent, interestingly enough, in his communications addressed to the emperor) included a number of accusations. The clergy were said to mistreat the Natives; Hieromonk Iuvenalii particularly, by then long dead, was said to have done so while in parts unknown. This accusation provided, much later, the basis for the fictitious account of Iuvenalii's activities enshrined in the literature courtesy of Ivan Petroff and Hubert H. Bancroft. Rezanov claimed that the Natives would welcome Russian settlements provided that no priests come and that the priests were lazy and inactive. He also, as noted earlier, ascribed to himself such measures instituted by the clergy as establishment and conduct of a school and an orphanage, study of Native languages, and agricultural experiments.

These statements must be contrasted with those made in Rezanov's letters to Hieromonk Gedeon and with letters sent by Gedeon to Rezanov (as well as Gedeon's other correspondence). In several communications addressed to Gedeon, Rezanov was highly complimentary to the clergy. In a letter to Gedeon dated 9 August 1805, he specifically commended the clergy for the excellent work they had done in agriculture and requested that he be provided with a description of experiments the clergy had conducted in growing a variety of crops. The information was provided, in detail. In another exchange, Rezanov refused any assistance to the churchmen, despite having informed Gedeon earlier that the company would provide whatever the clergy needed in terms of support (and to which Gedeon responded with a modest list, asking mainly for tools, clothing, and items with which to recompense Natives for labor). The beautification of the church in the future, wrote Gedeon, would depend entirely upon private donations by "benefactors and lovers of God."[46]

Interestingly, Rezanov did not mention that he was entrusted with delivering various items, including money in the sum of 6,816 rubles, 82¾ kopeks, for the mission, that Gedeon was receiving substantial salary from the synod, which was not delivered to him, and that the company was receiving and pocketing the very significant sum assigned to the mission by Catherine II (see above). As late as 1823, the imperial treasury sought to recover the embezzled sums or at least receive an accounting of any moneys expended on the mission's support.[47]

After Gedeon left Kodiak in 1807, the mission, now reduced to three men (Hieromonk Nektarii had been sent to Russia in 1806 because of ill health), carried on its work as best its members could. Father Herman was in charge. Gedeon, when leaving in 1807, appointed this humble monk to be head of mission. Revered in life by the Natives and many laborers, he impressed even high-ranking naval personnel, such as Golovnin and his officers.[48]

The activities of the remaining members of the mission were limited to the Kodiak archipelago. Brother Ioasaf continued to supervise agricultural activities and tended the church buildings until his death in 1823 (he was buried on Spruce Island). Hieromonk Afanasii continued as the priest at the Church of the Holy Resurrection, though he preferred to live on Afognak where he subsisted by fishing.

For a brief time, in 1810, it was expected that the Kodiak parish would be served by Prokopii Lavrov, the first Alaskan to become an Orthodox priest. In keeping with the ideal that a Native clergy should serve the emerging Alaskan Orthodox community, Lavrov was sent for theological education to Russia, was consecrated in 1809, and on 18 February 1810 assigned to the Kodiak parish. He was also expected to assume the directorship of the Kodiak school, museum, and library. He sailed aboard a company vessel from Okhotsk, but disembarked at Petropavlovsk-on-Kamchatskii from where he rendered a complaint against the company to his bishop. He was subjected to indignities on the part of the company's agent Staropogritskii, the provisions of his contract were not observed, his authority was challenged. The bishop found his complaints valid and supported him fully. Upon representations to the synod by Amvrosii, the Metropolitan of Novgorod and St. Petersburg who had succeeded Gavriil, the synod ordered Lavrov not to proceed to Kodiak. He was assigned in 1811 to a prestigious parish in Irkutsk.[49]

Afanasii remained until 1825, when he returned to Russia. He was replaced in 1824 by Father Frumentii Mordovskii, one of the three parish priests sent to Alaska under the company's Second Charter. Mordovskii served on Kodiak until 1833. Unpopular because of his feud with Father Herman, he was removed on the recommendation of Chief Manager Murav'iev during Wrangell's administration. Wrangell had the utmost respect for Father Herman. It was he who ordered in 1831 that the part of Spruce Island where Father Herman had his hermitage, now Monk's Lagoon, be called the New Valaam, ordered a chapel built there at company expense to replace the old one Father Herman had built many years earlier, and issued orders that no one could settle there without Father Herman's consent.

After the death of Father Herman in the winter of 1836, the activity of the spiritual mission in Alaska came to an end. The Orthodox community was now being served by parish clergy. The first to arrive, in 1816, was Father Aleksei Sokolov, who served the Orthodox at Novo-Arkhangel'sk. Before Father Sokolov's arrival, reader's services were conducted at the chapel by a company employee, Beliaev, beginning in 1808 (the exact date of the chapel's construction has not been established). Sokolov did not conduct missionary work among the Tlingit and for this reason was later criticized by Wrangell. In 1833, he replaced Father Mordovskii on Kodiak, and Ioann Veniaminov came to Novo-Arkhangel'sk from Unalaska in 1834.

Sokolov and Mordovskii had been found wanting for different reasons by many, but meanwhile two extraordinary churchmen came to Alaska as parish priests in the 1820s. Both men devoted their lives to the service of the church and the people. The first, arriving in 1824, was the renowned Ioann Veniaminov (1797–1871). Born in a Siberian village, son of a sacristan, he volunteered for service in the Aleutian Islands after a meeting in Irkutsk with Ivan Kriukov, former manager at Unalaska. He served as the parish priest for the eastern Aleutians, a parish that encompassed all the islands from the Shumagins in the east to Umnak in the west. He came with his family: his wife, his firstborn, a younger brother, and his mother. Six more children would be born in Alaska. One of the sons, Gavriil, born in Unalaska, would become a missionary to the peoples of the Lower Amur. Veniaminov's brother, Stephan, with his Unalaska Aleut wife, would later be a missionary serving Northern Kamchatka and working among the Koriak and the Chukchi. One of his daughters, Ekaterina, born in Sitka, would marry Il'ia Petelin, the first Orthodox priest to serve as missionary in the Yup'ik area, on the Nushagak River. When Veniaminov returned to Russia, after his wife's death in 1839, he became a monk, taking the name of Innokentii (Innocent), and on 31 December 1840 was consecrated bishop, to serve the newly established diocese of Kamchatka, the Kurils, and the Aleutian Islands.

Veniaminov returned to Alaska in his new capacity in 1843, and remained in residence until 1850. That year he became archbishop of Yakutsk and then, in 1868, metropolitan of Moscow and Kolomna, the head of the Russian Orthodox Church.[50]

FIGURE 71. **St. Innocent as bishop in 1840, from a portrait now lost. The original is in the State Museum of History and Culture of the Peoples of the North, Yakutsk, Sakha Republic (Yakutiia), Russian Federation.** *Courtesy State Museum of History and Culture of the Peoples of the North and the State Archive of the Sakha Republic.*

The second man was Iakov Netsvetov, himself of Aleut descent, the eldest son of a Russian Old Voyager and an Aleut, Mariia Alekseeva, of Atka. He served the central and western Aleutians, the Commander Islands, and the Kuril Islands from 1828 to 1844. That year, Netsvetov, now a widower, went at the request of Veniaminov (then Bishop Innokentii) to the Yukon River, to serve as missionary. There he worked until 1863 among the Yupiit of the Yukon, founding the Ikogmiut Mission (this Yup'ik settlement is now called Russian Mission), the Yupiit of the Kuskokwim, and the Athabaskans of the middle Yukon, Innoko, and lower Koyukuk. Replaced at the Ikogmiut Mission in 1863, he then came to Novo-Arkhangel'sk. Here he became the priest of the Church of the Holy Life-Creating Trinity, built in 1846 to 1848 for the Orthodox Tlingit of Sitka. He died in Novo-Arkhangel'sk 26 July 1864 and was buried at the entry to the Tlingit church.[51]

The contribution of Veniaminov and Netsvetov to the growth of the Orthodox faith in Alaska cannot be overestimated. Both men served the people with all

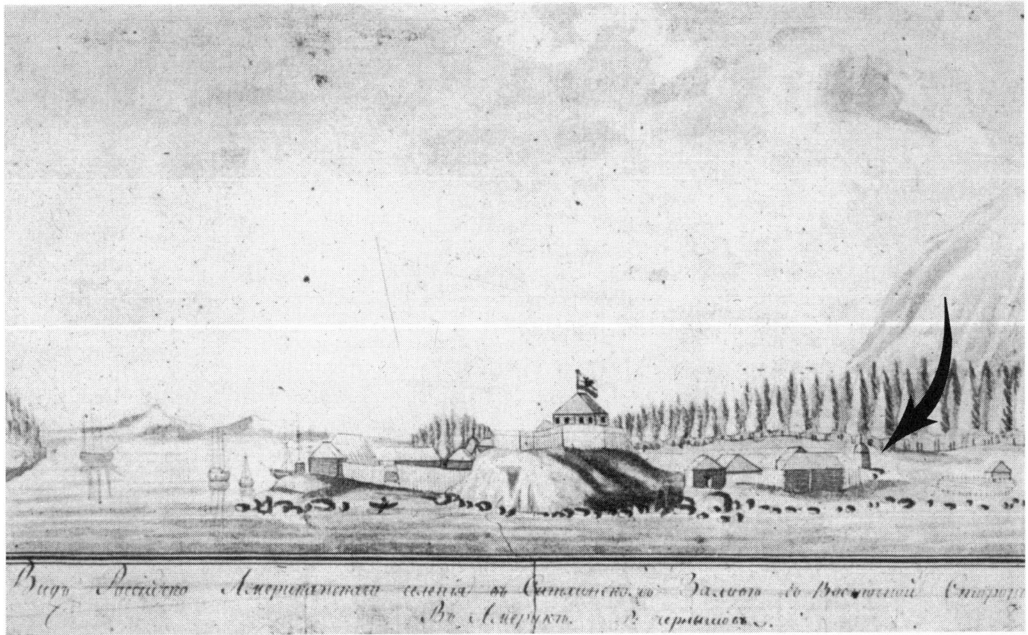

Figure 72. A drawing of Novo-Arkhangel'sk in or before 1809 by V. Chernyshov. On the right is a small structure topped by the Orthodox cross. This is the only known representation of the first Chapel of St. Michael the Archangel built in Baranov's time, soon after the reconquest of the area in 1804 (arrow added).

Original in RGAVMF, Fond 1331, op. 4, delo 133. Courtesy Richard A. Pierce.

Figure 73. This rare view of Sitka, 1828–1829, by Postels, a scientist attached to the Staniukovich-Litke expedition to the North Pacific, shows the first church of Novo-Arkhangel'sk, which was consecrated in 1816, incorporating a chapel built before 1808. Here Aleksei Sokolov ministered (1816–1833), as did Ioann Veniaminov (St. Innocent, Metropolitan of Moscow and Kolomna, 1834–1839).

Courtesy Richard A. Pierce.

FIGURE 74. **Sitka with view of the Cathedral of St. Michael, built in 1840–1845 by St. Innocent (Veniaminov). Sketch by W. Hamel, 1867.**
Courtesy University of California, Berkeley, Bancroft Library, George Davidson Collection, no. 1946.004-A.

FIGURE 75. **This building housed the offices of the diocese at Novo-Arkhangel'sk. Built in the 1840s by Bishop Innocent (Veniaminov), it has been restored by the National Park Service.**
Photo by Harvey Brandt.

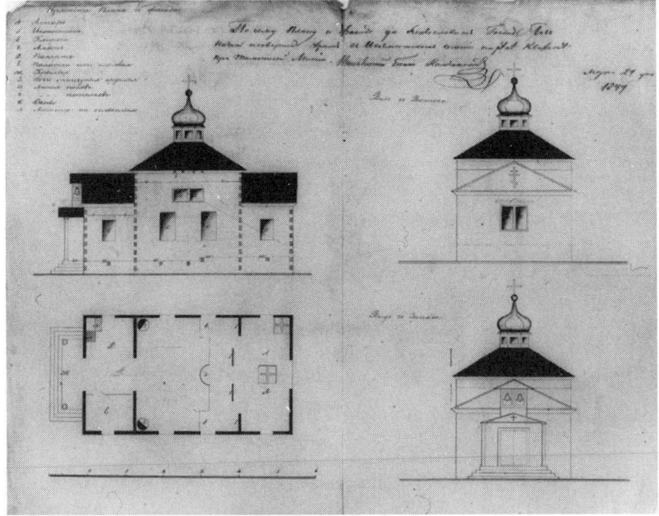

FIGURE 76. Historic plan of the Church of the Elevation of the Holy Cross at Ikogmiut (now Russian Mission), drawn by Fr. Iakov Netsvetov (St. Iakov, Enlightener of Alaska Native Peoples) of Atka.

Fr. Iakov was appointed as missionary in 1844 by St. Innocent to enlighten the people of Alaska's interior, the Yukon, and the Kuskokwim River basin.

As bishop, St. Innocent encouraged the building of chapels in Alaskan villages. By 1848, Fr. Iakov had designed the church and submitted the plans to St. Innocent. On 2 March 1849, St. Innocent issued a charter for construction of the church, and on 29 March 1849, endorsed the plans. The handwritten message reads: "Let the blessing of the Lord be given to commence and complete according to this plan the temple at the settlement of Ikogmiut on the river Kvikhpak [Yukon] at the local mission. [Signed] Innokentii, Bishop of Kamchatka."

The key on the upper left corner of the drawing reads: "Explanation of the plan and facade: (a) altar, (b) iconostasy, (c) cleros, (d) ambos, (e) porch, (f) tent or storage, (g) porch steps, (h) stoves, of iron, round, (i) floor level, (j) ceiling level, (k) windows, (l) stairwell to the belfry."

Original in Library of Congress, Manuscript Division, Alaskan Russian Church Archives, container DF 218 (microfilm reel 151). Courtesy University of Alaska Fairbanks, Rasmuson Library, Alaska and Polar Regions Department, Archives.

FIGURE 77. A sketch of the Church of the Elevation of the Holy Cross at Ikogmiut, the only representation of the original church. Artist unknown.

Courtesy Alaska Historical Library.

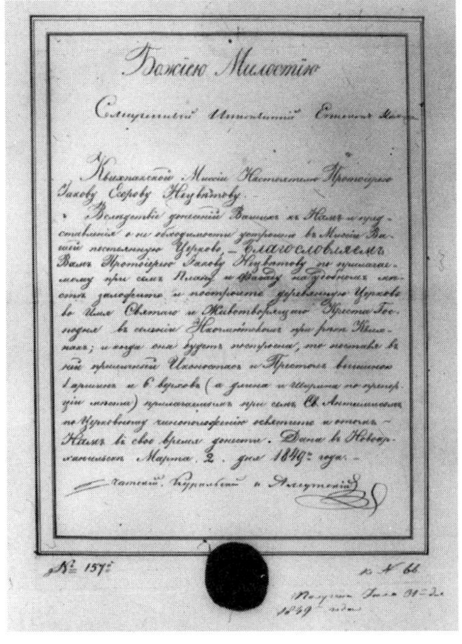

Божiею Милостiю

Благословляемъ

№ 157

FIGURE 78. The charter issued in 1849 by St. Innocent to Fr. Iakov Netsvetov to build the Church of the Elevation of the Holy Cross at Ikogmiut (now Russian Mission).

Original in Library of Congress, Manuscript Division, Alaskan Russian Church Archives, container DF 218 (microfilm reel 151). Courtesy University of Alaska Fairbanks, Rasmuson Library, Alaska and Polar Regions Department, Archives.

FIGURE 79. Fr. Iakov Netsvetov, now St. Iakov, Enlightener of Alaska Native Peoples, was buried at the entry of the Tlingit church in Sitka, where he was priest after leaving Ikogmiut. Two structures mark the place: one a small monument of stone in the form of a church, placed by the local Orthodox community, and the other a wooden shelter with a cupola crowned with the Orthodox cross, erected in the 1990s by the Diocese of Alaska (OCA).
Photo by Harvey Brandt.

FIGURE 80. Novo-Arkhangel'sk, 1851. Note the Tlingit church built into the palisade at far left.
Courtesy Richard A. Pierce.

FIGURE 81. Tlingit church, plan and elevation with an annotation by St. Innocent, 28 April 1846.

Courtesy Katerina Solovjova-Wessels.

Figure 82. Axonometric reconstruction of Tlingit church based upon historic drawings and sketches.
Courtesy Katerina Solovjova-Wessels.

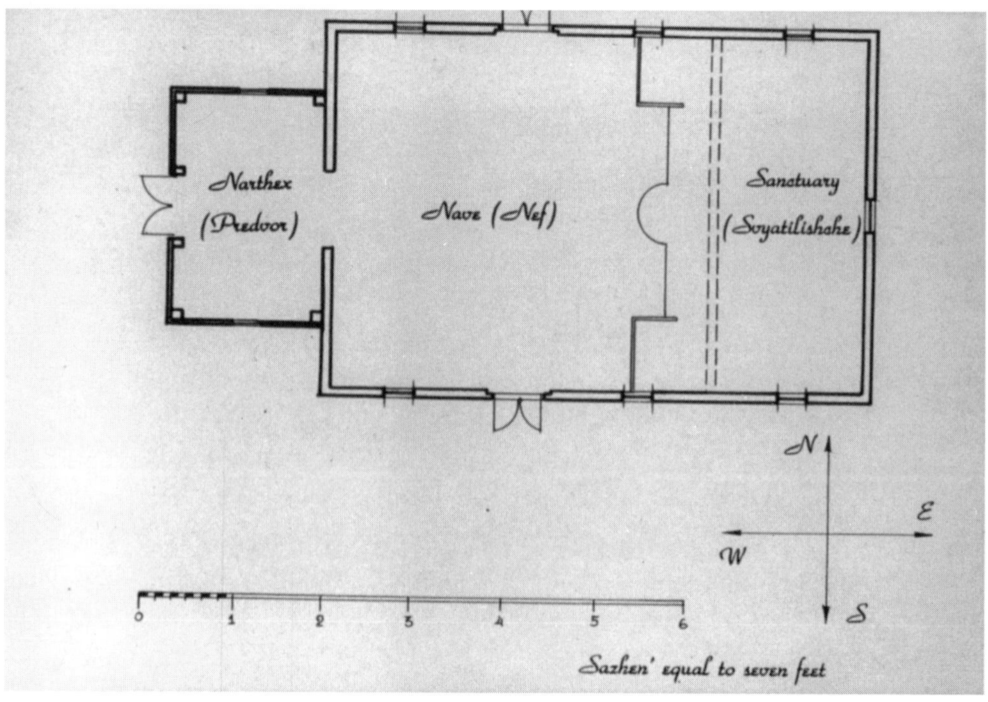

Figure 83. Reconstruction of the Tlingit church floor plan.
Courtesy Katerina Solovjova-Wessels.

their hearts. Both built churches, established schools, helped introduce smallpox vaccination, and translated and wrote original texts in Native languages. Their contribution to the linguistics of the Aleut, Alutiiq, Tlingit, and Yup'ik languages, and in creating Native literacy is acknowledged by scholars worldwide. Veniaminov began the linguistic work in Aleut and translations of scriptures and other sacred texts into Aleut soon after his arrival in the islands. He worked closely with Aleut elders and freely acknowledged their help in creating an Aleut alphabet. In particular, he recognized the toion of the Krenitzin Islands, Ivan Pan'kov of Akun.[52] Eventually, Veniaminov, having mastered the Aleut language, wrote *Indication of the Way to the Kingdom of Heaven* in Aleut. This composition has been translated into all major languages of the world, including many languages of the aboriginal people of Russia and Alaska, and is used in instruction in the faith in Orthodox churches worldwide.[53]

Father Iakov Netsvetov adapted the translations made by Veniaminov and Pan'kov to the central (Atkan) dialect and himself composed in Atkan Aleut several works of spiritual nature. He compiled the most extensive Atkan Aleut dictionary in existence. In his later life, on the Yukon, he was instrumental in creating Yup'ik script and taught Yup'ik students in their own language at Ikogmiut. The legacy of these men lives to this day. Aleuts are proud of their literacy that was created by Veniaminov and Netsvetov almost two centuries ago.[54] Both men produced students, but especially Netsvetov's pupils served as priests of the Orthodox Church in Alaska for many years. Lavrentii Salamatov, Zakharii Bel'kov, Innokentii Lestenkov, and Innokentii Shaiashnikov are but a few of the Alaska Native intellectuals who were guided by Father Iakov in their youth. This legacy is reflected in a number of Native priests who were sons, grandsons, and now are great-grandsons of St. Iakov's pupils.

Veniaminov was famed as a craftsman and mechanic. Some of his works were described by travelers who visited Sitka, and some survive and are exhibited in the Bishop's House, his residence and the diocesan offices and seminary he built in Sitka (now restored by the National Park Service). Netsvetov was an artist who painted icons, carved and decorated rood screens in churches and chapels, and carved church vessels and chandeliers (*panikadilo*) out of ivory. Unfortunately, none of his work survives.

Beginning in 1842, the Orthodox Church in Alaska enjoyed the presence of a resident bishop or, after 1850 when it was included in an archbishopric, of a bishop-vicar, and was supported, for the most part, by the company, by private donors (including members of the imperial family), and local communities. After 1867, the Russian state offered material support of the churches and of the schools the church continued to maintain, where education became trilingual: Native languages, Russian, and English were used. After the Russian Revolution of 1917, all outside support ceased.

After 1867, the church suffered from an attack by the mostly Protestant clergy newly interested in Alaska, led by the Presbyterian Sheldon Jackson. In some circles eradication of the Orthodox faith was considered a necessary prerequisite for Americanization of the Alaska Natives. More energy and money was spent in converting members of the Orthodox Church than on conversion of heathens.[55] To this end, the Orthodox Church was dealt with in most unflattering terms, including its characterization as nothing more than a regrettable superstition. This sentiment was shared (and is shared today) by many public school teachers and officials.[56] The Aleutian Islands became a province for Methodist missionary activities and Kodiak for the Baptists. The Tlingit area was the domain of the Presbyterians. Moravians were allowed on the Kuskokwim and the Episcopal and Roman Catholic missionaries in territories along the Yukon and its tributaries. In the face of mounting pressure from other denominations (and school teachers who were missionaries themselves) and from secular authorities in the American period, Orthodoxy became espoused by more conservative factions within the Native communities.[57] Among the Tlingit, of whom only small numbers converted to Orthodoxy during the Russian period,[58] mass conversions occurred during the American period.[59]

The shortage of priests was always (and continues to be) acute. In the absence of priests, Orthodoxy was maintained by often self-taught lay readers. Among the Tlingit, church brotherhoods often saw to it that reader's services were conducted. Today, in many communities reader's services are held on a regular basis, while a priest may visit monthly, or occasionally. Until very recent times reader's services were always held in the local Native language or in part in Slavonic. The clergy today, as in the days of Netsvetov and Veniaminov, are for the most part Alaska Natives. Financially, the churches and chapels are supported by the local village communities: no funds come from the outside at all. New churches are constructed by local volunteers.

The Orthodox Church, or as a filmmaker called it, this "Legacy of Faith,"[60] survived and persists against all odds. Today it is a vital institution in Alaska, and Orthodoxy is considered in many quarters to be a Native religion.[61] Will the Orthodox Church survive into the future? To judge by the village record of the past hundred years, the pride many Alaskans feel in their church, and the reception accorded the Patriarch of Moscow and all Russia during his visit to the state in the fall of 1993, it will.[62]

NOTES

1. This chapter is based in part on Lydia T. Black, "From Valaamo to Spruce Island: Russian Orthodoxy in Alaska, U.S.A.," in *Northern Religions and Shamanism*, ed. Mihály Hoppál and Juha Pentikainen (Budapest: Akadémiai Kiadó; Helsinki: Finnish Literature Society, 1992), 100–107. See also idem, "Put' na Novyi Valaam: Stanovlenie russkoi pravoslavnoi tserkvi na Aliaske," chap. 7 in *Osnovanie Russkoi Ameriki, 1732–1799*, vol. 1 of *Istoriia Russkoi Ameriki, 1732–1867*, ed. N. N. Bolkhovitinov (Moscow: "Mezhdunarodnye otnosheniia," 1997), 251–277.
2. Stepan Cherepanov, Report of 3 August 1762, in A. I. Andreev, ed., *Russkie otkrytiia* (1948), 117–118; Roza G. Liapunova, "Novyi dokument o rannikh plavaniiakh na Aleutskie ostrova ('Izvestiia' Fedora Afans'evicha Kul'kova, 1764 g.)," in *Strany i narody basseina Tikhogo okeana*, bk. 4, vol. 20 of *Strany i narody Vostoka* (Moscow: Izdatel'stvo "Nauka," 1979), 97–105.
3. Cherepanov, Report of 3 August 1762, in A. I. Andreev, ed., *Russkie otkrytiia* (1948), 117–118.
4. Gideon, *Round the World Voyage*, 60, 122.
5. See Lydia T. Black, "Peg Calendars of Alaska," in *Faces, Voices and Dreams: A Celebration of the Centennial of the Sheldon Jackson Museum, Sitka, Alaska, 1888–1988*, ed. Peter L. Corey (Juneau: Division of Alaska State Museums and Friends of Alaska State Museum, 1987), 97–100.
6. "Contract of the company of Moscow merchant Vasilii Serebrennikov September 15, 1773," in Makarova, *Russians on the Pacific*, 184–185. The passage quoted is my retranslation from the Russian edition (Makarova, *Russkie na Tikhom okeane*, 170).
7. Dmitrii Shabalin, foreman, watercolor of a Russian trading party on Hokkaido in 1779, manuscript, von Asch Collection, University of Göttingen, Germany. (See plate 6.)
8. Solov'ev's report to T. Shmalev (Kamchatka), 28 July 1766, in A. I. Andreev, ed., *Russkie otkrytiia* (1948), 148.
9. Original in the library of Sheldon Jackson College, Sitka, Alaska.
10. Based on material by Black, "Promyshlenniki . . . Who Were They?"

11. I. P. Sirotnitskii, ed., "Varlaam Shalamov," *Nashe nasledie* 3–4 (1988): 54–102. This article consists of the reminiscences of Varlaam Shalamov, son of Tikhon Shalamov, a Komi, descendant of a long line of Komi shamans. Tikhon Shalamov served in the early 1900s as an Orthodox priest on Kodiak, returning to Russia to serve in his native region. Material put at my disposal by Gennadii I. Shevelev, Moscow and Vologda.

12. "Rossiiskaia istoriia: Nechto o 'piatinakh Novgorodskikh,'" *Severnyi arkhiv* 11, no. 3 (1827): 191–192; V. A. Zaitsev, *Belomorskii Sever: Religiia, svobodomyslie, ateizm* (Arkhangel'sk: Severo-zapadnoe knizhnoe izdatel'stvo, 1983).

13. On the faith of the Russian common people, see Pierre Pascal, *The Religion of the Russian People*, trans. from French by Rowan Williams, foreword by Alexander Schmemann (Crestwood, N.Y.: St. Vladimir's Seminary Press, 1976); and Donald W. Treadgold, "The Peasant and Religion," in *The Peasant in Nineteenth-Century Russia*, ed. Wayne S. Vucinich (Stanford, Calif.: Stanford University Press, 1968), 72–107.

14. See the works of Soterios Mousalimas, Michael Oleksa, and Richard L. Dauenhauer as cited in note 19 (below) and elsewhere. Related ideas, especially in regard to shamans incorporated into Orthodoxy and syncretism of Yup'ik Eskimo and Orthodox beliefs and practices, have been expressed in several publications by noted anthropologist Ann Fienup-Riordan, e.g., "The Mask: The Eye of the Dance," *Arctic Anthropology* 24, no. 2 (1987): 40–55.

15. Edward W. Nelson, "The Eskimo About Bering Strait," in *18th Annual Report of the Bureau of American Ethnology, 1896–1897* (Washington, D.C., 1899; reprint, with introduction by W. W. Fitzhugh and addenda, Washington, D.C.: Smithsonian Institution Press, 1984), 421–422.

16. John Ledyard, *John Ledyard's Journal of Captain Cook's Last Voyage*, ed. James Kenneth Munford (Corvallis: Oregon State University Press, 1963), 95.

17. Among those chrizmated was the wife of Vasilii Merkul'iev, Shelikhov's trusted employee, baptized by Natalia Shelikhov.

18. Sivtsov's report to Captain Billings, with appended list of those baptized, chrizmated, and of marriages performed. Russian State Naval Archive (RGAVMF), Fond 214, op. 1, delo 28, fols. 80r–84v.

19. Soterios A. Mousalimas, "Shamans of Old in Southern Alaska," in *Shamans, Past and Present: Proceedings of the Symposium, 12th ICAE, 1988*, ed. Mihály Hoppál and Otto von Sadovszky (Budapest: Hungarian Academy of Sciences; Los Angeles: ISTOR, 1989), 307–316; idem, "Russian Orthodox Missionaries and Southern Alaskan Shamans: Interactions and Analysis," in *Russia in North America: Proceedings of the 2nd International Conference on Russian America, Sitka, Alaska, August 19–22, 1987*, ed. Richard A. Pierce (Kingston, Ontario; Fairbanks, Alaska: Limestone Press, 1990), 314–321; idem, "The Transition from Shamanism to Russian Orthodoxy in Alaska" (D.Phil., Faculty of Theology, University of Oxford, 1992); idem, *The Transition from Shamanism to Russian Orthodoxy in Alaska* (Providence, R.I.: Berghahn Books, 1995); idem, *From Mask to Icon: Transformation in the Arctic* (Brookline, Mass.: Holy Cross Orthodox Press, 2003); Michael Oleksa, ed., *Alaskan Missionary Spirituality* (New York and Mahwah, N.J.: Paulist Press, 1987), 10–11.

20. See Dauenhauer, "Education in Russian America," 155–163; Michael E. Krauss, "Alaska Native Languages in Russian America," in *Russian America: The Forgotten Frontier*, ed. Barbara S. Smith and Redmond J. Barnett (Tacoma: Washington State Historical Society, 1990), 205–213. A very important contribution, which includes instructions to priests by Bishop Innokentii (Veniaminov), is Barbara S. Smith, *Orthodoxy and Native Americans: The Alaska Mission*, Historical Society Occasional Papers, no. 1 (Syosset, N.Y.: St. Vladimir's Press for Historical Society, Orthodox Church in America, Crestwood, New York, 1980).

21. A most important work on syncretism in Alaska is Sergei Kan, *Symbolic Immortality: The Tlingit Potlatch of the Nineteenth Century* (Washington, D.C.: Smithsonian Institution Press, 1989). See also Kan's "Memory Eternal." On Orthodox-Yup'ik syncretism, see Ann Fienup-Riordan, "Selaviq: A Yup'ik Transformation of a Russian Orthodox Tradition," in *Eskimo Essays: Yup'ik Lives and How We See Them* (New Brunswick, N.J.: Rutgers University Press, 1990), 94–122; and idem,

"Following the Star: From the Ukraine to the Yukon," in *Russian America: The Forgotten Frontier*, ed. Barbara S. Smith and Redmond J. Barnett (Tacoma: Washington State Historical Society, 1990), 227–235; see also the film of Alexie Isaac, prod., "Following the Star" (Bethel, Alaska: KYUK-TV, 1987). A more general approach is taken by Ronald K. Inouye, "Starring and Slava: A Legacy of Russian America," in *Russia in North America: Proceedings of the 2nd International Conference on Russian America, Sitka, Alaska, August 19–22, 1987*, ed. Richard A. Pierce (Kingston, Ontario; Fairbanks, Alaska: Limestone Press, 1990), 358–378. No work has been done on syncretism in masking festivals, which are still held in Alaska between Orthodox Christmas and New Year (after the end of masking, participants purify themselves in the sweat bath and then go to communion). There is also no specialized study of correspondences in symbolic forms, though brief mentions are found in the literature. On correspondences in world view, especially in the spiritualization of nature, see Michael J. Oleksa, "Three Saints Bay and the Evolution of Aleut Identity," prepared for U.S. Department of Interior Heritage and Conservation Service, HCRS Village Histories Project, January 1981, revised and expanded March 1982. See also Lydia T. Black, "Religious Syncretism as Cultural Dynamic," in *Circumpolar Religion and Ecology: An Anthropology of the North*, ed. Takashi Irimoto and Takako Yamada (Tokyo: University of Tokyo, 1994), 213–220.

22. Shelikhov to Samoilov, 4 May 1786, in A. I. Andreev, ed., *Russkie otkrytiia* (1948), 199 (doc. 14), and Shelikhov to Governor General Iakobii, 19 April 1787, in ibid., 211 (doc. 18).
23. Shelikhov to Delarov, 30 August 1789, in ibid., 289 (doc. 31).
24. Pavlov, ed., *K istorii Rossiisko-amerikanskoi kompanii*, 35.
25. Russian State Historical Archive (RGIA), St. Petersburg, Fond 796, op. 74, delo 210, fols. 1r–2v.
26. Lydia T. Black, "Put' na Novyi Valaam"; idem, *Orthodoxy in Alaska: Christianization of Alaska; Veniaminov's Stewardship; Orthodoxy in Alaska after 1867*, Distinguished Lectures, no. 6 (Berkeley, Calif.: Patriarch Athenagoras Orthodox Institute at the Graduate Theological Union, 1998); A. L'vov, "Kratkiia istoricheskiia svedeniia ob uchrezhdenii v Severnoi Amerike pravoslavnoi missii, ob osnovanii Kad'iakskoi eparkhii i o deiatel'nosti tam pervykh missionerov," *Tserkovnyia vedomosti* 38, supplement (1894).
27. Russian State Naval Archive (RGAVMF), Papers of Count Kushelev, Fond 198, op. 1, delo 79, fol. 44v; on the death of Dmitrii Avdeev see Filip Kashevarov, [Answers to Kiril Khlebnikov's questions], fol. 8v; on Dmitrii Popov see Veniaminov, *Notes*, 234 n.
28. Shelikhov to Baranov, 9 August 1794, in A. I. Andreev, ed., *Russkie otkrytiia* (1948), 342; Russian State Historical Archive (RGIA), Fond 796, op. 74, delo 210, fols. 10r–10v.
29. Russian State Historical Archive (RGIA), Fond 796, op. 74, delo 210, fols. 37r–40v, *nastavlenie*; ibid., fols. 41–46, instruction.
30. Russian State Historical Archive (RGIA), Fond 796, op. 74, delo 210, fol. 49v.
31. Shelikhov to Baranov, 9 August 1794, in A. I. Andreev, ed., *Russkie otkrytiia* (1948), 336.
32. The list of these thirty families is in the Papers of Count Kushelev, Russian State Naval Archive (RGAVMF), Fond 1331, op. 4, delo 125, but the Kashevarovs are not listed; it is possible that the Kashevarovs were personal serfs of Golikov, and were not considered part of the "settler" party.
33. The Papers of Irkutsk Diocese Pertaining to the American Mission (in Russian State Historical Archive [RGIA], Fond 796, op. 74, delo 210) contain several references to lists of those baptized, those chrizmated, and of marriages performed, but the lists themselves are not in this file. In particular, such a list dated 18 November 1795 and received by the Bishop of Irkutsk and Nerchinsk 23 January 1796, is mentioned; similarly, there are references to a list brought in 1797 by Hieromonk Makarii, but neither list could be located. Further search of the archival materials pertaining to the mission is indicated.
34. Russian State Historical Archive (RGIA), Fond 796, op. 74, delo 210, fols. 211r–212v.
35. Baranov to Shelikhov, 20 May 1795, in Tikhmenev, *A History*, vol. 2, 71.
36. Makarii's letter to the Ruling Synod of the Orthodox Church, 5 October 1797, photostat of manuscript in the former Golder Collection, Russia: the Ruling Synod, Manuscript Division, Library

of Congress, Washington, D.C. The story of floggings for insufficient catch was told in August 1991 by Nikolai Galaktionoff of Unalaska at the Unalaska conference to commemorate the 250th anniversary of the Bering-Chirikov voyage of 1741.

37. Irkutsk State Regional Archive, Papers of the Irkutsk Consistory, Fond 50, op. 7, bundle 12, delo 55, fol. 4.

38. Response to Emperor Paul's instructions, Kodiak Office to Navigator Petrov, 12 October 1802, in Tikhmenev, *A History*, vol. 2, 132–134.

39. Russian State Historical Archive (RGIA), Fond 796, op. 74, delo 210, fol. 199, 13 October 1797. One wonders if this is not a pointer to the fact that Shelikhov's heirs had Paul's ear. For Instruction to Ioasaf, see fols. 201–202. Ioasaf's reply is his description of Kodiak Island, preserved in several manuscript copies in various archives, including the Russian State Historical Archive (RGIA), Fond 796, delo 210, fols. 225–243 (each page countersigned by Ioasaf); Russian State Naval Archive (RGAVMF), Papers of Count Kushelev; the von Asch Papers, University of Göttingen, Germany; and the Yudin Collection, Manuscript Division, Library of Congress. An abridged version was published anonymously in 1805 in Russian; for an English translation of the latter, see Black, "Konyag," 79–87.

40. Ioasaf to Shelikhov, 18 May 1795, Yudin Collection, Manuscript Division, Library of Congress, Washington, D.C.

41. The entrenched notion that Iuvenalii was killed in the Iliamna Lake area by Athabaskans rests on faulty sources, notably on a spurious "journal" attributed to Iuvenalii but in actuality a falsification by Ivan Petroff, then assistant to the historian Hubert H. Bancroft. See Lydia T. Black, "The Daily Journal of Reverend Father Juvenal: A Cautionary Tale," *Ethnohistory* 28, no. 1 (Winter 1981): 33–58. For citation of documentary evidence and Yup'ik oral tradition about the killing of Iuvenalii at Quinhagak, see Michael J. Oleksa, "The Death of Hieromonk Juvenaly," *St. Vladimir Theological Quarterly* 30, no. 3 (1986): 231–268; and idem, "The Death of Hieromonk Juvenaly," in *Russia in North America: Proceedings of the 2nd International Conference on Russian America, Sitka, Alaska, August 19–22, 1987*, ed. Richard A. Pierce (Kingston, Ontario; Fairbanks, Alaska: Limestone Press, 1990), 322–357.

42. Baranov to Larionov, 24 July 1800, in Tikhmenev, *A History*, vol. 2, 115–116, 118 (doc. 29).

43. Baranov to Larionov, 24 July 1800, in ibid., 121 (doc. 30).

44. Baranov to Larionov, 22 March 1801, in ibid., 124 (doc. 31).

45. Ibid., 124–127 (doc. 31).

46. Rezanov to Board of Directors, 6 November 1805, in Tikhmenev, *A History*, vol. 2, 167–169 (doc. 42); Gideon, *Round the World Voyage*, 72–101, 106–112. On Gedeon's commission, see ibid., 128–130. On misappropriation of church funds advanced by the synod (in care of Rezanov) see ibid., 144–146.

47. The treasury calculated that the company owed it 16,004 rubles and 8¾ kopeks of moneys issued for the mission and embezzled (Russian State Historical Archive [RGIA], Fond 797, op. 104, delo 1266, fols. 1r–1v, and ibid., delo 5447, fols. 1r–58v).

48. A brief acquaintance with this monk left such an impression on the young Lt. Ianovskii, who by his own admission was a liberal thinker tinged with anticlericalism, that in later life Ianovskii himself became a monk and wrote extensively about Father Herman. Among the people, beliefs grew about Father Herman's benevolent powers to heal, to stop a tidal wave, to save the people from forest fire, to predict the future. He was called a saint by the people long before the church recognized him as such. The icon of this man, protector of the Natives, caretaker of the sick during the most severe epidemics, helper of those in need, always there when one needed spiritual help, will be found today in every Orthodox home in Alaska.

    Frank A. Golder was the first to call Herman a saint in print; see his *Father Herman: Alaska's Saint* (Platina, Calif.: Orthodox Christian Books and Icons, 1910; reprint, San Francisco: Orthodox Christian Books and Icons, 1968). The most recent "life" of St. Herman is Sergei Korsun's *Prepodobnyi German Aliaskinskii: Zhizneopisanie* (Jordonville, N.Y.: Holy Trinity Monastery, 2002). For other references see Vsevolod Rochcau, *St. Herman of Alaska and the Defense of Alaskan Native Peoples*, offprint from *St. Vladimir Theological Seminary* 16, no. 1 (1972); Ann Elizabeth Williams, "Father Herman: Syncretic Symbol of Divine Legitimation" (master's thesis, University of Alaska Fairbanks, 1993); and Mousalimas, "The Transition from Shamanism to Russian Orthodoxy" (1992). See also a novel by Edward Opheim, a resident of Spruce Island, *Old Mike of Monk's Lagoon* (New York: Vantage Press, 1981).

49. Russian State Historical Archive (RGIA), Fond 797, op. 2, delo 4928, fols. 1–14.

50. Glorified in 1977, St. Innocent is revered by the Aleuts as their spiritual father to this day. In 1975, Father Ismael Gromoff, an Aleut of St. Paul Island, writing for the children of Unalaska about Veniaminov's life and his death in Moscow, said: "Did he think of his children, our Father, in his great age and blindness? Did he remember us living here on our green islands?" Aleuts certainly remember him. For a concise biography of St. Innocent in English, see Lydia Black, ed., *A Good and Faithful Servant: The Year of Saint Innocent, an Exhibit Commemorating the Bicentenial of the Birth of Ioann Veniaminov, 1797–1997* (Fairbanks: University of Alaska Fairbanks and Alaska State Veniaminov Bicentennial Committee, 1997).

51. Father Iakov Netsvetov is now acknowledged to be one of Alaska's Orthodox saints. His glorification was celebrated in Anchorage in October of 1994.

52. Lydia T. Black, "Ivan Pan'kov: An Architect of Aleut Literacy," *Arctic Anthropology* 14, no. 1 (1977): 94–107, reprinted with an addendum in *Orthodox Alaska* 7, no. 4 (Fall 1978): 1–33, and in *Interpreting Alaska's History*, ed. M. Mangusso and Stephen Haycox (Anchorage: Alaska Pacific University Press, 1989), 86–109.

53. Veniaminov's handwritten translation into Russian of his original composition in Aleut is preserved in the Alaska State Historical Library, Juneau.

54. Richard L. Dauenhauer, "The Spiritual Epiphany of Aleut" (Alaska Native Foundation, Center for Equality of Opportunity in Schooling, September 1978), reprinted in *Orthodox Alaska* 8, no. 1 (1979): 13–42.

55. A good summary is provided by Michael Oleksa in part 3 of his *Orthodox Alaska: A Theology of Mission* (Crestwood, N.Y.: St. Vladimir's Seminary Press, 1992).

56. See, for example, Albert E. Watkins, "A Historical Study of the Russian Orthodox Church in Alaska" (master's thesis, University of Alaska Fairbanks, Dept. of Education, 1961), "Conclusions," especially p. 122.

57. Wendell H. Oswalt, *Mission of Change in Alaska: Eskimos and Moravians on the Kuskokwim* (San Marino, Calif.: Huntington Library, 1963); idem, *Bashful No Longer: An Alaskan Eskimo Ethnohistory, 1778–1988* (Norman: University of Oklahoma Press, 1990); Martha L. McCollough, "Yup'ik Responses to Russian Orthodoxy and Moravian Missionaries in the Lower Kuskokwim Region of Southwestern Alaska" (master's thesis, University of Alaska Fairbanks, 1988).

58. A. V. Grinev, *Indeitsy tlinkity v period Russkoi Ameriki (1741–1867 gg.)* (Novosibirsk: Izdatel'stvo "Nauka," 1991), 227–232.

59. Sergei Kan, "Russian Orthodox Missionaries," and idem, "Russian Orthodox Brotherhoods."

60. Joseph Riley, prod., "Legacy of Faith: The Russian Orthodox Church in Alaska" (Fairbanks, Alaska: KUAC-TV, 1987).

61. Robert R. Rathburn, "The Russian Orthodox Church: A Mechanism for Maintaining Ethnic Identity" (master's thesis, Sacramento State College, California, 1970); idem, "The Russian Orthodox Church as a Native Institution among the Koniag Eskimo of Kodiak Island, Alaska," *Arctic Anthropology* 18, no. 1 (1981): 12–22; Nancy Yaw Davis, "The Role of the Russian Orthodox Church in Five Pacific Eskimo Villages as Revealed by the Earthquake," in *The Great Alaska Earthquake of 1964: Human Ecology*, National Research Council, Division of Earth Sciences, Committee on the Alaska Earthquake (Washington, D.C.: National Academy of Sciences, 1970), 125–146; idem, "Contemporary Pacific Eskimo," in *Arctic*, ed. David Damas, vol. 5 of *Handbook of North American Indians*, ed. William C. Sturtevant (Washington, D.C.: Smithsonian Institution, 1984), 198–204;

Edward Hosley, "The Kolchan Athapaskans of the Upper Kuskokwim," 1966, Rasmuson Library, University of Alaska Fairbanks.

62. Patriarch of Moscow and all Russia Alexii II visited Anchorage, Kodiak, and Sitka, Alaska. Services were held in Aleut, Tlingit, Yup'ik, Slavonic, and English. Church-related items by Native artists were presented as gifts to the patriarch: an icon of St. Herman of Alaska, executed in beadwork by Old Harbor Alutiiq artist Eleanor Naumoff; maniples and epitrachelion, which the patriarch wore celebrating vespers, by the Tlingit master bead embroidery artist Emma Marks; a toion staff carved from driftwood with an ivory knob in the shape of a seal head by a young Aleut carver; and a carved ivory cross by a self-taught Yup'ik ivory carver.

FIGURE 84. Nicholas I (1796–1855), emperor of Russia 1825–1855. The period of his rule is believed by many to have been Russian America's "golden age."

Courtesy Slavic and Baltic Division, New York Public Library, Astor, Lenox, and Tilden Foundations.

Chapter Fourteen

The Company Under the Three Charters

1799–1862

The Russian-American Company operated "Under the Patronage of His Imperial Majesty" since the First Charter granted in 1799 by Emperor Paul. Implicit was the understanding that in return for the monopoly to the rights of usufruct in the American territory claimed by Russia and in the Kuril archipelago, the Russian-American Company would serve not merely its pure commercial interests but also the interests of the state.

The First Charter was formulated on the basis of an agreement concluded in 1798 between the main shareholders of the Golikov-Shelikhov Company (foremost among whom was Natalia Shelikhov) and the Myl'nikov Company. The charter contained eleven points outlining the privileges granted, which included the definition of the territory where the company was authorized to conduct its business to the exclusion of all other parties and the right to expand this territory south of latitude 55°, and specified that the rights of usufruct extended not only to the surface resources (including timber, elsewhere not permitted to be cut without admiralty authorization), but also subsurface, that is, mineral rights. The second part of the official documents signed by Emperor Paul contained the very few regulations under which the company was to operate. These concerned mostly eligibility for buying into the company (all citizens of the empire were eligible to do so), capital, the original number of shares to be put up for public sale, and the seat of the main office (Irkutsk).

All documents pertaining to the formation of the company were made public through the Ruling Senate in St. Petersburg 19 July 1799 and in Moscow on 11 August 1799. On 2 December 1799, Emperor Paul confirmed Rezanov, whose title was now "Actual State Councillor," as company correspondent authorized to represent the company before government agencies. The charter, privileges, and regulations, as amended on recommendations of the ministry of commerce (valuation of shares at 500 rubles, transfer of the main office to St. Petersburg approved 19 October 1800), were confirmed by Emperor Alexander I in August of 1801. He was the first member of the imperial family to buy twenty shares, for a contribution of 10,000 rubles, to "express support for this very valuable enterprise." The shares held by members of the imperial family were assigned to charity for the benefit of the needy. After the privileges and regulations were confirmed by Alexander I following his accession to the throne, all documents were published in 1802.[1] The charter was valid for twenty years.

Emperor Alexander I renewed the company's privileges on 13 September 1821 for another twenty years, "with appropriate supplements and amendments."[2] These amended privileges were outlined in twenty paragraphs (versus the eleven of the First Charter). The territory within which the company held exclusive right of usufruct was specified in greater detail, to include the northern extremity of Vancouver Island, at 51° N latitude, Bering Strait, all the islands along the Eastern Siberian seaboard and along the Kurils to the island of Urup at 45°50' N. The company was still empowered to explore beyond these limits, but could not establish settlements outside of the specified territorial extent without imperial permission. Access to the territory by foreigners was forbidden. Maritime trade could be conducted by the company in the territory of foreign nations, except China: "the Company ships may not stop at her coasts."

Rights of employees eligible to perform state services were outlined in detail. Promotion rights of those employees who belonged to classes not eligible for such service, but who held positions of authority within the company, were also specified. The company had the right, as under its previous charter, to recruit employees throughout Russia who were free citizens (not serfs), was empowered to obtain passports of one to seven years' validity for the hired men, but was obliged to pay the local and state taxes for each employee. The company could not be compelled to repatriate to Russia either employees whose contracts expired but who wished to remain in America, or those employees who were in debt to the company. However, the company had to submit written documentation that the employees agreed to remain in further service in America out of their free will. If the company found an employee guilty of a violation of labor discipline, the management could bring the case to a court of law, where imperial laws would be applied, but the employees had the right of appeal to the Ruling Senate within six months of a court's ruling. The company was required to provide its employees with both winter and summer quarters which were healthy and convenient. The company was obligated at all times to provide its employees with subsistence so that "there is no lack in food or clothing." The company was obligated to provide health care, the services of trained physicians, and medicines. The company was obligated to keep track of children born of lawful unions between Russians and Natives, and when the employee left America, his family, including all the children, was to be repatriated to Russia with him.

The regulations governing company activities were considerably expanded (to seventy articles) and there was a special section dealing with the government's supervision of company activities. Company obligations to the government were outlined in articles thirty-five through sixty-two. While the company was obligated to preserve the integrity of the territory, it was to avoid any actions that could jeopardize Russia's relations with foreign powers. Treaties concluded with various foreign powers were to be scrupulously observed. In any matters involving foreign powers that were not strictly of local colonial interest, the company was to defer to the government. The company was to be mindful of state interests and act strictly within the regulations contained in the charter. The company was to report to the imperial government through, and be accountable to, the minister of finance. The company was obligated to maintain, at all times, a sufficient number of priests and church-servitors to serve the needs of the people under its jurisdiction and establish and maintain church buildings wherever a number of Russian subjects were in residence.

The status of the creoles (discussed above in chapter 12) was defined. The Natives inhabiting the archipelagos within the territory were recognized as imperial subjects, on the same basis as all other Russian citizens. They were considered as constituting a special estate "as long as they reside in the colonies and as long as they have not acquired membership in another estate through personal achievement or through other circumstances" (art. 43). They were free of all state taxes, iasak, or any other state obligations. The company was strictly forbidden to demand any of those (except limited labor service against recompense as defined in art. 51). The company was to keep records of population fluctuations and of the number of people who accepted baptism, and was to report these statistics to the government. Article forty-seven specified: "The islanders are governed by their own lineage chiefs under supervision of the leaders [*starshiny*] selected by the company *from among the best of their Russian employees*" (emphasis added). The leaders' duties (art. 48) included dispute settlement, dealing with complaints, and rendering aid in case of need, jointly if circumstances demanded. The company was obligated to ensure that the islanders had ample land for their needs and was to demonstrate the "advantages of [settled?] community life and means to enjoy the same." Article fifty stated: "Everything of which an islander is possessed, through his own labors, inheritance, bought or obtained in trade, constitutes his inalienable property and anyone attempting to dispossess him or offer him personal insult is to be prosecuted to the fullest extent of the law." The islanders, however, were required to serve the company in sea mammal procurement (art. 51). But there were restrictions, in several aspects the same as those which applied to the draft of free peasantry for military service in Russia. The company was authorized to demand services from no more than fifty percent of the males in the age bracket of eighteen to fifty years. The hunters were to be recruited by the village chiefs from families that included more than one able-bodied male "so as not to leave wives and children without help and subsistence." The term of service could not exceed three years. The company was obligated to provide all Native men in its service with clothing, food, and boats and to pay them for the animals they obtained at a minimum of no less than one-fifth of what was paid in previous times to Russians for each animal skin. If a Native desired to remain in company employ for a longer term, the company was permitted to hire him on mutually agreed terms. Women and adolescents below the age of eighteen could be hired only by mutual agreement for a set wage. Natives not in company employ retained fishing and hunting rights and their catch became their inalienable property. They could sell the catch, but the furs could be sold only to the company in accordance with a price schedule approved by the government.

The Natives occupying Alaska's mainland coasts and interior were treated somewhat differently. The regulations stated that, as the company's main business was fur procurement, there was no need to penetrate the interior or subjugate the people who inhabited the mainland coasts. Any factories (posts) the company wished to establish to enhance trade with the aboriginal peoples were to be built only with their express consent. Their independence was not to be violated or threatened, and the company was held responsible for maintaining good relations. The company was expressly forbidden to demand from the aboriginal peoples any tribute, iasak, tax, or any other form of involuntary giving. Under no circumstances were hostages to be taken by force. The government recognized that hostage giving existed because of a previously established custom. If any hostages were offered voluntarily, they were to be maintained well and not offered any insults or injuries. Any people who wished to move to Russian establishments were to be permitted to do so.

As far as government oversight was concerned, this was the province of the minister of finance. This official was responsible for taking immediate action should the company in any way violate any of the terms of the charter or the regulations. He was also responsible for dealing with other ministries which might have differences with the company. The government did not deem it necessary at this point to establish governmental agencies in the colonies. To ensure compliance with the regulations and to effect oversight, therefore, the chief manager of the colony had to be appointed from among senior naval officers, to serve for five years. Article sixty-eight specified particular concerns of the government with respect to colonial affairs that the chief manager had to address:

1. Is anyone being detained in the Colonies against his will?
2. Do the employees receive all to which they are entitled by the terms of their contracts?
3. Do they receive from the company all assistance to which they are entitled and how does the company treat them? [Poor treatment of employees was expected to be rectified.]
4. Does the company treat the aboriginal inhabitants, creoles and independent neighboring peoples as prescribed?
5. Does the company have clandestine forbidden relations with foreign vessels or powers?

In all of the above, the government assigned oversight responsibility to the chief manager. For this reason he could not participate in any commerce whatsoever, but would enjoy an appropriate salary set by the company.

Naval vessels dispatched from Russian ports to Alaska were authorized to carry company cargo. Their captains were to report to the chief manager. The captains of such naval vessels were authorized to seize any foreign vessels illegally trading in the Russian territories. All naval personnel were forbidden to engage in any trade.

Though the exclusive right to exploit Alaska's resources was extended, the obligations imposed on the company to provide social services to its employees and restrictions imposed in regard to use of Native labor had grown considerably. This trend continued when the charter was renewed for the third time in 1841 by Emperor Nicholas I.[3] The charter went into effect 1 January 1842 and was valid for another twenty years. New, contemporary bylaws were established, passed by the minister of finance, and approved by the emperor. The territory that the company had the right to exploit was now defined in accordance with the international treaties of 1824 and 1825 with the United States and Great Britain, respectively. The company's accountability to the finance minister, and specifically the responsibilities and accountability of the main office, were spelled out in detail. Colonial management was outlined in a separate chapter (ch. 7). A colonial managerial council was created to serve under the chief manager. The latter was to be a senior naval officer, selected from a slate of candidates and confirmed by the emperor. With respect to naval vessels calling at the colony, his status was that of a port commander. With respect to military officers, the relative rank was operable. The right of company vessels to call at foreign ports was expanded to include five Chinese harbors, among them Canton and Shanghai, provided no opium whatsoever was on board.

A significant new departure was an attempt to deal with administration of the law. As before, in all major criminal cases (felonies), preliminary investigation was to be conducted by the colonial managerial council or by a special commission appointed in each case. The findings, the accused, evidence, and witnesses, if warranted, were to be dispatched to the nearest location in metropolitan Russia where there were regular courts. Misdemeanors were to be handled by the chief manager when needed, with assistance of the council or of a special commission. If the accused was found guilty, the chief manager was to impose punishment. These punishments were outlined in article 153: (1) reprimand; (2) severe reprimand; (3) salary reduction; (4) assignment to a less desirable, less important position; (5) dismissal; (6) deportation to Russia prior to expiration of contract.

In general, the chief manager's sphere of authority was spelled out (art. 150) and limitations to his power and authority were stated. Specifically, the chief manager could not change wages and salaries and payments for furs without approval by the main office. His duties were prescribed and priorities stated. Foremost was the duty to maintain the integrity of the colonial territory, defend its borders, and deal with border disputes observing the ground rules according to all foreign treaties. The chief manager's second duty was to protect the rights and property of all individuals in the territory. He was also responsible for ensuring the rights of company employees. As before, no one could be detained in the colony against his will, and all contractual obligations were to be fulfilled. In addition, the chief manager was made responsible for preventing excessive employee indebtedness to the company. He was also responsible for protection of the rights of the aboriginal peoples: they were not to be oppressed or violated in any manner, and, in addition, the chief manager was made responsible for measures to be taken to improve their condition and avoid degradation. In the latter category was the introduction of luxury items incompatible with the aboriginal lifestyle and which could lead to the abandonment of age-old customary skills, crafts, and practices that served the population well. This provision was roundly criticized in the Russian press in the subsequent polemic about the company's role with respect to the aboriginal peoples. One government inspector, for example, criticized insufficiency of bread distribution to the Natives. It was taken for granted that they would much prefer bread to the "stinking and repulsive" dried fish—a food considered a delicacy even today.

Exemplary behavioral standards were prescribed. The chief manager was also made responsible for providing to the employees suitable recreational opportunities and activities. He was to be held accountable for the maintenance in appropriate condition of churches, hospitals, schools, mills, barracks, storage, and other structures. He was to see to it that the education of children was conducted in a manner that would "truly benefit the younger generation." Moral and value standards were understood under this rubric, but, remarkably, this article spelled out that the educational program was not to neglect aboriginal skills such as the handling of small watercraft, particularly kayaks, and shooting of both rifles and bows and arrows.

The status of the chief manager was for the first time defined vis-à-vis outsiders: it was that of a civilian provincial governor.

Chapter eight of the charter defined the various ranks the government recognized among the colony's populations, both immigrant labor and Native. For Russians hired by the company, colonial service was equated with that of active state duty, including military service. For these reasons the company was once again authorized to hire free and state peasants, over twenty-one years of age, or, in provinces where a lottery was employed to select draftees, those who were by this means freed of military service. Aboriginal peoples within the area in the colony where settlements were founded were to be called "settled peoples of different origin" (inorodtsy). Outside of this immediate area, aboriginal peoples who were Christians carried no special designation. The non-Christians were called "peoples of different faith" (inovertsy). All were considered Russian subjects, on a par with all the peoples of Russia. They enjoyed the protection of the laws and had the obligation to obey the same. They were free of all taxation and state services, except that they could sell furs only to the company. A significant difference was the regulation stating that while the aboriginal communities were to be governed by their own chiefs, superintended by "the best of the Russian employees" (a wording essentially unchanged from the Second Charter), the chief manager was given the power to choose chiefs, and the office of the chief was defined as nonhereditary. Chiefs who served in that capacity for fifteen years or more carried the title of chief (toion) lifelong, even in retirement. How this regulation was applied is not clear. The evidence suggests that very seldom did the chief manager invoke the power to choose, and never arbitrarily. Usually, he confirmed in office chiefs who were chosen by their communities. Section five dealt with "peoples of different origin" who were independent of colonial administration. They were entitled to ask the colonial management for protection and defense. If asked, the management was under obligation to provide such assistance. The company was prohibited from expanding its settlements into their territories. The relationship with them was limited to that of trade, the barter of European goods for local products. If it was deemed necessary to have a trading outpost, such outpost could be established only with the express consent of the local peoples. No tribute of any kind was to be demanded or accepted. And finally, trade in alcohol and firearms was expressly forbidden. Alcohol in limited quantity, one shot glass at most, was permitted to be offered to honored guests at meals, feasts, and entertainments.

The stress on defense and maintenance of territorial integrity was dictated, no doubt, by the changing international situation. Particularly, Russian relations with Great Britain had been deteriorating since the 1820s. Russian and British interests clashed in the Middle East, the Mediterranean, in Persia (now Iran) and Afghanistan, in Central Asia (as Britain feared Russian penetration into India), and in the Far East where Britain was engaged in penetrating China, eventually resulting in the Opium Wars. The Chinese situation dictated a renewed Russian interest in the Lower Amur region and Sakhalin Island. A rapprochement with the United States was desirable, particularly since the U.S. annexation of Oregon and then California in the 1840s and the emergence of the United States as a Pacific power. In many aspects governmental and company interests regarding international relations were in harmony, but in others, these interests were significantly divergent.

Company activities were not limited to Alaska. The company owned and operated trading posts and offices in Kamchatka and on the Okhotsk Sea, where between 1840 and 1845 its navigators were instrumental in transferring the port facilities from Okhotsk to Aian, and the company spearheaded the surveying and establishment of a land route from Yakutsk to Aian. It also conducted fur sealing operations in the Shantar Islands, as well as sea otter hunting in the Kurils. Thus, company navigators had been active in exploration and charting of the Okhotsk Sea coasts for several decades in tandem with the explorations conducted by the Russian navy. Naturally, the Amur estuary did not escape their attention. P. T. Koz'min, in command of the company vessel *Aktsiia*, explored and charted the southwestern shores of the Sea of Okhotsk in 1829–1831. This work was continued in later years. A. M. Gavrilov charted the Bay of Aian and explored the Amur delta in 1845–1846. This was followed up in 1848–1849 by a naval expedition under the command of Captain G. I. Nevel'skoi and by the later Amur expedition of 1850–1855, when N. K. Boshniak founded Emperor Nicholas I Harbor (formerly called Imperatorskaia and then Sovetskaia Gavan').[4] From 1847 on, the moving power in Russian imperial expansion on the Amur was N. N. Murav'iev (Murav'iev-Amurskii). In 1849, a special committee authorized a navy expedition to explore and chart the delta. The government proposed to use the Russian-American Company for the preliminary investigation of the feasibility of Russian navigation along the Amur River in order not to arouse suspicions of aggression on the part of the Chinese government. The post established by Nevel'skoi in 1850 at the mouth of the Amur was also to be presented as a trading post of the Russian-American Company.[5] Count Nesselrode, Russia's foreign minister and state chancellor, instructed the company on the ends sought and means to be employed and directed Murav'iev, governor-general of eastern Siberia, to assist the company. In 1853, the Russian-American Company, at the government's urging, with assistance and cooperation from the navy, established a Russian presence through occupation on Sakhalin Island.[6] In the 1850s, the company actively supported navy expeditions to Japan under Admiral Putiatin (1852–1855 and 1858–1859), which resulted in the conclusion of formal treaties between Japan and Russia. The treaty concluded by Putiatin in 1858 "governed relations between Russia and Japan until 1904."[7] Company activities in the Amur region, however, were terminated soon after the end of the Crimean War.[8]

A naval patrol was authorized 29 January 1849 in the Sea of Okhotsk to keep an eye on foreign shipping but especially to be on the lookout for British presence. The management of the Russian-American Company had been requesting naval patrols in the North Pacific (the Bering and Okhotsk seas) since the early 1840s. While the government was concerned with the growth of British power in China and feared British expansion into the North Pacific, the company was mostly concerned with the massive presence of American whaling vessels. In 1835, Captain Folger, commanding the vessel *Ganges* out of Nantucket, was whaling off the island of Kodiak, where he took the first Pacific right whales (initiating what a U.S. Commissioner of Fish and Fisheries in 1878 called "the Golden Age" of American whaling).[9] By 1841, at least fifty American vessels were taking whales in what the company considered Russian waters, and in 1842 more than 200 American whalers were reported in waters off the eastern Aleutians and Alaska Peninsula, both on the Pacific and Bering Sea sides.[10] The Northwest Coast (southern Alaska) whaling grounds became in that decade the most important field exploited by American whalers. By 1843, Americans were taking bowhead whales off the Kamchatkan coast. In 1845, 263 American whaling vessels "were fishing exclusively in seas under the jurisdiction of the Russian-American Company while about 200 vessels visited the Sea of Okhotsk annually."[11] In 1848, Roys, in command of the *Superior*, sailed through Bering Strait (using Russian charts he had purchased in Kamchatka three years earlier) and opened the rich bowhead whaling fishery in the Arctic.[12] The next year, 154 American whaling vessels sailed through Bering Strait.

The Russian-American Company and the Russian government had cause to worry. The whalers, not above poaching fur seals en route to or from the arctic whaling grounds or trading with Natives, also took valuable walrus ivory in the north, in the process slaughtering enormous numbers of walrus. Soon they had established trading networks in the north, dispensing alcohol and firearms, and in some measure syphoning off the flow of fur goods from the Alaskan interior. Of particular concern to the company, Yankee whalers put in at Chamisso Island, Kotzebue Sound, a point from which the Russians reached the Native trading fair on the Buckland River. They also were putting in at St. Lawrence Island and along the coast of the Chukchi Peninsula and developing extensive trade with the local Eskimos and Chukchi. English names were bestowed on bays, coastal features, and settlements on the Chukchi Peninsula, and soon Americans began to establish outposts on its shores. This American influence was to continue well into the twentieth century.

Thus, the Russian government's concerns about infringement of its territorial rights in this area, and not only by the Americans, were well grounded. British naval vessels had become active in Bering Strait and along Alaska's arctic shore in the course of the so-called Franklin Search. The famous British explorer of the Arctic, Sir John Franklin, had sailed on his last expedition in 1845 in the continuous search for the Northwest Passage. After two harrowing winters in the high Arctic and Franklin's death in 1847, the expedition's survivors abandoned their two ships in April 1848. None of them reached safety. The search for the two vessels, begun in 1847, would continue for well over a decade. In 1848, HMS *Herald* (commanded by Captain Kellett) arrived at Petropavlovsk on Kamchatka and sailed for Norton Sound, Alaska, and from there to Kotzebue Sound. Kellett left the Arctic in the fall and sailed south along the coast of South America, then in May 1849 to Hawaii, and from there returned to the Bering Strait region. The *Herald* was joined there by her consort, the *Plover*, Captain Moore commanding. In 1850, four more British vessels were in Russian waters, among them the *Enterprise*, Captain Collinson commanding. By the end of July the *Enterprise* passed the Aleutians, on 11 August sighted St. Lawrence Island, and continued northward to Cape Lisburne and then to Wainwright, to rendezvous with the *Herald* and the *Plover*. Collinson linked up with Moore of the *Plover* in Grantley Harbor and also with the *Herald*. Collinson instructed Moore to visit St. Lawrence Bay on the Chukchi Peninsula and St. Lawrence Island each season. The *Investigator*, Captain McClure commanding, also met with the *Herald* and the *Plover*. During these voyages, purportedly as part of their search, the British were dispatching shore parties. The Russians took a rather cynical view of the humanitarian aims of this prolonged activity in their territory, which included charting and mapping. They rather suspected that the real goal of the British navy captains was geopolitical reconnaissance and tried to keep an eye on their doings by sending a vessel of their own to Kotzebue Sound and beyond, and also through the Native personnel whom the British borrowed as guides, kayakers, etc. In fact, the concern was so great that a detailed chart showing the tracks of British vessels participating in the Franklin search in Alaskan waters was included in the company's annual report. The British questioning about trading conditions, relations with the Natives, and other aspects of Russian operations in the north aroused suspicions even among the local managers, such as the manager of the St. Michael outpost on Norton Sound.[13]

In any case, the Russian-American Company by 1845 was pressing for a patrol vessel. The company was ready to provide a vessel, but requested from the government the right for the ship to fly the imperial navy flag. This request was refused, though the Russian government informed the United States that a sea patrol was being instituted in view of the American whalers' violations of earlier international agreements signed by the two countries. Vandalism and violence by shore parties is believed to have been widespread. Etholen, acting on his own in 1843, dispatched an armed company vessel "to supervise" American whalers off Kodiak.[14] The company captains assigned to this duty were repeatedly warned, as was the chief manager, to handle matters carefully and not to provoke any international incidents (the three-mile territorial limit was at the time in the process of becoming the standard advocated by maritime powers who argued for "freedom of the sea"). The navy provided estimates for the equipment and maintenance of a cruiser, the costs to be borne by the company; the company found the cost prohibitive. In the matter of naval patrols in the Bering Sea and off the coast of Alaska, the company and the government were far apart. Only in 1850 did the navy order the corvette *Olivutsa* to Alaskan waters. In the end, in 1853, the government instructed the naval patrol vessels that they had only a watching brief and were merely to prevent the whalers from entering inner bays or from whaling nearer than three Italian miles offshore.[15]

In addition to the complicated international situation, the company was facing the need to reorient itself to a very different economic situation worldwide. Fur procurement alone could not sustain the company's profitability under market conditions of the mid-nineteenth century. The collapse of the China market in the wake of the Opium Wars, the competition—perhaps one could say dominance—of the Hudson's Bay Company in the European markets (except in the sale of fur seal skins in London and the United States), and the Crimean War (when shipment of furs from Alaska to Russia was not possible), all dictated that alternative resources be exploited. The company paid ever-increasing attention to mineral exploration and began to develop alternative enterprises such as timber, coal, and commercial fishing and whaling.

Earlier, the company had undertaken to introduce a whaling industry in the colony and in 1833 had invited an American, Thomas Barton, to organize this enterprise. He was based in Kodiak, and had no more than indifferent success. In 1846, establishment of the Russian whale fishery found support among government officials of eastern Siberia, and on 13 December 1850 a whaling subsidiary of the Russian-American Company came into being. It was called the Russian-Finnish Whaling Company (*Rossiisko-Finliandskaia kitolovnaia kompaniia*) with headquarters at Abo (modern Turku) in Finland. They outfitted the first whaling vessel, the *Suomi*, in the summer of 1851. A company representative was sent to Bremen to study whaling port facilities with the object of identifying and then establishing all that was needed at Abo. An American whaling boat, with a complete set of whaling equipment, was purchased as a model for boat and equipment development. The *Suomi* whaled in the Sea of Okhotsk in 1852 and 1853, returning to Bremen on 5 April 1854. The skipper, unaware that the Crimean War had broken out, barely escaped capture in an English port. Because the management was uncertain about the international situation and concerned with the duration of the war, the vessel was sold. A second vessel, the *Turku*, had been launched in 1852. In 1854, she put in at Petropavlovsk, where she wintered, and in 1855 sailed for Kodiak and then to Novo-Arkhangel'sk, seeking safety from French and British naval vessels. This vessel returned to Bremen in 1857. A third vessel, the *Aian*, sailed in 1853 and whaled out of Hawaii, sailing to Kamchatka in 1854. She was captured and burned with her entire cargo by the British and French in Avacha Bay. After the war the whaling company built another vessel, the *Count Berg*, several subsidiary vessels stationed in the Sea of Okhotsk, and some so-called shore whaling stations. Nevertheless, all the operations of this whaling subsidiary had little, if any, impact on the economy of Russian Alaska.[16]

Trade with Hawaii was revived at this time. Wood products, timber, and fish were shipped to Hawaii, and beginning in 1849 some Russian manufactured goods were sent also. Sugar, molasses, and salt in quantity were brought from Hawaii. Salt was even supplied to Kamchatka via Alaska. However, this trade was interrupted by the Crimean War, as was the whale fishery, and in later years only fish was shipped to Hawaii. The outlook for trade with American California was also good. In 1848, surplus goods were shipped from Alaska to San Francisco, where they were marketed without any trouble. American businessmen also looked toward establishing trade with Russia's American possession. The most profitable proved to be the ice trade. The first contract for ice shipments to California was concluded in 1851 with the Union Ice Company. The following year, 250 tons of Novo-Arkhangel'sk ice were sold to the California Ice Company at $75 per ton and shipped to San Francisco. In 1853, the American-Russian Commercial Company was incorporated in San Francisco for the Alaska trade. This company, "possibly a blind for provisioning Alaska during the Crimean War, worked through the great Russian-American Company" according to twentieth-century commentator Richard O. Cummings, was responsible for constructing ice storage facilities at Novo-Arkhangel'sk, for providing ice-cutting machinery, and for loading the ice on vessels. From the beginning, the Russians realized that no dependable ice supply could be obtained on Sitka (Baranof Island), and therefore ice production was established on Woody Island, off Kodiak, beginning in 1852.[17] In 1868, the Russian-American Company sold its interest in the ice company to Hutchinson, Kohl, and Company, forerunner of the Alaska Commercial Company. Ice production continued at Woody Island through 1879 and possibly the effort went on at reduced capacity as late as 1890.[18]

Coal deposits had been known to exist in various coastal regions of Alaska since the eighteenth century. For a time, coal deposits on Unga were worked to provide fuel for Russian-American Company steamers and for use in Sitka. But only one deposit, that in Cook Inlet, was exploited by the Russians for export. In 1852, mining engineer Doroshin specifically tested the quality of various coal deposits and recommended that they be exploited commercially. In 1853, Enoch Hjalmar Furuhjelm, educated in Germany at the prestigious Freiberg School of Mines, joined the Russian-American Company and went to Alaska to develop the coal industry. In 1854, Beverley Sanders, American businessman, negotiated in St. Petersburg a twenty-year agreement which expanded the Alaska commerce to include timber, coal, and fish.[19] By 1859, Coal Village on English Bay, where coal deposits had been found in 1786, was a bustling, busy town with twenty dwellings, a church, stables, cattle yards, blacksmith shop, foundry, sawmill, and various subsidiary structures. For a short while it became the third-largest Russian establishment in Alaska. Annual production of coal was 5,000 tons. The workers were free hired laborers; the myth that convicts in chains worked the mines there can be traced once again to that indefatigable inventor of historical fictions, Ivan Petroff. In any case, their employment did not last long. Coal was discovered in British Columbia, California, and Oregon. It was not profitable to transport coal from Alaska to American and Canadian settlements in competition with these more convenient sources. The English Bay mine was closed in 1865.[20]

The company also had limited success with fish export, largely because the only method of preservation available at the time was salting (canning was yet to come into commercial use). The market for salt fish was rather limited.

In fur procurement, in addition to the changing market conditions, the company faced ever-growing competition, particularly in Alaska's interior. The flow of furs through Native trade networks across the northern continental divide and from there to the Chukchi Peninsula and Siberian trade fairs was significant, so much so that in 1842 Etholen contemplated establishing a trading post in Kotzebue Sound to intercept this flow and ordered that Siberian goods, such as reindeer clothing, sea mammal oil, and blubber, be stocked and used as trade goods in the company's northern outposts.[21]

In 1847, Alexander Murray founded a Hudson's Bay Company trading post on the middle reaches of the Yukon. There is good evidence that he and his successors were well aware that Fort Yukon, as the post has been known ever since, was within Russian territory. The Russians became aware of this move almost immediately through Native networks. The then-manager of the Nulato outpost, Vasilii Deriabin, even wrote a note addressed to the manager at Fort Yukon inquiring why the British were there. Murray acknowledged receipt of the note and then forwarded it to London, where it was translated rather inadequately and left without response.[22] The British offered better terms than the Russians for furs. In particular, they were trading modern British rifles to the Natives. Soon these weapons were being traded among the Natives on the lower Yukon, lower Kuskokwim, and Copper Rivers. In addition, American vessels were trading arms and gunpowder illegally to the Natives, and sometimes these were resold to the Russians.[23]

The international rivalry for the trade of Alaska's interior soon affected Native intertribal relations. Rivalry for control of trade routes and of the lucrative middleman role

Figure 85. View of the settlement at the coal mines in Kenai Bay (Cook Inlet).
Courtesy University of Alaska Fairbanks, Rasmuson Library, Alaska and Polar Regions Department, Archives, Historical Photographs.

in the fur trade erupted in several bloody confrontations, of which the best known is the so-called Nulato Massacre of 4 February 1851. Represented usually in English and American literature as an "anti-Russian uprising," it was in reality the culmination of a Native trade war. The Athabaskans of the Upper Koyukuk River attacked the Athabaskan village at Nulato, where an inviting-in feast (potlatch) was in progress, with the leaders and important men of many villages attending. The Native village was destroyed, and casualties among the Natives, mostly men, were very high indeed.[24] British surgeon Edward Adams, a member of one of the Franklin Search crews who was at St. Michael Redoubt at the time, rushed to Nulato to render aid. His shipmate from HMS *Enterprise*, Lt. Barnard, was visiting Nulato at the time and died of wounds received during the attack. Adams reported fifty-three Athabaskan men, women, and children killed.[25] According to Orthodox Church records kept at Ikogmiut, fifteen Christians but many more non-Christians were among the dead. Of the Christians killed, five were children or teenagers and four were women. Native oral tradition puts the number much higher than does Adams, and the victims are believed to have been predominantly men. The Russians, who for a decade had maintained excellent relations with the local groups, were shocked. The death of Nulato manager Deriabin, who was very popular and married to a local woman, was hard to accept. The operation of the trading post, however, was restored almost immediately. Fur procurement there continued to 1868, largely through Native middlemen and the Native fur trading rendezvous and networks. The rendezvous were reached out of Nulato and other outposts on the Yukon by annual boat trips up the Yukon River, certainly as far as its confluence with the Tanana and, according to Native oral tradition, as far as the modern Yukon Flats.

FIGURE 86. A drawing of Ozerskoi Redoubt, which no longer exists, showing the fish processing station, the mill, and the chapel, by W. Hamel, U.S. Coast Survey Expedition to Alaska under George Davidson.
Courtesy University of California, Berkeley, Bancroft Library, George Davidson Collection.

The most severe blows came with the outbreak of the Crimean War between Russia and Turkey in the fall of 1853. After the Russians defeated the Turkish fleet, Britain and France entered the conflict on the side of Turkey in March 1854. From then on, these two Western European nations would be Russia's main adversaries. The war ended in 1856, after the death of Nicholas I, when the new tsar, Alexander II, signed the Peace Treaty of Paris, which left Russia in an extremely weakened position.

Long before the outbreak of hostilities, Russian-American Company management had grave concerns about Alaska's vulnerability. The colony had no defenses to speak of; there were no Russian troops in Alaska at all. Should the English choose to attack the territory, especially from the sea, the management doubted it could be defended. In view of the activity by British naval vessels in Alaskan waters, the tone and mood in English ruling circles as expressed in the British press,[26] and suspected increased British anti-Russian agitation among the northwest coastal Natives out of Vancouver Island, the management harbored few illusions. And not only Alaska seemed to be a potentially easy prey to enemy action: at the beginning of 1854, Petropavlovsk, Russia's major port on Kamchatka, had a garrison numbering only fifty men.[27] That there would be enemy action in the Pacific seemed inevitable, as Britain and her ally France feared a Russian-American alliance, anti-British in character, which might threaten Britain's position in the North Pacific. Actually, the British and French naval squadrons in the Pacific had orders, issued beforehand, to go into action as soon as they were notified that Britain and France had entered the war.[28] In 1855, after the combined British-French force was repulsed at Petropavlovsk, their strength was increased to twelve combat vessels. The British continued to fear that an alliance would be concluded and were also taking seriously rumors that Americans were outfitting privateers to aid the Russians. Russia, undoubtedly, would have welcomed an American alliance, but had to be content with the convention on marine neutrality concluded 10 (22) July 1854, modeled on the "armed neutrality" declaration by Russia in 1780.[29] Anticipating British entry into the war, the Russian-American Company approached the Hudson's Bay Company with a view toward concluding their own convention of neutrality. The agreement was concluded and approved by both governments, but the government of Great Britain insisted that neutralization applied only to the colonial territories. The agreement was not to extend to the high seas; Russian-American Company ships and their cargoes were subject to seizure, and Russia's Alaskan ports to a sea blockade. The Russian government agreed that Hudson's Bay Company establishments would not be attacked. To cover its bets, the management entered into the agreement with the American-Russian Commercial Company mentioned above.[30]

The year after the Crimean War broke out, 1854, the government, for the first time in the history of Russian America, provided troops for the defense of Novo-Arkhangel'sk, the point where it was expected the British would attack. The troops, ninety-nine men and two officers of the Siberian Line Battalion, arrived 22 September from Aian aboard the ship *Imperator Nikolai I*. The garrison was increased to 180 in 1855, the year the English-French naval squadron cruised near Sitka (Baranof) Island, but did not attack. In subsequent years, the number of men fluctuated between 150 and 180, the number of officers between two and three. Officers and men drew double pay and a substantial food allowance. With little for the soldiers to do at Novo-Arkhangel'sk, the company obtained permission to use them as part of the labor force (the labor shortage never did end).[31]

Only one company installation, that on the island of Urup in the Kuril Islands, was attacked. In August 1855, two frigates, the *Pique* (English) and the *Sibylle* (French), bombarded the settlement and sent out shore parties. Most of the personnel escaped, though the manager was captured, along with the office clerk and a Yakut laborer.[32] The losses in this skirmish were minimal. However, substantial losses occurred because of the disruption of fur shipments to markets and interference with company shipping. In 1854 alone, the circumnavigating vessel *Sitkha*, out of Hamburg, Conradi commanding, was taken at the entrance to Avacha Bay by the Anglo-French squadron attacking Petropavlovsk. The second circumnavigating vessel, *Kamchatka*, under command of Ridell, was entering San Francisco harbor, having avoided enemy vessels along the California coast, when it encountered an English frigate. The vessel was saved by an American steamship that had been sent out by Kostromitinov, the company agent at San Francisco, to take the *Kamchatka* in tow. To avoid capture, the ship remained in San Francisco harbor until the end of hostilities. Similarly, the ship *Imperator Nikolai I*, arriving at San Francisco 1 January 1855, was bottled up there. In 1855, the brig *Okhotsk*, Iuselius commanding, was intercepted 16 July near the Amur estuary by a British steam-powered vessel. Unable to repel large boarding parties or escape to sea, Iuselius set fire to the powder magazine and stove in his brig's hull below the water line. He and part of the crew escaped, but two longboats carrying a number of the sailors were captured. At Aian, in 1855, the British destroyed a vessel under construction. These losses added to the loss of vessels registered to the Russian-Finnish Whaling Company already mentioned. A new screw-driven vessel, ordered in Europe in 1853, could not arrive in the colonies before 1857, nor could the ship *Tsesarevich*.

From just before the outbreak of the war and throughout its course, the colonial administration was not the best. Mikhail Teben'kov, who succeeded Etholen in 1845, was the last for some time to serve a full five-year term. A snob and a man of limited vision, he had a long service experience in Alaska, returning to active duty in the navy in 1851 and eventually earning flag rank. He was succeeded by even lesser men: Rozenberg, Rudakov, and Voevodskii filled the post between 1850 and 1859.

After Teben'kov left office, the new chief managers failed to give inviting-in feasts (potlatches), which their predecessors had offered more or less regularly. Rozenberg proved especially inept at maintaining good relationships with the Tlingit. In 1850, he threatened to close the market if the Tlingit did not behave with greater respect. In response, the Tlingit attempted to storm the palisade surrounding the Russian establishment.[33] In 1852, because of Rozenberg's indecision and failure to act when warned of an impending planned massacre, the local Sitka Tlingit slaughtered visiting Tlingit from the Stikine area whom they had invited to a feast. The Russians were later blamed by the Stikine people for failing to protect the lives of their men. This inaction may also have created the perception that the Russians were weak. Whereas earlier the Stikine Tlingit respected the Russians and accepted them as arbitrators in disputes with the Hudson's Bay Company people,[34] now there were scattered attacks upon Russian personnel (not necessarily Russians) close to Sitka.

Rozenberg left his office early, in 1853, and the position of chief manager was temporarily filled by Aleksandr Rudakov, who was replaced in 1854 by Stepan Voevodskii. It was he who managed the colony in the difficult years of the Crimean War. Perhaps because the Russians suspected that the British would agitate Natives against the Russians, Voevodskii appears to have been extraordinarily suspicious of the Tlingit. For example, he forbade their free entry into Novo-Arkhangel'sk for marketing.[35] On 10 March 1855, the Tlingit attacked and wounded one of the sailors guarding the firewood supply. Apparently, a group of Tlingit intended to help themselves to the wood, and the men on duty tried to prevent the theft. Voevodskii demanded that the Tlingit leaders expel the guilty from the settlement under the walls of Novo-Arkhangel'sk, in perpetuity. This preemptory demand was refused, and the Tlingit began to arm themselves. Warning cannon shots fired from one of the batteries were ignored. Russians rushed to the walls and mounted a defense. A general firefight erupted. The Tlingit took the church built but recently for their use and fired upon the Russians from its windows. The fight lasted over two hours, but eventually the Russians won, despite losing seven dead and fifteen wounded. The Tlingit losses are not known; Voevodskii estimated that they lost about fifty fighters.[36] Voevodskii lost no time requesting an increase in the strength of the Siberian Line Battalion detachment assigned to Novo-Arkhangel'sk.

After 1855 Russian-Tlingit relations returned to normal, and until 1867 there was no more violence. Indeed, in 1867, a Tlingit leader, speaking to an American officer, characterized the Russians as "good friends" and expressed the hope that the Americans would prove to be the same.[37]

Voevodskii was replaced in 1859 by a very able governor, Johan Hampus Furuhjelm (a Finn, a future vice admiral and military governor of Russia's Far East). During his tenure, in 1862, the Third Charter expired. Though the company was negotiating with the government for a new charter, and though Furuhjelm set about restoring the company's affairs in the colony to better order, the government had different views. In 1853, Murav'iev-Amurskii had made representations to Emperor Nicholas I about the need to strengthen Russia's position in the Far East, in view of the dangerous international situation. He mentioned that "it should be borne in mind that sooner or later we will have to yield our North American possession to [the United States]." During the Crimean War the idea that America should acquire Alaska was presented, through William McKendree Gwin, to President Pierce, who immediately declared himself in favor of such a purchase.[38] The Russians in Alaska did not realize how near the inevitable end was.

NOTES

1. Russia, *Pod vysochaishim Ego Imperatorskago Velichestva pokrovitel'stvom Rossiisko-Amerikanskoi kompanii glavnago pravleniia Akt i vysochaishe darovannyia onoi kompanii pravila s priobshcheniem prilichnykh k onomu uzakonenii* (St. Petersburg: Imperatorskaia akademiia nauk, 1802).
2. The text of the company's Second Charter, with attendant regulations and privileges, is found in P. A. Tikhmenev, Appendix to *Istoricheskoe obozrenie obrazovaniia Rossiisko-Amerikanskoi kompanii i deistvii eiia do nastoiashchago vremeni*, vol. 1 (St. Petersburg: Edvard Veimar, 1861), 40–61 (docs. 7 and 8).
3. The text of the company's Third Charter is found in P. A. Tikhmenev, Appendix [1] to *Istoricheskoe obozrenie obrazovaniia Rossiisko-Amerikanskoi kompanii i deistvii eiia do nastoiashchago vremeni*, vol. 2 (St. Petersburg: Edvard Veimar, 1863), 11–63 (doc. 2). On the progressive trend in regard to treatment of and regulated interaction with the Natives, see David S. Case, "The Russian Legacy of the Alaska Native Claims," in *Russian America: The Forgotten Frontier*, ed. Barbara S. Smith and Redmond J. Barnett (Tacoma: Washington State Historical Society, 1990), 237–243; and [Vladimir Gsovski], *Russian Administration of Alaska and Status of the Alaska Natives*, 81st Cong., 2d sess., 1950, S. Doc. 152.
4. Petr Shumakher, "K istorii priobreteniia Amura," *Russkii arkhiv* 3 (1878): 257–342.

5. Shumakher, "K istorii," 262–264; Sladkovsky, *The Long Road*, 172–175; P. A. Tikhmenev, *A History of the Russian-American Company*, vol. 1, trans. and ed. Richard A. Pierce and Alton S. Donnelly (Seattle: University of Washington Press, 1978), 270–298.
6. Tikhmenev, *A History*, vol. 1, 299–314.
7. The company stressed its support of the Putiatin embassies in several documents and memoranda presented to the government in the course of negotiations for the extension of the monopoly charter. On Putiatin's expeditions to Japan, see Lensen, *Russian Push*, 308–354.
8. Tikhmenev, *A History*, vol. 1, 298.
9. Alexander Starbuck, *History of the American Whale Fishery* (Secaucus, N.J.: Castle Books, 1989), 98. This is a reprint of part 4 of *Report of the United States Commission on Fish and Fisheries* (Washington, D.C.: Government Printing Office, 1878). See also Walter S. Tower, *A History of the American Whale Fishery*, Series in Political Economy and Public Law, no. 20 (Philadelphia: University of Pennsylvania, 1907), 50.
10. 9 January 1846, Captain 2nd Rank Mashin, Kamchatka Commander, to Governor-General of Eastern Siberia, cited after Bolkhovitinov, *Russko-amerikanskie otnosheniia* (1990), 60. See also Tikhmenev, *A History*, vol. 1, 315–318.
11. Kushner, *Conflict on the Northwest Coast*, 82; Bolkhovitinov, *Russko-amerikanskie otnosheniia* (1990), 61.
12. John R. Bockstoce, *Whales, Ice, and Men: The History of Whaling in the Western Arctic* (Seattle: University of Washington Press in association with the New Bedford Whaling Museum, Massachusetts, 1986), 21–26.
13. Arndt, "Dynamics of the Fur Trade," 97–102.
14. Tikhmenev, *A History*, vol. 1, 317–318.
15. Ibid., 320.
16. Rossiisko-finliandskaia kitolovnaia kompaniia, *Otchet Rossiisko-finliandskoi kitolovnoi kompanii, s uchrezhdeniia do iskhoda 1858 g.* (St. Petersburg, 1858); excerpts in *Morskoi sbornik* 39, no. 2 (1859): 27–33; Tikhmenev, *A History*, vol. 1, 321–326.
17. Richard O. Cummings, *The American Ice Harvests: A Historical Study in Technology, 1800–1918* (Berkeley and Los Angeles: University of California Press, 1949), 56; Timothy L. Dilliplane, "Industries in Russian America," in *Russian America: The Forgotten Frontier*, ed. Barbara S. Smith and Redmond J. Barnett (Tacoma: Washingon State Historical Society, 1990), 131–143.
18. E. L. Keithahn, "Alaska Ice, Inc.," in *Alaska and Its History*, ed. Morgan B. Sherwood (Seattle: University of Washington Press, 1967), 173–186; Gary Stevens, "The Woody Island Ice Company," in *Russia in North America: Proceedings of the 2nd International Conference on Russian America, Sitka, Alaska, August 19–22, 1987*, ed. Richard A. Pierce (Kingston, Ontario; Fairbanks, Alaska: Limestone Press, 1990), 192–212.
19. Kushner, *Conflict on the Northwest Coast*, 121; Bolkhovitinov, *Russko-amerikanskie otnosheniia* (1990), 76–83.
20. Richard A. Pierce, "The Russian Coal Mine on the Kenai," *Alaska Journal* 5, no. 2 (1975): 104–108; Dilliplane, "Industries in Russian America," 132–136; Black and Pierce, "Russian America and the Finns," 28.
21. Chief Manager Etolin to Lt. Zagoskin, RAC, Communications Sent, vol. 22, no. 166, 27 April 1843, fols. 119v–120v, National Archives, Washington D.C.; Arndt, "Russian Exploration," 102.
22. Arndt, "Russian-American Company Trade," 183–184, 190 n. 3.
23. Arndt, "Dynamics of the Fur Trade," 80 n. 38, 100, 121; Zagoskin, *Puteshestviia*, 278. In the English-language edition of Zagoskin (*Lieutenant Zagoskin's Travels*, 268), the passage is mistranslated to indicate that Natives bought guns in the Interior and traded them to the Cook Inlet area, whereas the Russian edition actually states that Natives from the Interior were lured to Cook Inlet by the powder and guns being sold there.

24. Miranda Wright, "The Last Great Indian War (Nulato 1851)" (master's thesis, University of Alaska Fairbanks, 1995).
25. Edward Adams, "Journal Kept Ashore in and near St. Michael's, Alaska, 12 October 1850–3 July 1851," Collinson's Franklin Search expedition, 1850–1855, Manuscript 1115, Scott Polar Research Institute, Cambridge, England. Microfilm copy, Alaska and Polar Regions Department, Elmer E. Rasmuson Library, University of Alaska Fairbanks. On Nulato oral tradition, see Julius Jette, "Particulars of Nulato, Alaska, Massacre," typescript of manuscript dated 28 January 1914, Alaska and Polar Regions Department, Elmer E. Rasmuson Library, University of Alaska Fairbanks (published in part in *The Farthest-North Collegian*, 1 February 1936: 3, 7); Lydia Black, unpublished field data, Nulato, 1986; Miranda Wright, "The Last Great Indian War." Extensive analyses are presented by Arndt, "Dynamics of the Fur Trade," 103–108, and by Frederica de Laguna, *Travels Among the Dena: Exploring Alaska's Yukon Valley* (Seattle: University of Washington Press, 2000), 170–188.
26. The growth of tensions between Great Britain and Russia prior to the Crimean War is presented excellently by John Howes Gleason, *The Genesis of Russophobia in Great Britain: A Study of Interaction of Policy and Opinion* (Cambridge, Mass.: Harvard University Press, 1950; reprint, New York: Octagon Books, 1972). Related matters are discussed by M. S. Anderson, *Britain's Discovery of Russia, 1553–1815* (Toronto: Macmillan Company of Canada; New York: St. Martin's Press, 1958).
27. Barry M. Gough, *The Royal Navy and the Northwest Coast of North America, 1810–1914: A Study of British Maritime Ascendancy* (1971; reprint, Vancouver: University of British Columbia Press, 1974), 110.
28. Ibid., 112.
29. Bolkhovitinov, *Russko-amerikanskie otnosheniia* (1990), 89–91; Alan Dowty, *The Limits of American Isolation: The United States and the Crimean War* (New York: New York University Press, 1971).
30. Bolkhovitinov, *Russko-amerikanskie otnosheniia* (1990), 94–95.
31. Tikhmenev, *A History*, vol. 1, 371; Alexandra Kalmykow, *Administration of Alaska by the Russians on the Eve of Its Transfer to the United States* (master's thesis, Columbia University, 1947), microfilm in collections of Alaska and Polar Regions Department, Elmer E. Rasmuson Library, University of Alaska Fairbanks.
32. Rossiisko-amerikanskaia kompaniia, *Otchet Rossiisko-amerikanskoi kompanii za 1856g.* (St. Petersburg, 1857).
33. Grinev, *Indeitsy tlinkity*, 163.
34. Arndt, "Russian Relations"; Grinev, *Indeitsy tlinkity*, 163–166.
35. Grinev, *Indeitsy tlinkity*, 167.
36. Ibid., 285–286.
37. U.S. Department of State, *Russian America*, 40th Cong., 2d sess., 1868, H. Ex. Doc. 177.
38. Quoted after Bolkhovitinov, *Russko-amerikanskie otnosheniia* (1990), 92.

FIGURE 87. Alexander II (1818–1881), emperor of Russia 1855–1881.
Courtesy Slavic and Baltic Division, New York Public Library, Astor, Lenox, and Tilden Foundations.

CHAPTER FIFTEEN

And the Flag Was Ordered Down

IN THE LAST DECADE BEFORE ALASKA WAS SOLD TO THE UNITED STATES, following the upheavals and financial difficulties caused by the Crimean War, life in the colonies stabilized, and the company's affairs were on the mend. It is not clear whether Chief Manager Furuhjelm, a navy man holding the rank of full captain, was aware at the time of his appointment that the government was seriously contemplating withdrawal from the American colonies, though it is probable that he did know. The topic was being widely discussed in naval circles, and by company directors and shareholders. Shortly before his departure for the colony, Furuhjelm met in St. Petersburg with Wrangell, former chief manager of Alaska (and since 1855, minister of the navy). Wrangell had been consulted as early as 1857 on the subject of disengagement in America by Chancellor of State Gorchakov, when the Lord High Admiral, Grand Duke Konstantin, first raised the question. Wrangell, who, along with five other members of his family, held shares in the Russian-American Company, pointed out the profitability of the enterprise and potential value of Alaska's resources. It was he who at the time calculated the sum for potential indemnity for losses, which for the United States would be "a paltry sum."[1] Furuhjelm met also with Eduard Stoeckl, then on leave in Russia, who was minister to the United States and chief negotiator for Russia in the sale of Alaska.[2]

Nevertheless, upon his arrival in Alaska, Furuhjelm set about stabilizing the situation. The matter of withdrawal was far from settled and, no doubt, like others before and after him, Furuhjelm was most impressed with the richness of Alaska's natural resources. He probably also noticed that in reality things in Alaska did not appear as bleak as they had been painted by the company's opponents in Russia. Under his leadership, relations with the Tlingit soon improved significantly, Native trade on the Northwest Coast was revitalized, fish and ice were produced for export, and shipbuilding was a going concern. The first steamboat built in Alaska was launched on 12 March 1860. After the sale of Alaska, sold and remodeled and renamed *Rose*, she sailed for many years in Puget Sound and then returned to Alaska to end her days in the service of the Alaska Oil and Guano Company.

The financial position of the company was improving and the prospects, now focusing on such natural resources as timber, fish, coal, and other minerals (with fur procurement a ready fallback line), were bright. Fur resources were intact and maintained by a rigorous conservation program. On this subject, Captain W. A. Howard, commanding the U.S. Revenue Steamer *Lincoln*, the first to be dispatched to Alaska in 1867, and the

FIGURE 88. The *Baranov,* first steamer built in Alaska, ca. 1862. Renamed the *Rose* after 1867.
From E. W. Wright, ed., 1895, p. 161.

FIGURE 89. St. Paul in the Pribilof Islands, ca. 1873. Artist Henry W. Elliott.

first man to be appointed Special Treasury Agent for Alaska, later reported to the Hon. Hugh McCullough, secretary of the treasury:

> I would very respectfully call the attention of the department to the magnificent trade opened by this transfer, and consequently lost to Russia and Great Britain, but which, if unprotected by legislation, will in a very few years be entirely lost to us. The Russian American Fur Company protects in a most careful manner the "fur bearing animals," killing only the males of a certain age, never exceeding the number necessary for the supply of the market.

Captain Howard went on to explain how the fur seal herds were utilized with a view toward the future and mentioned the protective measures observed to maintain the sea otter population.[3] Ironically, in Russia, the critics of the company, the liberals in favor of laissez-faire economics, had been attacking these same conservation practices in the press. Among them was Aleksandr Kashevarov, a creole from Alaska, now the head of the navy's hydrographic office.[4]

Thus in 1859, when Furuhjelm took office, company affairs were prospering and fur procurement, especially of sea mammals, was a well-managed mainstay of the company's business. The international situation, however, was growing ever more complicated.

The Crimean War saw a concentration of British naval power in the North Pacific, and soon thereafter a permanent naval base with facilities at Esquimalt, Vancouver Island (a Crown colony since 1849), was in place.[5] During this period, too, gold was discovered in British Columbia, first in the Queen Charlotte Islands, Haida Indian territory claimed by the British and soon patrolled by the Royal Navy, and later on the Frazer and Stikine Rivers, the latter southernmost Tlingit territory. Fearful of potential consequences of a gold rush, the British increased their naval presence on the Northwest Coast and on 2 August 1858 Parliament created the new Crown Colony of British Columbia. Access to the Stikine River was, of course, part of Russian-American possessions and controlled by the terms of the international convention of 1825. A British warship called at Sitka, where her captain discussed matters with Furuhjelm and then sailed to the Stikine River.[6] Furuhjelm dispatched Russian vessels to the area in 1862 and 1863, when the Russians mediated Indian unrest and assisted some destitute miners. Their mining experts, among them the engineer Andreev, examined the gold strikes and reported on the numbers who were flocking to British Columbia, predominantly from the United States Pacific coast. The Russian-American Company and the government, well aware that gold was present in Alaska, were much concerned that the influx of gold seekers would spill across the international boundary. At one point the company proposed that gold seekers be permitted to operate in Alaska provided they pay a certain fee.[7]

The colonial chief manager worried about unmanageable hordes of profit-seekers invading the territory illegally. The government in St. Petersburg worried that the foreign powers of Great Britain and the United States might develop designs upon Russian America. But for the rank and file of Russian personnel, and for the Native inhabitants of the territory, life was running smoothly. There was peace, supplies were flowing once again, and everyday life was orderly. Life even offered a few pleasures. In the capital, Novo-Arkhangel'sk, social life was rather fine.

There were three churches in town, the finest the Cathedral of St. Michael the Archangel, consecrated in 1848 when it replaced the old church built during the Baranov era. It

Figure 90. An early lighthouse at Sitka. From a drawing by I. F. Vasil'iev, 1809, detail on harbor chart. Inscription reads "A view of the lighthouse on Maiachnyi Island."

Original in RGAVMF, Fond 1331, op. 4, delo 133. Courtesy Richard A. Pierce.

was, as one of the first Americans to come to Novo-Arkhangel'sk in 1867 wrote, "of blue slate color, the roof and dome a deep green, and the window frames and doors white." The church bell tower had a clock (now gone). "As a structure it would do credit to any New England town," wrote the American observer.[8] The Lutheran church built during the tenure of Chief Manager Etholen (1840–1845) and the Tlingit Church of the Holy Resurrection[9] served different congregations. There were several schools. The hospital, and the associated out-patient clinic and pharmacy, served annually close to 2,000 persons, of all states and conditions. There were other amenities such as steam baths, public gardens, and tea houses nearby. An excellent library, which contained several thousand volumes in most European languages, ranging in subject matter from mathematics and navigation to art and literature, had existed since the time of Baranov. A museum of natural history and ethnography could compete with many institutions in major European and American cities. Russian scholar I. G. Voznesenskii, on a scientific expedition from 1839 to 1849 in Alaska, California, and eastern Siberia, who collected natural history and ethnographic specimens for the Imperial Academy of Sciences in St. Petersburg, made a duplicate collection for the Novo-Arkhangel'sk museum (its collections were pilfered during American military rule in Alaska).[10]

There was a lighthouse, an observatory, and a meteorological station. In 1867, George Davidson, United States Coastal Survey, author of the first *Coast Pilot* for Alaska (1868), obtained from Chief Manager Maksutov printed records for the fourteen years preceding, including temperatures, rainfall, barometric pressure, etc.[11] There was no jail (in the American period, the barracks of the Siberian Battalion soon were converted into a jail). There were workshops, foundries, grain and saw mills. Private residences were situated on side streets "with planked sidewalks." All streets in Novo-Arkhangel'sk, where it rains much of the year, had board sidewalks. Most of the company buildings were painted yellow, and their sheet-iron roofs were painted red. "Every edifice, large and small, is built of hewn logs, hewn, in the better class of houses, so as to leave no crevices, with the external and internal walls so well dressed as to be suitable for painting or papering."[12]

There were clubs where gentlemen gathered regularly for billiards and card games. There were musical evenings, dances, at which parlor games were played, and family evenings attended by the ladies who brought along their handwork (embroidery, knitting,

FIGURE 91. Exterior view of "Baranoff's Castle," the residence of the Russian-American Company's colonial chief managers. Baranov did not live in this particular structure. The chief manager's house was rebuilt several times.

From Andrews, 1922, facing p. 60.

FIGURE 92. Interior view of "Baranoff's Castle," Sitka, ca. 1893.

Courtesy Richard A. Pierce.

etc.) and at which no wine whatsoever was served.[13] When important visitors came and on important holidays, balls were given by the chief manager and his lady at their residence. This building was greatly admired by some visitors and found wanting by others. Golovin, on his inspection tour, described it in his letters to his family as "hideous."[14]

It was also the custom that the chief manager entertain officers of the vessels and higher company officials for dinner at his residence. Official dinners were attended by the ladies. There was no racial discrimination whatsoever; rank and class mattered, not the color of one's skin or the shape of one's eyes.

These social customs did not escape the attention of company critics. Admiral A. A. Popov, commander of the Russian navy's Pacific squadron, wrote in 1862 to Admiral-General and Grand Duke Konstantin about the company's extravagant squandering of resources on such pastimes. He particularly cited a lavish ball given at Novo-Arkhangel'sk which was attended by more than forty ladies.[15]

Simpler pleasures included berry and mushroom picking, picnics, and boating. In winter, when ice was on the lake, there was skating and, always, visits to the hot springs.

Contrary to many exaggerated official statements (often at odds with their private ones) by brief visitors to Novo-Arkhangel'sk, such as Admiral Popov and navy inspector Golovin, residents did not live in a constant state of fear, under siege by the Tlingit.[16] The relations between the Russians and the Tlingit had improved considerably since the outbreak of violence in the 1850s. Trade flourished, town market was held daily, and local Tlingit dignitaries and visiting parties were entertained by the officials, privately and at feasts imitating Tlingit traditional customs given by the chief manager himself. Informal mixing at public occasions or at such events as ice skating parties and private visiting occurred on a daily basis. Tlingits were often of service to Russian officials: for example, Golovin, in 1860, was planning to send his private mail through Tlingit intermediaries to British Columbia, whence it would be dispatched to St. Petersburg much earlier than by the next vessel out of Sitka.

On the other hand, the Tlingit asked the Russians to assist them: on several occasions the Russians were called in to mediate in Native intergroup disputes. Sometimes they put a stop to incipient hostilities by showing superior might. Such was the case in 1860

FIGURE 93. Sitka, 1869, during the American military occupation.
From Andrews, 1922, facing p. 77.

when Furuhjelm stopped a potentially major conflict between the Sitkans and visitors from Yakutat, which grew out of a knife fight between a visitor and a local man. After tempers cooled, Furuhjelm assisted in a dispute settlement by means of exchanging indemnity payments.

In general, Tlingit leaders were offered respect. When the governmental inspectors Kostlivtsev and Golovin arrived in Novo-Arkhangel'sk in 1860, local Tlingit leaders were presented to them and were received with the customary ceremonial observances.[17]

In humbler homes and in outlying settlements, men in their leisure hours read books, newspapers, and journals that came into their possession (many subscribed to a variety of Russian periodicals, but delivery was rather slow, only once or twice a year), played chess and the card games commonly played in Russian villages. Accordions and fiddles were favorite musical instruments, and Russian songs and folk dances were a favorite form of entertainment (and are in evidence even today). A traditional pastime was storytelling. Russian folktales were soon retold in many Alaska Native languages and entered Native folklore. Children's games were also widespread. We shall never know who taught the children's games, but many Russian games are played to this day in Alaska, such as *lapta*, still played on Kodiak Island and called now "Russian baseball."[18] Ice skating, sledding, skiing and ski making, Evenk-type dog breeding practices, Kamchadal and Evenk dog sleds and harness and joinery, and smithing were adopted from the Russians by several Native groups.

Good works were not forgotten. Auctions to benefit orphanages, schools, and the poor were held in Novo-Arkhangel'sk. Sometimes handicrafts made by girls attending the boarding school there were auctioned off.

In many villages vegetables were grown, mostly root crops and potatoes, cattle were kept, and at district headquarters, such as at Korovin Bay on Atka Island in the central Aleutians, emergency food supplies were put up for everyone's use in times of food shortages:

> It was a big house in which no one lived, just for food, an ordinary Aleut house in which they used to store food for the winter, it is said.... But towards winter—at the end of this month (September)—when the weather generally changes, the food which had been stored was distributed to the hungry people, to everyone. This happened every month, but even though there were many people, it did not end before winter was over, it is said.[19]

Food was abundant, though it was not what American and European visitors were used to. Navy inspector Golovin, in Novo-Arkhangel'sk in 1860, was nauseated by the view of dry fish and refused to eat halibut or even to taste the crab meat offered to him by locals as a delicacy.[21] It was he who reported hardship suffered by the Natives because of an insufficient availability of baked bread.

The smallpox outbreak of 1862–1863 was checked through a well-administered vaccination program, this time an effort well accepted by the Native population.

Company profits were up and a period of stability and prosperity was in the air. In fact, Golovin wrote to his relatives:

> It is said that after our departure the company's shares dropped in value; those who would sell their shares are fools, indeed. Had I any money, I would immediately buy as many shares as possible, being sure of a great profit in a short time. It is possible that

> the fall of the share price is the result of speculation by some gentlemen who are fishing in troubled waters. If that is so, their calculations are very good.[21]

In the Russian capital, however, the decision to disengage was already a foregone conclusion. It was delayed, first of all, by the necessity to observe the terms of the Third Charter (expiring in 1862), and to honor international commercial contracts into which the Russian-American Company had entered and which were to expire only *after* 1862.[22] The arguments for disengagement were focused, in the main, on the impossibility of defense against foreign powers (notably Great Britain), bolstered by wildly exaggerated or nonexistent dangers: Native attacks, an influx of Indians from Western American territories, the emigration of Mormons and of hordes of gold seekers and unruly whalers. The second line of attack was criticism of the company's activities in the American territory. This criticism derived from the general, dominant, liberal public opinion of the times, which encompassed not only support for laissez-faire economics (for example, the attack on the company's conservation practices as measures infringing on individual freedom), but also the notion of the civilizing mission of the advanced nations, the "White Man's Burden." For example, in the proposal for reorganization of the territorial administration in America, the company was charged with not doing its share in civilizing the Natives, particularly with failure to Russianize Native men.[23] Another critic, Captain I. A. Shestakov, in a memorandum dated 7 February 1860, entitled "On the cession of our American colonies to the United States," charged that the company "in 60 years of its rule did not move the natives at all to advance along the path of moral development."[24] Exploitation of Russian employees was also a hotly debated topic, as were infringements, real or fancied, of their civil rights (it must be remembered that this was the age of reform, with serfdom and all forms of corporal punishment, especially flogging, abolished by 1861). One of these infringements was considered to be the prohibition of free importation of alcohol into the colony. In 1863, the proposal for reorganization would ask for free importation of alcohol, with payment of a license fee, and the regulated free sale of alcohol to all.

Figure 94. Head of the Admiralty, Admiral-General Konstantin, brother of Tsar Alexander II, advocated retreat from Alaska and eventually won.
Courtesy New York Public Library, Slavic and Baltic Division, Astor, Lenox, and Tilden Foundations.

For such reasons and other reasons of his own, such as the desire to focus Russian strength on the newly acquired Amur and Far East maritime regions, Tsar Alexander's brother, Admiral-General Konstantin, proposed in 1858 that an inspection team be sent to Alaska to evaluate the company's handling of its trust. The inspection team was created in 1859 and traveled to Alaska in 1860. It consisted of Councillor Kostlivtsev representing the ministry of finance, which was responsible for the oversight of Russian-American Company activities, and his assistant, Captain Golovin, representing the ministry of the navy but appointed personally by the admiral-general.[25]

The commissioners came with preconceived notions about the situation in Alaska, were prejudiced against the company, and their superiors expected them, especially Golovin, to recommend liquidation of the company.[26] Instead, faced with the real situation, they recognized that the company was economically viable and had good prospects for future development and that the situation of the Native population did not even come close to enslavement, as had been charged by the polemical press in Russia. In fact, both found much good to say about the state of affairs in Alaska, especially privately.[27]

In particular, Kostlivtsev's report made it clear that the company's financial affairs were nowhere near the brink of bankruptcy, as some critics charged. In fact, for the decade ending in 1860 (which included the years of the Crimean War when the company suffered tremendous losses and when its activities had to be curtailed) the net profit was substantial, even after debt service and expenses, which included provision of social services such as education and medical services, pensions and disability benefits, and support of the Orthodox Church and now the military garrison. Of the net profit, ten percent was earmarked for the capital fund, half a percent for the poor, and the rest was paid out in dividends. Kostlivtsev noted that the company had paid dividends each year since its inception in 1798 (prior to the issuance of the First Charter of 1799).[28] In 1861, 145,229 rubles in silver were paid out as dividends, with 31,656.51 rubles remaining in the dividend fund.[29] Both Kostlivtsev and Golovin recommended *against* liquidation of the company, in spite of considerable pressure exercised by some people in high places. They did recommend certain reforms and limitations of the company's privileges, and both found it necessary to stress the military vulnerability of the colonies.

The government then proceeded to discuss proposals for company and colony reorganization and reform, many of very drastic character. But this development was not a retreat from the position adopted earlier by Emperor Alexander II and his brother Konstantin. It was a temporary retrenchment in light of the fact that in 1861 civil war broke out in the United States, and any discussions of the transfer of sovereignty over Alaska had to await cessation of hostilities. In 1861–1862, no one could predict the outcome or the date when hostilities would end. The company charter was expiring and the time was opportune to change the ground rules under which the company operated. In particular, the government proposed to establish administration of the territory independent of the company, a system of courts independent both of colonial administration and the company, and complete self-rule, based on free elections of their leaders, for local communities, Native as well as colonial settlers. Some proposals recommended that the entire territory be opened to settlement (to which the company responded that this was a sure way to create Russian-Native conflicts), that the company fur procurement rights be limited to the Aleutian and Kodiak archipelagos and Prince William Sound, while the Alexander Archipelago and the mainland would be open for fur procurement to all, regardless of their estate, Russian or Native origin. Further, it was recommended that the rights to exploit other natural resources, such as fish, timber, coal, and mineral wealth, be taken away from the company and opened to all Russian subjects, native-born or former foreign nationals who became Russian subjects in perpetuity. While several proposals advanced at the time would have severely limited the company's privileges, none of its responsibilities were to be abolished; in fact, they were to be increased. The company would be responsible for the support of military forces to be stationed in Alaska for protection against territorial encroachment. In 1865, the draft of such new bylaws governing company activity was approved by governmental agencies. This proposal was not as drastic as that proposed in 1863, but incorporated many recommendations made by the Kostlivtsev-Golovin inspection team and included in the report of the governmental Committee for Reorganization of the Colonies (published in 1863).

Following a shareholders' meeting at which these matters were discussed, the company objected to many provisions. The company won one very important point: the privileges to procure furs throughout Alaska were, in the end, not rescinded. Two decisions, one dated 14 June 1865 and the other 2 April 1866, indicated that the privileges might be extended for another charter period of twenty years.[30]

In Alaska, meanwhile, life went on as usual. In 1864, Furuhjelm was replaced by his second-in-command, Prince Dmitrii Maksutov, who had lived in Alaska since 1859. Three children were born to him and his wife at Novo-Arkhangel'sk, and his wife died there. On leave in St. Petersburg in 1863, or recalled there for consultation, Maksutov argued against the sale of Alaska. It was his fate, however, to preside over Russian withdrawal from the American continent. He returned to Alaska as acting governor in 1864 (bringing with him his second wife), with instructions to develop Alaskan resources in fish, timber, and minerals, including copper, and to establish regular mail service to the colony via San Francisco and Victoria in British Columbia. The new charter had not been granted, and the company operated under a temporary extension of the previous one.

In the main, Maksutov continued the management policies established under his predecessor. Every effort was made to diffuse criticism at home and to prove the company's profitability. In particular, the company defended its treatment of the Natives, pointing out that according to the ten censuses conducted prior to 1862, the population was increasing and that at least in those areas where records were kept, net births were greater than the net number of deaths. The company cooperated with the Imperial Academy of Sciences, and when a Tlingit versed in the languages of the peoples inhabiting the areas just across the British Columbia border traveled to St. Petersburg at his own request (to learn about Russia), he was put in touch with Academician Radlov, famous for his linguistic work. The vocabularies Radlov collected survive and constitute an important source on languages that today are nearly extinct.[31] The company sent sea cow skeletons and other examples of Alaskan fauna to the imperial museums, and in 1862 participated in the World Exhibition in London.

The company also attempted to streamline its management. The system of district offices had been abolished in the late 1840s, making all outposts accountable directly to Novo-Arkhangel'sk, and efforts to develop a more efficient communication system went forward. Development of new industries was a constant concern. Maksutov even prepared a plan for such development.[32] New markets for furs were constantly sought, as the Chinese market at Kiakhta grew less and less viable and the majority of furs were now shipped directly to St. Petersburg for Russian and European markets. An attempt to develop a market in New York proved unsatisfactory, and efforts in this direction were suspended. In fur procurement Maksutov followed Furuhjelm's emphasis on the interior trade, though here, too, he streamlined the operation, closing three stations in 1866, one on the Copper River, one on the Kuskokwim, and one, the Andreevskaia Odinochka, near modern St. Marys on the lower Yukon.

Russians were well informed about the courses of the major rivers, the Yukon and the Kuskokwim, as is clearly demonstrated by the map published in 1860 as an appendix to the company's annual report for 1859. Fort Yukon is shown correctly within Alaska's boundary and Hudson's Bay Company outposts on the Pelly and Mackenzie Rivers are indicated. In 1862, Ivan Lukin, son of the late manager of Kolmakovskii Redoubt on the Kuskokwim, went on the chief manager's orders to the upper Yukon to reconnoiter British activities there. It is possible that he had made similar trips at other dates. After 1867 Ivan Lukin joined forces with an American independent fur trader named Bean; Bean later married Lukin's daughter Anastasia.[33] They pioneered the independent fur trade on the Tanana River, and for several years were successful in withstanding competition from the Alaska Commercial Company.

Ivan Lukin was on hand at St. Michael when an American team, a detachment of the Western Union Telegraph Expedition, arrived there. He made himself available (on orders from the chief manager) and was promptly engaged as a guide to the upper Yukon. Lukin's acquaintance with Bean dates to this engagement.[34]

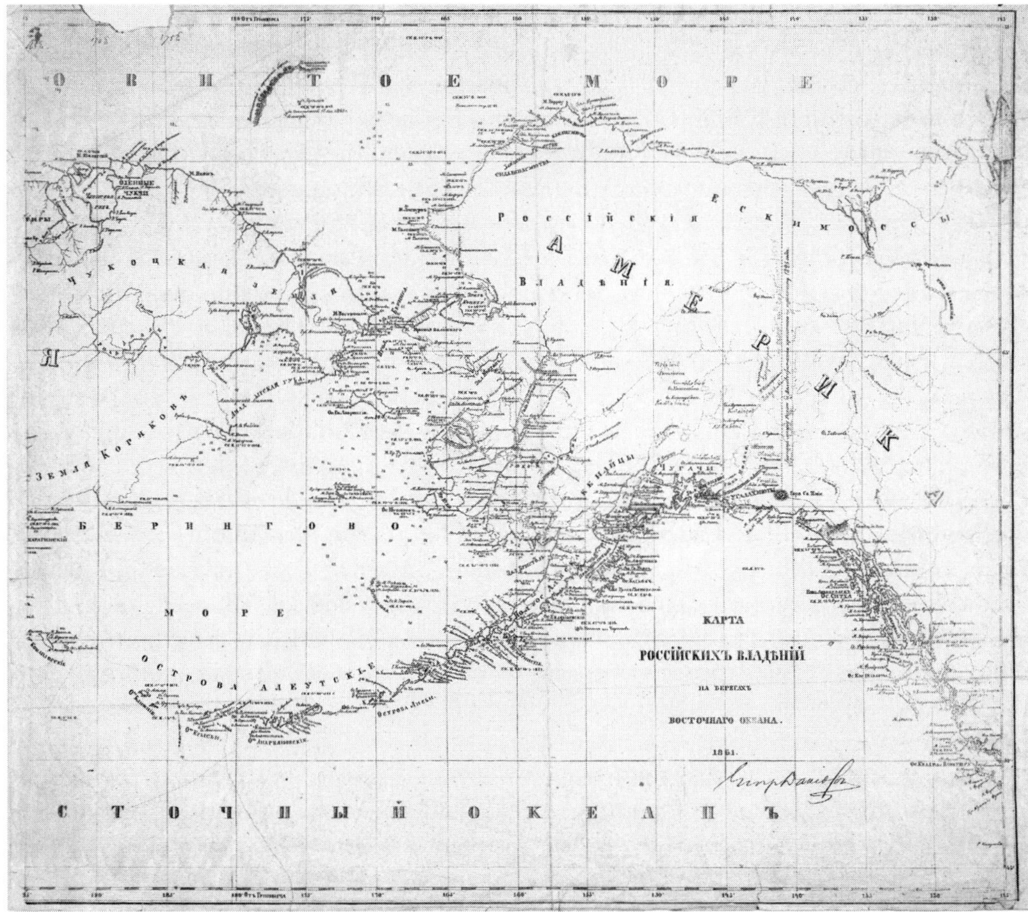

FIGURE 95. Map of Russian possessions on the shores of the Eastern (Pacific) Ocean, 1861. Identical to the eastern two-thirds of a map published in 1860 in the Russian-American Company's annual report for 1859, it depicts the entire course of the Yukon River and Russia's awareness that the Hudson's Bay Company's Fort Yukon was located within Russian territory.

Courtesy University of Alaska Fairbanks, Rasmuson Library, Alaska and Polar Regions Department, Rare Maps, no. G4370 1861 K37.

It can be argued that the project to establish a telegraph line from the United States through Canada and Alaska to Siberia, thence to St. Petersburg and thus to Europe, represented in some aspects the American private interests in Alaska's acquisition. Some scholars believe the project actually facilitated the purchase.[35] The telegraph line was proposed by Perry McDonough Collins, an advocate of close economic cooperation between the United States business community and Russia, who saw great opportunities for commerce in the Russian Far East. Well connected in American political circles, Collins, designated by Congress as United States agent for the Amur River, found support among influential Russians as well, such as the governor-general of Eastern Siberia, Murav'iev-Amurskii. He traveled down the entire length of the Amur River and his book about the journey was published in 1860. The United States Congress approved the telegraph project in 1864.[36] Collins Overland Line, a subsidiary of the Western Union Telegraph Company, was created and the enterprise called the Western Union Telegraph Expedition commenced in 1865, soon after the end of the Civil War.

Colonel Charles S. Bulkley, former chief of the United States Signal Service, was in charge of the preliminary surveys and construction work.[37] Several bright young men such as William H. Dall and Henry W. Elliott, who after 1867 became known as experts on Alaska, were recruited.[38] Elliott was in charge of the detachment working in British Columbia and sailed down the Stikine River to its mouth and then by canoe to Sitka. Richard J. Bush and George Kennan served with a detachment working in Siberia and in the Amur region.[39] The Alaska team was headed by Major Robert Kennicott. They sailed out of San Francisco aboard the bark *Golden Gate*, armed with cannon and commanded by a member of the United States Revenue Cutter Service, Captain Charles M. Scammon.[40] The vessel, accompanied by the *George S. Wright,* put in at Sitka 7 August (Gregorian calendar) 1865 where the party stayed for ten days. Some members of the party found Russian hospitality very pleasant; others, like Lt. Henry Martyn Bannister, kept to themselves: "I suppose the whole time I was on shore in Sitka would not exceed ¾ of an hour," he wrote on 13 August.[41] They visited Unga in the Shumagin Islands, where Bannister assessed the potential of coal deposits. The Americans then proceeded to St. Michael. From there they traveled overland to Unalakleet and from there to the Yukon, to the Russian outpost of Nulato. Kennicott died on the Yukon in 1866. Dall, in the summer of 1867, traveled upstream to Fort Yukon. He was accompanied by Frederick Whymper and several locally hired men, among them Ketchum and Lebarge, names later known in the Interior fur trade and the initial gold strikes. The expedition lasted until the fall of 1867, though the project was canceled in 1866 when the transatlantic telegraph cable was completed. By then Alaska was United States territory.

It is impossible to say what the feelings and thoughts were of the last chief manager of Russian America when the expedition arrived and carried its probe deep into Alaskan territory. Perhaps he anticipated the end against which he strove so valiantly. And the end was coming. The United States, once again one nation, her territory extending from the Atlantic to the Pacific, was following her Manifest Destiny. In St. Petersburg, a sympathetic government, friendly to the Americans, believed that soon the United States would dominate the entire North American continent. It was moving to transfer sovereignty over Alaska to the United States to remove a possible cause of misunderstanding and conflict between the two nations.[42] Baron von Stoeckl, representing Russia in Washington, was given full authority to negotiate. The price tag originally calculated as a just indemnity for the loss to the Russian-American Company was a face-saving device. The Alaska Treaty was signed at four o'clock in the morning 18 March (30 March by the Gregorian calendar) 1867.[43] Ratification followed, without any difficulties in Russia, with some delays and possibly bribery in the United States. By the terms of the treaty, ratification had to be achieved within three months from the signing, or by 30 June 1867.[44]

It would be weeks, even months, before the people of the territory would be notified about this event that was to change their lives forever. In May Maksutov was notified by a telegram from Stoeckl that Alaskan ports were to be opened to all American shipping. The U.S. Revenue Steamer *Lincoln* was dispatched to Alaska in July 1867. This vessel took part in the transfer of jurisdiction ceremonies in October at Sitka.[45] Commissioners to effect the transfer of jurisdiction were appointed, General Lovell H. Rousseau to represent the United States and Captain A. I. Peshchurov to represent Russia. Captain 2d Rank F. F. Koskul' was appointed a special representative to assist the chief manager in the repatriation of company personnel and in the disposal of company property.[46] Many American officials labored under the illusion that Russian occupation of Alaska was bolstered by substantial military presence and were concerned with immediate transfer of "all military posts" to the United States as government property. Stoeckl had to write to Secretary William Seward that Russia never had any military presence outside of Sitka, and even there only a small contingent, whose barracks would be turned over for the use of the American garrison. Major General Halleck, in command of the Military Division of the Pacific, envisioned taking possession as a military occupation, and proposed the immediate establishment of at least four military posts, each of company strength. Halleck envisioned that "should *our Indian system* be introduced there, Indian wars must inevitably follow, and instead of a few *companies* for its military occupation as many *regiments* will be called for."

It was Halleck who recommended that "the name 'Alaska' be used to designate the military district or department that will be organized there."[47] Also on Halleck's recommendation, Alaska was declared for some purposes Indian territory.

An important question was private property rights, especially rights to land, the real estate. In his instructions to General Davis, who had been appointed to command the new military district, Major General Halleck stated, "it is a well established principle of international law that a change of sovereignty involves no change in the rights of private property, whether of individuals or of municipal corporations." Unfortunately, Russian land tenure rested not on formalities, and certainly not on formal documents, but on the right of occupancy and use. American authorities, at the highest level, were concerned with titles to land. Councillor Kostlivtsev submitted a "Memorandum" in which he set out the Russian land tenure concepts as pertaining to Alaska's Natives: "neither the government nor the company had ever had any influence upon the mode of division of lands between said natives, who, to the present time, use such lands in perfect freedom, without any foreign influence or restrictions." In relation to the Aleuts of the Aleutian archipelago, he stated that the lands are "used by right of prescription, never interrupted by any foreign violation or interference." The Tlingit and their neighbors along the southeast coast were independent and here "no attempts were ever made and no necessity ever occurred to introduce any system of land-ownership." As far as settlers were concerned, first occupancy and use constituted title without any formalities. If the United States deemed such titles necessary with respect to Russian settlers and creoles, then colonial administrators should issue licenses to dwellings, yards, and houses as private property, while meadows, woods, and streams would be designated communal property "of each separate locality."[48]

Unfortunately, by the fall of 1867 no documents certifying ownership existed anywhere in Alaska. And they were needed, indeed. Land-hungry speculators were already standing in the wings. On 21 April 1867, there was formed in Philadelphia "the Pioneer association for the civilization of the lately acquired Russian American Territory (now America)," whose object was "selling and making permanent homes for the citizens of the United States."[49] These men were not alone. As Captain Howard of the Revenue Steamer *Lincoln* reported on 17 August 1867, unscrupulous, land-grabbing individuals were on shore in Sitka staking out claims in the town two months before the territory was officially transferred to the United States. This was done in total disregard of instructions issued by General Halleck to Davis to safeguard the civil rights of all and to respect the rights to private property. Howard wrote:

> and I regret exceedingly that he [Chief Manager Maksutov] and the people should be annoyed by a set of unprincipled scoundrels, calling themselves Americans, from Victoria, who are taking up claims by staking off lots throughout the town, including even the governor's garden and the church and the church property.[50]

Though church property specifically was guaranteed by the treaty, these would-be pioneers were followed by many scoundrels, and the churches of Sitka, Kodiak, Unalaska, and elsewhere lost (and continue to lose) lands without compensation both to governmental agencies and to private individuals and institutions. (Recently, an Athabaskan community on the Alaska Peninsula bought back its chapel and cemetery grounds from a squatter, who had claimed the land under the Homestead Act, with moneys that could have been spent for many much-needed projects. They despaired winning the case in the courts: decisions of courts in Alaska in favor of the Native community have been routinely administratively reversed in Washington.)

On the day when the flag of the Russian-American Company was lowered, and the Stars and Stripes ran up the flagpole on Governor's Hill in the city now renamed Sitka, Russian citizens had little to celebrate and much to fear.

That day Sitka harbor was crowded as United States Navy vessels continued to arrive. First came, on 9 October 1867, the *John L. Stephens.* General Jefferson Davis, appointed Commander of the Alaska Military District, was on board. Then came the *Ossippee*, the *Resaca*, and the *Jamestown.* General Rousseau, the United States commissioner, and Captains Peshchurov and Koskul', representing Russia, were on board the *Ossippee*, which came into the harbor on 18 October. General Davis pressed for the transfer to take place immediately. In the afternoon of the same day Russian troops, 100 soldiers of the Siberian Line Battalion, were hastily assembled in front of the chief manager's residence. United States troops in battalion strength, led by General Davis, commanded by Brevet Major C. O. Wood, Ninth Infantry, formed up on the other side of the flagstaff. A twenty-man honor guard brought up the United States flag, sent for the occasion by the U.S. State Department. American spectators from the vessels in port numbered over a hundred, and perhaps sixty other civilians. Few Russian subjects attended the ceremony. Tlingit watched from the sea, from their canoes. About 3:30 PM the commissioners and Prince Maksutov appeared and took up their places. Promptly at 4:00 PM, Captain Peshchurov ordered down the Russian flag that waved from a 100-foot flagpole. The American and Russian ships began firing salutes. About a third of the way down the mast the flag caught on a yardarm; it was released by a Russian sailor and fell onto the fixed bayonets of the Siberians. Peshchurov formally transferred the sovereignty over Alaska to General Rousseau, who accepted on behalf of the United States. The American flag was run up the flagstaff by General Rousseau's fifteen-year-old son. The Russian batteries offered a salute to which American vessels responded. Russian America was no more.[51]

Within three years, few of her subjects not native to the land would remain.[52] Many of those who remained would be dispossessed. The proud creoles would become the contemptible half-breeds. The Natives would become wards of the state and would not gain their civil rights as citizens of the United States until the twentieth century. For many, the ground they lost would be regained only with the passage of the Alaska Native Claims Settlement Act of 1971.

Has the Russian heritage survived in Alaska? On the surface not much is left, and few modern-day Alaskans know the early history of their state. Few are curious about the strange Russian place names on Alaska's map, though these are numerous. The architectural landmarks are gone, for the most part. The few that remain attract predominantly out-of-state and foreign tourists. Traces of Russian folk tales are found in the folklore of some Alaska Natives, but these are usually told in Native languages and inaccessible to a wider audience. A few bearers of Russian surnames attempt to trace their descent. Still fewer seek the hometowns of their early ancestors in Russia. St. Lawrence Island Yupiit have gained a right to visit their relatives on the Chukchi Peninsula, and Aleuts hope to gain this right and visit their kin on the Commander Islands. But the legacy of faith embodied in the Orthodox Church is strong.

"Americanization of Alaska," to borrow the phrase from a contemporary historian, demanded eradication of Russian culture, foremost the Orthodox religion. Sheldon Jackson and his supporters, such as Reverend S. Hall Young, saw this as necessary and Jackson predicted (in 1899) that the "days of [the] Orthodox Church are numbered" and "that in twenty-five years from now there will not be any Orthodox church members left in Alaska."[53] He was wrong. While merchants and their entourage have vanished from the scene, the Orthodox Church has survived, cherished by Native villagers, fostered by Native readers, Native clergymen, and their *matushka*s (the clerics' wives). In fact, after seventy years of Marxist-inspired religious persecution in Russia, in 1993 Kamchatka welcomed Aleuts carrying the holy symbols of Orthodoxy.[54] The Light of the Spirit remains.

NOTES

1. New company bylaws and a list of shareholders at the time of the granting of the Third Charter were authorized by the Emperor on 10 October 1844 at Gatchina and published that year in St. Petersburg. On Wrangell's opinion rendered in response to a query by Gorchakov, see Bolkhovitinov, *Russko-amerikanskie otnosheniia* (1990), 104–109.
2. Pierce, *Builders of Alaska*, 40–41.
3. U.S. Department of State, *Russian America*, 213.
4. A. Kashevarov, "Chto takoe zapusk i promysel pushnykh zverei v Rossiisko-amerikanskikh koloniiakh," *Morskoi sbornik* 58, no. 4 (1862): 86–92; response by the Russian-American Company (Rossiisko-amerikanskaia kompaniia), "Zamechaniia Glavnago Pravleniia Rossiisko-amerikanskoi kompanii," *Morskoi sbornik* 59, no. 6 (1862): 1–8; and rebuttal by Kashevarov, "Otvet na zamechaniia Glavnago Pravleniia Rossiisko-amerikanskoi ko.," *Morskoi sbornik* 62, no. 9 (1862): 151–168.

Captain Howard's words were not heeded. Immediately following the transfer of Alaska to U.S. jurisdiction, a free-for-all killing of fur seals ensued not only on the rookeries but also pelagically, at sea, during the herd's migration. Skippers of fur-hunting vessels fought each other with arms. Two years later, in 1869, the United States moved to restrict the taking of fur seals and to control the harvest on the Russian model. Senate Bill S 32, "To Prevent the Extermination of fur-bearing animals of Alaska," was introduced 15 March 1869. The House version was HR 305. It concerned only the Pribilof fur seals. The Secretary of the Treasury was authorized to lease the islands to a private company. In 1870, the lease was granted to the Alaska Commercial Company (Miscellaneous Records, Secretary of the Treasury, 1868–1903, National Archives, Washington, D.C., microcopy 720, roll 25). Still later, the fur seal harvest was managed on behalf of the United States by government agents appointed by the Treasury (this lasted until the 1970s).

It took much longer to realize that sea otters were brought to the verge of extinction within the twenty years after the territorial transfer. Individual sea otter hunters settled en masse on the Alaska Peninsula, Kodiak, and the Shumagin Islands. When the government reserved the right of taking sea otters to the Natives, many of these hunters married Native women. By 1886 Aleuts appealed to President Cleveland protesting this practice and also protesting the taking of sea otters with breech-loading rifles. In 1897, Captain C. L. Hooper, commander of the Bering Sea fleet, pleaded for reinstatement of the Russian sea otter conservation practices. In 1911, when sea otters had disappeared from Alaskan waters, an international total ban on the taking of sea otters was enacted.

5. Gough, *Royal Navy*, 128–130.

6. Ibid., 146–148.

7. Bolkhovitinov, *Russko-amerikanskie otnosheniia* (1990), 201. From Okun in 1939 to Bolkhovitinov writing at present, Russian historians who have meticulously examined the available documents believe that Russia was aware of the presence of gold deposits in Alaska and tried not to advertise such knowledge for fear of being overrun. American historians, among them Richard A. Pierce, maintain that Russians were ignorant of Alaska's mineral wealth. I agree with the opinion of Bolkhovitinov et al., but I believe that the extent of Alaskan gold deposits was not truly appreciated.

8. Del Norte, Special Correspondent of the *Alta*, 17 October 1867, in U.S. Department of State, *Russian America*, 69.

9. Earlier known as the Church of the Holy Life-Creating Trinity.

10. The collection disappeared during the time Alaska was under American military administration. Apparently, part of the collection came into the hands of Captain Edward G. Fast on the staff of General Davis, who exhibited it in Chicago and later (1869) sold it to the Peabody Museum, Harvard University. See Edward G. Fast, *Catalogue of Antiquities and Curiosities Collected in the Territory of Alaska by Edward G. Fast... Consisting of More Than 2000 Most Valuable and Unique Specimens of Antiquity... also a Collection of Remarkable Fire Arms, a Large Geological Collection, etc., etc. Now on Exhibition at the Clinton Hall Art Galleries* (New York: Leavitt, Strebeigh and Co., 1869); William H. Dall, "The Native Tribes of Alaska," *Proceedings, American Association for the Advancement of Science, August 1885, Ann Arbor*, vol. 34 (Salem, Mass.: Salem Press, 1885).

11. Report by George Davidson, 30 November 1867, San Francisco, in U.S. Department of State, *Russian America*, 224.

12. Del Norte, in U.S. Department of State, *Russian America*, 69. See also Clarence L. Andrews, *The Story of Sitka, the Historic Outpost of the Northwest Coast, the Chief Factory of the Russian American Company* (Seattle: Lowman and Hanford, 1922); Sophia Cracroft, *Lady Franklin Visits Sitka, Alaska, 1870: The Journal of Sophia Cracroft, Sir John Franklin's Niece*, ed. R. N. DeArmond (Anchorage: Alaska Historical Society, 1981).

13. Letter of P. N. Golovin to his mother and sister, Novo-Arkhangel'sk, 27 November 1860, in P. N. Golovin, "Iz putevykh pisem P. N. Golovina," *Morskoi sbornik* 66, no. 5 (1863): 178. These letters are available in English translation as P. N. Golovin, *Civil and Savage Encounters*, trans. and ed. Basil Dmytryshyn and E. A. P. Crownhart-Vaughan (Portland: Press of the Oregon Historical Society, 1983).

14. Ibid. There is a movement here in Alaska to recreate this building.

15. Bolkhovitinov, *Russko-amerikanskie otnosheniia* (1990), 132.
16. Grinev, *Indeitsy tlinkity*, 170–172.
17. Golovin's letter from Sitka to his mother and sister, dated 17 December 1860, published as part of Golovin, "Iz putevykh pisem," *Morskoi sbornik* 66, no. 5 (1863): 178–180; no. 6 (1863): 288–291.
18. Lydia T. Black, "Fusion of Cultures and Meeting of the Frontiers: In Memory of Ordinary People" (paper presented at conference "Meeting of Frontiers," University of Alaska Fairbanks, Fairbanks, Alaska, May 17–19, 2001), published online at http://international.loc.gov/intldl/mtfhtml.
19. Snigaroff, *Niiĝuĝis maqax̂tazaqangis*, 8–10.
20. Golovin to his mother and sister, 17 December 1860, Novo-Arkhangel'sk, in Golovin, "Iz putevykh pisem," *Morskoi sbornik* 66, no. 6 (1863): 281–282.
21. Ibid., 288.
22. Bolkhovitinov, *Russko-amerikanskie otnosheniia* (1990), 108–109.
23. "Memorandum [*zapiska*] in the matter of revision of the by-laws of the Russian-American Company and organization of the Russian American Colonies," addressed by the Ministry of Finance to State Council, dated 26 December 1863, with appendices (St. Petersburg).
24. Bolkhovitinov, *Russko-amerikanskie otnosheniia* (1990), 116. Bolkhovitinov points out that, ever since Frank A. Golder's pioneering work in 1920 concerning the sale of Alaska to the United States, the authorship of this memorandum has been ascribed to Admiral Popov. He proves authorship by Shestakov (ibid., 115–116).
25. Russia, Departament Vneshnei torgovli, *Doklad komiteta ob ustroistve russkikh amerikanskikh kolonii*, 2 vols. (St. Petersburg: Departament Vneshnei torgovli, 1863).
26. This prejudicial frame of mind was noted earlier by Alexandra Kalmykow, *Administration of Alaska*.
27. Bolkhovitinov notes that the *published* versions of their reports, especially that of Golovin, were carefully censored and some of their favorable remarks eliminated (*Russko-amerikanskie otnosheniia* [1990], 129–136).
28. Russia, Departament Vneshnei torgovli, *Doklad komiteta ob ustroistve*.
29. Rossiisko-amerikanskaia kompaniia, *Otchet Rossiisko-amerikanskoi kompanii za 1861 g.* (St. Petersburg, 1862).
30. Bolkhovitinov, *Russko-amerikanskie otnosheniia* (1990), 138–142.
31. These vocabularies have been recently provided to the Alaska Native Language Center, University of Alaska Fairbanks, by our Russian colleagues and are undergoing study by a Tlingit-language specialist.
32. Arndt, "Russian Exploration," 106–107.
33. The Beans had two children. After Anastasia died, Bean went to Chicago and remarried. The second Mrs. Bean's death, at the hands of an Athabaskan, has entered Alaskan lore. For an account based on Bean family papers, see Alden S. Bean, "Trade and Treachery on the Yukon, 1870–1878" (paper presented to Mr. Bennett, Northwestern University, in partial fulfillment of requirements for the course Business History, May 1966, copyright 1985; copy in collections of Rasmuson Library, University of Alaska Fairbanks).
34. Bean was a Western Union Telegraph Expedition underling.
35. Stuart Ramsay Tompkins, *Alaska: Promyshlennik and Sourdough* (Norman: University of Oklahoma Press, 1945), 182; Charles Vevier, "The Collins Overland Line and American Continentalism," in *Alaska and Its History*, ed. Morgan B. Sherwood (Seattle: University of Washington Press, 1967), 209–230; Richard A. Pierce, preface to *Life on the Yukon, 1865–1867*, by George R. Adams (Kingston, Ontario: Limestone Press, 1982), iv; James Alton James, *The First Scientific Exploration of Russian America and the Purchase of Alaska* (Evanston and Chicago: Northwestern University, 1942), 23 (this latter work is full of errors of fact and clichés, as far as Russian America is concerned).

36. Perry McDonough Collins, *A Voyage Down the Amoor* (New York: Appleton and Company, 1860). See also U.S. Congress, House of Representatives, *Explorations of the Amoor River: Letter from the Secretary of State, in Answer to a Resolution of the House, Calling for Information Relative to the Explorations of the Amoor River*, 35th Cong., 1st sess., 1858, H. Ex. Doc. 98. On Russian support for Collins's project, see Bolkhovitinov, *Russko-amerikanskie otnosheniia* (1990), 143–166. The U.S. Congress authorized the telegraph project (PL-199, 1 July 1864, 38th Cong., 1st sess.) by *An Act to Encourage and Facilitate Telegraphic Communication between the Eastern and Western Continents, U.S. Statutes At Large* 13 (1864): 340–341.

37. Col. Bulkley's papers await careful scholarly examination.

38. On the Scientific Corps of the Western Union Telegraph Expedition, see chap. 1 and on the role and assessment of W. H. Dall (with which not all scholars agree) see chap. 2 of Morgan B. Sherwood, *Exploration of Alaska, 1865–1900* (New Haven: Yale University Press, 1965), 15–56.

39. Bush and Kennan published two very different accounts of their sojourn in Siberia, though both served with the same outfit. Compare Richard J. Bush's *Reindeer, Dogs, and Snow-shoes: A Journal of Siberian Travel and Explorations Made in the Years 1865, 1866, and 1867* (New York: Harper and Brothers, 1871) with George Kennan's *Tent Life in Siberia, and Adventures among the Koraks and Other Tribes in Kamchatka and Northern Asia* (London: S. Low, Son and Marston, 1870). Kennan was the head of the Siberian team.

40. George R. Adams, *Life on the Yukon, 1865–1867*, ed. Richard A. Pierce (Kingston, Ontario: Limestone Press, 1982), 22–23.

41. See Bannister's journal in James, *First Scientific Exploration*, 174.

42. Frank A. Golder was the first scholar to put forward this view, never refuted by responsible scholarship. See Frank A. Golder, "The Attitude of the Russian Government toward Alaska," in *The Pacific Ocean in History*, ed. H. M. Stephens (New York: Macmillan, 1917; reprinted in *Alaska Journal* 1, no. 2 [1971]: 53–55, 59). See also Golder's "The Purchase of Alaska," *American Historical Review* 25, no. 3 (1920): 411–425.

43. Bolkhovitinov, *Russko-amerikanskie otnosheniia* (1990), 220.

44. David Hunter Miller, *The Alaska Treaty*, 120.

45. U.S. Coast Survey, "Report of Assistant George Davidson Relative to the Resources and Coast Features of Alaska Territory," in *Report of the Superintendent of the United States Coast Survey, Showing the Progress of the Survey during the Year 1867*, 40th Cong., 2d sess., 1869, H. Ex. Doc. 275, 187–329 and charts. See also U.S. Department of State, *Russian America*.

46. Bolkhovitinov, *Russko-amerikanskie otnosheniia* (1990), 265–267.

47. Clay to Seward, 5 July 1867; Stoeckl to Seward, 20 August 1867; and Halleck to Major General Townsend, 22 May 1867, in U.S. Department of State, *Russian America*, 17–18, 21, 56–58.

48. Kostlivtsev, "memorandum" in translation by S. N. Buynitzky, in ibid., 22–24.

49. U.S. Department of State, *Russian America*, 43.

50. Report by Howard to Secretary of the Treasury McCollough, Sitka, 18 August 1867, in U.S. Department of State, *Russian America*, 197.

51. This account follows that of Del Norte and the report of General Davis, in U.S. Department of State, *Russian America*.

52. According to Clarence L. Andrews (*Story of Sitka*, 78 n), 168 persons left aboard the *Tsaritsa* 14 December 1867; on 8 December 1868 the *Winged Arrow*, bound for St. Petersburg, carried 300 persons. The number of persons sailing on other vessels has not been established.

53. Quoted after Oleksa, *Orthodox Alaska*, 182; see also Ted C. Hinckley, *The Americanization of Alaska, 1867–1897* (Palo Alto, Calif.: Pacific Books, 1972).

55. Cf. chap. 4, note 14, and chap. 13, note 62. The 1993 event at the site of Nizhne-Kamchatsk, abandoned but now in the process of resettlement, was witnessed by the author.

Bibliography

ARCHIVAL SOURCES CONSULTED

Alaska State Historical Library, Juneau, Alaska: Russia Miscellaneous; Vinokouroff Collection; Dolgopolov Collection.

Archive of Russia's Foreign Policy (AVPRI; Arkhiv vneshnei politiki Rossii), Moscow: Fond Rossiisko-Amerikanskoi kompanii, "Portfeli Millera" and collection of charts and maps.

Archive of the Russian Geographic Society, St. Petersburg.

AVPRI *see* Archive of Russia's Foreign Policy.

Clarence L. Andrews Papers, Archives, Alaska and Polar Regions Department, Rasmuson Library, University of Alaska Fairbanks.

Dolgopolov Collection, private collection in possession of Richard A. Pierce, Limestone Press, Kingston, Ontario.

Golder Collection, Manuscript Division, Library of Congress, Washington, D.C., and University of Washington, Seattle. Available on microfilm. Note that the Golder Collection materials held at the Library of Congress were recently reorganized and the photostats from Russian archives are now filed under the appropriate Russian imperial ministry or office, such as Ministry of the Navy, etc.

Irkutsk State Regional Archive, Irkutsk, Russia: Records of the Orthodox Churches, Irkutsk Diocese.

National Archives, Washington, D.C.: Records of the Russian-American Company, Microfilm Group 11; Miscellaneous Records, Secretary of the Treasury, 1868–1903, Microcopy 720, Roll 25.

Records of the Russian Orthodox Church in Alaska, Manuscript Division, Library of Congress, Washington, D.C. Available on microfilm.

Records of the Russian Orthodox Church of Alaska, St. Herman Orthodox Seminary, Kodiak, Alaska. Available on microfilm.

RGADA *see* Russian State Archive of Ancient Documents.

RGAVMF *see* Russian State Naval Archive.

RGIA *see* Russian State Historical Archive.

Russian State Archive of Ancient Documents (RGADA), Moscow: Fond 796.

Russian State Historical Archive (RGIA), St. Petersburg: Fond 1374.

Russian State Naval Archive (RGAVMF), St. Petersburg: Fond 166; Fond 198; Fond 213; Fond 214; Fond 870.

Scott Polar Research Institute, Cambridge, England: Franklin Search collections.

Shur Collection, Archives, Alaska and Polar Regions Department, Rasmuson Library, University of Alaska Fairbanks (this collection consists of microfilm copies of documents from Russian archives pertaining to Alaska).

State Public Library, St. Petersburg, Russia (formerly the M. E. Saltykov–Shchedrin State Public Library): Manuscript Division, Fond Adelunga.

State Regional Archive of Perm', Russia.

University of Göttingen Library, Göttingen, Germany: Rare Books and Manuscripts, von Asch Collection.

Yudin Collection, Manuscript Division, Library of Congress, Washington, D.C.

BIBLIOGRAPHY

Adams, Edward
1850–51 "Journal Kept Ashore in and near St. Michael's, Alaska, 12 October 1850–3 July 1851." Collinson's Franklin Search expedition, 1850–1855, Manuscript 1115, Scott Polar Research Institute, Cambridge, England. Microfilm copy, Alaska and Polar Regions Department, Elmer E. Rasmuson Library, University of Alaska Fairbanks.

Adams, George R.
1982 *Life on the Yukon, 1865–1867*, ed. Richard A. Pierce. Kingston, Ontario: Limestone Press.

Afonsky, Gregory, Bishop of Sitka and Alaska
1977 *A History of the Orthodox Church in Alaska (1794–1917)*. Kodiak, Alaska: St. Herman Theological Seminary.

Alaska History Research Project
1938 *Documents Relative to the History of Alaska*. 16 vols. College, Alaska.

Aleksandrov, V. A.
1964 *Russkoe naselenie Sibiri XVII–nachala XVIII v. (Eniseiskii krai)*. Trudy Instituta etnografii, n.s., vol. 87. Moscow: Izdatel'stvo "Nauka."

Alekseev, A. I.
1958 *Okhotsk—kolybel' russkogo Tikhookeanskogo flota*. Khabarovsk: Khabarovskoe knizhnoe izdatel'stvo.

Anderson, M. S.
1958 *Britain's Discovery of Russia, 1553–1815*. Toronto: Macmillan Company of Canada; New York: St. Martin's Press.

Andreev, A. I.
1960 *Ocherki po istochnikovedeniiu Sibiri*. Vol. 1, *XVII vek*. Moscow and Leningrad: Izdatel'stvo "Nauka."
1965 *Ocherki po istochnikovedeniiu Sibiri*. Vol. 2, *XVIII vek (pervaia polovina)*. Moscow and Leningrad: Izdatel'stvo "Nauka."

Andreev, Aleksandr I., ed. and comp.
1944 *Russkie otkrytiia v Tikhom okeane i Severnoi Amerike v XVIII–XIX vekakh*. Moscow and Leningrad: Izdatel'stvo Akademii nauk SSSR. Translated by Carl Ginsberg under the title *Russian Discoveries in the Pacific and in North America in the Eighteenth and Nineteenth Centuries: A Collection of Materials* (Ann Arbor, Mich.: J. W. Edwards for American Council of Learned Societies, 1952).
1948 *Russkie otkrytiia v Tikhom okeane i Severnoi Amerike v XVIII veke*. Moscow: Ogiz.

Andreev, V.
1893 "Dokumenty po ekspeditsii kapitan-komandora Beringa v Ameriku v 1741." *Morskoi sbornik* 255, no. 5.

Andrews, Clarence L.
n.d. Unpublished biography of Baranov. Archives, Rasmuson Library, University of Alaska Fairbanks.
1922 *The Story of Sitka, the Historic Outpost of the Northwest Coast, the Chief Factory of the Russian American Company*. Seattle: Lowman and Hanford.

Archer, Christon I.
1992 "The Political and Military Context of the Spanish Advance into the Pacific Northwest." In *Spain and the Northwest Coast: Essays in Recognition of the Bicentennial of the Malaspina Expedition, 1791–1792*, ed. Robin Inglis, 9–28. Vancouver, B.C.: Vancouver Maritime Museum.

Arkhiv Admirala P. V. Chichagova
1885 St. Petersburg.

Armstrong, Terence E.
1965 *Russian Settlement in the North*. Cambridge, England: Cambridge University Press.
1983 "Bering's Expeditions." In *Studies in Russian Historical Geography*, ed. J. H. Bater and R. A. French. Vol. 2, 175–195. London: Academic Press.

Arndt, Katherine L.
1985 "The Russian-American Company and the Smallpox Epidemic of 1835 to 1840." Paper presented at twelfth annual meeting of the Alaska Anthropological Association, Anchorage, 2 March 1985.
1988 "Russian Relations with the Stikine Tlingit, 1833–1867." *Alaska History* 3, no. 1: 27–43.
1990 "Russian-American Company Trade on the Middle Yukon River, 1839–1867." In *Russia in North America: Proceedings of the 2nd International Conference on Russian America, Sitka, Alaska, August 19–22, 1987*, ed. Richard A. Pierce, 180–192. Kingston, Ontario; Fairbanks, Alaska: Limestone Press.
1990 "Russian Exploration and Trade in Alaska's Interior." In *Russian America: The Forgotten Frontier*, ed. Barbara S. Smith and Redmond J. Barnett, 95–107. Tacoma: Washington State Historical Society.
1996 "Dynamics of the Fur Trade on the Middle Yukon River, Alaska, 1837–1867." Ph.D. diss., University of Alaska Fairbanks.
1996 "Released to Reside Forever in the Colonies: Founding of a Russian-American Company Retirement Settlement at Ninilchik, Alaska." In *Adventures through Time: Readings in the Anthropology of Cook Inlet*, ed. N. Y. Davis and W. E. Davis, 237–250. Anchorage, Alaska: Cook Inlet Historical Society.
2000 "Preserving the Future Hunt: The Russian-American Company and Marine Mammal Conservation Policies." Paper presented at Cook

Inlet Historical Society Symposium "Science Under Sail: Russian Exploration in the North Pacific, 1728–1867," Anchorage, Alaska, October 2000.

Arndt, Katherine L., and Richard A. Pierce
2003 *A Construction History of Sitka, Alaska, as Documented in the Records of the Russian-American Company.* 2nd ed. Sitka National Historical Park Historical Context Study. Anchorage, Alaska: U.S. Department of the Interior, National Park Service, Alaska Support Office and Sitka National Historical Park.

Artem'iev, A. R.
1994 "Iz istorii osvoeniia russkimi ostrova Sitkha (Baranova)." Paper presented at the international conference "Bridges of Science Between North America and Russian Far East," 25–27 August 1994, Anchorage, Alaska, and Vladivostok, Russia.

A. S. [A. Sokolov?]
1848 "Iaponskoe sudno 1806 goda." *Morskoi sbornik* 1: 484–486.

Avdeeva-Polevaia, Ekaterina
1837 *Zapiski i zamechaniia o Sibiri, s prilozheniem starinnykh russkikh pesen.* Moscow: N. Stepanov. Reprinted in *Zapiski irkutskikh zhitelei*, comp. and ed. M. D. Sergeev, 7–124. Irkutsk: Vostochno-Sibirskoe knizhnoe izdatel'stvo, 1990.

Avrich, Paul
1972 *Russian Rebels, 1600–1800.* New York: W. W. Norton and Company.

Avril, Ph.
1697 *Voyage en divers états d'Europe et d'Asie.* Paris. Cited after S. V. Bakhrushin, "Russkoe prodvizhenie za Ural," in *S. V. Bakhrushin: Nauchnye trudy*, vol. 3, pt. 1 (Moscow: Izdatel'stvo Akademii nauk SSSR), 157 n. 42.

Bagrow, Leo
1947 "Sparwenfeld's Map of Siberia." *Imago Mundi* 4: 65–70.
1952 "The First Russian Maps of Siberia and Their Influence on the West-European Cartography of N.E. Asia." *Imago Mundi* 9: 83–93.
1975 *A History of the Cartography of Russia Up to 1800.* Edited by Henry W. Castner. 2 vols. Wolfe Island, Ontario: Walker Press.

Bailey, Berkley B., and Geoffrey C. Orth
1990 "Novo-Aleksandrovskii Redoubt: Hagemeister Island." In *Russia in North America: Proceedings of the 2nd International Conference on Russian America, Sitka, Alaska, August 19–22, 1987*, ed. Richard A. Pierce, 413–425. Kingston, Ontario; Fairbanks, Alaska: Limestone Press.

Bakhrushin, S. V.
1922 "Istoricheskii ocherk zaseleniia Sibiri do poloviny XIX veka." In *Ocherki po istorii kolonizatsii Severa i Sibiri*, 2: 18–83. Petrograd.
1941 "Voenno-promyshlennye ekspeditsii torgovykh liudei v Sibiri." *Istoricheskie zapiski* (Moscow) 10: 167–179.
1951 "Snariazhenie russkikh promyshlennikov v Sibiri v XVII v." In *Istoricheskii pamiatnik russkogo arkticheskogo moreplavaniia XVII v.*, ed. A. P. Okladnikov and D. M. Pinkenson. Moscow and Leningrad.
1954 "Agenty russkikh torgovykh liudei XVII v." In *S. V. Bakhrushin: Nauchnye trudy*, vol. 2, 134–153. Moscow: Izdatel'stvo Akademii nauk SSSR.
1954 "Promyshlennye predpriiatiia russkikh torgovykh liudei v XVII v." In *S. V. Bakhrushin: Nauchnye trudy*, vol. 2, 224–255. Moscow: Izdatel'stvo Akademii nauk SSSR.
1954 "Torgovye krest'iane v XVII v." In *S. V. Bakhrushin: Nauchnye trudy*, vol. 2, 118–133. Moscow: Izdatel'stvo Akademii nauk SSSR.
1955 "Iasak v Sibiri v XVII v." In *S. V. Bakhrushin: Nauchnye trudy*, vol. 3, pt. 2, 49–85. Moscow: Izdatel'stvo Akademii nauk SSSR.
1955 "Legenda o Vasilii Mangazeiskom." In *S. V. Bakhrushin: Nauchnye trudy*, vol. 3, pt. 1, 331–354. Moscow: Izdatel'stvo Akademii nauk SSSR.
1955 "Mangazeiskaia mirskaia obshchina v XVII v." In *S. V. Bakhrushin: Nauchnye trudy*, vol. 3, pt. 1, 297–330. Moscow: Izdatel'stvo Akademii nauk SSSR.
1955 "Ostiatskie i vogul'skie kniazhestva v XVI–XVII vv." In *S. V. Bakhrushin: Nauchnye trudy*, vol. 3, pt. 2, 86–152. Moscow: Izdatel'stvo Akademii nauk SSSR.
1955 "Pokruta na sobolinykh promyslakh XVII v." In *S. V. Bakhrushin: Nauchnye trudy*, vol. 3, pt. 1, 198–211. Moscow: Izdatel'stvo Akademii nauk SSSR.
1955 "Puti v Sibir' v XVI–XVII vv." In *S. V. Bakhrushin: Nauchnye trudy*, vol. 3, pt. 1, 72–136. Moscow: Izdatel'stvo Akademii nauk SSSR.
1955 "Puti v Vostochnuiu Sibir'." In *S. V. Bakhrushin: Nauchnye trudy*, vol. 3, pt. 1, 111–136. Moscow: Izdatel'stvo Akademii nauk SSSR.
1955 "Russkoe prodvizhenie za Ural." In *S. V. Bakhrushin: Nauchnye trudy*, vol. 3, pt. 1, 137–160. Moscow: Izdatel'stvo Akademii nauk SSSR.
1955 "Torgi gostia Nikitina v Sibiri i Kitae." In *S. V. Bakhrushin: Nauchnye trudy*, vol. 3, pt. 1, 226–251. Moscow: Izdatel'stvo Akademii nauk SSSR.

Bancroft, Hubert Howe
1886 *History of Alaska, 1730–1885.* San Francisco: A. L. Bancroft and Company. Reprint, Darien, Conn.: Hafner Publishing Company, 1970.

Barashkova, V. S.
1983 "Torgovlia ryboi i sol'iu belozerskikh posadskikh liudei i krest'ian v kontse XVI–nachale XVII v." In *Promyshlennost' i torgovlia v Rossii XVII–XVIII vv.*, ed. A. A. Preobrazhenskii, 192–201. Moscow: Izdatel'stvo "Nauka."

Barratt, Glynn

1981 *Russia in Pacific Waters, 1715–1825.* Vancouver: University of British Columbia Press.

Bashkina, Nina N., N. N. Bolkhovitinov, J. H. Brown, et al., eds.

1980 *The United States and Russia: The Beginning of Relations, 1765–1815.* Washington, D.C.: U.S. Government Printing Office.

Bassin, Mark

1988 "Expansion and Colonialism on the Eastern Frontier: Views of Siberia and the Far East in Pre-Petrine Russia." *Journal of Historical Geography* 14, no. 1: 3–21.

Bean, Alden S.

1966 "Trade and Treachery on the Yukon, 1870–1878." Paper presented to Mr. Bennett, Northwestern University, in partial fulfillment of requirements for the course Business History, May 1966. Copyright 1985. Copy in collections of Rasmuson Library, University of Alaska Fairbanks.

Beechey, Frederick W.

1831 *Narrative of a Voyage to the Pacific and Beering's Strait, to Co-operate with the Polar Expeditions: Performed in His Majesty's Ship* Blossom, *under the Command of Captain F. W. Beechey, R. N.,...in the Years 1825, 26, 27, 28.* 2 pts. London: Henry Colburn and Richard Bentley.

Belomorskii, Osip

1858 "Vzgliad na zapasy ptitselovnago promysla v Pomor'ie." *Morskoi sbornik* 36, no. 8: 121–140.

Belov, M. I.

1948 *Semeon Dezhnev, 1648–1948: K stoletiiu otkrytiia proliva mezhdu Aziei i Amerikoi.* Moscow-Leningrad.

1949 "Istoricheskoe plavanie Semeona Dezhneva." *Izvestiia Vsesoiuznogo geograficheskogo obshchestva* 79: 459–472.

1951 "Arkticheskie plavaniia i ustroistva russkikh morskikh sudov v XVII veke." In *Istoricheskii pamiatnik arkticheskogo moreplavaniia XVII veka: Arkheologicheskie nakhodki na ostrove Faddeia i na beregu zaliva Simsa*, 63–80. Leningrad and Moscow: Izdatel'stvo Glavsevmorputi.

1952 *Russkie morekhody v Ledovitom i Tikhom okeanakh.* Moscow-Leningrad: Glavsevmorput'.

1955 *Semeon Dezhnev.* 2nd rev. ed. Moscow: Morskoi transport.

1956 *Arkticheskoe moreplavanie s drevneishikh vremen do serediny XIX veka.* Vol. 1 of *Istoriia otkrytiia i osvoeniia Severnogo morskogo puti*, ed. Ia. Ia. Gakkel', A. P. Okladnikov, and M. B. Chernenko. Moscow: Morskoi transport.

1957 "Novye dannye o sluzhbakh Vladimira Atlasova i pervykh pokhodakh russkikh na Kamchatku." *Letopis' Severa* 2: 89–106.

1957 "Semeon Dezhnev i amerikanskaia literatura." *Izvestiia Vsesoiuznogo geograficheskogo obshchestva* 89: 482–485.

1963 "Novoe li eto slovo o plavanii S. I. Dezhneva?" *Izvestiia Vsesoiuznogo geograficheskogo obshchestva* 95: 443–446.

1969 *Mangazeia.* Leningrad: Gidrometeoizdat.

1973 *Podvig Semeona Dezhneva.* 3d rev. ed. Moscow: Mysl'.

Belov, M. I., ed.

1964 *Russkie arkticheskie ekspeditsii XVII–XX vv.* Leningrad: Gidrometeorologicheskoe izdatel'stvo.

Belov, M. I., O. V. Ovsiannikov, and V. F. Starkov

1981 *Mangazeia.* 2 pts. Leningrad: Gidrometeoizdat; Moscow: Izdatel'stvo "Nauka."

Benyowsky [Beniovskii], Mauritius Augustus

1790 *Memoirs and Travels of Mauritius Augustus Count de Benyowsky.* Translated from a French printed version by W. Nicholson. London: G.G.J. and J. Robinson.

Berg, L. S.

1946 *Ocherki po istorii russkikh geograficheskikh otkrytii.* Moscow and Leningrad: Izdatel'stvo Akademii nauk SSSR.

1946 *Otkrytie Kamchatki i ekspeditsii Beringa 1725–1742 gg.* Moscow and Leningrad: Izdatel'stvo Akademii nauk SSSR.

1949 *Ocherki po istorii russkikh geograficheskikh otkrytii.* 2d rev. and enl. ed. Moscow and Leningrad: Izdatel'stvo Akademii nauk SSSR.

Bering Sea Tribunal of Arbitration

1895 *Fur Seal Arbitration, Proceedings of the Tribunal of Arbitration, Convened at Paris.* 16 vols. Washington, D.C.

Berkh, Vasilii N.

1819 "Puteshestvie kozach'iago golovy Afanasiia Shestakova, i pokhod maiora Pavlutskago v 1729 i 1730 godakh." *Syn Otechestva* 54, no. 20: 3–17.

1821 "Pobeg grafa Ben'iovskago iz Kamchatki vo Frantsiiu." *Syn Otechestva* 71, no. 27: 3–23; 71, no. 28: 49–79.

1823 *Khronologicheskaia istoriia otkrytiia Aleutskikh ostrovov, ili podvigi Rossiiskogo kupechestva.* St. Petersburg: N. Grech. Translated by Dmitri Krenov, ed. Richard A. Pierce, under the title *A Chronological History of the Discovery of the Aleutian Islands, or, The Exploits of Russian Merchants with a Supplement of Historical Data on the Fur Trade* (Kingston, Ontario: Limestone Press, 1974).

1828 "Dopolnenie k zhizneopisaniiu M. V. Lomonosova." *Moskovskii telegraf* 11. Cited after V. A. Perevalov, *Lomonosov i Arktika* (Moscow and Leningrad: Izdatel'stvo Glavsevmorputi, 1949), 232 n. 1.

Bernshtam, T. A.

1978 *Pomory: Formirovanie gruppy i sistema khoziaistva.* Leningrad: Izdatel'stvo "Nauka."

Bernshtam, T. A., and K. V. Chistov, eds.

1986 *Russkii Sever: Problemy etnokul'turnoi istorii, etnografii, fol'kloristiki.* Leningrad: Izdatel'stvo "Nauka."

Black, Lydia T.

1977 "Ivan Pan'kov: An Architect of Aleut Literacy." *Arctic Anthropology* 14, no. 1: 94–107. Reprinted with addendum in *Orthodox Alaska* (Fall 1978): 1–33, and in *Interpreting Alaska's History*, ed. M. Mangusso and Stephen Haycox, Anchorage: Alaska Pacific University Press, 1989, 86–109.

1977 "The Konyag (The Inhabitants of the Island of Kodiak) by Ioasaf [Bolotov], 1794–1799, and by Gideon, 1804–1807." *Arctic Anthropology* 14, no. 2: 79–108.

1979 "The Question of Maps: Exploration of the Bering Sea in the Eighteenth Century." In *The Sea in Alaska's Past: Conference Proceedings*, 6–50. History and Archaeology Publications Series, no. 25. Anchorage: Office of History and Archaeology, Alaska Division of Parks.

1981 "The Daily Journal of Reverend Father Juvenal: A Cautionary Tale." *Ethnohistory* 28, no. 1 (Winter): 33–58.

1981 "The Nature of Evil: Of Whales and Sea Otters." In *Indians, Animals, and the Fur Trade: A Critique of "Keepers of the Game,"* ed. Shepard Krech III, 111–153. Athens, Ga.: University of Georgia Press.

1984 *Atkha: An Ethnohistory of the Western Aleutians.* Kingston, Ontario: Limestone Press.

1987 "Peg Calendars of Alaska." In *Faces, Voices, and Dreams: A Celebration of the Centennial of the Sheldon Jackson Museum, Sitka, Alaska, 1888–1988*, ed. Peter L. Corey, 97–100. Juneau: Division of Alaska State Museums and Friends of Alaska State Museum.

1990 "Creoles in Russian America." *Pacifica* 2, no. 2: 142–155.

1991 *Glory Remembered: Wooden Headgear of Alaska Sea Hunters.* Juneau: Alaska State Museums.

1991 *The Lovtsov Atlas of the North Pacific Ocean.* Kingston, Ontario; Fairbanks, Alaska: Limestone Press.

1992 "From Valaamo to Spruce Island: Russian Orthodoxy in Alaska, U.S.A." In *Northern Religions and Shamanism*, ed. Mihály Hoppál and Juha Pentikainen, 100–107. Budapest: Akadémiai Kiadó; Helsinki: Finnish Literature Society.

1992 "Promyshlenniki... Who Were They?" In *Bering and Chirikov: The American Voyages and Their Impact*, ed. O. W. Frost, 279–290. Anchorage: Alaska Historical Society.

1992 "The Russian Conquest of Kodiak." *Anthropological Papers of the University of Alaska* 24, nos. 1–2: 165–182.

1992 "The Russians Were Coming...." In *Spain and the North Pacific Coast: Essays in Recognition of the Bicentennial of the Malaspina Expedition, 1791–1792*, ed. Robin Inglis, 29–34. Vancouver, B.C.: Vancouver Maritime Museum.

1994 "Religious Syncretism as Cultural Dynamic." In *Circumpolar Religion and Ecology: An Anthropology of the North*, ed. Takashi Irimoto and Takako Yamada, 213–220. Tokyo: University of Tokyo Press.

1997 "Put' na Novyi Valaam: Stanovlenie russkoi pravoslavnoi tserkvi na Aliaske." In *Osnovanie Russkoi Ameriki, 1732–1799*, 251–277. Vol. 1 of *Istoriia Russkoi Ameriki, 1732–1867*, ed. N. N. Bolkhovitinov. Moscow: "Mezhdunarodnye otnosheniia."

[1998] *Orthodoxy in Alaska: Christianization of Alaska; Veniaminov's Stewardship; Orthodoxy in Alaska after 1867.* Distinguished Lectures, no. 6. Berkeley, Calif.: Patriarch Athenagoras Orthodox Institute at the Graduate Theological Union.

1999 "The Imperial Navy, V. M. Golovnin, and Baranov's Removal." Paper presented at International Conference Dedicated to the 200th Anniversary of the Formation of the Russian-American Company and to the Investigation of American Civilization as a Historical Phenomenon, Center for North American Studies, Institute of World History, Russian Academy of Sciences, Moscow, 6–9 September 1999.

2000 "The Best Route to America Lies Across the Pole." Paper presented at Cook Inlet Historical Society Symposium "Science Under Sail: Russian Exploration in the North Pacific, 1728–1867," Anchorage, Alaska, October 2000. Forthcoming in the symposium proceedings.

2001 "Fusion of Cultures and Meeting of the Frontiers: In Memory of Ordinary People." Paper presented at conference "Meeting of Frontiers," University of Alaska Fairbanks, Fairbanks, Alaska, May 17–19, 2001. Published online at Library of Congress website, section "Meeting of Frontiers," http://international.loc.gov/intldl/mtfhtml.

Black, Lydia, ed.

1997 *A Good and Faithful Servant: The Year of Saint Innocent, an Exhibit Commemorating the Bicentennial of the Birth of Ioann Veniaminov, 1797–1997.* Fairbanks: University of Alaska Fairbanks and Alaska State Veniaminov Bicentennial Committee.

Black, Lydia T., and Richard A. Pierce

1991 "Russian America and the Finns." *Terra* 29, nos. 2–3 (December–May): 18–29.

Bludov, D. N.

1865 "Zapiska o bunte Beniovskago v pol'zu kniazia Pavla Petrovicha." *Russkii arkhiv* 4: 657–680.

Bockstoce, John R.

1986 *Whales, Ice, and Men: The History of Whaling in the Western Arctic.* Seattle: University of

Washington Press in association with the New Bedford Whaling Museum, Massachusetts.

Bolkhovitinov, N. N.
1975 *The Beginnings of Russian-American Relations, 1775–1815.* Translated by Elena Levin with introduction by L. H. Butterfield. Cambridge, Mass.: Harvard University Press. Originally published as *Stanovlenie russko-amerikanskikh otnoshenii, 1775–1815* (Moscow: Izdatel'stvo "Nauka," 1966).
1975 *Russko-amerikanskie otnosheniia, 1815–1832 gg.* Moscow: Izdatel'stvo "Nauka."
1990 *Russko-Amerikanskie otnosheniia i prodazha Aliaski, 1834–1867.* Moscow: Izdatel'stvo "Nauka." Translated by Richard A. Pierce under the title *Russian-American Relations and the Sale of Alaska, 1834–1867* (Kingston, Ontario; Fairbanks, Alaska: Limestone Press, 1996).

Bolkhovitinov, N. N., ed.
1997–1999 *Istoriia Russkoi Ameriki, 1732–1867.* 3 vols. Moscow: "Mezhdunarodnye otnosheniia."

Bolotov, Archimandrite Ioasaf
[1797?] "Kratkiia ob"iasneniia sdelannye sootvetstvenno zapiske prislannoi ot Sviateishago Pravitel'stvuiushchago Sinoda, ob Amerikanskom ostrove Kadiake." Yudin Collection and Russian collections (formerly Golder Collection), Manuscript Division, Library of Congress. Photostat. Original in Russian State Naval Archive, St. Petersburg.
1805 "Kratkiia opisanie ob Amerikanskom ostrove Kad'iake." *Drug prosviashcheniia* 10: 89–106.

Breitfus, L. L.
1905 *Morskoi zverinyi promysel v Belom more i severnom Ledovitom okeane.* St. Petersburg.

Breitfuss, L.
1939 "Early Maps of North-Eastern Asia and of the Lands around the North Pacific: Controversy between G. F. Müller and N. Delisle." *Imago Mundi* 3: 87–99.

Brooks, Charles Wolcott
1875 "Report of Japanese Vessels Wrecked in the North Pacific Ocean, from the Earliest Records to the Present Time." *Proceedings of the California Academy of Sciences* 6: 50–66.

Bunak, V. V., ed.
1965 *Proiskhozhdenie i etnicheskaia istoriia russkogo naroda po antropologicheskim dannym.* Trudy Instituta Etnografii, n.s., 88. Moscow: Izdatel'stvo "Nauka."

Bush, Richard J.
1871 *Reindeer, Dogs, and Snow-shoes: A Journal of Siberian Travel and Explorations Made in the Years 1865, 1866, and 1867.* New York: Harper and Brothers.

Butsinskii, P. N.
1889 *Zaselenie Sibiri i byt pervykh eia nasel'nikov.* Kharkov: Tipografiia Gubernskago Pravleniia.

Bychkov, Oleg V.
1990 "Russian Fur Gathering Traditions in the Eighteenth Century." *Pacifica* 2, no. 2: 80–87.
1994 "Russian Hunters in Eastern Siberia in the Seventeenth Century: Lifestyle and Economy." Translated by Mina Jacobs. *Arctic Anthropology* 31, no. 1: 72–85.

Case, David S.
1990 "The Russian Legacy of the Alaska Native Claims." In *Russian America: The Forgotten Frontier*, ed. Barbara S. Smith and Redmond J. Barnett, 237–243. Tacoma: Washington State Historical Society.

Cherevko, K. E.
1975 "Ignatii Kozyrevskii—avtor opisaniia Iaponskago gosudarstva." *Problemy Dal'nego Vostoka* 2.

Chernenko, M. B.
1957 "Puteshestviia po Chukotskoi zemle i plavanie na Aliasku kazach'ego sotnika Ivana Kobeleva v 1779 i 1789–1791 gg." *Letopis' Severa* 2: 121–141.

Cheshkova, Lydia
1992 "Kartushi starykh morekhodov." *Vokrug sveta* 3 (March): 14–20.

Chevigny, Hector
1937 *Lost Empire: The Life and Adventures of Nikolai Petrovich Rezanov.* Portland, Ore.: Binfords and Mort.
1942 *Lord of Alaska: Baranov and the Russian Adventure.* New York: Viking Press.

Chistov, K. V., and T. A. Bernshtam, eds.
1981 *Russkii Sever: Problemy etnografii i fol'klora.* Leningrad: Izdatel'stvo "Nauka."

Choris, Louis
1822 *Voyage pittoresque autour du Monde.* Paris: Impr. de Firmin Didot.

Chulkov, Mikhail
1785 *Istoricheskoe opisanie rossiiskoi kommertsii pri vsekh portakh i granitsakh ot drevneishikh vremen do nyne nastoiashchago i vsekh preimushchestvennykh uzakonenii po onoi Gosudaria Imperatora Petra Velikago i nyne blagopoluchno tsarstvuiushchei Gosudariny Imperatritsy Ekateriny Velikoi.* Vol. 3. Moscow: Universitetskaia tipografiia N. Novikova.

Collins, Perry McDonough
1860 *A Voyage Down the Amoor.* New York: Appleton and Company.

Cook, Warren L.
1973 *Flood Tide of Empire: Spain and the Pacific Northwest, 1543–1819.* New Haven: Yale University Press.

Conway, Sir Martin
1906 *No Man's Land: A History of Spitsbergen from its Discovery in 1596 to the Beginning of the Scientific Exploration of the Country.* Cambridge: Cambridge University Press.

Corney, Peter
1896 *Voyages in the Northern Pacific: Narrative of Several Trading Voyages from 1813 to 1818, between the Northwest Coast of America, the Hawaiian Islands and China, with a Description of the Russian Establishments on the Northwest Coast.* Honolulu: Thos. G. Thrum.

Coxe, William
1780 *Account of the Russian Discoveries between Asia and America, to which are added, The Conquest of Siberia, and The History of the Transactions and Commerce between Russia and China.* London: T. Cadell.

Cracroft, Sophia
1981 *Lady Franklin Visits Sitka, Alaska, 1870: The Journal of Sophia Cracroft, Sir John Franklin's Niece.* Edited by R. N. DeArmond. Anchorage: Alaska Historical Society.

Culin, Stewart
1920 "The Wreck of the Wakamiya Maru." *Asia* 20, May: 365–372, 436; 20, June: 505–512; 20, July: 583–588; 20, Aug.: 704–711; 20, Sept.: 807–814.

Cummings, Richard O.
1949 *The American Ice Harvests: A Historical Study in Technology, 1800–1918.* Berkeley and Los Angeles: University of California Press.

Dall, William H.
1870 *Alaska and Its Resources.* Boston: Lee and Shepard. Facsimile reprint, New York: Arno Press and New York Times, 1970.
1885 "The Native Tribes of Alaska." *Proceedings, American Association for the Advancement of Science, August 1885, Ann Arbor.* Vol. 34. Salem, Mass.: Salem Press.
1890 "A Critical Review of Bering's First Expedition, 1725–30, Together with a Translation of His Original Report on It (with a Map)." *National Geographic Magazine* 2: 111–167.
1891 "Notes on an Original Manuscript Chart of Bering's Expedition of 1725–1730, and on an Original Manuscript Chart of His Second Expedition; Together with a Summary of a Journal of the First Expedition, Kept by Peter Chaplin, and Now First Rendered into English from Bergh's Russian Version." Appendix 19 in *Report of the Superintendent of the U.S. Coast and Geodetic Survey Showing the Progress of Work During the Fiscal Year Ending with June, 1890*, 759–774. Washington, D.C.: Government Printing Office.

Dauenhauer, Nora Marks, and Richard Dauenhauer
1990 "The Battles of Sitka, 1802 and 1804, from Tlingit, Russian, and Other Points of View." In *Russia in North America: Proceedings of the 2nd International Conference on Russian America, Sitka, Alaska, August 19–22, 1987*, ed. Richard A. Pierce, 6–24. Kingston, Ontario; Fairbanks, Alaska: Limestone Press.

Dauenhauer, Richard L.
1978 "The Spiritual Epiphany of Aleut." Alaska Native Foundation, Center for Equality of Opportunity in Schooling, September 1978. Reprinted in *Orthodox Alaska* 8, no. 1 (1979): 13–42.
1990 "Education in Russian America." In *Russian America: The Forgotten Frontier*, ed. Barbara S. Smith and Redmond J. Barnett, 155–163. Tacoma: Washington State Historical Society.
1996 *Conflicting Visions in Alaskan Education.* 3d ed. Fairbanks: University of Alaska Press.

Dauenhauer, Richard, and Nora Marks Dauenhauer
2002 "Collisions in Tlingit America: Tlingit Interpreters and the Russian-American Company." Paper presented at the conference "Worlds in Collision: Critically Analyzing Aboriginal and European Contact Narratives," University of Victoria, Victoria, B.C., Canada, February 21–24, 2002.

David, Andrew C. F.
1990 "Russian Charts and Captain Cook's Third Voyage." *The Map Collector* 52 (Autumn): 2–6.

Davidson, George
1901 *The Tracks and Landfalls of Bering and Chirikof on the Northwest Coast of America. From the Point of Their Separation in Latitude 49° 10', Longitude 176° 40' West, to Their Return to the Same Meridian. June, July, August, September, October, 1741.* San Francisco: John Partridge.

Davis, Nancy Yaw
1970 "The Role of the Russian Orthodox Church in Five Pacific Eskimo Villages as Revealed by the Earthquake." In *The Great Alaska Earthquake of 1964: Human Ecology*, National Research Council, Division of Earth Sciences, Committee on the Alaska Earthquake, 125–146. Washington, D.C.: National Academy of Sciences.
1984 "Contemporary Pacific Eskimo." In *Arctic*, ed. David Damas, 198–204. Vol. 5 of *Handbook of North American Indians*, ed. William C. Sturtevant. Washington, D.C.: Smithsonian Institution.

Davydov, G. I.
1810–1812 *Dvukratnoe puteshestvie v Ameriku morskikh ofitserov Khvostova i Davydova, pisannoe sim poslednim.* 2 pts. St. Petersburg: Morskaia tipografiia. Translated by Colin Bearne, ed. Richard A. Pierce, under the title *Two Voyages to Russian America, 1802–1807* (Kingston, Ontario: Limestone Press, 1977).

Demin, L. M.
1990 *Semen Dezhnev.* Moscow: "Molodaia gvardiia."

Dilliplane, Timothy L.
1990 "Industries in Russian America." In *Russian America: The Forgotten Frontier*, ed. Barbara S.

Smith and Redmond J. Barnett, 131–143. Tacoma: Washingon State Historical Society.

Divin, V. A.

1979 *Russkaia Tikhookeanskaia epopeia.* Khabarovsk: Khabarovskoe knizhnoe izdatel'stvo.

1993 *The Great Russian Navigator A. I. Chirikov.* Translated and annotated by Raymond H. Fisher. Fairbanks: University of Alaska Press.

Dixon, George, ed.

1789 *A Voyage Round the World; But More Particularly to the North-West Coast of America: Performed in 1785, 1786, 1787, and 1788 in the* King George *and* Queen Charlotte, *Captains Portlock and Dixon.* London: George Goulding.

Dmitriev, A. A.

1896 *Istoricheskii ocherk Permskago kraia.* Perm': Gubernskaia zemskaia uprava.

Dmitriev, Aleksandr

1889–1900 *Permskaia starina: Sbornik istoricheskikh statei i materialov preimushchestvenno o Permskom krae.* 2 vols., 8 pts. Perm'.

Dowty, Alan

1971 *The Limits of American Isolation: The United States and the Crimean War.* New York: New York University Press.

Dumond, Don E.

1996 "Poison in the Cup: The South Alaskan Smallpox Epidemic of 1835." *University of Oregon Anthropological Papers* 52: 117–129.

Dvoichenko-Markova, E.

1955 *Benjamin Franklin and Count M. A. Beniowski.* Philadelphia.

Dyson, George

1986 *Baidarka.* Edmonds, Wash.: Alaska Northwest Publishing Company.

Efimov, A. V.

1948 *Iz istorii russkikh ekspeditsii na Tikhom okeane, pervaia polovina XVIII veka.* Moscow: Voennoe izdatel'stvo Ministerstva vooruzhennykh sil Soiuza SSR.

1949 *Iz istorii velikikh russkikh geograficheskikh otkrytii.* Abridged and revised ed. Moscow.

1950 *Iz istorii velikikh russkikh geograficheskikh otkrytii v Severnom Ledovitom i Tikhom okeanakh XVII–pervaia polovina XVIII v.* Moscow: Gosudarstvennoe izdatel'stvo geograficheskoi literatury.

1951 "Dokumenty ob otkrytiiakh russkikh zemleprokhodtsev i poliarnykh morekhodov v XVII veke na severo-vostoke Azii." In *Otkrytiia russkikh zemleprokhodtsev i poliarnykh morekhodov XVII veka na severo-vostoke Azii: Sbornik dokumentov*, comp. N. S. Orlova, ed. A. V. Efimov, 6–48. Moscow: Gosudarstvennoe izdatel'stvo geograficheskoi literatury.

1971 *Iz istorii velikikh russkikh geograficheskikh otkrytii.* Moscow: Izdatel'stvo "Nauka."

Efimov, A. V., ed.

1951 *Otkrytiia russkikh zemleprokhodtsev i poliarnykh morekhodov XVII veka na severo-vostoke Azii: Sbornik dokumentov.* Compiled by N. S. Orlova. Moscow: Gosudarstvennoe izdatel'stvo geograficheskoi literatury.

1964 *Atlas of Geographical Discoveries in Siberia and North-Western America, XVII–XVIII Centuries.* From material compiled by A. V. Efimov, M. I. Belov, and O. M. Medushevskaia. Moscow: Izdatel'stvo "Nauka."

Elert, A. Kh.

1990 *Ekspeditsionnye materialy G. F. Millera kak istochnik po istorii Sibiri.* Novosibirsk: Izdatel'stvo "Nauka."

Emerov, B. D.

1962 "K istorii kitoboinogo promysla na russkom Severe." *Letopis' Severa* 3: 188–200.

Engelhardt, A. P.

1899 *A Russian Province of the North.* Translated by Henry Cooke. Westminster: Archibald Constable and Company.

Farrelly, T. S.

1944 "A Lost Colony of Novgorod in Alaska." *Slavonic and East European Review* 22 (October): 33–38.

Fast, Edward G.

1869 *Catalogue of Antiquities and Curiosities Collected in the Territory of Alaska by Edward G. Fast... Consisting of More Than 2000 Most Valuable and Unique Specimens of Antiquity... also a Collection of Remarkable Fire Arms, a Large Geological Collection, etc., etc. Now on Exhibition at the Clinton Hall Art Galleries.* New York: Leavitt, Strebeigh and Co.

Fedorova, S. G.

1964 "K voprosu o rannikh russkikh poseleniiakh na Aliaske." *Letopis' Severa* 4: 97–112 and table.

1967 "Flag Rossiisko-Amerikanskoi kompanii." In *Ot Aliaski do Ognennoi Zemli*, 121–129. Moscow: Izdatel'stvo "Nauka."

1971 *Russkoe naselenie Aliaski i Kalifornii: Konets XVIII veka–1867 g.* Moscow: Izdatel'stvo "Nauka." Translated and edited by Richard A. Pierce and Alton S. Donnelly under the title *The Russian Population in Alaska and California, Late 18th Century–1867* (Kingston, Ontario: Limestone Press, 1973).

1979, 1982 "Shturmany Ivany Vasil'evy i ikh rol' v izuchenii Aliaski (pervaia polovina XIX v.)." *Letopis' Severa* 9: 167–210; 10: 141–160.

1981 "Russkoe nasledie v sud'bakh korennogo naseleniia Aliaski." In *Traditsionnye kul'tury severnoi Sibiri i Severnoi Ameriki*, 244–266. Moscow: Izdatel'stvo "Nauka." Volume translated under the title *Cultures of the Bering Sea Region: Papers from an International Symposium,* ed. Henry N. Michael and James W. VanStone (ACLS/AN SSSR and New York: IREX, 1983).

Fienup-Riordan, Ann
1987 "The Mask: The Eye of the Dance." *Arctic Anthropology* 24, no. 2: 40–55.
1990 "Following the Star: From the Ukraine to the Yukon." In *Russian America: The Forgotten Frontier*, ed. Barbara S. Smith and Redmond J. Barnett, 227–235. Tacoma: Washington State Historical Society.
1990 "Selaviq: A Yup'ik Transformation of a Russian Orthodox Tradition." In *Eskimo Essays: Yup'ik Lives and How We See Them*, by Ann Fienup-Riordan, 94–122. New Brunswick, N.J.: Rutgers University Press.

Fisher, Raymond H.
1943 *The Russian Fur Trade, 1550–1700.* Berkeley and Los Angeles: University of California Press.
1956 "Semen Dezhnev and Professor Golder." *Pacific Historical Review* 25: 281–292.
1973 "Dezhnev's Voyage of 1648 in the Light of Soviet Scholarship." *Terrae incognitae* 1: 7–26.
1977 *Bering's Voyages: Whither and Why.* Seattle: University of Washington Press.
1981 *The Voyage of Semen Dezhnev in 1648: Bering's Precursor, with Selected Documents.* London: Hakluyt Society.
1984 "The Early Cartography of the Bering Strait Region." *Arctic* 37, no. 4: 574–589.
1990 "Imperial Russia Moves Overseas: An Overview." In *Russia in North America: Proceedings of the 2nd International Conference on Russian America, Sitka, Alaska, August 19–22, 1987*, ed. Richard A. Pierce, 71–78. Kingston, Ontario; Fairbanks, Alaska: Limestone Press.

Fitzhugh, William W., and Aron Crowell, eds.
1988 *Crossroads of Continents: Cultures of Siberia and Alaska.* Washington, D.C.: Smithsonian Institution Press.

Fjodorova, Tatjana [Fedorova, Tat'iana S.], Birgit Leick Lampe, Sigurd Rambusch, and Tage Sørensen
1999 *Martin Spangsberg: En dansk opdagelsesrejsende i russisk tjeneste.* Esbjerg, Denmark: Rosendahls Forlag. Translated under the title *Martin Spangsberg: A Danish Explorer in Russian Service* (Esbjerg, Denmark: Fiskeri- og Søfartsmuseet, 2002).

Fortuine, Robert
1990 "Health and Medical Care in Russian America." In *Russian America: The Forgotten Frontier*, ed. Barbara S. Smith and Redmond J. Barnett, 121–129. Tacoma: Washington State Historical Society.

Foust, Clifford M.
1969 *Muscovite and Mandarin: Russia's Trade with China and Its Setting, 1727–1805.* Chapel Hill: University of North Carolina Press.

Friz, Iakov Iakovlevich
1822 "Khronologicheskaia letopis' goroda Ustiuga Velikago." *Severnyi arkhiv* 11 (June): 321–332; 12 (June): 402–412; 13 (June): 19–29; 13 (July): 103–118, 221–234.

Frost, Alan
1992 "British Ambitions and the Western Coasts of the Americas, 1763–1793." In *Spain and the Northwest Coast: Essays in Recognition of the Bicentennial of the Malaspina Expedition, 1791–1792*, ed. Robin Inglis, 35–45. Vancouver, B.C.: Vancouver Maritime Museum.

Frost, O. W.
1990 "Adam Olearius, the Greenland Eskimos, and the First Slaughter of Bering Island Sea Cows, 1742: An Elucidation of a Statement in Steller's Journal." In *Russia in North America: Proceedings of the 2nd International Conference on Russian America, Sitka, Alaska, August 19–22, 1987*, ed. Richard A. Pierce, 121–135. Kingston, Ontario; Fairbanks, Alaska: Limestone Press.

Frost, O. W., ed.
1992 *Bering and Chirikov: The American Voyages and Their Impact.* Anchorage: Alaska Historical Society.

Gibson, James R.
1969 *Feeding the Russian Fur Trade: Provisionment of the Okhotsk Seaboard and the Kamchatka Peninsula, 1639–1856.* Madison: University of Wisconsin Press.
1975 "Bostonians and Muscovites on the Northwest Coast, 1788–1841." In *The Western Shore: Oregon Country Essays Honoring the American Revolution*, ed. Thomas Vaughan, 81–119. Portland: Oregon Historical Society.
1976 *Imperial Russia in Frontier America: The Changing Geography of Supply of Russian America, 1784–1867.* New York: Oxford University Press.
1983 "Smallpox on the Northwest Coast, 1835–1838." *BC Studies* 56 (Winter 1982–1983): 61–81.
1987 "Russian Dependence upon the Natives of Alaska." In *Russia's American Colony*, ed. S. Frederick Starr, 77–104. Durham: Duke University Press.
1990 "The 'Russian Contract': The Agreement of 1838 between the Hudson's Bay and Russian-American Companies." In *Russia in North America: Proceedings of the 2nd International Conference on Russian America, Sitka, Alaska, August 19–22, 1987*, ed. Richard A. Pierce, 157–180. Kingston, Ontario; Fairbanks, Alaska: Limestone Press.
1992 *Otter Skins, Boston Ships, and China Goods: The Maritime Fur Trade of the Northwest Coast, 1785–1841.* Seattle: University of Washington Press.

Gideon [Gedeon], Hieromonk

1989 *The Round the World Voyage of Hieromonk Gideon, 1803–1809.* Translated, with introduction and notes, by Lydia T. Black, ed. Richard A. Pierce. Kingston, Ontario; Fairbanks, Alaska: Limestone Press.

Gleason, John Howes

1950 *The Genesis of Russophobia in Great Britain: A Study of Interaction of Policy and Opinion.* Cambridge: Harvard University Press. Reprint, New York: Octagon Books, 1972.

Glushankov, I. V.

1969 "Aleutskaia ekspeditsiia Krenitsyna i Levasheva." *Priroda* 12: 84–92. Translated by Mary Sadouski and Richard A. Pierce under the title "The Aleutian Expedition of Krenitsyn and Levashov," *Alaska Journal* 3, no. 4 (1973): 204–210.

Gmelin, Johann Georg

1751–1752 *D. Johann Georg Gmelins... Reise durch Sibirien, von dem Jahr 1733 bis 1743.* 4 vols. Göttingen.

Gol'denberg, L. A.

1979 *Katorzhanin—sibirskii gubernator: Zhizn' i trudy F. I. Soimonova.* Magadan: Magadanskoe knizhnoe izdatel'stvo.

1980 "Karta Shestakova 1724 g." In *Ispol'zovanie starykh kart v geograficheskikh i istoricheskikh issledovaniiakh.* Moscow: Moskovskii filial Geograficheskogo obshchestva.

1984 *Mezhdu dvumia ekspeditsiiami Beringa.* Magadan: Magadanskoe knizhnoe izdatel'stvo.

Golder, Frank A.

1910 *Father Herman: Alaska's Saint.* Platina, Calif.: Orthodox Christian Books and Icons. Reprint, San Francisco: Orthodox Christian Books and Icons, 1968.

1910 "Some reasons for doubting Deshnev's voyage." *The Geographical Journal* (London) 36: 81–83.

1914 *Russian Expansion on the Pacific, 1641–1850: An Account of the earliest and later expeditions made by the Russians along the Pacific coast of Asia and North America; including some related expeditions to the Arctic regions.* Cleveland: Arthur H. Clark Co. Reprint, Gloucester, Mass.: Peter Smith, 1960.

1917 "The Attitude of the Russian Government Toward Alaska." In *The Pacific Ocean in History*, ed. H. M. Stephens. New York: Macmillan. Reprinted in *Alaska Journal* 1, no. 2 (1971): 53–55, 59.

1920 "The Purchase of Alaska." *American Historical Review* 25, no. 3: 411–425.

1922 *Bering's Voyages: An Account of the Efforts of the Russians to Determine the Relation of Asia and America.* Vol. 1, *The Log Books and Official Reports of the First and Second Expeditions, 1725–1730 and 1733–1742, with a Chart of the Second Voyage by Ellsworth P. Bertholf.* New York: American Geographic Society of New York.

1925 *Bering's Voyages: An Account of the Efforts of the Russians to Determine the Relation of Asia and America.* Vol. 2, *Steller's Journal of the Sea Voyage from Kamchatka to America and Return on the Second Expedition, 1741–1742*, translated and in part annotated by Leonhard Stejneger. New York: American Geographic Society of New York.

Golovin, P. N.

1863 "Iz putevykh pisem P. N. Golovina." *Morskoi sbornik* 66, no. 5: 101–182; 66, no. 6: 275–340. Translated and ed. by Basil Dmytryshyn and E. A. P. Crownhart-Vaughan under the title *Civil and Savage Encounters* (Portland: Press of the Oregon Historical Society, 1983).

Golovnin, V. M.

1851 *Zapiski Vasiliia Mikhailovicha Golovnina v plenu u iapontsev v 1811, 1812 i 1813 godakh i zhizneopisanie avtora.* St. Petersburg: N. Grech.

1986 "Memorandum of Captain 2nd Rank Golovnin on the Condition of the Aleuts in the Settlements of the Russian-American Company and its *Promyshlenniki.*" Translated by Katherine L. Arndt. *Alaska History* 1, no. 2: 59–71.

Gough, Barry M.

1971 *The Royal Navy and the Northwest Coast of North America, 1810–1914: A Study of British Maritime Ascendancy.* Reprint, Vancouver: University of British Columbia Press, 1974.

1980 *Distant Dominion: Britain and the Northwest Coast of North America, 1579–1809.* Vancouver: University of British Columbia Press.

Grekov, V. I.

1960 *Ocherki po istorii russkikh geograficheskikh issledovanii v 1725–1765 gg.* Moscow: Izdatel'stvo Akademii nauk SSSR.

Grinev, A. V.

1987 "Zabytaia ekspeditsiia Dmitriia Tarkhanova na Mednuiu reku." *Sovetskaia etnografiia*, 1987, no. 4: 88–110. Translated by Richard Bland under the title "The Forgotten Expedition of Dmitrii Tarkhanov on the Copper River," *Alaska History* 12, no. 1 (1997): 1–17.

1989 "The Eyak Indians and the Fate of a Russian Settlement at Yakutat." *European Review of Native American Studies* 3, no. 2: 1–6.

1991 *Indeitsy tlinkity v period Russkoi Ameriki (1741–1867 gg.).* Novosibirsk: Izdatel'stvo "Nauka."

[Gsovski, Vladimir]

1950 *Russian Administration of Alaska and Status of the Alaska Natives.* Prepared by the Chief of the Foreign Law Section, Law Library of the Library of Congress. 81st Cong., 2d sess., S. Doc. 152.

Gurvich, I. S.
1963 "Russkie na severo-vostoke Sibiri v XVII v." In *Sibirskii etnograficheskii sbornik* 5. Trudy Instituta etnografii, n.s., vol. 84, 71–91. Moscow: Izdatel'stvo Akademii nauk SSSR.
1970 "Aleuty Komandorskikh ostrovov." *Sovetskaia etnografiia*, no. 5: 112–123.

Hanable, William S.
1973 "New Russia." *Alaska Journal* 3, no. 2: 77–80.

Hinckley, Ted C.
1972 *The Americanization of Alaska, 1867–1897.* Palo Alto, Calif.: Pacific Books.

Hooper, C. L.
1897 *A Report on the Sea-Otter Banks of Alaska.* Washington, D.C.: Government Printing Office.

Hosley, Edward
1966 "The Kolchan Athapaskans of the Upper Kuskokwim." Manuscript, Rasmuson Library, University of Alaska Fairbanks.

Howay, F. W.
1973 *A List of Trading Vessels in the Maritime Fur Trade, 1785–1825*, ed. Richard A. Pierce. Kingston, Ontario: Limestone Press.

Huggins, Eli Lundy
1981 *Kodiak and Afognak Life, 1868–1870.* Kingston, Ontario: Limestone Press.

Inglis, Robin
1992 "The Effect of Lapérouse on Spanish Thinking about the Northwest Coast." In *Spain and the North Pacific Coast: Essays in Recognition of the Bicentennial of the Malaspina Expedition, 1791–1792*, ed. Robin Inglis, 46–52. Vancouver, B.C.: Vancouver Maritime Museum.

Inglis, Robin, ed.
1992 *Spain and the North Pacific Coast: Essays in Recognition of the Bicentennial of the Malaspina Expedition, 1791–1792.* Vancouver, B.C.: Vancouver Maritime Museum.

Innokentii, Saint, Metropolitan of Moscow and Kolomna: *see* Veniaminov, Ioann

Inouye, Ronald K.
1990 "Starring and Slava: A Legacy of Russian America." In *Russia in North America: Proceedings of the 2nd International Conference on Russian America, Sitka, Alaska, August 19–22, 1987*, ed. Richard A. Pierce, 358–378. Kingston, Ontario; Fairbanks, Alaska: Limestone Press.

Isaac, Alexie, prod.
1987 "Following the Star." Bethel, Alaska: KYUK-TV.

Istomin, Alexei A.
1992 *The Indians at the Ross Settlement According to the Census by Kuskov, 1820–1821.* Fort Ross, Calif.: Fort Ross Interpretive Association.

Iverson, Eve
1998 *The Romance of Nikolai Rezanov and Concepción Argüello: A Literary Legend and Its Effect on California History*, ed. Richard A. Pierce. Kingston, Ontario: Limestone Press.

"Iz"iasnenie o sposobakh k proizvedeniiu Rossiiskoi kommertsii iz Orenburga s Bukharskoiu, a iz onoi i s Indiiskimi oblastiami"
1763 *Ezhemesiachnyia sochineniia i izvestiia o uchenykh delakh* 18, no. 2 (July–December): 401–408.

Izmailov, Gerasim
Ships' logs. Russian State Naval Archive (RGAVMF), St. Petersburg, Russia. Fond 214, op. 1, delo 28.

J.L.S. [pseud.]
1776 *Neue Nachrichten von denen neuentdekten Insuln in der See zwischen Asien und Amerika; aus mitgetheilten Urkunden und Auszügen verfasset.* Hamburg and Leipzig: Friedrich Ludwig Gleditsch.

James, James Alton
1942 *The First Scientific Exploration of Russian America and the Purchase of Alaska.* Evanston and Chicago: Northwestern University.

Jette, Julius
1914 "Particulars of Nulato, Alaska, Massacre." Typescript of manuscript dated 28 January 1914, Alaska and Polar Regions Department, Elmer E. Rasmuson Library, University of Alaska Fairbanks. Published in part in *The Farthest-North Collegian* 1 February 1936: 3, 7.

Kalashnikov, Ivan
1905 "Zapiski irkutskago zhitelia." *Russkaia starina* 7: 187–251; 8: 384–409; 9: 609–646. Reprinted in *Zapiski irkutskikh zhitelei*, comp. and ed. M. D. Sergeev, 257–396. Irkutsk: Vostochno-Sibirskoe knizhnoe izdatel'stvo, 1990.

Kalmykow, Alexandra
1947 *Administration of Alaska by the Russians on the Eve of Its Transfer to the United States.* Master's thesis, Columbia University. Microfilm in collections of Alaska and Polar Regions Department, Elmer E. Rasmuson Library, University of Alaska Fairbanks.

Kamenetskaia, R. V.
1986 "Russkie starozhily poliarnogo areala." In *Russkii Sever: Problemy etnokul'turnoi istorii, etnografii, fol'kloristiki*, ed. T. A. Bernshtam and K. V. Chistov, 67–81. Leningrad: Izdatel'stvo "Nauka."

Kan, Sergei
1985 "Russian Orthodox Brotherhoods among the Tlingit: Missionary Goals and Native Response." *Ethnohistory* 32, no. 3: 196–222.
1987 "Memory Eternal: Orthodox Christianity and the Tlingit Mortuary Complex." *Arctic Anthropology* 24, no. 1: 32–55.

1989 *Symbolic Immortality: The Tlingit Potlatch of the Nineteenth Century.* Washington, D.C.: Smithsonian Institution Press.

1991 "Russian Orthodox Missionaries and the Tlingit Indians of Alaska, 1880–1900." In *New Dimensions in Ethnohistory: Papers of the Second Laurier Conference on Ethnohistory and Ethnology*, ed. Barry Gough and Laird Christie, 128–160. Hull, Quebec: Canadian Museum of Civilization.

Kari, James

Dena'ina traditions. Unpublished papers, Alaska Native Language Center, University of Alaska Fairbanks.

Kashevarov, A. [Aleksandr Filipovich]

1862 "Chto takoe zapusk i promysel pushnykh zverei v Rossiisko-amerikanskikh koloniiakh." *Morskoi sbornik* 58, no. 4: 86–92.

1862 "Otvet na zamechaniia Glavnago Pravleniia Rossiisko-amerikanskoi ko." *Morskoi sbornik* 62, no. 9: 151–168.

Kashevarov, Filip

1822 [Answers to Kiril Khlebnikov's questions on the history of the Russian American colonies, 10 June 1822]. Shur Collection, reel 2, item 13. Archives, Alaska and Polar Regions Department, Rasmuson Library, University of Alaska Fairbanks. Microfilm. Original in State Archive of the Perm' Region, Perm', Russia, Fond 445, op. 1, delo 75.

Kazantsev, I. P., ed.

1911 *Irkutskiia letopisi.* Irkutsk.

Keithahn, E. L.

1967 "Alaska Ice, Inc." In *Alaska and Its History*, ed. Morgan B. Sherwood, 173–186. Seattle: University of Washington Press.

Kennan, George

1870 *Tent Life in Siberia, and Adventures Among the Koraks and Other Tribes in Kamchatka and Northern Asia.* London: S. Low, Son and Marston.

Kerner, Robert J.

1948 *The Urge to the Sea.* Berkeley and Los Angeles: University of California Press.

Ketz, James A., and Katherine L. Arndt

1987 "The Russian-American Company and Development of the Alaskan Copper River Fur Trade." In *Le Castor Fait Tout: Selected Papers of the Fifth North American Fur Trade Conference, 1985*, ed. Bruce G. Trigger, Toby Morantz, and Louise Dechêne, 438–455. Montreal: Lake St. Louis Historical Society.

Keuning, Johannes

1954 "Nicolaas Witsen as Cartographer." *Imago Mundi* 11: 95–110.

Khlebnikov, Kiril T.

1827 "Travel Notes aboard the Brig *Kiakhta* along the Islands of Andreianov, Bering, Near, and Rat [Islands] District, by Manager of the Novoarkhangel'sk Office Khlebnikov, the Year 1827." Unpublished translation by Lydia T. Black made from a microfilmed copy (reel 6, item 52) in the Shur Collection, Archives, Alaska and Polar Regions Department, Rasmuson Library, University of Alaska Fairbanks. Original Russian manuscript in Archive of the Russian Geographic Society, Razriad 99, delo 34.

1833 "Pervonachal'noe poselenie Russkikh v Amerike." *Raduga*, Special supplement, 2: 313; 3: 15–24; 5: 69–85.

1835 *Zhizneopisanie Aleksandra Andreevicha Baranova, glavnago pravitelia Rossiiskikh kolonii v Amerike.* St. Petersburg: Morskaia tipografiia. Translated by Colin Bearne, ed. Richard A. Pierce, under the title *Baranov: Chief Manager of the Russian Colonies in America* (Kingston, Ontario: Limestone Press, 1973).

1979 *Russkaia Amerika v neopublikovannykh zapiskakh K. T. Khlebnikova.* Edited by R. G. Liapunova and S. G. Fedorova. Leningrad: Izdatel'stvo "Nauka." Translated by Marina Ramsay, ed. Richard A. Pierce, under the title *Notes on Russian America, Parts II–V: Kad'iak, Unalashka, Atkha, the Pribylovs* (Kingston, Ontario; Fairbanks, Alaska: Limestone Press, 1994).

1985 *Russkaia Amerika v "zapiskakh" Kirila Khlebnikova: Novo-Arkhangel'sk.* Edited by Svetlana G. Fedorova. Moscow: Izdatel'stvo "Nauka." Translated by Serge LeComte and Richard Pierce, ed. Richard Pierce, under the title *Notes on Russian America, Part I: Novo-Arkhangel'sk* (Kingston, Ontario; Fairbanks, Alaska: Limestone Press, 1994).

Khoroshkevich, A. L.

1963 *Torgovlia Velikogo Novgoroda s pribaltikoi i zapadnoi Evropoi v XIV–XV vekakh.* Moscow: Izdatel'stvo Akademii nauk SSSR.

King, Judith E.

1964 *Seals of the World.* London: Trustees of the British Museum (Natural History).

Kirchner, Walther

1966 *Commercial Relations between Russia and Europe, 1400 to 1800: Collected Essays.* Bloomington: Indiana University.

Kolesnikov, P. A.

1983 "Promyslovo-remeslennaia deiatel'nost' severnogo krest'ianstva v XVIII v." In *Promyshlennost' i torgovlia v Rossii XVII–XVIII vv.*, ed. A. A. Preobrazhenskii, 138–153. Moscow: Izdatel'stvo "Nauka."

Konakov, N. D.

1979 *Vodnye sredstva soobshcheniia naroda komi.* Seriia preprintov "Nauchnye doklady," no. 45. Syktyvkar: Akademiia nauk SSSR, Komi filial.

1983 *Komi: Okhotniki i rybolovy vo vtoroi polovine XIX–nachale XX v.* Moscow: Izdatel'stvo "Nauka."

1984 *Etnicheskaia ekologiia i traditsionnaia kul'tura komi.* Seriia preprintov "Nauchnye doklady," no. 107. Syktyvkar: Akademiia nauk SSSR, Komi filial.

Konakov, N. D., ed.

1989 *Genezis i evoliutsiia traditsionnoi kul'tury komi.* Trudy Instituta iazyka, literatury i istorii, no. 43. Syktyvkar: Akademiia nauk SSSR, Ural'skoe otdelenie, Komi nauchnyi tsentr.

Konrad, N. I., ed.

1961 *Orosiyakoku suymudan (Sny o Rossii).* Japanese text transcribed, translated into Russian, annotated, and with an introduction by V. M. Konstantinov. Moscow: Izdatel'stvo vostochnoi literatury.

Kordt, V. A.

1931 *Materialy po istorii kartografii Ukrainy.* Kiev: Izdatel'stvo Akademii nauk.

Korsun, Sergei, comp.

2002 *Prepodobnyi German Aliaskinskii: Zhizneopisanie.* Jordanville, N.Y.: Holy Trinity Monastery.

Kovalevsky, Maxime

1891 *Modern Customs and Ancient Laws of Russia, Being the Ilchester Lectures for 1889–1890.* Oxford. Reprint, New York: Burt Franklin, 1970.

Krauss, Michael E.

1990 "Alaska Native Languages in Russian America." In *Russian America: The Forgotten Frontier,* ed. Barbara S. Smith and Redmond J. Barnett, 205–213. Tacoma, Wash.: Washington State Historical Society.

Kristi, R. A., and L. A. Sitnikov

1988 "Novoe ob istorii osvoeniia severnoi chasti basseina Tikhogo okeana (stat'ia pervaia)." In *Istochniki po istorii Sibiri dosovetskogo perioda: Sbornik naychnykh trudov,* ed. N. N. Pokrovskii, 163–197. Novosibirsk: Izdatel'stvo "Nauka," Sibirskoe otdelenie.

Kriuchkova, M. N.

1997 *Pravitel' Russkoi Ameriki i ego potomki.* Kargopol': Izdatel'stvo "Gramota."

Kushner, Howard I.

1970 *American-Russian Rivalry in the Pacific Northwest, 1790–1867.* Ann Arbor, Mich.: University Microfilms.

1975 *Conflict on the Northwest Coast: American-Russian Rivalry in the Pacific Northwest, 1790–1867.* Westport, Conn.: Greenwood Press.

Kuza, A. V.

1975 "Novgorodskaia zemlia." In *Drevnerusskie kniazhestva X–XIII vv.,* ed. L. G. Beskrovnyi, 144–201. Moscow: Izdatel'stvo "Nauka."

Laguna, Frederica de

1972 *Under Mount St. Elias: The History and Culture of the Yakutat Tlingit.* Smithsonian Contributions to Anthropology, vol. 7. 3 pts. Washington, D.C.: Smithsonian Institution Press.

2000 *Travels Among the Dena: Exploring Alaska's Yukon Valley.* Seattle: University of Washington Press.

Lain, B. D.

1976 "The Decline of Russian America's Colonial Society." *Western Historical Quarterly* (April): 143–153.

Langsdorff, Georg Heinrich von

1993 *Remarks and Observations on a Voyage around the World from 1803 to 1807.* Translated and annotated by Victoria Joan Moessner, ed. Richard A. Pierce. Kingston, Ontario; Fairbanks, Alaska: Limestone Press. Originally published in German as *Bemerkungen aus einer Reise um die Welt* (Frankfurt am Mayn: Friedrich Wilmans, 1812).

Lantzeff, George V.

1943 *Siberia in the Seventeenth Century: A Study of the Colonial Administration.* Berkeley and Los Angeles: University of California Press.

Lantzeff, George V., and Richard A. Pierce

1973 *Eastward to Empire: Exploration and Conquest on the Russian Open Frontier, to 1750.* Montreal: McGill-Queen's University Press.

La Pérouse, Jean-François Galaup

1797 *Voyage de La Pérouse autour du Monde, publié conformément au décrêt du 22 avril 1791, et rédigé par M.L.A. Milet-Mureau.* 4 vols., atlas. Paris: Imprimerie de la République.

1798 *Charts and Plates to La Pérouse's Voyage.* London: G. G. and J. Robinson.

1798 *A Voyage Round the World, Performed in the Years 1785, 1786, 1787, and 1788 by the "Boussole" and "Astrolabe" under the command of J. F. G. de la Pérouse.* 2 vols. London: Printed for J. Stockdale.

Lashuk, L. P.

1972 *Formirovanie narodnosti komi.* Moscow: Izdatel'stvo Moskovskogo gosudarstvennogo universiteta.

Lavrentsova, T. D.

1964 "Podlinnye dokumenty o plavanii S. I. Dezhneva." In *Russkie arkticheskie ekspeditsii XVII–XX vv.,* ed. M. I. Belov, 127–143. Leningrad: Gidrometeorologicheskoe izdatel'stvo.

Laws of the Russian Empire: see Russia. *Polnoe sobranie zakonov.*

Lazarev, A. P.

1950 *Zapiski o plavanii voennogo shliupa* Blagonamerennogo *v Beringov proliv i vokrug sveta dlia otkrytii v 1819, 1820, 1821 i 1822 godakh, vedennye gvardeiskogo ekipazha leitenantom*

A. P. Lazarevym. Moscow: Gosudarstvennoe izdatel'stvo geograficheskoi literatury.

Lebedev, D. M.
1951 *Plavanie A. I. Chirikova na paketbote "Sv. Pavel" k poberezh'iam Ameriki, s prilozheniem zhurnala 1741 g.* Moscow: Izdatel'stvo Akademii nauk SSSR.

Ledyard, John
1963 *John Ledyard's Journal of Captain Cook's Last Voyage*, ed. James Kenneth Munford, introduction by Sinclair A. Hitchings. Corvallis: Oregon State University Press.

Len'kov, V. D., G. L. Silant'iev, and A. K. Staniukovich
1988 *Komandorskii lager' ekspeditsii Beringa (opyt kompleksnogo izucheniia).* Moscow: Izdatel'stvo "Nauka." Translated by Katherine L. Arndt, ed. O. W. Frost, under the title *The Komandorskii Camp of the Bering Expedition (An Experiment in Complex Study)* (Anchorage: Alaska Historical Society, 1992).

Lensen, George Alexander
1950 "Early Russo-Japanese Relations." *Far Eastern Quarterly* 10, no. 1 (November): 2–37.
1954 *Report from Hokkaido: The Remains of Russian Culture in Northern Japan.* Hakodate, Japan: Municipal Library of Hakodate.
1971 *The Russian Push Toward Japan: Russo-Japanese Relations, 1697–1875.* New York: Octagon Books.

Lesseps, Jean Baptiste Barthelemy
1790 *Journal historique du voyage de M. de Lesseps, Consul de France, employé dans l'expédition de M. le comte de la Pérouse, en qualité d'interprète du Roi: Depuis l'instant où il a quitté les frégates Françoises au port Saint-Pierre & Saint-Paul du Kamtschatka, jusqu'à son arrivée en France, le 17 octobre 1788.* 2 vols. Paris: Imprimerie Royale.
1790 *Travels in Kamtschatka, during the Years 1787 and 1788.* 2 vols. London: J. Johnson.

Levenshtern, E. E.
2003 *Vokrug sveta s Ivanom Kruzenshternom: Dnevnik leitenanta "Nadezhdy" (1803–1806). Samoe polnoe opisanie pervogo rossiiskogo krugosvetnogo puteshestviia.* Compiled by A. V. Kruzenshtern, O. M. Fedorova, and T. K. Shafranovskaia, translated by T. K. Shafranovskaia. St. Petersburg: TsKP VMF.

Liapunova, Roza G.
1971 "Etnograficheskoe znachenie ekspeditsii kapitanov P. K. Krenitsyna i M. D. Levashova na Aleutskie ostrova (1764–1769)." *Sovetskaia etnografiia*, no. 6: 67–78.
1979 "Novyi dokument o rannikh plavaniiakh na Aleutskie ostrova ('Izvestiia' Fedora Afanas'evicha Kul'kova, 1764 g.)." In *Strany i narody basseina Tikhogo okeana*, 97–105. Bk. 4, vol. 20 of *Strany i narody Vostoka.* Moscow: Izdatel'stvo "Nauka."
1979 "Zapiski ieromonakha Gedeona (1803–1807)—odin iz istochnikov po istorii i etnografii Russkoi Ameriki." In *Problemy istorii i etnografii Ameriki*, 215–229. Moscow: Izdatel'stvo "Nauka."
1990 "The Aleuts Before Contact with the Russians: Some Demographic and Cultural Aspects." *Pacifica* 2, no. 2 (November): 8–23.

Lindenau, Ia. I.
1983 *Opisanie narodov Sibiri (pervaia polovina XVIII veka): Istoriko-etnograficheskie materialy o narodakh Sibiri i Severo-Vostoka.* Translated from the German manuscript, ed. Z. D. Titova. Magadan: Magadanskoe knizhnoe izdatel'stvo.

Lisianskii, Iurii
1947 *Puteshestvie vokrug sveta na korable "Neva" v 1803–1806 godakh.* Moscow: Gosudarstvennoe izdatel'stvo geograficheskoi literatury.

Lomonosov, Mikhail
1952 *Trudy po russkoi istorii, obshchestvenno-ekonomicheskim voprosam i geografii, 1747–1765 gg.* Vol. 6. Moscow and Leningrad: Izdatel'stvo Akademii nauk SSSR.

Löwenstern, Hermann Ludwig von (*see also* Levenshtern, E. E.)
2003 *The First Russian Voyage around the World: The Journal of Hermann Ludwig von Löwenstern, 1803–1806.* Translated by Victoria Joan Moessner. Fairbanks: University of Alaska Press.

L'vov, A.
1894 "Kratkiia istoricheskiia svedeniia ob uchrezhdenii v Severnoi Amerike pravoslavnoi missii, ob osnovanii Kad'iakskoi eparkhii i o deiatel'nosti tam pervykh missionerov." *Tserkovnyia vedomosti* 38, supplement.

Machinskii, D. A.
1986 "Etnosotsial'nye i etnokul'turnye protsessy v Severnoi Rusi (period zarozhdeniia drevnerusskoi narodnosti)." In *Russkii Sever: Problemy etnokul'turnoi istorii, etnografii, fol'kloristiki*, ed. T. A. Bernshtam and K. V. Chistov, 3–29. Leningrad: Izdatel'stvo "Nauka."

Makarova, Raisa
1968 *Russkie na Tikhom okeane vo vtoroi polovine XVIII veka.* Moscow: Izdatel'stvo "Nauka." Translated and ed. Richard A. Pierce and Alton S. Donnelly under the title *Russians on the Pacific, 1763–1799* (Kingston, Ontario: Limestone Press, 1975).

Malloy, Mary
1994 *"Boston Men" on the Northwest Coast: Commerce, Collecting, and Cultural Perceptions in the American Maritime Fur Trade, 1788–1844.* Ann Arbor, Mich.: UMI Dissertation Services.
1998 *"Boston Men" on the Northwest Coast: The American Maritime Fur Trade, 1788–1844.*

Kingston, Ontario; Fairbanks, Alaska: Limestone Press.

McCollough, Martha L.

1988 "Yup'ik Responses to Russian Orthodoxy and Moravian Missionaries in the Lower Kuskokwim Region of Southwestern Alaska." Master's thesis, University of Alaska Fairbanks.

McGrail, Sean, and Eric Kentley, eds.

1985 *Sewn Plank Boats: Archaeological and Ethnographic Papers Based on Those Presented to a Conference at Greenwich in November, 1984.* Archaeological Series, no. 10. BAR International Series, no. 276. Greenwich, United Kingdom: National Maritime Museum.

Meares, John

1790 *Voyages Made in the Years 1788 and 1789 from China to the North West Coast of America, to Which Are Prefixed, an Introductory Narrative of a Voyage Performed in 1786, from Bengal, in the Ship* Nootka; *Observations on the Probable Existence of a North West Passage; and Some Account of the Trade Between the North West Coast of America and China, and the Latter Country and Great Britain.* London: Logographic Press.

Medushevskaia, O. M.

1952 "Russkie geograficheskie otkrytiia na Tikhom okeane i v Severnoi Amerike (50-e—nachalo 80-kh godov XVIII v.)." Ph.D. diss., Moscow State University.

Menzies, Archibald

1993 *The Alaska Travel Journal of Archibald Menzies, 1793–1794.* Edited by Wallace M. Olson, with list of botanical collections by John F. Thilenius. Fairbanks: University of Alaska Press.

Merck, Carl Heinrich

1980 *Siberia and Northwestern America, 1788–1792: The Journal of Carl Heinrich Merck, Naturalist with the Russian Scientific Expedition Led by Captains Joseph Billings and Gavriil Sarychev.* Translated from the German manuscript by Fritz Jaensch, ed. Richard A. Pierce. Kingston, Ontario: Limestone Press.

Merzon, A. Ts., and Iu. A. Tikhonov

1960 *Rynok Ustiuga Velikogo v period skladyvaniia vserossiiskogo rynka (XVII vek).* Moscow: Izdatel'stvo Akademii nauk SSSR.

Miller, David Hunter

1981 *The Alaska Treaty.* Kingston, Ontario: Limestone Press.

Miller, G. F.: *see* Müller, Gerhard Friedrich

Mirsky, Jeannette

1970 *To the Arctic! The Story of Northern Exploration from Earliest Times to the Present.* Chicago: University of Chicago Press.

Moore, Katrina H.

1979 "Spain Claims Alaska, 1775: Spanish Exploration of the Alaskan Coast." In *The Sea in Alaska's Past: Conference Proceedings*, 62–74. History and Archaeology Publications Series, no. 25. Anchorage: Office of History and Archaeology, Alaska Division of Parks.

Morrell, Benjamin, Jr.

1832 *A Narrative of Four Voyages, to the South Sea, North and South Pacific Ocean, Chinese Sea, Ethiopic and Southern Atlantic Ocean, Indian and Antarctic Ocean: From the Year 1822 to 1831.* New York: J. & J. Harper.

Mortimer, George

1791 *Observations and Remarks Made During a Voyage to the Islands of Tenerife, Amsterdam, Maria's Islands near Van Diemen's Land; Otaheite, Sandwich Islands; Owhyhee, the Fox Islands on the North West Coast of America, Tinian, and from thence to Canton in the Brig* Mercury, *Commanded by John Henry Cox, Esq.* Dublin: Printed for J. Byrne et al.

Mousalimas, Soterios A.

1989 "Shamans of Old in Southern Alaska." In *Shamans, Past and Present: Proceedings of the Symposium, 12th ICAE, 1988*, eds. Mihály Hoppál and Otto von Sadovszky, 307–316. Budapest: Hungarian Academy of Sciences; Los Angeles: ISTOR.

1990 "Russian Orthodox Missionaries and Southern Alaskan Shamans: Interactions and Analysis." In *Russia in North America: Proceedings of the 2nd International Conference on Russian America, Sitka, Alaska, August 19–22, 1987*, ed. Richard A. Pierce, 314–321. Kingston, Ontario; Fairbanks, Alaska: Limestone Press.

1992 "The Transition from Shamanism to Russian Orthodoxy in Alaska." D.Phil., Faculty of Theology, Oxford.

1993 "A Question of the 'Chugach Shaman' (Alaska): An Enquiry into Ecstasy and Continuity." In *Shamans and Cultures: Regional Aspects of Shamanism. Selected Papers from the 1st Conference of the International Society for Shamanistic Research*, ed. Mihály Hoppál, Keith Howard, et al., 147–159. Budapest: Hungarian Academy of Sciences; Los Angeles: ISTOR.

1995 *The Transition from Shamanism to Russian Orthodoxy in Alaska.* Providence, R.I.: Berghahn Books.

2003 *From Mask to Icon: Transformation in the Arctic.* Brookline, Mass.: Holy Cross Orthodox Press.

[Müller, Gerhard Friedrich]

1754 *A Letter from a Russian Sea-Officer, to a Person of Distinction at the Court of St. Petersburgh; containing His Remarks upon Mr. de l'Isle's Chart and Memoir, relative to the New Discoveries Northward and Eastward from Kamtschatka. Together with Some Observations on that Letter by Arthur Dobbs, Esq.; Governor of North-Carolina. To which is added, Mr. de l'Isle's Explanatory*

Memoir on his Chart Published at Paris and now Translated from the Original French. London.

Müller, Gerhard Friedrich
1758 *Nachrichten von Seereisen und zur See gemachten Entdeckungen, die von Russland aus langt den Kuesten des Eismeeres und auf dem ostlichen Westmeere gegen Japan und Amerika geschehen sind*. St. Petersburg: Akademiia nauk. Published in Russian under the title "Opisanie morskikh puteshestvii po Ledovitomu i po Vostochnomu moriu s Rossiiskoi storony uchinennykh," *Sochineniia i perevody k pol'ze uveseleniiu sluzhashchiia*, 1758, Jan.: 3–27; 1758, Feb.: 99–120; 1758, Mar.: 195–212; 1758, Apr.: 291–325; 1758, May: 387–409; 1758, July: 9–32; 1758, Aug.: 99–129; 1758, Sept.: 195–232; 1758, Oct.: 309–336; 1758, Nov.: 394–424. Published in English under the title *Voyages from Asia to America, for Completing Discoveries of the North West Coast of America* (London: T. Jeffreys, 1761; 2d ed. 1764).
1793 "Nachrichten von den neuesten Schiffahrten im Eissmeer und in der Kamtschatkischen See, seit dem Jahr 1742; da die zweite Kamtschatkische Ekspedition aufgehört hat: Ein Stück aus der regierungs-Geschichte der grosser Kayserinn Katharina II." *Neue nordische Beyträge* 5: 15–104.
1986 *Bering's Voyages: The Reports from Russia by Gerhard Friedrich Müller*. Translated with commentary by Carol Urness. Fairbanks: University of Alaska Press. Originally published as *Nachrichten von Seereisen, und zur See gemachten Entdeckungen, die von Russland aus langt den Kuesten des Eismeeres und auf dem ostlichen Weltmeere gegen Japon und Amerika geschehen sind* (St. Petersburg: Akademiia nauk, 1758).

Napalkov, A., et al., eds.
1989 *Rodniki parmy*. Syktykvar: Komi knizhnoe izdatel'stvo.

Narochnitskii, A. L., et al., eds.
1984 *Russkie ekspeditsii po izucheniiu severnoi chasti Tikhogo okeana v pervoi polovine XVIII v. (sbornik dokumentov)*. Compiled by T. S. Fedorova, L. V. Glazunova, A. E. Ioffe, and L. I. Spiridonova. Vol. 1 of *Issledovaniia russkikh na Tikhom okeane v XVIII–pervoi polovine XIX v.* Moscow: Izdatel'stvo "Nauka."
1989 *Russkie ekspeditsii po izucheniiu severnoi chasti Tikhogo okeana vo vtoroi polovine XVIII v. (sbornik dokumentov)*. Compiled by T. S. Fedorova, L. V. Glazunova, and G. N. Fedorova. Vol. 2 of *Issledovaniia russkikh na Tikhom okeane v XVIII–pervoi polovine XIX v.* Moscow: Izdatel'stvo "Nauka."
1994 *Rossiisko-amerikanskaia kompaniia i izuchenie Tikhookeanskogo Severa, 1799–1815 (sbornik dokumentov)*. Compiled by L. I. Spiridonova, A. E. Ioffe, and N. N. Bolkhovitinov. Vol. 3 of *Issledovaniia russkikh na Tikhom okeane v XVIII–pervoi polovine XIX v.* Moscow: Izdatel'stvo "Nauka."

"Navigatskiia shkoly Sibiri"
1850 *Zapiski Gidrograficheskago departamenta Morskago ministerstva* 8: 563–573.

Nelson, Edward W.
1899 "The Eskimo About Bering Strait." In *18th Annual Report of the Bureau of American Ethnology, 1896–1897*. Washington, D.C. Reprint, with introduction by W. W. Fitzhugh and addenda, Washington, D.C.: Smithsonian Institution Press, 1984.

Netsvetov, Iakov
1980 *The Journals of Iakov Netsvetov: The Atkha Years, 1828–1844*. Translated, with introduction and supplementary material, by Lydia T. Black, ed. Richard A. Pierce. Kingston, Ontario: Limestone Press.
1984 *The Journals of Iakov Netsvetov: The Yukon Years, 1844–1863*. Translated, with notes and additional material, by Lydia T. Black, ed. Richard A. Pierce. Kingston, Ontario: Limestone Press.

Oborin, V. A.
1983 "Permskie posadskie liudi v XVI–XVIII vv. (k voprosu o formirovanii torgovo-promyshlennoi verkhushki)." In *Promyshlennost' i torgovlia v Rossii XVII–XVIII vv.*, ed. A. A. Preobrazhenskii, 27–42. Moscow: Izdatel'stvo "Nauka."

Odintsov, V. A., and V. F. Starkov
1985 "Nekotorye problemy arkticheskogo moreplavaniia i pokhody russkikh na arkhipelag Spitsbergen." *Letopis' Severa* 11: 147–161.

Ogloblin, N. N.
1890 *Semeon Dezhnev*. St. Petersburg.
1890 "Semeon Dezhnev (1638–1671): Novye dannye i peresmotr starykh." *Zhurnal Ministerstva narodnago prosveshcheniia*, no. 12.
1890 " 'Zhenskii vopros' v Sibiri v XVII veke." *Istoricheskii vestnik* (July): 194–207.
1891 "Pervyi iaponets v Rossii, 1701–1705 gg." *Russkaia starina* 72, no. 10: 11–24.
1891 "Smert' S. Dezhneva v Moskve v 1673 g." *Bibliograf*, nos. 3–4.
1903 "Vostochno-Sibirskie poliarnye morekhody XVII veka." *Zhurnal Ministerstva narodnago prosveshcheniia*, no. 5: 38–62.

O'Grady, Alix
2001 *From the Baltic to Russian America, 1829–1836*. Edited by Richard A. Pierce. Kingston, Ontario: Limestone Press.

"Okhotsk (po zapiskam G. Savina, 1846 goda)"
1851 *Zapiski Gidrograficheskago departamenta Morskago ministerstva* 9: 148–161 with map.

Okladnikov, A. P., Z. V. Gogolev, and E. A. Ashchepkov
1977 *Drevnii Zashiversk: Drevnerusskii zapoliarnyi gorod*. Moscow: Izdatel'stvo "Nauka."

Okun [Okun'], S. B.
1935 *Kolonial'naia politika tsarizma na Kamchatke i Chukotke v XVIII veke: Sbornik arkhivnykh materialov*. Eds. Ia. P. Al'kor and A. K. Drezen. Leningrad: Institut narodov Severa, TsIK SSSR.
1951 *The Russian-American Company*. Edited by B. D. Grekov, translated from the Russian by Carl Ginsburg, preface by Robert J. Kerner. Cambridge, Mass.: Harvard University Press. Originally published in Russian under the title *Rossiisko-amerikanskaia kompaniia* (Moscow and Leningrad: Gosudarstvennoe sotsial'no-ekonomicheskoe izdatel'stvo, 1939).

Oleksa, Michael J.
1982 "Three Saints Bay and the Evolution of the Aleut Identity." Prepared for U.S. Department of Interior Heritage and Conservation Service, HCRS Village Histories Project, 19 January 1981, revised and expanded March 1982. Typescript.
1986 "The Death of Hieromonk Juvenaly." *St. Vladimir Theological Quarterly* 30, no. 3: 231–268.
1990 "The Creoles and Their Contributions to the Development of Alaska." In *Russian America: The Forgotten Frontier*, ed. Barbara S. Smith and Redmond J. Barnett, 185–195. Tacoma: Washington State Historical Society.
1990 "The Death of Hieromonk Juvenaly." In *Russia in North America: Proceedings of the 2nd International Conference on Russian America, Sitka, Alaska, August 19–22, 1987*, ed. Richard A. Pierce, 322–357. Kingston, Ontario; Fairbanks, Alaska: Limestone Press.
1992 *Orthodox Alaska: A Theology of Mission*. Crestwood, N.Y.: St. Vladimir's Seminary Press.

Oleksa, Michael, ed.
1987 *Alaskan Missionary Spirituality*. New York and Mahwah, N.J.: Paulist Press.

Olson, Wallace M.
1991 *The Tlingit: An Introduction to Their Culture and History*. 2d ed. Auke Bay, Alaska: Heritage Research.
2002 *Through Spanish Eyes: Spanish Voyages to Alaska, 1774–1792*. Auke Bay, Alaska: Heritage Research.

Opheim, Edward
1981 *Old Mike of Monk's Lagoon*. New York: Vantage Press.

Orth, Donald J.
1967 *Dictionary of Alaska Place Names*. Geological Survey Professional Paper 567. Washington, D.C.: U. S. Government Printing Office. Reprint, with minor revisions, Washington, D.C.: Government Printing Office, 1971.

Oswalt, Wendell H.
1963 *Mission of Change in Alaska: Eskimos and Moravians on the Kuskokwim*. San Marino, Calif.: Huntington Library.
1990 *Bashful No Longer: An Alaskan Eskimo Ethnohistory, 1778–1988*. Norman: University of Oklahoma Press.

Owens, Kenneth N.
1990 "Timofei Tarakanov: Frontiersman for the Tsar." In *Russia in North America: Proceedings of the 2nd International Conference on Russian America, Sitka, Alaska, August 19–22, 1987*, ed. Richard A. Pierce, 136–143. Kingston, Ontario; Fairbanks, Alaska: Limestone Press.

Owens, Kenneth N., and Alton S. Donnelly
1985 *The Wreck of the* Sv. Nikolai. Portland, Ore.: Western Imprints, The Press of the Oregon Historical Society.

Ozertskovskoi, N.
1793 "Opisanie morzhovago promysla." In *Sobranie sochinenii, vybrannykh iz mesiatsoslovov na raznye gody*. Pt. 10. St. Petersburg: Imperatorskaia akademiia nauk.

Pallas, Peter S.
1781 "Bericht von der in den Jahren 1768 und 1769 auf allerhöchsten Befehl der russischen Monarchinn unter Anführung des Capitains Krenitzyn und Lieutenants Lewaschef von Kamtschatka nach den neuentdeckten Inseln und bis an Aläska oder das feste Land von America vollbrachten Seereise." *Neue nordische Beyträge* 1, no. 2: 249–272.
1781 "Kurze Beschreibung der sogenannten Kupferinsel (Mednoi ostrof) im Kamtschatkischen Meere." *Neue nordische Beyträge* 2: 302–307.

Pamiatniki Sibirskoi istorii XVIII veka
1882 Vol. 1, *1700–1713*. St. Petersburg: Tipografiia Ministerstva vnutrennikh del.
1885 Vol. 2, *1713–1724*. St. Petersburg: Tipografiia Ministerstvo vnutrennikh del.

Partnow, Patricia
1993 "Alutiiq Ethnicity." Ph.D. diss., University of Alaska Fairbanks.

Pascal, Pierre
1976 *The Religion of the Russian People*. Translated from the French by Rowan Williams, foreword by Alexander Schmemann. Crestwood, N.Y.: St. Vladimir's Seminary Press.

Paseniuk, Leonid M.
1978 "Pokhozhdeniia barona Beniovskogo: Istoriko-biograficheskii ocherk." In *Kamchatka*, 109–166. Petropavlovsk-Kamchatskii.
1988 "Miatezhnaia sud'ba skital'tsa." In *Belye nochi na reke Mamontovoi*, 194–302. Kransodarsk knizhnoe izdatel'stvo.
1995 "Morekhod Gerasim Izmailov." In *Amerikanskii ezhegodnik 1994*, 96–115. Moscow: Izdatel'stvo "Nauka."

Pavlov, P. N.
1972 *Pushnoi promysel v Sibiri XVII v.* Krasnoiarsk: Krasnoiarskii gosudarstvennyi pedagogicheskii institut.
1974 *Promyslovaia kolonizatsiia Sibiri v XVII v.* Krasnoiarsk: Krasnoiarskii gosudarstvennyi pedagogicheskii institut.

Pavlov, P. N., ed.
1957 *K istorii Rossiisko-amerikanskoi kompanii.* Krasnoiarsk: Krasnoiarskii gosudarstvennyi arkhiv; Krasnoiarskii gosudarstvennyi pedagogicheskii institut. Translated by Marina Ramsay, ed. Richard A. Pierce, under the title *Documents on the History of the Russian-American Company* (Kingston, Ontario: Limestone Press, 1976).

Pekarskii, P.
1866 "O rechi v pamiat' Lomonosova, proiznesennoi v Akademii nauk doktorom LeKlerkom." *Zapiski Imperatorskoi akademii nauk* 10, no. 2: 178–187.
1869 "Arkhivnye razyskaniia ob izobrazhenii nesushchestvuiushchago nyne zhivotnago *Rhytina borealis* (so snimkom starinnago izobrazheniia *Rhytina borealis*)." *Zapiski Imperatorskoi akademii nauk* (St. Petersburg) 15, suppl. 1: 1–33.

Perevalov, V. A.
1949 *Lomonosov i Arktika.* Moscow and Leningrad: Izdatel'stvo Glavsevmorputi.

Petrov, Aleksandr Iu.
1997 "Obrazovanie Rossiisko-amerikanskoi kompanii (1795–1799)." Chap. 9 in *Osnovanie Russkoi Ameriki, 1732–1799*, vol. 1 of *Istoriia Russkoi Ameriki, 1732–1867*, ed. N. N. Bolkhovitinov, 322–363. Moscow: "Mezhdunarodnye otnosheniia."
2000 *Obrazovanie Rossiisko-amerikanskoi kompanii.* Moscow: Izdatel'stvo "Nauka."

Phipps, Constantine John
1774 *The Journal of a Voyage Undertaken by Order of His Present Majesty, for Making Discoveries Towards the North Pole by the Hon. Commodore Phipps, and Captain Lutwidge, in his Majesty's Sloops* Racehorse *and* Carcase*: To Which is Prefixed an Account of the Several Voyages Undertaken for the Discovery of a North-East Passage to China and Japan.* London: Printed for F. Newbery.
1774 *A Voyage Towards the North Pole Undertaken by His Majesty's Command, 1773.* London: Nourse. Reprint, Dublin: Sleater et al., 1775; Whitby, Yorkshire: Caedmon of Whitby Press, 1978.

Pierce, Richard A.
1965 *Russia's Hawaiian Adventure, 1815–1817.* Berkeley and Los Angeles: University of California Press.
1975 "The Russian Coal Mine on the Kenai." *Alaska Journal* 5, no. 2: 104–108.
1982 Preface to *Life on the Yukon, 1865–1867*, by George R. Adams. Kingston, Ontario: Limestone Press.
1985 "Hector Chevigny: Historian of Russian America." *Alaska Journal* 15, no. 4: 33–37.
1986 *Builders of Alaska: The Russian Governors, 1818–1867.* Kingston, Ontario: Limestone Press.
1990 *Russian America: A Biographical Dictionary.* Kingston, Ontario; Fairbanks, Alaska: Limestone Press.
1990 "The Russian American Company Currency." In *Russian America: The Forgotten Frontier*, ed. Barbara S. Smith and Redmond J. Barnett, 145–153. Tacoma: Washington State Historical Society.

Pierce, Richard A., ed.
1972 *Rezanov Reconnoiters California, 1806: A New Translation of Rezanov's Letter, Parts of Lieutenant Khvostov's Log of the Ship* Juno*, and Dr. Georg von Langsdorff Observations.* San Francisco: Book Club of California.
1984 *The Russian-American Company: Correspondence of the Governors, Communications Sent, 1818.* Translated by Richard A. Pierce. Kingston, Ontario: Limestone Press.
1990 *Russia in North America: Proceedings of the 2nd International Conference on Russian America, Sitka, Alaska, August 19–22, 1987.* Kingston, Ontario; Fairbanks, Alaska: Limestone Press.

Pierce, Richard A., and J. H. Winslow, eds.
1979 *H.M.S.* Sulphur *on the Northwest and California Coasts, 1837 and 1839.* Kingston, Ontario: Limestone Press.

Platonov, S. F.
1923 "Inozemtsy na Russkom Severe v XVI–XVII vv." In *Ocherki po istorii kolonizatsii Severa i Sibiri.* Petrograd.
1923 "Proshloe russkogo severa." In *Ocherki po istorii kolonizatsii Severa i Sibiri.* Petrograd.

Pokrovskii, A., comp. and ed.
1941 *Ekspeditsiia Beringa (sbornik dokumentov).* Moscow: Glavnoe arkhivnoe upravlenie NKVD SSSR.

Polevoi, Boris P.
1959 *Pervootkryvateli Sakhalina.* Iuzhno-Sakhalinsk: Sakhalinskoe khizhnoe izdatel'stvo.
1962 "O mestopolozhenii pervogo russkogo poseleniia na Kolyme." *Doklady Instituta geografii Sibiri i Dal'nego Vostoka* 2: 66–75.
1963 "Novyi dokument o pervom russkom pokhode na Tikhii okean." *Trudy Tomskogo kraevedcheskogo muzeia* 6, no. 2: 27.
1964 "K istorii formirovaniia geograficheskikh predstavlenii o severo-vostochnoi okonechnosti Azii v XVII v." In *Sibirskii geograficheskii sbornik*, 3, 224–270. Moscow and Leningrad: Akademiia nauk SSSR, Sibirskoe otdelenie, Institut geografii Sibiri i Dal'nego Vostoka.

1964 "Zabytyi pokhod I. M. Rubtsa na Kamchatku v 60-kh gg. XVII veka." *Izvestiia Akademii nauk SSSR (seriia geograficheskaia)* 4: 130–135.

1965 "O tochnom tekste dvukh otpisok Semeona Dezhneva 1655 goda." *Izvestiia Akademii nauk SSSR (seriia geograficheskaia)* 2: 101–111.

1966 "Nakhodka chelobit'ia pervootkryvatelei Kolymy." In *Ekonomika, upravlenie i kul'tura Sibiri XVI–XIX vv.*, ed. Oleg N. Vilkov, 285–291. Novosibirsk: Izdatel'stvo "Nauka."

1967 "Iz istorii otkrytiia severo-zapadnoi chasti Ameriki (ot pervogo izvestiia sibirskikh zemleprokhodtsev ob Aliaske do petrovskogo plana poiska morskogo puti k Amerike)." In *Ot Aliaski do Ognennoi Zemli*, 107–120. Moscow: Izdatel'stvo "Nauka."

1970 "O karte 'Kamchadalii' I. B. Gomana." *Izvestiia Akademii nauk SSSR (seriia geograficheskaia)* 1: 99–105.

1970 "O 'Pogyche'—Pokhache (o samom rannem russkom izvestii, otnosiashchemsia k sovremennoi Kamchatskoi oblasti)." *Voprosy geografii Kamchatki* 6: 82–86.

1970 "Soobshchenie Dezhneva o 'Bol'shom kamennom nose' i proiskhozhdenie ego lozhnogo tolkovaniia." *Izvestiia Akademii nauk SSSR (seriia geograficheskaia)* 6: 150–158.

1981 "Plaval li I. M. Rubets ot Leny do Kamchatki v 1662 g.?" In *Istoriia nauki* 6, 130–140. Izvestiia Akademii nauk SSSR. Seriia geograficheskaia. Moscow: Izdatel'stvo Akademii nauk SSSR.

1991 "Pervyi russkii pokhod na Tikhii okean v 1639–1641 gg., v svete etnograficheskikh dannykh." *Sovetskaia etnografiia*, no. 3: 56–69.

1993 "Zabytoe plavanie s Leny do r. Kamchatki v 1661–1662 gg. Itogi arkhivnykh izyskanii 1948–1991 gg." *Izvestiia Rossiiskogo geograficheskogo obshchestva* 125, no. 2: 35–42.

1997 "Predystoriia Russkoi Ameriki." In *Osnovanie Russkoi Ameriki, 1732–1799*, 12–51. Vol. 1 of *Istoriia Russkoi Ameriki, 1732–1867*, ed. N. N. Bolkhovitinov. Moscow: "Mezhdunarodnye otnosheniia."

Politov, V. V.

1978 *Iarensk: istoricheskii ocherk*. Leningrad: Izdatel'stvo "Nauka."

Polonskii, A.

n.d. "Perechen' puteshestvii russkikh promyshlennikov v Vostochnom okeane." Archive of the Russian Geographic Society, St. Petersburg, r. 60, op. 1, no. 2.

1850 "Pokhod geodezista Mikhaila Gvozdeva v Beringov proliv, 1732 goda." *Morskoi sbornik* 4 (November): 389–402.

1871 "Kurily." *Zapiski Imperatorskago russkago geograficheskago obshchestva* 4: 369–576.

Portlock, Nathaniel

1789 *A Voyage Round the World; But More Particularly to the North-West Coast of America: Performed in 1785, 1786, 1787, and 1788, in the* King George *and* Queen Charlotte, *Captains Portlock and Dixon*. London: John Stockdale and George Goulding.

Postnikov, Aleksei V. [Alexey V.]

2000 *Russkaia Amerika v geograficheskikh opisaniiakh i na kartakh*. St. Petersburg: "Dmitrii Bulanin."

2002 "The Sale of Alaska and the International Expedition to Effect Telegraph Link between North America and Europe via Siberia." *Archives Internationales d'histoire des sciences* 52: 237–276.

Rathburn, Robert R.

1970 "The Russian Orthodox Church: A Mechanism for Maintaining Ethnic Identity." Master's thesis, Sacramento State College, California.

1981 "The Russian Orthodox Church as a Native Institution among the Koniag Eskimo of Kodiak Island, Alaska." *Arctic Anthropology* 18, no. 1: 12–22.

Ray, Dorothy Jean

1964 "Kauwerak: Lost Village of Alaska." *The Beaver* 295 (Autumn): 4–13.

1975 *The Eskimos of Bering Strait, 1650–1898*. Seattle: University of Washington Press.

1983 "The Kheuveren Legend." In *Ethnohistory in the Arctic: The Bering Strait Eskimo*, 67–77. Kingston, Ontario: Limestone Press.

Records of the Russian-American Company

1818–1867 Correspondence of the Governors-General, Communications Sent. 49 vols. National Archives, Washington, D.C.

Riasanovsky, Nicholas V.

1977 *A History of Russia*. 3d ed. New York: Oxford University Press.

Richards, Rhys

1991 *Captain Simon Metcalfe: Pioneer Fur Trader in the Pacific Northwest, Hawaii and China, 1787–1794*. Edited by Richard A. Pierce. Kingston, Ontario: Limestone Press.

Riley, Joseph, prod.

1987 "Legacy of Faith: The Russian Orthodox Church in Alaska." Fairbanks, Alaska: KUAC-TV.

Robertson, William

1777 *The History of America*. 2 vols. London: W. Strahan, T. Cadell.

Rochcau, Vsevolod

1972 *St. Herman of Alaska and the Defense of Alaskan Native Peoples*. Offprint from *St. Vladimir Theological Seminary* 16, no. 1.

"Rossiiskaia istoriia: Nechto o 'piatinakh Novgorodskikh' i v osobennosti o strane, izvestnoi izdrevle pod imenem 'Vagi.'"

1827 *Severnyi arkhiv* 9: 3–34; 10: 89–120; 11: 189–209; 12: 271–289.

Rossiisko-amerikanskaia kompaniia
1857 *Otchet Rossiisko-amerikanskoi kompanii za 1856 g.* St. Petersburg.
1862 *Otchet Rossiisko-amerikanskoi kompanii za 1861 g.* St. Petersburg.
1862 "Zamechaniia Glavnago Pravleniia Rossiisko-amerikanskoi kompanii." *Morskoi sbornik* 59, no. 6: 1–8.

Rossiisko-finliandskaia kitolovnaia kompaniia
1858 *Otchet Rossiisko-finliandskoi kitolovnoi kompanii, s uchrezhdeniia do iskhoda 1858 g.* St. Petersburg. Excerpts reprinted in *Morskoi sbornik* 39, no. 2 (1859): 27–33.

Russia
1802 *Pod vysochaishim Ego Imperatorskago Velichestva pokrovitel'stvom Rossiisko-Amerikanskoi kompanii glavnago pravleniia Akt i vysochaishe darovannyia onoi kompanii pravila s priobshcheniem prilichnykh k onomu uzakonenii.* St. Petersburg: Imperatorskaia akademiia nauk.
1830–1839 *Polnoe sobranie zakonov Rossiiskoi imperii. Sobr. 1, s 1649 goda po 12 dekabria 1825.* 45 vols. St. Petersburg.
1863 "Memorandum [*zapiska*] in the matter of revision of the by-laws of the Russian-American Company and organization of the Russian American Colonies" (in Russian). Addressed by the Ministry of Finance to State Council, dated 26 December 1863, with appendices. St. Petersburg.

Russia. Departament Vneshnei torgovli
1863–1864 *Doklad komiteta ob ustroistve russkikh amerikanskikh kolonii.* 2 vols. St. Petersburg: Departament Vneshnei torgovli.

Russia. Gosudarstvennyi admiralteiskii departament
1815 "Nekotoryia izvestiia ob Okhotskom porte i uezde onago, dostavlennyia kapitan-leitenantom Minitskim v 1809 godu." *Zapiski izdavaemyia Gosudarstvennym admiralteiskim departamentom otnosiashchiiasia k moreplavaniiu, naukam i slovesnosti* 3, no. 3: 87–103.
1815 "Prodolzhenie izvestii ob Okhotskom porte, dostavlennykh kapitan-leitenantom Minitskim v 1811 godu." *Zapiski izdavaemyia Gosudarstvennym admiralteiskim departamentom otnosiashchiiasia k moreplavaniiu, naukam i slovesnosti* 3, no. 5: 137–150.
1824 "Ob Okhotskom porte." *Zapiski izdavaemyia Gosudarstvennym admiralteiskim departamentom otnosiashchiiasia k moreplavaniiu, naukam i slovesnosti* 7, no. 3: 86–97.

Rybina, E. A.
1978 *Arkheologicheskie ocherki istorii novgorodskoi torgovli X–XIV vv.* Moscow: Izdatel'stvo Moskovskogo gosudarstvennogo universiteta.

Samoilov, V. A.
1945 *Semen Dezhnev i ego vremia, s prilozheniem otpisok chelobitnykh Semeona Dezhneva o ego pokhodakh i otkrytiiakh.* Moscow: Glavsevmorput'.

Sarafian, Winston L.
1971 *Russian-American Company Employee Policies and Practices, 1799–1867.* Ann Arbor, Mich.: University Microfilms.

Sarychev, Gavriil A.
1802 *Puteshestvie flota kapitana Sarycheva po severovostochnoi chasti Sibiri, Ledovitomu moriu i Vostochnomu okeanu...pod nachal'stvom flota kapitana Billingsa s 1785 po 1793 god.* Atlas. St. Petersburg: Tipografiia Shnora.

Savel'eva, E. A.
1971 *Perm' Vychegodskaia: K voprosu o proiskhozhdenii naroda komi.* Moscow: Izdatel'stvo "Nauka."

Savva, Metropolitan
[1853?] "Letopis'." In *Vestnik Russkago geograficheskago obshchestva za 1853.* Vol. 2, pt. 7. Cited in A. S. Sgibnev, "Istoricheskii ocherk glavneishikh sobytii v Kamchatke s 1650 po 1856 g.," *Morskoi sbornik* 101, no. 4 (1869): 65–142.

Schuhmacher, W. Wilfried
1979 "Aftermath of the Sitka Massacre of 1802: Contemporary Documents with an Introduction and Afterword by W. Wilfried Schuhmacher." *Alaska Journal* 9, no. 1: 58–61.

Semenov, V. A.
1986 *Etnografiia komi (zyrian).* Syktyvkar: Permskii universitet.

Serbina, K. N.
1945 "Kniga Bolshogo Chertezha i ego redaktsiia." *Istoricheskie zapiski* 14: 129–147.
1947 "Istochniki knigi Bolshogo Chertezha." *Istoricheskie zapiski* 23: 290–324.
1950 *Kniga Bolshomu Chertezhu.* Moscow and Leningrad.

Serbina, K. N., ed.
1950 *Ustiuzhskii letopisnyi svod (arkhangelogorodskii letopisets).* Moscow-Leningrad: Izdatel'stvo Akademii nauk SSSR.

Sgibnev, A. S.
1868 "Bol'shoi kamchatskii nariad (ekspeditsiia El'china)." *Morskoi sbornik* 99, no. 12 (December): 131–139.
1868 "Ob obuchenii v Rossii iaponskomu iazyku." *Morskoi sbornik* 99, no. 12: 55–61.
1869 "Istoricheskii ocherk glavneishikh sobytii v Kamchatke s 1650 po 1856 g." 5 parts. *Morskoi sbornik* 101, no. 4: 65–142; 102, no. 5: 53–84; 102, no. 6: 37–69; 103, no. 7: 1–129; 103, no. 8: 33–110.
1869 "Materialy dlia istorii Kamchatki: Ekspeditsiia Shestakova." *Morskoi sbornik* 100, no. 2: 1–34.
1869 "Okhotskii port s 1649 po 1852 g. (istoricheskii ocherk)." *Morskoi sbornik* 105, no. 11: 1–92; 105, no. 12: 1–63.
1869 "Popytki russkikh k zavedeniiu torgovykh snoshenii s Iaponieiu v XVIII i nachale XIX stoletii." *Morskoi sbornik* 101, no. 1: 37–72.

1869 "Vedomost' sudam Sibirskoi flotilii s 1714 po 1853 god." *Morskoi sbornik* 105, no. 12: 55–63.
1876 "Bunt Ben'iovskago v Kamchatke v 1771 g." *Russkaia starina* 15, no. 3: 526–547; 15, no. 4: 757–769.
1876 "Skorniakov-Pisarev i Dev'ier v Sibiri: 1727–1743." *Russkaia starina* 2 (February): 444–450.

Shalkop, Antoinette, trans. and ed.
1979 *The Wreck of the* Neva. Anchorage: Alaska Historical Society and Sitka Historical Society.

Shelikhov, Grigorii I.
1981 *A Voyage to America, 1783–1786*. Translated by Marina Ramsay, ed. Richard A. Pierce. Kingston, Ontario: Limestone Press. Originally published in Russian in two parts under the titles *Rossiiskago kuptsa Grigor'ia Shelikhova stranstvovanie s 1783 po 1787 god iz Okhotska po Vostochnomu okeanu k Amerikanskim beregam* (St. Petersburg, 1791) and *Rossiiskago kuptsa Grigor'ia Shelikhova prodolzhenie stranstvovaniia po vostochnomu okeanu k Amerikanskim beregam v 1788 godu* (St. Petersburg, 1792).

Shemelin, Fedor
1816–1818 *Zhurnal pervago puteshestviia rossiian vokrug Zemnago shara*. 2 pts. St. Petersburg: Meditsinskaia tipografiia.

Sherwood, Morgan B.
1965 *Exploration of Alaska, 1865–1900*. New Haven: Yale University Press.

Shishenko, Vasilii, comp.
1881–82 *Permskaia letopis' s 1263–1881 g*. 2 pts. Perm': Gubernskaia zemskaia uprava.

Shumakher, Petr
1878 "K istorii priobreteniia Amura." *Russkii arkhiv* 3: 257–342.

Sirotnitskii, I. P., ed.
1988 "Varlaam Shalamov." *Nashe nasledie* 3–4: 54–102.

Sirridge, Agnes T.
1954 "Spanish, British and French Activities in the Sea Otter Trade of the Far North Pacific, 1774–1790." Ph.D. diss., St. Louis University.

Sitnikov, L. A.
1990 *Grigorii Shelikhov*. Irkutsk: Vostochno-Sibirskoe knizhnoe izdatel'stvo.

Sladkovsky, M. I.
1981 *The Long Road: Sino-Russian Economic Contacts from Ancient Times to 1917*. Translation of the revised Russian text by Liv Tudge. Moscow: Progress Publishers. Originally published in Russian under the title *Istoriia torgovo-ekonomicheskikh otnoshenii narodov Rossii s Kitaem do 1917 goda* (Moscow: Izdatel'stvo "Nauka," 1974).

Smirnov, N. G.
1992 *Gosudarstvo solntsa*, introduction by Ia. Svet. Moscow: Respublika. Originally published Moscow: Gosudarstvennoe izdatel'stvo, 1928.

Smith, Barbara S.
1980 *Orthodoxy and Native Americans: The Alaska Mission*. Historical Society Occasional Papers, no. 1. Syosset, N.Y.: St. Vladimir's Seminary Press for Historical Society, Orthodox Church in America, Crestwood.

Smyshliaev, D., comp.
1876 *Istochniki i posobiia dlia izucheniia Permskago kraia*. Perm': Gubernskaia zemskaia uprava.

Snigaroff, Cedor L.
1979 *Niiĝuĝis maqax̂tazaqangis: Atkan Historical Traditions Told in 1952 by Cedor L. Snigaroff*. Translated and ed. by Knut Bergsland. 2d rev. ed. Fairbanks: Alaska Native Language Center, University of Alaska Fairbanks.

[Soimonov, F. I.]
1761 "Drevniaia poslovitsa: Sibir'—zolotoe dno." *Sochineniia i perevody k pol'ze i uveseleniiu sluzhashchiia* 14, no. 3 (November): 449–467.
1764 "Prodolzhenie o drevnei poslovitse: Sibir'—zolotoe dno." *Ezhemesiachnyia sochineniia i izvestiia o uchenykh delakh* 19, no. 2 (January–June): 44–59.

Sokolov, A.
1847 "Proekt Lomonosova i ekspeditsiia Chichagova 1765 i 1766 goda." *Zapiski Gidrograficheskago departamenta Morskago ministerstva* 5: 240–251.
1848 "Raznye svedeniia otnosiashchiiasia k ekspeditsii Chichagova." *Zapiski Gidrograficheskago departamenta Morskago ministerstva* 6: 100–141.
1851 "Pervyi pokhod russkikh k Amerike 1732 goda." *Zapiski Gidrograficheskago departamenta Morskago ministerstva* 9: 78–107.
1851 "Raznye svedeniia otnosiashchiiasia k ekspeditsii Chichagova." *Zapiski Gidrograficheskago departamenta Morskago ministerstva* 9: 108–147.
1851 "Severnaia ekspeditsiia 1733–1741 godov." *Zapiski Gidrograficheskago departamenta Morskago minsterstva* 9: 190–469 and charts.
1852 "Ekspeditsiia k Aleutskim ostrovam kapitanov Krenitsyna i Levashova, 1764–1769 gg." *Zapiski Gidrograficheskago departamenta Morskago ministerstva* 10: 70–103.
1852 "Khvostov i Davydov." *Zapiski Gidrograficheskago departamenta Morskago ministerstva* 10: 391–433.
1853 "Khvostov i Davydov." *Morskoi sbornik* 9, no. 5: 349–357.

Spasskii, G.
1822 "Opisanie Mednago ostrova, lezhashchago v Kamchatskom more i proizvodimykh na onom gornykh rabot." *Sibirskii vestnik* 18: 281–290, map.

Staniukovich, A. K., and P. Yu. Chernosvitov
1994 "Investigation of the Earliest Settlement with Stone Tools on the Commander Islands." *Arctic Anthropology* 31, no. 2: 45–56.

Starbuck, Alexander
1989 *History of the American Whale Fishery.* Secaucus, N.J.: Castle Books. Reprint of part 4 of *Report of the United States Commission on Fish and Fisheries* (Washington, D.C.: U.S. Government Printing Office, 1878).

Starkov, Vadim, et al.
1983 "Russkie poseleniia XVI v. na Spitzbergene." *Vestnik Akademii nauk SSSR*, no. 12: 109–113.

Steller, Georg Wilhelm
1793 *Reise von Kamtschatka nach Amerika mit dem Commandeur-Capitän Bering.* St. Petersburg: Johann Zacharias Logan. Facsimile reprint, edited by Hanno Beck, Stuttgart: F. A. Brockhaus, 1974.
1793 "Tagebuch seiner Seereise aus dem Petripauls Hafen in Kamtschatka bis an die westlichen Küsten von Amerika und seiner Begebenheiten auf der Rückreise." *Neue nordische Beyträge zur physikalischen und geographischen Erd- und Völkerbeschreibung, Naturgeschichte und Ökonomie* 5: 129–236; 6: 1–26.
1984 *Steller's Manuscript Journal: Facsimile Edition and Transliteration.* Edited by O. W. Frost, with transliteration by Margritt A. Engel and Karen Willmore. Alaska Historical Commission Studies in History, no. 114. Anchorage: Alaska Historical Commission.
1988 *Journal of a Voyage with Bering, 1741–1742.* Edited, with introduction, by O. W. Frost, translated from the German by Margritt A. Engel and O. W. Frost. Stanford, Calif.: Stanford University Press. Originally published as *Reise von Kamtschatka nach Amerika mit dem Commandeur-Capitän Bering* (St. Petersburg: Johann Zacharias Logan, 1793).

Stevens, Gary
1990 "The Woody Island Ice Company." In *Russia in North America: Proceedings of the 2nd International Conference on Russian America, Sitka, Alaska, August 19–22, 1987*, ed. Richard A. Pierce, 192–212. Kingston, Ontario; Fairbanks, Alaska: Limestone Press.

Storå, Nils
1987 "Russian Walrus Hunting in Spitsbergen." *Etudes/Inuit/Studies* 11, no. 2: 117–137.

Strange, James
1928 *James Strange's Journal and Narrative of the Commercial Expedition from Bombay to the North-West Coast of America together with a Chart Showing the Tract of the Expedition with an Introduction by A. V. Venkatarama Ayyar, Curator, Madras Record Office.* Madras: Government Press.

Surnik, A. P.
1993 "Rezanov's Documents in G. V. Yudin's Collection." Paper presented at Second St. Innocent Readings, Russia and Russian America, Petropavlovsk-Kamchatskii, Russia, 9–11 August 1993.

Sverdlov, L. M.
1990 "Odin iz putei vozmozhnogo proniknoveniia russkikh na Aliasku v XVII veke." Russian Geographic Society at the Russian Academy of Sciences, Moscow. Typescript.
1991 "When Was Alaska Settled by Russians?" *Soviet Life* (September).
1992 "Russkoe poselenie na Aliaske v XVII v.?" *Priroda* 4: 67–69.

Taylor, E. G. R.
1955 "John Dee and the Map of North-East Asia." *Imago Mundi* 12: 103–106.

Tikhmenev, P. A.
1861–1863 *Istoricheskoe obozrenie obrazovaniia Rossiisko-Amerikanskoi kompanii i deistvii eiia do nastoiashchago vremeni.* 2 vols. St. Petersburg: Edvard Veimar.
1978 *A History of the Russian-American Company.* Vol. 1. Translated and ed. by Richard A. Pierce and Alton S. Donnelly. Seattle: University of Washington Press.
1979 *A History of the Russian American Company.* Vol. 2, *Documents.* Translated by Dmitri Krenov, ed. Richard A. Pierce and Alton S. Donnelly. Kingston, Ontario: Limestone Press.

Titov, A. A.
1889 *Letopis' Velikoustiuzhskaia.* Pt. 1. Moscow: A. K. Trapeznikov.
[1905?] *Letopis' Velikoustiuzhskaia.* Pt. 2. Moscow: Bragin.

Tompkins, Stuart Ramsay
1945 *Alaska: Promyshlennik and Sourdough.* Norman: University of Oklahoma Press.

Tompkins, S. R., and M. L. Moorhead
1949 "Russia's Approach to America." *British Columbia Historical Quarterly*, (April/July/October). Cited after S. G. Fedorova, *Russkoe naselenie Aliaski i Kalifornii: Konets XVIII veka–1867 g.* (Moscow: Izdatel'stvo "Nauka," 1973), 18.

Tower, Walter S.
1907 *A History of the American Whale Fishery.* Series in Political Economy and Public Law, no. 20. Philadelphia: University of Pennsylvania.

Townsend, Joan B.
1965 *Ethnohistory and Culture of the Iliamna Tanaina.* Ann Arbor, Mich.: University Microfilms.
1983 "Firearms Against Native Arms: A Study in Comparative Efficiencies with an Alaskan Example." *Arctic Anthropology* 20, no. 2: 1–33.

Treadgold, Donald W.

1968 "The Peasant and Religion." In *The Peasant in Nineteenth-Century Russia*, ed. Wayne S. Vucinich, 72–107. Stanford, Calif.: Stanford University Press.

United States

1864 *An Act to Encourage and Facilitate Telegraphic Communication between the Eastern and Western Continents. U.S. Statutes At Large* 13: 340–341.

United States. Coast Survey

1869 "Report of Assistant George Davidson Relative to the Resources and the Coast Features of Alaska Territory." In *Report of the Superintendent of the United States Coast Survey, Showing the Progress of the Survey during the Year 1867*, 187–329, charts. 40th Cong., 2d sess., H. Ex. Doc. 275.

United States. Congress. House of Representatives

1858 *Explorations of the Amoor River: Letter from the Secretary of State, in Answer to a Resolution of the House, Calling for Information Relative to the Explorations of the Amoor River.* 35th Cong., 1st sess., H. Ex. Doc. 98.

United States. Department of Commerce. Coast and Geodetic Survey

1954 *United States Coast Pilot 9: Alaska, Cape Spencer to Arctic Ocean.* 6th edition. Washington, D.C.: U. S. Government Printing Office.

United States. Department of State

1868 *Russian America.* 40th Cong., 2d sess., H. Ex. Doc. 177.

Urness, Carol

1986 *Bering's First Expedition: A Re-examination Based on Eighteenth-Century Books, Maps, and Manuscripts.* New York: Garland Press.

1990 "Joseph Nicholas Delisle's Map for Bering's Second Kamchatka Expedition." In *Russia in North America: Proceedings of the 2nd International Conference on Russian America, Sitka, Alaska, August 19–22, 1987*, ed. Richard A. Pierce, 79–101. Kingston, Ontario; Fairbanks, Alaska: Limestone Press.

Vancouver, George

1967 *A Voyage of Discovery to the North Pacific Ocean and around the World.* 3 vols., and charts. New York: DaCapo Press. Originally printed in London for G. G. and J. Robinson, 1798.

VanStone, James W., ed.

1973 *V. S. Khromchenko's Coastal Explorations in Southwestern Alaska, 1822.* Translated by David H. Kraus. Fieldiana: Anthropology, vol. 64. Chicago: Field Museum of Natural History.

1988 *Russian Exploration in Southwest Alaska: The Travel Journals of Petr Korsakovskiy (1818) and Ivan Ya. Vasilev (1829).* Translated by David H. Kraus. Fairbanks: University of Alaska Press.

Vasil'iev, Ivan F.

1814 "Vypiska iz zhurnala puteshestviia shturmana Ivana Vasil'ieva k ostrovam Aleutskim v 1811 i 1812 godakh. [Soobshchil] direktor Irkutskago uchilishcha Ivan Miller." *Kazanskie izvestiia*, no. 11.

1816 "Vypiska iz zhurnala puteshestviia shturmana Ivana Vasil'ieva k ostrovam Aleutskim v 1811 i 1812 godakh. [Soobshchil] direktor Irkutskago uchilishcha Ivan Miller." *Dukh zhurnalov* 14, no. 41: 675–684; 15, no. 42: 721–732; 15, no. 43: 757–766.

Veniaminov, Ioann

1840 *Zapiski ob ostrovakh Unalashkinskago otdela.* St. Petersburg: Rossiisko-amerikanskaia kompaniia. Translated by Lydia T. Black and R. H. Geoghegan, ed. Richard A. Pierce, under the title *Notes on the Islands of the Unalashka District* (Fairbanks: Elmer E. Rasmuson Library Translation Program, University of Alaska Fairbanks; Kingston, Ontario: Limestone Press, 1984).

1857 "Sostoianie russkoi pravoslavnoi tserkvi v Rossiiskoi Amerike." In *Pamiatnik trudov pravoslavnykh blagovestnikov russkikh s 1793 po 1853 goda*, ed. Aleksandr Sturdza. Moscow: Got'ie. Originally published under the same title in *Zhurnal Ministerstva narodnago prosveshcheniia* 26, no. 6 (1840).

Vernadsky, George

1943 *Ancient Russia.* Vol. 1 of *A History of Russia.* New Haven: Yale University Press.

1948 *Kievan Russia.* Vol. 2 of *A History of Russia.* New Haven: Yale University Press.

1951 *A History of Russia.* 3d rev. ed. New Haven: Yale University Press.

1969 *The Tsardom of Moscow, 1547–1682.* Vol. 5, parts 1 and 2, of *A History of Russia.* New Haven: Yale University Press.

Vevier, Charles

1967 "The Collins Overland Line and American Continentalism." In *Alaska and Its History*, ed. Morgan B. Sherwood, 209–230. Seattle: University of Washington Press.

Vucinich, Wayne W., ed.

1968 *The Peasant in Nineteenth-Century Russia.* Stanford, Calif.: Stanford University Press.

"Vzgliad na torgovliu proizvodimuiu chrez Okhotskii port"

1823 *Severnyi arkhiv* 7, no. 13 (July): 28–45.

Watkins, Albert E.

1961 "A Historical Study of the Russian Orthodox Church in Alaska." Master's thesis, University of Alaska, Fairbanks, Dept. of Education.

Waxell, Sven

1940 *Vtoraia Kamchatskaia ekspeditsiia Vitusa Beringa.* Translated from the German manuscript by Iu. I. Bronshtein, edited by A. I. Andreev. Leningrad and Moscow: Glavsevmorput'.

1952 *The American Expedition*. Translated from the Danish version of Johan Skalberg by M. A. Michael. London: William Hodge.

Wheeler, Mary

1971 "Empires in Conflict and Cooperation: The 'Bostonians' and the Russian-American Company." *Pacific Historical Review* 40, no. 4: 419–441.

Whitmore, Frank C., Jr., and L. M. Gard, Jr.

1977 *Steller's Sea Cow (*Hydrodamalis gigas*) of Late Pleistocene Age from Amchitka, Aleutian Islands, Alaska*. Geological Survey Professional Paper 1036. Washington, D.C.: U.S. Government Printing Office.

Williams, Ann Elizabeth

1993 "Father Herman: Syncretic Symbol of Divine Legitimation." Master's thesis, University of Alaska Fairbanks.

Wright, E. W., ed.

1895 *Lewis and Dryden's Marine History of the Pacific Northwest*. Portland, Ore.: Lewis and Dryen Publishing.

Wright, Miranda

1995 "The Last Great Indian War (Nulato 1851)." Master's thesis, University of Alaska Fairbanks.

Zagoskin, Lavrentii Alekseevich

1844 Manuscript journal and report submitted to the Chief Manager of the Russian-American Company. Records of the Russian-American Company, vol. 82, National Archives, Washington, D.C. Microfilm Group 11, Reel 77.

1846 "Redut Sviatago Mikhaila v iuzhnoi chasti Nortonova zaliva." *Zapiski Gidrograficheskago departamenta Morskago ministerstva* 4: 86–101.

1847 "Puteshestvie i otkrytiia leitenanta Zagoskina v Russkoi Amerike." *Biblioteka dlia chteniia* 83, no. 3: 29–102, 145–190; 84, no. 3: 1–64, 115–156.

1847–1848 *Peshekhodnaia opis' chasti Russkikh vladenii v Amerike proizvedennaia leitenantom L. Zagoskinym*. 2 pts. St. Petersburg.

1956 *Puteshestviia i issledovaniia leitenanta Lavrentiia Zagoskina v Russkoi Amerike v 1842–1844 gg*. Edited by M. B. Chernenko, G. A. Agranat, and E. E. Blomkvist. Moscow: Gosudarstvennoe izdatel'stvo geograficheskoi literatury. Translated by Penelope Rainey, ed. Henry N. Michael, under the title *Lieutenant Zagoskin's Travels in Russian America, 1842–1844*, Anthropology of the North: Translations from Russian Sources, no. 7 (Toronto: University of Toronto Press for Arctic Institute of North America, 1967).

Zagoskin, N. P.

1910 *Russkie vodnye puti i sudovoe delo v dopetrovskoi Rusi (Materialy dlia opisaniia russkikh rek i istorii uluchsheniia ikh sudokhodnykh uslovii)*, no. 16. Kazan'.

Zaitsev, V. A.

1983 *Belomorskii Sever: Religiia, svobodomyslie, ateizm*. Arkhangel'sk: Severo-zapadnoe knizhnoe izdatel'stvo.

"Zapiska o bunte, proizvedennom Beniovskim v Bol'sheretskom ostroge i posledstviiakh onago"

1865 *Russkii arkhiv* 4: 417–438.

"Zapiski kantseliarista Riumina o prikliucheniiakh ego s Beniovskim"

1822 *Severnyi arkhiv* 2, no. 5: 375–394; 2, no. 6: 447–462; 2, no. 7: 3–18.

"Zapiski P. V. Chichagova"

1886 *Russkaia starina* 50: 221–252, 463–488.

Zenzinov, Vladimir Mikhailovich

1913 *Russkoe ust'e Iakutskoi oblasti, Verkhoianskago okruga*. Moscow: P. P. Riabushinskii.

Zherebtsov, L. N.

1982 *Istoriko-kul'turnye vzaimootnosheniia komi s sosednimi narodami*. Moscow: Izdatel'stvo "Nauka."

Zubov, N. N.

1954 *Otechestvennye moreplavateli—issledovateli morei i okeanov*. Moscow: Gosudarstvennoe izdatel'stvo geograficheskoi literatury.

Zviagin, V. N., Sh. M. Musaev, and A. K. Staniukovich

1995 *Vitus Ionassen Bering, 1681–1741: Medico-kriminalisticheskii portret*. Baku: Azerbaidzhanskoe gosudarstvennoe izdatel'stvo.

Index

Page numbers in italics refer to illustrations.

C